Frommer's®

Washington, D.C. with Kids

10th Edition

WILEY
Wiley Publishing, Inc.

ABOUT THE AUTHOR

Beth Rubin has written extensively on family topics for over 25 years and has lived in the Washington, D.C., area since the early 1960s. During that time, she has played tour guide to her own two children and grandchildren as well as the offspring of numerous friends and relatives. Her experience and tell-it-like-it-is style make this well-researched book indispensable to anyone living in or visiting the nation's capital with kids in tow.

Published by:

WILEY PUBLISHING, INC.

111 River St.
Hoboken, NJ 07030-5774

ISBN 978-0-470-55612-2

Editor: Chris Summers (with Jennifer Reilly)
Production Editor: Lindsay Conner
Cartographer: Roberta Stockwell
Photo Editor: Richard Fox
Production by Wiley Indianapolis Composition Services

Front cover photo: Tian Tian Giant Panda in National Zoo © Ken Ross / Viestiphoto.com.
Back cover photo: Boy jumping by Reflecting Pool © JupiterImages / Getty Images.

For information on our other products and services or to obtain technical support, please contact our Customer Care Department within the U.S. at 877/762-2974, outside the U.S. at 317/572-3993 or fax 317/572-4002.

Wiley also publishes its books in a variety of electronic formats. Some content that appears in print may not be available in electronic formats.

Manufactured in the United States of America

5 4 3 2 1

CONTENTS

5 FAMILY-FRIENDLY RESTAURANTS 77

6 EXPLORING WASHINGTON, D.C. WITH YOUR KIDS 112

7 NEIGHBORHOOD STROLLS 187

8 FOR THE ACTIVE FAMILY 196

9 SHOPPING FOR THE WHOLE FAMILY 220

10 ENTERTAINMENT FOR THE WHOLE FAMILY 238

11 SIDE TRIPS FROM WASHINGTON, D.C. 254

12 FAST FACTS 288

INDEX 297

LIST OF MAPS

ACKNOWLEDGMENTS

My gratitude goes to Frommer's editors Jennifer Reilly and Chris Summers for keeping me on the straight and narrow, the many D.C. folks who assisted me in uncovering the latest and greatest info about the nation's capital, and my wonderful family and friends for their support through it all.

HOW TO CONTACT US

In researching this book, we discovered many wonderful places—hotels, restaurants, shops, and more. We're sure you'll find others. Please tell us about them, so we can share the information with your fellow travelers in upcoming editions. If you were disappointed with a recommendation, we'd love to know that, too. Please write to:

Frommer's Washington, D.C. with Kids, 10th Edition
Wiley Publishing, Inc. • 111 River St. • Hoboken, NJ 07030-5774

AN ADDITIONAL NOTE

Please be advised that travel information is subject to change at any time—and this is especially true of prices. We therefore suggest that you write or call ahead for confirmation when making your travel plans. The authors, editors, and publisher cannot be held responsible for the experiences of readers while traveling. Your safety is important to us, however, so we encourage you to stay alert and be aware of your surroundings. Keep a close eye on cameras, purses, and wallets, all favorite targets of thieves and pickpockets.

FROMMER'S STAR RATINGS, ICONS & ABBREVIATIONS

Every hotel, restaurant, and attraction listing in this guide has been ranked for quality, value, service, amenities, and special features using a **star-rating system.** In country, state, and regional guides, we also rate towns and regions to help you narrow down your choices and budget your time accordingly. Hotels and restaurants are rated on a scale of zero (recommended) to three stars (exceptional). Attractions, shopping, nightlife, towns, and regions are rated according to the following scale: zero stars (recommended), one star (highly recommended), two stars (very highly recommended), and three stars (must-see).

In addition to the star-rating system, we also use **six feature icons** that point you to the great deals, in-the-know advice, and unique experiences that separate travelers from tourists. Throughout the book, look for:

Finds	Special finds—those places only insiders know about
Fun Facts	Fun facts—details that make travelers more informed and their trips more fun
Kids	Best bets for kids, and advice for the whole family
Moments	Special moments—those experiences that memories are made of
Overrated	Places or experiences not worth your time or money
Tips	Insider tips—great ways to save time and money
Value	Great values—where to get the best deals

The following **abbreviations** are used for credit cards:

AE American Express	**DISC** Discover	**V** Visa
DC Diners Club	**MC** MasterCard	

TRAVEL RESOURCES AT FROMMERS.COM

Frommer's travel resources don't end with this guide. **Frommers.com** has travel information on more than 4,000 destinations. We update features regularly, giving you access to the most current trip-planning information and the best airfare, lodging, and car-rental bargains. You can also listen to podcasts, connect with other Frommers.com members through our active-reader forums, share your travel photos, read blogs from guidebook editors and fellow travelers, and much more.

1

How to Feel Like a Washington, D.C. Family

I moved to Washington, D.C., as a dewy-eyed college student—before the Kennedy Center or Metro; before Watergate, Iran-Contragate, Monicagate, Iraqgate, or WMD (Weapons of Mass Destruction). I grabbed a B.A. from George Washington University in Foggy Bottom, married a native, and then found a job with a trade association—a polite term for lobbying groups. After a few years, I traded downtown traffic and bureaucracy for suburban diaper duty and freelancing. Raising two children a dozen miles from the National Mall had its perks. Whenever the kids grew restless—and, in later years, during school vacations—I bundled them into the car and we headed to D.C. Back then, there were few resources targeted to families visiting the nation's capital. So we were trailblazers in a way, discovering the wonders of Washington, D.C., by the seat of our pants (and, sometimes, diapers). Armed with a map and a Frommer's guidebook, we found out which museum exhibits had the most kid appeal and where to let off steam. We learned the best and worst times to visit the popular attractions and where to get a quick and cheap meal. An inveterate note-taker, I shared my notebooks with local friends and out-of-town visitors. Little did I know that I had sown the seeds for a guidebook. With the kids in school full time and bored with baking brownies for PTA functions, I began writing travel features in 1980. A decade later I parlayed my knowledge and our family's experiences into *Frommer's Washington D.C. with Kids,* here in its 10th edition.

Since I first set foot on a D.C. street more than 45 years ago, I've lived through more scandals than I can count, endured Potomac Fever and worsening D.C. traffic, and survived the administrations of 10 presidents. I was at one of the Washington Senators' final baseball games in 1971 and at one of the Washington Nationals' first games in 2005. The kids are now grown and are parents themselves. In the blink of an eye, I morphed into the grandmother of four munchkins whom I delight in introducing to the wonders of the nation's capital. Heaven knows my step is a bit slower, and I have more silver in my hair than in my jewelry box. Restaurants, hotels, dress codes—and many of the major players—have come and gone. But some things haven't changed. I still get a thrill on Capitol Hill. And when I walk past the White House. Or visit the newest zoo babies at the National Zoo. Or take in a world-class exhibition at one of the myriad museums or galleries. And whenever I'm downtown with the family, if you dig into my backpack, you'll still find—tucked beneath the tissues and snacks and crayons—my notepad and pen.

There's no doubt that living in or visiting the Center of the Free World can be an exciting and educational experience. Washington produces and employs more spin-doctors than anywhere else on the planet. This is not only the nation's capital, but also the *world* capital of security leaks. This is where congressional investigations, protests, spies, filibusters, motorcades, and national debts in the zillions are as commonplace as crabs in the Chesapeake Bay—or corn in Iowa. It's a place where our presidents take the oath of office outside the Capitol and subsequently lie in state in its Rotunda. D.C. is where protestors and special-interest groups converge to exercise their rights to free speech and assembly. Washington is where today's rumors bump noses with tomorrow's headlines—and coverups. What better place for children to learn the inner workings of our unique, if at times confounding, form of government?

If you scratch the District's grimy bureaucratic surface, you'll uncover a cosmopolitan city that is rich in history—a microcosm of the American experience and a living classroom. No wonder it's a top travel destination for families. For most of us who live in the Washington metropolitan area, D.C. is less about executive privilege, multibillion-dollar budgets, federal buyouts, and votes than it is about *home*—a vibrant multicultural city where we work, play, and raise our kids. A place where families fly kites on the Mall or listen to free concerts from front-row blankets on the Capitol lawn. Where we pause, in awe, to watch the president's motorcade pass by, even if we dislike the current president's policies (or the president). We frequently spot—on city streets, in restaurants, shops, and theaters—legislators, media moguls, and Hollywood celebs. We never tire of visiting the city's magnificent landmarks, sights, and diverse neighborhoods, whether on foot or via Metro, bicycle, open-air tram, cruise boat, or kayak.

Washington, D.C., is just another place on the map. And it's like nowhere else.

Kids and Washington, D.C., go together like peanut butter and jelly. Little wonder, then, that children of all ages come to know and love the fascinating international playground that is the nation's capital. Washington has broad, tree-lined boulevards, numerous parks and recreational areas, and multiethnic shops and restaurants, not to mention a host of attractions (historic and new), waiting to be discovered and rediscovered. The nation's capital is a natural as a family vacation destination. Not bad for a 69-square-mile parcel of former swampland!

Some 16.6 million visitors traveled to Washington in 2008, with double-digit growth from international visitors. Rest assured, the District pulls out all the stops to extend a friendly hand to families. Local hotels bend over backward to cater to families by offering special rates and perks to those with kids in tow. And restaurants go out of their way to please pint-size patrons, with kids' menus, half portions, crayons—and sometimes free food. It's no accident that thousands of buses and planeloads of schoolchildren arrive annually from all over the world. Where else can kids visit the president's house, touch a moon rock, view the city from atop a 555-foot obelisk, and cruise the Potomac on a luxury yacht or the C&O Canal on a mule-drawn boat—all within minutes of the U.S. Capitol? And that's just for openers!

Despite the staggering number of museums and federal buildings, much of downtown Washington resembles an enormous park. First-time visitors are quick to note the abundance of greenery cozying up to all the marble and granite. In fact, gardens, fountains, and parks hug most major sightseeing attractions. The area known as the National Mall (stretching for 2 miles from the U.S. Capitol to the Lincoln Memorial) is the perfect site for chasing pigeons or flying a kite. Anyone with kids knows that they have short attention spans and typically get bored and antsy after an hour in a museum. These same kids, cranky from being cooped up and longing for physical activity, can exit almost any museum in D.C. onto a glorified yard and let loose.

Compared with other urban areas, both in the United States and abroad, Washington's skyline is surprisingly and refreshingly uncluttered. You can thank the Founding Fathers for that: Because the original city planners declared that no building could be higher than the dome of the U.S. Capitol, the height of commercial buildings is strictly regulated to 110 feet. And if you've visited other major cities recently, you'll be pleased to discover that Washington's foremost tourist areas are clean and safe.

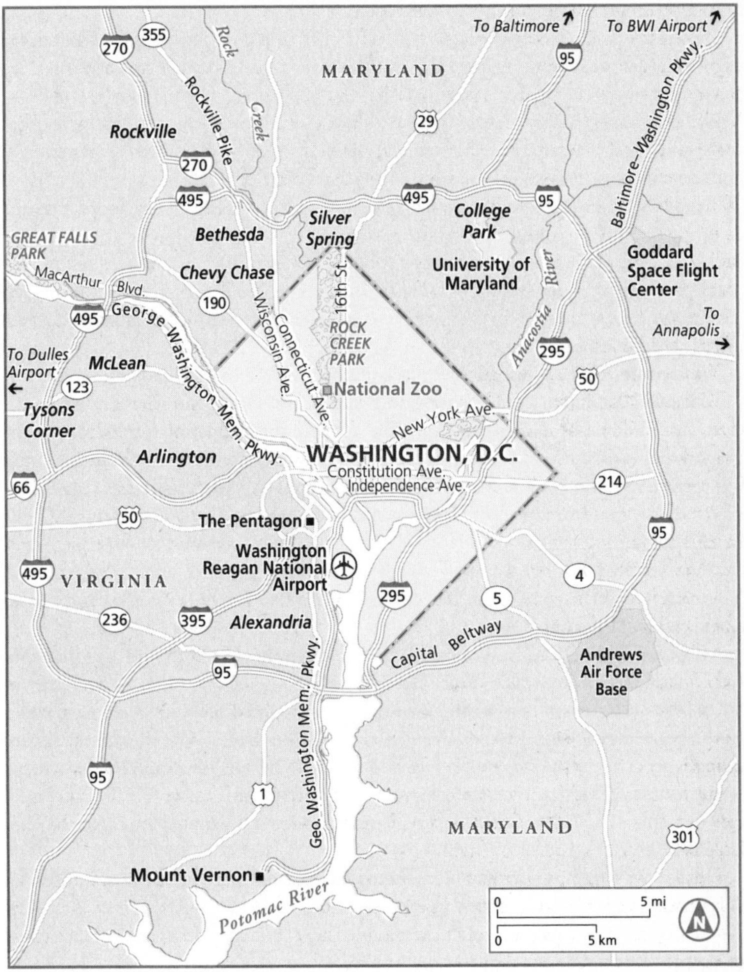

Getting around D.C. is a breeze. All major attractions are accessible by the Metro, the public rail/bus system. Despite the occasional delay, the subways are clean, safe, and surprisingly graffiti free. They're also quiet. It's easy to navigate the city with kids on the Metro, even if they're in strollers. Some stations are at hotels, shops, and food courts listed in this book. Most are within a couple of blocks of your destination. And except for a few neighborhoods, where you're not apt to be in the first place, you can unleash older children to wander on their own. Teenagers will enjoy exploring areas such as Georgetown and Old Town Alexandria, which are uniquely appealing to this age group.

You don't need a degree in accounting—or a huge budget—to plan a D.C. vacation! Prices for food, lodging, and entertainment compare favorably with those of other tourist meccas around the United States and around the world. If you've recently been to New York, London, Los Angeles, or Rome, you'll find Washington a relative bargain—even if you can't sleep for free in the White House and have pillow fights with Malia and Sasha. Families also find that they can eat well in a wide variety of kid-friendly Washington restaurants without breaking the bank. Best of all, almost all the major attractions are free. Try that in New York or Paris!

Tourism is the second-largest industry in D.C. The first, as you might have guessed, is the federal government. The "natives" (sort of an inside joke, because so many residents come from somewhere else) are friendly, helpful, and eager to make visitors feel at home. Washington is, after all, everyone's home, and it tends to engender a sense of belonging to short-term guests as well as longtime residents.

Although D.C.'s citizens enjoy many perks, they have suffered, one way or another, because of local politics. Here's why. According to the Constitution, Congress has the power to "exercise exclusive legislation . . . over the seat of the Government of the United States." Believe it or not, before 1961 and the passage of the 23rd Amendment, residents of the District could not vote in national elections. Under the Reorganization of 1967, the president appointed a mayor and a nine-member council to govern the District.

In 1970, Congress okayed legislation for a delegate to represent the District in the House of Representatives, but here's the catch: This rep can vote on committees but not on legislation on the House floor. When we went to press, the House Rules Committee was working on legislative details, introduced in February 2009, that will give D.C.'s congressional rep the right to vote on legislation on the House floor.

Although Washington has had an elected mayor and city council since 1975, Congress continues its tight reign over the D.C. budget, like many parents over their kids' allowances.

Kids who'll snooze their way through American history class wake up when they tour the Capitol, White House, and other federal buildings. Being there and seeing for themselves where laws are enacted, where the president lives, and where the government works leave a mark on young minds—one that won't soon be erased. Those who live and work in the District share an immense feeling of pride. Chances are, it will rub off on you and yours during your visit.

1 FAVORITE WASHINGTON, D.C. FAMILY EXPERIENCES

- **Watching the Fourth of July Fireworks on the Mall.** You can't beat the setting of the Washington Monument grounds, National Mall, or west front of the Capitol for observing the nation's birthday. A concert by the National Symphony Orchestra, culminating in the *1812 Overture,* accompanies the magnificent pyrotechnic display. See p. 118 for a map of the Mall.
- **Seeing the Sunset Behind the Lincoln Memorial.** Make sure your camera is primed and ready to snap for one of Mother Nature's better shows. The west front section of the Capitol is the best vantage point for a sweeping view across the Mall to the Lincoln Memorial and beyond.
- **Catching a Free Concert on the Capitol Lawn.** Memorial Day and Labor

Day weekends and July 4th, local families toting blankets and chairs camp on the Capitol lawn to hear a free concert by the National Symphony Orchestra and songs by a megastar or two, and then join in the traditional singalong. See "Calendar of Kids' Favorite Events," in chapter 2, for more information.

- **Row, Row, Rowing Your Boat on the Potomac.** Don't go home without viewing Washington's waterfront and several major sights from an appropriate conveyance: rowboat, canoe, or kayak. Or let someone else play captain on a river cruise. Equally fun is pedaling a two- or four-seater around the Tidal Basin before visiting the Jefferson and FDR memorials. See "Boating," under "Outdoor Activities," in chapter 8.
- **Picnicking on the Mall.** Grab takeout from a food court, restaurant, food emporium (Whole Foods, Dean & Deluca, Trader Joe's), or street vendor to enjoy on the Mall. There's plenty of room on the 2-mile parcel between the Capitol and Lincoln Memorial. See p. 118.
- **Looking Up Your Congressional Representative or Senator.** Stop and say hello to the folks who partake in those lengthy and boring filibusters, battle the pigheaded opposition, and work long days (and often nights). Tell him/her how you feel—how you *really feel*—about important issues. Be prepared: You may end up shaking hands with an administrative assistant who looks about 12. Research your representatives or senators at www.senate.gov or www.house.gov, or call © **202/224-3121.** See p. 156 for more information on visiting the U.S. Capitol.
- **Spying on the Giant Pandas at the National Zoo.** Tai Shan, born July 9, 2005, was due to move to China in the first quarter of 2010. His parents, Mei Shang and Tian Tian, are scheduled to leave lat in 2010. With any luck, and before packing their bags, they will produce a baby panda (via artificial insemination) spring-summer 2010. Meanwhile, use the zoo's Panda Cam. See p. 138.
- **Taking Pictures of the Cherry Blossoms.** Forget about buying those touched-up postcards. Make your own. Photos of the cherry blossoms, the White House, or other famous D.C. sights make stunning cards to mail or e-mail to friends and family. My grandkids bring disposable cameras to record their own memories.
- **Listening to a Military Band Concert.** March yourself over to a free military band concert, and salute the red, white, and blue. The concerts are held two or three evenings a week in summer at several D.C. venues and Arlington Memorial Cemetery. See "Military Band Concerts," under "Music," in chapter 10.
- **Seeing a Free Movie on the Mall.** Families blanket the Washington Monument grounds summer evenings for "Screen on the Green," free screenings of classics, such as *Rebel Without a Cause* and *Close Encounters of the Third Kind,* under the stars. See p. 251.
- **Getting a Bird's-Eye View from the Washington Monument.** Order timed passes in advance and thrill to a panorama of downtown D.C.; Arlington, Virginia; and beyond. Yes, it is touristy, and yes, it is usually crowded. And those with altitude issues may not want to linger. Go anyway. If you've been during the day, go at night. You may not recognize the sights, but the view is spectacular! See p. 146.
- **Reading the Charters of Freedom at the Archives.** A moving experience awaits visitors, especially first-timers, regardless of their hailing port. Avoid lines and make reservations to see the Declaration of Independence, Constitution, and Bill of Rights in the National Archives Building. See p. 166.

- **Experiencing America the Beautiful and the History of Flight in *To Fly* at the Air and Space Museum's IMAX Theater.** What is it about this movie that debuted in 1976? Crowds still line up to view it. My eyes still mist over at the breathtaking photography—and I've seen it more than a dozen times. See p. 125.

2 BEST HOTEL BETS

- **Most Family-Friendly Hotel near the Mall:** The **JW Marriott,** 1331 Pennsylvania Ave. NW (✆ **202/393-2000**), and **L'Enfant Plaza,** 480 L'Enfant Plaza SW (✆ **202/484-1000**), are each less than a 10-minute walk to the Mall. Both offer plenty of family perks, along with nearby sightseeing, dining, and shopping opportunities. And both have direct access to the Metro, so no raindrops need fall on your heads. See p. 58.
- **Most Child-Pampering Hotel:** The **Four Seasons,** 2800 Pennsylvania Ave. NW (✆ **800/332-3442** or 202/342-0444), does not discriminate, pampering children every bit as much as their parents. Some of the hotel's kid-spoiling tactics include personalized cookies, bucket of bath toys, coloring books and crayons, and "sushi" (Rice Krispies treats rolled with gummy bears). See p. 64.
- **Most Fun for Kids 5 and Older:** The **Helix,** 1430 Rhode Island Ave. NW (✆ **800/706-1202** or 202/462-9001), knows how to create the right atmosphere for young-at-heart fun-seekers. When was the last time you had a pillow fight? Well, get on the stick! Request the Family Bunk Room for four, with a king and double-decker bed (top single, bottom double), and battle it out for the top berth. See p. 62.
- **Best Views: L'Enfant Plaza,** 480 L'Enfant Plaza SW (✆ **202/484-1000**), has rooms that enjoy views of the Potomac River; Arlington, Virginia; and Georgetown. See p. 59 Some top-floor rooms of the **Omni Shoreham,** 2500 Calvert St. NW (✆ **202/234-0700**), overlook Rock Creek Park and/or downtown. See p. 67.
- **Best Value for Families:** The **Hotel Harrington,** 11th and E streets NW (✆ **202/628-8140**), is a centrally located, family-run property with three restaurants and double, triple, and quad rooms. Don't expect bells and whistles (or room service), but for location and value, you can't beat it. See p. 61.
- **Best Suite Deals: Georgetown Suites Washington D.C.,** 2500 Pennsylvania Ave. NW (✆ **877/736-2500** or 202/333-8060), is a short walk from the Foggy Bottom Metro and has lots more to recommend it—kids 18 and under stay free in the same suite (with a separate bedroom), and the hotel offers complimentary cribs, strollers, and expanded continental breakfast daily. Pets are welcome, too. You'll find a Trader Joe's across the street and a slew of neighborhood restaurants within a few blocks. See p. 66.
- **Best Bargain for Families: Hostelling International–Washington, D.C.,** 1009 11th St. NW, at K Street (✆ **202/737-2333**). If you don't mind roughing it a bit, staying here is a bargain and makes for a unique family experience not far from the action. Kids 2 and under are free if they share a parent's bed. A pool table and piano are available to guests and special family activities are gratis. See p. 56.
- **Hippest Bathrooms:** The **Helix,** 1430 Rhode Island Ave. NW (✆ **800/706-1202** or 202/462-9001). Better than a

jolt of java in the morning are the Helix's minimalist, crayon-colored bathrooms. What? A bathroom without a traditional vanity? Where does the water go? And how does it get there? This could be the most fun your family members have ever had brushing their teeth. See p. 62.

- **Most Peace and Quiet: Morrison-Clark Historic Hotel,** 1015 L St. NW (btw. 11th St. and Massachusetts Ave.; ✆ **800/332-7898** or 202/898-1200). Opt for a room with a porch or balcony overlooking the garden courtyard. Stay here for a genteel experience that's a tad off the beaten path yet convenient to the Metro and the sights. Kids 16 and under stay free with a parent, and weekend breakfast is complimentary. See p. 56.
- **Coolest Decor: Helix,** 1430 Rhode Island Ave. NW (✆ **800/706-1202** or 202/462-9001). In a town that takes itself too seriously, here are royal blue and orange countertops, curtained platform beds, floating entertainment centers, lava lamps, and Pop Rocks in the honor bar. This is hotel as entertainment. See p. 62.
- **Best Pool: L'Enfant Plaza,** 480 L'Enfant Plaza (✆ **202/484-1000**). The attractive outdoor pool (covered in the winter) is surrounded by potted flowering plants and has plenty of seating. Many families request a room off the pool. (This also provides front-row seating for watching the Fourth of July fireworks!) See p. 59.
- **Best Hotel Food Deal for Kids:** At the **Grand Hyatt at Washington Convention Center,** 1000 H St. NW (✆ **800/233-1234** or 202/582-1234), kids 3 and under eat for free in the Grand Cafe; kids 12 and under can order from the kids' menu or from the regular menu for half price. See p. 57.
- **Most Welcoming to Pets:** The **Hotel Monaco Alexandria,** in Old Town, 480 King St., Alexandria, Virginia (✆ **703/549-6080**), hosts Doggy Happy Hour every Tuesday and Thursday from 5 to 8pm, April through October. Bring Fido for water and biscuits, while you enjoy drinks, light fare, and pooch-watching in the brick courtyard. See p. 72.
- **Best for Athletic Families:** The jocks and jockettes in your family will love the **Omni Shoreham,** 2500 Calvert St. NW (✆ **202/234-0700**), for its oversize outdoor pool and extensive grounds for power walks or jogs. Exit the hotel's back door to Rock Creek Park's 10 miles of hiking and biking trails and its 1.5-mile fitness course with 18 exercise stations. You can also walk to the zoo. See p. 67.

3 BEST DINING BETS

- **Best Burgers: Five Guys** has raised the bar on fast food. I like 'em so much, I have their number programmed into my cell phone. Try these D.C. locations: 1645 Connecticut Ave. NW (Dupont Circle; ✆ **202/328-3483**), 1825 Eye St. NW (downtown; ✆ **202/223-2737**), 808 H St. (Chinatown, near Verizon Center; ✆ **202/393-2900**), 1335 Wisconsin Ave. (Georgetown; ✆ **202/337-0400**), 13th and F streets NW (Eat at National Place, downtown; ✆ **202/393-2135**). And order fries with that! In the Maryland suburbs, try **Houston's Woodmont Grille,** 7715 Woodmont Ave., which consistently serves the best burgers in the area. Go at off times or bring a copy of *War and Peace* to read while you wait.
- **Best Hot Dogs: Nathan's,** the top "dawgs" introduced in 1916 in NYC, get my vote. Try one at Flamers, in the

Food Court at the Ronald Reagan Building and International Trade Center, 1300 Pennsylvania Ave. NW (✆ **202/842-0027**), or Union Station, 50 Massachusetts Ave. NW (✆ **202/289-1908**). Runner-up goes to **Sabrett's.** Just look for the carts with the blue and yellow umbrellas, downtown and near the Mall. See p. 85.

- **Best Kids' Menu:** I wish I were a kid again so I could order from the kids' menu at the **Austin Grill,** 750 E St. NW (✆ **202/393-3776**). For $7, *los niños* can have a taco, enchilada, quesadilla, or nachos, or a burger, grilled cheese, or PB&J with a drink and a side dish. Ice cream is only $2 more. On Tuesdays, kids eat free. Honest! See p. 87.
- **Best Place for Politicking:** Head for the exclusive **Senate Dining Room** (✆ **202/224-2350**), in the U.S. Capitol, to rub elbows with U.S. senators and order a tureen of famous Senate Bean Soup, which, after many years, is still a deal at $6. You'll need a "request letter," and men must wear a suit and tie to experience this D.C. moment. See the introduction to the "Capitol Hill" section of chapter 5 for more information.
- **Best Pizza: Pizzeria Paradiso,** at 2003 P St. NW (✆ **202/223-1245**) and 3282 M St. NW (✆ **202/337-1245**), is *the* place for wood-oven-baked classic pizza. I usually stick to the basic Margherita or Quattro Formaggi (four cheeses)—pizza this good doesn't need extra toppings. See p. 102.
- **Best Tex-Mex: Austin Grill,** 750 E St. NW, between 7th and 8th streets (✆ **202/393-3776**), and in the Maryland and Virginia burbs, has a varied menu of *deliciosa* Tex-Mex favorites, and margaritas for Mom and Dad. *¡Muy bueno!* See p. 87.
- **Best Food Court:** The **Food Court** at the **Ronald Reagan Building and International Trade Center,** 1300 Pennsylvania Ave. NW (✆ **202/312-1300**), near the Federal Triangle Metro station, is a centrally located refueling spot (less than a 10-min. walk from the Washington Monument or the Mall) for hungry sightseers. Belly up to one of the stands for hamburgers, hot dogs, chicken, salads, deli, Cajun, wraps, subs, smoothies, gelato, and ethnic fare (pizza, sushi, dim sum, and filled pita). From spring through fall, you can take lunch outside, where there's free entertainment. On Capitol Hill, you will find similar fare, with even more selections (plus all those trains and shops), at **Union Station,** 50 Massachusetts Ave. NE (✆ **202/371-9441**). See p. 84.
- **Best Restaurant for Teens:** A trip to the **Hard Rock Cafe,** 999 E St. NW, next to Ford's Theatre (✆ **202/737-ROCK** [7625]), will make you a hero to your kids. Here, you can ogle (depending on your age) one of Michael Jackson's leather jackets, an autographed Stones photo, or one of Chuck Berry's guitars. This will take your mind off the food, which is okay but nothing to write a song about. See p. 87.
- **Best Ice Cream: Gifford's,** 555 11th St. NW (✆ **202/347-7755**). Also in Chevy Chase, Bethesda, and Rockville, Maryland, Gifford's has been pleasing generations of area ice-cream lovers for decades with its rich ice cream treats. Try the hot fudge or Swiss sundaes or double-dip cone. See p. 89. Behind by a nose, but missing the local flavor, is any one of **Ben & Jerry's** six D.C. locations. See p. 85.
- **Best Ice Cream Parlor: Thomas Sweet** ("Sweet's" to locals), 3214 P St. NW (at Wisconsin Ave.; ✆ **202/337-0616**), reminds me of my youth, and the Malt Shoppe in Archie comics. The ice cream is made on the premises, and a kids size single-dip ice cream cone is $3; a large single-dip, $4. Quite a deal in this day and age. See p. 97.

- **Best Milkshake: Chick & Ruth's Delly,** 165 Main St., Annapolis, Maryland (✆ **410/269-6737**), makes the kind of thick shakes and malts of which poetry is written. If you have to ask how much ice cream goes into these monsters, you shouldn't go here. Your family could share one of these giant-size babies and leave some in the glass. See p. 275.
- **Best Breakfast: The Market Lunch** (in Eastern Market), 225 7th St. SE (✆ **202/547-8444**), is the place for "Bluebucks" (buckwheat blueberry pancakes) and local Capitol Hill ambience. You may have to wait, but that's part of the experience. See p. 84. For hearty breakfast platters—bacon and eggs, omelets, and the like—head to **Afterwords Cafe,** 1517 Connecticut Ave. NW (✆ **202/387-1462;** p. 100), or **Luna Grill & Diner,** 1301 Connecticut Ave. NW (✆ **202/835-2280;** p. 100). If you want more formal trappings (for example, tablecloths), make a reservation at the **Old Ebbitt Grill,** 675 15th St. NW (✆ **202/347-4801**). See p. 90.
- **Best Place for a Picnic:** Tote that hamper or brown bag to the **National Mall,** between 4th and 7th streets NW. For picnicking alfresco, you can't beat the area between the Washington Monument and the Capitol. The mall itself is mostly dirt, from years of abuse—all those feet treading on the grass. So find a bench or sit on the museum steps. When in Georgetown, go to **Washington Harbour Park,** at the foot of Wisconsin Avenue (btw. K St. and the river). See p. 118.
- **Best Waterfront Dining:** Friends, we have a three-way tie here. **Sequoia,** 3000 K St. (✆ **202/944-4200**), perched on the Potomac in Georgetown, has a drop-dead view of the riverfront and pretty good food. At the **Chart House,** 1 Cameron St., Alexandria, Virginia (✆ **703/684-5080**), on another part of the Potomac, you can drool over the yachts, along with your coconut shrimp. **Cantler's Riverside Inn,** 458 Forest Beach Rd., Annapolis, Maryland (✆ **410/757-1311**), is situated on picturesque Mill Creek and is *the* place to go for steamed Maryland blue crabs. See p. 188, 263, and 275, respectively.
- **Best Selection: America,** 50 Massachusetts Ave. NE at Union Station (✆ **202/685-9555**), serves tasty takes on regional favorites and comfort food (meatloaf, steak, pizza, pork chops, ribs, burgers, wraps, soups, and sandwiches). Few, other than our Washington Redskins' linebackers, can finish the oversize portions here. Let the kids split an order, or doggie-bag the leftovers. See p. 84.
- **Best Romantic Restaurant (for a Night When You Hire a Sitter):** The **Sea Catch Restaurant and Raw Bar,** at Canal Square, 1054 31st St. NW, Georgetown (✆ **202/337-8855**), has seating overlooking the picturesque C&O Canal. Many think the restaurant serves the best seafood in D.C. Enjoy drinks and tapas, and a primo view of downtown, at **POV (Point of View),** on the top floor of the W Washington hotel, 515 15th St. NW (✆ **202/661-2400**). Make a reservation for a coveted outdoor table as soon as you plan your escape. See p. 94 and 90.

4 BEST OF THE BEST

- **Best Place to Run Around:** Head for the **National Mall** (you can't miss it—just step outside almost any Smithsonian museum) or Washington Harbour Park, on the Potomac River, at Wisconsin Avenue and K Street. If you have time, go to **Rock Creek Park,** at 5200 Glover Rd. NW (© **202/426-6829**), where you may also ride bikes or horses, play tennis or golf, gaze at the stars, swing, slide, hike, or rent a boat on the C&O Canal or Potomac. See p. 204.

- **Best Views: The Washington Monument,** 15th Street and Constitution Avenue NW (© **202/426-6841**), can't be beat. Order timed passes, so you don't have to wait in line. See p. 146. You'll rarely have a wait at the **Old Post Office,** 1100 Pennsylvania Ave. NW (© **202/289-4224**). Take the elevator to the clock tower for a panoramic view of downtown and beyond. See p. 164. The **National Cathedral,** Massachusetts and Wisconsin avenues NW (© **202/537-6200**), is a bit out of the way, but the view from the Pilgrim Observation Gallery is spectacular. See p. 152.
- **Best Ride for Kids:** Both the **Carousel on the Mall,** 1000 Jefferson Dr. SW (on the Mall outside the Smithsonian "Castle"; © **202/633-1000**), and the **Dentzel Carousel** at Glen Echo Park, MacArthur Boulevard at Goldsborough Road, Glen Echo, Maryland (© **301/492-6282**), get my vote. See "Carousels," under "Rides for Children," in chapter 8.
- **Best Souvenirs:** For D.C.-inspired mementoes—shirts, hats, books, mugs, paperweights—go to **Souvenir City,** 1001 K St. NW (btw. 10th and 11th sts.; © **202/638-1836**). For museum-quality souvenirs go to any museum store. See p. 237.
- **Best Toy Store: Barston's Child's Play,** 5536 Connecticut Ave. (© **202/244-3602**), and **Sullivan's,** 3412 Wisconsin Ave. NW (© **202/362-1343**), get my vote and have stood the test of time. Both are in the Friendship Heights neighborhood, because that's where a large number of affluent D.C. families live. Though they're a bit out of the way if you're staying in downtown D.C., the stores are well stocked and excel at giving their young customers one-on-one attention. (For this toy shopper, they are a refreshing alternative to the large, impersonal toy "factories," where customer service is far from the number-one concern.) See p. 236.
- **Best History Lesson:** For older kids, sitting in the **House or Senate galleries at the U.S. Capitol,** East Capitol Street and 1st Street NE (© **202/225-6827**), when either is in session, is to view history in the making. Bear in mind that the House and Senate are not in session all the time. You can check the local papers or the Capitol website to see what is on the docket. See p. 156.
- **Most Unusual Tours: D.C. Ducks,** Union Station, 50 Massachusetts Ave. NE (© **202/966-DUCK** [3825]), departs Union Station to tour various Washington, D.C., sights on land and sea (the Potomac River) in refurbished World War II amphibious vehicles. With precocious kids 10 and older, take the 2-hour **Spy City Tour,** cosponsored by the International Spy Museum and Grayline, Tuesdays and Saturdays at 10am (800 F St. NW; © **202/EYE-SPY-U** [393-7798]). See p. 218 and 173.

2

Planning a Family Trip to Washington, D.C.

Logistics take on a whole new meaning when you're dealing with a group—nothing is simple when the needs of the many must be taken into account, as happens with most (successful) family vacations. Happily, I've trooped all over Washington, D.C. on your behalf, and thought long and hard about the details so that you won't have to work too hard to devise a terrific trip to suit your own entourage.

1 WHEN TO GO

For obvious reasons, you'll probably plan your visit for spring or summer, when the kids are out of school. That's fine, but understand that the warm-weather months are when Washington is most crowded. One exception: Late August is beyond quiet. Although summer is the best time to take advantage of numerous free outdoor events and reduced hotel rates, the heat and humidity can wilt a cactus. However, if you dress appropriately and sightsee early or late in the day, you'll fare well.

July and August are the warmest months, with average highs in the mid-80s (mid-20s Celsius). This is not to say that it won't heat up to the mid-90s (mid-30s Celsius)—it does with disturbing regularity and oppressively high humidity. Fortunately, all the public buildings, restaurants, and hotels in Washington are air-conditioned, and many hotels have swimming pools.

If your kids are preschoolers or budding geniuses who can afford to miss school (or are lucky enough to have a fall break), fall is a lovely time to visit. The weather is usually pleasant and mild, and you can enjoy the city while the rest of the world is at home, at work, or at school. In winter, hotel prices usually dip around the Christmas holidays, and lines at attractions are shorter.

Highs in December, January, and February are in the mid-40s (around 5°C), with lows around 30°F (–1°C). Again, these are averages. The rainfall is evenly distributed throughout the year, so don't leave home without a raincoat.

Average Monthly Temperatures

	Jan	Feb	Mar	Apr	May	June	July	Aug	Sept	Oct	Nov	Dec
Avg. High (°F)	45	44	53	64	75	83	87	84	78	68	55	45
Avg. High (°C)	7	7	12	18	24	28	31	29	26	20	13	7
Avg. Low (°F)	27	28	35	44	55	63	68	66	60	48	38	30
Avg. Low (°C)	–3	–2	2	7	13	17	20	19	16	9	3	–1

CALENDAR OF KIDS' FAVORITE EVENTS

Whether you decide to visit Washington in June or in January or any time in between, you'll find a wide range of special events to enhance your sightseeing. Most are free. For the latest information before you leave home, contact the **Washington, D.C. Convention & Tourism Corporation,** 901 7th St. NW, 4th Floor, Washington, DC 20001 (✆ **202/789-7000;** www.washington.org), and request the quarterly "Calendar of Events" brochure.

The **D.C. Visitor Information Center,** in the Ronald Reagan Building, 1300 Pennsylvania Ave., is a one-stop shop for brochures and information (✆ **866/DC-IS-FUN** [324-7386]; www.dcvisit.com).

The **White House Visitors Center,** on the southeast corner of 15th and E streets NW, is open daily from 7:30am to 4pm. Stop in to view the 30-minute video and see the exhibits about the home's architecture, history, and first families (✆ **202/208-1631;** www.whitehouse.gov). Also consult the "Weekend" magazine of the *Washington Post* every Friday. Before you attend a special event, it's smart to call and verify the time and location. Some changes and cancellations are inevitable.

For a listing of events beyond those here, see http://events.frommers.com.

January

Martin Luther King, Jr.'s Birthday. This national holiday is celebrated the third Monday in January, with speeches, dance performances, and choral presentations citywide, as well as a wreath-laying ceremony at the Lincoln Memorial. Check local newspapers for free commemorative events, or call ✆ **202/619-7222** (www.nps.gov).

Robert E. Lee's Birthday Bash. Lee's birthday is observed January 19 at Arlington House, in Arlington National Cemetery, and the free celebration features 19th-century music, food, and memorabilia (✆ **703/607-8000;** www.arlingtoncemetery.org). You can also visit the **Lee-Fendall House,** at 614 Oronoco St., in Old Town Alexandria (✆ **703/548-1789;** www.leefendallhouse.org).

Inauguration Day. This monumental event is held on January 20 of every fourth year when the president is sworn in at the West Front of the Capitol. The next presidential inauguration will be January 20, 2013. A colorful and *very* lengthy parade follows the ceremony from the Capitol to the White House along Pennsylvania Avenue. Admission is free.

February

Black History Month. This is observed by museums, libraries, and recreation centers, with special exhibits, events, and performances to celebrate African-American contributions to American life. Check local newspapers and magazines for events, or call ✆ **202/633-1000.**

Abraham Lincoln's Birthday. A moving wreath-laying ceremony and reading of the *Gettysburg Address* at the Lincoln Memorial on February 12 commemorate the birthday of the 16th U.S. president. Admission is free. It's truly inspiring (✆ **202/426-6841;** www.nps.gov).

Chinese New Year Parade. Although younger kids might be frightened by the firecrackers, the colorful street parade of lions and dragons, dancers, and music-makers through Chinatown (H St. NW, btw. 5th and 7th sts.) is great family fun. After the parade, fill up on dumplings and duck (Peking, of course) at one of Chinatown's many restaurants. ***Note:*** Sometimes the Chinese New Year starts in late January. Blame it on the moon.

George Washington's Birthday. The father of our country's birthday is celebrated with a parade through Old Town Alexandria's historic district on the Saturday closest to his February 22 birthday. The free parade begins at Wilkes and St. Asaph streets. Wear your finest white stockings and a powdered wig (✆ **703/746-3301** or 800/388-9119; www.visitalexandriava.com). On February 22, a free ceremony is held at the Washington Monument (✆ **202/426-6841;** www.nps.gov). George Washington's Mount Vernon estate features a free family celebration on Presidents' Day, on the third Monday of the month (✆ **703/780-2000;** www.mountvernon.org).

March

St. Patrick's Day Parades. On the Sunday before St. Patty's Day (on Mar 17, when it falls on a Sun), it's top o' the mornin' at the festive afternoon parade down Constitution Avenue, from 7th to 17th streets NW, with floats, bagpipes, bands, and dancers (✆ **202/637-2474;** www.dcstpatsparade.com). Old Town Alexandria also celebrates the wearin' of the green with a procession down King Street (✆ **703/237-2199;** www.ballyshaners.org).

Ringling Bros. and Barnum & Bailey Circus. The "Greatest Show on Earth" pitches its tent at the Verizon Center and the Patriot Center, Fairfax, Virginia, for several weeks of thrills and chills extending into April. Treat your kids, if they've never been (✆ **703/448-4000;** www.ringling.com).

Smithsonian Kite Festival. Breeze on down to the Washington Monument grounds for this free annual event, which draws kite makers from all over the country. Prizes and trophies are awarded for homemade kites, but you must register between 10am and noon (✆ **202/633-1000;** www.kitefestival.org).

National Cherry Blossom Festival. If you hit this right—no snow, no gale winds, no August-in-spring weather—the vision of thousands of cherry trees blooming around the Tidal Basin will take your breath away. There is a parade of floats with cherry-blossom princesses from each state, free concerts, a marathon, a Japanese lantern-lighting ceremony, and fireworks (✆ **877/44BLOOM** [442-5666]; www.nationalcherryblossomfestival.org). Late March to early April. See "Parks, Gardens & Other Wide-Open Spaces," in chapter 8, for more about the famed trees.

April

White House Easter Egg Roll. Children 8 and under, accompanied by an adult, are invited on Easter Monday to the South Lawn of the White House, where free eggs and entertainment are dished out. Although there's a crunch of people and eggshells, your kids might find the event "egg-citing." No yolk! Line up early at the southeast gate of the White House on East Executive Avenue. Admission is free. Call ✆ **202/456-1414** (www.whitehouse.gov) for the latest information before putting on your bunny ears.

Thomas Jefferson's Birthday. On April 13, gather at the Jefferson Memorial to honor the birthday of this Renaissance man and third U.S. president, with military drills and a wreath-laying ceremony. Admission is free (✆ **202/426-6841;** www.nps.gov/theje).

White House Garden Tour. Tour the Children's Garden, with its bronze impressions of the hands and feet of White House children and grandchildren among the tulips and azaleas, and the executive mansion's public rooms. Line up at least an hour before this weekend event. Admission is free. Call ✆ **202/456-1414** (www.whitehouse.gov) for information before going.

William Shakespeare's Birthday. The bard's birthday is celebrated the Saturday closest to April 23 at the Folger Shakespeare Library, 201 E. Capitol St. SE, with music, theater, children's events, and food. Admission is free (✆ **202/544-4600;** www.folger.edu).

May

National Cathedral Flower Mart. Children's games, flower booths, entertainment, and food spring up on the grounds of the majestic National Cathedral, Wisconsin Avenue and Woodley Road NW, during the first weekend of the month. An extensive selection of herbs is for sale (✆ **202/537-6200;** www.cathedral.org).

Air Show at Andrews AFB. Go ballistic over the Army's Golden Knights parachute team and an aerial show by the Air Force Thunderbirds in their F-16s at this weekend open house at Andrews Air Force Base, in Camp Springs, Maryland. Kids can climb aboard aircraft and tanks. Admission is free. Go early, allow plenty of driving time, and bring earplugs (✆ **301/981-1110** or 888/231-4058; www.andrews.am.af.mil).

Memorial Day Concert. The Sunday of Memorial Day weekend, Washington's own National Symphony Orchestra serenades you on the West Lawn of the Capitol. Bring a blanket. Admission is free (✆ **202/416-8100;** www.kennedy-center.org/nso).

Memorial Day Ceremonies. Witness wreath-laying ceremonies in Arlington Cemetery at the Kennedy gravesite and the Tomb of the Unknowns, and services at the Memorial Amphitheater accompanied by military bands. (✆ **703/607-8000;** www.arlingtoncemetery.org).

More Wreath-Laying Ceremonies. These ceremonies take place at the Vietnam and Korean War Veterans memorials, just south of 21st Street and Constitution Avenue NW (✆ **202/426-6841;** www.nps.gov/vive), and at the Navy Memorial, Pennsylvania Avenue, between 7th and 9th streets NW (✆ **202/737-2300;** www.navymemorial.org).

June

Civil War Living History Day. Take a torchlight tour of Union and Confederate camps, and watch "soldiers" in Civil War uniforms reenact a battle and perform drill competitions at Fort Ward Museum and Park, 4301 W. Braddock Rd., Alexandria, Virginia. Admission is free (✆ **703/838-4242;** www.oha.historicalexandria.gov).

Alexandria Red Cross Waterfront Festival. Tall ships berth at Alexandria's historic waterfront during this family oriented weekend (the second or third weekend of June), featuring games, refreshments, entertainment, arts and crafts, and the blessing of the fleet. Adults $10 in advance, $15 at gate; children 3 to 12, up to 2 free with paying adult; additional kids $5 each; 2 and under free (✆ **703/549-8300;** www.waterfrontfestival.org).

Juneteenth Jubilee. Storytellers, infantry-reenactment groups, clowns, and magicians commemorate the day Texas slaves learned of the Emancipation Proclamation. Admission is free. Check the *Washington Post* and other local papers for location, which changes from year to year (www.19thofjune.com).

Festival of American Folklife. One of the most popular annual events in the nation's capital, the 10-day folk life festival on the Mall is filled with music, crafts, and ethnic foods reflecting America's rich multicultural heritage. Admission is free (✆ **202/633-1000;** www.folklike.si.edu). ***Note:*** The festival spills over into July.

National Capital Barbecue Battle. Bring your appetite to the grandest pork barrel of them all (usually held the fourth weekend of the month). Local restaurants pit their pork against each other for a rib-roaring good time sauced with cooking demonstrations and music. Adults $10; children 6 to 12 $5; 5 and under free. Barbecue central is Pennsylvania Avenue NW, between 9th and 14th streets (✆ **202/828-3099;** www.bbqdc.com).

Greater Washington Soap Box Derby. Drivers between 9 and 16 years old coast down Capitol Hill in their aerodynamic vehicles at this traffic-stopping event that has taken place annually for more than 65 years. Admission is free (www.dcsoapboxderby.org).

July

Independence Day Celebrations. The nation's capital celebrates its birthday in grand style, beginning with a 12:30pm parade along Constitution Avenue, from 7th to 17th streets NW (✆ **800/215-6405;** www.july4thparade.com). Enjoy entertainment all afternoon at the Sylvan Theatre, on the Washington Monument grounds (✆ **202/426-6841**). At 8pm, the National Symphony plays on the Capitol's West Lawn (✆ **202/416-8100;** www.kennedy-center.org/nso), and a fantastic fireworks display starts at about 9:20pm (✆ **202/426-6841;** www.nps.gov). Bring something to sit on. Admission is free. Check newspapers July 3 and 4 for details.

Fiesta D.C. A parade along Mt. Pleasant Street, between Park Road and Harvard Street, takes place the last Sunday of the month. Enjoy entertainment, arts and crafts, and delicious international foods between 11am and 7pm (✆ **202/232-4393;** www.fiestadc.org).

Farm Tours. The last weekend of the month, about a dozen Montgomery County, Maryland, farms open their doors and stalls to visitors. If your kids think eggs hatch in little corrugated cartons, bring them here. Some farms offer hayrides, pony rides, and other special activities—and it's an opportunity to buy just-picked produce. Admission is free (✆ **301/590-2823;** www.montgomerycountymd.gov).

August

Renaissance Festival. Crownsville, Maryland (about 30 miles from downtown), is the site of a 16th-century fair, with jousting matches, magicians, wandering minstrels, and crafts. A special children's area has pony rides, a zoo, and Tudor-era amusements. Armor up on weekends from late August to mid-October. Free for kids under 12 on Children's Weekend; always free for kids under 7. Otherwise, $18 adults; $15 seniors (62 and older); $8 children 7 to 15 (✆ **800/266-7304;** www.rennfest.com).

U.S. Army Band's *1812 Overture*. The Salute Gun Platoon of the 3rd U.S. Infantry provides the noisy finale to this patriotic free concert by the U.S. Army Band at the Sylvan Theatre, Washington Monument grounds (✆ **202/619-7222;** www.usarmyband.com).

Labor Day Concert. The National Symphony bids adieu to summer, even though it's usually still hot as blazes, with a free concert on the West Lawn of the Capitol (✆ **202/619-7222;** www.kennedy-center.org/nso).

International Children's Festival. Rain or shine, the sun will be out at Wolf Trap Farm Park in Vienna, Virginia, where crafts, music, dance workshops, and performances delight families. Admission is $10 adults and teens; $6 children and seniors; kids 2 and under free (✆ **703/255-1900;** www.wolftrap.org).

College Park Airport Open House and Air Fair. Fly over here with your crew for airplane and helicopter rides, an air show, and exhibits at the area's oldest airport, at 1909 Corporal Frank Scott Dr., College Park, Maryland (✆ **301/864-5844;** www.collegeparkairport.org).

Virginia Scottish Games. One of the largest Scottish festivals in the United States features Highland dancing, fiddling competitions, a heptathlon, animal events (sheep shearing and other activities), and plenty of long-winded bagpipers, and takes place midmonth. After years at Episcopal High School in Alexandria, Virginia, the event moved in 2007 to Sky Meadows State Park, in Delaplane, Virginia. Admission for adults $18; children 5 to 12 $5; 4 and under free (✆ **703/912-1943;** www.vascottishgames.org).

Constitution Day Commemoration. On September 17, at the National Archives, Constitution Avenue at 8th Street NW, pay your respects to the Constitution on the anniversary of its signing. A naturalization program and honor-guard ceremonies are part of the day's free events (✆ **866/272-6272;** www.archives.gov).

Rock Creek Park Day. Children's activities, environmental and recreational exhibits, foods, crafts, and music highlight the celebration of Washington's largest park, which reached the ripe old age of 120 in 2010. The free event is usually held on the Saturday closest to September 25, the park's birthday (✆ **202/895-6070;** www.nps.gov/rocr).

Folger Open House. Here's a chance to go behind the scenes in a theater. Inspect costumes and scenery, and watch a rehearsal in the Shakespeare Theatre (an authentic model of an Elizabethan theater) at the Folger Library, 201 E. Capitol St. SE. Admission is free (✆ **202/544-4600;** www.folger.edu).

Kennedy Center Open House Arts Festival. Treat your senses to a free musical celebration by more than 40 entertainers (musicians, musical groups, vocalists, choral groups, mimes, and dancers), who appear in every nook and cranny of the "Ken Cen" (✆ **202/467-4600;** www.kennedy-center.org).

Black Family Reunion Celebration. Gospel music, ethnic treats, dancing, and craft demonstrations take place on the National Mall. Admission is free (✆ **202/383-9114;** www.ncnw.org).

Greek Fall Festival. Games for kids, a Greek buffet, arts and crafts, jewelry, and Oriental rugs are featured at this lively free bazaar at Saint Sophia Cathedral, 36th Street and Massachusetts Avenue NW. Music and dancing take place after 5pm (✆ **202/333-4730;** www.saintsophiawashington.org).

October

Sugarloaf's Autumn Crafts Festival. Puppet shows, storytelling, and a petting zoo will keep the youngsters happy while grown-ups shop for holiday gifts and souvenirs sold by 400 artists and craftspeople at the Montgomery County Fairgrounds in Gaithersburg, Maryland (✆ **301/963-3247;** www.sugarloafcrafts.com).

U.S. Navy Birthday Concert. Wear your dress blues to the DAR Constitution Hall, 1776 D St. NW, for the annual concert celebrating the navy's birthday (235 years old in 2010). It's free, but tickets (four maximum per request) must be ordered in September. Send a self-addressed, stamped envelope to Navy Birthday Tickets, U.S. Navy Band, P.O. Box 70271, Washington, DC 20024-0271. For information, contact ✆ **202/433-2525** (www.navyband.navy.mil).

White House Fall Garden Tour. One weekend this month, the public is invited to visit the Rose Garden, South

Lawn, and beautiful beds of multihued chrysanthemums, as well as some of the White House's public rooms, while enjoying the upbeat sounds of military bands. Line up at the southeast gate, E Street and East Executive Avenue, an hour before the free tour starts (✆ **202/456-7041;** www.whitehouse.gov).

Theodore Roosevelt's Birthday. Even if you forgot to send a card, on the Saturday closest to T. R.'s birthday (Oct 27), you can celebrate on the island named after him, with free nature programs, island tours, and special kids' entertainment. No food is available on the island, but you can picnic outside. Theodore Roosevelt Island is off the G. W. Parkway, north of Roosevelt Bridge (✆ **703/289-2500;** www.nps.gov/this).

NOVEMBER

Veterans' Day Ceremonies. Military music accompanies a solemn ceremony honoring the nation's war dead. The Memorial Amphitheater, at Arlington National Cemetery, is the service site where the president or another high-ranking official lays a wreath at the Tomb of the Unknown Soldier (✆ **202/619-7222;** www.nps.gov or www.arlingtoncemetery.org).

DECEMBER

Festival of Music and Lights. More than 200,000 twinkling bulbs sparkle and gleam on the greenery at the Washington Mormon Temple in Kensington, Maryland, through Twelfth Night. Free concerts are held nightly until New Year's Eve (✆ **301/588-0650;** www.lds.org).

Scottish Christmas Walk. A parade through historic Old Town Alexandria, Virginia, includes Celtic activities for children, tartan-clad bagpipers and Highland dancers, and house tours (✆ **703/549-0111;** www.campagnacenter.org).

Old Town Christmas Candlelight Tours. Several historic homes, dressed in period decorations, are opened up to visitors. Music, colonial dancing, and refreshments add to the festive atmosphere. Tickets are $20 adults; $15 seniors (65 and older); $5 kids 6 to 17 (✆ **703/838-4242;** http://oha.alexandriava.gov).

Holiday Celebration. Decorated Christmas trees, holiday crafts, ethnic food, stories, and music at the Smithsonian's National Museum of American History demonstrate how Americans celebrate Christmas, Hanukkah, Kwanzaa, and New Year's. Join the holiday fun at the Smithsonian (✆ **202/633-1000;** www.si.edu).

People's Christmas Tree Lighting. The People's Christmas Tree, towering some 60 feet, is lighted each year on the west side of the Capitol to herald the holiday season. There's music, too, at this free event (✆ **202/224-3069;** www.capitolholidaytree.org).

National Christmas Tree Lighting and Pageant of Peace. Every year on the Ellipse (btw. the White House and Constitution Ave.), one or more members of the First Family throws the switch that lights the nation's blue spruce Christmas tree and 57 Scotch pine siblings, representing the 50 states, the District of Columbia, and the six U.S. territories. Free musical and choral performances take place every evening from 6 to 9pm, except Christmas, through December 30 (✆ **202/619-7222;** www.nps.gov).

U.S. Navy Band Holiday Concert. A free concert awaits all holiday revelers at DAR Constitution Hall, 1776 D St. NW. Reservations are required (✆ **202/433-6090;** www.navyband.navy.mil).

Kennedy Center Holiday Celebrations. Since its opening in 1971, the

Kennedy Center has been celebrating the holidays in grand style. The festivities include a *Messiah* Singalong, Hanukkah Festival, Christmas Eve and New Year's Eve programs, and concerts by local children's choruses. Many events are free (✆ **202/467-4600;** www.kennedy-center.org).

2 ENTRY REQUIREMENTS

PASSPORTS

Virtually every air traveler entering the U.S. is required to show a passport. All persons, including U.S. citizens, traveling by air between the United States and Canada, Mexico, Central and South America, the Caribbean, and Bermuda are required to present a valid passport. U.S. and Canadian citizens entering the U.S. at land and sea ports of entry from within the western hemisphere will need to present government-issued proof of citizenship, such as a birth certificate, along with a government-issued photo ID, such as a driver's license. A passport is not required for U.S. or Canadian citizens entering by land or sea, but it is highly encouraged to carry one.

VISAS

The U.S. Department of State has a **Visa Waiver Program (VWP)** allowing citizens of the following countries to enter the United States without a visa for stays of up to 90 days: Andorra, Australia, Austria, Belgium, Brunei, Czech Republic, Denmark, Estonia, Finland, France, Germany, Hungary, Iceland, Ireland, Italy, Japan, Latvia, Liechtenstein, Lithuania, Luxembourg, Malta, Monaco, the Netherlands, New Zealand, Norway, Portugal, Republic of Korea, San Marino, Singapore, Slovakia, Slovenia, Spain, Sweden, Switzerland, and the United Kingdom. (***Note:*** This list was accurate at press time; for the most up-to-date list of countries in the VWP, consult http://travel.state.gov/visa.) Even though a visa isn't necessary, in an effort to help U.S. officials check travelers against terror watch lists before they arrive at U.S. borders, visitors from VWP countries must register online through the **Electronic System for Travel Authorization (ESTA)** before boarding a plane or a boat to the U.S. Travelers will complete an electronic application providing basic personal and travel eligibility information. The Department of Homeland Security recommends filling out the form at least 3 days before traveling. Authorizations will be valid for up to 2 years or until the traveler's passport expires, whichever comes first. Currently, there is no fee for the online application. ***Note:*** Any passport issued on or after October 26, 2006, by a VWP country must be an **e-Passport** for VWP travelers to be eligible to enter the U.S. without a visa. Citizens of these nations also need to present a round-trip air or cruise ticket upon arrival. E-Passports contain computer chips capable of storing biometric information, such as the required digital photograph of the holder. If your passport doesn't have this feature, you can still travel without a visa if it is a valid passport issued before October 26, 2005, and includes a machine-readable zone, or between October 26, 2005, and October 25, 2006, and includes a digital photograph. For more information, go to http://travel.state.gov/visa. Canadian citizens may enter the United States without visas; they will need to show passports (if traveling by air) and proof of residence, however.

Citizens of all other countries must have (1) a valid passport that expires at least 6 months later than the scheduled end of their visit to the U.S., and (2) a tourist visa.

To find out if you need a Visa to travel to the U.S., go to www.travel.state.gov to see your country's requirements. For information on obtaining a visa, see "Visas" (p. 292).

CUSTOMS

What You Can Bring Into the U.S.

Every visitor older than 21 years of age may bring in, free of duty, the following: (1) 1 liter of wine or hard liquor; (2) 200 cigarettes, 100 cigars (but not from Cuba), or 3 pounds of smoking tobacco; and (3) $100 worth of gifts. These exemptions are offered to travelers who spend at least 72 hours in the United States and who have not claimed them within the preceding 6 months. It is forbidden to bring into the country almost any meat products (including canned, fresh, and dried meat products such as bullion, soup mixes, and more). Generally, condiments including vinegars, oils, spices, coffee, tea, and some cheeses and baked goods are permitted. Avoid rice products, as rice can often harbor insects. Bringing fruits and vegetables is not advised, though not prohibited. Customs will allow produce depending on where you got it and where you're going after you arrive in the U.S. International visitors may carry in or out up to $10,000 in U.S. or foreign currency with no formalities; larger sums must be declared to U.S. Customs on entering or leaving, which includes filing form CM 4790. For details regarding U.S. Customs and Border Protection, consult your nearest U.S. embassy or consulate, or **U.S. Customs** (www.customs.gov).

What You Can Take Home from Washington, D.C.

For information on what you're allowed to bring home, contact one of the following agencies:

U.S. Citizens: U.S. Customs & Border Protection (CBP), 1300 Pennsylvania Ave., NW, Washington, DC 20229 (✆ **877/287-8667;** www.cbp.gov).

Canadian Citizens: Canada Border Services Agency (✆ **800/461-9999** in Canada, or 204/983-3500; www.cbsa-asfc.gc.ca).

U.K. Citizens: HM Customs & Excise at ✆ **0845/010-9000** (from outside the U.K., 020/8929-0152), or consult their website at **www.hmce.gov.uk**.

Australian Citizens: Australian Customs Service at ✆ **1300/363-263,** or log on to **www.customs.gov.au**.

New Zealand Citizens: New Zealand Customs, The Customhouse, 17–21 Whitmore St., Box 2218, Wellington (✆ **04/473-6099** or 0800/428-786; www.customs.govt.nz).

MEDICAL REQUIREMENTS

Unless you're arriving from an area known to be suffering from an epidemic (particularly cholera or yellow fever), inoculations or vaccinations are not required for entry into the United States.

3 GETTING THERE

BY PLANE

Three airports serve the Washington, D.C. area. General information follows that should help you determine which airport is your best bet. See chapter 12, "Fast Facts," for the listing of airlines that travel to Washington, D.C. and their websites, p. 293.

A note for **international visitors:** Some large airlines offer transatlantic or transpacific passengers special discount tickets under the name **Visit USA,** which allows

Show & Tell: Getting the Kids Interested in D.C.

Successful family vacations don't just happen serendipitously. Below are some suggestions to get them involved and excited for your trip. If you follow these simple guidelines, your family should have a good time and will fill several scrapbooks with happy memories:

- **Help your children gather information about the nation's capital.** Supplement your kids' knowledge of D.C. by borrowing from the library or purchasing a basic book about the city and reading it with them nightly before your trip.
- **Think small.** Prioritize your sightseeing objectives, leaving time for recreational and spontaneous activities such as chasing squirrels and eating ice cream.
- Of course, as a family vacation destination, Washington is anything but boring and yucky. Your mission, should you decide to accept it, is **to get your kids so fired up** about the impending trip that they probably won't sleep the night before you leave home.
- **Plan ahead and allow every family member input** in organizing your sightseeing schedule. Contact your congressional rep if you wish to do the following: Eat lunch in the members' dining room or take VIP tours of the Capitol, White House (groups of 10 or more only), Kennedy Center, Bureau of Engraving and Printing, or FBI Building (if or when it reopens—no date had been set when this book went to press, so check before your visit: ✆ **202/324-3447;** www.fbi.gov). Doing so will allow you to tour with a smaller group. Passes are limited, and 6 months before your visit is not too soon to write. Send your request, with the dates of your trip, names of people in your party, your phone number, and mailing address, to your senator, c/o U.S. Senate, Washington, DC 20510, or your representative, c/o U.S. House of Representatives, Washington, DC 20515. If you're not sure to whom you should write, call the **Capitol Switchboard** (✆ **202/224-3121**), or visit www.house.gov or www.senate.gov. If you're coming for the National Cherry Blossom Festival and want to view the blossoms from the water, reserve a paddleboat ($10 per hour for a two-passenger boat; $18 per hour for a four-passenger boat) a month or two in advance (www.tidalbasinpeddleboats.com).
- Encourage older children to visit the **Washington, D.C. Convention and Tourism Corporation** site, at www.washington.org, for free brochures and maps. Invite them to read chapter 6 of this guide and write down the attractions that most interest them. They can request information about any of the **Smithsonian**'s museums by visiting www.si.edu.
- Under your supervision, your children can also **send away for maps and guidebooks**—you know that kids love to receive mail. Numerous Washington, D.C. videos and DVDs are available at video stores, from your library, or online. Viewing one or more of these is sure to whet your family's travel appetite.

mostly one-way travel from one U.S. destination to another at very low prices. Unavailable in the U.S., these discount tickets must be purchased abroad in conjunction with your international fare. If Washington, D.C. is just one of the places you're visiting in the United States, you might want to check out the Visit USA program, which might prove the easiest, fastest, and cheapest way for you to see the country.

Ronald Reagan Washington National Airport (DCA) lies 4 miles south of D.C., across the Potomac River in Virginia, a trip of only a few minutes by car, 15 to 20 minutes by Metro in non-rush-hour traffic. Its proximity to the District and its direct access to the Metro rail system are reasons why you might want to fly into National.

Approximately 12 airlines serve this airport, which has nonstop flights to 69 U.S. cities, plus Nassau, Bermuda, Montreal, and Toronto. Nearly all nonstop flights are to and from cities located within 1,250 miles from Washington. The exceptions are flights between National and Phoenix, Denver, Las Vegas, Seattle, Los Angeles, and Salt Lake City. Among the airlines serving National Airport are **Air Canada, American, Continental, Delta, Northwest, United,** and **US Airways,** and discount airlines **Frontier** and **AirTran.** Delta and US Airways operate shuttles that together offer hourly or nearly hourly flights between National and Boston's Logan Airport, and National and New York's LaGuardia Airport.

The Metropolitan Washington Airports Authority oversees both National and Dulles airports, so the website is the same for the two facilities: www.mwaa.com. Check there for airport information, or call ✆ **703/417-8000.** For Metro information, call ✆ **202/637-7000.**

Washington Dulles International Airport (IAD) is 26 miles outside the capital, in Chantilly, Virginia, a 35- to 45-minute ride to downtown in non-rush-hour traffic. Of the three airports, Dulles handles more daily flights, with more than 30 airlines flying nonstop to 127 destinations, including 43 foreign cities. And though the airport is not as convenient to the heart of Washington as National, it's more convenient than BWI (see below), thanks to an uncongested airport access road that travels half the distance toward Washington.

Dulles continues its decades-long expansion. Plans include an underground airport train system and station, replacing the cumbersome mobile lounges that until now have transported most travelers to and from the main and midfield terminals. The project's other improvements feature a pedestrian walkway between the main terminal and concourses A and B and, eventually, the addition of a fifth runway that will more than triple its annual passenger traffic to 55 million.

Among Dulles's major domestic airlines are **American, Continental, Delta, Northwest, United,** and **US Airways,** and discount airlines **AirTran, JetBlue, Southwest, Ted,** and **Virgin America.** The airport's major international airlines include **Aeroflot, Air Canada, British Airways, Aer Lingus, Air France, Lufthansa, Virgin Atlantic, ANA Airways,** and **Saudi Arabian Airlines.**

Last but not least is **Baltimore–Washington International Thurgood Marshall Airport (BWI),** which is located about 45 minutes from downtown, a few miles outside of Baltimore. A vast expansion has added 11 gates to a newly improved concourse, skywalks from parking garages to terminals, and tripled the number of parking spaces. One factor especially accounts for this tremendous growth, the same that recommends BWI to travelers: the major presence of **Southwest Airlines,** whose bargain fares and flights to nearly 40 cities seem to offer something for everyone. (Southwest also serves Dulles Airport, but in a much smaller capacity.)

In all, about 14 airlines serve BWI, flying nonstop to 70 destinations, including five foreign cities. Major domestic airlines include **American, Continental, Delta, Northwest, United,** and **US Airways,** and discount airlines **AirTran, Southwest,** and **USA 3000.** Major international airlines include **British Airways** and **Air Canada.**

Call ✆ **800/435-9294** for airport information, or point your browser to www.bwiairport.com.

Getting into Town from the Airport

Several shuttle services serve D.C.'s airports. Departures from the airports run about every 20 minutes or as needed. For transit to the airport, all require reservations, usually 24 hours in advance. Payment is by cash or credit card.

The **"Super Shuttle"** (✆ **800/258-3826,** 202/296-6662, or 410/859-0800 in Baltimore; www.supershuttle.com) offers door-to-door service between Dulles, Reagan National, and BWI airports and the metropolitan D.C. area 24 hours a day. Call for pricing, which is based on ZIP code. To give you an example, the fare from Reagan National Airport to the White House zip code is $12, plus a $1 fuel surcharge; $8 for each additional passenger 3 and older ($45 for entire van up to seven passengers). Kids 2 years and under ride for free. On arrival, board the Super Shuttle blue van at the airport. If you're going back to the airport, you'll need to make reservations 24 hours in advance.

Maryland Shuttle and Sedan (✆ **800/590-0000** or 301/230-0000; www.marylandshuttle.com) serves all three airports 24 hours a day. The fare from Bethesda to Reagan National Airport is $25 to $27 (depending on zip code); from Bethesda to Dulles, $25 to $27; Bethesda to BWI, $31. Book at least 24 hours ahead or pay an additional $8 fee.

RONALD REAGAN WASHINGTON NATIONAL AIRPORT (REAGAN NATIONAL OR "NATIONAL") Just across the Potomac River in Virginia, National Airport is about a 15- to 30-minute taxi ride from downtown in non-rush-hour traffic and costs about $20; it's much less via the Metro, depending on where you're staying, and you'll have to do some walking. This is the most convenient airport to downtown (less than 5 miles), but it's also the most congested. In the wake of the September 11, 2001, terrorist attacks, heightened security dictates arriving at the airport 1½ hours before your departing flight (2 hr. for international). Be sure to carry a photo ID. Without it, you will be denied boarding for your flight. You will probably be required to remove your shoes when passing through the scanner, so you may want to wear slip-ons. (For what it's worth, I've found the security checkpoints at D.C.-area airports to run much more smoothly than others in the nation.) The stunning glass-and-steel main terminal designed by Cesar Pelli has 54 skylighted domes and a five-story glass wall overlooking the Potomac River. If you've got time to kill, the view from Gate 43 is primo.

Covered pedestrian bridges connect the Metro station and the terminal. Of course, the best parking spaces—112 of them right next to the terminal—are reserved for VIPs: senators, congressional reps, and local politicians. That's right! We pay their salaries *and* for their optimum parking spaces!

In the vast commercial space, 40 shops, 25 eateries, and 30 retail carts vie for travelers' wallets. There's even a meditation room near the baggage claim area so that you can compose yourself if your flight out is canceled or delayed.

For airport information, call ✆ **703/417-8000** (www.mwaa.com).

Shuttle service is provided by some hotels. Check to see if yours is one of them. A taxi from National to downtown

Washington, D.C. costs about $20 for the first person, plus various charges depending on time of day, number of passengers, and pieces of luggage (www.dctaxi.dc.gov). Trains on **Metro's Blue and Yellow lines** stop at National. The **Metro** is the quickest way to get to many locations in the District and beyond because local roads are notoriously bottlenecked. Count on a 15- to 20-minute ride into D.C. To help you, maps, fares, and traveling times are posted at every stop. Trains run Sunday through Thursday 5am to midnight, Friday 5am to 3am, and Saturday 7am to 3am (✆ **202/637-7000;** phone line open Mon–Fri 6am–10:30pm, Sat–Sun 8am–10:30pm).

The **Super Shuttle** (✆ **800/258-3826**) departs Reagan National every 20 to 30 minutes for D.C. hotels. The fare to central D.C. is $12 for the first person, $8 for each additional passenger 3 and older; free for kids 2 and under. You must make a reservation, however, for the return trip to the airport.

WASHINGTON DULLES INTERNATIONAL AIRPORT (DULLES) This airport is located in Chantilly, Virginia, about 30 miles and a 35- to 45-minute ride to downtown D.C. in non-rush-hour traffic. The main Eero Saarinen–designed terminal is an architectural marvel. It is also huge. Two midfield terminals (A-B and C-D) are reached by mobile lounges. For airport information, call ✆ **703/572-2700** (www.mwaa.com).

A **taxi** from Dulles to downtown Washington costs $51 to $58.

The **Super Shuttle** (✆ **800/258-3826;** www.supershuttle.com) serves downtown D.C. from Dulles (also Reagan National). The fare from Dulles to the JW Marriott, for example, is $27 for the first person, and $8 for each additional person 3 and older (free for kids 2 and under). With a large group (up to seven passengers), you can save by booking the entire van for $70. Vans depart the airport on demand, about every 20 to 30 minutes. Make reservations at least 24 hours ahead for your return to the airport via phone or online: reservations@supershuttle.com.Metrobus makes hourly runs to the L'Enfant Plaza (D.C.) and Rosslyn (Arlington, Virginia) Metro Stations for only $3. The ride takes about 50 minutes (✆ **202/637-7000;** www.wmata.com).

The **Washington Flyer Shuttle** (✆ **703/685-1400;** www.washfly.com) provides daily express bus service between the West Falls Church (Virginia) Metro station and Dulles and takes from 20 to 30 minutes. The bus operates about 70 times per day weekdays, 50 times on weekends and holidays. Buy tickets at the Arrivals level, Ground Transportation Center. The fare between the West Falls Church Metro and Dulles is $9 one-way, $16 round-trip.

BALTIMORE–WASHINGTON INTERNATIONAL AIRPORT (BWI) One of the nation's largest airports, BWI is a few miles south of Baltimore, Maryland, 34 miles to the heart of downtown D.C., and about a 45-minute ride. It survived some growing pains and is, without a doubt, the most user-friendly of the three airports serving Washington. BWI is a hub for Southwest (with 178 flights daily to 35 nonstop U.S. destinations), the best airline on the planet, in my opinion. The Southwest concourse is home to umpteen Southwest ticket counters, a food court, and retail shops.

BWI sports a two-level observation gallery, with computerized interactive displays and a Smithsonian Museum Shop. If you have time to kill, sink into one of the comfortable leatherette chairs in front of the 147-foot-wide window, and marvel at the takeoffs and landings. By punching a flight number into one of the computer displays, your kids can learn the altitude, speed, and location of the plane of their choice. For airport information, visit www.bwiairport.com.

The Super Shuttle from BWI to D.C. is $35 for the first passenger and $12 for each additional passenger 3 and older; you can lease the whole van for $100.

Taxi fare from BWI to downtown Washington is about $80 per family.

The **BWI Express/B30 bus** goes to the Greenbelt Metro station on Metro's Green line, about a 20-minute ride. From Greenbelt, it is about a 20-minute ride to downtown D.C. There are 25 departures weekdays, 21 on weekends, and it's still only $3. Go to the lower level of the International Pier/Concourse E, and follow signs to Public Transportation. For details, call ✆ **202/637-7000** (www.wmata.com).

Train service is available daily on **Amtrak** (✆ **800/USA-RAIL**) and weekdays on **MARC** (✆ **800/325-RAIL**), at the BWI Airport Station, 5 minutes from the airport. A **courtesy shuttle** runs every 15 to 20 minutes between the airport and the train station, weekdays between 6am and midnight. Weekend service tends to be less regular.

BY TRAIN

Amtrak (✆ **800/872-7245;** www.amtrak.com) offers daily service to Washington from several East Coast, Midwest, and West Coast cities. Travelers from the far West change trains in Chicago or New Orleans. Amtrak's high-speed Acela trains travel as fast as 150 miles per hour along the Northeast Corridor, linking Boston, New York, and Washington. The Acela cuts about 15 to 30 minutes off the usual 3¾-hour ride between New York and Washington, and as much as an hour off the trip between Boston and Washington.

Although Amtrak is the most efficient way to get to D.C. from New York and points in between, it has had some problems in recent years, mostly owing to financial woes, aging equipment, and cutbacks. On a Regional train, the round-trip fare between New York and Washington ranges from $67 to $111 one-way. The Acela Express, which is about 15 to 20 minutes faster, ranges from $125 to $188 one-way (not worth it unless you're on an expense account, in my opinion). Children get a discount, especially in summer. Bear in mind that some weekend and holiday blackouts might apply, so check when you call. Between Boston and Washington, the round-trip Regional fares range from $162 to $270 round-trip; on the Acela Express, from $374 to $468 round-trip. Yikes! You could practically hire a chauffeured limo for that. Yes, it's cheaper to fly, but I'd rather walk than contend with Boston Logan Airport. Kids up to age 15 pay half the adult rate when accompanied by a fare-paying passenger 18 or older. Every adult passenger is allowed two children's-fare tickets. **Seniors** 62 and older are entitled to a 15% discount. **AAA** members get a 10% discount. Also ask about special fares and promotions, especially in summer. There is a 5% discount for booking online. Passengers with disabilities are entitled to a 15% reduction on regular one-way coach fares. Children with disabilities between the ages of 2 and 15 can travel for 50% of the fare for adults with disabilities. The discount does not apply to the Metroliner.

If you arrive by Amtrak, your first glimpse of Washington will be **Union Station,** at Massachusetts Avenue NE and North Capitol Street, a stone's throw from the U.S. Capitol. Your kids might want to spend their entire vacation here, among the food court, shops, and restaurants. There's **Metro** service right in the building, and **taxis** are plentiful. **MARC** (Maryland Rural Commuter System) and **Virginia Railway Express** arrive and depart from here, too. Many Amtrak trains also stop at the **New Carrollton Station** in Lanham, Maryland, about 15 to 20 minutes by rail and 20 minutes by car from Union Station. Long-term parking is more readily available at New Carrollton, but be advised it may still fill early on weekday mornings. If you're staying in the Maryland suburbs, taking Amtrak to New Carrollton is more convenient than Union Station.

Most kids enjoy train travel because it's less confining than a car or a plane, and it's fun visiting the snack bar. Consider giving your children a food allowance to last the entire trip so they don't bug you every few minutes. Also, Amtrak is not known for its snack-bar cuisine. When I take my grandkids on the train, I bring sandwiches from home and let them buy drinks and snacks.

Maryland Rural Commuter System (MARC) operates trains between Union Station in Washington, BWI Airport, and downtown Baltimore Monday through Friday (© **800/325-RAIL** [7245]).

BY CAR

Most visitors arrive in Washington by car. Although a car is helpful if you want to take excursions to many points outside the city, it can be a real liability in the downtown area. You might want to consider leaving the car at home and renting one for day trips outside the city.

Washington's streets are congested, and its drivers—many of whom learned to drive elsewhere or not at all—follow many different rules of the road. The result can be less than pleasant. In addition, **parking** in most sectors is expensive or nonexistent. (At some hotels, parking is included in the room rate. Find out in advance, or you might be unpleasantly surprised by having to shell out up to $30 a day. You should also ask if there is and additional charge for in-out privileges.) If your sightseeing plans are restricted to the city and close-in environs, leave the family buggy at home; you'll have a far better time. The District's efficient subway system will transport your brood to within a short walk of all the major attractions.

Like it or not, whether you are arriving from the north (I-270, I-95, I-295), south (I-95, Rte. 1, Rte. 301), east (Rte. 50/301, Rte. 450), or west (Rte. 7, Rte. 50, I-66, Rte. 29/211), you will run into the **Capital Beltway** (hereinafter known as the **Beltway**). This 66-mile road encircles Washington, D.C. (some think like a noose) and has 56 interchanges that intersect with all the major approach routes to the city. Sometimes more than 600,000 cars per day travel the Beltway, and gridlock is not uncommon, especially between 6 and 9am and 3 and 7pm. The eastern segment of the Beltway is part of I-95, which joins Baltimore, Maryland, to the north and Richmond, Virginia, to the south.

To confuse you, the rest is designated I-495, but mercifully dual I-495/I-95 signs are posted. Before you leave home, study a map; make sure you have directions from the intersection of the Beltway and whichever interstate or road you will be traveling to your destination.

To further challenge those driving into the D.C. metropolitan area, Maryland's exits correspond to the nearest milepost. Virginia's are numbered consecutively. Go figure. People have been known to drive the entire 66 miles of the Beltway before realizing that they've missed their exit. You don't want to spend your vacation this way; there's no room service and not much of a view.

North of the city, I-270 links the Maryland suburbs with I-70 at Frederick. To the southwest, I-66 and U.S. 50 connect with the Virginia segment of I-495. If you're a member of **AAA,** request a Trip-Tik and other pertinent information (© **800/222-4357** or 703/222-6000) before you depart.

If you want to take day trips from the D.C. area by car, you can rent a car from one of the many national car-rental companies with offices in D.C. Try **Alamo** (© 800/462-5266; www.alamo.com), **Avis** (© 800/230-4898; www.avis.com), **Budget** (© 800/527-0700; www.budget.com), **Dollar** (© 800/800-3665; www.dollar.com), **Hertz** (© 800/654-3131; www.hertz.com), or **National** (© 800/227-7368; www.nationalcar.com).

BY BUS

Bus travel is often the most economical form of public transit for short hops between U.S. cities, but it's certainly not an option for everyone (particularly when Amtrak, which is far more luxurious, offers similar rates). **Greyhound** (✆ **800/231-2222;** www.greyhound.com) is the sole nationwide bus line. International visitors can obtain information about the **Greyhound North American Discovery Pass.** The pass can be obtained from foreign travel agents or through www.discoverypass.com, for unlimited travel and stopovers in the U.S. and Canada.

4 MONEY & COSTS

CURRENCY

The Value of the Dollar vs. Other Popular Currencies

US$	Can$	UK£	Euro (€)	Aus$	NZ$
$1	C$1.6	£0.66	€0.73	A$1.31	NZ$1.65

The most common bills are the $1 (a "buck"), $5, $10, and $20 denominations. There are also $2 bills (seldom encountered), $50 bills, and $100 bills (the last two are usually not welcome as payment for small purchases).

Coins come in seven denominations: 1¢ (1 cent, or a penny); 5¢ (5 cents, or a nickel); 10¢ (10 cents, or a dime); 25¢ (25 cents, or a quarter); 50¢ (50 cents, or a half dollar); the gold-colored Sacagawea coin, worth $1; and the rare silver dollar.

If you've traveled in other U.S. cities or internationally you'll be pleasantly surprised by how far your travel dollar stretches in the nation's capital. Washington hotels and restaurants roll out the red carpet to families, offering special rates and discounts to those traveling with munchkins. The government may not be able to balance its budget, but rest assured you'll go home with coins jingling in your pocket. Best of all, most of the museums and sights in D.C. are free. Try that in New York, Paris, or Hong Kong.

ATMS

Nationwide, the easiest and best way to get cash away from home is from an ATM (automated teller machine), sometimes referred to as a "cash machine," or "cashpoint." The **Cirrus** (✆ **800/424-7787;** www.mastercard.com) and **PLUS** (✆ **800/843-7587;** www.visa.com) networks span the country. Go to your bank card's website to find ATM locations throughout D.C. Be sure you know your daily withdrawal limit before you depart.

Note: Many banks impose a fee every time you use a card at another bank's ATM, and that fee is often higher for international transactions (up to $5 or more) than for domestic ones (where they're rarely more than $2). In addition, the bank from which you withdraw cash may charge its own fee. To compare banks' ATM fees within the U.S., use **www.bankrate.com**. Visitors from outside the U.S. should also find out whether their bank assesses a 1% to 3% fee on charges incurred abroad.

CREDIT CARDS

Credit cards are the most widely used form of payment in the United States: **Visa** (Barclaycard in Britain), **MasterCard** (Eurocard in Europe, Access in Britain, Chargex in Canada), **American Express,**

What Things Cost in Washington, D.C.

Taxi from National Airport to JW Marriott	$20
Taxi from Dulles Airport (Virginia) to JW Marriott	$55
Taxi from BWI Airport to JW Marriott	$79
Super Shuttle (family of four) from Dulles Airport (Virginia) to downtown hotel	$51
Metro ride	$1.35–$4.50
Taxi	$6.50
Lunch for one at the Air and Space Museum (inexpensive)	$8–$10
Lunch (hot dog, soda, and potato chips) from street vendor	$4–$5
Dinner for one at America (moderate)	$15–$30
Dinner for one at Bullfeathers (inexpensive)	$12–$20
Ice-cream cone	$2.50–$3.75
Admission to National Zoological Park	Free
Movie ticket (adult matinee before 6pm)	$7.50–$9
Movie ticket (adult evening)	$7.50–$10
Movie ticket (child)	$7.50

Diners Club, and **Discover.** They also provide a convenient record of all your expenses, and offer relatively good exchange rates. You can withdraw cash advances from your credit cards at banks or ATMs, but high fees make credit card cash advances a pricey way to get cash.

It's highly recommended that you travel with at least one major credit card. You must have a credit card to rent a car, and hotels and airlines usually require a credit card imprint as a deposit against expenses.

TRAVELER'S CHECKS

Though credit cards and debit cards are more often used, traveler's checks are still widely accepted in the U.S. Foreign visitors should make sure that traveler's checks are denominated in U.S. dollars; foreign-currency checks are often difficult to exchange.

5 HEALTH

The biggest medical challenges you're liable to encounter are indigestion and other travel-related digestive problems. It seems to go with the territory. Usually taking a mild antacid and watching your diet will do the trick. In summer always wear sunscreen with SPF 30, sunglasses, and a hat that shades your face. The sun can be intense from May to September. The heat and humidity in summer trouble some people and can cause dehydration. Be sure to drink plenty of nonalcoholic fluids, especially water.

Several hospitals serve Washington, D.C. If you are in extreme distress and feel you need to go to an emergency room, the most centrally located (and also with a good reputation) is George Washington University Hospital, 901 23rd St. NW (✆ **202/715-4911** for emergency room; 202/715-4000 for general information). If you need an ambulance, dial 911, and tell the dispatcher your exact location. If you're unsure, ask a traveling companion or someone with a clear head to get on the phone.

If your children require **medication,** pack plenty in a carry-on bag. You'll also want a **first-aid kit**—small basic kits are available at most pharmacies and supermarkets, or call your physician or local Red Cross chapter for a recommendation. In addition, remember grown-up and children's-strength aspirin, a thermometer, cough syrup, a plastic cup, flexible straws, baby wipes, a plastic spoon, a night light, and pacifiers. Be prepared for **motion sickness.** Make sure you have a bottle of liquid Dramamine close at hand when traveling. Kids who are fine in a car could get sick on a boat, plane, or train, and vice versa.

If you or the kids wear **eyeglasses,** by all means bring backups. If extra pairs are unavailable, bring the prescriptions. You can't sightsee if you can't see!

Before you leave, get a list of your **kids' inoculations** and the dates they were administered from your pediatrician. In an emergency, you're not apt to remember this information.

If possible, before you leave home, obtain the name of a **Washington, D.C. pediatrician** from your hometown physician or relatives or friends in the Washington area. Or ask your hotel concierge for recommendations. If you have a problem that does not require a doctor, go to the nearest pharmacy. Don't quote me, but sometimes the pharmacist can be more helpful than a doctor. And you won't have to wait nearly as long. A pharmacist can recommend over-the-counter meds and dispense other advice. Some pharmacies/drugstores are open round-the-clock.

If you are caring for someone else's child, make sure that the child's parent or guardian has filled out and signed a **notarized letter** giving you the legal right to authorize medical and surgical treatment. Basically, it should say, "So-and-So has the right to authorize medical/surgical treatment after all attempts to reach parents fail." According to one hospital spokesman, though, "No invasive treatment will be done unless a parent can be notified; in case of a life-threatening emergency, doctors will take responsibility until the parent can be notified." Doctors and lawyers say that these forms will "facilitate treatment," even though they might not be legally binding. If you have custodial care of a child with divorced parents, it's wise to get forms from both parents.

The United States **Centers for Disease Control and Prevention** (✆ **800/311-3435;** www.cdc.gov) provides up-to-date information on health hazards by region or country and offers tips on food safety.

WHAT TO DO IF YOU GET SICK AWAY FROM HOME

I list **hospitals** and **emergency numbers** under "Fast Facts," p. 289.

If you suffer from a chronic illness, consult your doctor before your departure. Pack **prescription medications** in your carry-on luggage, and carry them in their original containers, with pharmacy labels—otherwise they won't make it through airport security. Visitors from outside the U.S. should carry generic names of prescription drugs. For U.S. travelers, most reliable health-care plans provide coverage if you get sick away from home. Foreign visitors may have to pay all medical costs upfront and be reimbursed later. See "Medical Insurance," under "Travel Insurance," above.

6 SAFETY

Although the number of violent crimes has declined in recent years, being cautious is always smart. Rest assured that the areas in which you'll be spending most, if not all, of your time are relatively safe. To help ensure that your family has a safe visit, stay out of dark and deserted areas, and don't wander aimlessly. Criminals are known to prey on those who appear defenseless, so be alert to what's going on around you, and walk purposefully. If your children are young, hold their hands. Make sure your family has a plan if you are separated. Kids old enough to understand should know the name and address of their hotel.

Always lock your hotel room, car doors, and trunk. Wear a money belt under your clothes, and hold on to your purse in a restaurant; don't drape it over a chair back or put it on an empty seat. When you buy something, put your money and credit cards away, and secure your wallet before you go out on the street. Leave expensive jewelry at home; what you do bring, don't flash. If approached by a panhandler, say "Sorry, no" and keep walking.

For the latest information on safe travel in the U.S. and throughout the world, go to the Department of State Advisory website: http://travel.state.gov.

General Suggestions If you're in doubt about which neighborhoods in D.C. are safe, don't hesitate to make inquiries with the hotel front-desk staff or the local tourist office. Avoid deserted areas, especially at night, and don't go into public parks after dark unless there's a concert or similar occasion that will attract a crowd.

A welcome presence on D.C. streets is the group of friendly and helpful goodwill ambassadors dressed in bright red jackets with the **SAM (Safety and Maintenance)** insignia and/or "Downtown D.C." logo on their caps. Known as **SAMs,** they give directions; advise on dining, shopping, and sights; and will walk you to your Metro station, hotel, or car. Equipped with walkie-talkies, they work closely with the Metropolitan Police. Should you see any suspicious behavior, report it to them. For more information, check the **Business Improvement District website** (www.downtowndc.org).

Discuss with your kids what they should do if they get separated from you during the trip. Some parents dress their kids in bright colors when they're sightseeing. You might want to take a tip from preschool groups on field trips and have your very young ones carry a card in their pocket or wear a name tag that includes the name and phone number of your hotel and your cellphone number.

When you check into your room, give the kids a little time to settle in before rushing off to an activity. Find the nearest fire exits, and discuss the do's and don'ts of fire safety. If there isn't a card in the room describing emergency procedures, ask for one at the front desk. Before turning in, some families pack a small bag or sack with emergency items: a flashlight, an extra room key, wallets, and the like. If there's a fire drill in the middle of the night, you'll be good to go in a matter of seconds.

7 SPECIALIZED TRAVEL RESOURCES

FAMILY TRAVEL

How to Take Great Trips with Your Kids (The Harvard Common Press) is full of good general advice that can apply to travel anywhere.

Recommended family travel websites include **Family Travel Forum** (www.familytravelforum.com), a comprehensive site that offers customized trip planning; **Family Travel Network** (www.familytravelnetwork.com), an online magazine providing travel tips; **TravelWithYourKids.com** (www.travelwithyourkids.com), a comprehensive site, written by parents for parents, offering sound advice for long-distance and international travel with children.

For more good travel info, pick up a copy of *The Unofficial Guide to the Mid-Atlantic with Kids* or *Frommer's 500 Places to Take Your Kids Before They Grow Up* (both Wiley Publishing).

TRAVELERS WITH DISABILITIES

Washington welcomes visitors with physical disabilities with open arms and relatively few obstacles. Most of the museums, monuments, and public buildings—as well as many theaters and restaurants—are accessible to travelers with disabilities. The Metro, the public transportation system, is rated among the nation's best for accommodating those with disabilities. The **Washington Metropolitan Transit Authority** publishes a free guide on the Metro's bus and rail system accessibility (✆ **202/962-6464;** TDD 202/638-3780; www.wmata.com). Each Metro station is equipped with an elevator (complete with Braille number plates) to train platforms, and rail cars are fully accessible. Punctuated rubber tiles lead up to the granite-lined platform edge to warn visually impaired Metro riders that they are nearing the tracks. Train operators make station and onboard announcements of train destinations and stops.

The **Washington, D.C. Convention and Tourism Corporation** publishes a fact sheet detailing general accessibility around town. For a free copy, call ✆ **202/789-7000** (www.washington.org), or write to WCTC, 901 7th St. NW, 4th Floor, Washington, DC 20001.

Regular **Tourmobile** trams (see "Getting Around," in chapter 3) are accessible to visitors with disabilities. The company also operates special vans for immobile travelers, complete with wheelchair lifts. Call a day ahead to ensure that the van is available for you when you arrive. For information, call ✆ **202/554-5100.**

All Smithsonian museum buildings are accessible to visitors in wheelchairs. A free, comprehensive publication called "Smithsonian Access" lists all services available to visitors with disabilities, including parking, building access, sign-language interpreters, and more. To obtain a copy, call ✆ **202/357-2700** or TTY 202/357-1729.

The Lincoln, Jefferson, and Vietnam memorials and the Washington Monument are equipped to accommodate visitors with disabilities; wheelchairs are also kept on the premises. Call ahead to other sightseeing attractions for accessibility information and special services (✆ **202/426-6841**).

Call your senator or representative to arrange wheelchair-accessible tours of the Capitol; special tours for the hearing- and seeing-impaired can also be arranged. If you need further information on these tours, call ✆ **202/224-4048.**

Most of the large performing-arts venues in town offer special services for special-needs audience members, ranging from headphones for the hearing-impaired to large-print programs to wheelchair-accessible seats. Most also offer specially priced tickets for patrons with physical disabilities.

GAY & LESBIAN TRAVELERS

Washington, D.C. is relatively hospitable to gays. The most gay-friendly neighborhood is probably Dupont Circle. You might check out this website for specifics: www.vacation.away.com/washington.

The International Gay and Lesbian Travel Association (IGLTA; ✆ **800/448-8550** or 954/776-2626; www.iglta.org) is the trade association for the gay and lesbian travel industry, and offers an online directory of gay- and lesbian-friendly travel businesses and tour operators.

SENIOR TRAVEL

Members of **AARP,** 601 E St. NW, Washington, DC 20049 (✆ **888/687-2277;**

www.aarp.org), get discounts on hotels, airfares, and car rentals. AARP offers members a wide range of benefits, including *AARP: The Magazine* and a monthly newsletter. Anyone over 50 can join.

The U.S. National Park Service offers an **America the Beautiful—National Park and Federal Recreational Lands Pass—Senior Pass** (formerly the **Golden Age Passport**), which gives seniors 62 years or older lifetime entrance to all properties administered by the National Park Service—national parks, monuments, historic sites, recreation areas, and national wildlife refuges—for a one-time processing fee of $10. For more information, go to www.nps.gov/fees_passes.htm or call ✆ **888/467-2757.**

8 SUSTAINABLE TOURISM

In some respects, Washington, D.C. has always been ahead of the curve when it comes to green-friendly endeavors. It was Pierre L'Enfant, in 1791, after all, whose vision for the city included a network of parks, an expansive "public walk," beautiful gardens, and sweeping vistas. The capital today stays true to L'Enfant's plan, as anyone can see who has strolled the 2-mile long National Mall, biked through the 2,000-acre Rock Creek Park (the nation's oldest urban park), or picnicked on a verdant spot overlooking the Potomac River. The National Park Service maintains 70% of the city's land; when you count the parkland in the surrounding metropolitan area, the total exceeds 230,000 acres.

The capital continues to build upon its green foundation. Consider these facts:

Not only is D.C. the nation's most walkable city, but it also has the greatest number of walkable urban places per

General Resources for Green Travel

The following websites provide valuable wide-ranging information on sustainable travel. For a list of even more sustainable resources, as well as tips and explanations on how to make your travel greener, visit www.frommers.com/planning.

- **Responsible Travel** (www.responsibletravel.com) is a great source of sustainable travel ideas; the site is run by a spokesperson for ethical tourism in the travel industry. **Sustainable Travel International** (www.sustainabletravelinternational.org) promotes ethical tourism practices, and manages an extensive directory of sustainable properties and tour operators around the world.
- **Carbonfund** (www.carbonfund.org), **TerraPass** (www.terrapass.org), and **Carbon Neutral** (www.carbonneutral.org) provide info on "carbon offsetting," or offsetting the greenhouse gas emitted during flights.
- **Volunteer International** (www.volunteerinternational.org) has a list of questions to help you determine the intentions and the nature of a volunteer program. For general info on volunteer travel, visit **www.volunteerabroad.org** and **www.idealist.org**.

capita, according to the Brookings Institution. Biking, always popular here as recreation, is increasingly a transportation choice, and the city has responded: the District recently added 40 new miles of bike lanes to city streets and has partnered with **SmartBike DC** (www.smartbikedc.com), a self-service bike rental program, America's first, to avail SmartBike subscribers (there's a $40 annual fee) of bikes, kept at stations throughout the city. By the time you read this, more than 500 bikes at 50 locations should be on hand.

D.C.'s excellent public transportation system (see "Getting Around," earlier in this chapter) provides another inducement for drivers to leave their cars behind, and the picture gets even better, when it comes to the many Metrobuses and D.C. Circulator buses that run on clean-burning natural gas.

The list goes on, whether we're talking about construction—Washington, D.C. was the first major city to require developers to adhere to guidelines established by the U.S. Green Building Council—or hotel trends—most D.C. hotels are incorporating eco-friendly practices into their daily operations and many, like the **Willard InterContinental** (p. 60), go even further, adopting nearby parks, for instance, and helping to maintain them. If participating in the environmental movement is important to you, you'll have countless opportunities to do so when you travel to the capital. To make it easy for you, I've included specific information about the eco-friendly practices of hotels, restaurants, and attractions in their descriptions within corresponding chapters.

9 STAYING CONNECTED

TELEPHONES & CELLPHONES

If you are American and own a **cellphone,** bring your phone with you to D.C., making sure first, of course, that your cellphone service does not charge excessively—or at all—for long-distance calls. In fact, if you are from outside the country and own an international cellphone with service that covers the Washington area, bring that phone along. The point is that hotels often charge outrageous fees for each long-distance or local call you make using the phone in your hotel room.

AT&T, Verizon, Sprint, and T-Mobile are among the cellphone networks operating in Washington, D.C., so there's a good chance that you'll have full coverage anywhere in the city—except, possibly on the subway, where Verizon is the sole provider of wireless service. You can expect reception to be generally excellent, but maybe not during certain special events, say, the inauguration of President Barack Obama, when cellphone use was off the charts and affected connections.

International visitors should check their **GSM (Global System for Mobile Communications) wireless network,** to see where GSM phones and text messaging work in the U.S.; go to the website www.t-mobile.com/coverage.

In any case, take a look at your wireless company's coverage map on its website before heading out. If you know your phone won't work here, or if you don't have a cellphone, you have several options.

You can **rent** a phone before you leave home from **InTouch USA** (© **800/872-7626** in the U.S., 703/222-7161 outside the U.S.; www.intouchusa.com).

You can use a **public pay telephone,** although these are increasingly hard to find. Many public pay phones at airports now accept American Express, MasterCard, and Visa credit cards. **Local calls** made from pay phones in most locales cost 35¢. (No pennies, please.)

You can **buy** a phone once you arrive. All three Washington-area airports sell cellphones and SIM cards. Look for the **Airport Wireless** shops at Dulles International Airport (✆ **703/661-0411**), National Airport (✆ **703/417-3983**), and BWI Airport (✆ **410/691-0262**).

You can purchase a pay-as-you-go phone from all sorts of places, from Amazon.com to any Verizon store. In D.C., Verizon has a store at Union Station (✆ **202/682-9475**) and another at 1314 F St. NW (✆ **202/624-0072**), to name just two convenient locations.

Your final option is to buy **prepaid calling cards,** which are sold at convenience and grocery stores, post offices, and pharmacies, in denominations up to $50. These calling cards can be useful to anyone, but they come in handy, especially if you're a traveler from abroad; the cards can be the least expensive way to call home.

Most long-distance and international calls can be dialed directly from any phone. **For calls within the United States and to Canada,** dial 1 followed by the area code and the seven-digit number. **For other international calls,** dial 011 followed by the country code (44 to the U.K., 61 to Australia, and 64 to New Zealand), the city code, and the number you are calling.

Calls to area codes **800, 888, 877,** and **866** are toll-free. However, calls to area codes **700** and **900** (chat lines, bulletin boards, "dating" services, and so on) can be very expensive—usually a charge of 95¢ to $3 or more per minute, and they sometimes have minimum charges that can run as high as $15 or more.

For **reversed-charge or collect calls,** and for person-to-person calls, dial the number 0 and then the area code and number; an operator will come on the line, and you should specify whether you are calling collect, person-to-person, or both. If your operator-assisted call is international, ask for the overseas operator.

For **local directory assistance** ("information"), dial 411; for long-distance information, dial 1, then the appropriate area code and 555-1212.

INTERNET/E-MAIL

When you're in Washington, D.C. without your trusty computer and want to check e-mail messages, try these cyber cafes: **cyberSTOPcafe,** 1513 17th St NW (at P St.; ✆ **202/234-2470;** Mon–Thurs 7am–midnight, Sat–Sun 8am–midnight); **Kramerbooks and Afterwords Cafe,** 1517 Connecticut Ave NW (near Dupont Circle; ✆ **202/387-1462**). To find others, ask your concierge or visit **www.cybercaptive.com** and **www.cybercafe.com**. Also, public libraries usually allow visitors free access to their computers with Internet access.

Most major airports have **Internet kiosks** that provide basic Web access for a per-minute fee that's usually higher than cybercafe prices. Check out copy shops, such as **FedEx,** which offers computer stations with fully loaded software (as well as Wi-Fi).

WITH YOUR OWN COMPUTER

More and more hotels, resorts, airports, cafes, and retailers are going Wi-Fi (wireless fidelity), becoming "hotspots" that offer free high-speed Wi-Fi access or charge a small fee for usage. Wi-Fi is found in campgrounds, RV parks, and even entire towns. Most laptops sold today have built-in wireless capability. To find public Wi-Fi hotspots at your destination, go to **www.jiwire.com**; its Hotspot Finder holds the world's largest directory of public wireless hotspots.

For dial-up access, most business-class hotels in the U.S. offer dataports for laptop modems, and many hotels in D.C. now offer free high-speed Internet access.

Wherever you go, bring a **connection kit** of the right power and phone adapters, a spare phone cord, and a spare Ethernet network cable—or find out whether your hotel supplies them to guests. For electrical current conversions, see "Electricity," in chapter 12, "Fast Facts."

Getting to Know Washington, D.C.

Welcome! You and your family are about to embark on an adventure in one of the most inspiring and captivating cities in the world. The nation's capital is distinguished by an eclectic style: Old South mixes with high-tech, marble and granite blend with cherry blossoms and magnolias, ethnic festivals meld with presidential inaugurals, and the nation's history bumps noses with tomorrow's headlines. With so much to see and do, there is little doubt that you and your children will have fun discovering the many facets of this enchanting and enigmatic city.

1 ORIENTATION

IMPORTANT INFORMATION RESOURCES

For general information about Washington attractions, events, and accommodations before you leave home, visit **http://washington.org**. While in D.C. go to the **D.C. Visitor Information Center** run by the D.C. Chamber of Commerce in the Ronald Reagan Building, 1300 Pennsylvania Ave. NW (✆ **866/DC-IS-FUN** [324-7386]). It's conveniently located at the Federal Triangle Metro stop.

For information on **Maryland attractions and lodging,** call ✆ **866/639-3526** or visit www.visitmaryland.org. For information on **Arlington, Virginia,** call ✆ **703/228-3000** or visit the Arlington Convention and Visitors Service online at www.arlingtonva.us; for **Alexandria, Virginia,** call ✆ **800/388-9119** or 703/746-3301 or go to www.visitalexandriava.com.

The White House Visitor Center, at the southeast corner of 15th and E streets NW (✆ **202/**456-7041**;** www.whitehouse.gov), has information about the White House (and restrooms, too). The Visitor Center is open daily from 7:30am to 4pm; closed Thanksgiving, December 25, and January 1.

The White House is open for tours Tuesday through Saturday, 7:30am to 12:30pm, only to groups of 10 or more with reservations provided by their congressional representative or senator. Meanwhile, at the Visitor Center you can watch the video "Within These Walls," which some find more satisfying than an actual visit to the presidential home. For Smithsonian Visitor Information, stop between 9am and 5:30pm daily at the Smithsonian Information Center, 1000 Jefferson Dr. SW, Washington, DC 20560 (✆ **202/633-1000**), or visit www.si.edu/visit. Also check out **www.gosmithsonian.com**. A listing of Smithsonian exhibits and activities appears every Friday in the "Weekend" magazine of the *Washington Post.*

If you need help sorting out mixed-up tickets, retrieving lost baggage, or locating lost family members, the **Travelers Aid Society** will come to the rescue. Besides maintaining desks at Washington Dulles International Airport, Main Terminal Baggage Claim area (✆ **703/572-7350**), and Reagan National, Terminal B Baggage Claim area (✆ **703/417-3975**), the society has a booth across from the Amtrak information desk in Union

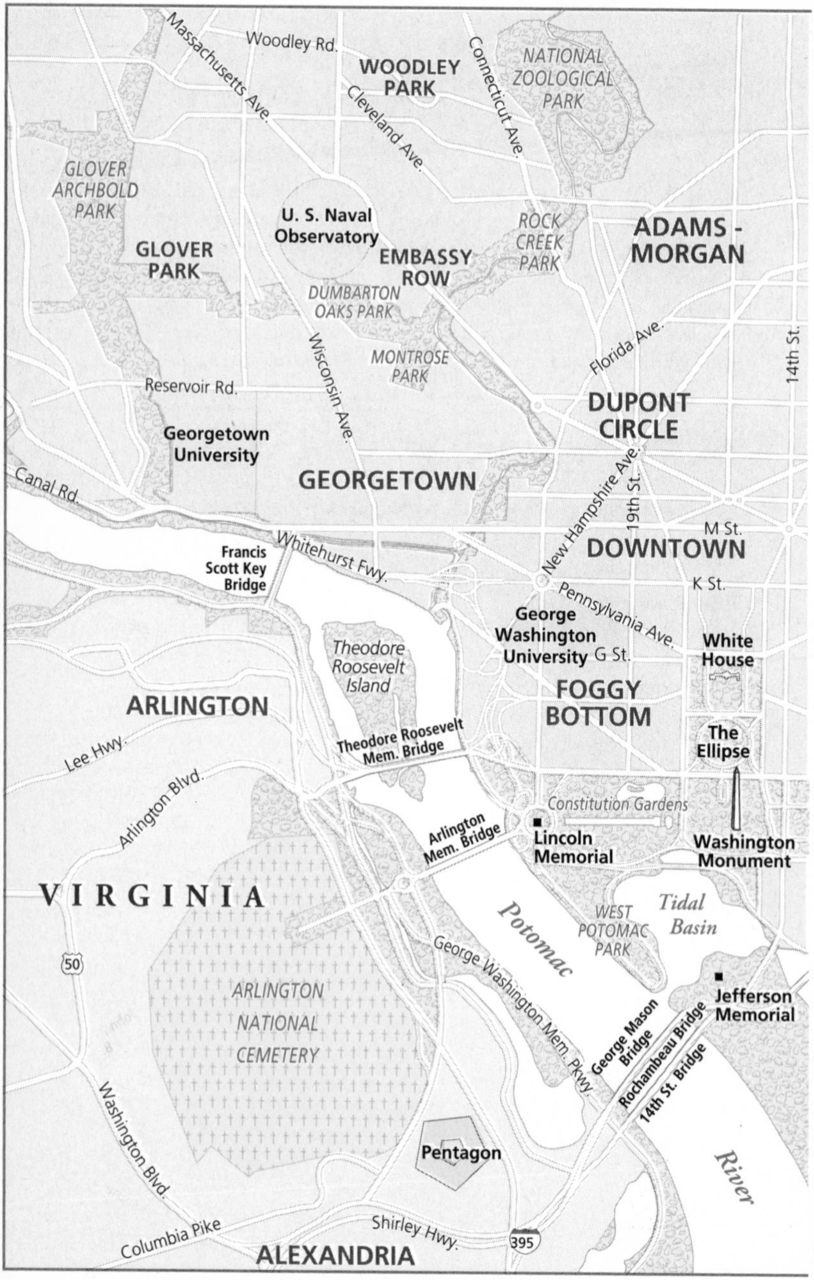
Massachusetts Ave.
Woodley Rd.
WOODLEY PARK
Connecticut Ave.
NATIONAL ZOOLOGICAL PARK
Cleveland Ave.
GLOVER ARCHBOLD PARK
U. S. Naval Observatory
ROCK CREEK PARK
ADAMS - MORGAN
GLOVER PARK
EMBASSY ROW
DUMBARTON OAKS PARK
Florida Ave.
14th St.
MONTROSE PARK
Wisconsin Ave.
Reservoir Rd.
DUPONT CIRCLE
Georgetown University
GEORGETOWN
Canal Rd.
New Hampshire Ave.
19th St.
M St.
DOWNTOWN
Whitehurst Fwy.
Francis Scott Key Bridge
K St.
Pennsylvania Ave.
George Washington University
G St.
White House
Theodore Roosevelt Island
FOGGY BOTTOM
ARLINGTON
The Ellipse
Theodore Roosevelt Mem. Bridge
Lee Hwy.
Arlington Blvd.
Constitution Gardens
Arlington Mem. Bridge
Lincoln Memorial
Washington Monument
VIRGINIA
Potomac
Tidal Basin
WEST POTOMAC PARK
50
George Washington Mem. Pkwy.
Jefferson Memorial
ARLINGTON NATIONAL CEMETERY
George Mason Bridge
Rochambeau Bridge
14th St. Bridge
Washington Blvd.
Pentagon
River
Columbia Pike
Shirley Hwy.
395
ALEXANDRIA

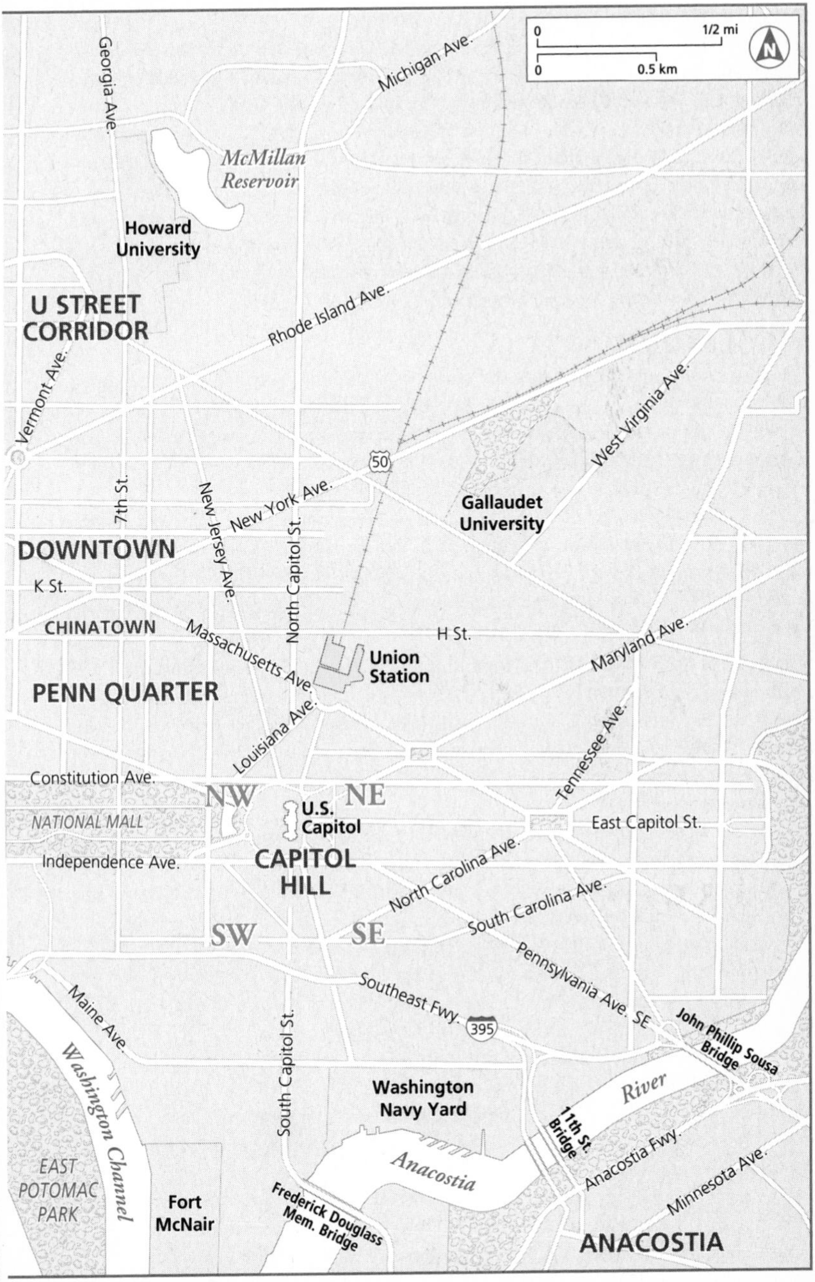

0
1/2 mi
0
0.5 km
N
Georgia Ave.
Michigan Ave.
McMillan Reservoir
Howard University
U STREET CORRIDOR
Rhode Island Ave.
Vermont Ave.
West Virginia Ave.
50
7th St.
New Jersey Ave.
New York Ave.
North Capitol St.
Gallaudet University
DOWNTOWN
K St.
CHINATOWN
Massachusetts Ave.
H St.
Union Station
Maryland Ave.
PENN QUARTER
Louisiana Ave.
Tennessee Ave.
Constitution Ave.
NW
NE
U.S. Capitol
NATIONAL MALL
East Capitol St.
Independence Ave.
CAPITOL HILL
North Carolina Ave.
South Carolina Ave.
SW
SE
Pennsylvania Ave. SE
Southeast Fwy.
395
Maine Ave.
South Capitol St.
John Phillip Sousa Bridge
Washington Channel
Washington Navy Yard
River
11th St. Bridge
Anacostia
Anacostia Fwy.
EAST POTOMAC PARK
Fort McNair
Frederick Douglass Mem. Bridge
Minnesota Ave.
ANACOSTIA

Station, 50 Massachusetts Ave. NE, at North Capitol Street (© **202/371-1937;** www.travelersaid.org). In Baltimore, Travelers Aid operates out of the Samaritan Center, 19 W. Franklin St. (© **410/659-4020**).

To find out what's going on day by day, see Washington's two daily newspapers, the ***Washington Post*** (the Thurs "Weekly" section and Fri "Weekend" magazine are especially helpful) and the ***Washington Times.*** The spirited weekly ***City Paper*** is published every Thursday and is available at all Metro stations and 1,300 D.C. shops and restaurants. ***Washington Jewish Week*** comes out every Thursday. If you're staying in the suburbs, look for the Friday edition of the ***Journal*** newspapers (no relation to the *Wall Street Journal*), which are chockablock with things to do and see. The monthly ***Washingtonian*** magazine lists area events, previews major happenings, and reviews restaurants; also look for ***Washington Flyer*** magazine (available free at the airports) and ***Where*** magazine (available at downtown hotels and newsstands).

CITY LAYOUT

The District of Columbia is shaped like a baseball diamond—but with a chunk missing, as if someone took a big bite out of the field between third base and home.

The District was originally laid out on a grid. Pay attention to a few general rules, and you should have little difficulty finding your way around. Refer to the "Washington, D.C. at a Glance" map, in this chapter, while digesting the following.

The U.S. Capitol marks the center of the city, which is divided into quadrants: **Northeast (NE), Northwest (NW), Southeast (SE),** and **Southwest (SW).** All addresses are followed by one of the four designations. *Pay attention to them:* The same address can (and often does) appear in all four quadrants of the city. Most tourist attractions are in either the NW or SW quadrant.

MAIN ARTERIES & STREETS **North Capitol Street** and **South Capitol Street** run north and south, respectively, from the Capitol. **East Capitol Street**—you guessed it—divides the city into north and south. Easy, right? Unfortunately, it's here that the plot thickens: Where you would logically expect to find West Capitol Street is the area known as the **National Mall.** The north side of the Mall is **Constitution Avenue;** the south side is **Independence Avenue.**

Lettered streets above and below (north and south of, if you prefer) East Capitol Street run east and west and are named **alphabetically,** beginning with A Street. Just to keep things interesting, there is no B or J Street, although Constitution, on the north side of the Mall, and Independence, on the south side, avenues are the equivalent of B Street. I understand that Pierre L'Enfant, who laid out the city, omitted J Street because the "I" and "J" too closely resembled each other in old-style printing.

Numbered streets run north and south, so theoretically at least, there's a 1st Street (NE and SE; NW and SW) on either side of the Capitol.

State-named avenues (now we're getting to the fun part!) radiate from the Capitol like the spokes of a wheel, all bearing state names. They slice diagonally through the numbered and lettered streets, creating a host of circles—and sometimes havoc. If you're new in town, it is possible to drive several times around these circles before finding the continuation of the street you were on.

The primary artery is **Pennsylvania Avenue,** scene of parades, inaugurations, and other splashy events. Pennsylvania Avenue runs between the Capitol and the White House, and then continues on a northwest trajectory from the White House to Georgetown. In the original plan, the president was supposed to have an uninterrupted view of the Capitol Building from the White House. But Andrew Jackson placed the Treasury Building between the White House and the Capitol, blocking off the presidential vista.

Pennsylvania Avenue, between 15th and 17th streets NW, fronting the White House, is closed to cars. To handle the traffic snarls caused by this 2-block closing, H Street is one-way eastbound, between 13th and 19th streets NW; I Street is one-way westbound, between 11th and 21st streets NW. If you're driving, good luck—you'll need it.

Constitution Avenue is north of and parallels **Independence Avenue.** It runs east–west, flanking the U.S. Capitol and the Mall with its many major museums (and important government buildings to the north and south), the Washington Monument, the Ellipse, and the White House (to the north), and continues past the Reflecting Pool to the Lincoln Memorial and the Potomac River. Until the late 1800s, when Tiber Creek ran through town (down what is now Constitution Ave.) to meet the Potomac, the entire area was a malaria-infested swamp. You can be sure D.C. had trouble drawing tourists then. In fact, it had trouble drawing anyone, and D.C. was considered a hard-luck post. For many politicians, it still is.

Washington's longest avenue, **Massachusetts Avenue,** runs north of and parallel to Pennsylvania Avenue. Along this street, heading northwest, you'll find Union Station, Dupont Circle, and Embassy Row. Farther still, you'll see the Naval Observatory (the vice president's residence is on the premises), Washington National Cathedral, and American University. Then Massachusetts Avenue just keeps going, right into Maryland.

Connecticut Avenue, running more directly north, starts at Lafayette Square near the White House. Heading north, it cuts through Dupont Circle and Rock Creek Park, past the National Zoo's main entrance, through a mostly residential neighborhood and then well into suburban Maryland. Between K Street and Dupont Circle, it's lined with casual and elegant eateries alike, shops, and high-rise office and apartment buildings, a little bit like New York's Fifth Avenue. **Wisconsin Avenue,** from the point where it crosses M Street, creates Georgetown's main intersection. Antiques shops, trendy boutiques, restaurants, and pubs all vie for attention. Yet on the side streets, lined with lovely Georgian and Federal homes, Georgetown manages to maintain its almost-European charm. Wisconsin Avenue continues into Chevy Chase and Bethesda, Maryland. In Rockville, it becomes Rockville Pike/Route 355. Farther north, it is Frederick Avenue/Route 355.

FINDING AN ADDRESS Finding an address in Washington, D.C. is easy—once you get the hang of it. In any four-digit address, the first two digits indicate the nearest lower-numbered cross street. For example, 1750 K St. NW is between 17th and 18th streets in the northwest quadrant of the city. In a three-digit address, look at the first digit. A restaurant at 620 H St. NW would be between 6th and 7th streets.

The digits of state-named avenues refer to the nearest numbered street. For example, 1600 Pennsylvania Ave. NW is on Pennsylvania Avenue at 16th Street.

Finding an address on a numbered street is a little stickier. First, assume that the addresses between A and B streets are numbered in the 100s, between B and C in the 200s, between C and D in the 300s, and so on. Now suppose that you're looking for 808 17th St. NW. Following this line of reasoning, the first digit in 808 signifies eight letters or blocks away from A Street, so start counting! If you come up with H, you're a winner: 808 17th St. is between H and I streets. This will become a game to your kids, who will find your destination while you're still deciding whether you're in SW or NW.

THE NEIGHBORHOODS IN BRIEF

To help you get acquainted with the city, the following alphabetical rundown will give you a preview of Washington's major sightseeing areas.

ADAMS MORGAN Centered on 18th Street and Columbia Road NW, colorful, vibrant, multiethnic Adams Morgan is host to international shops, restaurants, and music clubs. Whether you hunger for Ethiopian, Italian, Latin American, or fast food, family appetites will be well satisfied. You'll encounter fewer briefcases and buttoned-down shirts and minds here than in any other sector of the city. Parking can be a problem, especially on weekends. Although the 15- to 20-minute walk from the nearest Metro is fine in nice weather, I don't recommend it after dark. Be safe, and take the DC Circulator that runs every 10 minutes between Woodley Park Metro (24th and Calvert streets NW) and McPherson Square Metro (14th and I streets), Sunday through Thursday 7am to midnight, Friday and Saturday 7am to 3:30pm. After dark, take a taxi.

CAPITOL HILL Known affectionately as "the Hill," this area encompasses much more than just the awe-inspiring U.S. Capitol. Bounded by the western side of the Capitol to the west, H Street NE to the north, RFK Stadium to the east, and the Southwest Freeway (I-395) to the south, it is home to the Library of Congress, the Folger Shakespeare Library and Elizabethan Theatre, Union Station, the U.S. Botanic Garden and the Eastern Market, always a family favorite. Many restaurants in this part of town are especially kid-friendly.

CONVENTION CENTER/PENN QUARTER This neighborhood is a happening place with hotels, shops, and restaurants near the Verizon Center (for sports events and concerts by major stars) and the Convention Center at 8th Street and Mt. Vernon Place NW (the sixth largest in the country). For business travelers and vacationers alike, it is convenient to Metro Center (the transfer station for Metro's Red, Orange, and Blue lines), within walking distance of the FBI Building, the International Spy Museum, the National Museum of American Art and National Portrait Gallery, Chinatown, Ford's Theatre, and plenty of restaurants to accommodate all those conventioneers. Hotels catering to business travelers frequently offer great weekend rates and perks for families.

DOWNTOWN Geographically spread out, D.C.'s downtown centers on Connecticut Avenue and K Street NW, and extends east to 7th Street, west to 22nd Street, north to P Street, and south to Pennsylvania Avenue. The heart of the business community beats here. Although the White House and most of historic Pennsylvania Avenue are here, there are fewer attractions than in other sectors. However, it is four or fewer Metro stops to the sights on the National Mall and Capitol Hill. You'll find in this cosmopolitan area many of the city's finest restaurants, national retail chains (Ann Taylor, Banana Republic, The Gap), and street vendors hawking everything from soft pretzels to designer knockoffs.

DUPONT CIRCLE Dupont Circle (the neighborhood) surrounds Dupont Circle (the traffic circle and park). The park—and, by extension, the neighborhood—is distinguished by an abundance of squirrels and pigeons, young people with multipierced body parts, and ongoing chess games between seniors. Radiating from the intersection of Connecticut and Massachusetts avenues NW lies an area colored by the many artistic types and free spirits who reside there. One of my favorite art museums, the Phillips Collection, is here, along with smaller galleries, diverse restaurants, boutiques, and bookstores. I heartily endorse it for sipping, supping, shopping, and people-watching.

FOGGY BOTTOM An industrial center in the 18th century, Foggy Bottom lies west of the White House and stretches about 10 blocks to the foot of Georgetown. Pennsylvania Avenue and Constitution Avenue are its northern and southern perimeters. The area is villagelike, with row houses and postage-stamp-size gardens fronting brick-walked, tree-lined streets. Foggy Bottom derives much of its panache and international flavor from the State Department, the International Monetary Fund, the Kennedy Center for the Performing Arts, and George Washington University.

GEORGETOWN Long a favorite tourist draw, this bustling area, once a prosperous tobacco port, radiates from the intersection of Wisconsin Avenue and M Street NW. Georgetown's riverfront setting, Georgian and Federal architecture, boutiques, and wealth of restaurants draw visitors of all ages. Sightseeing attractions include the C&O Canal, the pre-Revolutionary Old Stone House, and the magnificent Dumbarton Oaks Gardens and Museum. On a riverfront parcel below the Whitehurst Freeway, you'll find the Washington Harbor Complex, with restaurants, and a scenic park and promenade. The Georgetown University campus perches on a hill in the western corner of this vibrant neighborhood. Dining outdoors, walking, biking, taking a river cruise, and renting a boat on the canal are all popular warm-weather respites. Georgetown is always packed on weekends. Go to www.georgetowndc.com for help planning your visit.

THE MALL Your kids will think you're crazy when you tell them they can't buy clothing or electronics at this "Mall." They can, however, visit most of the Smithsonian museums and galleries, the Lincoln Memorial, the Washington Monument, and the Vietnam, Korean War Veterans, and WWII memorials, *and* shop for souvenirs. You also can take a ride on an antique carousel, watch the Fourth of July fireworks, or catch a free outdoor summertime concert or movie. This parklike rectangle between the Capitol and Lincoln Memorial attracts kite fliers, joggers, Frisbee-tossers, inline skaters, and picnickers.

2 GETTING AROUND

BY PUBLIC TRANSPORTATION

Because Washington's Metrorail subway system is generally reliable, efficient, clean, and quiet (it's even carpeted!), your kids might want to spend their whole visit riding underground.

Getting to Georgetown

The good news: Getting to Georgetown is much easier than it has been in the past—and you have a number of ways to get there. The **Georgetown Metro Connection** (✆ **202/625-RIDE** [7433]; www.georgetowndc.com), a privately run shuttle service, buses visitors from the Dupont Circle and Rosslyn, Virginia Metro stations, making various stops in Georgetown. Ask the driver for the stop nearest your destination. Daily hours of operation are 7am to midnight. The one-way fare is $1 (50¢ if you have a SmarTrip card), 25¢ seniors, free kids 4 and under (www.commuterdirect.com). The **D.C. Circulator** bus runs between Union Station and Georgetown every 10 minutes from 7am to 9pm. Additional service is provided weekday evenings between 9pm and midnight, Friday and Saturday 9pm to 2am, between 17th and I streets NW (Farragut West Metro station) and Wisconsin Avenue and Whitehaven Street. One-way fares are $1, 50¢ seniors/persons with disabilities, free kids 4 and under. You can also catch a **Metrobus** (nos. 30, 32, 34, or 36) near the Foggy Bottom Metro station, but it usually takes longer than the Georgetown Connection or Circulator.

DISCOUNT PASSES Metro offers a **One-Day Pass,** a good deal at $7.80 per person. It can be used after 9:30am weekdays and all day Saturday, Sunday, and federal holidays. If you're stickin' around for a while, the **7-Day Fast Pass** is $39 good for unlimited travel (all hours) on 7 consecutive days. Metrobus offers passes for commuters and other frequent riders, but D.C. isn't a bus-riding-friendly city like New York. You can purchase the passes at any station or at the **Washington Metropolitan Area Transit Authority,** 600 5th St. NW (✆ **202/637-7000;** www.wmata.com). Kids 4 and under always ride free on the Metro. Senior citizens (65 and older) and persons with disabilities, with valid proof, ride the Metrorail and the Metrobus for a reduced fare.

BY SUBWAY **Metrorail (Metro),** Washington's subway system, the second busiest in the nation, opened in 1976. The system has 86 stations on 106 miles of track blanketing the metropolitan area (which includes the Maryland and Virginia suburbs); it's graffiti free, streamlined, and attractive, with air-conditioning and comfortable, upholstered seats. Signs at both ends of the cars tell the name of the last station on the line. Kids can sit in the first seat of the first car and note the train's speed and eye the control panel in the operator's compartment.

Metro is relatively quiet, and most stations are 2 or 3 minutes apart, so you're never more than a short walk from the major attractions. The system has few dark nooks and crannies in the stations to shelter criminals, and Metro Transit Police (MTPD) constantly monitor and patrol the trains and stations.

Most cars have been replaced over the years, but the escalators and elevators have been showing the aches and pains of old age. If the escalators are "sick" at your station, and you're not up to walking, ride the elevator. When riding the escalator with a small child, stand to the right, hold your child's hand, and don't allow your youngster to sit on the step. Unfortunately, accidents occasionally do happen.

Pick up a **Pocket Guide** in any station, and tuck it in your bag or use it as a bookmark for easy retrieval. Call ✆ **202/637-7000** with your questions, or go to www.metroopens doors.com. The five Metro lines—Red, Blue, Orange, Yellow, and Green—operate Sunday through Thursday from 5am to midnight, Friday from 5am to 3am, Saturday from 7am to 3am, and Sunday from 7am to midnight. A weekend schedule is usually adopted on holidays, and evening hours are sometimes extended for special events such as the Fourth of July festivities on the Mall. Trains run about every 10 to 12 minutes, more frequently during peak times, and less so after 8pm. Marking the entrance to every Metro station is a narrow brown column inscribed with the letter "M." Below the "M" is a colored stripe or stripes that tell you which line or lines operate there. Station names also appear in Braille on the columns at all Metro stops. The stationmaster will answer any routing or fare-card questions you might have. For a map of each Metro station, with streets, key buildings, and sights, visit **Stationmasters** online at www.stationmasters.com. Your ticket to ride is a computerized fare card from the intimidating-looking machines near the entrance. (If it takes you a while to figure out the system, welcome to the club.) You may also purchase a fare card—in $10, $15, or $20 denominations—online. Under the distance-based fare system, you pay the minimum, "Reduced Fare" ($1.35–$2.35) during non–rush hours (9:30am–3pm and after 7pm weekdays; all day Sat, Sun, and holidays up to 2am), and the "Regular Fare" during rush hours (5–9:30am and 3–7pm weekdays, and 2am–closing weekends). The minimum fare is $1.65; the maximum is $4.50. Fares are posted beneath the large colored map or the stationmaster's window. The machines take nickels, dimes, quarters, bills up to $20, and credit and debit

Get Smart

SmarTrip is a rechargeable card that can also be used for Metro fares, bus fares, and transfers. If you plan to park in a Metro station lot, in most cases, you will need a SmarTrip card to get out. However, in Anacostia, Franconia-Springfield, Largo Town Center, New Carrollton, Shady Grove, and Vienna/Fairfax–GMU, cash and credit cards are accepted. The cost of a SmarTrip card is $30 (includes $25 in value on the card and a $5 processing fee), if you order one via snail mail *before* you leave home (✆ **888/762-7874;** www.wmata.com). You can also purchase one from a Metrorail vending machine (next to the fare-card machines; no service fees) or at the Metro Sales Office at 12th and F St. NW, weekdays 7:30am to 7:30pm and Saturday noon to 6pm. (Are you having fun yet?) You can add up to $300 value with a credit card. To gain access to Metro, just swipe the SmarTrip card over the SmarTrip icon on the turnstile. If you live in the area or are a frequent visitor, this is the way to go.

cards. ***Warning:*** Change is returned in coins up to $5. If you feed the machine a $10 bill for a $1.20 fare, you'll be walking around with $3.80 in coins. ***Money-saver:*** Purchase a round-trip fare card, when possible, to save time. On your last day in D.C., plan carefully. There are no cash refunds on amounts showing on your fare card.

You can buy multiple fare cards of the same value with one transaction. If you arrive at a destination and your fare card comes up short, add what's necessary at an Exitfare machine near the exit gate.

Because you need a fare card to enter and exit most stations, keep it handy for reinsertion at your destination. If you will be transferring to a Metrobus, you will receive a 50¢ discount, if you have a SmarTrip card when boarding the Metrobus. Otherwise, you'll pay the full fare of $1.35. ***Tip:*** SmarTrip cards can be purchased online at www.wmata.com or at Metro Sales Offices. The one at Metro Center, 12th and F St. NW is open weekdays 7:30am to 7:30pm and Saturday noon to 6pm.

BY BUS You don't have to be a genius to figure out the **Metrobus** system, but it helps. For complete information, be sure to visit www.metroopensdoors.com.

The 13,000 stops on the 1,500-square-mile route (operating on all major D.C. arteries and in the Virginia and Maryland suburbs) are indicated by red, white, and blue signs. However, the signs—at best—just tell you what buses pull into a given stop, not where they go. For routing information, call ✆ **202/637-7000.** Using a computer, a transit-information agent can tell you the most efficient route from where you are to where you want to go (using bus and/or subway) almost instantly. Calls are taken daily between 6am and 10:30pm, but the line is often busy. A voice-response information system is available at the same number 24 hours a day. You can also get routing and fare information online at www.wmata.com. All you have to do is key in where you are coming from, your destination, and the time you want to go or arrive.

If you travel the same route frequently and would like a free map and time schedule, ask the bus driver, or call ✆ **202/637-7000** and request one. Information about free parking in Metrobus fringe lots is also available from this number.

The fare on regular routes is $1.25 using a SmarTrip card, $1.35 in cash (exact change); $3 for express routes with SmarTrip, $3.10 in cash; and transferring from Metrorail to Metrobus and vice-versa is 50¢ less with a SmarTrip card. Bus-to-bus transfers are free within a 3-hour time period with a SmarTrip card. (***Note:*** You will pay the going fare when transferring from bus to rail—no special deals here.) There are additional charges for travel into the Maryland and Virginia suburbs. Bus drivers are not equipped to make change, so be sure to carry exact change or use a SmarTrip card, which looks like a credit card. If you'll be riding a lot in 1 day, purchase a 1-day regional bus pass from the bus driver. The pass costs $3 and is good on most buses in the D.C. area. Other passes include zones in Virginia or Maryland.

Most buses operate daily around the clock. Service is very frequent on weekdays (especially during rush hours), but less so on weekends and late at night. There's a full bus-information center (the **Metro Sales Facility**) at the Metro Center Station (12th and F sts.), where tokens and special bus tickets are available.

Up to two children 4 and under ride free with a paying passenger on the Metrorail and the Metrobus alike, and there are reduced fares for senior citizens (✆ **202/962-1245**) and travelers with disabilities (✆ **202/962-1245**). Finally, if you leave something on a bus, on a train, or in a station, call **Lost and Found** (✆ **202/962-1195;** www.wmata.com).

The **Georgetown Metro Connection** shuttle is operated by a collective of Georgetown businesses (www.georgetowndc.com). Blue buses run from the Dupont Circle (19th St. at Sunderland Place) and Rosslyn (VA) Metro stations to various stops along M Street and Wisconsin Avenue. The one-way fare is $1 (50¢ with a SmarTrip card). The **Circulator** (✆ **202/962-1423;** www.dccirculator.com) shuttle bus was introduced to alleviate downtown congestion. The large buses (with three doors) run every 10 minutes from 7am to midnight, on an east–west loop between Union Station and Georgetown and a north–south loop between the Convention Center and southwest waterfront. The fare is $1 one-way, 50¢ seniors/disabled, free kids 4 and under. Pay with exact change or a SmarTrip card. Purchase tickets at the sidewalk fare meters along the routes. Ask about 1-day, 3-day, and 5-day passes.

BY CAR

Unless you absolutely have to, **don't drive in D.C.** Washington vies with Los Angeles for worst commuter traffic in the country. Driving a car is especially nightmarish during rush hour (Mon–Fri from about 6–10am and 3–7pm) and in the spring and summer seasons, when traffic jams are the norm—and only a smidge better at other times of the day and year. Not only is traffic bad, but D.C.'s many one-way streets and circles habitually confound motorists. If you don't swallow anything else in this guidebook, please accept on blind faith (and my 47 years of living in the area) that you'll waste precious time crawling through Washington's heavily trafficked downtown streets. To see some attractions in Virginia and Maryland, you may need wheels. Otherwise, you'll be better served using the comprehensive public transportation system and walking. At *all times,* street parking is very limited, and parking lots are ruinously expensive. If you're driving into D.C. for the day, you might want to park in Union Station's ample garage and then board the Metro or take the Circulator or a taxi to your destination.

All the major car-rental companies, however, are represented here. Some handy phone numbers are: **Budget** (✆ **800/527-0700**), **Hertz** (✆ **800/654-3131**), **Thrifty** (✆ **800/367-2277**), **Avis** (✆ **800/331-1212**), and **Alamo** (✆ **800/327-9633**).

BY TAXI

After years of an inscrutable zone system that confounded locals and visitors for decades, on May 1, 2008 D.C.'s 6,000 taxicabs switched to a meter system like that in other U.S. cities. The minimum fare ("drop rate") is $3 and rises with distance traveled and time spent idling in traffic. A $1 surcharge is added for travel that commences weekdays during morning and evening rush hours (7–9am and 4–6:30pm). After the first sixth of a mile, riders will pay 25¢ for each additional sixth of a mile. Riders will pay an additional 25¢ for every minute the taxi is stuck in traffic or inches forward at less than 10 miles an hour. During snow emergencies add 25% to the fare. (That's why my mantra remains, "take Metro or walk.")

For more information, go to the D.C. Taxicab Commission website, **www.dctaxi.dc.gov**.

If you want to hire a taxi for an hour or more, the hourly rate is $25 for the first hour (or portion) and $5 for each additional quarter hour. The driver's identification card must, by law, be displayed on the cab's right-side sun visor.

Be careful: There's a $1.50 charge for each additional passenger (6 and older) after the first. If you want to stop en route, it'll cost you $1 for under 5 minutes, and the stop can't be more than 5 blocks from your destination (honest). The baggage-handling rate for one piece of luggage is 50¢. Trunks and large articles cost $2. Tipping is up to you, but the going rate is 10% to 15% of the fare.

I'm proud to say I have not ridden in a D.C. cab for 4 years. Unless it's late at night, you have a disability, or you're in an iffy neighborhood, walk whenever possible or take the Metro.

When your destination is an out-of-district address (such as the airport); the fare is also based on mileage covered—$2 for the first mile or part of a mile, and 70¢ for each additional half mile or part. You can call ✆ **202/331-1671** to find out what the rate should be between any point in D.C. and an address in Virginia or Maryland.

If you decide to go for broke, it's generally easy to hail a taxi; there are about 9,000 cabs, and drivers are allowed to pick up as many passengers as can comfortably fit (provided that the new passenger doesn't take the first passenger more than 5 blocks out of the way). In bad weather or when I'm in a hurry, I walk to the nearest hotel or museum where cabs are usually lined up. If your group is small, you can count on sharing the taxi. You can also call a taxi, although there is a $2 charge for doing so. Try **Diamond Cab Company** (✆ **202/387-6200**), **Yellow Cab** (✆ **202/544-1212**), or **Capitol Cab** (✆ **202/546-2400**). They're three of the oldest and most reputable companies. If you have a complaint, note the driver's name and cab number, and call the **Taxicab Complaint Office** (✆ **202/645-6018**).

BY TOURMOBILE

If you're visiting Washington for the first time, consider the Tourmobile, a National Park Service concession. It's an ideal way to get an overview of the major attractions. The open-air, blue-and-white sightseeing trams run on routes along the Mall and as far out as Arlington Cemetery and even (with coach service) Mount Vernon.

The full-day **American Heritage Tour** (Washington and Arlington Cemetery) visits 17 sites on or near the Mall and four sites at Arlington Cemetery: the Visitor Center, the grave sites of John and Robert Kennedy and Jacqueline Kennedy Onassis, the Tomb of the Unknowns, and Arlington House. One fare allows you to use the trams for a full day.

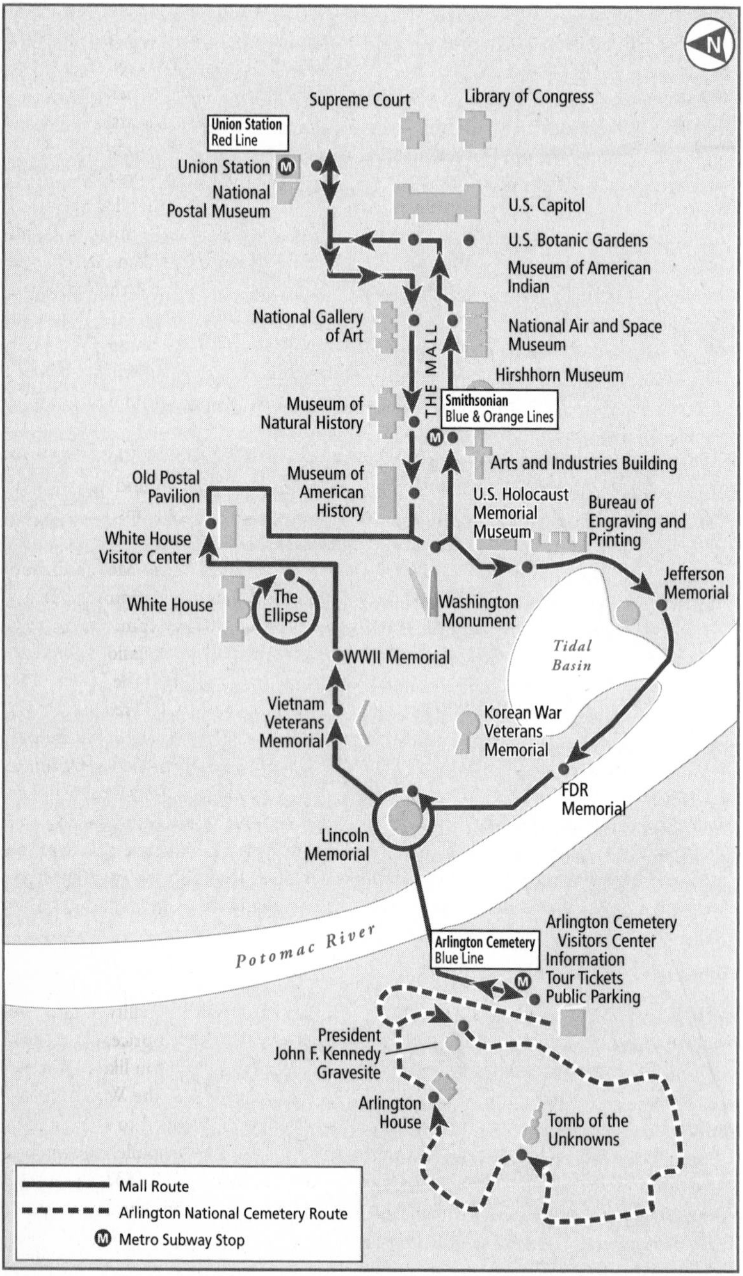
N
Supreme Court
Library of Congress
Union Station
Red Line
Union Station
National
Postal Museum
U.S. Capitol
U.S. Botanic Gardens
Museum of American
Indian
National Gallery
of Art
National Air and Space
Museum
THE MALL
Hirshhorn Museum
Museum of
Natural History
Smithsonian
Blue & Orange Lines
Arts and Industries Building
Old Postal
Pavilion
Museum of
American
History
U.S. Holocaust
Memorial
Museum
Bureau of
Engraving and
Printing
White House
Visitor Center
Jefferson
Memorial
White House
The
Ellipse
Washington
Monument
Tidal
Basin
WWII Memorial
Vietnam
Veterans
Memorial
Korean War
Veterans
Memorial
FDR
Memorial
Lincoln
Memorial
Potomac River
Arlington Cemetery
Blue Line
Arlington Cemetery
Visitors Center
Information
Tour Tickets
Public Parking
President
John F. Kennedy
Gravesite
Arlington
House
Tomb of the
Unknowns
Mall Route
Arlington National Cemetery Route
Metro Subway Stop

The cost is $27 for age 12 and older; $13 for children 3 to 11. A 2-day pass is $35 for 12 and older, and $17 for ages 3 to 11. For **Arlington Cemetery** only, adults pay $7.50; children ages 3 to 11, $3.75. You may order American Heritage Tour tickets a day ahead at Ticketmaster (www.ticketmaster.com). The price is the same, but you'll have to pay a service fee of $2.50. You may board vehicles at any of 23 popular locations. If you wish to pay by credit card, ticket kiosks are located at the Washington Monument (1401 Jefferson Dr. NW), Arlington Cemetery, and Union Station (50 Massachusetts Ave. NE, in the main hall). Otherwise, you pay the driver with cash or traveler's checks only when you board. Along the route, you may get off at any stop to visit monuments or buildings. When you finish exploring each area, you step aboard the next Tourmobile that comes along. The trams travel in a loop, serving each stop about every 20 to 30 minutes. Trams follow "figure-8" circuits from the Capitol to Arlington and back. Children under 3 ride free. If you're traveling with very young children or elderly grandparents, the 2-day pass makes a lot of sense.

Along the route, the savvy guides regale visitors with colorful commentary. They will also answer your questions. It might seem like a lot of money to plunk down at one time, but I think it's well spent. With kids in tow, you can cover a lot of ground with comfort and ease.

Tourmobiles operate year-round, daily from approximately 9am to 4:30pm. Summer hours are usually extended to 6:30pm, but you can expect seasonal and year-to-year variations. For further Tourmobile information, including a full list of stops, call ✆ **202/554-5100** or visit the website www.tourmobile.com.

Tourmobile also runs seasonal round-trip tours (lasting about 4 hr.) to **Mount Vernon** (mid-June through Labor Day). Coaches depart from the Arlington National Cemetery Visitor Center and the Washington Monument at 10am, noon, and 2pm. The price is $32 for those 12 and older, $16 for children 3 to 11, and includes admission to Mount Vernon. Make a reservation at least half an hour before departure time at the Washington Monument Tourmobile stop or Arlington Cemetery Visitor Center. The **Frederick Douglass Tour** is another seasonal offering (mid-June to Labor Day). It includes a guided tour of Frederick Douglass's home, Cedar Hill. Call for reservations and departure times. The adult fare is $7; children ages 3 to 11 pay $3.50, which includes admission. The seasonal (mid-Mar to mid-Nov) Twilight Tour of the presidential monuments, war memorials, and Capitol is $30 for adults, $15 for kids 3 to 11. Purchase tickets at the Tourmobile kiosk in Union Station (50 Massachusetts Ave. NE), also the 7pm departure point for the tour. I think kids under 9 or 10 will be bored silly. Why pay for them to sleep?

BY OLD TOWN TROLLEY TOURS

Similar to Tourmobile, and very competitive in terms of price and quality, is the **Old Town Trolley** (✆ **202/832-9800;** www.historictours.com). For a fixed price, you can get on and off these green-and-orange open-air vehicles as many times as you like at 17 locations in the District, including Union Station, the Old Post Office, the White House, National Cathedral, and other popular sites. The trolley is not licensed to stop directly on the Mall, and that is the primary difference between it and Tourmobile. The trolleys operate daily between 9am and 4:30pm, later in summer. Cost is $35 ($32 online) for riders 12 and older, $18 ($16 online) for kids 4 to 11, and free for children 3 and under.

The full narrated tour takes about 2 hours, and trolleys come by every 20 to 30 minutes, beginning at 9am.

Tickets can be purchased in Union Station (50 Massachusetts Ave. NE, in the main hall). Or book online, save 10%, and present your e-ticket when you board.

For additional tour information, see chapter 6.

Family-Friendly Accommodations

When it comes to choosing a place to stay with your kids, look for a hotel that is convenient to the Metro, sightseeing attractions, restaurants, and amusements. A complimentary terry-cloth robe and 24-hour room service might turn you on, but such amenities are of little consequence to youngsters. What's important to them is that they're close to food and fun: If there's a refrigerator, restaurant, snack machine, pool, or shopping nearby, your kids will be happy staying almost anywhere.

Budget-minded traveling families will be happy to know that many of the District's large hotel chains not only have kitchenettes but offer inexpensive alternatives to full-service restaurants such as coffee bars, fast-food kiosks, or shops that carry snacks and light fare right in their lobbies.

Make sure your kids know the difference between food taken *into* the rooms and food taken out of them. Guests pay dearly for food or beverages from stocked refrigerators and minibars. If there's no lock on yours, tell your kids that the contents are off-limits unless they clear it with you first.

Many D.C. hotels have an indoor or outdoor pool (covered in winter for year-round swimming) with a poolside beverage or snack bar. And nearly all hotels have on-site or nearby fitness clubs. Some are complimentary, some charge a fee. Of course, kids must be accompanied by an adult at the pool or health/fitness club. Many guest rooms offer complimentary premium channels or charge a small fee for pay-per-view movies and/or video games, so there should be enough to keep your tot entertained when you're not out and about in the city.

Depending on your budget, the selection of places to stay in Washington, D.C. is wide indeed. For those who prefer to leave the city at night (or find the city options filled up), I've included several hotels in the Maryland and Virginia suburbs. The following suggestions cover a broad spectrum, from super-duper luxury hotels to budget alternatives. All, with a few exceptions, are within easy walking distance of the Metro, and all have something (in most cases, several somethings) that makes them attractive to kids. If you can't swing a $4,000-a-night Presidential Suite or room with a view of the Capitol, don't despair. You won't be spending that much time in your room anyway. At day's end, flopping into a bed—even one with a few lumps—will spell relief.

GETTING THE MOST FOR YOUR DOLLAR

To get the best value for your travel dollar, stay away from the District during the high season, which runs from late March to mid-June, when prices are at their highest. To save the most, visit between mid-June and Labor Day, when Congress and your kids are on vacation. The trade-off for a summer visit is Washington's notorious heat and humidity. Most years, hotels offer family incentive packages and summer savings. These hotel packages include accommodations, admission to a private museum and/or tickets to a performance, and a welcome gift for the kiddies. As of 2009, rates started around $109 per

Take Time to Total Taxes

When you're budgeting for your vacation, remember the hefty hotel-room tax: It's 14.5% in the District. On a $200 room, that's an extra $29 per night.

night. History—and 19 years penning this book—has taught me that great deals will be in effect in subsequent summers. Call ✆ **202/789-7000** or go to www.washington.org for information on this or other bargains. The weeks during Thanksgiving and Christmas are usually slow, followed by January and February—and rates typically fall then as well. The trade-off for lower prices and fewer tourists: cold, damp weather. If you can live without cherry blossoms, definitely avoid the 2-week festival in late March and early April; it's an expensive and crowded time to visit D.C. And owing to Mother Nature's quirkiness, the blossoms often peak before or after the festival anyway.

Weekday rates can drop 30% to 50% on weekends; depending on occupancy, you might be able to cash in on weekdays as well. Hotels sometimes run unadvertised special promotions, but you won't find out about them if you don't ask. So speak up when you make a reservation.

Many experienced travelers believe you'll be quoted a better rate if you call a hotel directly instead of reserving through its toll-free number or at the website. It's always a good idea to print out your confirmation page and bring it with you in case you need proof of your reservation. When quoted a price, don't be afraid to ask if anything else is available for less. There's probably no point trying this around cherry-blossom time, but it's amazing what reservations clerks will come up with when you tell them you're going to shop around.

It's no secret that in most cases accommodations in the suburbs are less expensive than in D.C. But as usual, there's a trade-off for the lower prices. I think there's a lot to be said for waking up in a city and having the attractions at your fingertips (maybe even a view of the Potomac or U.S. Capitol from your hotel) instead of having to commute into the city and getting stuck with a view of a highway or shopping mall. The only exception, to my mind, is Old Town Alexandria, which is a worthwhile destination all by itself—and also convenient to D.C.

HELPING HANDS

For information on accommodations, try the **Washington, D.C. Convention and Tourism Corporation,** 901 7th St. NW, 4th Floor, Washington, DC 20001 (✆ **202/789-7000;** www.washington.org); or **Washington D.C. Hotels,** 1730 Rhode Island Ave. NW, Washington, DC 20036 (✆ **800/847-4832** or 202/452-1270; www.washingtondchotels.com). If you're more comfortable with someone else negotiating for you, contact **Capitol Reservations,** 1730 Rhode Island Ave. NW, Washington, DC 20036 (✆ **800/847-4832** or 202/452-1270; www.capitolreservaitons.com). They've been assisting D.C. visitors for 25 years and handle hotels in all price ranges. They are privy to discounts because of their high-volume business. Additionally, they screen all the hotels they use for cleanliness and to make sure they're in safe neighborhoods.

Groups that will occupy 10 or more rooms should know about **U.S.A. Groups** (✆ **800/872-4777** or 703/440-9704; www.usagroups.net). This free service represents hotel rooms at almost every property in the Washington, D.C. and suburban Virginia/

Tips Handy Hotel Reviews

I find www.tripadvisor.com a helpful site when I'm planning a trip. If most of the reviewers' comments are good or better, experience has taught me to discount the lone review that trashes the hotel. There's no pleasing some people.

Maryland region, and will work hard to find the best accommodations at the rates you request, saving your group valuable time and money.

BED & BREAKFASTS

Staying in a B&B can enhance your family's visit if your kids are past the age when they feel compelled to touch everything, and if you like personalized service and meeting and greeting other visitors in an intimate setting. The downside is that you might not be near a Metro station and will have to rely more on taxis and buses. I personally love B&Bs but think families with young children are better served by staying in a hotel. Rooms in B&Bs run the gamut from pint-size rooms (with the john down the hall) to suites accessorized with antiques in historic buildings.

I've listed a reservations service and suggest reserving as early as possible to get the best selection of locations and lowest rates. And be sure to specify your needs and preferences: For instance, discuss children; pets; smoking policy; preferred locations (do you require convenient public transportation?); parking; availability of TV, phone and Wi-Fi, breakfast (Continental? Full? None?); and your choice of payment.

B&B Reservation Service

Bed & Breakfast Accommodations Ltd., 1339 14th St. NW, Washington, DC 20005 (✆ **877/893-3233,** 202/328-3510; fax 413/582-9669; www.BedandBreakfastDC.com), is a reservation service for more than 35 B&Bs, furnished apartments, and vacation rentals in the D.C. area. Rates are from a basic unit for $65 to accommodations with Jacuzzi tubs and a private balcony for $265. Many properties have complimentary Wi-Fi and off-street parking. Ask about off-season or longer-stay discounts. Most major credit cards are accepted.

1 CAPITOL HILL

After living in the D.C. area for more than 45 years, I still get a thrill every time I see the Capitol, especially when it is lit like a beacon at night. If you stay here, you, too, can find your thrill on Capitol Hill and be close to the area's many attractions and family-friendly restaurants. ***A word of warning:*** Although my "Hill" friends accuse me of being overly cautious, I maintain that walking on side streets in this neighborhood after dark is not a smart idea. However, walking near the hotels and restaurants listed in this book should be fine, if it's not too late at night. Kids like to stay in this area because of its proximity to Union Station, the Capitol (and U.S. Botanic Garden), the Supreme Court, the Library of Congress, bustling Eastern Market, and attractions at or near the eastern end of the Mall—Air and Space and American Indian museums, the Newseum, and National Gallery of Art (East and West buildings).

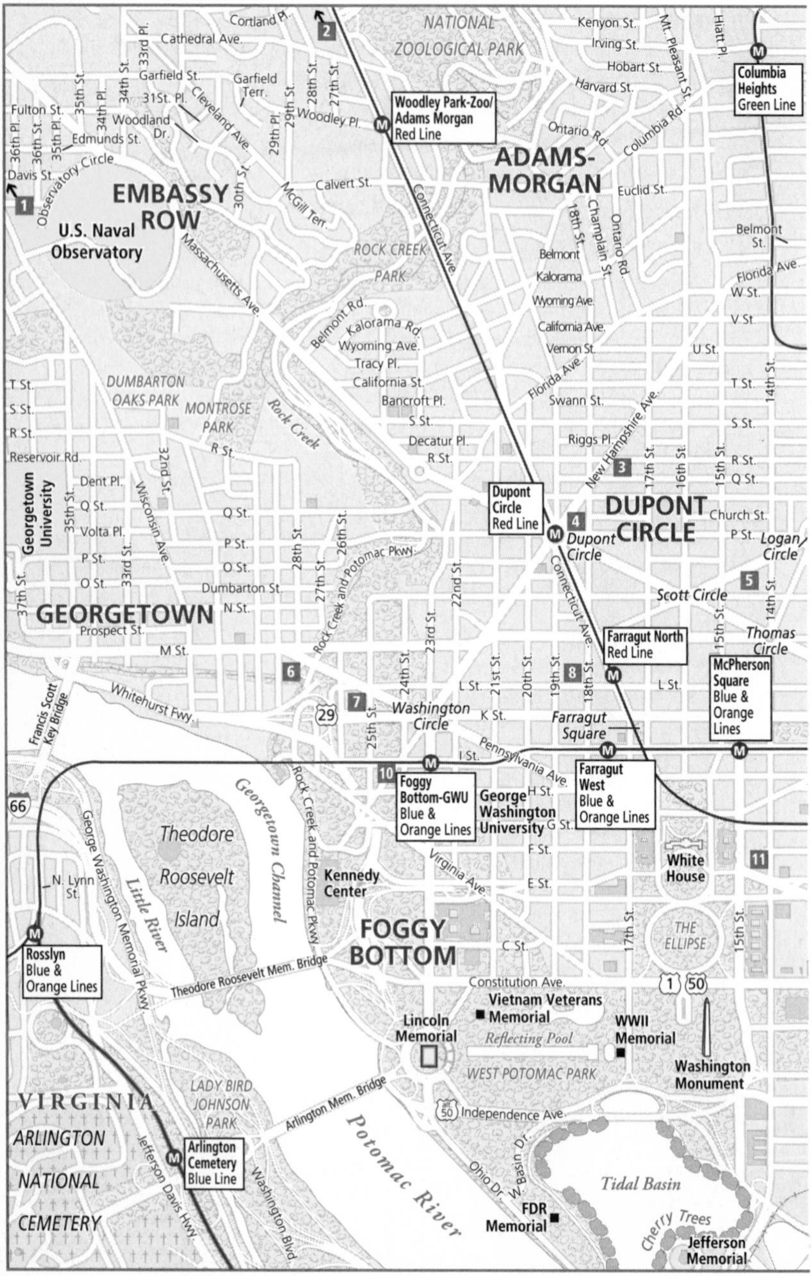
NATIONAL ZOOLOGICAL PARK
Woodley Park-Zoo/ Adams Morgan Red Line
Columbia Heights Green Line
ADAMS-MORGAN
EMBASSY ROW
U.S. Naval Observatory
ROCK CREEK PARK
DUMBARTON OAKS PARK
MONTROSE PARK
Rock Creek
Georgetown University
GEORGETOWN
Dupont Circle Red Line
Dupont Circle
DUPONT CIRCLE
Logan Circle
Scott Circle
Thomas Circle
Farragut North Red Line
McPherson Square Blue & Orange Lines
Washington Circle
Farragut Square
Farragut West Blue & Orange Lines
Foggy Bottom-GWU Blue & Orange Lines
George Washington University
White House
THE ELLIPSE
Theodore Roosevelt Island
Little River
Georgetown Channel
Kennedy Center
FOGGY BOTTOM
Rosslyn Blue & Orange Lines
Theodore Roosevelt Mem. Bridge
Francis Scott Key Bridge
Whitehurst Fwy.
Constitution Ave.
Vietnam Veterans Memorial
Lincoln Memorial
Reflecting Pool
WWII Memorial
Washington Monument
WEST POTOMAC PARK
LADY BIRD JOHNSON PARK
VIRGINIA
ARLINGTON NATIONAL CEMETERY
Arlington Cemetery Blue Line
Arlington Mem. Bridge
Potomac River
Independence Ave.
Tidal Basin
Cherry Trees
FDR Memorial
Jefferson Memorial
Connecticut Ave.
Massachusetts Ave.
Wisconsin Ave.
New Hampshire Ave.
Pennsylvania Ave.
Virginia Ave.
Florida Ave.
Rock Creek and Potomac Pkwy.
George Washington Memorial Pkwy.
Jefferson Davis Hwy.
Washington Blvd.
1
2
3
4
5
6
7
8
10
11

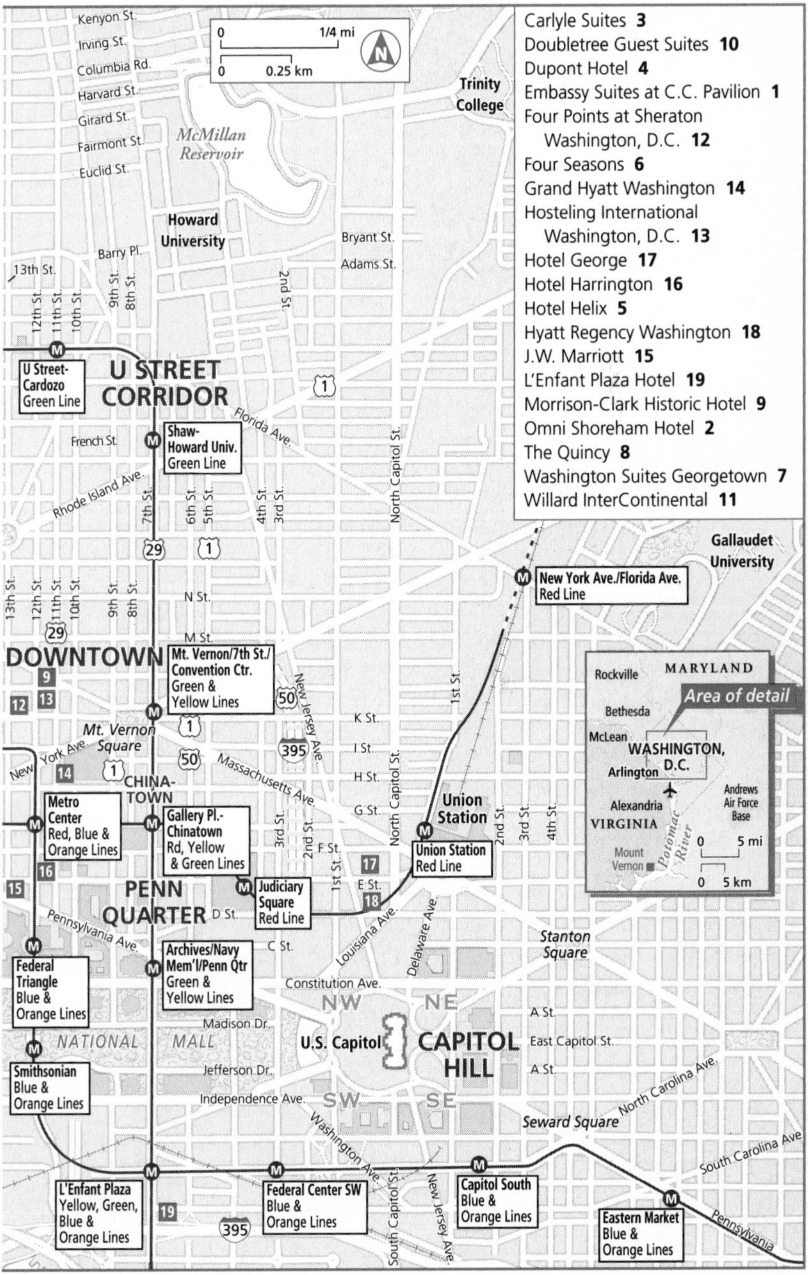
Carlyle Suites 3
Doubletree Guest Suites 10
Dupont Hotel 4
Embassy Suites at C.C. Pavilion 1
Four Points at Sheraton Washington, D.C. 12
Four Seasons 6
Grand Hyatt Washington 14
Hosteling International Washington, D.C. 13
Hotel George 17
Hotel Harrington 16
Hotel Helix 5
Hyatt Regency Washington 18
J.W. Marriott 15
L'Enfant Plaza Hotel 19
Morrison-Clark Historic Hotel 9
Omni Shoreham Hotel 2
The Quincy 8
Washington Suites Georgetown 7
Willard InterContinental 11
0 1/4 mi
0 0.25 km
N
Kenyon St.
Irving St.
Columbia Rd.
Harvard St.
Girard St.
Fairmont St.
Euclid St.
McMillan Reservoir
Trinity College
Howard University
Barry Pl.
Bryant St.
Adams St.
13th St.
12th St.
11th St.
10th St.
9th St.
8th St.
2nd St.
U Street-Cardozo Green Line
U STREET CORRIDOR
Florida Ave.
French St.
Shaw-Howard Univ. Green Line
Rhode Island Ave.
7th St.
6th St.
5th St.
4th St.
3rd St.
North Capitol St.
Gallaudet University
New York Ave./Florida Ave. Red Line
N St.
M St.
DOWNTOWN
Mt. Vernon/7th St./Convention Ctr. Green & Yellow Lines
New Jersey Ave.
1st St.
K St.
I St.
H St.
G St.
F St.
E St.
D St.
C St.
Mt. Vernon Square
New York Ave.
Massachusetts Ave.
CHINA-TOWN
Metro Center Red, Blue & Orange Lines
Gallery Pl.-Chinatown Rd, Yellow & Green Lines
Union Station
Union Station Red Line
2nd St.
3rd St.
4th St.
MARYLAND
Rockville
Area of detail
Bethesda
McLean
WASHINGTON, D.C.
Arlington
Alexandria
VIRGINIA
Andrews Air Force Base
Potomac River
Mount Vernon
0 5 mi
0 5 km
PENN QUARTER
Judiciary Square Red Line
Louisiana Ave.
Delaware Ave.
Pennsylvania Ave.
Stanton Square
Federal Triangle Blue & Orange Lines
Archives/Navy Mem'l/Penn Qtr Green & Yellow Lines
Constitution Ave.
NW
NE
A St.
Madison Dr.
NATIONAL MALL
U.S. Capitol
CAPITOL HILL
East Capitol St.
Smithsonian Blue & Orange Lines
Jefferson Dr.
Independence Ave.
SW
SE
North Carolina Ave.
Seward Square
Washington Ave.
South Carolina Ave.
L'Enfant Plaza Yellow, Green, Blue & Orange Lines
Federal Center SW Blue & Orange Lines
South Capitol St.
New Jersey Ave.
Capitol South Blue & Orange Lines
Eastern Market Blue & Orange Lines
Pennsylvania

EXPENSIVE

Hotel George ★★ Finds Two blocks from the Capitol and Union Station, the eight-story Hotel George occupies a pre–Depression era building, but there's nothing depressing about the accommodations or service. Contemporary-style paintings of G. W. hang in the hip two-story glass, chrome, and limestone lobby. The guest rooms are uncluttered and spare but soothing in shades of tasteful beige. Floor-to-ceiling cherry cabinets conceal dresser drawers, closet space, and a refreshment center. The upholstered lounge chairs with ottomans and armchairs do much to soften the decor's hard edges. Business types can use the T1 lines for free Internet access. Wi-Fi is available for a fee; complimentary for members of the Kimpton In-Touch Loyalty Program. Unwind with a choice movie on one of the complimentary premium stations (Nintendo is extra). Bathrooms (most with tub and shower; eight with shower only) are a symphony of gray-and-white marble and black granite.

Families can spread out by booking an adjoining parlor room (the hotel has two) with a double-size Murphy bed. The George Suite is a one-bedroom suite with separate living room, wet bar, powder room, dressing area, Jacuzzi, and shower.

Award-winning **Bistro Bis,** open for brunch, lunch, and dinner, is appropriate for younger kids at lunch only. The kitchen will gladly prepare "child-friendly" food for your tots. Dining choices abound in Union Station, with its myriad restaurants and Food Court, and elsewhere on Capitol Hill.

15 E St. NW, Washington, DC 20001. ✆ **800/576-8331** or 202/347-4200. Fax 202/347-4213. www.hotelgeorge.com. 139 units. $199–$519 double. Weekend/seasonal specials. Kids 17 and under stay free. Crib free, rollaway $25. AE, DISC, MC, V. Valet garage parking $40 (in-and-out privileges). Metro: Union Station. **Amenities:** Restaurant; fitness center; room service. *In room:* A/C, TV/DVD, Internet, minibar.

Hyatt Regency Washington ★★ A convenient Capitol Hill location and special perks make the Hyatt a perennial favorite for families. You can book a second room for the kids at half price, and the restaurants and room service have special kids' menus. The 5-story atrium lobby was remodeled in 2008, the 834 rooms and suites back in 2005.

The hotel is within walking distance of the Metro, the U.S. Capitol, National Mall, and other Hill attractions. Depending on which Smithsonian museum you're visiting, it's a 10- to 20-minute walk.

Some rooms have showers only, so if you're a bubble-bath fan, be sure to state your preference.

The indoor heated lap pool (in a two-story glass atrium) is sure to attract your kids' attention, as will the hotel's complimentary fitness center. Children of any age are welcome at the pool, although those under 16 must be accompanied by a parent. In the atrium lobby, the open and airy **Article One–American Grill** (& Lounge) is family-appropriate for breakfast, lunch, and dinner. The **Lounge** has nine flatscreen televisions; you can order light fare.

400 New Jersey Ave. NW, Washington, DC 20001. ✆ **800/233-1234** or 202/737-1234. Fax 202/737-5773. www.washington.hyatt.com. 834 units. Mon–Fri $139–$429 double, Regency Club $75 extra; Sat–Sun from $139 single or double. Children under 18 stay free in parent's room. Crib free. Weekend and seasonal specials; AAA discounts. AE, DISC, MC, V. Valet parking $41 (in-and-out privileges). Metro: Union Station. **Amenities:** Restaurant; coffee shop; bar; babysitting; concierge; complimentary fitness center; room service; indoor pool. *In room:* A/C, TV, fax, Wi-Fi (fee), ADA equipment for guests with disabilities.

2 CONVENTION CENTER

Weekdays this area is frequented mostly by local business types and conventioneers. The Verizon Center (which hosts sports events and concerts) and Walter E. Washington Convention Center at 8th Street and Mt. Vernon Place NW have spawned new office and residential complexes, hotels, and restaurants. What the neighborhood lacks in charm it makes up in convenience; it's within walking distance of Ford's Theatre, the Spy Museum, Metro Center (a hub for the Blue, Orange, and Red Lines), Macy's, Barnes & Noble, and scores of restaurants. Hearty souls hoof it the 7 or 8 blocks to the Mall attractions, but you can catch a train at the nearby Metro Center (12th and G sts. NW).

VERY EXPENSIVE

Four Points by Sheraton Washington D.C. Downtown ★★ The Sheraton is convenient to the Convention Center (about 3 blocks) and within walking distance of many downtown attractions. Each room come with a minifridge and complimentary in-room high-speed Internet access and bottled water. A view of something more pleasing than an elevator shaft is by request only—unless you book a suite.

The neighborhood has turned around in the past few years (for the better) and the location is just 3 blocks to the Metro Center, where you can hop a train on three of Metro's five lines. Walk to Ford's Theatre, the Smithsonian American Art Museum, the Shops at National Place, the Mall, the Verizon Center for a sports event or rock concert, downtown shopping, and scores of restaurants. A small indoor rooftop swimming pool with a sundeck (but no lifeguard) is more than adequate for cooling off after pounding the pavement. Or get reenergized in the fitness center.

The hotel restaurant, the **District Grille,** serves American cuisine, breakfast, lunch, and dinner daily. Many favorite family-friendly restaurants—Hard Rock Cafe, T.G.I. Friday's, Capitol City Brewing Co.—are within a few blocks, as are such high-end restaurants as **Acadiana** (see "Restaurants," p. 86), which welcomes well-behaved kids 8 and older, maybe because Executive Chef Jeff Tunks has young children and understands their finicky eating habits and small stomachs. With preteens and older, try D.C. Coast, Bobby Van's Steak House, and Brasserie Beck. Too pooped to peep or dress for dinner? Call room service.

1201 K St. NW, Washington, DC 20005. ✆ **202/289-7600.** Fax 202/349-2215. www.starwoodhotels.com/fourpoints. 265 units. $109–$459 double. Children under 18 stay free in parent's room. Crib free. AE, DC, DISC, MC, V. Valet parking $35 (in-and-out privileges; limited parking facilities, with maximum height restrictions: 6 ft. 8 in.). Metro: Metro Center or McPherson Sq. **Amenities:** Restaurant; lounge; concierge; 24-hr. fitness center; small indoor pool; room service. *In room:* A/C, TV, Internet.

A Room-Service Alternative

Too tired to dine out? Families staying near the Convention Center can order a pie via phone or online from **Domino's Pizza,** at 1300 L St. NW (✆ **202/216-0057;** www.dominos.com).

EXPENSIVE

Morrison-Clark Historic Hotel ★★★ Finds The Morrison-Clark Historic Hotel, listed on the National Register of Historic Places, is a top choice, if you appreciate charm and vintage ambience. The former 1860s homes of David Morrison and Reuben Clark, two prominent (and wealthy) Washingtonians, form the basis for the hotel. Beginning in 1923, the Morrison house served as headquarters for the Women's Army & Navy League (for enlisted men). The Clark home was annexed and, in 1972, the combined/dual property began housing military women. After substantial renovations, the property opened as a hotel in 1987. You too can be part of Morrison-Clark history and enjoy the Victorian entry parlor, beautifully decorated guest rooms—individualized with wicker, antiques, original art, and fresh bouquets—and southern-style courtyard. All 54 Victorian rooms (some of which have a Carrera marble nonworking fireplace) have one queen or two double beds, and some accommodations have bougainvillea-draped trellised balconies or private porches that open onto a courtyard garden and fountain. Most of the parlor suites are done in French country style, with down duvets, and have separate living areas with sofa beds.

Among the offerings on the full southern-style breakfast served daily ($8–$12) are fresh fruits and juices, egg dishes, pancakes, grits and ham, and the signature crab omelet. A basket of baked muffins and biscuits is included. After the pastries and croissants, step (or waddle) into the complimentary on-site fitness center for damage control. Gratis daily newspapers, twice-a-day maid service with Belgian chocolates at bed turndown, and complimentary overnight shoeshines are but a few of the extras at the Morrison-Clark. The management is gracious about accepting children of all ages.

The hotel's noted restaurant is open daily. The chef shops for fresh ingredients at the Eastern Market, and the kitchen will gladly split orders or prepare half orders for kids. Dine in the courtyard, weather permitting.

1015 L St. NW. (btw. 11th St. and Massachusetts Ave.), Washington, DC 20001. ✆ **800/332-7898** or 202/898-1200. Fax 202/289-8579. www.morrisonclark.com. Mon–Fri $159–$379 single; Sat–Sun from $139–$159 single or double. Rates include continental breakfast. Children 16 and under stay free in parent's room. Crib $20, rollaway $20. Extra person $20. Internet specials sometimes available; group rates available. AE, DC, DISC, MC, V. Valet parking $28. Metro: Metro Center (walk east 1 block on F or G St. NW to left at 11th St., continue 4 blocks, and cross Mass. Ave) or Mount Vernon Square (closer, but fewer trains). Take a taxi late at night. **Amenities:** Restaurant; babysitting; concierge; fitness club; room service. *In room:* A/C, TV, minibar, hair dryer.

INEXPENSIVE

Hostelling International–Washington, D.C. ★ Value I know of no other way to stay in D.C. this inexpensively, unless you sleep in a Metro station, and I don't recommend that—it's noisy, uncomfortable, and illegal. Opt instead for a bed in Hostelling International (HI), which offers dorm-style and private rooms in a renovated downtown building. The lobby was updated in 2008, with environmentally friendly (low voc) paint, new floors, a pool table, and piano. A guitar is available for hostellers to use. In 2009, all guest rooms and hallways were spruced up with eco-conscious carpets (low voc, made from recycled materials, and 100% recyclable) and low voc paint. A new library/reading room was completed in late 2009. Despite the no-frills decor, you can stay connected via high-speed modem lines (fee) and free Wi-Fi. The rooms are cheerful and bright and more than adequate. The area teems with new office buildings and trendy condos. The location, just 3 blocks north of the Metro Center stop, is extremely convenient. The big question is: Can your family survive without an in-room TV? The good news: The hostel's television room has a 60-inch big-screen TV with 150 channels, DVD/VCR, and loads of free movies available to borrow anytime. For a breath of fresh air, step onto the outdoor patio.

The dorm rooms—all air-conditioned—have 4 to 10 beds; private rooms have 2 twin beds. Clean, recently renovated bathrooms are down the hall. Although some of the dorm rooms are coed, most are for men or women, so couples may be separated, with sons sleeping in the same dorm as fathers and daughters with their mothers. If you rent all the beds in one room, families can stay together. For everyone's safety and comfort, families traveling with children under 18 are required to stay in rooms without other hostellers. The hostel provides linens, pillows, blankets, towels, soap, and shampoo/conditioner. All you have to do is bring your clothes, toothpaste and toothbrush, and this guidebook. A gift shop sells toiletries and souvenirs in case you forgot something essential.

Upon registering, you'll be given a local area map and calendar of free events and activities around town. The HI also offers free special activities for guests—walking tours, concerts, free pasta nights, movies, and more. And the knowledgeable volunteers at the information desk are available to help you with sightseeing and other travel questions. The hostel also has a comfortable lounge, storage lockers, covered parking for bicycles, and a self-service Laundromat. All public areas and rooms are accessible to travelers with disabilities, and all guest rooms are nonsmoking.

To cut costs further, you can shop for groceries at the Capitol Supermarket on 11th St., between M and N streets, and prepare your meals in the huge fully equipped self-service kitchen, and eat in the shared dining room. Enjoy a hearty free breakfast here (one helping per person, please) before heading for the National Mall. Ideally, your kids will meet some interesting international visitors who will spark their interest in learning about other countries.

1009 11th St. NW, at K St., Washington, DC 20001. ✆ **202/737-2333.** Fax 202/737-1508. www.HIWashingtondc.org. 250 beds. $29–$42 HI members; add $3 per person, per night for nonmembers (yearly membership is $28 per adult). Rates include all taxes. Children 2 and under free (if they sleep in the same bed). Free continental breakfast. No cribs. MC. V. Parking is in public lots, some street parking available. Metro: Metro Center, McPherson Sq., Gallery Place. **Amenities:** Lounge; large-screen TV/DVD/VCR w/ movie library. *In room:* A/C.

3 DOWNTOWN

If you stay in this area, you can roll out of bed and onto the White House lawn. Well, *almost.* Most of the top sights (such as the Smithsonian museums, presidential memorials, and U.S. Capitol) are within walking distance or just a few stops away on the Metro. You'll be in the thick of things and also have your pick of restaurants and shopping. You'll usually pay top dollar for accommodations at a downtown hotel, but you can't beat the convenience. And if your time is limited, wouldn't you rather spend it *in* rather than traveling *to* a museum?

VERY EXPENSIVE

Grand Hyatt Washington ★★ The Grand Hyatt, in the vibrant Penn Quarter, is within walking distance of the Spy Museum, where you can test your family's espionage skills, the Smithsonian American Art Museum, the White House, the National Mall, the Newseum, the FBI Building (if or when it ever reopens for tours), Ford's Theatre and the Petersen House, Chinatown, the Verizon Center (sports and entertainment complex), and lots of restaurants and shopping. Five dining options are onsite. Large, well-appointed rooms surround a stunning 12-story, glass-enclosed atrium filled with light and greenery. Direct underground access to the Metro Center is a huge plus in nasty weather, and the **Old Town Trolley** (p. 47) stops right outside.

As part of the weekend family program, kids 18 and under (traveling with a parent or guardian) get their own room at half price, as well as dining breaks. After a tough day of sightseeing, they can unwind in the indoor pool (children must be accompanied by an adult). Kids can test the latest Nintendo Wii games or watch sports on high-def plasma screens over burgers, hot dogs, chicken fingers, wings, or nachos in the **Grand Slam** sports bar (with a parent or guardian). If the troops are restless, watch an in-room movie or borrow a board game at the front desk. The Grand Hyatt is a nonsmoking hotel. Complimentary minifridges, cribs, and rollaways are available upon request. For a quiet dinner *à deux,* ask the concierge to arrange for a bonded babysitter. You can breakfast or lunch on American fare in the airy **Grand Café** (daily 6:30am–2pm), where kids 3 and under eat free; those 12 and under can order from the adult menu for half price or choose items from the Johnny Venture children's menu. The **Zephyr Deli** and full-service **Starbucks** are open for a quick or grab-and-go breakfast, lunch (sandwiches, pizza, salads), and snacks, weekdays from 6:30am to 2:30pm and weekends from 6:30am to 1:30pm. Pick up sandwiches and picnic on the Mall or in your room, if you return for a midday siesta.

1000 H St. NW, Washington, DC 20001. ✆ **800/233-1234** or 202/582-1234. Fax 202/637-4781. www.grandwashington.hyatt.com. 888 units. $149–$340 double. Children under 18 stay free in parent's room or get their own room for half price Sat–Sun. Special family weekend rates. Crib and rollaway free. Grand Club available; AAA discounts. AE, DISC, MC, V. Self-parking $24, valet parking $30 (in-and-out privileges for valet service). Metro: Metro Center. **Amenities:** 4 restaurants; 3 bars; babysitting (outside company); concierge; on-site health club with steam and sauna; indoor pool; room service. *In room:* A/C, TV, hair dryer.

EXPENSIVE

JW Marriott ★★ One look at the large, opulent lobby and you know the Marriott family has come a *long* way since opening a root-beer stand on 14th Street in 1927. The lobby underwent a major face-lift in 2007. Guests can plug laptops, cameras, and iPods into the new 32-inch flatscreen TVs. Go ahead, e-mail and watch a movie simultaneously on the split screen. Guest rooms wear a sleek, sophisticated look. Bedding is top of the line. Attractive as the Marriott is, it's easy to become disoriented. One end of the lobby flows into Eat at National Place (a convenient 575-seat food court with Quizno's, Five Guys, and other eateries), making things a bit more confusing, so keep a sharp eye on younger kids.

The hotel boasts a great location; the Metro Center, with trains on the Blue, Orange, and Red lines, is just a block away, and there are plenty of sights, restaurants, and shopping nearby as well. The pool and health club will keep kids occupied when you're not out sightseeing. The rooms are light and bright, with a king or two double beds, a good-size dresser, a desk and chair, two phones, and a high-definition TV with cable and premium movie channels. Suites have kitchenettes. Bathrooms are generous in size. Kids can get On Demand movies for a fee. (For this, you traveled to Washington?) A limited number of rooms have a view of the Washington Monument or Pennsylvania Avenue rather than a courtyard. Go ahead and ask; you don't ask, you don't get.

Weekend visitors should ask about special packages, which can include full complimentary breakfasts and late checkouts. Kids stay free, and those 5 and under eat free from the special kids' menu in the hotel restaurants.

The lounge-restaurant, **1331,** open for lunch and dinner, features Continental/Asian fusion cuisine, formal atmosphere, and high prices. Watch the Pennsylvania Avenue traffic from **The Avenue Grill,** open for breakfast, lunch, and dinner. The Starbucks opens at 6am and offers coffee, pastries, fruits, and fresh juices. At lunch, head next door to eat at National Place or the Reagan Building food court (a block away). For dinner, a host of suitable restaurants is also within a short walk or Metro ride.

1331 Pennsylvania Ave. NW (at E St.), Washington, DC 20004. ✆ **800/228-9290** or 202/393-2000. Fax 202/626-6991. www.marriotthotels.com. 738 units. Mon–Fri $239–$469 double; ask about weekend/special rates. Children under 16 stay free in parent's room. Cribs and rollaways free. AE, DC, DISC, MC, V. Valet garage parking $39 (in-and-out privileges). Metro: Metro Center (F St. exit). **Amenities:** 2 restaurants; 2 bars; coffee shop; babysitting; concierge; health club with hot tub and sauna; indoor swimming pool; room service. *In room:* A/C, TV, minibar, hair dryer.

L'Enfant Plaza Hotel ★★★ This hotel is great for families with children. First of all, it's less than a 10-minute walk to the National Air and Space Museum and other Smithsonian museums on the National Mall. Don't feel like walking? The steps off the lobby lead to a Metro station; the Smithsonian station is just a stop away, and the Washington Nationals Baseball Stadium is two stops. The Shopping Promenade, a lackluster mall below the hotel, has 30 tenants, including a pharmacy, some clothing stores, and a McDonald's.

The lobby is quiet and elegant; the staff is professional, gracious, and courteous. As part of the "We Love Kids!" program, children receive a cool welcome gift on arrival. In 2009, parents who bought the Spy Package received 4 VIP Spy Museum tickets and a Spy book. We can't promise that this will be ongoing, but we're hoping. Family board games and DVDs are available for free at the front desk. Children can also order from a special kids' menu in the restaurant.

Large, cushy guest rooms with elegant furnishings contain either two doubles or a king. Suites come with kitchenettes. Rooms take up the top four floors of the 15-story office building. The 14th- and 15th-floor rooms have balconies. Great views here range from the Washington Monument to the Washington Cathedral.

The outdoor pool is a knockout, as nice as those at resorts, with plenty of chaises and chairs. In winter, the pool area is covered with a bubble. A lifeguard is on duty from 9am to 8pm.

A 5-minute walk over a pedestrian-only bridge will lead you to the waterfront, where you can board the *Spirit of Washington* cruise to Mount Vernon, inspect the seafood stands along Maine Avenue, eat in one of several riverside restaurants, or ogle the pleasure craft in the marina. This neighborhood, although convenient to the Mall, is less than ideal for late-night strolling. I suggest taking the Metro or a taxi back to the hotel at night.

The riverfront is a great place to exercise your family pooch. You can bring up to two dogs, as long as you abide by the leash and clean-up rules. There is a $25 per pet per night charge and a $250 refundable deposit.

The **American Grill** serves breakfast, lunch, and dinner on the lobby level. A kids' menu for 12 and under has items for $4 to $7. Business types frequent the **Foggy Brew Pub,** with pub fare. The **Lobby** Lounge offers more than 50 types of martinis for the grown-ups.

480 L'Enfant Plaza SW, Washington, DC 20024. ✆ **800/635-5065** or 202/484-1000. Fax 202/646-4456. www.lenfantplazahotel.com. 370 units. $329 double Mon–Fri; $475 suite. Sat–Sun specials from $109; ask about packages. Children under 18 stay free in parent's room. Crib free; rollaway $20. AE, DC, DISC, MC, V. Valet garage parking $30 plus tax (in-and-out privileges). Metro: L'Enfant Plaza. Pets accepted. **Amenities:** Restaurant; 2 bars; concierge; fully equipped health club complimentary to adults (Nautilus equipment, weights, aerobic classes, and on-call masseuse); outdoor pool (covered Sept–May); room service. *In room:* A/C, TV w/pay movies, hair dryer, Wi-Fi.

Willard InterContinental Hotel ★★ Stay at the Willard and you'll get your fill of history without leaving the elegant premises. President-elect Lincoln checked in for a spell after rumors of an assassination plot. (Maybe he should have stayed.) Ulysses S. Grant met with influence peddlers in the lobby and added "lobbyist" to the lexicon. Julia Ward Howe penned the words of "The Battle Hymn of the Republic" in her room. Willard history is well-documented in the hotel's museum. Not a bad way for your kids to expand their minds.

The opulent 12-story hotel—just 1 block from the White House Visitor Center, 2 blocks from the White House and National Museum of American History—is a short walk to most Mall museums, the presidential monuments and memorials. The hotel itself has a colorful history—opening, closing, falling into disrepair, reopening again in 1986. Members of royalty, the international business community, and discriminating leisure travelers stay here for the location, old-world setting, and impeccable service.

Rooms are oversized by D.C. standards and traditional in decor—and the windows open! The hotel, relying 100% on wind energy, is a leader in Sustainable Hospitality and received the 2009 D.C. Mayor's Environmental Excellence Award, among others.

Onsite is a Café du Parc, serving French bistro fare indoors and on a shaded courtyard. The kids' coloring-book menu (at breakfast, lunch, and dinner) introduces young diners to French. Around Christmas, the hotel offers families a Nutcracker package, which includes front orchestra seats for the Washington Ballet's Nutcracker, this version set in Georgetown. Mom can slip into the Red Door Spa on the second floor for a milk bath, massage, microdermabrasion, or makeover, while the children settle down with a movie (DVD players in most rooms), check e-mail, or watch an international channel on TV.

Willard InterContinental Washington, 1401 Pennsylvania Ave. NW (btw. 14th & 15th sts.), Washington, D.C. 20004. ✆ **800/827-1747** or 202/628-9100. www.washington.intercontinental.com. 333 units. $299–$4,100 per night double. Breakfast with some packages. Seasonal rates. Credit cards: AE, DISC, MC, Visa. Pets allowed $100 (must sign a pet waiver). Valet parking $35 (in-and-out privileges). Metro: Metro Center. **Amenities:** Restaurant; bar; 24-hour concierge; Red Door Spa (full spa and fitness facility, face and body treatments); Wi-Fi. *In room:* TV, CD player, DVD players (suites only), iDock music systems (suites only), Internet, minibar.

MODERATE

The Quincy ★ Value Visitors enjoy classic comfort in an attractive contemporary setting at the all-suites Quincy, a boutique hotel just four Metro stops from the Smithsonian museums. You have your pick of three basic room types: king (king bed, non-pullout sectional sofa, no kitchen, larger living area); double (two double beds, sofa, some with kitchens, some without); and queen (queen bed, pullout sofa, some with kitchens, some without). The double or queen works best for a family. Each "suite" is actually one large (400-sq.-ft.) room with bed(s), kitchenette/kitchen or not, comfortable sofa, oversize desk with ergonomic chair, flatscreen TV, two phones, and complimentary Wi-Fi. Wooden window blinds are attractive and practical. Sumptuous duvets cover the comfy, plush pillow-top mattresses. Guests receive turndown service at night and delivery of the *Washington Post* each morning. The small lobby is a minimalist's dream and serviceable. Bring Fifi or Fido if you like, but you'll pay an additional $150 per stay, whether you check in for 1 night or 1 week.

You can walk to the White House, National Geographic Society Museum, or Renwick Gallery in 10 minutes. The Corcoran is 15 minutes away. From there it's another 10 minutes to the Mall. Upscale dining and shopping establishments line Connecticut Avenue 2 blocks away. Vendors hawk fast food, clothing, and souvenirs outside Connecticut Avenue/K Street office buildings. In exchange for a refundable deposit, kids can borrow games (Twister, Trouble, Checkers, Taboo and such) from the front desk.

On site is the family-friendly **Mackey's Public House,** serving Irish fare (see chapter 5); **Recessions II** is for grown-ups. Nearby are Au Bon Pain (1801 L St.), Corner Bakery (1828 L St.), and the very delish and very pricey Morton's steakhouse (1050 Connecticut Ave. NW).

1823 L St. NW, Washington, DC 20036. ✆ **800/424-2970** or 202/223-4320. Fax 202/223-8546. www.thequincy.com. 99 studio suites. Mon–Fri $169–$239 double; Sat–Sun $129–$189 double. Children under 16 stay free in parent's room. Extra person $20. Crib or rollaway $20. Weekend packages available. AE, DC, DISC, MC, V. Valet parking $28 (in-and-out privileges), free meter parking Fri night to Sun. Metro: Farragut North or Farragut West. Pets (under 25 lb.) allowed $150 per stay. **Amenities:** 2 restaurants; free passes to the nearby Bally's Total Fitness; room service. *In room:* A/C, TV, kitchenette or kitchen (full kitchen w/4-burner stove, microwave, and full-size refrigerator in 28 of the 99 suites).

INEXPENSIVE

Hotel Harrington (Value) Little wonder that this old-timer is still truckin' after so many years. The price is right, and the location is prime. It's 5 blocks from the White House, and an easy walk to the Newseum, Ford's Theatre, Eat at National Place, the Old Post Office Pavilion (with a food court), Ronald Reagan Building (Food Court and free midday music most days), the National Aquarium, and several Smithsonian museums. The Metro Center, with three of the five Metro lines (Red, Blue, and Orange), is 2 blocks away. The Harrington has been family owned since 1914 and is still one of the best deals around. Note, though, that due to the great prices, this hotel is often filled with school groups. And you've probably heard that kids make noise. So bring earplugs or turn up your iPod.

Make no mistake, you'll know you're in an older hotel, but the high-ceilinged rooms are clean and updated annually with new carpets and drapes. Closets and bathrooms are small; some bathrooms have a shower only. Most rooms have a desk and chair, and all rooms have a TV with complimentary CNN and HBO. Small refrigerators are standard in some rooms. Otherwise, request one and stock it with snacks from the CVS Pharmacy at 13th Street and Pennsylvania Avenue NW. Triples and quads are ideal for families, with different bed configurations (queen and twin) and two bathrooms. Extra-large family rooms sleep up to six people. Deluxe family rooms sleep four and are suitable for families with older children; a folding privacy door separates the two rooms. Three restaurants offer reasonably priced fare on site, or you can take the money you're saving by staying here and go splurge at the nearby Hard Rock Cafe. Board games (free) and movies are available for family entertainment. Have the kids ask for a souvenir paper airplane Harrington Hawk. (The owner of the hotel is a plane buff.)

The no-frills **Harriet's Restaurant** and **Harry's Pub** (with sidewalk tables in good weather) serve basic down-home fare. **Ollie's Trolley** is a good choice for a quick burger, fries, and shake.

436 11th St. NW (at E St.) Washington, DC 20004. ✆ **800/424-8532** or 202/628-8140. Fax 202/347-3924. www.hotel-harrington.com. 245 units. $129–$135 double; $165–$189 triple and quad. Crib free. AE, DC, DISC, MC, V. Self-parking in nearby garage $15 (in-and-out privileges; cars and minivans only). Metro: Metro Center. **Amenities:** 3 restaurants; nearby health club. *In room:* A/C, TV.

4 DUPONT CIRCLE

Dupont Circle has a free-spirited, neighborhood feel to it and is more colorful and unbuttoned than "official" Washington. Dupont Circle (the park) lends itself to people-watching and pigeon-chasing. It's a gathering place for musicians, office workers, and families with benches, grass, and an awesome marble fountain commemorating Civil War rear admiral Samuel Francis DuPont. Also, you'll find great "local" restaurants around here. The area east of Dupont Circle around 14th and P streets has made quite a comeback in recent years.

Stay here if your kids are interested in browsing farmers' markets (every Sun, rain or shine, year round), boutiques, bookstores, and art galleries (the Phillips is a gem). I think the few extra minutes on the Metro to the Mall attractions are worth it. Most of the hotels are less pricey than their closer-in counterparts and less apt to host conventioneers.

EXPENSIVE

The Dupont Hotel ★★ Part of the prestigious Doyle Collection, The Dupont Hotel opened in March 2009 and offers guests a prime location in a residential 'hood just 1 block from the Metro and easy access to the major downtown sites. Kids 11 and under stay free in the same room with parents. A plus for families is Dupont Circle (the small park) where you can play, picnic, read, watch some serious chess games, listen to music (live and manufactured), or catch the spray from the large fountain. Stay here and you're a block from one of the city's more colorful and extensive weekend farmers' markets. A Zen-like feeling prevails in the hotel rooms and public areas. The only exception is the bar off the lobby. Because it's not a place to bring children, it's not a problem. Understated luxury and excellent service prevail. Though average in size, rooms are extremely well designed to make the best possible use of the space. Adjoining rooms are available for families. The quietest rooms are on the top floors and face away from Dupont Circle. The decor is minimalist with Oriental accents; the furnishings sumptuous. Great attention has been lavished on the details, such as the heated tile bathroom floors and slender gooseneck lamps on both sides of the beds for late-night reading. And the elevators are fast, no 5-minute waits. Dine in the pleasant first-floor cafe, where there's a kids' menu; or the chef will prepare half-portions, if you ask. Breakfast is included in some packages; ask about others.

Otherwise, you can fall into one of the many family restaurants in the 'hood. The Luna Grill and Afterwards Cafe are excellent choices for hearty, reasonably priced fare at breakfast and lunch. Hank's Oyster Bar serves award-winning seafood in a casual setting. (See chapter 5, Dupont Circle, p. 98)

The Dupont Hotel, 1500 New Hampshire Ave. NW. ✆ **800/423-6953** or 202/483-6000. www.doylecollection.com/dupont. Mon–Fri $199–$429; Sat–Sun $149–$429, double. AE, DISC, MC, V. Pets under 20 lbs. accepted $150 (plus tax). Valet parking $32 (in-and-out privileges). Limited street parking. Metro: Dupont Circle (either exit). **Amenities:** Restaurant; bar/lounge; babysitting; concierge; Level 9 (executive level), exercise room onsite; fully equipped health club offsite; outdoor pool at nearby Courtyard by Marriott Washington, D.C. (summer only; complimentary); Internet in common areas. *In-room:* A/C, TV/DVD or TV/VCR, fridge, hair dryer, minibar, mp3 docking station, iPod docking station.

Hotel Helix ★ This hip boutique hotel, part of the popular Kimpton Group, attracts people in the arts, lobbyists, and sybarites. Standard guest rooms are a blend of funk, minimalist, pop art, and psychedelic decor. Think orange bathroom vanities, electric blue and lime green built-in room accessories, a freestanding entertainment center, sheer fabric that pulls around platform beds covered in faux fur, and Pop Rocks, wax lips, and PEZ dispensers in the honor bar.

Specialty rooms include Zone Rooms, which include a separate curtained space with an amazingly comfortable Euro-style chair and ottoman and lava lamp—all very conducive to "zoning" out. Flex Rooms, built with the health enthusiast in mind, have a separate workout area with cardio and yoga equipment and a 12" TV. Bunk Rooms, ideal for a family of four, are intended for fun-seekers, such as those into postmidnight pillow fights. The top bunk is a twin; the bottom opens up to a full-size bed. There's also a 27-inch TV in the bunk room with a DVD player; a Nintendo Wii is available on request at the front desk, based on availability. Across the room is a king-size bed and another TV for Mom and Dad. To ensure your beauty sleep, ask for a room on one of the higher floors (the Helix has 10). To the right of the lobby (where complimentary champagne or wine is served to adult guests from 5–6pm every afternoon) is the **Helix Lounge** for cocktails and American-style light fare kicked up a notch. Nearly everything is kid-friendly, especially the Burger Royale with Cheese and Mac & Cheese. Brunch is served weekends. With kids, you want to be out of here by 7 or 8pm. (Do stick your head in here after dark. It's a scene.) The "Bring 'em Along" family package in a bunk room starts at $179 and includes board games, a pizza party with two large pizzas, two pints of Häagen-Dazs ice cream, and more. The only drawback I see here is the 15-minute walk to the Metro at McPherson Square or Dupont Circle. Those who have trouble getting around should plan on using a taxi or consider staying in a hotel closer to a Metro station. Otherwise, the neighborhood is a walker's and voyeur's delight.

1430 Rhode Island Ave. NW, Washington, DC 20005. ✆ **800/706-1202** or 202/462-9001. Fax 202/332-3519. www.hotelhelix.com. 178 units. $99–$500 double. Weekend and seasonal specials. Children under 18 free in parent's room. Crib and rollaway free. AE, MC, V. Valet garage parking $33 (in-and-out privileges). Metro: McPherson Square or Dupont Circle. Pets accepted (no charge). **Amenities:** Helix Lounge (bar/restaurant); on-site workout room (complimentary passes to the YMCA and its pool are available). *In room:* A/C, TV, minibar, Wi-Fi.

MODERATE

Carlyle Suites This eight-story, all-suite hotel, 3 blocks from the Dupont Circle Metro, sits on a residential street (by D.C. standards) near restaurants, shops, and galleries. One of the district's top family attractions, the National Geographic Museum at Explorers Hall, is 6 blocks away.

The Carlyle Suites, distinguished by its Art Deco exterior and lobby, has lots going for it besides its location. Rooms have two Tempur-Pedic double beds and a sofa bed, or a Tempur-Pedic king and sofa bed—ample space for a family of four. Large closets, a dining and sitting area, a fully equipped kitchen, workspaces with cordless phones, complimentary high-speed Internet access and Wi-Fi, add to the Carlyle's panache. And kids under 18 stay free with a parent. Pets are welcome (no Burmese pythons, please), but please let the hotel know you're bringing a pet when you make your reservation. A small Safeway market is 2 blocks away, at 1701 Corcoran St. NW. Load up on supplies, and your family can eat meals in the room, if you choose, or snack while enjoying a movie on complimentary cable with 66 channels, including HBO and Showtime. Tables and chairs are set in a courtyard off the lobby for relaxing or writing postcards.

The hotel restaurant, **Twist Dupont Circle,** offers year-round outdoor dining on a glass-enclosed patio with a retractable roof. Come for the ample breakfast buffet to fortify your family before you set out. Items from the kids menu are sure to fill little tummies at any meal. If you prefer to relax and eat in your room, an extensive menu is available for dinner. The **Twist Bar,** with light fare and cocktails, is open from 4pm until midnight. Within an easy walk are plenty of family-friendly restaurants and cafes.

1731 New Hampshire Ave. NW (btw. R and S sts.), Washington, DC 20009. ✆ **202/234-3200.** Fax 202/387-0085. www.carlylesuites.com. 170 efficiency suites. $129–$359 suite. Children under 18 stay free in parent's room. Crib and rollaway free. Extra person $20. Weekend packages available. AE, DC, MC, V. Limited free parking. Metro: Dupont Circle (Q St. exit). Pets (75 lb. or under) accepted. **Amenities:** Restaurant; babysitting by prior arrangement; concierge services; free access to the nearby (5 blocks) adults-only Washington Sports Club. *In room:* A/C, flatscreen TV, hair dryer, Internet access and Wi-Fi.

5 GEORGETOWN

A small, sophisticated riverfront town within the city, Georgetown draws locals and out-of-towners with its fine Georgian architecture, hundreds of restaurants and shops, and party atmosphere (especially evenings and weekends). Younger kids seem to enjoy the activity (people, cars, lots to look at). Of all D.C.'s neighborhoods, however, it is the least accessible to the Metro. For that reason, I am recommending only one hotel in Georgetown—because it is so special. The nearest Metro station is Foggy Bottom; from there, you can take the D.C. Circulator (Georgetown-Union Station route; ✆ **202/962-1423**; www.dccirculator.com). Another option is the Georgetown Metro Connection (✆ **202/625-RIDE** [7433]; www.georgetowndc.com/shuttle.php), which runs every 10 to 15 minutes and makes numerous stops between the Dupont Circle and Rosslyn (Arlington, VA) Metro stations. See the "Getting to Georgetown" sidebar in chapter 3 for details.

Four Seasons ★★★ I'm surprised that the management of this elegant hotel can coax guests to leave after experiencing the TLC that the Four Seasons is famous for worldwide. Business and entertainment types, heads of state, and royalty have frequented the hotel regularly since it opened in 1979. Families who choose to stay here will enjoy the same service afforded sultans and silver-screen stars.

Some visitors have checked in empty-handed (I don't suggest it) and been outfitted within hours—even at night.

After a $40-million renovation, the West Wing (no, not *that* one) reopened in January 2009, just in time for the Presidential Inauguration. If you want to book the Royal Suite (bullet-proof glass, private entrance, and closed-caption security system), it can be converted into a three-bedroom suite. Or, bring the grandparents and distant cousins, and the entire wing can be closed off, giving you eight bedrooms. The East Wing was renovated and reconfigured in 2005. As a result, the majority of the rooms are 50% larger.

Most rooms overlook Rock Creek Park and the C&O Canal. It's a short walk to Washington Harbor, with restaurants, a multiplex movie theater, and a lovely park on the Potomac, 10 minutes or less to Georgetown's concentration of shops, restaurants, and historic homes.

At check-in children receive personalized cookies and milk and "sushi" made of rice crispy treats rolled in gummy worms or popcorn—and a natural soda. Bathrooms of kids 6 and under will be decorated in a duck motif; 9 and under will find a coloring book and crayons on the desk. Kids 9 to 12 receive a *Kids Guide to Washington* and *National Geographic* magazine. Teens receive a Fandex on the U.S. presidents or Washington, D.C.; and teen girls get a current issue of *Teen Vogue.* Ooh la-la. There is a kids' menu in **Seasons** restaurant (breakfast and lunch) and a wireless laptop for checking e-mail messages.

The concierge will secure a bonded babysitter, if you want to dine *a deux* in Bourbon Steak, the hotel's high-profile restaurant, or partake of Georgetown nightlife without the kiddies.

The health club is 12,500 square feet of state-of-the-art luxury. Water toys are kept poolside for little squirts. Children under 16 must be accompanied by an adult at the pool, in the whirlpool, and at the fitness club.

The lobby, renovated in 2009, invites relaxation with an interior winter garden, stone fireplace, and library with books on nature, gardening, and art.

2800 Pennsylvania Ave. NW, Washington, DC 20007. ✆ **800/332-3442** or 202/342-0444. Fax 202/944-2076. www.fourseasons.com. 211 units (including 25 suites). Mon–Fri from $545 double to $15,000 for the 1-bedroom 4,000-sq-ft. Royal Suite; Sat–Sun from $395 double. Children under 16 stay free in parent's room. Crib and rollaway free. Ask about special and seasonal packages. AE, DC, DISC, MC, V. Valet parking $42 plus tax. Metro: Foggy Bottom, and then Georgetown Connection shuttle. Pets (under 15 lb.) accepted. **Amenities:** Restaurant; bar; CD and video games library; children's programs; concierge; fully equipped state-of-the-art fitness club; indoor heated pool and whirlpool; sauna; spa; room service. *In room:* A/C, TV, hair dryer, minibar.

6 FOGGY BOTTOM

In the West End of the city between Georgetown and the White House, Foggy Bottom is distinguished by its relatively quiet tree-lined streets and Lilliputian row houses. The sophisticated international/cultural/college-town air is generated by the State Department, the Kennedy Center, and George Washington University. Stay here, and you'll be able to walk to concerts and plays, as well as free performances (daily at 6pm) on the Millennium Stage of the Kennedy Center. Pinstripers, students, artistic types, and old-timers populate the neighborhood after dark. Charming Foggy Bottom is within walking distance of Georgetown and accessible to D.C.'s sights via the Metro station at 23rd and I streets NW.

EXPENSIVE

Doubletree Guest Suites Washington, DC ★ A warm bag of chocolate chip cookies welcomes visitors to the Doubletree, situated in picturesque Foggy Bottom, a stone's throw from George Washington University, the Department of State, and the Kennedy Center. The hotel attracts leisure travelers as well as dark suits and performing artists needing to hunker down for a while. Stay here and you may run into someone starring in a play, concert, or dance performance. They like the Doubletree for its convenience, low profile (no paparazzi), and affordability. So will you. Other big pluses at Doubletree Guest Suites (other than those yummy cookies) are space and privacy, and a 5-minute walk to Foggy Bottom Metro. You can also walk to Georgetown for shopping, dining, and a boat ride or stroll on the C&O Canal. The hotel rooms were completely redone in 2008—stem to stern, with new kitchens and living room furniture, new sofa beds, and flatscreen TVs. The suites have a separate living room with a sofa bed, a bedroom with king or two queen beds, two phone lines, a walk-in closet, and wireless Internet connection. The look is clean and comfortable, if a bit institutional for my taste.

Each kitchen has a microwave, full-size stainless steel refrigerator, dishwasher, stove, cookware, toaster, coffeemaker, and service (silverware) for four. Stock up on snacks at the Safeway in the Watergate, 2½ blocks away. A complimentary continental breakfast is served in the lobby weekends only. Room service is available mornings and evenings.

Cool off in the small rooftop pool and relax on the sundeck, open seasonally from Memorial Day through Labor Day. It's too small to do laps, but it's big enough for a cooling dunk. If you're combining business with pleasure, the voicemail, dataports, and Wi-Fi come in handy.

801 New Hampshire Ave. NW, Washington, DC 20037. ✆ **800/424-2900** or 202/785-2000. Fax 202/785-9485. http://doubletree1.hilton.com. 103 suites. $129–$450 suite. Children under 18 stay free in parent's room. Continental breakfast included in Sat–Sun rates. Crib free; rollaway $20. Extra person $20 each. Weekend and special packages available. Monthly rates. AE, DC, DISC, MC, V. Valet parking $30 plus tax (in-and-out privileges) per day. Metro: Foggy Bottom, then walk 1 block south on New Hampshire Ave. (toward the Kennedy Center). Pets (up to 75 lb.) accepted $20 per day. **Amenities:** Pool; room service. *In room:* A/C, TV, hair dryer.

Georgetown Suites Washington D.C. ★ Walk to the heart of Georgetown, the Kennedy Center, and the White House from this kid-friendly hotel. During the most recent renovations (2008), new carpeting, wall coverings, mattresses, and flatscreen HD TVs were added. Each unit is over 600 square feet (large by D.C. standards), with a living/dining area with pullout sofa, separate bedroom/vanity area, full kitchen (refrigerator, stove, dishwasher, microwave, coffeemaker, dishes, pots and pans, and utensils), and bathroom. The workout room has rubber floors (no padded walls), an elliptical treadmill, free weights, and a flatscreen TV. The freebies include warm, freshly baked cookies upon check-in, high-speed wired and wireless Internet access, continental breakfast (daily), use of cribs and strollers, and a daily newspaper. Save a bundle at mealtime and shop for produce, groceries, bakery items, and prepared foods at my all-time fave grocery store, Trader Joe's, a block away at 1101 25th St. NW, between L and M sts. (✆ **202/296-1921**). As part of the hotel's eco-friendliness, guests driving hybrid cars receive a discount on parking. In addition, each unit has a recycling receptacle and eco-friendly bath products; guests have the option of using sheets and towels for more than 1 day. Everyone is invited to the weekly manager's reception Tuesdays from 6 to 7pm for complimentary appetizers and beverages. Veg out and watch an On Demand movie with the children until they fall asleep.

There's a pleasant tree-lined patio off the rear of the lobby, and dozens of restaurants are within a few blocks. **Five Guys** (prize-winning burgers and fries) is half a mile away in Georgetown (1335 Wisconsin Ave.). **Johnny Rockets,** fast food with 1950s ambience, is just 6 blocks away on M Street. **Kinkead's,** one of the best restaurants in the entire city, is a short walk (not recommended for very young children at dinner). And who can resist **T.G.I. Friday's,** also nearby, for satisfying family fare? **Marshall's Restaurant,** a casual neighborhood drop-in kind of place, is just three doors away at 2524 L St. NW. There are a Ben & Jerry's and a Häagen-Dazs a few blocks away in Georgetown to satisfy your sweet tooth (or teeth). If you're taking your kids to look at colleges, the hotel is just a 5-minute stroll to George Washington University (you're practically on campus) and about a mile east of Georgetown University.

2500 Pennsylvania Ave. NW, Washington, DC 20037. ✆ **877/736-2500** or 202/333-8060. Fax 202/338-3818. www.wsgdc.com. 124 suites. $119–$309 suite. Children under 18 stay free in parent's room. Rates include Continental breakfast. Crib and stroller free. Extra person $20. Weekend and Family Fun packages available online. Extended-stay rates available. AE, DISC, MC, V. Valet parking $30 per day. Metro: Foggy Bottom, then walk north on 23rd St. 1½ blocks, left at Pennsylvania Ave. 2 blocks. Pets accepted $20 per day. **Amenities:** Weekly manager's reception; fitness room (adults only); high-speed Internet access. *In room:* A/C, TV, full kitchen.

7 UPPER NORTHWEST

The northwest pocket of the city borders Chevy Chase, Maryland. Like Neverland, it's not on any map and is more a state of mind. The neighborhood is largely residential, with many of the District's most expensive homes, and shopping and restaurants that cater to a sophisticated and discriminating clientele. Stay here, and you'll have a 20-minute Metro ride to the Mall. But you'll be only a Metro station or two away (in some cases, a walk) from the National Zoo, a must-see with kids.

EXPENSIVE

Embassy Suites at the Chevy Chase Pavilion ★★ At this property in the Chevy Chase Pavilion, guests enjoy a full, free, cooked-to-order, delicious breakfast, which is sufficient enough reason to relocate, in my opinion. More than $6 million in renovations were completed in January 2009, including flatscreen HD televisions, an expanded fiberoptic entertainment system, and cordless phones in the living room. Suites consist of a bedroom with a king bed or two doubles and a separate living room with a sofa bed. There are two flatscreen HD TVs with HBO, pay-per-view movies, and more than 60 combined TV/music channels (25 high-def TV channels); high-speed Internet access (daily fee); and a wet bar and refrigerator, so the munchkins need never go hungry. The hotel is within walking distance of scores of restaurants and more excellent shopping at Bloomingdale's, Mazza Gallerie (with Neiman Marcus and Filene's Basement), Lord & Taylor, Saks, and Tiffany & Co.

After a tough day of sightseeing, swim in the rooftop indoor pool, relax in the Jacuzzi, or work out in the fully equipped health club (kids must be accompanied by an adult). Then unwind with a complimentary cocktail.

Stay dry with underground access to the Friendship Heights Metro station. From there, it's only a 15-minute ride to downtown. Shopping downstairs in the multilevel Chevy Chase Pavilion is fairly lackluster (some might say "dying" or "in transition"), with the exception of Stein Mart and J. Crew. But there is a Washington Sports Club (hotel guests receive discounted admission) and a **Cheesecake Factory,** with California cuisine and 35 varieties of cheesecake, plus specialty pastas and gourmet pizza baked in a wood-burning oven. **Maggiano's,** half a block away on Wisconsin Avenue, has super Italian fare and huge portions. The front room is down-home casual for a quick bite with little ones. Several other restaurants are within easy walking distance.

4300 Military Rd. NW (at Wisconsin Ave.), Washington, DC 20015. ✆ **800/EMBASSY** [362-2779] or 202/362-9300. Fax 202/686-3405. www.embassysuitesdc.com. 198 suites. Mon–Fri $249–$349 suite; Sat–Sun $159–$249 suite. Rates include breakfast and cocktails. Children 18 and under stay free in parent's room. Crib free; rollaway $10. Ask about the Georgette Klinger spa special (guests already receive a 15% discount). Weekend, AAA, family, and seasonal packages available. AE, DC, DISC, MC, V. Garage self-parking $24 per day. Metro: Friendship Heights (Western Ave. exit). **Amenities:** Restaurant; health club; Jacuzzi; indoor pool; room service. *In room:* A/C, TV, hair dryer, refrigerator.

Omni Shoreham Hotel ★★ The dowager queen of D.C. hotels—a member of Historic Hotels of America and Great Resorts and Hotels—celebrates its 80th birthday in 2010. She's looking remarkably well for an octogenarian. When this hotel was just the plain-old Shoreham, it provided the setting for Perle Mesta's celebrated parties, numerous inaugural balls, and Harry Truman's poker games. Adjacent to Rock Creek Park, the Omni

Shoreham is a self-contained 11-acre resort in a residential neighborhood off Connecticut Avenue, about 300 feet from the Metro and less than 15 minutes from downtown. The cavernous lobby is usually filled with conventioneers weekdays. If you think bigger is better, and if yours is a family of fitness freaks, look no further. At day's end, cool off in the large outdoor pool (Apr–Oct), work out in the health club (charge for users 16 years of age and older), or stroll through the gardens. If you crave more exercise, head out the hotel's back door into Rock Creek Park, with hiking, biking, and jogging trails, and a fitness course.

Renovations to the guest rooms were completed in 2008. The new "regal" look features a gold-and-plum color scheme, cherry-ton furniture, granite countertops, and new luxury bedding. Marble-floor bathrooms and myriad amenities aside, the best thing about the Omni Shoreham is its location—you can walk to the National Zoo.

Please note that prices here vary widely depending on availability, the season, and whether you stay on a weekday or a weekend. So you could pay anything from a bargain rate ($129 when the hotel runs a weekend special) to top dollar ($450 for a suite).

Robert's restaurant may look fancy with its Versailles-like high ceilings and oversize mirror-paneled walls but it serves mostly American cuisine at breakfast, lunch, and dinner and is exceedingly kid-friendly (high chairs, booster seats, an all-day kids menu and breakfast buffet—only $5.95 for kids 5–10, free 4 and under). **Morsels,** a European gourmet carryout, is in the lobby. The adults-only **Marquee Bar and Lounge** is a martini-and-cigar bar serving imported beers on tap. A pool bar, located on the pool deck, is open seasonally and features light fare and beverage service.

2500 Calvert St. NW (at Connecticut Ave.), Washington, DC 20008. ✆ **800/THE-OMNI** [843-6664] or 202/234-0700. Fax 202/265-7972. www.omnihotels.com. 834 units. $129–$309 double; $229–$450 suite. Children under 18 stay free in parent's room. Crib free; rollaway $25. Extra person $25. Family and weekend packages available. AE, DC, DISC, MC, V. Garage self-parking $22; valet $26 (in-and-out privileges). Metro: Woodley Park–Zoo/Adams Morgan; then walk south 1½ blocks and cross Calvert St. **Amenities:** 2 restaurants; bar; babysitting; concierge; 1.5-mile fitness course with 18 exercise stations (in Rock Creek Park); spacious health club & spa with sauna, CYBEX equipment; outdoor pool; 10 miles of jogging, hiking, and bicycle trails; video checkout; room service. *In room:* A/C, TV, Wi-Fi.

8 SUBURBAN MARYLAND

The Montgomery County suburbs of Chevy Chase and Bethesda are largely residential and well known for their fine shopping, restaurants, kid-filled vans, and gridlock. The Metro ride into D.C. is 20 to 30 minutes, depending on where you stay in Chevy Chase (closer in) or Bethesda. Don't even think of driving into the District if you stay in Maryland. You could fly to Europe faster. Due east, in Prince George's County, is Lanham, a commercial/industrial area with numerous hotels and family-friendly restaurants. Stay here, and you'll be 1 mile from Amtrak (20 min. to Union Station) and the New Carrollton Metro (20 min. to the Smithsonian station).

BETHESDA

I remember when Bethesda was a sleepy suburban village. That was way back in the '70s and before. These days, it is overbuilt and overpopulated with people, office buildings, and cars. The once-bucolic small town is now a traffic-choked minimegalopolis. The big draws in Bethesda are its excellent restaurants (ethnic and American) in all price ranges, almost all of which are within walking distance of the hotels listed below. The Metro ride to downtown D.C. is about 30 minutes.

Expensive

Hyatt Regency Bethesda ★ Providing top-notch facilities at a convenient suburban location atop the Bethesda Metro, the Hyatt Regency Bethesda delivers the goods to vacationing families staying in this safe, happening 'hood of restaurants, shopping, movies, music, and live theater.

As Yogi Berra used to say, you'll get "déjà vu all over again" when you enter the large, plant-filled, open-atrium lobby, with its requisite bar. Many find comfort in the familiar. And it is eye-catching.

The guest rooms and bathrooms are large and sumptuous, with a king or two double beds, plenty of closet and drawer space. Some have balconies/terraces. Unfortunately, the views are mostly of commercial downtown Bethesda. When making reservations, ask for the best family rate available. And the best view.

Your kids will spend nary a dull moment here. The hotel has a large, glass-enclosed, heated rooftop indoor pool (Mon–Fri 6am–10pm; Sat–Sun and holidays 4–8pm), a newly renovated, complimentary health club open 24/7 (you'll have to go with them), and a family-style restaurant. An 11-screen movie theater is within walking distance, as are more than 150 restaurants and Gifford's ice cream parlor. Imagination Stage, producing children's theatrical events, is about 5 blocks from the hotel (at 4908 Auburn Ave.). Check with the concierge for details.

The hotel's family-friendly **Daily Grill** is open for breakfast, lunch, dinner, and Sunday brunch. **Morton's** (steakhouse) is open for dinner nightly, reservations are highly recommended (more info in Restaurants, p. 93). The **Concours Lobby Lounge** has coffee-bar service every morning from 6am and beverages and appetizers from 4pm until closing. Bethesda has more restaurants than you can shake a stick at, representing just about every ethnic persuasion. For cheap eats and local color, go to the nearby **Tastee Diner,** open 24/7 (see description in Restaurants, p. 107). Ask the concierge for suggestions. Chevy Chase (Bloomingdale's, numerous specialty shops, Mazza Gallerie, Chevy Chase Pavilion), and White Flint Mall (with Bloomies, Lord & Taylor, Border's, and numerous specialty shops) are about equidistant by car or Metro.

1 Bethesda Metro Center (Wisconsin Ave. and Old Georgetown Rd.), Bethesda, MD 20814. ✆ **800/233-1234** or 301/657-1234. Fax 301/657-6453. www.bethesda.hyatt.com. 390 units. Mon–Fri $215–$350 double, $150 additional for an executive suite; Sat–Sun $109–$189 double; $25 for each additional person. Children 18 and under stay free in parent's room. Crib and rollaway (fee). Special weekend, family, AAA, and senior packages available. AE, DC, DISC, MC, V. Self-parking per day Mon–Fri $15, Sat–Sun $12; valet parking per day Mon–Fri $20, Sat–Sun $17 (in-and-out privileges). Metro: Bethesda. **Amenities:** 2 restaurants; bar; babysitting; concierge; newly renovated 24/7 health club; heated indoor pool; room service. *In room:* A/C, TV, hair dryer, Wi-Fi (fee).

CHEVY CHASE

Chevy Chase is synonymous with *upscale.* Well-heeled professionals and their families live in the affluent bedroom community full of large, older homes. Kid-friendly restaurants and shopping—quality department and specialty stores, and designer boutiques—serve discerning residents and visitors alike.

Moderate

Marriott Courtyard Inn Chevy Chase Brand, spanking new in July 2009, this Courtyard, like most, is frequented by business types. But don't let that dissuade you. It's an ideal location for families who want to vacate the city at night and mix heavy doses of shopping with their sightseeing. Stroll over to Bloomingdale's, Saks Fifth

Avenue, Lord & Taylor, Gucci, Brooks Brothers, Yves St. Laurent, and Mazza Gallerie (with Neiman Marcus, Filene's Basement, and many upscale boutiques and specialty stores). When you run out of money and want to head downtown for some free sightseeing, the Friendship Heights Metro is only 2 blocks away. Rooms (king or two queens) are attractive and well appointed, with excellent lighting, an oversize desk and ergonomic chair, and a 42" high-def, flatscreen TV.

Traffic from Wisconsin Avenue may disturb light sleepers. Inquire about a quiet room away from the street and/or on an upper floor when you make a reservation. A lifeguard watches over the third-floor outdoor pool open May to September, and guests have use of the on-site fitness center. While you're working out, the younger kids can enjoy an in-room movie or their favorite sports on the big TV. Using 100% renewable energy, this property is the first Gold LEED (LEadership in Energy and Design) candidate in Montgomery County, Maryland.

If you're hungry any time of the day or night, the lobby **Market** is open—would you believe, 24/7—for take-away, premade sandwiches, snacks, and beverages. A hearty, made-to-order breakfast is complimentary. The **Bistro** is open daily and has a kids' menu with items $6 to $10. It's convenient, if you're wiped out from sightseeing, but the food is nothing to write home about and you can do better in this 'hood. A slew of family restaurants is within walking distance. Clyde's, the Cheesecake Factory, and Chadwick's all welcome families. As part of one Courtyard package, Mom will receive a $50 gift certificate toward a visit to the Elizabeth Arden Red Door Spa, 2 blocks away.

Other special packages include Tickets to a Movie (includes dinner and movie tickets).

5520 Wisconsin Ave., Chevy Chase, MD 20815. ✆ **301/656-1500.** Fax 301/656-5045. www.courtyardchevychase.com. 214 units. Mon–Fri $119–$239; Sat–Sun $109 and up double. Crib free; rollaway $15 per night. Children 18 and under stay free in parent's room. Rates include breakfast. Ask about special rates and packages. AE, DISC, MC, V. Self-parking $15 (in-and-out privileges). Metro: Friendship Heights. **Amenities:** Restaurant; carryout; bar; fitness center; outdoor pool. *In room:* A/C, TV, clock w/iPod docking stations, minifridge, Wi-Fi.

LANHAM

Lanham is commercial, with businesses, office parks, and lots of reasonably priced restaurants. It's a bit off the beaten path, yet only 1 mile from the New Carrollton Metro/Amtrak station. From there, it's a 20-minute ride on the Marc commuter train (weekdays only) to Union Station, or 25 minutes to the Smithsonian Metro station on the Mall. For many families, the low hotel rates outweigh any inconvenience and the lackluster neighborhood. You might want a car if you stay here, however. Without it, you'll be limited to the hotel restaurant once you return from D.C. Of course, you can always take a taxi to a nearby restaurant.

Inexpensive

Best Western Capital Beltway (Value) Located in Prince George's County, near the intersection of Route 450 and the Beltway (495), the Best Western provides complimentary van service (daily 8am–8pm, on the hour) to the New Carrollton Metro station, just 1 mile away. There, you can board a train and be in the heart of downtown D.C. in 20 minutes or head to Six Flags, just 5 miles away. Fed-Ex field is only 9 miles, if you score tickets to a Redskins game or a concert. The hotel is equidistant (20 miles) from BWI and Reagan National airports and 2 miles from NASA's Goddard Space Flight Center, with a visitor center, exhibits, a gift shop, model rocket launches, and other family events.

The spacious two-story lobby is bright and comfortable, accented with stained-glass panels. A small gift shop is off the lobby. A heated indoor pool with a retractable roof is open year-round. The roof is open from Memorial Day weekend to early September. Each room has a 25-inch TV; microwaves and refrigerators are available on request for a small charge. Telephones have free local calls and long-distance access. Sixth-floor rooms have king beds; other floors have two doubles each—perfect for a family of four whose kids have not yet had a growth spurt. Traffic noise from the Beltway is a dull hum (at these prices, it's worth investing in earplugs). The quietest quarters are poolside and odd-numbered rooms.

Neptune's, on the lobby level, serves a free breakfast buffet daily from 7 to 10am. Within a 5-minute drive are oodles of fast-food and sit-down restaurants such as Jerry's Seafood, Red Lobster, and Ledo Pizza. Nearby Greenbelt and New Carrollton have dozens more. Because this, for the most part, is a nonresidential neighborhood, I don't suggest a walk after dark.

5910 Princess Garden Pkwy., Lanham, MD 20708. ✆ **800/866-4458** or 301/459-1000. Fax 301/459-1526. www.bestwestern.com/capitalbeltway. 169 units. From $90–$109 double. Children 17 and under stay free in parent's room. Rates include breakfast. Crib complimentary; rollaway $25 per night. Ask about spring and summer family specials. AE, DC, DISC, MC, V. Free parking. Shuttle service to Metro. Metro: New Carrollton. **Amenities:** Restaurant; bar; fitness room; heated indoor pool. *In room:* A/C, TV, hair dryer, Internet, Wi-Fi.

9 SUBURBAN VIRGINIA

The Virginia suburbs are marked by old and new neighborhoods, fine shopping, restaurants, too many high-rises, and gridlock. If you travel into the District on Metro—a 10- to 30-minute ride, depending on where you're staying (Rosslyn is closest, Vienna is farthest)—you won't have to fight the traffic. If you need to be near the airport and close to D.C. there are a number of dependable options. Less than a mile away from Reagan National are the **Crowne Plaza Hotel Washington National Airport,** 1480 Crystal Dr., Arlington, Virginia (✆ **800/970-4891** or 703/416-1600; www.crowneplaza.com) and **Holiday Inn National Airport,** 2650 Jefferson Davis Hwy., Arlington, Virginia (✆ **703/684-7200** or 877/643-4614; www.holidayinn.com).

Maryland and Virginia residents continue to trade barbs over the up- and downsides of living in their respective states. I break out in hives when I cross the border into northern Virginia. It reminds me of L.A.—sprawl and congestion—but without the palm trees and the Pacific. But don't let that deter you.

ARLINGTON

Arlington National Cemetery and the Pentagon are in Arlington, which extends westward from the Potomac River between McLean (north) and Alexandria (south). With easy access to D.C. via Metro and the Key, Roosevelt, and Memorial bridges, the area is attractive to visitors and residents alike. The closest of D.C.'s bedroom communities, Arlington consists of older, established neighborhoods, high-rise condos and office buildings, and shopping center after shopping center. Area shopaholics favor Fashion Centre at Pentagon City, with 160 stores (including Macy's and Nordstrom), a multiplex theater, and several restaurants.

Embassy Suites Crystal City ★ Except on weekends and in summer, business types account for most of this hotel's clientele. I'm surprised that more families don't stay here year-round. If you stay in Crystal City—a future world of multistoried offices, residences, restaurants, and shopping—you'll be able to board a train and be downtown (Yellow or Blue lines) or at Arlington Cemetery (Blue line) within 10 minutes, depending on the day's agenda. It's also 2 minutes away from the Air Force Memorial. The hotel's free shuttle can take you to Reagan National Airport (very convenient with kids and luggage), the Pentagon City Metro station, or Fashion Centre at Pentagon City (four stories of shopping, with Macy's, Nordstrom, Gymboree, The Children's Place, and Gap Kids, among others, plus 13 eateries in the Food Court and a number of "proper" sit-down restaurants).

Comfortable and attractive furnishings and a spacious bathroom distinguish suites. Not enough can be said about the merits of having the kids sleep in a separate room with their own TV—worth twice the price, in my mind.

After a full day downtown, relax on the sundeck or watch the kids swim in the indoor pool. Breakfast and late-afternoon cocktails are complimentary. The **Crystal Grille,** nestled in a tropical setting off the atrium, is open for (complimentary) breakfast, as well as lunch and dinner. At lunch and dinner, the kids' menu has five items to choose from, ranging from $5 to $10.

1300 Jefferson Davis Hwy., Arlington, VA 22202. ✆ **703/979-9799.** www.embassysuites.com. 267 suites. Mon–Fri $170–$275 suite; Sat–Sun from $119 suite. Rates include full, cooked-to-order breakfast and manager's reception cocktails daily. Children 18 and under stay free in parent's room. Crib free; rollaway $30. Special weekend packages from $110; ask about AAA, AARP rates. AE, DC, DISC, MC, V. Garage self-parking $21. Metro: Crystal City or Pentagon City. **Amenities:** Restaurant; exercise equipment; fully equipped health club offsite; hot tub; indoor pool (outdoor pool available at nearby Courtyard by Marriott Washington, D.C., summer only); Internet; sauna; transportation to Reagan National Airport, nearby shopping, and Metro station (blue and yellow lines). *In room:* A/C, TV, fridge, hair dryer.

OLD TOWN ALEXANDRIA

I've been enjoying Old Town's charms and riverfront location since I was a college student, not long after George Washington was a surveyor's assistant in the neighborhood. All I can say is, it keeps getting better and better. A destination unto itself, Old Town is convenient to Reagan National Airport and Arlington National Cemetery. The major D.C. sights are just six stops (about 20 min.) away on the Yellow Line to L'Enfant Plaza. Cruise on the Potomac to Mount Vernon or Georgetown; roam the Torpedo Factory and watch skilled craftspeople and artists creating new works; take a historic walking tour; shop 'til you drop in one-of-a-kind boutiques; bike the Georgetown Memorial Parkway or paddle on the river; enjoy family- and pocketbook-friendly dining; or explore the country's early history on a self-guided or guided walking tour.

Expensive

Hotel Monaco Alexandria ★★ Location, location, location! One of the newest jewels in the Kimpton crown, the Hotel Monaco Alexandria opened in January 2008. My two eldest grandkids and I had a ball when we spent a night here recently. The staff's friendliness and enthusiasm was contagious. After checking in, we walked to sights and restaurants; a rare treat for suburbanites who rely on wheels for getting around. Enjoy the stylish, sumptuous furnishings (some rooms have a Jacuzzi), for which Kimpton is known, at this premiere location in one of the area's hottest 'hoods. If your kids miss their pets, they can borrow a goldfish to keep them company during their stay. (Actually, Fido is welcome here: One of Old Town's happenings is the Doggie Happy Hour at the Monaco on Tues and Thurs from 5–8pm, Apr–Oct—weather permitting—on the hotel patio.) After a day's sightseeing, a dip in the indoor pool provides an ideal cool-down for overheated tykes. If you have a sitter or feel comfortable leaving them to watch a movie on the flatscreen LCD television, slip downstairs for dinner a deux in **Jackson 20,** the onsite restaurant. It's open for breakfast, lunch, and dinner and welcomes families. The name pays tribute to Andrew J. and features regional American cuisine with a menu that changes seasonally. The menu showcases produce from local farms and fish from local waters.

480 King St., Alexandria, VA 22134. ✆ **703/549-6080.** www.monaco-alexandria.com. 241 units. $159–$599 double. Kids 17 and under stay free in parent's room. Crib free; rollaway $15. Extra person $25. AE, DC, DISC, MC V. Valet parking $20 (in-and-out privileges). Metro: King St., then free Old Town shuttle. **Amenities:** Restaurant; concierge service; on-site fitness center; indoor pool; room service. *In room:* A/C, 37" flatscreen LCD TV, hair dryer, minibar, Wi-Fi (complimentary to members of Kimpton In-Touch program).

VIENNA

Vienna, despite its lovely residential neighborhoods, is better known as a landscape of shopping (malls, strip shopping centers, and stand-alones), too-tall office buildings (developers love this area!), restaurants, and gridlock most of the time. It's about 15 minutes by car from Wolf Trap Park for the Performing Arts, which features great live entertainment and family activities spring to fall. Stay here, and you'll have a half-hour ride on Metro into the city yet be just minutes from world-class shopping. Families flock to Tysons Corner Center for their kids' clothes, shoes, electronics, videos, music, games, and toys. It's one of the most successful malls in the country and, as you might expect, has several restaurants and a multiplex movie theater. You could easily spend a day here. Many do.

Expensive

Embassy Suites Tysons Corner Let Embassy Suites be your chauffeur. About 12 miles from the heart of D.C., this hotel has a shuttle that will ferry you to restaurants and shopping within 3 miles of the hotel. The shuttle is available from 7am to 11pm. If you return from sightseeing hungry or want to shop with your kids, you can leave the buggy in the lot and just sit back and relax—navigating suburban Virginia roads is not for amateurs.

If you stay at an Embassy Suites, you and your kids won't be tripping over one another. There's a lot to be said for that, especially when you're spending every waking moment in one another's company. Each suite has a king bed in the bedroom and a queen sleeper sofa in the living room; they all overlook the lushly landscaped atrium. New bedding and bathroom upgrades were completed in 2009. The bedroom and living room each have a TV with free HBO and cable, and On Command video. Every morning, your family can look forward to a full, cooked-to-order American breakfast; evenings, wind down at the complimentary 2-hour manager's reception (drinks and munchies), in the Atrium Lounge. Please note that the weekend rate is sometimes half the weekday rate, putting the hotel in the "Inexpensive" category if you arrive on Friday and depart on Sunday.

The Metro is not within walking distance, but the hotel provides free transportation to the Dunn Loring station. It's about a 10-minute ride to the Metro station and—attention shoppers!—a 5-minute ride to Tysons Corner Center and Tysons II (mall). Drivers will find plenty of on-site complimentary parking.

Carnevale Cafe serves American fare in a casual setting and has a kids' menu.

8517 Leesburg Pike, Vienna, VA 22182. ✆ **800/EMBASSY** (362-2779) or 703/883-0707. Fax 703/760-9842. www.tysonscorner.embassysuites.com. 234 suites. Mon–Fri $189–$289 suite; Sat–Sun $99–$149 suite. Children 16 and under stay free in parent's room. Rates include breakfast. Crib free; rollaway $25. Extra person $20. Several packages available. AE, DC, DISC, MC, V. Free self-parking. Metro: Dunn Loring. **Amenities:** Restaurant; heated indoor pool; on-site health club; large hot tub; room service; transportation to Metro station. *In room:* A/C, TV, fridge, hair dryer, minibar.

Moderate

Sheraton Premiere at Tysons Corner The Sheraton Premiere offers luxury accommodations with all the frills. Located 12 miles from Washington (at I-495, I-66, and Dulles Toll Road), Dulles Airport is about 8 miles away; Reagan is 15 miles. The facilities, service, and food are all first class. Ten suites, including the Presidential Suite, overlook Virginia's Blue Ridge Mountains.

The location is convenient to kid magnets: Wolf Trap Center for the Performing Arts, Tysons Corner and Tysons II, Build-A-Bear Workshop, 18 movie theaters, and numerous restaurants. Complimentary transportation to the Dunn Loring Metro is provided Saturday and Sunday on the hour, from 7am to 10pm. From Dunn Loring to the hotel, service is on the half hour, from 7:30am to 10:30pm. Please note that this schedule can and does change frequently, so be sure to ask when you check in.

Comfortable armchairs, seven computer stations with webcams, and 1 hour of free high-speed Internet access were added during the lobby renovation in 2008. **Ashgrove's** is the Sheraton's family-friendly restaurant for informal dining for breakfast and lunch. Kids are welcome anytime. At lunch, children can order from their own menu, which includes grilled cheese, chicken tenders, pizza, hamburgers, and peanut butter and jelly with a banana happy face. All items are priced between $3 and $5. Dinner is available at **First Impressions,** the lobby bar serving light fare. At dinner, I think families are better served by restaurants in and around Tysons Corner (mall).

661 Leesburg Pike, Vienna, VA 22182. ✆ **800/325-3535** or 703/448-1234. Fax 703/893-8193. www.sheraton.com/tysonscorner. 443 units. Mon–Fri $149–$229 double, $250–$400 suite; Sat–Sun from $79 double. Children under 12 stay free in parent's room. Crib free; rollaway $15. Extra person $15. Weekly rates and promotional packages are available. AE, DC, DISC, MC, V. Free parking. Metro: Dunn Loring or West Falls Church. **Amenities:** Restaurant; lobby bar; fitness center with exercise equipment, weights, hot tub, sauna, and Lifecycles; indoor and outdoor pool (approximately Memorial Day–Labor Day) with lifeguard; 2 racquetball courts; room service. *In room:* A/C, TV, hair dryer, Internet.

10 CAMPGROUNDS

If you're an outdoorsy family, consider staying in one of Maryland's or Virginia's many campgrounds. Here are two of the closest and best equipped.

Aquia Pines Camp Resort ★ Value The heavily wooded Aquia Pines lies 1 mile from exit 143A off I-95, about 35 miles south of D.C. and 10 miles north of George Washington's boyhood home, Fredericksburg. It's the Virginia campground most convenient to D.C.'s sights. The bathrooms are so clean that the National Campground Association once photographed them for a training film. Now that's clean!

Those who want to rough it less might consider renting 1 of the 30 deluxe campsites with Wi-Fi and cable TV, or a modest cabin consisting of one room with a double bed, two bunk beds, and a porch. You'll have to use the campground restrooms, and linen service is provided for a fee. Or you can opt for one of three deluxe cabins with a full bathroom (with shower and tub), air-conditioning, a kitchenette, and cable TV.

A Wal-Mart and two supermarkets are 1 mile from the campground (a third is 2 miles away), and an on-site store sells the essentials. So if you forgot the marshmallows, your stay won't be spoiled. Pets are welcome, but *not* in the cabins. Because the nearest Metro station is 25 miles away, Mount Vernon is about 30 miles away, and Washington is 35 miles away, the Aquia Pines owner (with 24 years experience) recommends driving to D.C. and parking in a lot or using Virginia Rail Express. Two **Virginia Rail Express** stations (www.vre.org), with ample parking, are each 6 miles from Aquia Pines. Trains on the Fredericksburg Line run weekdays only, with stops at L'Enfant Plaza and Union Station (25–30 min.). The fare to D.C. is $21 round-trip. (For more information, see chapter 3, "Getting to Know Washington, D.C."). Another option (in season): Visit Mount Vernon, with plenty of free parking; take a cruise to Georgetown, spend time there, and return to Mount Vernon late in the day.

3071 Jefferson Davis Hwy., Stafford, VA 22554. ✆ **540/659-3447.** www.aquiapines.com. 5 cabins; 100 campsites. Rates for 4 persons, unless otherwise noted. $42 tent, no hookup ($5 each additional guest); $42 water and electricity; $48 water, electricity, sewer; $55 campsites with cable/phone hookup; $53 rustic cabin; $118 luxury cabin (1–5 persons). Extra cabin guests $10 each per night. DISC, MC, V. Pets accepted except in cabins. Metro: Franconia/Springfield (also Virginia Rail Express train). **Amenities:** General store; free firewood; minigolf; playground w/basketball court; large outdoor pool; pool table; showers; picnic tables; Wi-Fi.

Cherry Hill Park ★ (Value) This 58-acre campground lies just 10 miles from downtown Washington, with easy access via I-95. Be warned that purists searching for Walden Pond will hardly consider staying here a back-to-nature experience once they see all the amenities.

First off, unlike many campgrounds that are open only in the summer, this one is open year-round. April through October, food service is available at the poolside cafe. And when was the last time you "roughed it" with a walk-in beach-style pool, separate kids' pool, basketball court, play areas with age-appropriate equipment, nature trails, fishing ponds (catch and release), hot tub, sauna, sundeck, large-screen TV lounge with fireplace, game rooms, 30-plus washers and dryers, and tour options? Hey, there's even a concierge onboard to serve you, and dog walkers are available to take Poochy for a walk while you're sightseeing. Ask about motorcoach charters into D.C. and the once-a-week (in season) Night Tour. The Gurevich family runs the place like a southern-style Borscht Belt resort, and you can enjoy line dancing (for a fee, unless you're just watching) every Wednesday night in the conference center. And it's just 20 minutes from Six Flags America. The trees and natural floral landscaping on the site's 58 acres help absorb the traffic drone from the nearby Beltway, but if you're light sleepers, it might be a good idea to pack earplugs.

Starlight Theatre offers free family-fare movies in season. Grab a bench or bring your chairs and be surrounded by six Bose speakers.

If you don't want to drive into D.C., the Greenbelt Metro station is only 3 miles away. Or catch the 83 Metrobus at the campground entrance (Cherry Hill Rd.) to the College

Park Metro station. The bus runs daily with service more frequent on weekdays than Saturday and Sunday.

9800 Cherry Hill Rd., College Park, MD 20740. ✆ **800/801-6449** or 301/937-7116. Fax 301/937-3110. www.cherryhillpark.com. 400 RV/tent campsites; 5 air-conditioned and heated trailers (2 trailers have 3 bedrooms for 6 people; the other 3 have 1 bedroom and a large living room, sleeps 6); 2 air-conditioned cabins (12×20 ft., sleeps 5); 1 yurt. $57 per RV (2 persons; $5 each extra person over 7), $62 pull-through sites, $67 premium campsite with brick patio and patio furniture; $42 tent camping (2 persons). $5 fee for each additional vehicle (1 car is included with each RV); trailers $120 (4 people, extra charge for extra people); yurt $85 (2-night minimum stay; bring your own bedding). Pets not allowed. Hookups include electric (20/30/50 amps), cable TV, water, and sewer. Ask about discounts. DISC, MC, V. **Amenities:** Exercise room with fitness classes; firewood; fishing pond; hot tub; miniature golf; play areas, including basketball court and nature trails; 2 pools; propane refills; sauna; Wi-Fi.

Family-Friendly Restaurants

More than 1,800 restaurants serve Washington, D.C. Owing to the diverse, international population, visitors can choose everything from burgers to pizza, USDA Prime aged beef to seafood; not to overlook the whole gamut of ethnic cuisines. I encourage you to be adventurous; your family's education doesn't end when you leave the Smithsonian. If you're raising your children on meat and potatoes, expand their gustatory horizons and try a Thai, Greek, Spanish, or African restaurant (check out the "Restaurants by Cuisine" listing, below). And if your family has never tasted fresh crabmeat, here's your opportunity to savor this delicious local specialty, harvested from the Chesapeake Bay from late spring through fall.

Most D.C. restaurants are family-friendly—so consider this chapter a sampling. Well-behaved kids who can sit still for an hour or longer are welcome at just about any restaurant in the city. However, when deciding where to dine with a very young child, please consider the appropriateness of your choice. Nobody wants to dress up and pay a lot of money in a fine restaurant to play peek-a-boo with an antsy tot at the next table. Kids who would rather blow bubbles into their milk than eat a square meal are served better by casual restaurants, fast food, or takeout. Consider what shape your kids are in, too. (They might not be on their best behavior after 14 museums in 2 days.)

The drinking age in D.C. is 21. No exceptions are made for almost-21-year-olds dining with adults, so don't even think of offering your offspring a sip of your cocktail. A single violation could close the restaurant for good.

To save time on days when you want to pack in as much downtown sightseeing as possible, eat in a museum or government restaurant or cafeteria. When you want simple, walk-away fare—hot dogs, chips, ice cream, and sodas—look for the pagoda-style roofs of the freestanding food-service kiosks nestled among the elms on the Mall. Or head for a food court in one of D.C.'s enclosed malls. Hey, this is Washington, so your brood can exercise their freedom of choice at these popular eateries. The selections are consistent and inexpensive. On a beautiful day, get it to go and picnic on the grass or on a park bench.

An interminable wait in a mobbed restaurant can sabotage an otherwise pleasant day. If you plan to dine at a peak time in a popular spot, bring along some crayons, scrap paper, and a few playthings, and have crackers or other snacks in your bag to pacify impatient little ones. If you don't have reservations and you want attentive service, try to get seated before noon or after 2pm for lunch and no later than 6 or 6:30pm for dinner.

The tax on restaurant meals is a hefty 10% in the District.

A NOTE ON PRICES The following reviews include a range of specific menu prices as often as possible. I've also categorized the restaurants as very expensive, expensive, moderate, or inexpensive, based on rough estimates of what it would cost to feed a family of four: two adults and two children, assuming that one of the kids is young enough to be satisfied with either a kids' meal, a half portion, or just an appetizer. If this mythical family would have to spend $120 or more for dinner (excluding any bar tab), I've classed that restaurant as **very expensive ($$$$);** $75 to $120 as **expensive ($$$);** between $50 and $75 as **moderate ($$);** and under $50 being **inexpensive ($).**

1 RESTAURANTS BY CUISINE

Afternoon Tea

Café Promenade at Renaissance Mayflower Hotel (Downtown; $$$, p. 92)
Empress Lounge at Mandarin Oriental Hotel ★ (Downtown/Mall area; $$$, p. 92)
Washington National Cathedral ★★ (Upper Northwest; $$$, p. 105)

American

Afterwords Cafe at Kramerbooks (Dupont Circle; $, p. 100)
America ★★ (Capitol Hill; $–$$, p. 84)
Brickskeller (Dupont Circle; $–$$, p. 101)
Bullfeathers ★ (Capitol Hill; $–$$, p. 84)
Capitol City Brewing Co. (Convention Center; Capitol Hill; Arlington, Virginia; $–$$, p. 88)
Chadwicks (Upper Northwest, p. 103; Alexandria, Virginia; $–$$, p. 264)
Cheesecake Factory ★ (N. Bethesda, Maryland; Upper Northwest; $–$$, p. 104)
Chili's Grill & Bar ★ (Vienna, Virginia; $$, p. 110)
Clyde's ★ (Georgetown; Vienna, Virginia; $$, p. 94)
G Street Food ★ (Downtown; $, p. 91)
Garrett's (Georgetown; $$, p. 96)
Hamburger Hamlet ★ (Bethesda, Maryland; $–$$, p. 106)
Hard Rock Cafe ★ (Convention Center; $$, p. 87)
Houston's Woodmont Grille ★★ (Bethesda, Maryland; $–$$, p. 106)
Kinkead's ★★★ (Foggy Bottom; $$$–$$$$, p. 92)
Luna Grill & Diner ★ (Dupont Circle; Arlington, Virginia; $–$$, p. 100)
Mackey's Public House (Downtown; Arlington, Virginia $–$$, p. 90)
Market Lunch (Capitol Hill; $, p. 84)
Morton's ★★★ (Downtown; Georgetown; Annapolis, Maryland; Vienna, Virginia; $$$$, p. 93)
Old Ebbitt Grill ★ (Downtown; $$, p. 90)
Philadelphia Mike's ★ (Bethesda, Maryland; $, p. 107)
Tastee Diner ★ (Bethesda, Maryland; $, p. 107)

Bakery

Baked and Wired ★★ (Georgetown; $, p. 97)
Bread & Chocolate (Capitol Hill; Downtown; $, p. 92)
Firehook ★★ (Dupont Circle, et al; $, p. 98)
Vaccaro's (Downtown; $, p. 85)

Cajun/Creole

Acadiana ★★ (Convention Center; $$$–$$$$, p. 86)
Louisiana Kitchen ★ (Bethesda, Maryland; $–$$, p. 107)

Candies

Chocolate Chocolate (Downtown; $, p. 92)

Kron Chocolatier ★★(Upper Northwest; $, p. 104)

Chinese

Foong Lin ★(Bethesda, Maryland; $$, p. 105)

Tony Cheng's Seafood and Mongolian Barbecue (Convention Center; $$, p. 88)

Cookies & Cupcakes

Baked and Wired (Georgetown; $, p. 97)

Bread & Chocolate (Capitol Hill; Downtown; $, p. 92)

Hello Cupcake (Dupont Circle; $, p. 109)

Larry's Cookies (Capitol Hill; Downtown; $, p. 85)

Mrs. Field's (Georgetown; $, p. 97)

Red Velvet Cupcakery (Convention Center/Penn Quarter; $, p. 89)

Eclectic/Food Courts

Eat at National Place (Downtown; $, p. 91)

Food Court at the Old Post Office (Convention Center; $, p. 89)

Food Court at the Ronald Reagan Building and International Trade Center (Downtown; $, p. 91)

Food Court at Union Station ★(Capitol Hill; $, p. 84)

Market Lunch (Capitol Hill; $, p. 84)

German

Cafe Mozart (Convention Center; $$, p. 87)

Hot Dogs

Ben's Chili Bowl ★★(Adams Morgan-U St. Corridor; $, p. 101)

Ice Cream

Baskin-Robbins (Upper Northwest; $, p. 104)

Ben & Jerry's ★(Adams Morgan; Capitol Hill; Downtown; Dupont Circle; Georgetown; Upper Northwest; $, p. 85)

Cone E Island (Foggy Bottom; Vienna, Virginia; $, p. 93)

Gifford's ★(Convention Center; Bethesda, Chevy Chase, and Rockville, Maryland; $, p. 89)

Häagen-Dazs (Capitol Hill; Georgetown; $, p. 85)

Thomas Sweet ★(Georgetown; $, p. 97)

Irish

Mackey's Public House (Downtown; Arlington, Virginia; $–$$, p. 90)

Italian

Adams Morgan Spaghetti Garden ★ (Adams Morgan; $–$$, p. 102)

Filomena Ristorante ★(Georgetown; $$$, p. 94)

Otello ★(Dupont Circle; $$, p. 100)

Paolo's ★(Georgetown; $$, p. 97)

Pizzeria Paradiso ★(Dupont Circle; Georgetown; $, p. 102)

Light Fare

POV (Downtown; $, p. 90)

Mexican

El Tamarindo ★(Adams Morgan; $–$$, p. 103)

Rosa Mexicano ★(Convention Center, $–$$, p. 88)

Uncle Julio's Rio Grande Café (Bethesda, Gaithersburg, Maryland; Ballston, Reston, Virginia; $, p. 106)

Moroccan

Marrakesh ★(Convention Center; $$$–$$$$, p. 86)

Pan Asian

New Dynasty ★(Dupont Circle, $–$$, p. 101)

Pizza

Pizzeria Paradiso ★(Dupont Circle; Georgetown; $, p. 102)

Tips Eating Fast & Well

Many national and local chains serve Washington, D.C. Consider them for a quick, tasty, well-prepared meal that will fill your tummies without eating up your dining budget. Here are our favorites (figure $10 or less per person, no table service, and no alcohol, unless otherwise noted).

California Tortilla. Come here for yummy overstuffed tortillas, tacos, burritos, fajitas, salads. 728 7th St. NW (btw. 7th and 8th sts., Penn Quarter district of Downtown). www.californiatortilla.com.

Chick-fil-A. Locals cluck over the boneless chicken breast sandwiches, nuggets, waffle fries, and fresh-squeezed lemonade. 800 21st St. NW, on the GWU campus; several locations in the Maryland and Virginia suburbs. www.chick-fil-a.com.

Firehook. Grab a breakfast or lunch sandwich—on the b-e-s-t breads this side of Paris—and other homemade light fare, then tuck an award-winning loaf under your arm on the way out. 1909 Q St. NW (Dupont Circle, btw. 19th and 20th sts.; daily); 912 17th St., at I St. (near Farragut Square and White House; Mon–Fri); 441 4th St. (btw. D and I sts., near Judiciary Square; Mon–Fri); 555 13th St. (btw. E and F sts., near Warner Theatre and Shops at National Place; Mon–Fri); 401 F St., in National Building Museum (daily); 215 Pennsylvania Ave SE, on Capitol Hill (daily). www.firehook.com.

Five Guys. Our family loves Five Guys' tasty hand-formed hamburgers from fresh/never frozen meat and outstanding French fries (extra-crispy, please): plain, with ketchup, or doused with malt vinegar. 13th and F St (Shops at National Place), 1400 I St. NW (at 14th St.), 1825 I St. NW (btw. 18th and 19th sts.), 808 H St. NW (corner of 9th St.), 1645 Conn. Ave. (at M St.), 1335 Wisconsin Ave. (at Dumbarton Ave., in Georgetown); Reagan National Airport, and 107 N. Fayette St. (Old Town Alexandria, Virginia); numerous Maryland and Virginia locations are farther afield. www.fiveguys.com.

Fuddrucker's. Order your burger according to your appetite (they come in four sizes)—and don't forget onion rings and a thick milkshake to satisfy the basic food groups. 734 7th St. NW (btw. G and H sts.) and 1216 18th St. NW (at Jefferson Place, just off Connecticut Ave., near Dupont Circle); other locations in far-out suburban Maryland and Virginia. www.fuddruckers.com.

TGI Friday's. Friday's is good *any* day you have time to enjoy a sit-down meal. The multi-page menu includes small portions and a kids' menu. Friday's has table service and a full bar. Most items are $8 to $15. 2100 Pennsylvania Ave (at 21st St., GWU campus) and numerous locations in the Maryland and Virginia suburbs. www.tgifridays.com.

Ribs/Barbecue

Branded 72 ★★ (Rockville, Maryland; $–$$, p. 108)

Houston's Woodmont Grille ★★ (Bethesda, Maryland; Rockville, Maryland, $–$$, p. 106)

Old Glory (Georgetown; $, p. 96)

Red, Hot & Blue ★ (Arlington, Virginia; $$, p. 110)

Salvadoran

El Tamarindo ★ (Adams Morgan; $–$$, p. 103)

Sandwiches

Roy's Place ★★ (Gaithersburg, Maryland; $–$$, p. 108)

Seafood

Crisfield Seafood Restaurant ★ (Silver Spring, Maryland; $$, p. 108)

Hank's Oyster Bar ★★★ (Dupont Circle and Alexandria, Virginia; $$–$$$, p. 98)

Kinkead's ★★★ (Foggy Bottom; $$$–$$$$, p. 92)

Sea Catch Restaurant and Raw Bar ★ (Georgetown; $$$–$$$$, p. 94)

Southwestern

Chili's Grill & Bar ★ (Vienna, Virginia; $$, p. 110)

Steakhouses

Morton's ★★★ (Downtown; Georgetown; Annapolis, Maryland; Vienna, Virginia; $$$$, p. 93)

Tex-Mex

Austin Grill ★★ (Convention Center; Bethesda, Maryland; Alexandria and Springfield, Virginia; $$, p. 87)

Cactus Cantina ★ (Upper Northwest; $$, p. 103)

Thai

Jandara (Upper Northwest; $$, p. 104)

Viennese

Cafe Mozart (Convention Center; $$, p. 87)

2 CAPITOL HILL

Capitol Hill is surprisingly kid-friendly, probably because so many politicians, lobbyists, and their staffs live here with their families. If your stomach starts growling while you're touring the Capitol, Supreme Court, or Library of Congress, try one of their dining rooms or cafeterias for a quick meal or snack; you'll find listings for these in chapter 6.

Advance planning is required if your family wishes to slurp famed Senate bean soup (the recipe is more than 100 years old!) alongside legislators weekdays between 11:30am and 3pm. A bowl of soup costs $6 in the exclusive **Senate Dining Room** ★ in the U.S. Capitol. There are two hitches: (1) You must first secure a "request letter" from your senator, which you can pick up and bring to the dining room, or the senator's office can forward it directly to the dining room, and (2) men (ages 12 and older) are required to wear a suit and tie; and no hair rollers or flip-flops for women. For more information, contact the Senate Dining Room at ✆ **202/224-2350.** If these rules are too stringent, stop by the Capitol's basement snack bar (Room SB10; ✆ **202/224-5340**) for breakfast and lunch between 7:30am and 3pm. Soups, sandwiches, and specials cost $4 to $9 (How come they can keep the prices low here when the sky's the limit with government spending elsewhere?)

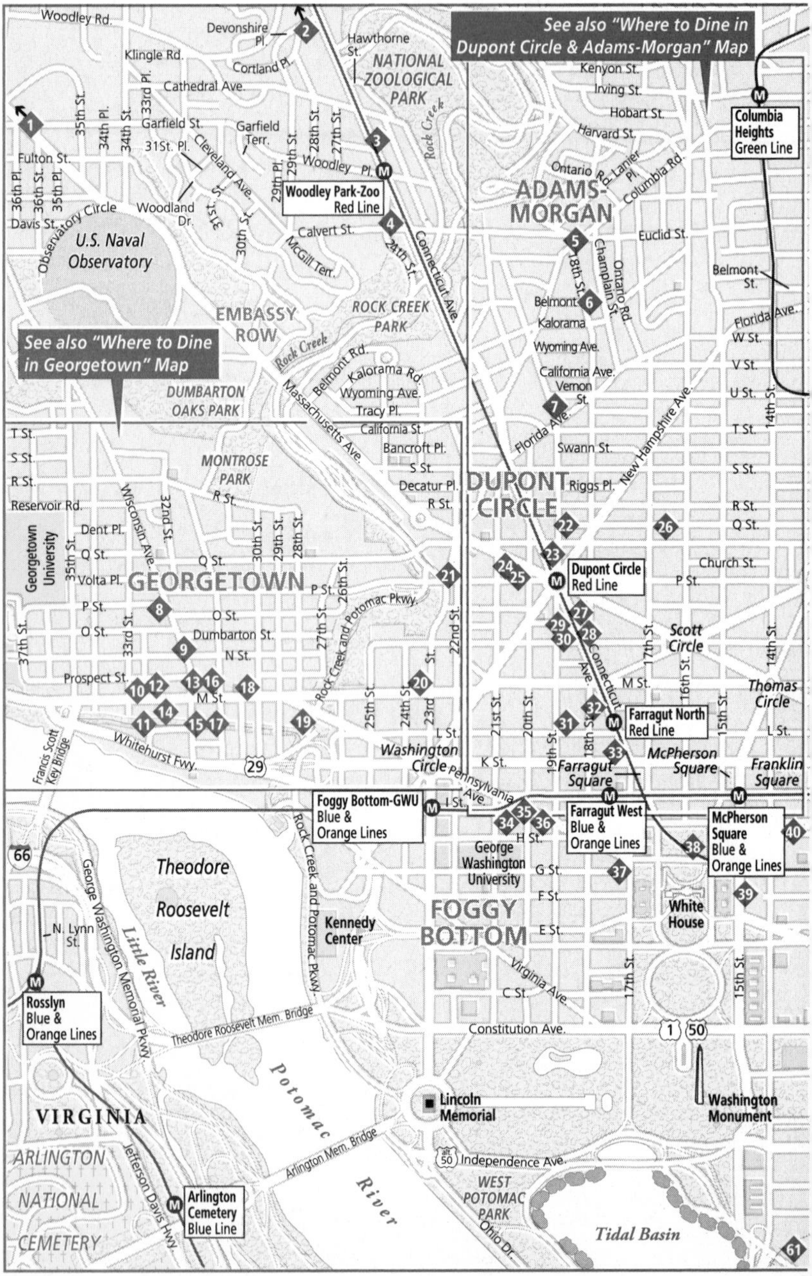

See also "Where to Dine in Dupont Circle & Adams-Morgan" Map
See also "Where to Dine in Georgetown" Map
NATIONAL ZOOLOGICAL PARK
ADAMS-MORGAN
U.S. Naval Observatory
EMBASSY ROW
ROCK CREEK PARK
DUMBARTON OAKS PARK
MONTROSE PARK
DUPONT CIRCLE
GEORGETOWN
Georgetown University
Woodley Park-Zoo Red Line
Columbia Heights Green Line
Dupont Circle Red Line
Farragut North Red Line
Farragut West Blue & Orange Lines
McPherson Square Blue & Orange Lines
Foggy Bottom-GWU Blue & Orange Lines
Rosslyn Blue & Orange Lines
Arlington Cemetery Blue Line
Washington Circle
Farragut Square
McPherson Square
Scott Circle
Thomas Circle
Franklin Square
George Washington University
FOGGY BOTTOM
Kennedy Center
White House
Theodore Roosevelt Island
Little River
Potomac River
VIRGINIA
ARLINGTON NATIONAL CEMETERY
Lincoln Memorial
Washington Monument
WEST POTOMAC PARK
Tidal Basin
Connecticut Ave.
Massachusetts Ave.
Wisconsin Ave.
New Hampshire Ave.
Pennsylvania Ave.
Virginia Ave.
Constitution Ave.
Independence Ave.
Florida Ave.
Whitehurst Fwy.
Rock Creek and Potomac Pkwy.
George Washington Memorial Pkwy.
Theodore Roosevelt Mem. Bridge
Arlington Mem. Bridge
Francis Scott Key Bridge
Jefferson Davis Hwy.
Ohio Dr.
Woodley Rd.
Klingle Rd.
Cathedral Ave.
Garfield St.
Fulton St.
Davis St.
Observatory Circle
Calvert St.
Euclid St.
Belmont St.
Kalorama Rd.
Wyoming Ave.
California St.
Swann St.
Riggs Pl.
Church St.
Prospect St.
Dumbarton St.
Constitution Ave.

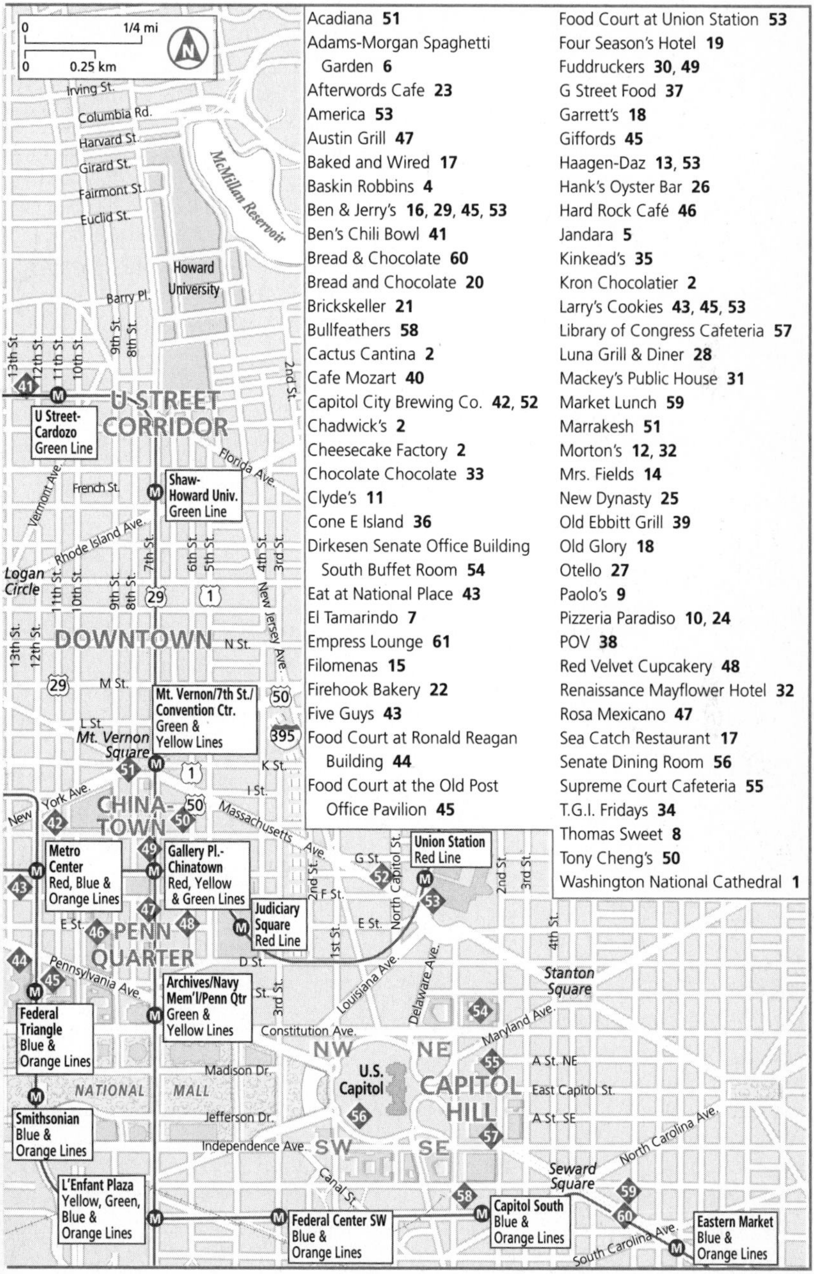
0 1/4 mi
0 0.25 km
N
Irving St.
Columbia Rd.
Harvard St.
Girard St.
Fairmont St.
Euclid St.
McMillan Reservoir
Howard University
Barry Pl.
9th St.
8th St.
13th St.
12th St.
11th St.
10th St.
2nd St.
U STREET CORRIDOR
U Street-Cardozo Green Line
Florida Ave.
Vermont Ave.
French St.
Shaw-Howard Univ. Green Line
Rhode Island Ave.
7th St.
6th St.
5th St.
4th St.
3rd St.
Logan Circle
New Jersey Ave.
DOWNTOWN
N St.
M St.
L St.
Mt. Vernon Square
Mt. Vernon/7th St./ Convention Ctr. Green & Yellow Lines
K St.
I St.
York Ave.
New
CHINA-TOWN
Massachusetts Ave.
Metro Center Red, Blue & Orange Lines
Gallery Pl.-Chinatown Red, Yellow & Green Lines
Union Station Red Line
G St.
North Capitol St.
F St.
E St.
PENN QUARTER
Judiciary Square Red Line
1st St.
D St.
Pennsylvania Ave.
Louisiana Ave.
Delaware Ave.
Stanton Square
Federal Triangle Blue & Orange Lines
Archives/Navy Mem'l/Penn Qtr Green & Yellow Lines
Constitution Ave.
Maryland Ave.
NW
NE
A St. NE
U.S. Capitol
CAPITOL HILL
East Capitol St.
NATIONAL MALL
Madison Dr.
Jefferson Dr.
A St. SE
Smithsonian Blue & Orange Lines
Independence Ave.
SW
SE
North Carolina Ave.
Canal St.
Seward Square
L'Enfant Plaza Yellow, Green, Blue & Orange Lines
Federal Center SW Blue & Orange Lines
Capitol South Blue & Orange Lines
South Carolina Ave.
Eastern Market Blue & Orange Lines

America ★★ Value AMERICAN Look no farther than the Navaho Fried Bread & Spicy Chicken (deep-fried dough filled with grilled chicken, guacamole, tomato, onion, lettuce, and salsa). If that doesn't fill your sails, how about sautéed lemon-pepper chicken, red beans and rice, a burger, soup, salad, sandwich, pasta, or comfort food along the lines of meatloaf, pork chops, Buffalo wings with celery sticks and blue cheese dip, or chicken pot pie? This cavernous, multilevel Union Station restaurant tries (and usually succeeds) to be all things to all diners. Kids can order chicken tenders, pizza, a hot dog, or spaghetti for $6.95 (includes a drink). Personal pizzas, quesadillas, and chili are plenty for most tykes. If you're a weekend Amtrak traveler, America is an ideal choice for Saturday and Sunday brunch (from 7:30am–4pm). Cheap insurance at busy times: Make a reservation online.

Union Station, 50 Massachusetts Ave. NE. ✆ **202/682-9555.** www.arkrestaurants.com. High chairs, booster seats, kids' menu, crayons. Reservations recommended at dinner. Most items $12–$18; kids' meal $6.95. AE, DC, DISC, MC, V. Sun–Thurs 11:30am, last seating at 9:30pm; Fri–Sat 11:30am, last seating at 10pm. Metro: Union Station.

Bullfeathers ★ AMERICAN Hamburgers, nachos, soups, sandwiches, and salads make this a popular spot for sippers and suppers of all ages. Just stick to the basics, and you won't be disappointed. If you are, let me know. Suits and Hill wannabes of all ages fill the place for happy hour and late at night; sometimes the line blurs between the two. Dining outdoors is a delight on a summer's eve. On Monday nights, burgers are half-price ($4)—that's with fries, as long as you order a drink. The bargain children's menu ($3.25–$5.25), for kiddies 10 and under, includes peanut-butter-and-jelly sandwiches, chicken, hot dogs, spaghetti, and a 3½-ounce kiddie burger, half the size of the Bullfeathers signature burger. Or they could order an appetizer of chicken wings, tempura shrimp, potato skins, or chicken tenders. Light fare and nightly beer specials are served in the saloon.

410 1st St. SE. ✆ **202/543-5005.** www.bullfeatherscapitolhill.com. High chairs, booster seats, kids' menu. Reservations recommended, particularly at lunch. Main courses $8–$12 lunch, $11–$21 dinner; kids' menu $3.25–$5.25. AE, DC, DISC, MC, V. Mon–Sat 11:15am–midnight. Metro: Capitol South.

Food Court at Union Station ★ Value ECLECTIC/FOOD COURT It's fun to case the myriad stands before making a selection at this bustling food court. Some of the best bets for youngsters are the all-beef European kosher hot dog at Frank & Stein, the deep-dish pizza at Mamma Ilardo's, and the charbroiled hamburger at Flamers. You will also find Tex-Mex, Greek, Indian, sushi, and wraps. Top off your visit to Union Station with some ice cream from Häagen-Dazs or Ben & Jerry's, or a cannoli or other mouth-watering pastry at Vaccaro's. Hey, have 'em all. I won't tell.

Union Station. 50 Massachusetts Ave. NE. ✆ **202/371-9441.** Reservations not accepted. Most items $4–$10. No credit cards. Mon–Sat 10am–9pm; Sun noon–6pm. Metro: Union Station.

Market Lunch Value AMERICAN/ECLECTIC/FOOD COURT Try the mouth-watering Bluebucks (blueberry buckwheat pancakes), egg sandwiches, or French toast for breakfast at this tiny eatery inside historic Eastern Market. If you want breakfast on Saturday, you must be in line before noon. After that, it's lunch only. The soft-shell crab (seasonal) sandwich on homemade bread is a lunchtime specialty, with the crab cake a close second (and favored by most kids). Some say servers are less than cordial. This isn't a fine-dining experience; the cooks are busy-busy and service is fast. Weather permitting, there's outdoor seating. The place jumps with hordes of shoppers hunting for bargains

On the Run

In a hurry? For a quick bite when you're on the go, grab a snack from a street vendor. My kids were raised on hot dogs, soft pretzels, and ice cream without ill effect. They even graduated from college, are gainfully employed, and became parents. Miracles never cease. D.C. has expanded and diversified its curbside offerings. Some vendors sell ethnic (Lebanese pita rollups, kabobs, Korean barbecue, and soul food) and vegetarian fare. I know eating healthy is a good thing, but I'm still a pushover for a **Sabrett's** hot dog with "the works." (So much tastier than the bland hot dogs from truck vendors.) Look for a pushcart with the blue-and-yellow Sabrett's logo umbrella.

Saturday; and the outdoor flea market Sunday, 10am to 5pm, across the street in the Hine School yard.

225 7th St. SE. ✆ **202/547-8444.** High chairs. Reservations not accepted. Breakfast $4–$8; lunch $6–$12. No credit cards. Wed–Fri 7:30am–2:30pm; Sat 8am–3pm; Sun 11am–3pm (lunch only). Metro: Eastern Market.

COOKIES, CUPCAKES, CANDY & ICE CREAM

Ben & Jerry's ICE CREAM ★ Who'd have thought that two young men dishing it out at a stand in Burlington, Vermont, would've created such an empire? Sample this rich, environmentally correct product, and you'll know why Ben and Jerry—and Unilever, who acquired B&J in 2000—are mooing all the way to the bank. It's expensive, but you get what you pay for. After lunch at Union Station or on your way to the Capitol, stop at the street-level counter and grab some Cookie Dough or Chunky Monkey in a waffle cone or dish. Ice cream doesn't get much better than this. Also at the Old Post Office, 1100 Pennsylvania Ave. (✆ **202/842-5882**); 1333 19th St. (at N St.), Dupont Circle (✆ **202/785-4882**); and 3135 M St. NW, in Georgetown (✆ **202/965-2222**).

Union Station, 50 Massachusetts Ave. NE. ✆ **202/842-2887.** www.benjerry.com. Most treats $4–$8. AE, DISC, MC, V. Daily 10am–10pm. Metro: Union Station.

Häagen-Dazs ICE CREAM Häagen-Dazs certainly rates up there with the best commercially produced ice cream anywhere. But it's pricey. I like to think of it as designer ice cream. The shop also has sundaes, shakes, smoothies, sorbets, and low-fat ice creams. There are other locations at 3120 M Street, in Georgetown (✆ **202/333-3433**), and 703 7th St., in Gallery Place (✆ **202/783-4711**).

Union Station, 50 Massachusetts Ave. NE. ✆ **202/789-0953.** Most treats $4–$8. AE, DISC, MC, V. Mon–Sat 10am–9pm; Sun noon–6pm. Metro: Union Station.

Larry's Cookies COOKIES Of the various cookie–brownie bars sold here, the "Special" is particularly heavenly because it marries brownie to chocolate chip cookie. These treats are sold by weight and will set you back about $2 apiece. Also at the Old Post Office Pavilion, 1100 Pennsylvania Ave. NW (✆ **202/682-1018**).

Union Station, 50 Massachusetts Ave. NE. ✆ **202/289-7586.** Cookies and brownies about $2 each. AE, MC, V. Mon–Sat 10am–9pm; Sun noon–6pm. Metro: Union Station.

Vaccaro's Bakery ★ The cookies are good but no match for the cannoli, in our family poll. Try a bag of miniatures (chocolate- and vanilla-cream filled). Get extras of your fave for a snack later. Also in Foggy Bottom, at 2000 Pennsylvania Ave. NW. (✆ **202/822-0904**).

Union Station, 50 Massachusetts Ave. NE ✆ **202/371-2855**. Cookies and pastry 35¢ and up. AE, MC, V. Mon–Sat 10am–9pm; Sun noon–6pm. Metro: Union Station.

3 CONVENTION CENTER

If you're staying in this area, visiting the Spy Museum, have tickets to an event at the Verizon Center, or just want to eat on 7th Street (in the Penn Quarter), with its multitude of restaurants, shops, and action, this is a logical neighborhood in which to dine. The choices are varied, and Chinatown, with the greatest concentration of Asian restaurants in the city, is here. You'll also find many other ethnic restaurants, hotel dining rooms, and coffee shops, and the favorite of many kids: the Hard Rock Cafe.

VERY EXPENSIVE

Acadiana ★★ CAJUN/CREOLE Even if you hopped a plane to the Big Easy, I doubt you would find better Louisiana-style cuisine than at Acadiana. Acadiana offers a sublime, consistent (and always filling) dining experience in the shadow of the Convention Center. Acadiana serves up scrumptious shrimp, oyster, and roast beef po' boys (subs/hoagies; lunch only); char-broiled oysters in garlic butter–Parmesan sauce (a meal unto itself); grilled seasonal fish; gumbo; NOLA-style barbecued shrimp (in a piquant sauce of garlic, lemon, Worcestershire and seasonings); grillades (veal medallions) with cheddar-cheese grits; snapper amandine; roast duck; and grilled tenderloin (if you insist) in a large, high-ceilinged room with window walls, chandeliers, and comfy upholstered banquettes. A three-course "Pre Event" menu is served between 5:30 and 6:30pm for $29. Unbuckle your belt and dip into the lemon doberge, chocolate bread pudding, or crème brûlée. Families are welcome anytime; if your kids are under 8, I suggest sticking to lunch or Sunday brunch. Because Chef Tunks has young kids, he understands young appetites and willingly makes substitutions to please junior clientele. Valet parking is available from 5:30pm to closing and at Sunday brunch for $7 (K St. side of restaurant); also, a large public lot is just across the street.

901 New York Ave. NW ✆ **202/408-8848.** www.acadianarestaurant.com. High chairs. Reservations recommended. Main courses lunch $12–$15, dinner $21–$28; Sun 3-course fixed-price brunch $32. AE, DC, DISC, MC, V. Mon–Thurs 11:30am–2:30pm, 5:30–10:30pm; Fri 11:30am–2:30pm, 5:30–11pm; Sat 5:30–11pm; Sun 11:30am–2:30pm, 5:30–9:30pm. Metro: Gallery Place–Chinatown (9th St. exit).

Marrakesh ★ MOROCCAN Okay, some consider it touristy and hokey, but dining at this lively, colorful oasis is an evening's entertainment and a fitting place to celebrate a special event. Sink into the pillowed banquettes and partake of the seven-course fixed-price dinner built around entrees of lamb, chicken, beef, and vegetarian dishes. At Marrakesh, eating is strictly a hands-on experience, accompanied by Moroccan music and belly dancing. Don't be surprised if someone in your party becomes part of the entertainment. It's a lot of fun and good value for the money (provided you don't order a lot of wine). If your kids need a high chair or a booster seat, they're too young to dine here. Plan on spending 3 hours for dinner. Valet parking costs $7.

617 New York Ave. NW. ✆ **202/393-9393.** www.marrakesh.us. Reservations required. Fixed-price dinner $31 per person; kids 12 and under half price Sun–Thurs. No credit cards; checks accepted. Daily 6–11pm. Metro: Gallery Place–Chinatown.

MODERATE

Austin Grill ★★TEX-MEX This place has a partylike atmosphere, with inexpensive Tex-Mex fare served in an unpretentious setting reminiscent of a Texas roadhouse. Try the house-braised *carnitas* (pork) fajitas or one of the popular combo plates, which include a mix of enchiladas, tacos, or tamales. You'll also find Texas chili and a selection of margaritas. The level of spiciness is noted on the menu to assist you when ordering for sensitive palates.

From the children's menu (with puzzles and a map and flag of Texas to color), kids can order a single taco, enchilada, quesadilla, nachos, burger; or grilled cheese or PB&J (those old Tex-Mex favorites!). All come with milk, juice, or soda and a side dish for $7. A scoop of ice cream is $2. Tuesdays, kids 10 and under eat free. During Happy Hour, Monday through Friday 2 to 7pm, things can get a bit boisterous. The restaurant is convenient to Ford's Theatre, the Newseum, the Spy Museum, the Smithsonian American Art Museum, and the Convention Center. In season, outside awnings and trees shade diners.

In Alexandria, Virginia, visit its location at 801 King St. (✆ **703/684-8969**). In Springfield, Virginia, there's one at 8430-A Old Keene Mill Rd. (✆ **703/644-3111**). The Bethesda, Maryland, location is at 7278 Woodmont Ave. (✆ **301/656-1366**). In Annapolis, there's one at Annapolis Mall, Jennifer Road and Route 450 (✆ **571-6688**); in Baltimore, at 2400 Boston St. (Canton, near Fells Point; ✆ **410/534-0606**).

750 E St. NW (btw. 7th and 8th sts). ✆ **202/393-3776.** www.austingrill.com. High chairs, booster seats, kids' menu, crayons. Reservations for 15 or more. Lunch entrees $7–$15; dinner $10–$18; kids' meal $7. AE, DC, DISC, MC, V. Mon–Thurs 11am–10pm; Fri–Sat 11am–11pm; Sun 11am–9:30pm. Metro: Gallery Place or Archives.

Cafe Mozart ★GERMAN/VIENNESE You could do a lot "wurst" than to dine at this *gemütlich* restaurant tucked behind a deli, where the *sauerbraten* (sweet-and-sour braised pot roast) and Wiener schnitzel (breaded veal cutlet) are almost as good as my grandmother's. Try the robust and tasty *unsere wuerste* (sausage) platters, served with potato salad and sauerkraut or red cabbage. Service is warm and friendly. On the menu for *kinder* (children) are hamburger, German hot dog, sandwiches, and linguine (!)—all with a side dish ($5.95–$6.95). They offer takeout and delivery service too. Live music is offered some nights. The monthly Opera Night is fun if your progeny are so inclined. Complimentary parking is available after 6pm on weeknights at the garage next door.

1331 H St. NW. ✆ **202/347-5732.** www.cafemozartgermandeli.com. High chairs, booster seats, kids' menu. Reservations recommended at dinner. Breakfast $3–$7; lunch $6.95–$20; dinner $16–$24; kids' menu $5.95–$6.95. AE, DC, DISC, MC, V. Mon–Fri 7am–10pm; Sat and holidays 9am–10pm; Sun 11am–10pm. Closed Thanksgiving, Dec 25, Jan 1. Metro: Metro Center or McPherson Sq.

Hard Rock Cafe ★AMERICAN Let the good times roll as you ogle Michael Jackson's red leather jacket from the video "Beat It," costumes worn by Britney Spears and No Doubt's Gwen Stefani, Mick Jagger's shirt from the Stones 1989 tour, and one of Chuck Berry's guitars. Nobody comes here just for the food, so stick to the basics: burger platters (real beef or veggie), sandwiches, and chicken salads. The jumbo combo appetizer (spring rolls, chicken wings, onion rings, potato skins, and chicken fingers with four dipping sauces) will feed little ones—for about a week. Or they can order off the kids' menu ($7.50; includes a beverage and refills). The hot-fudge brownie sundae will make you feel like dancin'. So will the 29 video monitors strategically placed throughout the restaurant. Go at off times unless you like lines. You'll be a hero to your kids for bringing them here. (If you're sensitive to noise, bring earplugs.)

999 E St. NW, next to Ford's Theatre. ✆ **202/737-ROCK** [7625]. www.hardrock.com. High chairs, booster seats, kids' menu. Reservations not accepted; arrange preferred seating 24 hr. in advance online. (You'll go to the head of the line when you arrive.) Main courses $9.95–$21. AE, DC DISC, MC, V. Sun–Thurs 11am–11pm; Fri–Sat 11am–midnight. Metro: Metro Center or Gallery Place/Chinatown.

Rosa Mexicano ★ MEXICAN Traditional folk crafts, tasteful decor, and wrap-around windows raise the eye appeal of this Mexican restaurant to a cut above Tex-Mex roadhouse ambience. On the Young Amigos menu, for kids 11 and under, are chicken fingers, tortilla roll (beef, chicken, or cheese), quesadillas, and layered tortilla pie. All are served with sweet potato fries and buttered corn, a soft drink or milk, and a scoop of vanilla ice cream for dessert ($7.50). The "Rock the Guac" program invites kids to learn that cooking is fun. How? They assist in making the restaurant's tableside guacamole and receive a complimentary souvenir apron. Just mention it when you make a reservation or when you show up.

Mama and papa can choose from a wide variety of *entradas* (appetizers); quesadillas, enchiladas, and tacos; *tortas* (sandwiches), and *pescado* (fish) or *carne* (meat) specialties. The menu changes seasonally to capitalize on local ingredients. (I get full just reading the menu.)

575 7th St. (in Penn Quarter). ✆ **202/783-5522.** www.rosamexicano.com. High chairs and boosters. Reservations recommended. Appetizers $4–$12; main courses lunch $11–$19, dinner $17–$27; brunch $9–$16; kids' menu $7.50. AE, DISC, MC, V. Mon–Wed 11:30am–10:30pm; Thurs–Sat 11:30am–11:30pm; Sun 11:30am–10pm. Metro: Gallery Place.

Tony Cheng's Seafood and Mongolian Barbecue CHINESE It takes a while to choose from the extensive menu (more than 200 items) of Szechuan, Cantonese, and Hunan dishes in this tablecloth—but unpretentious—restaurant. The dim sum alone, served upstairs every day at lunch, merits a visit. I've yet to meet the child who didn't cotton to dumplings. ***Note:*** The carts roll by on Saturday and Sunday (a fun part of the dim sum experience, I believe); from Monday through Friday, order dumplings off the menu. If you're on a budget, come at lunch and stick to the dim sum or daily specials (soup, main course, rice) for $10 to $13. Among the signature dishes served here are stir-fried crabs with ginger and scallions, and whole steamed sea bass. The kids can practice their prowess with chopsticks. If they grow bored, they can make faces at the fish in the large tanks. On the first floor is a buffet-style Mongolian barbecue. Not my cup of Oolong, but kids over 4 or 5 enjoy choosing the ingredients (meats, vegetables, sauces) for their meal and then watching the cook stir-fry the concoction on the giant grill. Frankly, I prefer to leave it to the pros in the kitchen, but that's your call.

619 H St. NW. ✆ **202/371-8669.** High chairs and boosters. Reservations recommended. Main courses $10–$12 lunch, $14–$20 dinner. AE, MC, V. Mon–Thurs and Sun 11am–11pm; Fri–Sat 11am–midnight. Metro: Gallery Place/Chinatown.

INEXPENSIVE

Capitol City Brewing Co. AMERICAN The first brewpub in D.C., Capitol City is noisy, fun, and reasonable—three good reasons to bring your half-pints and try one of *theirs.* Beer lovers will want to sample one of the microbrews made on the premises (I favor the amber). Point out the beer-making equipment, of interest to most youngsters. This is not the spot for an intimate conversation, but it's warm and welcoming to kids.

The basket of pretzels and mustard is a nice touch and—aren't they clever?—makes you *very* thirsty. The generous hamburgers are yummy and served with seasoned fries. Barbecued ribs have a strong following. The menu also includes seafood, jambalaya, and other Cajun/Creole favorites. The kids can order a corndog, hamburger, chicken tenders, or mac and cheese at $4.95 each (comes with fries, fruit, or a vegetable and a drink). A wait is not unusual at dinner and on weekends. Capitol City has another location at 2 Massachusetts Ave. NE (at the Postal Sq. Bldg.; ✆ **202/842-BEER** [2337]) and 2700 Quincy St., in Arlington, Virginia (✆ **703/578-3888**).

1100 New York Ave. NW (corner of H and 11th sts.). ✆ **202/628-2222.** www.capcitybrew.com. High chairs, booster seats, kids' menu. Reservations for 15 or more. Lunch and dinner $6.95–$15; kids' menu items $4.95. AE, DC, DISC, MC, V. Mon–Thurs 11am–midnight, Fri–Sat 11am–1am; Sun 11am–10pm. Metro: Metro Center.

Food Court at the Old Post Office Value ECLECTIC/FOOD COURT If you're sightseeing on the Mall or along Pennsylvania or Constitution avenues, duck in here for a quick meal or a snack in the International Food Court. You'll find everything from Indian and Asian fare to burgers and fries and bagels at the 14 food stands. Also save room for Ben & Jerry's ice cream or desserts at Temptations. Enjoy free entertainment most days, starting around noon and ending about 4 or 5pm.

1100 Pennsylvania Ave. NW. ✆ **202/289-4224.** Most items $4–$8. No credit cards. Fall/Winter: Mon–Sat 10am–7pm, Sun noon–6pm; Spring/Summer Mon–Sat 10am–8pm, Sun noon–7pm Metro: Federal Triangle.

COOKIES, CUPCAKES, CANDIES & ICE CREAM

Gifford's ★ ICE CREAM The Alpine Swiss chocolate and hot fudge sundaes are worthy of poetry. Owner Neal Lieberman (who has three young kids) has expanded the operation (begun as a family-owned chain in 1938), and Gifford's now has branches in D.C., Chevy Chase, Bethesda, and Rockville, Maryland. If you're tired of cups and regulation-size sugar cones, try the generous waffle cone. You'll find seating here for 18. Other locations, all in Maryland, are at: 21 Wisconsin Circle (Wisconsin and Western aves.), Chevy Chase; 7237 Woodmont Ave., Bethesda; and Rockville Town Square (100 Gibbs St.), Rockville.

555 11th St. NW (at 10th and E sts.). ✆ **202/347-7755.** Single-dip cone $4.15 (ouch!); Super Banana Split $7.65 (big enough to share with the team). MC, V. Sun–Thurs 11:30am–10pm; Fri–Sat 11:30am–11pm. Metro: Metro Center.

Red Velvet Cupcakery BAKERY Try the Morning Call (chocolate espresso cake, mocha buttercream), Key West (key lime cake, white chocolate buttercream), and/or Southern Belle (red velvet cake with whipped cream-cheese frosting). Grab a seat or get it to go.

675 E St. (at 7th St.). ✆ **202/347-7895.** www.redvelvetcupcakery.com. Sun–Thurs 11am–11pm, Fri–Sat 11am–1am. $3.25 each. Metro: Gallery Place.

4 DOWNTOWN

Visiting the Corcoran or Renwick late in the day? Celebrating a special occasion? With older kids, slip into one of the upscale restaurants on K Street NW, Washington's restaurant row, for a heady (and expensive) dining experience. If you have tickets to a show at the Warner or the National, try one of the many restaurants that have sprouted up in recent years on and around 7th Street, known as the "Penn Quarter" (near the Convention Center and Verizon Center). ***Please note:*** Downtown covers a large area, and the boundaries blur, so also see the "Convention Center" recommendations, above.

Mackey's Public House IRISH/AMERICAN For a taste of the Emerald Isle, head to Mackey's and snuggle up in a "snug" (tables separated by glass partitions for a modicum of privacy). Try the beer-battered fish and chips or corned beef and cabbage ($13 each). Or go for a burger, sandwich (the Reuben is yummy), salad, appetizer, or soup. Do try a side of mashed potatoes with roasted garlic or braised cabbage, and wash it down with one of Ireland's finest beers, including Guinness, Harp, and Smithwick's. An order of chicken tenders or Buffalo wings—perhaps with a side of homemade chips (fries)—will more than fill a wee one.

Avoid Mackey's Friday nights, especially with young children. That's when business types and students let down their hair, and things can get a bit rowdy. Outdoor seating is available, weather permitting. Another Mackey's (with free Wi-Fi) has opened in Crystal City (Arlington, Virginia), at 320 S. 23rd St. (✆ **703/412-1113**).

1823 L St. NW. ✆ **202/331-7667.** www.mackeyspub.com. High chairs. Sandwiches and entrees $9–$14. AE, MC, V. Mon 11:30am–midnight; Tues–Thurs 11:30am–2am; Sat noon–3am; Sun noon–8pm during football season only. Metro: Farragut North.

Old Ebbitt Grill ★ AMERICAN The Ebbitt is consistently good and open almost round the clock. Because this is around the corner from the White House and a primo power-breakfast scene, there could be more deals sealed here over eggs Benedict than behind closed doors in the Capitol. Lunch features overstuffed sandwiches, huge salads, and hot entrees. The location is convenient if you're in the White House 'hood or have tickets to a show. The staff has a rep for going overboard to please munchkins. The kids' coloring book–menu has 10 choices; all include milk or soda and ice cream with chocolate sauce or fruit for dessert for $6. (Wonder how many orders they get for fruit?) The large saloon appeals, with its polished wood, brass, and gaslights. Much of the menu changes daily, relying on local fresh goods (such as fish and seafood) and produce. You can keep your tab in the inexpensive-to-moderate range with something from the raw bar, an appetizer (portions are large), sandwich or a hamburger, or a sumptuous dessert—how about a chocolate layer cake with raspberry sauce and whipped cream? The **Ebbitt Express,** an onsite takeout, is open for breakfast and lunch Monday through Friday from 7:30am to 5pm (and you can order online!). Choices include soups, salads, pizza, pasta, and half-a-dozen entrees (most $8–$10). Consider this for dinner in your room, when a long day of sightseeing leaves you too tired to sit upright in a restaurant.

675 15th St. NW (btw. F and G sts). ✆ **202/347-4801.** www.ebbitt.com. High chairs, booster seats, kids' menu, crayons. Reservations recommended. Main courses breakfast (most items) $11–$14, brunch (Sat–Sun) $10–$15, lunch (most items) $11–$15, dinner (most items) $13–$17; kids' menu items $6. AE, DC, DISC, MC, V. Mon–Fri 7:30am–midnight (bar till 1am); Sat–Sun 8:30am–midnight (bar till 1am). Closed Dec 25. Metro: Metro Center.

POV (Point of View) LIGHT FARE/DESSERT The extraordinary view of downtown and environs is feast enough for most souls. Go anytime. See-through curtains are lowered in inclement weather. The prices match the location and cache of the W hotel (former site of the Hotel Washington). Graze on an appetizer, salad, sandwich, burger, or dessert (most items $10–$12). Specialty cocktails are $15 (ouch!), wine $9 to $15, beer $6. Chalk it up to a singular experience with a commanding view. The stunning black, white, and red decor gets my vote. You can almost touch the planes landing and taking off from National Airport. It might be fun to ask your kids how many buildings they can identify from this vantage point.

W Washington Hotel, 515 15th St. NW (at Pennsylvania Ave.). ✆ **202/661-2400.** High chairs. Reservations not accepted. All items $6–$25. AE, DC, DISC, MC, V. Daily 11:30am–1am. Metro: Metro Center.

INEXPENSIVE

Eat at National Place Value ECLECTIC/FOOD COURT This is a well-located refueling spot, about a 10-minute stroll from the National Mall/Pennsylvania Avenue/ Constitution Avenue sights; close to Ford's Theatre and Metro Center (transfer station for the Blue, Orange, and Red lines). Nibble your way through Five Guys (*yummy* award-winning hamburgers and fries), Kabuki (Japanese), Quizno's (sandwiches), Slice of Italy (pizza), Naan and Beyond (Indian), Mei Wah Express (Chinese), Amazon Café (sandwiches, wraps, salads), and Moe's Southwest Grill (burritos and tacos).

529 14th St. NW. Enter on F St. NW, btw. 13th and 14th sts., or via the J. W. Marriott. ✆ **202/662-7000.** Mon–Fri 10:30am–7pm; Sat 11am–5pm. Metro: Metro Center or Federal Triangle.

Food Court at the Ronald Reagan Building and International Trade Center Value ECLECTIC/FOOD COURT Conveniently located near the White House and a 10- to 15-minute stroll from the Mall museums, this food court, with 18 eateries, has seating for close to 1,000 and is in the same building as the Chamber of Commerce's D.C. Visitor Information Center. You'll find the usual selection of fast foods (hamburgers, chicken, salads, deli, wraps) and ethnic fare (pizza, Cajun, sushi, dim sum) in pleasing surroundings. (I'm surprised they don't serve ketchup sandwiches. Remember when Ronnie was in the White House and he recommended ketchup as a vegetable?) Before or after your meal, you may want to tour (on your own any time; with a guide Mon, Wed, and Fri at 11am) the vast glass, steel, and stone building—a stunning architectural feat. Check out the hunk of the Berlin Wall at the Woodrow Wilson Memorial Plaza entrance (at Pennsylvania Ave.). Also, there's free entertainment daily in summer noon to 1:30pm on Woodrow Wilson Plaza. Friday and Saturday evenings (year-round) at 7:30pm, you can catch the irreverent political satire of the Capitol Steps in the building's amphitheater. On a nasty day, this is a good choice, as the Metro entrance is accessible from the building.

1300 Pennsylvania Ave. NW. ✆ **202/312-1300.** www.itcdc.com. High chairs and booster seats. Mon–Fri 7am–7pm; Sat 11am–6pm; Mar–Aug Sun noon–5pm (closed Sun Sept–Feb). Metro: Federal Triangle.

G Street Food ★ AMERICAN Leave it to Mark Furstenberg, the revered creator of Marvelous Market and Breadline, who introduced designer breads and gourmet delights to D.C. several years ago. He's filled another downtown void. In September 2009, he opened G Street Food near the White House with a select menu of breakfast and lunch items that lure the we're-in-a-hurry, suit-and-iPhone brigade. (Customers order at the counter, then find a table or take it to the office.) But you don't need a suit—or an office—to eat here. Come for tasty egg-bread dishes, muffins, and coffee cake at breakfast, beyond-delish sandwiches, soups, salads and tartines at lunch. Everything is made from scratch—and tastes it. And most items are between $3 and $7. The hand-cut fries are worth a visit. It's a short walk from the White House, Washington Monument, Constitution Gardens (Vietnam Veterans Memorial, et al), DAR Museum, and Renwick Gallery. On your way out, buy a dessert for afternoon snacking. Seating is indoors and out (weather permitting).

G Street Food, 1706 G St. NW. ✆ **202/408-7474.** www.gstreeetfood.com. High chairs. No reservations. All items $2–$8. AE, MC, V. Mon–Fri only 7am–4pm. Metro: Farragut West or Farragut North.

Bread & Chocolate BAKERY/COOKIES Don't limit yourself to cookies here. Go ahead—sample the just-out-of-the-oven croissants and pastries, or enjoy a salad, sandwich, bowl of French onion soup au gratin, or hot entree in the dining area. Bread & Chocolate is open for breakfast, lunch, and dinner. Eat in or take out.

There is another branch at 5542 Connecticut Ave. NW (near the D.C.–Chevy Chase, Maryland line; ✆ **202/966-7413**).

2301 M St. NW. ✆ **202/833-8360.** www.breadandchocolate.net. High chairs, booster seats. Menu items $2–$9 (croissant or panini). AE, DISC, MC, V. Mon–Sat 7am–6pm; Sun 8am–6pm. Metro: Foggy Bottom, and then 3-block walk.

Chocolate Chocolate CANDIES Chocolate Chocolate: my two favorite words in the English language. The shop carries a sweet selection of imported and locally made candy. Among the goodies: hand-dipped chocolates ($17 per pound).

1050 Connecticut Ave. NW. ✆ **202/466-2190.** www.chocolatechocolatedc.com. Items 75¢–$1 and up for 1 piece of chocolate; $28 for a pound of imported Neuhaus truffles. AE, DISC, MC, V. Mon–Fri 10am–6pm; Sat 11am–4pm. Metro: Farragut North.

AFTERNOON TEA

Café Promenade The elegant Promenade makes a soothing setting for full tea (finger sandwiches, scones, biscuits, sweet bread, pastries, and tea) daily. Try this with mature preteens or older kids for a special grown-up treat.

In the Renaissance Mayflower Hotel, 1127 Connecticut Ave. NW. ✆ **202/347-3000.** Reservations recommended. Royal I tea $35 per person (with glass of champagne); Mayflower Tea $28 per person (no discounts for children). AE, DISC, DC, MC, V. Mon–Sat 3–5pm; Sun 3:30–5:30pm. Metro: Farragut North.

Empress Lounge ★ Rated tops in D.C. teas by aficionados who take their cuppa very seriously, guests partake of a variety of served teas and unlimited trips to the sumptuous dessert buffet for finger sandwiches, scones, muffins and, gulp, a chocolate fountain. If you haven't dipped fruit or cake chunks into warm liquid chocolate, you haven't lived. Forget about dinner—and dieting. Outdoor seating is available, weather permitting. ***Note:*** Lines can be long.

In the Mandarin Oriental Hotel, 1330 Maryland Ave. SW. ✆ **202/787-6868.** Reservations recommended. Tea is $32 for adults, $18 for kids 12 and under. AE, DISC, DC, MC, V. Thurs–Sun 2:30–4pm. Metro: Smithsonian.

5 FOGGY BOTTOM

Row houses fronted by brick sidewalks and postage-stamp-size gardens make Foggy Bottom one of the most attractive and distinctive neighborhoods in the city. If you have business at the Department of State, or you are attending a Kennedy Center or Lisner Auditorium performance, you've come to the right place.

VERY EXPENSIVE

Kinkead's ★★★ AMERICAN/SEAFOOD Many critics and patrons think this dining establishment serves the best seafood in the city. Kinkead's welcomes children, but frankly, it is not appropriate for kids under 8. And it's pricey. If you're ready to splurge, however, you're in for a treat. Award-winning chef Bob Kinkead presides over a kitchen that makes everything from scratch, even the mayonnaise, and depends on fresh and locally grown produce. Fish are harvested from local waters or are flown in fresh daily. Splurge on the entrees or keep costs in check with an appetizer-based meal. The New England–style clam chowder, fish and chips, and fried Ipswich clams rival any I've sampled in New England. For dessert, try the crème brûlée. Heck, try anything! The cafe/raw-bar area is cozier to my mind than upstairs. A tinkling piano adds atmosphere during the evening. If you have young children, I think you'll feel more comfortable (and so will other diners) if you sit here or in the enclosed courtyard. ***Tip:*** Come for lunch and enjoy the same wonderful food for considerably less. The clientele is comprised largely of locals, pols (the White House is 4 blocks away), and business types. After 5:30pm, there's valet parking for $5.

2000 Pennsylvania Ave. NW (entrance on I St., btw. 20th and 21st sts.). ✆ **202/296-7700.** www.kinkead.com. High chairs, booster seats. Reservations recommended. Main courses $15–$24 lunch; $30–$34 dinner. AE, DC, DISC, MC, V. Lunch Sun–Fri 11:30am–2:30pm; dinner daily Sun–Thurs 5:30–10pm, Fri–Sat 5:30–10:30. Metro: Foggy Bottom.

ICE CREAM

Cone E Island ICE CREAM Kids of all ages love the waffle cones, loaded with ice cream (Jack and Jill's and Hershey brands), hot fudge, and whipped cream. What's not to like? Loyal fans will tell you that it's well worth the cost and calories.

2000 Pennsylvania Ave. NW. ✆ **202/822-8460.** $3–$5.95 (1–3 scoops). No credit cards. Daily noon–midnight. Metro: Foggy Bottom, and then north on 23rd St.; right at Pennsylvania Ave. 3 blocks.

6 GEORGETOWN

Georgetown is one of Washington's most sophisticated neighborhoods and oft-visited tourist areas, with plenty of restaurants to choose from. You'll have little trouble finding one that serves your favorite cuisine. The Metro does not run into Georgetown, but you can take the Georgetown Metro Connection (✆ **202/625-RIDE** [7433]; www.georgetowndc.com/shuttle.php) from the following Metro stations: Dupont Circle and Rosslyn (Virginia). Each bus makes several stops. When you board, tell the driver where you're going, and ask for the stop closest to your destination. Another option is the D.C. Circulator, which runs between Union Station (Metro Red Line) and Georgetown. For more details, see chapter 3.

If you're out past 11pm, I suggest taking a taxi to your Metro station of choice or to your hotel. Call me a worrywart, but it's better to play it safe.

VERY EXPENSIVE

Morton's ★★★ AMERICAN/STEAKHOUSE Come here for one of the best steaks in town—in a town known for its steakhouses. While some Morton's fans prefer the veal chop, oversize lobsters, or prime rib, I'm a sucker for the steak and side orders of hash browns and fresh vegetables—enough for two or three servings. Soups, salads, and pastas are available for the less carnivorous and, along with daily specials, are a bit easier on the wallet than the main entrees. Well-mannered kids are welcome; no strollers are allowed in the restaurant, and two kids may want to share a portion. A surefire kid-pleaser is the chicken *goujonettes* (crispy chicken strips), served with fries. Be forewarned that lobster is market price (usually over $20 a pound)—it may be cheaper to drive to Maine. Check out the permanent collection of Leroy Neiman paintings while you're here. Valet parking is $9.

There's a downtown Morton's at 1050 Connecticut Ave. NW (at L St.; ✆ **202/955-5997**) and branches in Tysons Corner, Virginia (✆ **703/883-0800**); Arlington/Crystal City, at 1631 Crystal Square Arcade (✆ **703/4181444**); Reston, at 11956 Market St. (✆ **703/796-0128**); Annapolis, 100 Westgate Circle (✆ **410/280-1170**); and Baltimore, at the Sheraton Hotel, 300 S. Charles St. (✆ **410/547-8255**).

3251 Prospect St. NW (off Wisconsin Ave). ✆ **202/342-6258.** www.mortons.com. Reservations recommended. Main courses $26–$45. AE, DC, MC, V. Mon–Sat 5:30–11pm; Sun 5–10pm. Reston, Tysons, and Connecticut Ave. restaurants also serve lunch Mon–Fri 11:30am–2:30pm. Closed most major holidays. Metro: Foggy Bottom; then Georgetown Metro Connection or D.C. Circulator; or taxi.

EXPENSIVE

Filomena Ristorante ★ ITALIAN Even with a reservation, on Friday and Saturday nights you might have to wait, so eat early or go on a weeknight. At dinner, Filomena is appropriate for well-behaved kids 5 and older. At lunch, the restaurant is fine for most kids. (This is usually my daughter's first choice for a birthday lunch. She's 41 and very well behaved.) Try the panini (sandwich on a large roll). My fave: sausage, peppers, onions, and provolone. Or design your own calzone. The house-made pasta with your choice of a variety of delicious sauces is always delicious—and the kitchen is happy to prepare half-orders for bambinos. The linguine *cardinale* (lobster sauce) is *molto bene.* Or opt for one of the seafood, chicken, or veal entrees. Everybody's friendly, and the atmosphere is festive. It's not unusual to hear your neighbor's life story before the espresso arrives. Bill Clinton, Bush 41, Sandra Bullock, Harrison Ford, and Tom Cruise have dined here. Let's face it: They can afford to eat anywhere. Don't miss the home-baked desserts.

1063 Wisconsin Ave. NW (below M St.). ✆ **202/338-8800.** www.filomenadc.com. High chairs. Reservations recommended. Most main courses lunch $10–$13 ($18 buffet lunch Fri–Sat), dinner $13–$27; Sun brunch $16. AE, DC, DISC, MC, V. Daily 11:30am–11pm. Closed Jan 1, Thanksgiving, Dec 24 (evening), Dec 25. Metro: Foggy Bottom; then Georgetown Metro Connection or D.C. Circulator.

Sea Catch Restaurant and Raw Bar ★ SEAFOOD When you're in the mood to linger over seafood in a picturesque setting, reserve a canal-side table at this attractive stone-and-brick historic landmark, once a warehouse for goods transported on the C&O Canal. Pop some oysters or clams at the 40-foot marble raw bar to whet your appetite for seasonal specialties such as Dover sole, soft-shell crabs, crab cakes, grilled salmon, or lobster. A few meat and chicken entrees are also listed. Key lime pie, "triple X" decadent chocolate cake (one of my fave desserts *anywhere*), or cheesecake is a fitting finale. Well-behaved kids over 6 are welcome. If they don't like fish, they can have a large burger for lunch ($9) or a nut-crusted chicken breast with vegetables ($19) at dinner. There's free parking (3 hr.) at Constitution Parking Lot, 1054 31st St.

Canal Sq., 1054 31st St. NW, at M St. ✆ **202/337-8855.** www.seacatchrestaurant.com. High chairs. Reservations recommended. Main courses lunch $8–$18 (including sandwiches), dinner $23–$36. AE, DC, DISC, MC, V. Mon–Sat noon–3pm and 5:30–10pm. Metro: Foggy Bottom; then 20-min. walk, Georgetown Metro Connection, or D.C. Circulator.

MODERATE

Clyde's ★ AMERICAN The first Clyde's opened in 1963, shortly after the wheel was invented. Now the Clyde's family has grown to 16 (several in the hinterlands). Have brunch in the sunny Omelette Room, or head for the cheery Patio Room for a burger, sandwich, salad, or something more substantial from the menu, which changes daily and features seasonal favorites. At dinner, you can opt for bar food (burgers and such).

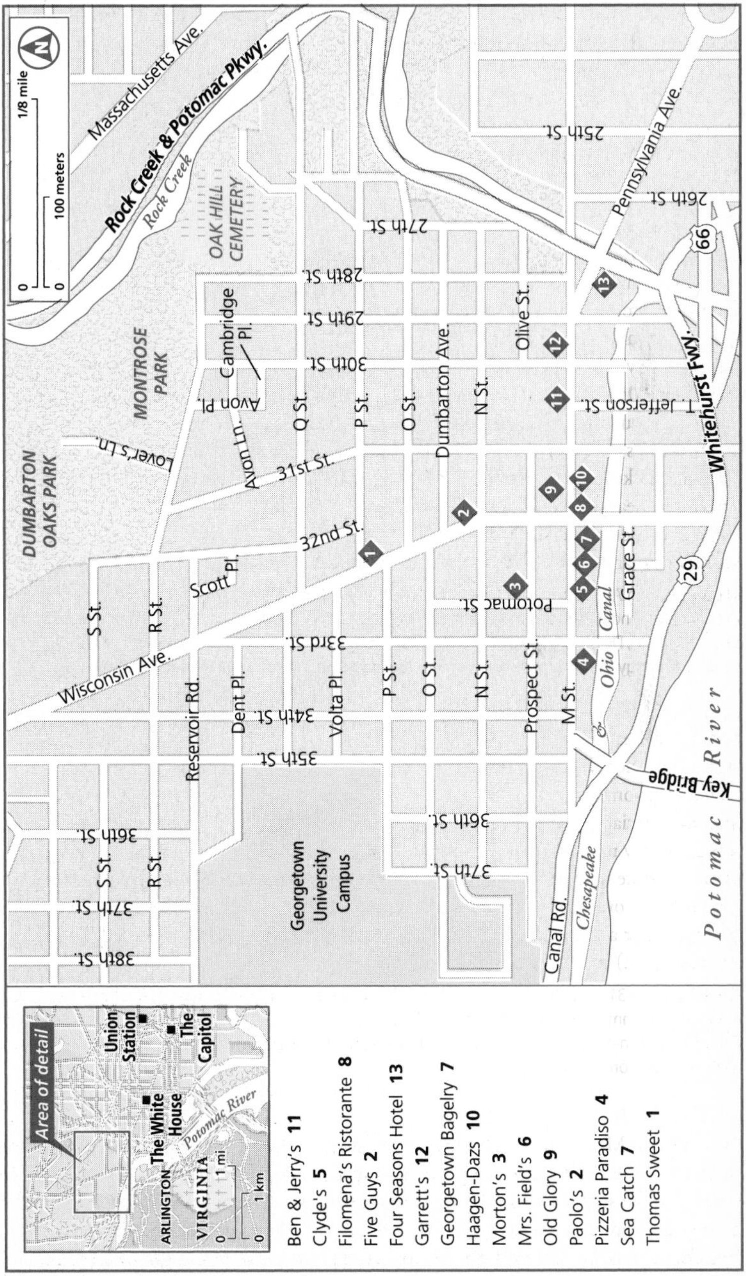
Ben & Jerry's 11
Clyde's 5
Filomena's Ristorante 8
Five Guys 2
Four Seasons Hotel 13
Garrett's 12
Georgetown Bagelry 7
Haagen-Dazs 10
Morton's 3
Mrs. Field's 6
Old Glory 9
Paolo's 2
Pizzeria Paradiso 4
Sea Catch 7
Thomas Sweet 1
Area of detail
ARLINGTON
VIRGINIA
The White House
Union Station
The Capitol
Potomac River
1 mi
1 km
100 meters
1/8 mile
N
Massachusetts Ave.
Rock Creek & Potomac Pkwy.
Rock Creek
OAK HILL CEMETERY
MONTROSE PARK
DUMBARTON OAKS PARK
Georgetown University Campus
Wisconsin Ave.
Pennsylvania Ave.
Whitehurst Fwy.
Key Bridge
Potomac River
Chesapeake & Ohio Canal
Canal Rd.
M St.
Prospect St.
N St.
O St.
P St.
Q St.
R St.
S St.
Dumbarton Ave.
Olive St.
Grace St.
Volta Pl.
Dent Pl.
Reservoir Rd.
Scott Pl.
Avon Ln.
Avon Pl.
Cambridge Pl.
Lover's Ln.
Potomac St.
T. Jefferson St.
25th St.
26th St.
27th St.
28th St.
29th St.
30th St.
31st St.
32nd St.
33rd St.
34th St.
35th St.
36th St.
37th St.
38th St.
29
66

All items on the kids' menu are $6 (burgers, chicken fingers, and pasta, among other choices) and include milk or a soft drink and a sundae or fruit. Each child receives a Busy Bag of small toys, crayons, and puzzle and coloring pages. Stay out of the bar area if you bring the children—or if you want to retain your hearing and your sanity.

Look for the monthly specials. For example, in October you could order a 1¼-pound lobster with fries and coleslaw for $19.

The 4 to 7pm "Afternoon Delights" snack menu at the bar was inspired by the 1976 Starland Vocal Band's hit song of the same name. Look for the gold record in the Patio Room. After shopping at Bloomingdale's, Mazza Gallery, Lord & Taylor, or Saks, stop at the Clyde's at 70 Wisconsin Circle, Chevy Chase, Maryland, near the Friendship Heights Metro station (✆ **301/951-9600**). You'll also find Clyde's at 707 7th St. NW, at H Street (✆ **202/349-3700**); in Alexandria (✆ **703/820-8300**); at the Mark Center, in Reston (✆ **703/787-6601**); and near Tyson's Corner in Vienna, Virginia (✆ **703/734-1901**).

3236 M St. NW. ✆ **202/333-9180.** www.clydes.com. High chairs, booster seats, kids' menu. Reservations strongly recommended. Bar food and lunch $10–$13; dinner main courses (most) $15–$18. AE, DC, DISC, MC, V. Mon–Thurs 10:30am–midnight; Fri–Sat 10am–1am; Sun 9am–10:30pm. Metro: Foggy Bottom; then 20-min. walk, Georgetown Metro Connection, or D.C. Circulator.

Garrett's AMERICAN **Value** Garrett's has been pleasing customers for more than 30 years. Thomas Sim Lee, the second governor of Maryland, built this tavern in what is now a National Historic Trust building. Locals belly up to the three copper-topped bars and feed one of the hottest jukeboxes around. Bypass the noisy bar scene downstairs, decorated with vintage train memorabilia, for a table on the glass-enclosed second-floor terrace. Kids under 10 can order a hot dog and fries, chicken tenders, spaghetti, or grilled cheese ($4.50), or parents can make kitchen requests for their kids. The "All Aboard Appetizers" include potato skins, Buffalo wings, nachos, and quesadillas—enough for a meal for small appetites. Soups, chili, burgers, and sandwiches are tasty alternatives. Or select a pasta and choose a sauce (Parmesan, white wine–garlic, marinara). Also check out the seafood chowder, other seafood dishes, and the delectable salads. The kitchen is flexible in this neighborhood watering hole and has been a longtime favorite of local families. Bring your laptop and check messages with the free Wi-Fi.

3003 M St. NW. ✆ **202/333-1033.** www.garrettsdc.com. High chairs, booster seats, kids' menu, crayons. Reservations recommended for 10 or more. Appetizers $5–$10; burgers and sandwiches $7–$10; main courses $11–$15; kids' menu $4.50. AE, DC, DISC, MC, V. Mon–Thurs 11:30am–10pm; Fri 11:30am–11pm; Sat noon–11pm; Sun noon–10:30pm. Metro: Foggy Bottom; then 15-min. walk, Georgetown Metro Connection, or D.C. Circulator.

Old Glory BARBECUE/RIBS What is it about eating with your hands? Maybe it's a link to our caveman roots. Who cares? Old Glory delivers delicious slow-cooked St. Louis–style (seasoned with dry-rub not wet sauce) ribs that are truly *finger-licking* good. Depending on your appetite, you can order a quarter, half, or a whole rack. Vying with the ribs is the pulled pork—on a platter with two side dishes—or piled high on a bun. The appetizers, sandwiches, and main dishes make for a satisfying meal that will stick to *your* ribs. Those who don't like to dirty their hands can put fork and knife to chicken, sliced beef brisket, ham, catfish, or a veggie main dish. Kids 10 and under may order a Kids Meal (burger, ribs, corndog, mac and cheese, or chicken tenders; or BBQ, grilled cheese, or PB&J sandwich), between 5 and 7pm. Each Kids' Meal comes with fries or carrots, a drink, and ice cream sundae. All for $5.95. Sunday and Monday, kids 10 and under eat free. Our family loves the food and the roadhouse ambience. Seating is on two floors, with an upstairs back patio.

3139 M St. NW (btw. 31st St. and Wisconsin Ave.). ✆ **202/337-3406.** www.oldglorybbq.com. High chairs, booster seats, kids menu. Reservations recommended for dinner. Main courses $6.95–$22 (full rack platter with 2 sides); Kid's Meal $5.95. Mon–Thurs 11:30am–2am; Fri–Sat 11:30am–3am; Sun 11am–2am (Sun brunch served 11am–3pm). Metro: Foggy Bottom; then 15-min. walk or Georgetown Metro Connection or D.C. Circulator.

Paolo's ★ ITALIAN Paolo's is a looker, and its beauty is more than skin deep. Munch the breadsticks with tapenade while deciding on one of the California-style pastas, signature pizzas cooked in a wood-burning oven, chicken or fish dishes, or a salad—all well seasoned and attractively served. House specialties include shrimp scampi and roasted chicken served with grilled veggies and roasted potatoes. Because Paolo's is a hot spot, especially on weekends, try it at off times. The kids' menu items average $8 (chicken tenders with pasta on the side; spaghetti, veggies on the side; or a personal pizza). During Happy Hour, Monday through Friday, 4 to 7pm, enjoy small plates (pizza, pasta, shrimp scampi, meatballs and such) for $3 to $6.

There are Paolo's branches in Reston, Virginia (✆ **703/318-8920**); Baltimore's Inner Harbor (✆ **410/539-7060**); and farther afield in Towson, Maryland (✆ **410/321-7000**).

1303 Wisconsin Ave. NW (btw. N and Dumbarton sts.). ✆ **202/333-7353.** www.paolosristorante.com. High chairs, booster seats, kids' menu, crayons and paper. Reservations recommended. Most main courses $12–$18. AE, DC, DISC, MC, V. Mon–Thurs 11am–11:30pm (pizza menu until 12:30am); Fri 11am–12:30am (pizza menu until 1:30am); Sat 10am–1:30am; Sun 10am–11:30pm (brunch till 3pm). Metro: Foggy Bottom; then 15-min. walk, Georgetown Metro Connection, or D.C. Circulator.

COOKIES, CUPCAKES, CANDY & ICE CREAM

In addition to the places listed below, there's a Ben & Jerry's at 2135 M St. NW (✆ **202/965-2222**), and a Häagen-Dazs (see p. 85).

Baked and Wired ★★ BAKERY This bakery and espresso/tea bar (not much bigger than a cookie tin) is known for its made-from-scratch blueberry muffins in parchment, cookie bars, brownies, cupcakes, and tarts to go. The yummy baked goods—as attractive to the eye as the palate—have been drawing loyal patrons since opening in 2001.

1052 Thomas Jefferson St. NW (btw. 30th and 31st sts., K and M sts.). ✆ **202/333-2500.** www.bakedandwired.com. Cupcakes $3.50; cookies $1.50. Mon–Fri 7am–7pm; Sat 8am–8pm; Sun 9am–7pm.

Mrs. Field's COOKIES These soft, chewy, chip-laden cookies are nearly as good as homemade, and the muffins are also excellent. They make the perfect bribe when you need one (with kids, that's about every 30 sec.).

Shops at Georgetown Park, Wisconsin Ave. and M St. NW. (3222 M St. NW). ✆ **202/337-5117.** $1.60 (including tax) per cookie. MC, V. Mon–Sat 10am–9pm; Sun noon–6pm. Metro: Foggy Bottom; then 15-min. walk, Georgetown Metro Connection, or D.C. Circulator.

Thomas Sweet ★ ICE CREAM **Finds** This old-style ice cream parlor, begun by two college friends (the original location is in Princeton, New Jersey), is a reincarnation of the "malt shoppe" in the Archie comics. The ice-cream-making operation (up to 135 flavors!) is located in the store, where it handles the large demand from area restaurants, some of the Smithsonian museums, and the White House. The best-selling "Blend In" is a customized mix of up to three toppings (fresh fruit, cookies, and candies) with any flavor of ice cream or yogurt. Some chocoholics think the bittersweet chocolate is the best in the world. Get your sugar rush while enjoying the passing parade of students, tourists, Brooks Brothers suits, and blue-haired ladies from a sidewalk table.

3214 P St. NW (at Wisconsin Ave.). ✆ **202/337-0616.** www.thomassweet.com. Single scoop kids' size $3, regular $4; banana split $6.60. No credit cards. Sun–Thurs 10am–10:30pm; Fri–Sat 10am–midnight. Metro: Foggy Bottom; then 15-min. walk, Georgetown Metro Connection, or D.C. Circulator.

7 DUPONT CIRCLE

Dupont Circle, Adams Morgan, and the U Street Corridor lend themselves to people-watching, shopping, and dining—often all at the same time. The restaurants reflect these neighborhoods' unzipped, diverse natures. Besides fine-dining establishments, you'll find bistro, diner, and pub fare, sandwiches, chili, pizza, hot dogs, wraps, and ice cream. Phew! How's that for diversity? There's also plenty of eye candy. What kid can turn down an opportunity to ogle pink hair and multipierced body parts? Dupont Circle (the park in the center of the rotary) is a good place to let the little darlings run around and create havoc (under supervision) and then fall into one of the many family-friendly restaurants within a few blocks of the park (and Metro stop).

In addition to the restaurants listed below, there's a Ben & Jerry's branch near Dupont Circle, at 1333 19th St (at N St.). See p. 85 for a full review.

MODERATE

Firehook ★★ BAKERY/CAFE "Born and bread" locally, the first Firehook opened in Old Town Alexandria in 1992. But this isn't a slick, cookie-cutter (ha!) chain. The cozy, neighborhood feel recalls a gentler era. Locals sip coffee, gossip, and work on laptops—or play Internet games. Classical music plays, and a sense of well-being pervades. ***Note:*** Kids must be old enough to sit on a chair, stool, or lap without falling over, as there are no high chairs or booster seats. No one will rush you if you want to linger. In a hurry? Get your order to go. For a quick and satisfying meal, come here in the morning for the breakfast sandwiches, croissants, rolls, muffins, brioche, flatbread, sweet rolls, yogurt/fruit/granola parfaits, and Danish (the cheese is killer!). At lunch, the salads, sandwiches, soups—all homemade, and all claiming no preservatives—are delicious. When your blood sugar is running low, stop for a pick-me-up. It's strictly self-serve. Did I say that the breads are outta sight? More than two dozen varieties are available every single day. Maybe one will fit in your luggage. For other locations, see the box "Eating Fast & Well," p. 80, earlier in this chapter.

1909 Q St. NW (btw. 19th and 20th sts.). ✆ **202/588-9296.** www.firehook.com. Breakfast $2–$6; lunch $4–$7. Mon–Fri 6:30am–9pm; Sat 7am–7pm; Sun 7am–7pm. Metro: Dupont Circle, then walk 1 block east on Q St.

Hank's Oyster Bar ★★★ SEAFOOD On a mild day, there's little that's more pleasurable than dining outdoors at Hank's and watching the passing scene between forkfuls of delectable seafood. Inside it may be warmer and drier, but it's also noisier. Come here for fresh oysters and clams on the half shell, jumbo shrimp cocktail, lobster bisque, fried Ipswich clams (not the bland and chewy strips), fried oyster po' boy (served with lettuce and tomato on French bread). My personal fave is the lobster roll (chunks of lobster meat bound with a little mayo and lemon juice piled in a New England-style buttered hot dog roll), served with Old Bay fries. OMG! Kids can busy themselves with the peel-and-eat shrimp, a small plate of popcorn shrimp, bowl of lobster bisque, or a single crab cake

Where to Dine in Dupont Circle, Adams Morgan & U Street Corridor

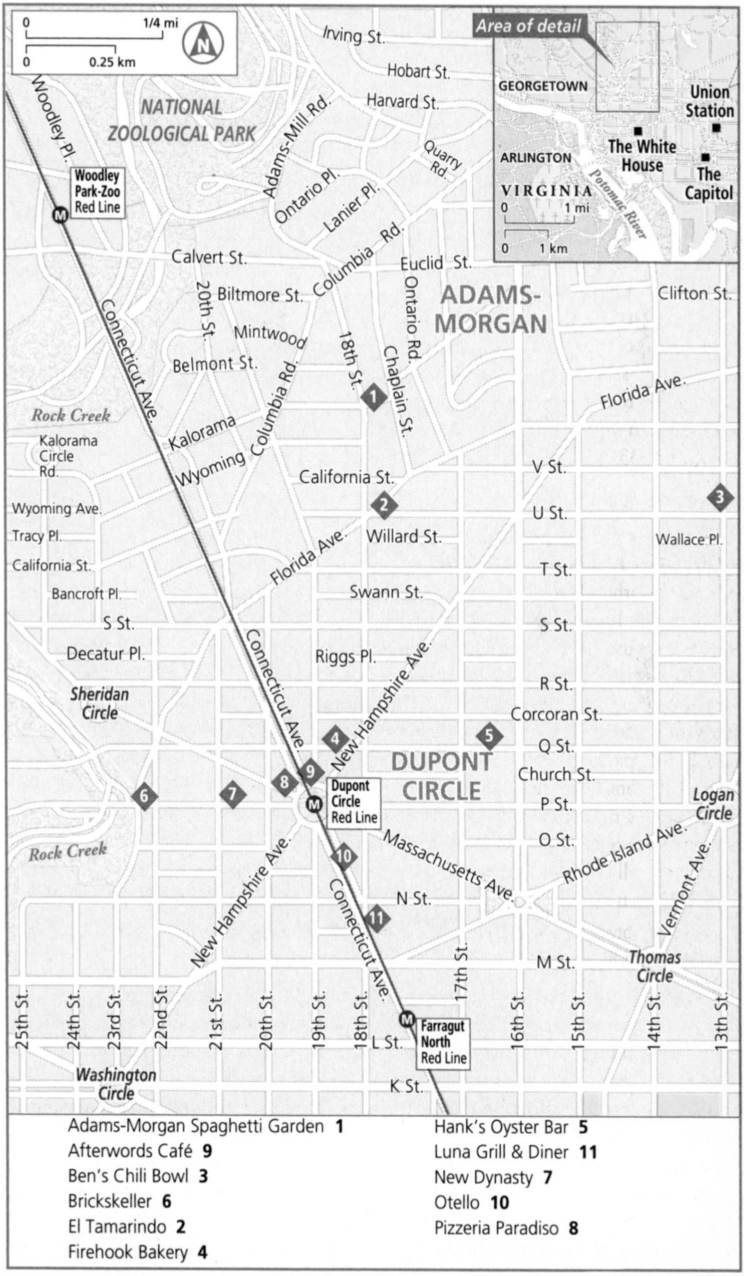

Adams-Morgan Spaghetti Garden **1**
Afterwords Café **9**
Ben's Chili Bowl **3**
Brickskeller **6**
El Tamarindo **2**
Firehook Bakery **4**
Hank's Oyster Bar **5**
Luna Grill & Diner **11**
New Dynasty **7**
Otello **10**
Pizzeria Paradiso **8**

($13). Carnivores can hunker down with one of the daily "Meat & 2 Sides" specials (blue-cheese encrusted steak, fried chicken, braised short ribs, for example). The buttermilk onion rings are one of life's necessities. Not for nuttin' has Hank's received numerous restaurant awards. Come early or late for dinner or plan to wait. It's first-come, first-served. A second Hank's is at 1026 King St. in Alexandria, Virginia (✆ **703/739-HANK** [4265]).

1624 Q St. NW (btw.16th & 17th sts.). ✆ **202/462-4265.** www.hanksdc.com. Booster seats and high chairs. No reservations. Appetizers $2–$12; main courses $13–$23. AE, DISC, MC, V. Sun–Tues 5:30–10pm; Wed–Sat 5:30–11pm; Sat–Sun brunch 11am–3pm. Metro: Dupont Circle (Q St. exit), then 2-block walk.

Luna Grill & Diner ★ AMERICAN Slide into a booth at the hip, retro Luna for delicious diner food with a funky-chic 'tude. Sip fresh-squeezed OJ with your bagel, cream cheese, and lox; granola and fruit; or steak and eggs at breakfast. (There's plenty of traditional breakfast fare, too.) Lunch and dinner entrees include salads, pasta, burgers, sides of mashed potatoes and gravy, nachos, and chicken wings. We're talking major comfort food: tasty, warm, and satisfying (the kitchen fills more orders for its roast turkey and meatloaf than anything else). Daily Blue Plate and Green Plate (vegetarian) specials are $8 to $11. On the kids' menu are miniburgers, pasta, chicken tenders, mac and cheese for $4 to $6 (side dish included). Most salads, sandwiches, pastas, meatloaf, and mashed potatoes are under $10. Luna has a second location at 4024 28th St., Arlington, Virginia (✆ **703/379-7173**).

1301 Connecticut Ave. NW (at N St.). ✆ **202/835-2280.** www.lunagrillanddiner.com. High chairs, booster seats. Reservations not accepted. Breakfast (most items) $5–$8; lunch $5–$8; dinner main course $9–$15. AE, DC, DISC, MC, V. Mon–Thurs 8am–10:30pm; Fri 8am–11:30pm; Sat 9am–11:30pm; Sun 9am–10pm. Metro: Dupont Circle (1 block) or Farragut North (3 blocks).

Otello ★ ITALIAN Otello is a friendly, family-operated neighborhood trattoria, more typical of those in New York than in D.C. The sauces taste freshly made and pack the right amount of punch. Seafood and veal are as fine as you'll find south of Baltimore's Little Italy. Have your favorite pasta, served with a variety of sauces. The *osso buco* (veal shanks in a well-seasoned sauce) is a house specialty. Kids are welcome (though babies and toddlers might upset your experience and other diners). Half portions are available for kids at half price. And the bruschetta (grilled Italian bread here topped with chopped tomatoes, basil, and mozzarella) is similar to pizza. A small antipasto, salad, and/or bowl of Pasta e Fagiole (pasta and bean soup) keeps the younger generation of my family happy.

1329 Connecticut Ave. NW. ✆ **202/429-0209.** www.otellodc.com. Booster seats. Reservations recommended. Main courses lunch $7–$13, dinner $17–$20. AE, DISC, DC, MC, V. Mon–Fri noon–2:30pm; Mon–Sat 5:30–10:30pm. Metro: Dupont Circle.

INEXPENSIVE

Afterwords Cafe at Kramerbooks AMERICAN After browsing at Kramerbooks, stop for a meal or snack at Afterwords, where the atmosphere is as bohemian as Washington allows itself to get, and you can devour a book or newspaper until your food comes. The menu changes seasonally, but the OJ is always freshly squeezed, and it seems to me that the food has improved over the years. Try an omelet served with potatoes and fresh fruit garnish, pancakes or waffles, eggs Benedict, and other delectable breakfast food. All come with muffins, coffee or tea, and a complimentary drink at brunch Saturday and Sunday. At other times, you'll find a full breakfast menu. At lunch and dinner, everything from salads, soup, sandwiches, pasta (always a safe bet), and vegetarian dishes to calorie-packed desserts, such as sour cream blackout cake and banana splits, is served.

For $19, you can order any three items to share off an extensive "Sharezies" (light fare/ appetizer) menu. And there is a Kids at the Cafe menu ("for folks under 4 feet") with favorites such as mac and cheese, grilled cheese, spaghetti, and hamburgers. If they're not up for a full breakfast, they can get a bagel and cream cheese ($2.95) or granola, milk, and fruit ($5.25). Wednesday through Saturday evenings, there's live music—folk, jazz, or blues. Grown-ups could indulge in a café signature martini or cocktail ($7–$10), draft or bottled beer ($6), or glass of wine ($6–$8) while the children enjoy ice-cream treats.

1517 Connecticut Ave. NW. (btw. Dupont Circle and Q St.). ✆ **202/387-1462.** High chairs, kids' menu. Reservations accepted for 6 or more. Appetizers $3.95–$7.75; most lunch and dinner main courses $10–$13; Sat–Sun breakfast/brunch $15–$17; kids' menu $4.75–$6.75. AE, MC, V. Mon–Thurs 7:30am–1am; continuously Fri 8am–Sun 1am. Metro: Dupont Circle.

Ben's Chili Bowl ★★ **Value** HOT DOGS/CHILI Make a beeline for Ben's—once a silent-movie house and pool hall—for a quintessential D.C. experience. Ben's has been serving its signature dogs, half-smokes, and secret-recipe chili to adoring fans since 1958, before President Obama was born. Speaking of the First Dude, he chowed down at Ben's shortly after relocating from Chicago. (Ben's is next door to the historic Lincoln Theatre, where Ella Fitzgerald and Nat King Cole, and D.C. natives Pearl Bailey and Duke Ellington, performed. Now it's a venue for top-draw music acts, films, and plays. Even when the line trails onto U Street, it moves quickly. ***Tip:*** My fave is a chili dog and fries (with chili and cheese, if I'm feeling especially perverse). If you're into healthy foods, Ben's offers several vegetarian dishes. You can eat at the counter; or order, and then grab a table or booth. It's cash only, but there's an ATM near the entrance.

1213 U St. NW (btw. 12th and 13th sts.). ✆ **202/667-0909.** www.benschilibowl.com. High chairs and booster seats. Most items $3.80–$5.20. No credit cards. Mon–Thurs 6am–2am; Fri 6am–4am; Sat 7am–4am; Sun 11am–11pm. Metro: U St./Cardozo.

Brickskeller **Value** AMERICAN At the corner of 22nd and P streets, the Brick serves pub fare in a setting reminiscent of *Cheers.* Dartboards on weekends and video games accessorize the place. During my college days in D.C., I spent some time here when my parents thought I was at the library. More than 1,000 kinds of beer (making this the *Guinness Book of World Records* holder for most different kinds of beer commercially available—who says D.C. is dull?) and an oldies-filled jukebox will nurture your nostalgia trip. Your underagers can play electronic games and munch on chicken tenders, burgers, nachos, potato skins with the works (sour cream, grated cheese, bacon), and other "light" fare. Vegetarians won't starve. Try the tempura vegetables, onion rings (made in-house), fries, and salads. The Brickskeller has been pleasing patrons for more than 45 years. Add your name to the list and stop by, maybe in conjunction with a visit to the Phillips Collection or a stroll through Dupont Circle.

1523 22nd St. NW. ✆ **202/293-1885.** www.thebrickskeller.com. High chairs, booster seats. Reservations accepted for 8 or more. Most items $7.95–$12. AE, DC, DISC, MC, V. Mon–Thurs 11:30am–2am; Fri 11:30am–3am; Sat 6pm–3am; Sun 6pm–2am. Kitchen closes 1 hr. before restaurant closes. Metro: Dupont Circle; walk west on P St. 2 blocks, then go right at 22nd St.

New Dynasty ★ **Value** PAN ASIAN Because it's very good and very reasonable, New Dynasty can fill up, especially at lunchtime. So go early or late for a quick, inexpensive meal of Asian food (Chinese, Thai, Vietnamese, Malaysian) in a no-frills setting, or for carryout—it's extremely good value. And the restaurant delivers to the immediate area. Imagine unwinding in your room and watching a movie with the kiddies while enjoying dinner for four for under $50. The menu is extensive; there's a wide range of appetizers and soups; rice and lo mein; and chicken, beef, shrimp, or tofu/vegetable dishes. Younger kids—always happy to eat with their fingers—will be content with an order of spring rolls, dumplings, fried wonton, or shrimp tempura (all under $5). Fancy it's not—but its tasty and dependable fare.

2020 P St. NW. ✆ **202/872-8889.** www.xingchow.com. High chairs, booster seats. Appetizers $2.50–$6; main courses $8–$1. MC, V. Mon–Fri 11am–10pm; Sat–Sun noon–10pm. Metro: Dupont Circle.

Pizzeria Paradiso ★ ITALIAN/PIZZA Pizzeria Paradiso moved to larger space in August 2009, just off Dupont Circle, where they still serve authentic, wood-oven-baked classic pizza worthy of an aria or two. Stick to the basic Margherita or Quattro Formaggi (four cheeses), if your arteries can handle it. On pizza this good, you don't need extra toppings. But that's your call. You can create your own pie from 37 toppings. Stop here for a quick bite when you're browsing Dupont Circle or visiting the Phillips Collection. There's seating for 75 indoors and on the side patio, and a couple of high chairs and booster seats. My favorite seat is at the counter, where I can watch the pizzas baking while I nosh on the complimentary Mediterranean olives. Hey, stand if you have to—the pizza is worth it. Not in the mood for pizza? Try a salad, bruschetta, or panini (sandwich) on really good bread. I like the lemonade—tart and slightly fizzy. There's a second, equally good location in Georgetown, at 3282 M St. NW (a stone's throw from the Shops at Georgetown Park and two doors from Dean & Deluca; ✆ **202/337-1245**).

2003 P St. NW. ✆ **202/223-1245.** www.eatyourpizza.com. High chairs and boosters. Reservations not accepted. $17 12-in. cheese pizza; additional toppings extra. DC, DISC, MC, V. Mon–Thurs 11:30am–11pm; Fri–Sat 11:30am–midnight; Sun noon–10pm. Metro: Dupont Circle, then walk 1½ blocks.

8 ADAMS MORGAN

Like most kids, I love Adams Morgan. It's colorful, vibrant, and edgy. I must warn you, however, that parking is next to impossible in the area, especially on weekends. The good news: You can take the Metro to the Woodley Park–Zoo/Adams Morgan station and walk 10 minutes across the Calvert Street Bridge (at Connecticut Ave. and Calvert St.) to 18th and Columbia Road NW. If you miss the last bus (with kids, I doubt it!), take a taxi. Do not walk. See the "Where to Dine in Dupont Circle, Adams Morgan & U-Street Corridor" map (p. 99) for locations of restaurants in this section.

MODERATE

Adams Morgan Spaghetti Garden ★ ITALIAN This might not be *Bon Apetit* magazine fare and, heaven knows, there are better (and much pricier) Italian restaurants downtown, but most of the hearty, large-portioned pasta dishes—lasagna, spaghetti, ravioli, and the like—are tasty and still priced between $9 and $13. Most chicken, veal, and shrimp are served with a side of spaghetti marinara for under $15. The pizza puttanesca is adorned with black olives, tomato, capers, and plenty of garlic. *Bellissima!* The second-floor rooftop dining area affords a view of one of the city's more interesting neighborhoods, although it's not open full time. The restaurant has a genuine family-friendly attitude and even modifies menu items, along with prices, for kids.

2317 18th St. NW (btw. Belmont and Kalorama rds.). ✆ **202/265-6665.** High chairs, booster seats, children's portions. Reservations for groups of 8 or more. Appetizers $3–$7; pasta main courses $9–$13; meat main courses $10–$15; children's spaghetti portions $4.95. AE, DISC, DC, MC, V. Tues–Thurs and Sun noon–midnight; Fri–Sat noon–2:30am. Closed Thanksgiving, Dec 25, Jan 1. Metro: Woodley Park–Zoo/Adams Morgan or Dupont Circle.

El Tamarindo ★ SALVADORAN/MEXICAN This neighborhood spot serves authentic Mexican and Salvadoran cooking that is hearty and reasonable. You can't go wrong with the chicken, beef, or shrimp fajitas. Kids can order a la carte items such as burritos, *pupusas* (tortillas filled with various items, only $2–$3 each), tamales, tostadas, chimichangas, and tacos. I've never been here when there weren't kids in abundance, and the prices are ridiculously low. The congenial atmosphere is gratis. The restaurant is open until the wee hours—perfect for quelling your teenagers' late-night munchies. If you're already in Adams Morgan, walk south on 18th Street (from Columbia Rd.) 4 blocks to Florida Ave. If you're here late, take a cab back to your hotel.

1785 Florida Ave. NW (near intersection of 18th and U sts.). ✆ **202/328-3660.** www.eltamarindodc.com. High chairs, booster seats. Reservations for 20 or more. Most appetizers $7–$8; main courses $10–$15. AE, DISC, MC, V. Mon–Thurs 11am–3am; Fri 11am–5am; Sat–Sun 10am–5am. Metro: U St./Cardozo, and then walk west on U St. 4 blocks.

9 UPPER NORTHWEST

Oodles of D.C. kids call this largely residential neighborhood home, so it's no surprise that the local restaurants cater to them (and the folks who pay for their french fries and braces). You'll find plenty of family-pleasing fare, especially in the burger, overstuffed-sandwich, and dessert categories.

MODERATE

Cactus Cantina ★ TEX-MEX This cozy cantina, decorated with twinkling lights and other tacky touches, is on busy Wisconsin Avenue (1 block from the National Cathedral and a short drive from the National Zoo). Except for the traffic hum, you could be on a dusty plain south of the border. Tex-Mex lovers drool at the mention of mesquite-grilled fajitas. The generous combination platters ($10) appease large appetites. Many applaud the *camarones* brochette, broiled cheese- and jalapeño-stuffed shrimp wrapped in bacon. The kids' menu offers nachos, quesadillas, enchiladas, and chicken nuggets (that's Mexican?); each is under $6. Sunday brunch features half a dozen entrees in the $8 to $12 range, such as huevos rancheros. Toast Cactus Cantina's ever-popular tortilla chips with a margarita, glass of sangria, or Dos Equis. Show up before 6pm for dinner, especially on weekends. Kids like to watch the glass-enclosed tortilla-making machine—which might have been dreamed up by Rube Goldberg. The dough is fed into the top and then cooked while being pulled through the machine.

3300 Wisconsin Ave. NW. ✆ **202/686-7222.** www.cactuscantina.com. High chairs, booster seats, kids' menu, crayons. Reservations at lunch Mon–Thurs for 10 or more, Fri–Sun 15 or more. Appetizers $4.95–$9.95; most main courses $9–$15; kids' menu, $3.75–$5.75. AE, DC, DISC, MC, V. Mon–Thurs 11am–11pm; Fri–Sat 11am–midnight; Sun 10:30am–11pm (brunch 10:30am–3pm). Metro: Tenleytown, then take any no. 30 bus south or 15-min. walk.

Chadwicks AMERICAN Going to Chadwicks is like visiting an old friend—an *old* old friend. The Friendship Heights Chadwicks has been welcoming diners since 1982. Children are greeted with crayons and their own menus to color. The service is friendly and prompt, and the cocktails are generous. The hamburgers and sandwiches are ample and tasty, and Sunday brunch (10am–4pm) is a bargain, with most entrees under $13. A shaded outdoor patio is pleasant and somewhat sheltered from automobile and bus fumes. On the kids' menu are grilled cheese, chicken fingers, hamburger/cheeseburger, or PB&J—all with fries—personal pizza, and pasta with tomato or *alfredo* (cream) sauce. Prices run from $2.95 to $3.50. Can you feed them this cheaply at home?

I've been receiving good reports on the grilled salmon served on field greens with glazed pecans, blue cheese, and balsamic vinaigrette dressing, as well as the Super Deal, an entree and beverage for $7.95, Monday through Friday from 11:30am to 4pm.

5247 Wisconsin Ave. NW, at Jenifer St. ✆ **202/362-8040.** High chairs, booster seats, kids' menu, crayons. Most main courses lunch under $9.95, dinner $10–$20; kids' menu items $2.95–$3.50. AE, DISC, MC, V. Mon–Sat 11:30am–midnight (bar later); Sun 10am–midnight. Metro: Friendship Heights.

The Cheesecake Factory ★ AMERICAN The California-based Cheesecake Factory blew in like a Santa Ana wind when the restaurant opened in 1991. Judging by the lines, this is no ill wind. The first-class fries are crunchy and greaseless, and the salads and chicken dishes are tasty and oversized. In fact, I rarely leave without a doggy bag. The extensive menu is worthy of framing. Many complain about the noise and the wait. And I'm one of the most vocal complainers. (Just ask my family.) I'll keep saying it until I'm blue in the face: Go very early, especially with easily tired young 'uns. Don't forget the real reason you came: to try at least 1 of the 35 kinds of cheesecake. The original (plain) is $6.50 a slice and enough for two. Be sure to save some room. There's no kids' menu, but the lengthy appetizer menu offers kid-pleasing taquitos, mini crab cakes, pot stickers (dumplings), and Roadside Sliders (miniburgers on Lilliputian-size buns). Outside D.C., try the Cheesecake Factory at White Flint Mall, in North Bethesda, Maryland (✆ **301/770-0999**); at Tysons Galleria, McLean, Virginia (✆ **703/506-9311**); or at the Inner Harbor, in Baltimore (✆ **410/234-3990**).

5345 Wisconsin Ave. NW (Chevy Chase Pavilion). ✆ **202/364-0500.** www.cheesecakefactory.com. High chairs, booster seats. Appetizers $5.95–$11; most main courses $11–$17; desserts $4.50–$8.95. AE, DISC, MC, V. Mon–Thurs 11:30am–11:30pm; Fri–Sat 11:30am–12:30am; Sun 10am–11pm. Metro: Friendship Heights.

Jandara THAI Point little ones to the appetizers such as barbecued chicken in peanut sauce, spring rolls, Thod Mun (deep-fried fish cakes), Goong Nang Pah (shrimp wrapped in egg roll "skin" and deep fried), or chicken satay—all mild in flavor. That ought to keep them you busy while you decide among the many fish, chicken, pork, and vegetarian main dishes. If your innards are heat-sensitive, ask your server to recommend some of the milder dishes—and stay way from menu items with the single and double chili icons. If you don't mind bus fumes, dine at a sidewalk table in nice weather. The sponge-painted walls in exotic colors and brass-colored accessories provide a pleasing setting for indoor dining. Jandara is a short walk from the Metro and the National Zoo.

2606 Connecticut Ave. NW, at Calvert St. ✆ **202/387-8876.** www.jandarathai.com. High chairs, booster seats. Appetizers $3.95–$7.95; main courses lunch $7–$11, dinner $10–$16. AE, DC, DISC, MC, V. Sun and Mon–Thurs 11am–10:30pm; Fri–Sat 11am–11pm. Metro: Woodley Park–Zoo/Adams Morgan.

ICE CREAM & CANDY

Baskin-Robbins ICE CREAM They must be doing something right, because this brand sells more ice cream than any other retail dealer in the country. The franchises are institutional, but like an old friend, they're there when you need them.

2604 Connecticut Ave. ✆ **202/483-4820.** www.baskinrobbins.com. Single dip $3; double dip $4.60 AE, MC, V. Daily 11am–10pm. Metro: Woodley Park–Zoo/Adams Morgan, then a 5-min. walk.

Kron Chocolatier ★★ CANDY In a recurring dream, I fall into a vat of Kron's melted bittersweet chocolate and live happily ever after. Try the Budapest cream truffles and chocolate-dipped strawberries, and you, too, will have sweet dreams. Kids will find their own favorites. Underground parking is free, with ticket validation.

Mazza Galleria, 5300 Wisconsin Ave. NW. ✆ **202/966-4946.** www.krondc.com. Most chocolates, almond toffee butter crunch, $17 per 11-ounce box or $1 per piece; truffles $26 per ½ pound. AE, MC, V. Mon–Fri 10am–8pm; Sat 10am–6pm; Sun noon–5pm; extended hours around Christmas. Metro: Friendship Heights.

AFTERNOON TEA

Washington National Cathedral ★★ Finds What a lovely setting in which to enjoy tea. The Tour and Tea is every Tuesday and Wednesday, with the tour departing from the west nave (Wisconsin Ave. entrance) at 1:30pm, followed by the tea at 2:45pm. Like love and marriage, you can't have one without the other: Tea can be taken only in conjunction with the tour. The cost is $25, regardless of age. I recommend this for patient, well-behaved kids 8 and older. Finger sandwiches, scones, and a variety of sweets are served on linen napery in the Cathedral tower gallery, with its wonderful view of the city. The teas are immensely popular and must be booked well in advance (often months). There is, however, a wait list, and last-minute cancellations sometimes occur.

Massachusetts and Wisconsin aves. NW. ✆ **202/537-8993.** www.cathedral.org/cathedral. Tour and Tea $25. MC, V. Tues–Wed at 1:30pm. Metro: Dupont Circle, then any northbound Mass. Ave. bus to Wisconsin Ave.

10 SUBURBAN MARYLAND

Years ago, if you lived in the suburbs and wanted a decent meal, you ventured downtown. Now there are so many restaurants ringing the Beltway that many diners prefer to stay put—as well they should. Suburban Maryland is crawling with restaurants. Knowing how much kids can eat (and how expensive it can be to feed them), we are recommending places that fall into the inexpensive to moderate range. We don't want you to go home broke. We want you to come back. In addition to the places listed below, there's a **Fuddruckers,** in Rockville, at 1592A Rockville Pike (✆ **301/468-3535**), and two **Five Guys,** 4829 Bethesda Ave. (✆ **301/657-0007**), and 10414 Auto Park Dr., both in Bethesda (in Expo Square; ✆ **301/365-9300**).

BETHESDA

Foong Lin ★ CHINESE An oldie and a goodie, this neighborhood restaurant has a friendly waitstaff, who are especially considerate to young families. Foong Lin consistently turns out delicious Cantonese, Hunan, and Szechuan favorites. At lunch, your choice of 1 of 18 entrees comes with a spring roll and rice for $6.25 to $7.95. I don't know about you, but I can't prepare a meal for that price. Most main dishes at dinner are $11 to $14. The lengthy menu of appetizers, soups, specialties, and a la carte beef, pork, chicken, seafood, and noodles might take a while to digest, but you'll find scores of items to tempt the kids. How about some tasty finger foods such as egg rolls and spring rolls, dumplings, chicken wings, or shrimp toast? If you're staying in Bethesda or Chevy Chase, delivery service is available within 3 miles from 4:30 to 10pm, with a $15 minimum order. The crispy whole fish is exceptional; see if you can talk the kids into trying it.

7710 Norfolk Ave., Bethesda, MD. ✆ **301/656-3427.** www.foonglin.com. High chairs, booster seats. Main courses lunch $6.95–$8.95, dinner $8.95–$18. AE, MC, V. Mon–Fri 11am–10:30pm; Sat 11am–11pm; Sun 11:30am–10pm. Closed Thanksgiving. Metro: Bethesda.

Uncle Julio's Rio Grande Café MEXICAN Build a better burrito and the world will beat a path to your door. Order a margarita, and dig into the warm tortilla chips and chunky salsa while the kids watch the Rube Goldberg contraption that produces around 400 tortillas an hour. The fajitas al carbon are *numero uno* for big appetites. On the kids' menu are "Lotta Enchilada," "Kidsadillas," nachos, tacos, and fajita, served with fresh fruit. All items are $5.50 to $6.25 (drink extra). Or maybe they would prefer an appetizer or an a la carte taco or burrito. I'm a sucker for the tortilla soup and chicken fajitas. If you have room, finish with honey-drenched sopapillas. *¡Que bueno!* Go at off times, especially on weekends or holidays.

There are branches in Gaithersburg, Maryland (✆ **240/632-2150**); Arlington, Virginia (✆ **703/266-7760**); Ballston, Virginia (✆ **703/528-3131**); and Reston, Virginia (✆ **703/904-0703**).

4870 Bethesda Ave. (Bethesda Row), Bethesda, MD. ✆ **301/656-2981.** High chairs, booster seats, kids' menu. Reservations not accepted. Appetizers $4.95–$14 (fajitas); most main courses $9.50–$20; Sun brunch $8.95–$14. AE, DC, DISC, MC, V. Sun and Mon–Thurs 11am–10:30pm; Fri–Sat 11am–11:30pm. Metro: Bethesda.

Hamburger Hamlet ★ AMERICAN Hamburger Hamlet has been attracting families since 1979. Children can amuse themselves with the restaurant-supplied crayons to draw on the white paper tablecloths until the grub comes. On the kids' menu (for those 12 and under): baby burger, chicken fingers, pasta, grilled cheese, and PB&J. Price is $5.25 and includes a beverage. For bigger appetites, I recommend sticking with the burgers (including turkey and vegetarian; from $9.95–$12), sandwiches, fish tacos, and fajitas. ***Tip:*** Portions are large. My favorite appetizer—more like a meal—remains Zucchini Zircles (batter-dipped and fried with an apricot dipping sauce). Youngsters might share the Baby Burger Sampler (four small burgers for $11). And then there's the Ultimate Hot Fudge Cake (fudgey layer cake, with vanilla ice cream, hot fudge, and whipped cream), served with extra spoons. Be prepared to wait 15 minutes or longer at prime time. In Gaithersburg, there's a branch in the Rio Center, at 9811 Washington Blvd. (✆ **301/417-0773**). In Virginia, you'll find one at Crystal City Underground (✆ **703/413-0422**) and one in Old Town Alexandria, at 109 S. St. Asaph St. (✆ **703/683-1776**).

10400 Old Georgetown Rd., Bethesda, MD. ✆ **301/897-5350.** www.hamburgerhamlet.com. High chairs, booster seats, kids' menu, crayons. Reservations accepted for 8 or more. Most main courses $8.95–$18 (most under $16); kids' menu items $5.25 (includes drink). AE, DC, DISC, MC, V. Mon–Thurs 11am–10:30pm; Fri–Sat 11am–11pm; Sun 11am–10pm (brunch until 2pm).

Houston's Woodmont Grill ★★ AMERICAN/RIBS/BARBECUE Houston's serves the best hickory-grilled hamburgers in the D.C. area (for $13). And the Metro stops in Bethesda, just a couple of blocks away. It's a short walk to Imagination Stage, with children's live theater. When the line is long (at peak lunch and dinner hours), put your name on the list and take a walk—to Outer Mongolia. Or solve the problem by eating early or late. The barbecued ribs ($26 for a full rack, with fries and coleslaw) and salads are outstanding; wash them down with a shake or a frosty mug of beer. There is no printed kids' menu. Just ask for a kids' meal: grilled cheese, hamburger, cheeseburger, or chicken tenders (all come with fries or any other side dish for $7; ribs are $8; soda included but fresh-squeezed juice or milk is extra). This clubby-looking restaurant is part of a chain extending from Atlanta to Phoenix to Chicago. Its popularity is easily understood: Houston's ambience is welcoming to all ages, and the food is fresh and good quality.

7715 Woodmont Ave., Bethesda, MD. ✆ **301/656-9755.** High chairs, booster seats. Reservations not accepted. Main courses (other than burgers) $19–$35. AE, MC, V. Tues–Sat 11am–11pm; Sun–Mon 11am–10pm.

Louisiana Kitchen ★ CAJUN/CREOLE Cajun, casual, and cheap, Louisiana Kitchen excels at New Orleans–style po' boys (aka subs, hoagies, and grinders), fish fritters, and gumbos. You can order small plates of most entrees ($8–$9). Pair it with a Dixie or Blackened Voodoo beer. For the kiddies' more sensitive palates, the menu includes unspicy chicken, fries, *calas* (fried rice balls), and crab balls (small crab cakes). Try one of the breakfast sandwiches or omelets, served from 7:30am to 2:30pm daily. The a la carte Saturday and Sunday brunch features pastries and pancakes, along with traditional N'awlins egg dishes such as eggs Sardou (poached eggs with spinach and artichoke hearts on an English muffin with hollandaise sauce) or *pain perdu* (French toast). You can stuff your craws with some mighty good eats for less than $12 in most instances, less for the children. There's a parking garage a block away.

4907 Cordell Ave., Bethesda, MD. ✆ **301/652-6945.** www.louisianabethesda.com. High chairs, booster seats. Reservations not accepted. Sandwiches and main dishes $5–$16; most items breakfast and Sat–Sun brunch $8–$12. MC, V. Mon–Thurs 7:30am–10pm; Fri–Sat 7:30am–11pm (Sat brunch 7:30am–2:30pm); Sun 9am–10pm (brunch until 2:30pm). Metro: Bethesda, then walk north 4 blocks on Old Georgetown Rd. and right 1 block.

Philadelphia Mike's ★ AMERICAN You'll have to order at the counter and share an oilcloth-covered table with strangers—but that's a small price to pay for the best cheesesteak sandwich (on warm, baked-on-the-premises bread) this side of South Philly. The cheesesteak sub comes small (6-in.: $5), medium (8-in.: $6), and large (14-in.: $8.55). Try one (grilled paper-thin steak slices and melted cheese with any or all extras—lettuce, tomato, fried onions, sweet peppers, hot peppers, and oil dressing), but please don't taint it with mayonnaise. In Philadelphia, that's a capital offense. The kids' meal comprises a burger, cheeseburger, or hot dog with fries and a drink for $4. Deli sandwiches and other hoagies, soups, and salads are on the menu, if you're cheesesteaked out. Call ahead and your order will be waiting. If you're staying in Bethesda, there's free delivery service. Free parking is offered in the rear of the building. Enter on Woodmont Avenue.

7732 Wisconsin Ave., Bethesda, MD. ✆ **301/656-0103.** www.phillymikesonline.com. High chairs, booster seats. All items under $9. AE, MC, V. Mon–Thurs 8am–9:30pm; Fri–Sat 8am–midnight; Sun 8am–8pm. Metro: Bethesda.

Tastee Diner ★ (Value) AMERICAN 'Round the clock, 7 days a week, 364 days a year (closed Christmas), the Tastee Diner is open for business. None of the new neon-and-chrome-plated establishments calling themselves diners holds a candle to the Tastee, which served its first creamed chipped-beef on toast in 1942. Come here for the hearty breakfasts, homemade chili and soups, sandwiches, and desserts. I'm in love with the Diner Home Fries (with onion, bacon, and melted cheese). I didn't say it was healthful, but it is delish. The kids' menu, for kids 12 and under ($3.90; no substitutions), is served all day and includes the one egg, one pancake, one strip of bacon combo; minipancakes (plain, blueberry, chocolate chip); hamburger; grilled cheese; spaghetti; and chicken tenders. The individual jukeboxes, colorful regulars, chatty short-order cooks, and bee-hived waitresses spell *Happy Days* (if you're old enough to remember). Elsewhere in Maryland, there are Tastee Diners in Silver Spring, at 8601 Cameron St. (✆ **301/589-8171**), and in Laurel, at 118 Washington Blvd. (U.S. 1; ✆ **301/953-7567**).

7731 Woodmont Ave., Bethesda, MD. ✆ **301/652-3970.** www.tasteediner.com. High chairs, booster seats, kids' menu, crayons. Reservations not accepted. Breakfast $4.95–$9.50; lunch $4.95–$9.95; dinner $6.95–$12. MC, V. Daily 24 hr. Closed Dec 25. Metro: Bethesda.

Ice Cream

There's a branch of **Ben & Jerry's** in Bethesda, at 4901-B Fairmont Avenue (✆ **301/652-2233**). See the full review on p. 85. Bethesda also has a branch of **Gifford's** ★, the family-owned chain that features hot fudge sundaes and other delights, at 7237 Woodmont Ave. (✆ **301/907-3436**). See the full review on p. 89.

GAITHERSBURG

Roy's Place ★★ Finds SANDWICHES A moment of silence, please, for Roy Passin, the colorful owner of Roy's Place, who passed away in May 2009. He trademarked more than 200 sandwiches and showed up at work—day in/day out—for more than 50 years. Granted, it's a trip from downtown D.C.; but, if you have the time or you are staying in suburban Maryland, it's worth it. The Dagwood-style sandwiches are delish and satisfying, and range in price from $7.15 for the Tyrol (brisket and horseradish sauce) to $23 for the five-decker Bender Schmender (with almost everything but the kitchen sink). The average sandwich price is $10 to $13. Roy's is fun, funky, and great for the frugally inclined. Our family (four generations strong) loves to come here. The decor is grandma's-attic chic. Allow time to digest the 23-page menu of zany sandwich combinations and permutations, such as The Nothing Burger (a plain hard roll with butter) and The Real Gasser (broiled knockwurst, cheese, onions, and relish on French bread). You may also order a hamburger, full dinner, meal-size salad, vegetarian 'wich, or 1 of 18 plain sandwiches for "chicken eaters" and "little chicken eaters" (kids). Kids' choices range from PB&J ($2.40) to a cheeseburger ($5.55). Several imported beers are offered on tap.

2 E. Diamond Ave., Gaithersburg, MD. ✆ **301/948-5548.** www.roysplacerestaurant.com. High chairs, booster seats. Menu prices 65¢–$22; most sandwiches $10–$13. AE, DC, DISC, MC, V. Mon–Sat 11:30am–10:30pm; Sun 11:30am–9pm. Directions: Rte. 355 north (the extension of Wisconsin Ave. and Rockville Pike) into Gaithersburg; cross the bridge; go left at Chestnut, and turn left on East Diamond to Roy's on left. Plenty of free parking in Roy's lot.

ROCKVILLE

Branded 72 (formerly O'Brien's Pit Barbecue) ★★ RIBS/BARBECUE Texas ribs, chopped pork, and barbecued beef brisket are top draws in this award-winning Western-style cafeteria and carryout, family owned since 1972. In my opinion, O'Brien's very best offering is the chopped pork sandwich with plenty of barbecue sauce and side dishes of smoky baked beans and coleslaw. Everything is slow-cooked in one of three wood-fired enclosed pits. Other top sandwich choices are the pit ham, beef, or sausage. Add two vegetables and Texas toast for a meal that's hard to finish, for $14 or less. If you're not into pork, try the smoked turkey or chicken breast. For the little ones, a Kids' Portion (mini barbecue sandwich, chicken fingers, or hot dog, with two mini side dishes and a drink) costs $4.95. The friendly waitstaff makes junior cowpokes feel right at home.

387 E. Gude Dr., Rockville, MD. ✆ **301/340-8596.** www.branded72.com. High chairs. Reservations not accepted. Items $8.50–$14. AE, DISC, MC, V. Sun–Thurs 11am–9pm; Fri–Sat 11am–9:30pm. Closed Thanksgiving, Christmas, Easter. Not convenient to Metro.

SILVER SPRING

Crisfield Seafood Restaurant ★ SEAFOOD The decor might be early restroom, but don't let it turn you off. This place has been in the Landis family since 1945 (that's no typo!). There is charm in the checkered floor and worn wooden countertop, where lone diners belly up for raw oysters and fried shrimp. Crisfield's serves some of the

How Sweet It Is

In my youth, I would buy cupcakes at Peter's Bakery for 5¢ each. Today that wouldn't cover a teaspoonful of sprinkles. Cupcake shops continue to pop up and show no signs of leaving the culinary landscape. Today's designer cupcake will set you back $2.75 to $3.50—what a chocolate layer cake would fetch in the good old days. Of course, you can't hold a whole cake in the palm of your hand. When you're out and about and you need a sugar fix, consider the following (all meticulously researched and personally recommended).

- **Baked and Wired** 1052 Thomas Jefferson St. NW, off M St., btw. 30th and 31st St. ✆ **202/333-2500.** www.bakedandwired.com. Mon–Fri 7am–7pm; Sat 8am–8pm; Sun 9am–7pm.
- **Georgetown Cupcake** 3301 M St. NW. ✆ **202/333-8448.** www.georgetowncupcake.com. Tues–Fri 11am–pm; Sat 11am–9pm; Sun noon–5.
- **Buzz on Slaters** 901 Slaters Lane, Alexandria, Virginia. ✆ **703/600-BUZZ [2899].** www.buzzonslaters.com. Daily 6am–midnight. Metro: Braddock Road, then 1 mile walk or DASH bus no. 4.
- **Hello Cupcake** 1361 Connecticut Ave. NW. ✆ **202/861-2253.** www.hellocupcakeonline.com. Mon–Thurs 10am–7pm; Fri–Sat 10am–9pm. Metro: Dupont Circle (south exit).
- **Red Velvet Cupcakery** 675 E. St. (at 7th St.). ✆ **202/347-7895.** www.redvelvetcupcakery.com. Sun–Thurs 11am–11pm; Fri–Sat 11am–1am.

freshest seafood west of the Chesapeake Bay. The cold seafood platter, fried combo platters, crab cakes, and baked stuffed fish and shrimp have been pleasing multiple generations since World War II. A personal favorite, if you can handle the butter: crab Norfolk. Kids 12 and under can order fried shrimp or fried chicken ($9), or chicken tenders with fries ($7). Avoid dinnertime on weekends or go early. Metered street parking is available; there's parking in an adjacent lot after 6pm.

8012 Georgia Ave., Silver Spring, MD. ✆ **301/589-1306.** www.crisfieldseafoodrestaurant.com. High chairs, booster seats. Reservations not accepted. Most main courses $16–$28; kids' menu $7–$9. AE, MC, V. Tues–Thurs 11am–9pm; Fri–Sat 11am–10pm; Sun noon–9pm. Metro: Silver Spring.

11 SUBURBAN VIRGINIA

A generation ago, the area near and beyond the Beltway was considered the "boonies." Those days are long past. The number of fast-food, pizza, pub, ethnic, and fine dining establishments continues to grow with the population and urban sprawl. Stay in this area, and you'll have as many restaurants from which to choose, as if you'd stayed in downtown D.C. In addition to the restaurants listed below, a **Maggiano's Little Italy** is located in Tysons Galleria (near the Ritz-Carlton), at 2001 International Dr., McLean (✆ **703/**

356-9000); you'll find a **Rio Grande Café** in Ballston, at 4301 N. Fairfax Dr. (✆ **703/528-3131**), and one in Reston, at 1827 Library St. (✆ **703/904-0703**). See the full review on p. 106. There's also a **Morton's** steakhouse in Vienna, at 8075 Leesburg Pike (✆ **703/883-0800**); see p. 93.

ALEXANDRIA

See the "Old Town Alexandria" section in chapter 11.

ARLINGTON

Red, Hot & Blue ★ RIBS/BARBECUE Some think it's easier to get into heaven than to snare a table at Red, Hot & Blue at peak time (after 6pm). The Memphis ribs, pulled-pig sandwiches, and onion loaf have a large following in these parts. A good buy is the rack of ribs for two, with two side dishes, for $22 (single rack is $19). Some platters include a few ribs, if you want to sample 'em. Your bill will fall in the inexpensive category if you skip the ribs and stick with the sandwiches, all $9 or less. If you order nothing else, try the onion ring loaf ($6). Those 10 and under can order a pulled-pork, brisket, or chicken sandwich; minicorndogs; grilled cheese; or chicken nuggets (Love Me Tenders) from the children's menu. All are served with fries or applesauce and a beverage. The place is nothing to look at. If you want beauty, go to the National Gallery. If you want great ribs, wet (with sauce) or dry, come here.

There is a RH&B at 4150 Chain Bridge Rd., Fairfax, Virginia (✆ **703/218-6989**); and an RH&B Express at 3014 Wilson Blvd., Clarendon (Arlington), Virginia (✆ **703/243-1510**). You can find branch restaurants in several towns in Virginia and Maryland (see the website for a full list).

1600 Wilson Blvd., Arlington, VA. ✆ **703/276-7427.** www.redhotandblue.com. High chairs, booster seats, kids' menu, crayons. Reservations not accepted. Most main courses (other than ribs) $10–$14; kids' items $5. AE, DC, DISC, MC, V. Sun–Thurs 11am–10pm; Fri–Sat 11am–11pm. Closed Thanksgiving, Dec 25. Metro: Rosslyn or Court House.

VIENNA

Clyde's ★ AMERICAN The burgers (I'm partial to the blue-cheese-and-bacon variety), ribs, pasta dishes, and salads are delish. The menu sometimes changes so the chef can utilize the freshest produce and seasonal items, such as locally caught seafood. And there are monthly specials that are a steal, based on what's fresh and available. In October 2009, lobster dinners (with french fries and coleslaw) were $18. The grown-up's menu has a full range of chicken, beef, fish, and pasta items, as well as specialties such as crab cakes. Big, brassy, and divided into four dining areas, Clyde's merits a look around on your way in or out. In the main dining room, kids might have questions about the naked ladies—excuse me, nudes—in the paintings.

8332 Leesburg Pike, Vienna, VA. ✆ **703/734-1901.** www.clydes.com. High chairs, booster seats, kids' menu, crayons. Reservations recommended. Main courses lunch $8.95–$14, dinner $11–$16 (more for beef); kids' menu items $6. AE, DC, DISC, MC, V. Mon–Sat 11am–11pm; Sun 10am–11pm (brunch 10am–4pm).

Chili's Grill & Bar ★ SOUTHWESTERN/AMERICAN Elegant it's not, but Chili's serves good food and loves families, which is probably why so many families love it. It's the kind of place where you don't have to keep reminding your kids to keep their voices down. Fajitas freaks, young and old, say that these are among the best in town ($13–$16). The burgers, well-seasoned fries, and salads are all tasty and generous, and many rate the barbecued ribs a ten. In late 2009, Chili's ran a special: "3 courses, 2 people, $20." It may not be gourmet fare, but, with kids, it fills the bill. The kids' menu has 10 choices—the usual suspects (hamburgers and hot dogs, mac and cheese, and the like). All come with a choice of sides and beverage. A zillion Chili's locations can be found throughout the Washington, D.C. suburbs. If you're staying in Virginia's Vienna/Tysons Corner area, this is a good choice. Ask the concierge/front desk for directions.

8051 Leesburg Pike, Vienna, VA. ✆ **703/734-9512.** www.chilis.com. High chairs, booster seats, kids' menu, crayons. Reservations not accepted. Most main courses $9–$15; kids' menu items $4.25–$6.70 (ribs). AE, DISC, MC, V. Mon–Thurs 11am–11pm; Fri–Sat 11am–midnight; Sun 11am–10pm.

6

Exploring Washington, D.C. with Your Kids

You could spend an entire lifetime discovering the wonders of Washington, D.C., but you probably have other things to do as well, such as working, eating, and paying bills. So be realistic and scale down your expectations. It's better to spend quality time on a few attractions than to dash through a multitude. (I am one of those type As who sometimes bites off more than she can chew. Please do as I say, not as I do.)

Look to your children when planning your itinerary, and be sure to factor in time for relaxing. Visit a few well-chosen sites and then let off steam in one of the city's many parks and recreational areas. Take a dunk in the hotel pool, or if shopping is your favorite sport, browse in one of the museum shops or glitzy indoor malls. Remember, this is a vacation, not an endurance contest!

Most museum websites have activities and interactives for kids. This is a wonderful way to get them interested in advance of their visit. You probably have your own preferred ways of getting your youngsters psyched for sightseeing. Some parents read their kids a relevant story the night before a visit. Others buy postcards on entering a museum or gallery and accompany their youngsters on a scavenger hunt to find the pictured object or work of art. Here's a tip from a savvy friend of mine. In museums, let the kids stop in the museum store *first* to look around and buy a souvenir. If logic prevails, you'll avoid the unpleasantness of having them bug you while you're viewing the exhibits.

If you're new at this, the best advice I can offer is not to overschedule. Young children have short attention spans. Preschoolers often get antsy after 20 minutes in a museum. When they do, it's fruitless to push them further. Catch a movie, puppet show, or theater presentation for a change of pace. Stop for a snack, rest, or get some fresh air. Then try again. You'll know when they've had it!

When you're on a tight schedule, concentrate your sightseeing in and around the downtown area known as the National Mall (see map on p. 118). Here, you will find the presidential monuments, most of the Smithsonian museums, the U.S. Capitol, the White House, and numerous other attractions—all free and within walking distance of each other.

SUGGESTED ITINERARIES

For Toddlers

Day 1

Run, don't walk, to the zoo. Go early, especially in the summer and on weekends. There's plenty to keep everyone occupied for several hours. Pack a picnic or buy lunch at one of the snack bars or the cafeteria/restaurant on the premises.

Day 2
Visit the dinosaurs, mammals, O. Orkin Insect Zoo, and North American Birds in the National Museum of Natural History. Inspect the outdoor Butterfly Habitat Garden (9th St., btw. Constitution Ave. and the Mall). Grab lunch in a museum eatery or from a street vendor. Eat outside, weather permitting. A pleasant dining alternative is the Food Court at the Ronald Reagan Building and International Trade Center, where there's free family entertainment most days. In the afternoon, return to the Natural History Museum or visit the Old Post Office Pavilion for a panoramic view of downtown and/or the Aquarium in the Commerce Department.

Day 3
Start out at one of the Smithsonian museums you've missed, such as the Air and Space Museum, where pilot and astronaut wannabes will be in their element. Have lunch in the Wright Place. Or move on to the Food Hall at Union Station and then visit the Postal Museum. Tuck in a siesta after lunch and then visit another Smithsonian museum. Mature 4- and 5-year-olds and older siblings will enjoy seeing a movie in the Air and Space Museum, but don't sit too close to the screen. The larger-than-life images and booming soundtrack might frighten younger kids. If time permits, and they are still upright, spend a half-hour or so looking around; that's about all kids this age can take. Have dinner near your hotel (or pick up takeout, spring for room service, or order in a pizza) and turn in early.

For 6- to 8-Year-Olds

Day 1
Hop on a Tourmobile tram, and after you've completed the loop and listened to the narrator's spiel, spend the afternoon visiting one or two sights that interested you most on the tour.

Day 2
Visit the Air and Space Museum in the morning and then have lunch at one of the museum eateries on the Mall. In the afternoon, tour the Hirshhorn, especially the outdoor sculpture garden, and then ride the carousel nearby. Cross the Mall to the Museum of Natural History for the dinosaurs, gems and minerals, and O. Orkin Insect Zoo. Cast an eye (but not a fishing line) into the tanks of the Commerce Department's Aquarium. Have dessert at the Old Post Office or the Ronald Reagan Building and International Trade Center—both close by. Or go back to your room and rest. You deserve it.

Day 3
At the Bureau of Engraving and Printing, see how money is made—literally. Pool your pennies for lunch and then visit the past at the DAR Museum's Children's Attic. If you're still rarin' to go, visit any or all of the presidential memorials: the Washington Monument or the Lincoln, Jefferson, and Roosevelt memorials. You might want to include, or substitute, the Vietnam and Korean War Veterans memorials. In the warm-weather months, rent a boat or bicycle, and paddle or pedal away the afternoon. In winter, ice-skate at the National Sculpture Garden or warm up in the Jungle at U.S. Botanic Garden. In summer, when Washington is at its steamiest, cool down in your hotel pool or chill in your room and watch a movie.

For 8- to 10-Year-Olds

Day 1
Start early and spend the morning at the Spy Museum, one of the most popular sites in all D.C. Splurge on lunch at the Hard Rock Cafe or grab a hot dog or slice of pizza from a street vendor. Visit spruced-up Ford's Theatre, which reopened in 2009, and the Petersen House across the street, where Lincoln died. Have a cupcake or ice cream then go back to

NATIONAL ZOOLOGICAL PARK
ADAMS-MORGAN
U.S. Naval Observatory
EMBASSY ROW
ROCK CREEK PARK
Rock Creek
DUMBARTON OAKS PARK
MONTROSE PARK
DUPONT CIRCLE
GEORGETOWN
Georgetown University
C & O Canal
Washington Circle
Scott Circle
Thomas Circle
Farragut Square
McPherson Square
Franklin Square
George Washington University
FOGGY BOTTOM
Kennedy Center
Theodore Roosevelt Island
Little River
White House
Lincoln Memorial
Washington Monument
WEST POTOMAC PARK
Tidal Basin
Cherry Trees
Jefferson Memorial
FDR Memorial
Potomac River
VIRGINIA
ARLINGTON NATIONAL CEMETERY
Woodley Park-Zoo Red Line
Columbia Heights Green Line
Dupont Circle Red Line
Farragut North Red Line
Farragut West Blue & Orange Lines
McPherson Square Blue & Orange Lines
Foggy Bottom-GWU Blue & Orange Lines
Rosslyn Blue & Orange Lines
Arlington Cemetery Blue Line
Cathedral Ave.
Garfield St.
Garfield Terr.
31St. Pl.
Cleveland Ave.
Fulton St.
Woodley Pl.
Observatory Circle
Woodland Dr.
Calvert St.
McGill Terr.
Connecticut Ave.
Irving St.
Hobart St.
Harvard St.
Ontario Rd.
Lanier Pl.
Columbia Rd.
Euclid St.
Belmont St.
Florida Ave.
W St.
V St.
U St.
T St.
S St.
R St.
Q St.
Church St.
P St.
Belmont Rd.
Kalorama Rd.
Wyoming Ave.
Tracy Pl.
California St.
Bancroft Pl.
Massachusetts Ave.
Decatur Pl.
Riggs Pl.
Swann St.
New Hampshire Ave.
Reservoir Rd.
Dent Pl.
Volta Pl.
O St.
Dumbarton St.
N St.
Prospect St.
M St.
Wisconsin Ave.
Rock Creek and Potomac Pkwy.
Whitehurst Fwy.
Francis Scott Key Bridge
L St.
K St.
I St.
H St.
G St.
F St.
E St.
C St.
Pennsylvania Ave.
Virginia Ave.
Constitution Ave.
Independence Ave.
Theodore Roosevelt Mem. Bridge
Arlington Mem. Bridge
George Washington Memorial Pkwy.
N. Lynn St.
Wilson Blvd.
Jefferson Davis Hwy.
Washington Blvd.
Ohio Dr.
West Basin Dr.
36th Pl.
36th St.
35th Pl.
35th St.
34th Pl.
34th St.
33rd Pl.
33rd St.
32nd St.
31st St.
30th St.
29th Pl.
29th St.
28th St.
27th St.
26th St.
25th St.
24th St.
23rd St.
22nd St.
21st St.
20th St.
19th St.
18th St.
17th St.
16th St.
15th St.
14th St.
37th St.
Champlain St.
Ontario Rd.
Belmont
Kalorama
Wyoming Ave.
California Ave.
Vernon St.
29
66
1
50

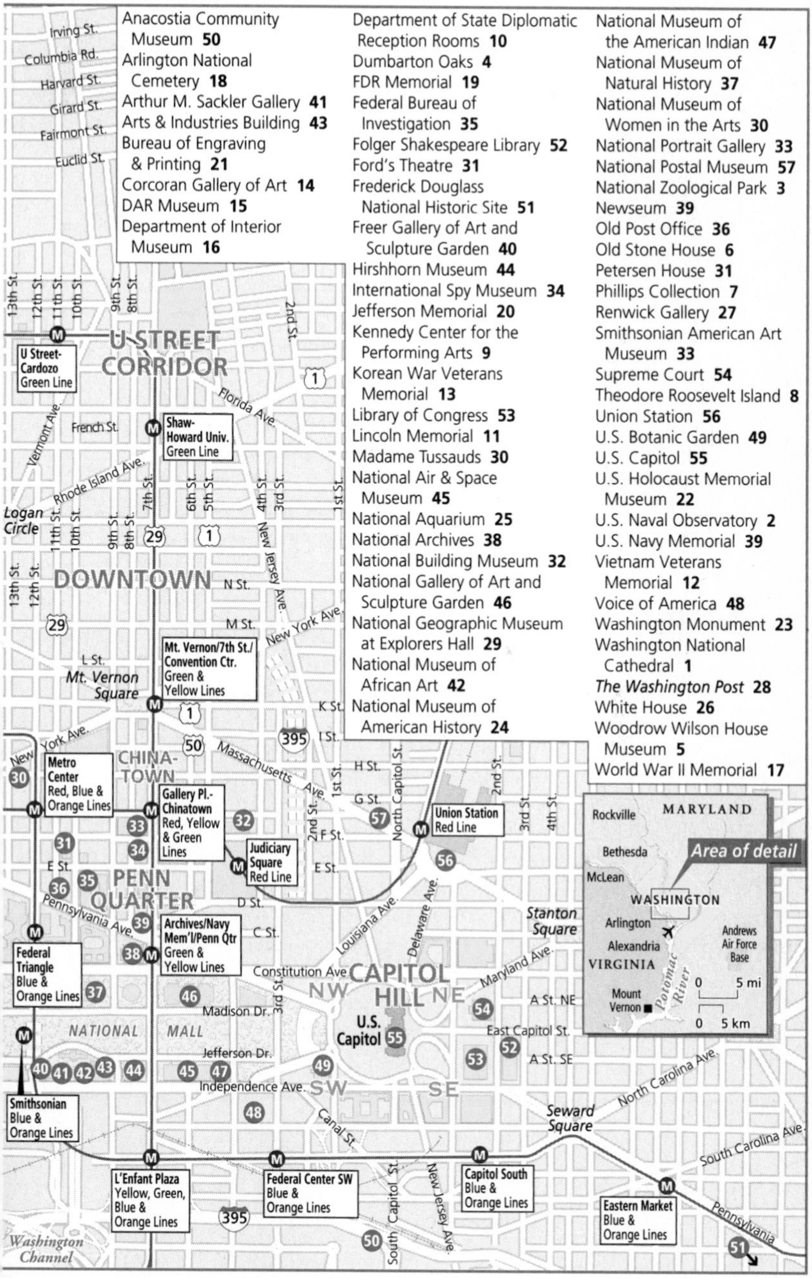
Anacostia Community Museum 50
Arlington National Cemetery 18
Arthur M. Sackler Gallery 41
Arts & Industries Building 43
Bureau of Engraving & Printing 21
Corcoran Gallery of Art 14
DAR Museum 15
Department of Interior Museum 16
Department of State Diplomatic Reception Rooms 10
Dumbarton Oaks 4
FDR Memorial 19
Federal Bureau of Investigation 35
Folger Shakespeare Library 52
Ford's Theatre 31
Frederick Douglass National Historic Site 51
Freer Gallery of Art and Sculpture Garden 40
Hirshhorn Museum 44
International Spy Museum 34
Jefferson Memorial 20
Kennedy Center for the Performing Arts 9
Korean War Veterans Memorial 13
Library of Congress 53
Lincoln Memorial 11
Madame Tussauds 30
National Air & Space Museum 45
National Aquarium 25
National Archives 38
National Building Museum 32
National Gallery of Art and Sculpture Garden 46
National Geographic Museum at Explorers Hall 29
National Museum of African Art 42
National Museum of American History 24
National Museum of the American Indian 47
National Museum of Natural History 37
National Museum of Women in the Arts 30
National Portrait Gallery 33
National Postal Museum 57
National Zoological Park 3
Newseum 39
Old Post Office 36
Old Stone House 6
Petersen House 31
Phillips Collection 7
Renwick Gallery 27
Smithsonian American Art Museum 33
Supreme Court 54
Theodore Roosevelt Island 8
Union Station 56
U.S. Botanic Garden 49
U.S. Capitol 55
U.S. Holocaust Memorial Museum 22
U.S. Naval Observatory 2
U.S. Navy Memorial 39
Vietnam Veterans Memorial 12
Voice of America 48
Washington Monument 23
Washington National Cathedral 1
The Washington Post 28
White House 26
Woodrow Wilson House Museum 5
World War II Memorial 17
U STREET CORRIDOR
DOWNTOWN
CHINA-TOWN
PENN QUARTER
CAPITOL HILL
NATIONAL MALL
Logan Circle
Mt. Vernon Square
Stanton Square
Seward Square
U.S. Capitol
U Street-Cardozo Green Line
Shaw-Howard Univ. Green Line
Mt. Vernon/7th St./Convention Ctr. Green & Yellow Lines
Metro Center Red, Blue & Orange Lines
Gallery Pl.-Chinatown Red, Yellow & Green Lines
Judiciary Square Red Line
Union Station Red Line
Archives/Navy Mem'l/Penn Qtr Green & Yellow Lines
Federal Triangle Blue & Orange Lines
Smithsonian Blue & Orange Lines
L'Enfant Plaza Yellow, Green, Blue & Orange Lines
Federal Center SW Blue & Orange Lines
Capitol South Blue & Orange Lines
Eastern Market Blue & Orange Lines
Washington Channel
MARYLAND
VIRGINIA
Rockville
Bethesda
McLean
WASHINGTON
Arlington
Alexandria
Andrews Air Force Base
Mount Vernon
Potomac River
Area of detail
0 5 mi
0 5 km

your hotel for a swim, or hop on the Metro and choose one of the following: Interact with the displays at the National Geographic Museum at Explorers Hall or U.S. Postal Museum, or stroll through Georgetown or Dupont Circle.

Day 2

Time for a Mall crawl. Start at the Air and Space Museum (be sure to buy movie tickets first) or go to the Museum of American History and visit the original Star-Spangled Banner, Kermit the Frog, Dorothy's ruby slippers, and Edison's light bulb. Have lunch in a Mall museum or at a nearby Food Court. In the afternoon, take Metro to the National Museum of the American Indian. Pick up a map at each information desk and concentrate on a few exhibits. In between, take pictures on the Mall or fly a kite (you can buy one in the Air and Space Museum's gift shop). Have dinner in or near your hotel or have dinner delivered and watch an in-room movie. Write postcards.

Day 3

Begin at the Museum of Natural History, Sant Ocean Hall. Awesome! Then visit the O. Orkin Insect Zoo where feeding times are 10:30am, 11:30am, and 1:30pm during the week, an hour later on weekends. Say hello to the dinosaurs, and gems and minerals. Lunch in the museum or Old Post Office Pavilion food court. Check out the nearby Aquarium, American History Museum, or Washington Monument. If you're tired or the weather is crummy, see the sights on a Tourmobile or Jolly Trolley tour. Have dinner and browse Union Station, or have dinner on Capitol Hill.

For Preteens

Day 1

Same as Day 1 for 8- to 10-year-olds. Stroll around Georgetown or Union Station. After dinner indulge in a yummy dessert, or catch a theater performance.

Day 2

Same as Day 2 for 8- to 10-year-olds. You might want to skip a Smithsonian museum or two and substitute the Newseum or Arlington National Cemetery. Or maybe your crew's idea of a good time is cruisin' Georgetown or an indoor mall for souvenirs. Or go to the Air and Space museum in the morning. If you have a car, drive to the Udvar-Hazy facility near Dulles Airport to see two huge hangars full of vintage flying machines and ascend the tower to view Dulles takeoffs and landings. Return to D.C. for dinner, and take a nighttime tour of the major sights, or visit the Washington Monument or Lincoln Memorial on your own.

Day 3

Same as Day 3 for 8- to 10-year-olds. After lunch, ride a bike, take a hike, or pick out something else you like. Or spend the morning and early afternoon visiting Mount Vernon (by boat in nice weather), then browse and have dinner in Alexandria's Old Town. Or return to D.C., see free entertainment (nightly at 6pm on the Kennedy Center Millennium Stage), catch a theater performance, or go to a sporting event (depending on the season—pro football, soccer, basketball, hockey, or baseball) or a concert at the Verizon Center, where interactive games allow you to test your sports skills. Too pooped to peep? Snuggle in bed with pizza and a cable movie.

Highlights for Kids: The Top Attractions by Age Group

Picking Washington's top-10 attractions for kids of different ages is next to impossible. Depending on your kids' ages and interests, your family's top 10 will probably include a mix of some of the following, along with selections listed in this chapter under "For Kids with Special Interests."

2 to 4 National Zoo, FDR Memorial, National Museum of Natural History (dinosaurs, O. Orkin Insect Zoo), National Aquarium, DAR Museum, National Museum of American History (first-floor machinery), National Air and Space Museum (planes suspended from ceiling, space station, and space capsule), Hains Point playground (East Potomac Park), carousel on the Mall, Hirshhorn Sculpture Garden, National Gallery Sculpture Garden, Constitution Gardens.

4 to 6 National Zoo, National Museum of Natural History, FDR Memorial, DAR Museum, National Air and Space Museum, National Gallery Sculpture Garden, National Museum of American History, Bureau of Engraving and Printing, National Gallery of Art Sculpture Garden or Hirshhorn Sculpture Garden, Oxon Hill Farm (Maryland), Hains Point playground (East Potomac Park), Rock Creek Park.

6 to 8 National Zoo, National Museum of Natural History, National Air and Space Museum, National Museum of American History, presidential monuments (Washington Monument, and Lincoln, Jefferson, and Franklin Delano Roosevelt memorials), Bureau of Engraving and Printing, DAR Museum, U.S. Postal Museum.

8 to 10 National Zoo, National Museum of Natural History, National Air and Space Museum, National Museum of American History, presidential monuments, the International Spy Museum, the Capitol, National Geographic Museum at Explorers Hall, Bureau of Engraving and Printing, National Museum of the American Indian.

10 and older National Zoo, National Museum of American History, National Museum of Natural History, National Air and Space Museum, presidential monuments, Mount Vernon, the National Museum of the American Indian, the Capitol, International Spy Museum, Newseum, Bureau of Engraving and Printing.

1 THE SMITHSONIAN INSTITUTION ★★★

According to the Greater Washington Board of Trade, "If all the treasures of the Smithsonian Institution were lined up in one long exhibit, and you spent 1 second looking at each item, it would take you more than 2½ years of around-the-clock touring to see them all." I haven't double-checked their computations, but you have to admit, the statistics are impressive. According to one poll, 40% of all Americans have visited the Smithsonian, the largest museum/research complex in the world.

Arthur M. Sackler Gallery **9**
Arts and Industries Building **12**
Freer Gallery of Art **8**
Hirshhorn Museum **13**
Hirshhorn Sculpture Garden **14**
National Archives **1**
National Gallery/East Building **7**
National Gallery/ West Building **6**
National Gallery Sculpture Garden and Ice Rink **5**
National Air and Space Museum **15**
National Museum of African Art **11**
National Museum of American History **3**
National Museum of Natural History **4**
Newseum **2**
Smithsonian Institution Building ("the Castle") **10**
U.S. Court House **7**

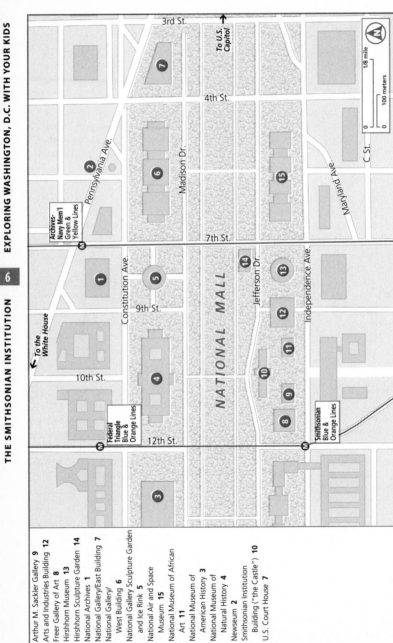

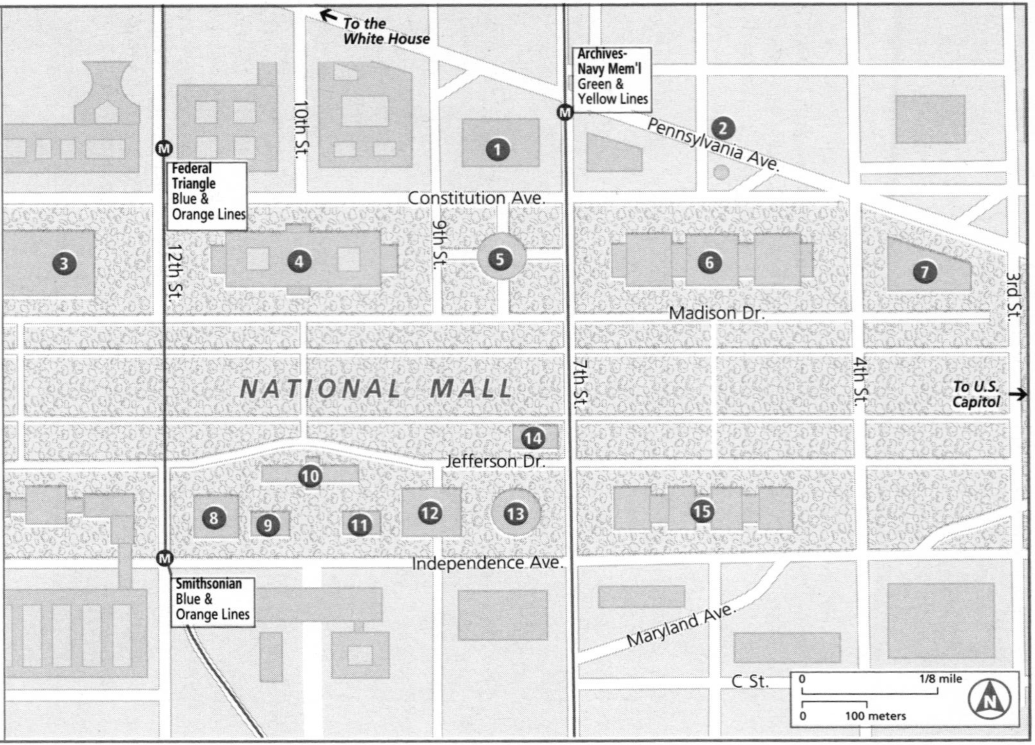

Break Time

If you find yourself on the Mall before the museums open, and you haven't had your cup of joe, slip into the Castle Café in the Castle, south entrance (Independence Ave.; ✆ **202/633-1000**), for coffee and a muffin. Also on the menu are soups, salads, sandwiches, espresso/cappuccino, gelato, and pastries. The cafe is open daily from 8:30am to 5pm. Prices are $2 to $7.

Like other cultural institutions adversely affected by cutbacks, the Smithsonian, in recent years, has sought funding from corporations and individuals—hence, the O. Orkin Insect Zoo and Janet Annenberg Hooker GGM (geology, gems, and minerals) Hall at the Museum of Natural History. Currently, the federal government supplies about 75% of the Smithsonian's revenues.

In 1846, when the willed funds of English scientist James Smithson (he died in 1829) were sent to the United States (105 bags of gold sovereigns, equal to about $500,000) to establish an institution "for the increase and diffusion of knowledge among men," he probably never imagined that today the Smithsonian conglomerate would house some 137 million artifacts and encompass 19 museums and galleries (plus the National Zoo) and become one of the world's major tourist attractions.

Visitors may request a print version of *Planning Your Smithsonian Visit* by contacting: Smithsonian Information, P.O. Box 37012, SI Building, Rm. 153, MRC 010, Washington, DC 20013-7012; or keep it simple and go to www.si.edu/visit.

For a full page of Smithsonian special events for the coming month, residents can turn to the "Smithsonian Sampler" in the *Washington Post Weekend* magazine, published the third Friday of every month. The Smithsonian museums are open from 10am to 5:30pm daily except December 25. "The Castle," with its visitor information center, is open from 8:30am to 5pm. Every year Congress votes whether to extend hours in spring and summer. Call ahead or check the website to avoid disappointment (✆ **202/633-1000;** www.si.edu).

Because one-third of the approximately 23 million people who visit the Smithsonian annually do so in June, July, and August, you might want to schedule your visit for any other month. Or arrive when the doors open or after 3pm. Or pack some chill pills. Bear in mind that Mondays are the quietest days and Saturdays and Sundays are the busiest; early morning and late afternoon are the least crowded. Tuck this Smithsonian information phone number in your wallet: ✆ **202/633-1000,** or ✆ **202/357-1729** for TDD (telecommunications device for the deaf).

Smithsonian Institution Building ("the Castle") **Ages 4 and up.** As I mentioned earlier, the Smithsonian Information Center in the Castle is a good place to begin your tour of D.C. The doors open at 8:30am so you can get to your first destination ahead of the crowds (theoretically, at least). You've heard of one-stop shopping? Consider this one-stop information gathering. Press a button on one of the video-display monitors to get information on the Smithsonian and more than 100 other attractions. About a dozen pages are devoted to kid-pleasing things to see and do. You might have trouble prying your progeny away from the monitors' highly imaginative and colorful graphics. Two electronic wall maps will help you get your bearing and plan your day. More than a dozen information specialists are on hand at the Castle to assist visitors from 8:30am to 5:30pm.

Also check the video screens mounted on the information desk where "Today at the Smithsonian" lists events and exhibits, and ask for **"10 Tips for Visiting the Smithsonian with Children,"** which includes a map, family highlights, and a quiz for kids—all free. In the gift shop, you can purchase a "Guide to the Nation's Capital," a detailed map with brief descriptions of the major museums and attractions. Not only is the map immensely helpful, but it also makes a nice souvenir.

In two orientation theaters, a 20-minute video is shown throughout the day, giving a Smithsonian overview. Guides printed in seven languages are available for foreign visitors. While you're at the Castle, you might want to inquire about the **Smithsonian Young Associate Program,** which offers workshops, films, and live performances for children throughout the year (✆ **202/633-3030**).

If you enter the Castle from Jefferson Drive (on the Mall), you'll find, on the left, the crypt bearing the remains of James Smithson. Although he died in Genoa, Italy, on June 26, 1829, he was brought to this spot—ironically, his first time on U.S. soil and his final resting place—in 1904.

Free walking tours of the Castle are given year-round, Monday and Friday at 9:30am, Saturday and Sunday at 9:30 and 10:30am, and may be of interest to children 9 and older.

Before you leave the Castle, make a quick sweep of the **Children's Room,** open daily from 10am to 5:30pm. The *trompe l'oeil* fantasy garden and skylights have been restored to their original state in the cozy, light-filled space. From here, you can exit to the Mall's **Enid A. Haupt Victorian Garden,** enchanting spring through fall and with benches for weary visitors.

1000 Jefferson Dr. SW. ✆ **202/633-1000,** or 202/359-2900 for a recording. www.si.edu. Free admission. Daily 8:30am–5:30pm. Closed Dec 25. Metro: Smithsonian.

Anacostia Community Museum **Ages 4 and up.** You have to cross Washington's lesser-known river, the Anacostia, to get to this Smithsonian facility, which focuses on local African-American art, culture, and history. Augmenting its permanent collection and changing exhibits, the Anacostia offers free family workshops and events several times a month. Past examples include a slide show, "Origins of Islamic Calligraphy," a hands-on workshop to create henna, and a tour of public art related to the African-American experience. "The African Presence in Mexico," showcasing the relationship between Africans and Mexicans in the U.S., is on view until July 4, 2010. Call the museum's education department (✆ **202/633-4875**) to find out about upcoming family activities, speakers, and guided tours offered Monday through Friday.

Visitors with reservations can take a guided walk along the George Washington Carver nature trail on the museum grounds. It's less than a third of a mile long, so even the

Tips — Where to Go When You Gotta Go

Three museums now have unisex or companion care restrooms: the National Air and Space Museum (near the cafeteria entrance), the National Museum of Natural History (in the East Court, off of the Rotunda), and the Hirshhorn Museum and Sculpture Garden (near the standard restrooms). Several more are planned in various museums. Stay tuned!

Arts & Industries Building Closure

The distinctive Victorian-style redbrick-and-sandstone building on the south side of the Mall opened in time for President Garfield's first inaugural ball in March 1881. Better known to visitors as the home of the Discovery Theater, a venue for top-notch children's theater, it will be closed to the public for several years while it undergoes renovation. As of October 2009, renovations had not yet begun and no date had been set for the reopening. Visitors can still ride the Carousel on the Mall outside the building.

youngest scouts in your party should be able to keep up the pace. You might want to tote snacks or lunch to eat in the picnic area, because there's no on-site restaurant, and the neighborhood surrounding the museum is not recommended for casual strolling.

1901 Fort Place SE. ✆ **202/633-4820**. www.anacostia.si.edu. Free admission. Daily 10am–5pm. Closed Dec 25. Metro: Anacostia, local exit, left to Howard St., and take the W-2 or W-3 bus from Howard St. to the museum entrance. Directions: Take I-395 north to I-295 south to Martin Luther King, Jr. Ave.; left on Morris Ave., which becomes Erie St., and then Fort Place.

Smithsonian Freer Gallery of Art and Arthur M. Sackler Gallery ★ Ages 8 and up. These two joined forces, as it were, and are also joined physically by an underground exhibition space. Both merit a visit if time permits. It is nearly impossible to visit the Freer and not be taken with the beauty of the museum itself, as well as its contents. As you emerge from the Mall exit of the Smithsonian Metro station, the stunning Renaissance-style facade of the Freer greets you. In a concerted effort to draw young people, the museum offers workbooks that challenge youngsters to examine what they see and to think critically and creatively.

Named for Detroit industrialist and art connoisseur Charles Lang Freer, who made a bundle from manufacturing the first railroad cars in the Midwest and became James McNeill Whistler's chief patron, the Freer houses the world's largest Whistler collection—more than 1,200 pieces. The museum is recognized internationally for its collection of Asian art spanning 6,000 years. To give you an idea of the breadth of the Freer's riches, at any given time, 10% or less of the museum's permanent collection is on view.

Among the treasures, and hands-down the best-known work, is Whistler's *Harmony in Blue and Gold: The Peacock Room.* The actual dining room you see was painted by Whistler between 1876 and 1877 for the British businessman Frederick Leyland, who engaged Whistler to redecorate his dining room around the artist's painting *The Princess from the Land of the Porcelain,* and a large collection of blue-and-white Oriental porcelain. Whistler's feelings about Leyland's failure to pay what he felt the job was worth are reflected in the mural of two peacocks over the sideboard.

Children over 10 may be intrigued to learn the story behind this extraordinary dining room, which has been moved, piece by piece, from London to Detroit to Washington, D.C. See if your children can find Whistler's trademark butterfly signature. (He left his imprint in four places in the room.)

Freer: Jefferson Dr. at 12th St. SW, on the south side of the Mall. ✆ **202/357-2104**. www.asia.si.edu. Free admission. Daily 10am–5:30pm. Closed Dec 25. Tours (both galleries) noon Thurs–Tues (never on Wed). Closed Dec 25. Metro: Smithsonian (Mall or Independence Ave. exits).

Activities That Don't Cost a Penny

- Watch the sun set behind the Lincoln Memorial.
- Ride to the top of the Washington Monument after dark.
- Warm up in the National Zoo's Amazonia rain forest exhibit or U.S. Botanic Garden.
- Attend a summertime concert on the Ellipse (behind the White House), at the Capitol (West Lawn), or at Navy Memorial Plaza (Pennsylvania Ave., btw. 7th and 9th sts.)
- Redesign the FBI Building, the ugliest structure in D.C.
- See who, or what, is buried in the crypt under the Capitol.
- Feel a tornado in the National Geographic Museum at Explorers Hall.
- Imagine how you'd spend the money printed in a day at the Bureau of Engraving and Printing.
- Find world heavyweight champion Joe Louis's grave at Arlington National Cemetery.
- Discover your favorite work of art in the Corcoran Gallery.
- Ask a Native American docent at the National Museum of the American Indian about his or her ancestry.
- Rename the works in the Hirshhorn Museum's or National Gallery's Sculpture Garden.
- Count the crystals in the Kennedy Center Opera House chandelier.
- Visit Kermit the Frog, George Washington in a toga, and Simba's mask (from "The Lion King" musical) at the Smithsonian National Museum of American History.
- Trace the origins of your family tree at the National Archives.
- Go in-line skating in front of the White House.

Arthur M. Sackler Gallery (of Asian and Near Eastern Art) **Ages 8 and up.** This museum is joined to the Freer by underground exhibition space, and shares a 4¼-acre underground museum complex with the National Museum of African Art. While Chinese bronzes, Southeast Asian sculpture, and Persian manuscripts might not appeal to your kids upon entering, they're sure to have a change of heart during their visit.

Children with an interest in ancient history or archaeology can see some of the oldest art ever made. Even the youngest visitors enjoy counting the fanciful animal forms among the intricate designs on 4,500-year-old bronze vessels in **"Arts of China."** You can pick up free family guides at the information desk. **ImaginAsia** refers to family programs cosponsored by the Sackler and Freer galleries aimed at children from 6 to 14 and their companions. ImaginAsia is held during the school year on most Saturdays and Sundays at 2pm. Admission is free. Ask about summer programs which, in past years, took place on Tuesdays, Wednesdays, and Thursdays. **Docent-led tours** are offered most days, except Wednesday and federal holidays, at noon, departing from the information desks of *both* museums. Call for the current schedule, museum programs, and exhibits (✆ **202/633-1000;** www.asia.si.edu). Or inquire at the information desk. Call or e-mail at least 4 weeks in advance to reserve group tours (✆ **202/633-1012;** asiatours@si.edu).

- Make up a story about Fragonard's *Young Girl Reading,* in the National Gallery's West Building.
- Skip rocks in the Tidal Basin.
- Find out what "Star Route" means in the National Postal Museum.
- Picnic along the Potomac River or behind the Old Stone House in Georgetown.
- See how long it takes to walk the length of the National Mall.
- Feed the ducks in Constitution Gardens.
- Hear a case before the Supreme Court (Oct–Apr).
- Enjoy the vista from the Washington National Cathedral's Pilgrim Observatory Gallery.
- Fly a kite on the Mall.
- Water the plants in the Children's Garden (spring–fall) at the U.S. Botanic Garden.
- Write a letter to the president.
- View downtown from the tower in the Old Post Office Pavilion.
- Sit in Albert Einstein's lap (2101 Constitution Ave. NW).
- Wish on a star at the Naval Observatory.
- Dip your toes in the Reflecting Pool.
- Explore the 2-mile nature trail in Glover Archbold Park.
- Identify the birds and planes over Theodore Roosevelt Island.
- Stroll along the Maine Avenue/Water Street SW waterfront, and choose your dream boat.
- Watch a polo match in West Potomac Park (Sun afternoon, late Apr–Oct, excluding Aug).

On the way out, visit the Victorian-style **Enid A. Haupt Garden** (p. 120), with its geometric parterre. On one side of the garden, you can enter a moon gate to an Asian garden; on the other, a small waterfall cascades into a smaller pond. The garden is open Memorial Day to Labor Day from 7am to 8pm; the rest of the year, it's open from 7am to 5:45pm.

1050 Independence Ave. SW. ✆ **202/633-1000.** www.asia.si.edu. Free admission. Daily 10am–5:30pm. Tours (both galleries) noon Thurs–Tues (never on Wed). Closed Dec 25. Metro: Smithsonian.

Hirshhorn Museum and Sculpture Garden ★★ **Ages 2 and up.** While other teenage boys were hanging out on the front stoop or getting into mischief, a young Latvian immigrant, Joseph Hirshhorn (1899–1981), was buying etchings in New York. The rest, as they say, is history. The museum bearing the mining magnate and art collector's name opened in 1974 with his little "gift" of mostly 20th-century art—2,000 pieces of sculpture and 4,000 paintings and drawings. When Hirshhorn died at the age of 82, additional works were bequeathed from his estate. The collection continues to receive gifts from other donors and is the fifth-most-visited art museum in the United States. Seems like yesterday that I attended the opening of this incredible museum. (I was 5

Break Time

At the Hirshhorn's **Full Circle Café,** surrounded by the sculpture garden on the south side of the Mall, at Independence Avenue and 8th Street SW, you'll find a self-service outdoor cafe with foot-long hot dogs, Italian sausage, vegetarian wraps, salads, snacks, iced beverages, and gelato. It's open daily from late spring through early fall from 11am to 3pm, weather permitting.

years old at the time. *If* you believe that, I have a monument I'd like to sell you.) Even kids who gag at the mention of going to an art museum find something to like at the Hirshhorn. Take preschoolers outside to the sculpture garden. The plaza provides an inviting and soft-edged setting for more than a dozen works, including Calder's black stabile, *Two Discs,* and Claes Oldenburg's *Geometric Mouse.* Your children should have something interesting to say about Lucio Fontana's billiard-ball-like spheres. Lie on the grass or rest on one of the benches amid the greenery and contemplate the scene. It's always the right time to ride the carousel, nearby on the Mall.

Note: Only a portion of the museum's works are on view at any one time. Kindergartners on up find the museum's doughnutlike inner space intriguing. They may become disoriented while traversing the concentric rings, but that's part of the fun. Paintings hang in the galleries of the outer circle, while sculptures and plenty of comfortable seating fill the inner circle (known as an ambulatory), where light pours in through floor-to-ceiling windows. If your family takes one mental postcard away from the Hirshhorn, I'll bet it will be Ron Mueck's ultrareal, much-larger-than-life sculpture, *Big Man.* Bearing an uncanny resemblance to Uncle Fester, the husky nude with a bald head looks like he's taking a "time out" on the lower level near the Warhols. On the second floor, look for *Guardian Angel* and works by Rodin and Degas. Ask your kids which of Matisse's *Heads of Jeanette* looks like you in the morning. An Alexander Calder motorized mobile usually turns youngsters' heads.

Older kids can explore on their own after viewing a short orientation film in the lower-level theater. They might like the portraits by Eakins and Sargent on the third floor before moving on to works by Bellows, Sloane, O'Keeffe, de Kooning, Pollock, and others. Many young people find the more abstract works appealing, even though "they don't look like anything." For a sweeping panorama of the Mall area, peer out the windows of the Abram Lerner Room for a view of the Old Post Office, National Archives, National Gallery (East and West), and U.S. Capitol.

At the information desk, pick up a free self-guided "Family Guide" with activities tied to specific works and ask about any films or special family programs taking place on the day of your visit. Between noon and 4pm, docents are on hand to assist you and/or lead you on an impromptu tour (lasting about 30 minutes). How cool is that? **Interpretive guides** ★★ are stationed throughout the museum to answer your questions about individual works of art and their artists. Don't be shy or self-conscious. As a teacher-friend of mine says, "The only stupid question is the one you don't ask." Just look for people wearing the badge with a big "?" Improv Art is a drop-in program for kids 5 to 11 and their families. Go to the Lower Level Improv Art Room for an activity sheet. Young at Art family workshops (for kids 6–12) and Gallery Tales for Tots (ages 3–5) take place on select weekends. Call to preregister at ✆ **202/633-3382.** Groups must preregister for group tours, which are usually conducted from 10:30am to 12:30pm. Regular scheduled tours of the sculpture garden are given only in summer, usually Monday through Saturday at 10:30am; dates vary, so be sure to ask. No tours are given on holidays. In the museum shop, you'll find posters, art books, and prints.

Independence Ave. and 7th St. SW, on the south side of the Mall. ✆ **202/633-1000.** www.hirshhorn.si.edu. Free admission. Daily 10am–5:30pm; Thurs May–Labor Day until 8pm; sculpture garden daily 7:30am–dusk; plaza daily 7:30am–dusk. Closed Dec 25. Metro: L'Enfant Plaza (Smithsonian exit) or Smithsonian.

National Air and Space Museum ★★★ **Ages 2 and up.** Longer than two football fields, the National Air and Space Museum is a huge pinkish marble monolith that opened July 1, 1976, in time for the U.S. Bicentennial. No, it's not much to look at from the outside; the magic begins when you enter. Inside, major historical and technological feats of air and space flight are documented in 23 exhibit areas.

Almost every specimen in the Air and Space Museum was flown or used to back up a craft, and this triggers excitement and a sense of immediacy in kids of all ages. The planes suspended from the ceiling appear to be in flight, and younger kids (young enough not to be embarrassed) might want to lie down and look straight up for the maximum effect. Before your family flies off in different directions, line up at the (Lockheed Martin) **IMAX Theater ★★** box office, and buy tickets ($8.75 adults, $7.25 ages 2–12, and $7.75 age 60 and over) for one of the special flight-related movies shown several times a day on the five-story IMAX screen. If you have time for only one, make it *To Fly,* the museum's inaugural film, which airs daily at least once. I've seen it more times than I can count, and I think it's safe to say that you won't ever forget it. With younger kids, I'd opt for *To Fly,* with a running time of a half-hour; shorter than the others. (See the "Films" section, in chapter 10, for details.) ***A tip:*** The first morning show (10:15am) and the last afternoon show (6pm) almost never sell out. Go early or late, and avoid disappointment. You may **order tickets ahead** at www.smithsonian.org/IMAX or ✆ **202/633-4629** (both with a service fee). Albert Einstein Planetarium show tickets (see below) are available from these outlets as well.

Next, if you're interested in catching a heavenly show, take an out-of-this-world journey at the **Albert Einstein Planetarium.** Buckle your seat belt and explore the Milky Way. Sky Vision, the planetarium's dual digital projection and surround sound system, will have you gripping your armrests. The special effects are awesome. The free 20-minute *One World, One Sky* is utterly beguiling and features Sesame Street characters on an exploration of the night sky. It's geared to younger children yet is enjoyable for kids of all ages. While tickets are free at the box office, you may want to play it safe and reserve them in advance (✆ **202/633-4629;** $2 fee). The other "flights" to the edge of the universe are appropriate for kids 5 and older.

I suggest buying your tickets for the planetarium shows (same prices as for the Air and Space shows, above) before you begin circling the exhibits. A free show, *The Stars Tonight,* airs daily at 11:30am.

Stop at the information desk for a floor plan and list of events. *I Spy in the Sky* is a self-guide for kids 3 to 5 and their parents. The museum hosts Family Days, usually Saturdays or Sundays, in conjunction with a specific exhibit, speaker, or aviation-related book signing. Activities may include a film, story time, short talk, and/or actors in period dress. To avoid wasting time and energy—this place is huge—note the exhibits that interest your crew most. Docent-led tours of the museum are held daily at 10:30am and 1pm. Call ahead for information on group tours. With kids under 6, it's best to see the highlights on your own. Tell 2- to 4-year-olds to "look up," because the overhead sights appeal to this age group the most.

Now we're ready to blast off. Start on the first floor with **"Milestones of Flight,"** in the two-level gallery at the museum's entrance (Gallery 100). If you view nothing else in this museum, make sure to see this permanent exhibition. There's a good reason why it occupies the museum's center stage. Highlights include Charles Lindbergh's *Spirit of St. Louis, Sputnik I,* John Glenn's *Friendship 7, Gemini 4,* the *Apollo 11* command module *Columbia, Pioneer 10,* Chuck (The Right Stuff) Yeager's *Bell X-1,* and *SpaceShipOne.* This remarkable craft is the first privately owned and operated spacecraft to fly more than 62 miles above Earth (it reached an altitude of 70 miles on Oct 4, 2004!). The 1903 *Wright Flyer* (the first airplane) was moved from the Milestones gallery where it hung for many years to the floor of "Early Flight" (Gallery 107) for closer inspection. Good move! When the line isn't too long, school-age kids love to walk through the Skylab Orbital Workshop, a backup for America's first space station. Check out the *Apollo* lunar module on the first floor's east end. "Explore the Universe" answers questions about the origins of the universe through artifacts (astrolabes, globes, and the like), telescopes, and digital technology (wide-field planetary cameras).

America by Air (Gallery 102) ★★ showcases the evolution of air travel in the 20th century. On display are a Curtiss Jenny, Boeing 247, and nose of a Boeing 747 that your kids can go in.

At the west end of the first floor kids can ride in one of six **Simulators** ★★ (Gallery 103). Daredevils can test their skills at performing barrel rolls in a sortie. Top Gun wannabes can engage in aerial combat in an F-4 Phantom II jet fighter. Reservations are not required but there is a fee of $7 for a ride in a simulator, $8 for an interactive simulator experience. Purchase tickets before boarding. You can get a discount at the IMAX box office, *if* you're also purchasing tickets to a film or planetarium show.

Make sure to see one of the museum's most successful educational projects ever, **"How Things Fly"** ★ (Gallery 109). The largely interactive exhibit makes principles of aerodynamics accessible to school-agers on up. The internal workings of a piston engine are revealed in the Continental cutaway. Aspects of lift and drag are provided by wind tunnels and computer activities. Climb into a full-size Cessna 150 and handle the controls regulating the wings and tail; learn about orbits and trajectories via computer. Sometimes docents or local high school or college students are on hand to demystify concepts for younger visitors.

"Looking at Earth" should appeal to the scientific-minded, with its aerial photographs and satellite imagery (Gallery 110). The Surveyor, Lunar Orbiter, and Ranger are hangared in the hall devoted to **"Lunar Exploration Vehicles"** (Gallery 112). In **"Rocketry and Space Flight"** (Gallery 113) are the *Vega,* flown by Amelia Earhart on the first transatlantic flight piloted by a woman, and spacesuits. Next door (Gallery 114) is devoted to the space race between the United States and the former Soviet Union. If you're interested in the rocketry and space-flight milestones and missions touched off by the Soviet Union's launching of *Sputnik* on October 4, 1957, **"Space Race"** has your name on it.

Tomorrow's astronauts will learn more about the early years of manned space flight in **"*Apollo* to the Moon"** (Gallery 210). The 40th anniversary of *Apollo 11* (July 16, 2009), a major milestone, is still being celebrated at the NASM. While the guidance and navigation aids, maps and charts, and full-size mock-up of a lunar-module cockpit and command module docking target will intrigue many, I found the razor and shave cream, sealed fruitcake, lunar rock, and water gun far more interesting (call me shallow). To better understand the origin of the voice in your car that directs you from Point A to Point B, check out the GPS exhibit (Gallery 213).

Break Time

The Wright Place Food Court (get it?), at the National Air and Space Museum, is perfect for kids. Here fast food has joined fast planes with standard golden arches fare from McDonald's, Boston Market (chicken and side dishes), and Donatos Pizzeria (small personal pizzas) at inflated prices. Hey, you're a captive audience unless you interrupt your museum visit and opt for street food or walk to a restaurant. Designed especially for the museum, the restaurant resembles a hangar with launching-pad-type scaffolding. It's open from 10am to 5pm. At the **Outdoor Kiosk** (west side of museum) you can grab a hot dog, potato chips, cold drinks, and ice cream between 10am and 5pm.

Touch down in the **Shuttle Shop and Museum Gift Shop** ★★ to pick up some freeze-dried ice cream sandwiches for snackin'. The selection of books, kites, models, posters, and T-shirts is one of the best in the city.

The **Steven F. Udvar–Hazy Center** ★★, near Washington Dulles International Airport in suburban Chantilly, Virginia, has been packing in visitors since opening in December 2003. There are two 10-story-high hangars (the tri-level Boeing Hangar for aircraft and the James S. McDonnell Space Hangar for rockets, spacecraft, and satellites). Together they house 80% of the national collection *not* displayed at the flagship museum on the Mall. ***A word of advice:*** This is one of the few destinations more easily accessible by car than by public transportation. Although the website suggests ways to get here—via rail and bus—I don't recommend it and suggest that you bite the bullet and rent a car for the day. It's worth it: This place is amazing.

Among the treasures are the *Enola Gay,* the space shuttle *Enterprise,* the shark-mouthed Curtiss P-40 Warhawk (flown in WWII), the Boeing 307 Stratoliner (first pressurized passenger plane), the Boeing 367-80 (first successful commercial jet), an Air France Concorde, and the Blackbird reconnaissance plane. Among the displayed artifacts are Lindbergh memorabilia and Amelia Earhart's flight suit. The Center also has a large-format theater, a flight simulator, restaurants, and gift shops.

Every June, the Center holds a "Become a Pilot Family Day" for families, with lots of hands-on stuff, huge cargo planes on the flight line, balloon rocket races, stories, and visits by astronauts. Hours are 10am to 5:30pm; admission is free and parking is $12. Perhaps more exciting to the kids is the Donald D. Engen observation tower for watching Dulles air traffic. Be forewarned that there's usually a line. An elevator carries about 15 voyeurs to and from the tower every 5 minutes. You can also catch a movie in the Airbus IMAX theater, or see the free film *Stars Tonight.* Purchase tickets at the IMAX or Einstein box office, or order ahead (a good idea, but with a $2 per-ticket fee; ✆ **877/932-4629** or 202/633-4629). Docent-led tours of the facility are held daily at 10:30am and 1pm. Because of heavy commuter traffic, I suggest doing this midday during the week or on a Saturday or Sunday morning. And please wear sturdy shoes. The floors are concrete.

Note: No food or drinks, other than bottled water, are allowed inside. If you have food, eat it or lose it before entering the museum.

For a free calendar of events, write to Calendar, National Air and Space Museum, Rm. 3733 MRC 321, Washington, DC 20560.

4th St. and Independence Ave. SW (enter at Independence Ave. or Jefferson Dr.). ✆ **202/633-1000.** www.nasm.si.edu. Free admission. Daily 10am–5:30pm; ask about extended summer hours. Closed Dec 25.

Metro: L'Enfant Plaza (Smithsonian Museums exit). Directions to Udvar-Hazy Center: I-495 (Beltway) to Dulles Toll Rd./Rte. 267, then exit 9A/Rte. 28 south; continue 3½ miles to Air & Space Museum Parkway, and follow signs.

National Museum of African Art ★ Ages 4 and up. Most kids over 5 will find the carved wooden masks and fertility dolls of particular interest here, the only museum in the United States dedicated solely to African art. The bovine gong on the first-floor landing is a hit with youngsters, especially after they discover what happens when they push the button next to it. The collection of mostly 19th- and 20th-century traditional arts and artifacts shares a tomblike space with the Arthur M. Sackler Gallery. More than 6,000 objects in the permanent collection are displayed in rotating exhibits. In 2004, the museum received the Walt Disney Co.–Tishman Collection (the late real estate magnate Paul Tishman had given his artwork to Disney). I've heard that many of the objects provided the inspiration for the creation of *The Lion King.* See if the 18th-century bronze mask, festooned with snakes and crocs and capped by an ominous-looking spike, is displayed during your visit. Ouch! In 2009, the "Artful Animals" exhibition (more than 100 colorful and playful renderings of our four-legged friends) focused on the individual animal's behavior and spiked kids imaginations. Similar exhibits are introduced every 10 to 12 months.

Usually one or two weekends a month (more often in summer) there's storytelling for kids focused on an individual country or special subject. Inquire at the information desk about the free gallery guide and other children's and family activities. In 2009, on Fridays at 10:30am, kids 5 to 10 were invited to "Let's Read About Africa," followed by an art activity, or to attend an author reading. Both introduce youngsters to African literature. Parents are invited to check the website for a schedule of family workshops, films, and storytelling. The **Warren M. Robbins Library** is open to researchers by appointment Monday through Friday from 8:45am to 5:15pm (✆ **202/633-4680**). The museum shop has crafts, artifacts, clothing, and jewelry.

950 Independence Ave. SW. ✆ **202/633-1000.** www.nmafa.si.edu. Free admission. Daily 10am–5:30pm; ask about extended summer hours. Closed Dec 25. Metro: Smithsonian (Mall or Independence Ave. exits).

National Museum of American History ★ Ages 2 and up. The museum reopened in November 2008 after a 2-year multimillion-dollar renovation. The building's interior is much brighter, and more appealing owing, in large part, to the addition of a multistory atrium filled with natural light. Major aspects of America's cultural, scientific, and technological history come alive here, intriguing kids of all ages. Three floors packed with exhibits that bridge more than 200 years—from the country's early days (the original Star-Spangled Banner that inspired our national anthem) to the present (Kermit the Frog, Dorothy's ruby slippers. Edison's light bulb, Archie and Edith Bunker's well-worn chairs and Muhammad Ali's boxing gloves)—provide a comprehensive overview of American social history. Bruce Willis's grungy undershirt from *Die Hard* is on display (no word on whether they fumigated it before displaying it). The museum also has Dustin Hoffman's artificial breast prosthesis from *Tootsie,* but I doubt it will ever occupy a display case. (Well, maybe when the ultraconservative right vacates D.C.) Don't try to cover the entire museum in one visit. First, at the information desks, pick up one or more of the museum's helpful **brochures and floor plans,** a Self-Guide of the museum's highlights and/or a Self-Guide for families with kids up to 5 years old at the information desks. Ask about the location of Interactive Carts in the museum. Manned (and womaned) by docents, these encourage active participation and are associated with museum exhibits.

Not to discourage you, but you could spend days here. To help with decision-making, here are some family-pleasing highlights. You're sure to discover your own favorites. I think the first floor of this museum is hot (or "cool," if you prefer), and so do most kids. On the first floor east, **"America on the Move"** tracks U.S. history through our changing transportation system—from the first railroad to California (1876) to 20th-century modes of getting around, all of which have impacted our daily lives. Among the wheeled vehicles are a Chicago Transit Authority L car, an electric streetcar, and huge steam locomotives, such as the 199-ton "1401" model that chugged through the late 19th and early 20th centuries. All are perennial kid-pleasers, as are the tractors and other farm machinery around the corner in the Hall of Agriculture. (I wouldn't mind parking the snazzy 1913 Model-T Ford in my driveway.) **Invention at Play** in the new Lemelson Center of Invention, first floor west, is awesome. My kids had to drag me away last time we visited. Come here to find out, through displays, artifacts, and interactives, about the yin and yang of play and creativity. Ever wonder about the people who created Post-its, Velcro, the microwave oven and other stuff we use in our daily lives—and usually take for granted? This is the place to find out. Kids can try their skill at surfboarding on a (stationery) Sailboard Simulator. In the adjacent Spark! Lab kids are encouraged by a smart and savvy staff to take part in numerous other hands-on activities to invent, experiment, and create. The inventions of the center's namesake, Jerome Lemelson, earned him more than 600 patents. Behind glass are some of his notebooks—filled with sketches and notes for toys that allow one a glimpse into his highly creative mind.

Get a thrill or two in a ride simulator opposite the Stars and Stripes Café. You can experience a roller-coaster ride and Grand Pix race without leaving the safety of the museum. You want to ride? You pay—$7 to be exact. I have a delicate constitution so I skipped this. My sources tell me it's a hoot and half (but not on a full stomach).

On the third floor east, **"The Price of Freedom: Americans at War,"** surveys U.S. military history from Colonial times until the present through interactive stations and multimedia presentations. In the Civil War section, visitors can watch a puppet play ("Give Me Liberty") or learn field maneuvers and drills (with docent assistance). There are loads of interactives throughout this mammoth exhibition. Let me know what you think. Call me sexist, but the guys in your group will probably enjoy seeing the Willy's Jeep from World War II and the UH-H1 Huey helicopter from Vietnam a lot more than the girls will. Pin a medal on the museum for attempting to show the harrowing effects of war on families and loved ones. I'm waiting to see how the museum will showcase the war in Iraq. Stay tuned.

Also on the third floor, and a respite from war games, is **"The American Presidency: A Glorious Burden."** It is fun, fun, fun, and also highly informative—chockablock with presidential memorabilia, videos, and interactives. Kids can gawk at Amy Carter's dollhouse, Chelsea Clinton's ballet slippers, and other items belonging to presidential offspring. Step up to the podium and deliver (part of) a presidential speech. Ogle Lincoln's office coat, Truman's gaudy sport shirt, photos from the 1945 Yalta Conference, peanut-shaped banks (a la Jimmy Carter), and Clinton's sax. Anyone 8 and older should connect with this.

Curators labored close to a year to catalogue, pack, and reassemble gourmet cooking diva **Julia Child's kitchen**—including utensils, dishes, and the sink. Known as "Bon Appetit! Julia Child's Kitchen at the Smithsonian," the kitchen served for 7 years as the set for Child's successful TV cooking series, *Bon Appetit!* The **Hands On Science Center,** part of the "Science in American Life" exhibition on the first floor, simplifies concepts

Break Time

Rest your weary feet and grab a snack or meal at the National Museum of American History's **Stars and Stripes Café** (new in 2008), on the lower level, for sandwiches, soups, salad bar, burgers, pizza, and dessert. Cash or credit cards accepted. With seating for 600, you shouldn't have a problem finding a spot. Open daily from 11am to 3pm. High chairs and boosters are available (✆ **202/633-1000**).

Growling stomachs and cranky tots can also be appeased in the Constitution Café on the first floor (✆ **202/633-1000**). Come for coffee, a light lunch, or dessert. It's adequate, it's convenient, and it's open during regular museum hours, 10am to 5:30pm.

for kids (according to the entrance sign) from "5 to 105." Don't drop off your kids and disappear. Children ages 5 through 12 must be accompanied by an adult. Under the supervision of docents, kids are invited to don neon safety goggles and take part in various experiments involving dry ice, DNA profiling, and pH levels of liquids—to name a few. Hours are seasonal, so please call ahead, visit the website, or ask when you arrive.

The museum's second floor is devoted to social and cultural history, such as the original **Star-Spangled Banner** (aka Old Glory) in its newly created, climate-and light-controlled gallery. It managed to survive the 1814 British attack on Fort McHenry in Baltimore, but it nearly succumbed to the ravages of light, air pollution, and 200 years when it was taken down in the 1990s. Speaking of flags, you can also view the flag that hung outside the Pentagon after the September 11, 2001, terrorist attacks.

In these enlightened times, you may want to peek at the exhibit **"First Ladies: Political Role and Public Image."** In addition to the gowns worn by presidential wives, plenty of First Lady memorabilia—photographs, jewelry, personal effects, and campaign mementos—are displayed, and the exhibit showcases the women's public and political roles.

The third floor is dedicated to popular culture, photography, textiles, and, last but not least, money—an interest all ages seem to share. The items change frequently in the **"Popular Culture"** exhibition, but you are bound to see one or more of the following: Dorothy's ruby slippers, Jim Henson's Kermit the Frog Muppet, Mr. Rogers' sweater, or basketball player Rebecca Lobo's U.S. Olympic team uniform.

Tours of the museum's highlights are at 10:15am and 1pm daily. Meet at either Welcome desk (Constitution Ave. or Mall entrance).

14th St. and Constitution Ave. NW, entrances on Constitution Ave. and Madison Dr. ✆ **202/633-1000.** www.americanhistory.si.edu. Free admission. Daily 10am–5:30pm. Closed Dec 25. Metro: Smithsonian (Mall exit) or Federal Triangle.

National Museum of the American Indian **Ages 4 and up.** Situated between the Air and Space Museum and the Capitol, the NMAI is a showcase for the culture, traditions, and history of American Indians (actually, "Native peoples" is considered correct) from North and South America. This enormous project succeeds on some levels and misses on others. Should you go? Absolutely. For starters, the massive sandstone exterior—situated close to so many ugly institutional federal buildings—is beyond impressive. Stroll the perimeter and note the plantings before you go in.

Once inside, my reactions after several visits—to the artifacts, paintings, and sculptures from two dozen tribes throughout North, Central, and South America—are still all over the map. How best to describe the overall effect? "Uneven" comes to mind. So does "disjointed." I leave it to you whether it satisfies visitors' curiosity about our nation's original forefathers. Blatantly missing, however, is any reference to the near obliteration of these indigenous peoples by the "civilized" white man. Okay, I'll step down from my soap box.

I suggest arriving early or late. School groups descend in waves weekdays between 10 and 11am and usually leave by 1:30 or 2pm. On weekends, get here when it opens, while locals are lolling over breakfast and running errands. To gain entrance, queue up in the General Entry line at the east entrance between 10am and 5pm, where you may have a short wait. Note the large screen over the Welcome Desk where *Welcome* is projected in many different languages. Here's where you can pick up info on special events as well as a **Family Guide** (also available on the website, www.nmai.si.edu, for preplanning; you'll find it under "Education"). The soaring atrium, when you first enter, is awe-inspiring. It often serves as a performance space. If you're pooped, rest on a bench and let the kids run around. One-hour tours of the highlights (fall, winter, spring) are Monday through Friday at 1 and 3pm, Saturday and Sunday at 11am, 1:30pm, and 3pm. In summer, the tours are Monday at 1:30 and 3pm; Tuesday through Sunday 11am, 1:30pm, and 3pm. Meet in the Potomac (atrium), first level.

Note: If you have questions, corral a docent in a green vest. Once you get your bearings, begin your visit on the fourth floor in the **Lelawi Theater,** where an introductory film is shown in-the-round on four fringed-cloth screens and overhead. Exhibitions on the fourth floor are dedicated to tribes of different areas, including videos, clothing, and artifacts from the Mayans (Yucatán Peninsula), Hoopas (California), Santa Clara pueblo (New Mexico), and Lakotas (South Dakota). The Lakota buffalo headdress is a must-see for kids. Also, point them toward the "projectile points" (more commonly known as arrowheads), colorful weavings, beaded objects, dolls, and interactives for identifying pieces of wood, pottery, and baskets.

To enhance your education about the Washington, D.C. area, see **Return to a Native Place: Algonquian Peoples of the Chesapeake,** which showcases through maps, artifacts, and interactive exhibits, the local Nanticoke, Pohatan, and Piscataway tribes who lived in the area long before European explorers set foot on North America.

On the third floor, numerous videos and exhibits attempt to capture the essence of "Our Lives," how various tribes live, work, and preserve their heritage. Except with older kids, I suggest targeting just one or two displays here, such as the colorful and extensive collection of Native peoples dolls. Also on the third floor is the Learning Center, which is open to the public daily for research (if you want help from a docent for "guided hands-on sessions," you must make an appointment).

Special events, such as films, speakers, live performances (by musicians, dancers, storytellers), and visits by children's authors such as Richard Van Camp of Canada's Dogrib Nation, are held in the first-level Rasmuson Theater, Atrium, and outdoor Welcome Plaza. Past performances included Navajo dancers, retelling of creation stories by an Amazon tribe from Columbia, the Alaska Native Arts and Culture Festival, and demonstrations of beadwork and basket making.

Mitsitam ("Let's eat" in the parlance of the local Piscataway and Delaware peoples), the museum cafe, is pleasing to the eye, palate, and pocketbook. The food is well above standard museum fare and offers choices for vegetarians and vegans. Dine on pumpkin cornbread, cedar-planked juniper salmon, fall squash and duck soup, herb-crusted lamb, and other dishes inspired by Native peoples from North, South, and Central America. Kids can get chicken tenders, a chili enchilada, or a burger for under $10. Seat them in front of the curved window wall, and they'll be so absorbed by the water splashing on rocks that they won't care what they eat. The cafe is open daily from 10am to 5pm. After 3pm, the menu is limited. Most main dishes are between $7.50 and $20.

4th St. and Independence Ave. SW. (btw. Air and Space and the Capitol). ✆ **202/633-1000.** www.nmai.si.edu. Free admission. Daily 10am–5:30pm; ask about extended summer hours. Closed Dec 25. Metro: L'Enfant Plaza or Smithsonian.

National Museum of Natural History ★★★ **Ages 2 and up.** I've always been partial to this museum (the most-visited museum in the world), and so are most kids. In summer, before you enter, I suggest walking around to the 9th Street side of the museum to see the outdoor **Butterfly Garden.**

Go first to the four-story, marble-pillared rotunda on the first floor and pick up a floor plan and calendar of events at the information desk. The child hasn't been born who won't ooh and aah over the 8-ton **African Bush Elephant,** which is more than 13 feet tall!

Dive into the **Sant Ocean Hall** for a multisensory experience that will knock your socks off.

Suspended from the ceiling is a replica of a Right Whale, which, in the wild, can reach a weight of 100 tons. The breadth and depth of this exhibition—panoramic photos, artifacts, videos, and interactives that encourage critical thinking about the oceans, which cover 70% of the earth's surface—will help young learners to understand the diverse and complex nature of our most valuable resource and the importance of maintaining our delicate interdependence. Kids are little sponges, as we know. And they can soak up knowledge about the differing natures of *Shores & Shallows, Coral Reefs,* and *Open Ocean* without getting their feet wet.

I urge two-legged mammals to hoof it to the **Family Hall of Mammals,** where mammalian evolution and adaptation are depicted in in-your-face exhibits—a gape-mouthed hippo, a leopard resting on a branch, and a Grevy's zebra at a watering hole are among the 274 specimens from Africa, South America, and North America, in settings akin to their natural habitats. My grandkids like this almost as much as the zoo. And unlike zoo

Break Time

The Atrium Café (a bright, six-story soaring space; sort of a Hyatt with fast food) is a glorified food court/cafeteria with standard lunch faves: burgers, hot dogs, fries, pizza, sandwiches, and wraps (Mon–Thurs 11am–3pm; Fri and Sun 11am–4pm; Sat 11am–5pm). **The Fossil Café** has a limited menu of sandwiches, soups, salads, desserts, and a coffee/espresso bar (10am–5pm). An **Ice Cream & Espresso Bar** is open daily 11am to 5pm. Not tempted? A short distance away is the **Food Court in the Old Post Office,** 11th Street and Pennsylvania Avenue NW. Of course, the food vendors parked end to end outside the museums are always an alternative.

animals, these are always awake (in a manner of speaking). While on safari, Theodore Roosevelt (the old Rough Rider) shot many of the African game animals in the dioramas. Taxidermists slaved long and hard to pump life, so to speak, into TR's white rhino, donated to the museum in 1909. This is a hands-on experience with plenty of interactives.

Make like a fly and buzz upstairs to the **O. Orkin Insect Zoo** ★, a living museum exhibit and a favorite with young and old alike. Leave your arachnophobia at the door before meeting the tarantulas. Pull up a chair to observe their table manners at feeding times, Tuesday through Friday at 10:30am, 11:30am, and 1:30pm. Bon Appetit! Hold a hissing cockroach. View bees swarming around their hive, watch ants building a colony, observe millipedes as long as stretch limos, and observe the amazing Amazon walking stick (as lanky as some NBA players).

The insect zoo, with many colorful visual aids, crawls with more than one million visitors annually. In one interactive display, kids can test their knowledge of insect camouflages. The youngest members of your colony are invited to crawl through a replica of an African termites' mound (in the wild, these mounds grow to 25 ft.!). You might go bug-eyed peering inside a model home for common household insects that most likely cohabitate with your family. Touch models of four insect heads in the Adaptation Section, and increase your knowledge of spider strategies and ants' sociability. The rainforest exhibit features giant cockroaches, leaf-cutter ants, and tropical plants.

Visit the **Butterfly Pavilion** and walk among these ethereal beauties. Purchase timed-entry tickets ($6) adjacent to the exhibit, at the IMAX theater box office or rotunda box office (both downstairs), or order online at www.tickets.com.

Remember *Jurassic Park?* In the **Dinosaur Hall,** get up close and personal with skeletons of the stegosaurus and triceratops, among others, and rare bones of juvenile dinosaurs. If you want to go eyeball to eyeball with *Quetzalcoatlus,* the largest flying reptile (here, suspended from the ceiling), climb the stairs, where you can also examine several oldies but goodies mounted on the wall. In the fossil collection, you'll find specimens of creatures that swam in the seas 600 million years ago and a 70-million-year-old dinosaur egg. Skeletons of dinosaurs that lived more than 100 million years ago are always big hits.

"African Voices" (due to close, unfortunately, in fall 2010) presents the diversity and influence of the African people, history, and culture—family, work, community, environment—through photos, artifacts, sculpture, pottery, and textiles. Interactive audio and video stations allow you to view a timeline and listen to folk tales, traditional songs, and oral histories. Nearby, and less exciting I think, are the exhibits devoted to Asian and Pacific cultures.

For a hands-on experience, take kids between 2 and 8 to the **Discovery Room,** where they can touch all but a few very fragile items, and explore and learn at their own pace. Among the room's treasures are large boxes of bones, reptile skins, and shells. There's a crocodile head and even a preserved rattlesnake in a jar. Discovery Room hours are Tuesday through Thursday noon to 2:30pm; Friday 10am to 2:30pm; and Saturday and Sunday 10:30am to 3:30pm. Just walk in. During busy times, get your free passes at the door. Closed Mondays.

You can also look for **Discover Stations** (mobile carts), set up throughout the museum, usually between 10:30am and noon. Here docents introduce young visitors to "object-based, problem-solving opportunities and experiences" that tie in to nearby exhibits.

Fun Facts A Gem of a Story

Talk about romancing the stone. The legendary **Hope Diamond,** once the eye of a Hindu idol in India, was stolen in the 17th century, and, as the story goes, the gods put a curse on all future wearers.

The stone was named for British gem collector Henry Philip Hope, who listed the gem in his 1839 catalog. The rock first caught socialite Evalyn Walsh McLean's eye in 1908, when she noticed it in the Constantinople harem of the sultan of the Ottoman Empire. McLean was on a 3-month honeymoon trip with her husband, Ned, whose family owned the *Washington Post.* Before McLean purchased the stone from jeweler Pierre Cartier for $184,000 in 1911, previous owners included Louis XIV, Louis XVI, and Marie Antoinette, who learned the hard way that diamonds aren't necessarily a girl's best friend.

McLean, the last person to wear the celebrated 45½-carat blue diamond, counted presidents and monarchs among her friends, owned several homes, and, on the surface, led a charmed life, once spending $48,000 for a dinner party in 1912. But it was a life marred by tragedy (or perhaps the curse of the Hope Diamond). Her husband went insane, the marriage dissolved, and then her eldest son was killed in an accident. Still, she continued to wear the diamond. She is reported to have said, "I always thought it was garish—until I owned it." Touché! In the wake of the Great Depression, financial ruin followed. In 1933, the *Post* was sold at auction to Eugene Meyer. The curse continued—in 1946, McLean's only daughter died of a drug overdose at the age of 24.

When McLean died in 1947, friends put the diamond in a cigar box. When no bank would accept it, it found a temporary haven in an FBI vault before being sold to jeweler Harry Winston in 1949 to pay McLean's estate taxes. Nine years later, Winston donated the gem to the Smithsonian. It is said that the mailman who delivered the gem to the Smithsonian had his leg crushed in a truck accident. Soon thereafter, his wife and dog died, and his house burned to the ground.

The **Janet Annenberg Hooker Hall of Geology, Gems, and Minerals** ★★ dazzles the eye and mind. The hall accommodates visitors in a hurry as well as those wanting to digest the exhibits and scores of interactive stations in depth. The centerpiece is the 45½-carat **Hope Diamond,** in the Harry Winston Gallery (named for the esteemed jeweler who purchased the diamond and donated it to the museum in 1958), valued at $100 million. (See the box "A Gem of a Story," above). Many visitors are surprised by its color—and size. What a rock! The most-visited object in all the Smithsonian museums got naked in September 2009 when it was divested of its original setting. In a hokey PR stunt to celebrate the rock's 50th anniversary at the Smithsonian, online voters got to choose the new setting which is slated to go on display in April 2010. I liked the old setting better; some things are better left alone. Among the other glittering treasures are diamond earrings, supposedly worn by Marie Antoinette on her final ride—to the guillotine—and a necklace that together comprise 374 diamonds and 15 emeralds. The displays of other gems and minerals, to my mind, upstage the polished gems.

In another section of the hall, a world map records the activity of every volcano and earthquake in the last 40 years, accompanied by sound effects. Kids (and you, too!) can pound the granite mounting of a seismograph that demonstrates the sensitivity of the instrument. In the dimly lit hall where four mines are re-created, watch the video of how gems and minerals are formed and mined; then peek through the window to catch a glimpse of another jewel: the National Mall.

Moon rocks brought back by the *Apollo* astronauts and a 1,371-pound meteorite are on display in the space devoted to Earth and the solar system. Visitors can access a computer linking various meteorites and craters.

The **Discovery Center** (as in Discovery Channel) encompasses a cafeteria-style restaurant, museum shop, and 500-seat Johnson IMAX Theater. In the **IMAX Theater** ★ you can view large-scale movies about the natural world. Put on your 3D glasses to witness the live-action nature dramas. *Wild Ocean* (in 3D) and *Night at the Museum: Battle of the Smithsonian* were featured late in 2009. Usually three or four films take turns on the big screen at any given time. Tickets are $8.75 for adults, $7.25 for kids 2 to 11, and $7.75 for seniors 60 and older. I strongly suggest ordering tickets ahead or buying them in the morning when the museum opens. For more information or to purchase tickets ahead, call ✆ **202/633-4629.**

The **Naturalist Center,** a research library/lab for families wishing to learn more about the natural world, is located at 741 Miller Dr. SE, Ste. G2, Leesburg, Virginia (✆ **800/729-7725** or 703/779-9712), about 35 miles from the museum. The center is open Tuesday through Saturday from 10:30am to 4pm; it's closed Sunday, Monday, and federal holidays.

Tours of the museum's highlights are offered Tuesday through Friday at 10:30am and 1:30pm. Meet at the African elephant in the rotunda.

During your visit, stop at the museum shops on the ground floor, open from 10am to 5:30pm. Look no further for a wide selection of crafts, jewelry, books, science kits, toys, posters, T-shirts, and more.

In the past, on Friday nights from 6am to 10pm, the public enjoyed live jazz (with well-behaved kids 10 and older) in the **Smithsonian Jazz Cafe** (✆ **202/633-7400;** www.mnh.si.edu/imax) from 6 to 10pm. Due to budget constraints, this program may or may not resume in 2010. My fingers are crossed.

10th St. and Constitution Ave. NW (2nd entrance on Madison Dr.). ✆ **202/633-1000.** www.nmnh.si.edu. Free admission. Daily 10am–5:30pm. Closed Dec 25. Metro: Smithsonian or Federal Triangle.

National Postal Museum ★★ Ages 4 and up. A joint project of the Postal Service and the Smithsonian Institution, the Postal Museum has the largest and most comprehensive collection of its kind in the world. It is a must stop for philatelists and anyone interested in postal-service history. A 1924 DeHavilland airmail plane suspended, along with others, from the ceiling of the 90-foot-high atrium greets visitors descending the escalators from the very ornate lobby entrance. At the information desk, pick up copies of "A Self-Guided Tour for Very Young Visitors" and "Check It Out!"

"Binding the Nation" covers early postal history from pre-Revolutionary days to the late 19th century. Did you know, for example, that Benjamin Franklin served as postmaster for the colonies? Or that he was fired? Find out why and lots more during your visit.

"Moving the Mail" explores the ways the postal service moves 600 million pieces per day. The amazing thing is that most of it is delivered (eventually). Aside from displays of stamps and postal documents, you'll see an 1850s stagecoach and replica of a Southern Railway mail car, complete with mailbags and sorting table. At one time, 32,000 railway mail clerks, considered the elite of the postal system, delivered 95% of the U.S. mail via rail. In the Philatelic Gallery, you can view every stamp issued since the mid-1800s. Little ones can pretend-drive a real mail truck, a highlight for the under-6 crowd.

"The Art of Cards and Letters" resonates. The focus here is on the role of personal mail in our daily lives. Think about it: letters home from soldiers, letters from anxious parents to kids at camp, letters from college kids asking for money. **"Customers and Communities"** takes the personal a step further with exhibits on how the mail-delivery system evolved in the 20th century to meet the needs of a growing population.

Half-hour drop-in guided tours are offered at 11am and 1pm. Groups (of 10 or more) must call at least 3 weeks ahead to schedule a tour (✆ **202/633-5534**). Family Days, which used to be given 1 Saturday afternoon a month, have been temporarily suspended. Check to see if they've been reinstated. When you're in the Union Station/Capitol Hill area, squeeze in this museum posthaste. It has my stamp of approval! (Sorry, I couldn't resist.)

2 Massachusetts Ave. NE (Washington City Post Office Bldg., next to Union Station). ✆ **202/633-1000,** or 202/357-2991 to schedule group tours. www.postalmuseum.si.edu. Free admission. Daily 10am–5:30pm. Closed Dec 25. Metro: Union Station (1st St. exit).

National Zoological Park ★★★ Ages 2 and up. More than 5,000 animals call the National Zoo home, and your children will probably want to see every one of them. Occupying 163 acres a few Metro stops from the White House, the zoo boasts many rare and endangered species and is perennially a premier attraction for families. On weekends, during school vacations, and in the summer, go early in the morning, not only because it's less crowded, but also because the animals are spunkier. Typically, they nap in the middle of the day (sounds good to me). In May and June, when the zoo residents become parents, it's an especially appealing time to bring your little ones. Speaking of babies, did you know that giraffes grow as much as an inch a day, doubling their height in their first year? And they usually stand and take their first steps within 10 minutes after they're born. (So how come it takes human babies 10 *months* or more?)

Olmsted Walk is the zoo's main drag, and more than 3 miles of trails crisscross the park. If you follow the helpful signs along the way, you won't get lost. The terrain is hilly, so leave your flip-flops under the bed and wear your most comfortable nonskid shoes. Be sure to lift up your kids in strollers so that they can see everything. If they don't get cranky along the way, you could easily spend half a day or longer here. Older kids, of

Tips Your Zoo Trip

1. Go early, especially if you drive. The parking lots often fill by 9:30am weekends, holidays, school vacations, and May through September. If you take Metro and want to beat the crowds, arrive between 8 to 10am or after 2pm weekdays; weekends, before 10am or after 4pm.
2. Before leaving home, print activity sheets at the Zoo's website and bring them with you. They will help you navigate and add to your child's experience.
3. Wear comfy, nonskid shoes.
4. Cater first to the youngest in your clan. Break frequently to snack, rest, and people-watch.

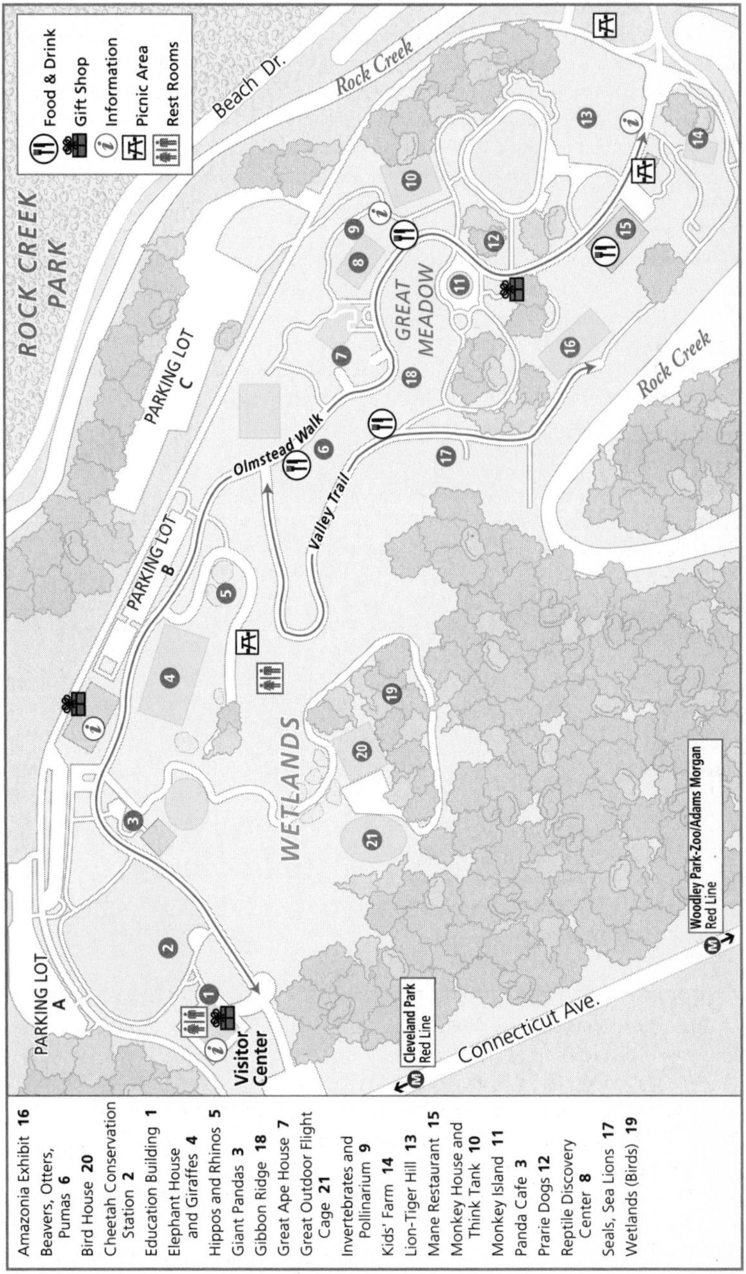
Amazonia Exhibit 16
Beavers, Otters, Pumas 6
Bird House 20
Cheetah Conservation Station 2
Education Building 1
Elephant House and Giraffes 4
Hippos and Rhinos 5
Giant Pandas 3
Gibbon Ridge 18
Great Ape House 7
Great Outdoor Flight Cage 21
Invertebrates and Pollinarium 9
Kids' Farm 14
Lion-Tiger Hill 13
Mane Restaurant 15
Monkey House and Think Tank 10
Monkey Island 11
Panda Cafe 3
Prarie Dogs 12
Reptile Discovery Center 8
Seals, Sea Lions 17
Wetlands (Birds) 19
Food & Drink
Gift Shop
Information
Picnic Area
Rest Rooms
ROCK CREEK PARK
Beach Dr.
Rock Creek
PARKING LOT A
PARKING LOT B
PARKING LOT C
Visitor Center
Olmstead Walk
Valley Trail
GREAT MEADOW
WETLANDS
Connecticut Ave.
Cleveland Park Red Line
Woodley Park-Zoo/Adams Morgan Red Line

course, can go on forever, and you'll probably be the one shouting "Uncle!" Before you visit, consider printing out activity sheets at the zoo's website. And the zoo recommends catering to the youngest in your clan first. Good idea!

Stop first at the information kiosk near the zoo's Connecticut Avenue entrance to pick up a map and check on any special programs—over a dozen most days that involve the animals' feeding, bathing, or training. On a recent visit I had the uncommon experience of watching a giant octopus feed. And I recommend it. In "How Do You Zoo?" ★, kids, under the watchful eye of docents, are invited to role-play in a zookeeper's office, commissary, vet hospital, and animal exhibit. Geared to 5- to 10-year-olds, it's open Saturday and Sunday from 10am to 4pm.

Pandas ★★ Mei Xiang (may-*shong,* "beautiful fragrance"), the female, and Tian Tian (t-*yen* t-*yen,* "more and more"), the male, arrived in December 6, 2000, and live in a 17,500-square-foot habitat, furnished largely with bamboo. Rumors to the contrary, that they met over the Internet, are untrue—they were chosen for their genetic compatibility. And here's proof: Giant panda Tai Shan ("peaceful mountain") celebrated his fourth birthday July 9, 2009, with a "cake" of fruits and bamboo frozen in beet juice and water. The goodies helped him to reach his full weight of close to 250 pounds. Because pandas are high-altitude dwellers, they can handle Washington's winters with aplomb. Summer's heat and humidity are a different story, so the zoo installed air-conditioned grottos and misting sprays. Thank you, zoo people. I had the thrill of viewing both on a hot summer's day. While the Internet is no sub for the real thing, before your visit, your kids might like to view these two on the pandacam at the zoo's website. The pandas' diet consists of about 50 pounds of bamboo a day, nutritious biscuits, carrots, and apples. The pandas live on the Asia Trail, along with red pandas, clouded leopards, sloth, and a giant Japanese salamander, about 5 feet long. (You wouldn't want to stumble upon him in your garden.)

Almost faster than a speeding bullet are the cheetahs, which usually race (weather permitting) between 9:30 and 10:30am in the zoo's **Cheetah Conservation Station,** which mirrors their African savanna home. You'll find them next to the visitor center. (In October 2007, the new **Cheetah Science Facility** opened at the zoo's Conservation and Research Center in Front Royal, Virginia, which will eventually house 14 to 20 cheetahs. Here the cats have more room to roam and run while scientists research their habits. So far, no visitors are allowed.) Nearby are the large land mammals: rhinos, hippos, giraffes, and elephants. The elephant training delights audiences at 11am most days. Expect some detours near the Elephant House which closed temporarily in September 2009 for completion of the Elephant Trails. When completed it will wend through woods, allowing the animals to move about more freely. (Do not be afraid. They will not be allowed

Bye-bye, Pandas

Say it isn't so! Tai Shan, the adorable 4-year-old panda born at the National Zoo, is scheduled to return to China in the first quarter of 2010. (Note: The Chinese government extended his "visa" twice.) Sources say Mei Shang and Tian Tian (Tai Shan's mom and dad) will follow later in 2010. But this is Washington—so who knows? Our fingers are crossed that attempts at artificial insemination will produce a new baby panda for the zoo. For the latest, go to: http://nationalzoo.si.edu/Animals/GiantPandas.

to mingle with visiting bipeds). When it reopens the Elephant House will be known as a Community Center and much more hospitable to their social nature. Follow Olmsted Walk (or the detour) to the large and small cats, apes, orangutans, gibbons, and reptiles. Try to catch the seal and sea lions' training demonstration at 11:30am (check first at the information desk), and stop to peek through the window in the otter pool for a close-up of these endearing animals' high jinks.

My grandkids love the **Bird House,** especially the colorful tropical birds that fly free in the Indoor Flight Room, an enclosed junglelike habitat. If you have field glasses, bring 'em. The Great Outdoor Flight Cage is a sky-high, mesh-enclosed hemisphere that your little chickadees will enjoy. Older kids and adults can carry their featherweight concerns to the Bird Resource Center at the rear of the Bird House and take a guided tour of a room where eggs incubate and zoo workers examine some of our ailing fine-feathered friends. Watch the flamingoes and other residents on the live webcams.

Bald eagles Sam (female) and Tioga (male) can't fly due to injuries sustained as fledglings, so this awesome pair sticks pretty close to the ground in the Bald Eagle Refuge (near the Mexican wolves and sea otters). This exhibit also houses hawks (also birds of prey), videos, and other information about the bald eagles. Take a look at the **American Prairie** exhibit, sure to have you humming "Home on the Range" in no time flat. Prairie dogs (actually rodents, but cute rodents) prowl the prairie grasses when they're not burrowing to escape the stares of funny-looking tourists. Roaming the range are two American Bison, named Ten Bears (a boy) and Kicking Bird (a girl), which weigh in at close to 2,000 pounds each.

The invertebrate exhibit features tanks of starfish, sponges, and crabs, as well as spiders—all displayed very much out in the open. Although grownups are occasionally turned off, children usually want to inspect the dirt-filled sandbox inhabited by a bunch of creepy-crawlers. Last time I checked, this exhibit was open Wednesday through Sunday only.

You won't find bipeds in pinstripe suits or pantyhose in the **Think Tank** here. Instead, in an awesome spectacle, Thursday through Sunday 10am to 4pm, you can watch orangutans ("orangs") commuting (much as they do in the wild) between the Great Ape House and the Think Tank along cables 45 feet above the main path. Daily demonstrations engage the public in three areas: language, tool use, and sociability. Along with macaques (an endangered breed from Indonesia), the orangutans demonstrate their problem-solving skills while scientists explain their behavioral-research findings to onlookers. As visitors, you are invited to participate in a variety of activities here.

Ever wonder why flowers are colorful? Or what butterflies eat? Find the answers to these questions and many more in the **Pollinarium** ★, also part of the zoo's BioPark exhibit.

Amazonia is an ideal cool-day escape. It's plenty steamy inside the re-created rain forest at the foot of Valley Trail. The exhibit supports a broad array of plants and animals. Enjoy an underwater view of the freshwater fish of the Amazon, some of which are 7 feet long.

Step into the **Amazonia Science Gallery,** adjacent to the Rainforest Exhibit, for a behind-the-scenes view of Smithsonian research on the biodiversity of the Amazon—and a chance to speak with the research scientists. Visitors can analyze their own voices and compare them to animal vocalizations as scientists and education specialists explain what they do and how they do it. In the **GeoSphere,** projectors, satellite imagery, and computer-generated information provide visual images that illustrate the Earth's geophysical process.

Near Amazonia and the Rock Creek Park entrance lies the **Kids' Farm** ★★ (geared to kids 3–8), with chickens, cows, donkeys, ducks, and goats—and a fly or two or three. Children can climb atop a giant rubber pizza with movable foam toppings and find out the sources of their favorite foods. Depending on staff availability and weather, kids can groom the donkeys and goats in the Caring Corral, typically open for about 1½ hours in the morning and again in the afternoon. For an update, ask at the information kiosk when you arrive.

"What if Adam and Eve were tempted by a fuzzy-tailed squirrel rather than a snake?" This is one of the questions posed in the **Reptile Discovery Center.** You have to admit it's a step up from "snake house." The many hands-on exhibits help to raise the biological literacy of zoo visitors and modify negative notions about reptiles and amphibians. The desired effect is nearly achieved by having reptile keepers and docents on hand to answer questions.

Immensely popular is the zoo's take on a slumber party, **"Snore & Roar,"** which takes place June through September. After an evening zoo tour with flashlights, the kids (6 and older) bed down in four-person tents near the lions and tigers, one adult for every three kids. (You didn't think you could just drop them off, did you?) The wait list is always long, so if you're interested, sign up in early April, when the dates and prices are posted.

Snack bars and ice-cream stands are scattered throughout the park. At the **Panda Cafe,** enjoy a fast-food break at tables with umbrellas. The **Panda Express Grill,** across from the Panda House, serves sandwiches, salads, cotton candy, and ice cream from 10am to 4pm, and accepts most credit cards. The **Mane Restaurant** is at the bottom of the hill, if you started at Connecticut Avenue. Hot dogs, hamburgers, and fresh salads are available. But many visitors prefer to bring sandwiches, buy drinks and ice cream, and dine alfresco at one of the zoo's grassy picnic areas.

Across the street from the main Connecticut Avenue entrance is a tavern that I recommend as superior to the zoo's food for humans; I can't speak for the elephants and orangutans. The **Zoo Bar Café** features yummy burgers and sandwiches and a children's menu. Filled with families at noon, at night the local animals take over, so then I suggest eating outdoors—or elsewhere.

The Zoo Store in the visitor center is open daily and carries a wide selection of zoo-related books on several reading levels, DVDs, stuffed (excuse me, "plush" is the correct term) animals, clothing, souvenirs, animal puzzles, post cards and (small, breakable) imported toys that probably won't last until nightfall. I wish this mass-produced stuff wasn't so expensive. (Maybe I'm turning into a cranky old coot.)

Beginning late June, a free summer concert series, Sunset Serenades, runs for five consecutive Thursdays, 6:30 to 8:30pm, on Lion/Tiger Hill. You can BYO or get supper to go at the Mane Restaurant and picnic while you listen.

3001 Connecticut Ave. NW. ✆ **202/633-4800,** or 202/633-3025 for weekend guided walking tours. www.nationalzoo.si.edu. Free admission. Buildings Apr 1–late Oct 10am–6pm, late Oct–late Mar 10am–4:30pm; grounds Apr 1–late Oct 6am–8pm, late Oct–Apr 1 6am–6pm; How Do You Zoo? Sat–Sun 10am–4pm; bookstore daily 9am–5pm. Closed Dec 25. Fee for parking based on length of visit, $10 for first hour, $15 for 2–3 hours up to $20 (for 4 or more hr.). Free parking for Friends of the National Zoo (FONZ) members; parking for visitors with disabilities in Lots A, B, and D; some street parking. Strollers rent for $9 single, $12 double for nonmembers plus a paid deposit, driver's license, or military ID. Pets are not allowed in the park. Metro: Cleveland Park (an easier walk) or Woodley Park–Zoo/Adams Morgan and then northbound L-2 or L-4 bus, or walk 1/3 mile uphill.

Renwick Gallery ★ **Ages 6 and up.** Washington's first private art museum was the original home of the Corcoran collection. The Renwick is a department of the Smithsonian American Art Museum. The gallery, in a stunning 19th-century French Second

Empire–style building, is a personal favorite of mine. The first floor exhibits, showcasing contemporary crafts and decorative arts, appeal to kids because they're 3D and usually colorful (blown glass, wooden objects, quilts, and so on). The second floor is devoted to works from the permanent collection, exhibited on a rotating basis. Most kids over 6 have at least a fleeting appreciation of the interior space. Especially impressive is the broad carpeted staircase leading to the second floor. You almost expect the trumpets to announce your arrival. The 90-foot **Victorian Grand Salon,** with its 38-foot skylight ceiling and wainscoted plum walls holding scores of paintings, is striking, even if you don't warm to the art.

Without a doubt, the most popular work in this museum for young people is Larry Fuente's whimsical ***Game Fish,*** an eye-catching sailfish trophy whose scales glitter with a colorful array of toys and game pieces. If you can lure the kids away, see if Patti Warashina's ***Convertible Car Kiln*** is displayed.

The Octagon Gallery was designed for Hiram Powers's nude, ***The Greek Slave*** (now in the Corcoran). Because of its prurient nature (for the Victorian era), viewing times were once different for men and women. Flanking the Octagon Gallery are exhibits of contemporary works, such as Wendell Castle's ***Ghost Clock,*** a remarkable example of *trompe l'oeil* imagery. The clock is actually a solid piece of carved mahogany. Honest!

Walking tours are Monday through Friday at noon, and Saturdays and Sundays at 1pm. Group tours must be scheduled at least 3 weeks in advance (© **202/633-8550**). The merchandise in the intimate museum shop—crafts, books, clothing—is well chosen and unique, a favorite of mine for gift buying, especially the art-inspired children's books.

Pennsylvania Ave., at 17th St. NW. © **202/633-1000.** www.americanart.si.edu/renwick. Free admission. Daily 10am–5:30pm. Closed Dec 25. Metro: Farragut North (K St. exit) or Farragut West (17th St. exit).

Smithsonian American Art Museum and National Portrait Gallery ★ Some things are worth waiting for. This is one of them. On July 4, 2006, the Donald W. Reynolds Center for American Art and Portraiture—for the sake of brevity, the Smithsonian American Art Museum, or "SAAM"—opened (with a price tag of $346 million) to great and well-deserved fanfare in the historic Old Patent Office Building. The building had been closed for several years, so that long overdue improvements could be made to outdated fire, electric, and communications systems, and major cosmetic surgery could be performed on the galleries. In the process, a large auditorium, cafe, museum stores, lots of interactives for kids, and handicapped accessibility were added.

Today few come here to check out the wiring. Do visit if time permits; you won't regret it. ***Note:*** Unlike the other Smithsonian museums, this one is open from 11:30am to 7pm. Many a visitor has showed up here at 10am and been disappointed. I love this place—with or without children. It inspires, enlightens, and educates—and speaks to all ages. (For what it's worth, my grandchildren think it's cool.) Hats off to the visionaries, architects, designers, planners, curators, and docents—oh, yes, and all the artists living and dead (hope I didn't leave out anyone).

The grown-ups will drool over portraits by 19th-century masters Gilbert Stuart, John Singleton Copley, Charles Wilson Peale, and their peers, the magnificent landscapes of the Hudson River School, works by late-19th-century impressionists (Childe Hassam, Mary Cassatt, et al.), Homer, Whistler, early-20th-century Sargent, and more contemporary fare representing the best in American drawing, printmaking and photography, folk and decorative arts. Your kids, on the other hand, will probably find George Caitlin's portraits of Plain Tribe Indians more to their liking, as well as the inventive, often colorful and whimsical folk art by such self-taught visionaries as James Hampton. If Hampton's *The Throne of the*

Where Children Can . . .

- Crawl through a replica of an African termites' mound—the O. Orkin Insect Zoo in the **National Museum of Natural History.**
- Enjoy free entertainment—**Kennedy Center Millennium Stage, Old Post Office,** and **Ronald Reagan International Trade Building.**
- Gin raw cotton—the Hands-On History Room in the **National Museum of American History.**
- Whisper and be heard clear across the room—the **U.S. Capitol's Statuary Hall.**
- Watch millions of dollars being printed—the **Bureau of Engraving and Printing.**
- Take a simulated orbital flight—Earth Station One, in the **National Geographic Museum.**
- View the model tarantula featured in the James Bond movie *Dr. No*—the **International Spy Museum.**
- Be dazzled by a 45$^1/_2$-carat diamond—the **National Museum of Natural History.**
- Sink their teeth into a freeze-dried ice cream sandwich—the **National Air and Space Museum's** gift shop.
- Pedal a boat next to two presidential monuments—the **Tidal Basin,** next to the Jefferson Memorial and the Franklin Delano Roosevelt Memorial.
- Touch a moon rock—the **National Air and Space Museum.**
- Sniff fragrant blossoms year-round—the **U.S. Botanic Garden.**
- Dress in colonial clothing—the **DAR Museum.**
- Watch a clock that always reads 7:22am—the **Petersen House,** where Lincoln died on April 15, 1865, at 7:22am.
- Ride a carousel in the heart of the city—outside the **Smithsonian's Arts and Industries Building.**
- Read the front pages of 80 major U.S. newspapers—the **Newseum.**
- Peer up at a 15-story ceiling—the **National Building Museum.**
- Pet a crab or fish—the **National Aquarium's** touch tank.
- Explore the oldest house in Washington—the **Old Stone House** in Georgetown.
- Dine with U.S. senators—the **Senate Dining Room** in the Capitol.
- Find the grave of the founder of the Smithsonian Institution—the **Smithsonian "Castle."**

Third Heaven doesn't make your socks roll up and down, I suggest a checkup. Kids dig Mr. Imagination's clever bottle-cap sculptures. (So do grown-ups.) Those old enough to read will surely enjoy Mike Wilkins' *Preamble*—50 license plates, one from each state, arranged to spell out (phonetically) the Preamble of the Constitution.

George Lucas and Steven Spielberg are loaning their individual Norman Rockwell collection of more than 50 drawings and paintings to the museum from July 10, 2010, to Jan. 2, 2011. "Telling Stories" is a way to introducing your kids to the artist who captured a gentler era in America.

Step into the magnificent glass-canopied Kogod Courtyard, the site of free Family Days (random Saturdays throughout the year). Past events included Hispanic folk dances with live music, and a celebration of the 1930s through music, dance, board games, and a screening of "Annie."

The museum shop is one of the most seductive in the entire Smithsonian system. It's chockfull of puzzles, books, notepads, creative toys, colored markers for the kids; posters, calendars, stationery, books, ties and scarves, unusual accessories, and tchotchkes big kids can't live without. I could easily do my annual holiday and special occasion shopping here. Hungry? Head for **The Courtyard Café,** in the atrium off the G St. entrance, for casual dining and a menu of specialty sandwiches, create-your-own salads, soup, desserts, beer and wine, hot and cold beverages; open daily 11:30am to 6:30pm (full menu until 4pm, "quick pick" from 4–6:30pm).

8th and F sts. NW. Smithsonian American Art Museum: ✆ **202/633-1000.** http://americanart.si.edu. National Portrait Gallery: ✆ **202/633-8300.** www.npg.si.edu. Free admission. Daily 11:30am–7pm. Closed Dec 25. Metro: Gallery Place.

2 MONUMENTS, MEMORIALS & THE NATIONAL CATHEDRAL

PRESIDENTIAL MONUMENTS

Four U.S. presidents have been honored with monuments in the nation's capital: George Washington, Abraham Lincoln, Thomas Jefferson, and Franklin Delano Roosevelt. Try to see them all. I could wax poetic on the feelings elicited by each, but you should find out for yourself.

Thomas Jefferson Memorial ★★★ Moments Ages 8 and up. Some students of history think that Jefferson was the Rodney Dangerfield of his time, in that he "got no respect." While the memorials to Washington and Lincoln enjoyed prestigious downtown addresses for quite a spell, in accordance with L'Enfant's plan, Mr. Jefferson wasn't appropriately honored until April 13 (his birthday) in 1943, when the Jefferson Memorial was dedicated.

Well, good things come to those who wait. On a parcel reclaimed from the Potomac, on line with the south axis of the White House, a memorial was erected similar to Rome's Pantheon. Jefferson so favored this architectural model that he used its columned rotunda design at the Virginia State Capitol, the University of Virginia, and Monticello, his home in Charlottesville, Virginia.

Park Your Questions with the Rangers

Please note that monuments and memorials are not staffed by park rangers 24/7. Rangers are usually on site to answer questions and give directions from 9 or 9:30am to 5 or 5:30pm; in summer, usually until 7:30pm or later.

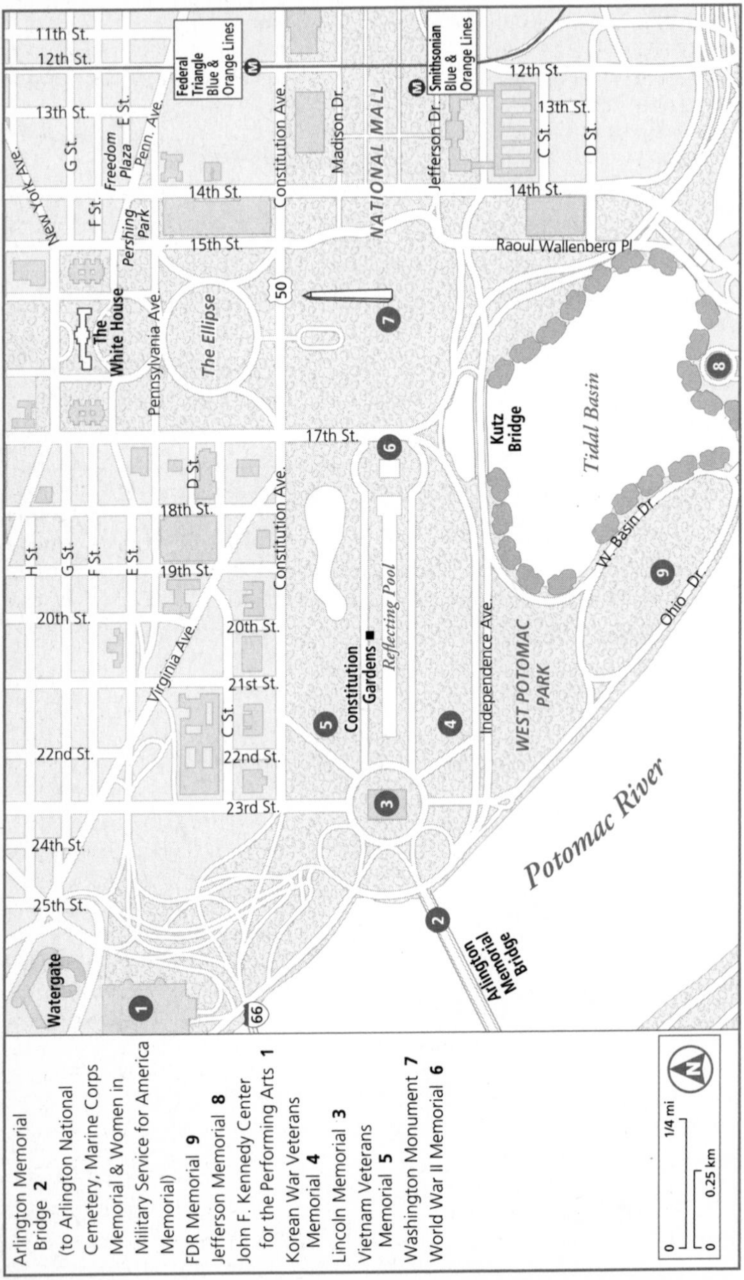
Arlington Memorial Bridge 2
(to Arlington National Cemetery, Marine Corps Memorial & Women in Military Service for America Memorial)
FDR Memorial 9
Jefferson Memorial 8
John F. Kennedy Center for the Performing Arts 1
Korean War Veterans Memorial 4
Lincoln Memorial 3
Vietnam Veterans Memorial 5
Washington Monument 7
World War II Memorial 6
0
1/4 mi
0
0.25 km
N
Watergate
Arlington Memorial Bridge
Potomac River
WEST POTOMAC PARK
Tidal Basin
Kutz Bridge
Constitution Gardens
Reflecting Pool
The Ellipse
The White House
NATIONAL MALL
Federal Triangle Blue & Orange Lines
Smithsonian Blue & Orange Lines
Freedom Plaza
Pershing Park
11th St.
12th St.
13th St.
14th St.
15th St.
17th St.
18th St.
19th St.
20th St.
21st St.
22nd St.
23rd St.
24th St.
25th St.
H St.
G St.
F St.
E St.
D St.
C St.
New York Ave.
Penn. Ave.
Pennsylvania Ave.
Virginia Ave.
Constitution Ave.
Madison Dr.
Jefferson Dr.
Independence Ave.
Raoul Wallenberg Pl.
W. Basin Dr.
Ohio Dr.
50
66

Above the entrance, he is seen standing before Benjamin Franklin, John Adams, Roger Sherman, and Robert Livingston, members of the committee appointed to write the Declaration of Independence. Engraved on the interior walls are inscriptions from Jefferson's writings that sum up his philosophies on freedom and government. History buffs might note that certain "liberties" were taken with the Declaration of Independence. There are 11 mistakes that can't be blamed on the typing pool. Can your family find them?

Consider renting a pedal boat on the Tidal Basin near the memorial (see p. 212, in chapter 8).

The Capitol, White House, Washington Monument, and Lincoln Memorial are visible from the steps, and it's a front-row seat for the Cherry Blossom Festival. After a visit to the memorial, you'll probably agree that Jefferson finally received the respect that he so richly deserved. For high drama, come at night and sit on the steps. If your kids don't think it's awesome, leave them home next time.

Tidal Basin, south end of 15th St. SW, in West Potomac Park. © **202/426-6821.** www.nps.gov/jeff. Free admission. Daily 8am–midnight. Closed Dec 25. Metro: Smithsonian, (Independence Ave. exit), then a 15-min. walk. Also accessible by car (limited parking), cab, or Tourmobile.

Lincoln Memorial ★★★ **Ages 4 and up.** I had an English professor who said if you weren't moved by the Lincoln Memorial, your heart had probably stopped.

If the only image that you hold of the 16th U.S. president is on a penny, toss it aside and come see this one. The 19-by-19-foot statue of a seated, contemplative Abraham Lincoln was designed by Daniel French. It took 28 blocks of marble and 4 years of carving to complete, and it is the focal point of the classically inspired monument by Henry Bacon.

A gleam in some politician's eye shortly after Lincoln's death in 1865, this Parthenon look-alike was not completed until 1922. The Doric columns number 36, one for each state in the Union at the time of Lincoln's death. The names are inscribed on the frieze over the colonnade. The names of the 48 states at the time of the memorial's dedication appear near the top of the monument, and a plaque for Alaska and Hawaii was added later.

The stirring words of Lincoln's "Gettysburg Address" and "Second Inaugural Address" are carved into the limestone walls, and above them allegorical murals by Jules Guérin represent North–South unity and the freeing of the slaves.

If you can come here at night, when the crowds thin out, I urge you to do so. From the rear of the memorial, gaze across the Potomac to Arlington National Cemetery and the eternal flame at John F. Kennedy's grave. From the steps, take in the reflecting pool, a nighttime mirror of the memorial, and past it to the Washington Monument, Mall, and Capitol. If the sight doesn't grab you, well, my English professor spoke the truth.

As the result of a project conceived by a group of high school students visiting from Scottsdale, Arizona, a visitor center opened in the once-gloomy basement of the memorial in 1994. Most striking in the minimuseum are photographs and film clips of history-making protests and civil-rights events that took place at the site, such as Marian Anderson's Easter 1939 concert after she, as an African-American woman, was barred from singing at DAR Constitution Hall, and Martin Luther King, Jr.'s 1963 "I Have a Dream" speech. Also on display are 13 marble tablets carved with Lincoln quotations and exhibits detailing the memorial's design and construction. The "Lincoln Legacy" is a permanent exhibition, open from 8am to midnight daily.

Before your visit, consider accessing a free interpretive Park Ranger talk via your telephone any time of the day or night. Just dial © **202/747-3420** to hear about Lincoln

A Little Piece of History

The little stone house on the southwest corner of 17th Street and Constitution Avenue was the lock keeper's house for L'Enfant's "Canal Through Tiber Creek" plan. L'Enfant envisioned a canal meandering along Constitution Avenue from the Potomac River in Georgetown, through the Ellipse, and east through the District before dipping south to the Anacostia River. Believe it or not, the canal was built and used until the coming of the railroads made it obsolete in the 1870s. The lock keeper's house is the only remnant still remaining of this piece of D.C. history.

Memorial programs organized around themes such as "The Life of Lincoln" and "The Gettysburg Address."

West of the Mall, at 23rd St. NW, btw. Constitution and Independence aves. NW. ✆ **202/426-6895.** www.nps.gov/linc. Free admission. Daily 24 hr. Park staff on duty 8am–midnight. Metro: Foggy Bottom.

Franklin Delano Roosevelt Memorial ★★★ Ages 6 and up. The newest of the presidential monuments was dedicated in May 1997. The length of three football fields, it lies on the western shore of the Tidal Basin, near the Jefferson Memorial. Entrances are at several points from the pathway along the Tidal Basin. It's about a 10-minute walk from the Smithsonian Metro station, longer from the Foggy Bottom station. The Tourmobile trams also stop here. I hesitate to recommend this, but limited street parking is available in front of the memorial. The parklike setting makes this a good place to bring kids.

Anchored by restrooms at both ends, the FDR monument is marked by imposing granite walls; fountains (the most aesthetically pleasing aspect of the monument, in my opinion); meditative areas; and bunkerlike areas evoking Roosevelt's first inauguration, the Great Depression, World War II, postwar optimism, and FDR's accomplishments.

Of interest to younger children, besides the awesome fountains, is the sculpture of FDR with his beloved dog Fala (here 3 ft. high), loyally depicted next to the president's feet. And it's a great photo op! A 39-ton statue of Eleanor Roosevelt stands at the entrance of Room Four. Mrs. Roosevelt is the first First Lady to be honored in a presidential memorial. Perhaps the most inspiring aspect of this latest stone homage to U.S. presidents is the view across the Tidal Basin to D.C.

An information center and bookshop (spring–summer 9am–6pm, fall–winter 9am–5pm) are located at the main entrance (south end). On display in the information center, among the Roosevelt memorabilia, is a replica of FDR's wheelchair, which he designed. A pamphlet containing the quotes etched in the granite walls of the memorial is a meaningful souvenir.

West Basin Dr., off Ohio Dr. SW (west side of the Tidal Basin). ✆ **202/376-6700.** www.nps.gov/fdrm. Free admission. Daily 8am–midnight. Closed Dec 25. Metro: Smithsonian (Independence Ave. exit).

Washington Monument ★★ Ages 6 and up. If you fly into Reagan National Airport, you will be treated to a supreme view of this monument. Standing 555 feet, 5 inches tall in its stocking feet, the marble-and-granite obelisk is an engineering marvel with walls that taper from 15 feet at the base to 18 inches at the top.

Note to parents with strollers: Park your stroller at the base. Once you see how tight space is at the top, you'll understand why.

Nearly half a century passed from its conception to the actual construction between 1848 and 1884—a story and a half, if you have the time and interest to research it. During the Civil War, the unfinished structure was known as Beef Depot Monument because cattle grazed the grounds before they were slaughtered. Another sidelight: The monument is not positioned exactly according to L'Enfant's plan. It had to be shifted eastward a tad because the original site was too marshy. That's a polite way of saying that D.C. was a varmint- and mosquito-infested swamp.

Designed by Robert Mills, architect of the Treasury and Old Patent Office buildings, the monument is two-tone, but not by original design. Notice how the stones darken about 150 feet from the base. During the construction of the monument, the Civil War as well as other matters put the building process on hold. When the government resumed the project in the 1870s, the "new" marble, mined from another part of the quarry, was darker. If you've ever tried to match paint, you'll understand the problem.

Heads up: At the top you may, as I do, experience a slight headache, sinus pressure, fullness in your ears, or other disquieting altitude-related symptoms. Rest assured, they'll disappear when you're back at sea level. The view is worth any minor discomfort.

Come on a weekday, if at all possible. Everyone 2 and older must have a free timed ticket. You can take a chance (a big chance) and pick up passes from the kiosk at 15th Street and Jefferson Drive, beginning at 8:30am and ending when they are gone (***Note:*** Lines form as early as 7:30am), or order ahead from the U.S. Park Service (✆ **800/967-2283,** 10am–10pm; http://reservations.nps.gov). There is a $1.50 per ticket fee. Visitors were once allowed to climb the 897 steps. Now you'll have to take the elevator—faster than in most apartment buildings—and you'll be at the top in a little over a minute. (There's a "Down The Steps Tour" for the hale and very hardy. It takes about an hour. Write and tell me about it.) The view is spectacular, especially after dark. For a singular Washington moment, watch the sun set behind the monument from the 14th Street (west) side of the Museum of American History.

The monument grounds are often the site of concerts and other special events in summer.

With the exception of water in a clear bottle, no food or beverages may be brought into the monument.

15th St. and Constitution Ave. NW. ✆ **202/426-6841.** www.nps.gov/wamo. Free admission. Daily 9am–4:45pm. Closed July 4th and Dec 25. Metro: Smithsonian.

WAR MEMORIALS

Arlington National Cemetery ★★ Moments **Ages 6 and up.** More than 216,000 American war dead are buried in the 612 acres of hallowed hills overlooking the nation's capital from the Virginia side of the Potomac River. Try to include this in your itinerary, especially if you have school-age children in tow—there is much to feed the mind and the spirit.

I urge you to stop first at the Visitor Center (at the cemetery entrance) for maps, exhibits, a bookstore, and restrooms. If anyone in your party requires a stroller or a wheelchair, it is strictly BYO. This cemetery is huge, so you may want to visit via **Tourmobile** tour buses (www.tourmobile.com), especially with younger children. Four million visitors enter Arlington National Cemetery annually to watch specially trained members of the 3rd Infantry Regiment from the adjacent Fort Myer guard stand sentinel day and night over the simple but inspiring white marble **Tomb of the Unknowns.** Four unidentified bodies from this century's four wars are interred here. The soldiers who stand guard are part of the nation's oldest military unit, known as the Old Guard; it dates

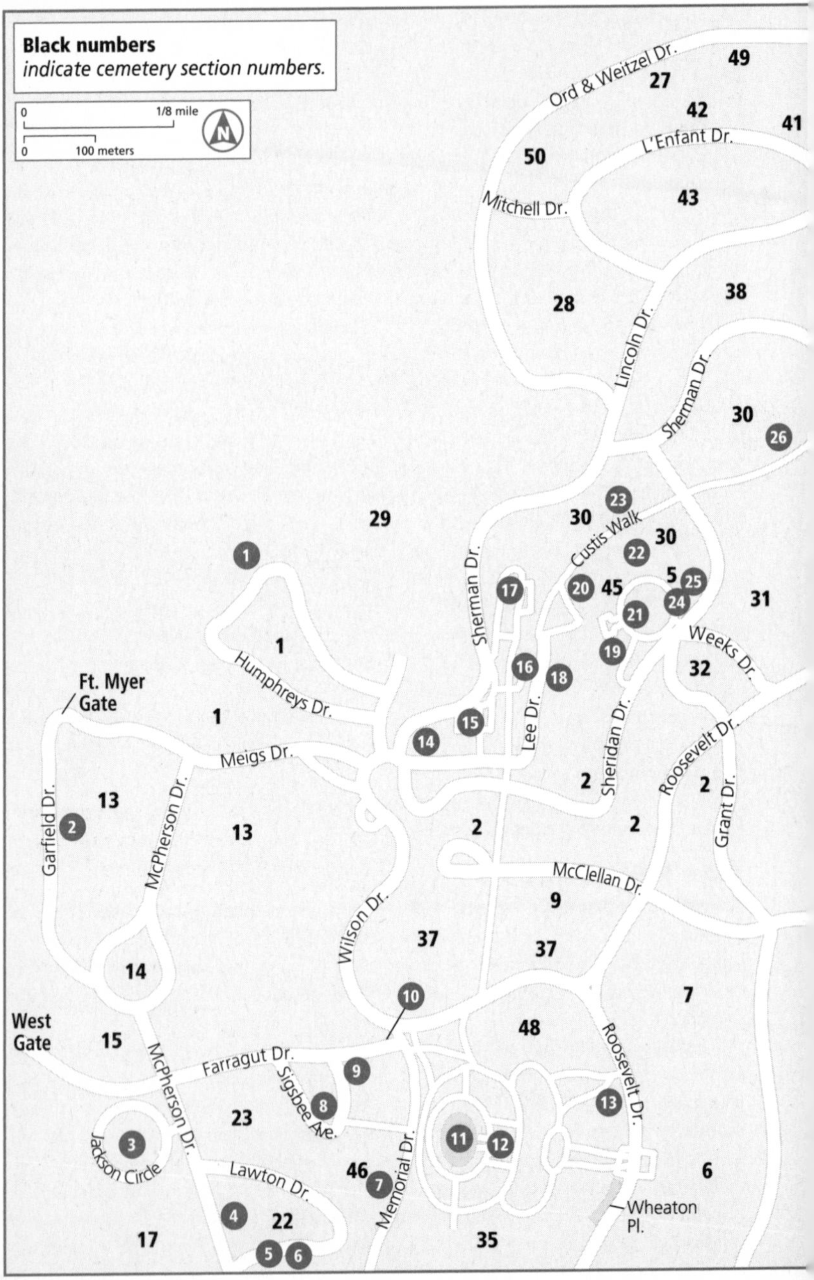
Black numbers
indicate cemetery section numbers.
0 1/8 mile
0 100 meters
N
Ord & Weitzel Dr.
49
27
42
41
L'Enfant Dr.
50
Mitchell Dr.
43
38
28
Lincoln Dr.
Sherman Dr.
30
26
23
29
30
Custis Walk
30
22
1
5
25
Sherman Dr.
17
20
45
24
31
21
Weeks Dr.
1
19
32
Humphreys Dr.
16
18
Ft. Myer Gate
1
15
Lee Dr.
Sheridan Dr.
Roosevelt Dr.
14
Meigs Dr.
2
2
13
Garfield Dr.
2
McPherson Dr.
13
2
2
Grant Dr.
McClellan Dr.
9
Wilson Dr.
37
37
14
10
7
West Gate
15
48
McPherson Dr.
Farragut Dr.
9
Sigsbee Ave.
8
13
Roosevelt Dr.
23
3
Jackson Circle
11
12
Memorial Dr.
Lawton Dr.
46
7
6
Wheaton Pl.
4
22
17
35
5
6

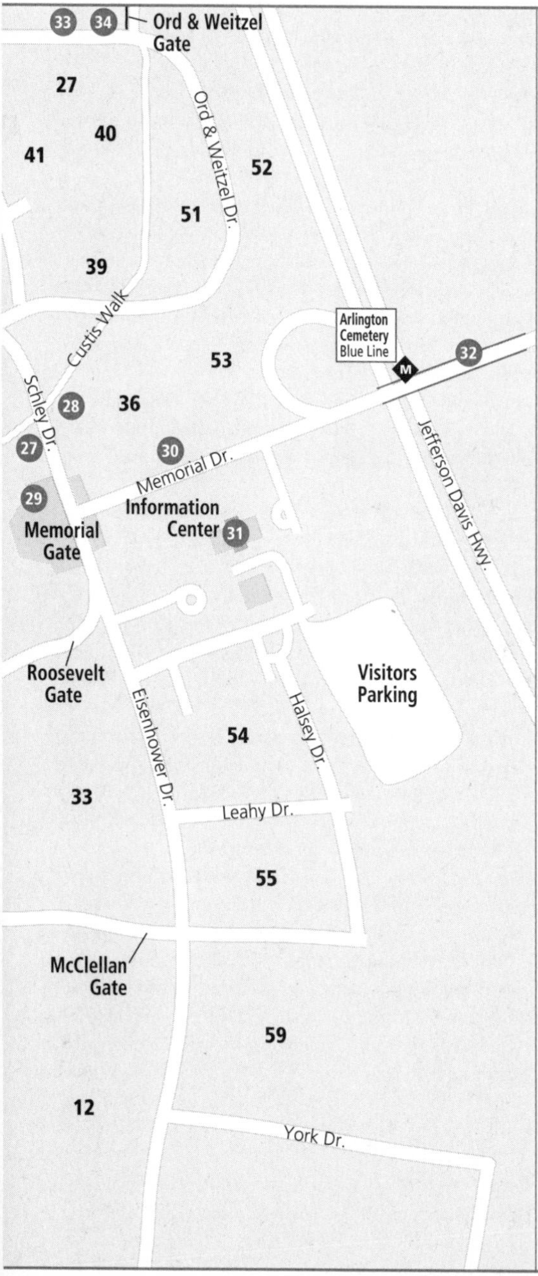

Arlington House **16**
Arlington Memorial Bridge **32**
Bradley (Gen. Omar Nelson) grave **27**
Byrd (Rear Adm. Richard, Jr.) statue **30**
Challenger Memorial **10**
Confederate Section/ Confederate Monument **3**
Douglas (Supreme Court Justice William O.) grave **22**
Dulles (Sec. of State) John Foster) grave **6**
Evers (Medgar) grave **28**
Holmes (Supreme Court Justice Oliver Wendell) grave **23**
Information Center **31**
Iwo Jima statue **34**
Kennedy (Pres. John F. and Jacqueline Kennedy Onassis) grave **21**
Kennedy (Sen. Robert F. and Sen Edward M.) grave **19**
Lee (Robert E.) Museum **17**
L'Enfant (Pierre Charles) grave **18**
Louis (Joe) grave **13**
Marshall (Supreme Court Justice Thurgood) grave **25**
Memorial Amphitheater **11**
Murphy (Audie) grave **7**
Netherlands Carillon **33**
Old Amphitheater **14**
Paderewski (Ignace Jan) marker **9**
Parks (James) grave **2**
Randolph (Mary) grave **20**
Rickover (Adm. Hyman G.) grave **24**
Rough Riders Monument **4**
Taft (Pres. William Howard) grave **26**
Tomb of the Unknown Civil War Dead **15**
Tomb of the Unknowns **12**
USS *Maine* mast **8**
Wainwright (Gen. Jonathan) grave **1**
Warren (Supreme Court Justice Earl) grave **5**
Women in Military Service For America Memorial **29**

from Colonial times. If you're close enough, you might notice that the soldiers' white gloves are wet. Before standing guard, they soak their gloves to better grip the wood handle of the bayonet-tipped M-14. The changing of the guard takes place every half-hour from April through September and every hour on the hour from October through March.

The **Memorial Amphitheater** is the setting for Memorial Day and Veterans' Day services. Junior historians interested in the Spanish–American War will want to see the mast from the USS *Maine* ("Remember the Maine") on the other side of Memorial Drive.

The imposing Greek Revival building at the top of the hill, **Arlington House,** once belonged to Gen. Robert E. Lee and Mary Randolph Curtis, who just happened to be Martha Washington's great-granddaughter. Lee was married here and lived in the neoclassical mansion until 1861 when he resigned from the U.S. Army to command the Northern Virginia Rebel Army. Four weeks later, the house was seized by Union troops. When the Union Army was looking for a burial site for its soldiers, Gen. Montgomery Meigs suggested that the war dead be buried "in Lee's backyard."

The government ultimately bought the property, and since 1933 the National Park Service has been cutting the grass and taking care of the furnishings. Check out the servants' quarters during the free self-guided tour (9:30am–4:30pm Oct–Mar; until 6pm Apr–Sept).

The marble, slate, and Cape Cod fieldstone gravesites of **John F. Kennedy,** 35th U.S. president, his wife, Jacqueline Kennedy Onassis, and two of their infant children lie off Sheridan Drive on the sloping lawn below Arlington House. At night, the Eternal Flame can be seen from the Rooftop Terrace of the Kennedy Center and several other D.C. vantage points. Sen. Robert Kennedy's and Sen. Edward M. (Teddy) Kennedy's graves lie close by, marked by simple white crosses. The site is best visited early in the morning before the masses arrive. JFK and William Howard Taft are the only U.S. presidents buried in Arlington.

Pierre L'Enfant was moved from a pauper's grave to his final resting place, near Arlington House, when it finally dawned on those in power that, despite his supposedly cantankerous disposition, L'Enfant did a bang-up job designing the capital city. Many newcomers (and old-timers, too) have trouble finding their way around D.C. and think that L'Enfant should have been left undisturbed in his original burial site.

The **Women in Military Service for America Memorial** (www.womensmemorial.org) honors the 1.8 million American women who have served in the military, from the American Revolution to the present. The memorial, dedicated October 18, 1997, incorporates the spruced-up neoclassical granite retaining/entrance wall designed in the 1920s by McKim, Mead & White. Carved from the hillside behind the semicircular wall are the computer registry, where visitors can access the personal recollections and photographs of over 250,000 U.S. servicewomen, a Hall of Honor, a theater, a conference center, 14 exhibit alcoves, and a gift shop. Kudos to retired Air Force Brig. Gen. Wilma L. Vaught, who oversaw the project for more than a decade, and on-site project manager Margaret Van Voast. The memorial is a fitting and long-overdue answer to "What did you do in the war, Mom?"

The **Marine Corps War Memorial** (www.nps.gov/gwmp/usmc.htm) and the statue of the Marines raising the flag over **Iwo Jima** are near the Ord-Weitzel Gate at the north end of the cemetery. The U.S. Marine Drum and Bugle Corps and Silent Drill team perform at the Iwo Jima Memorial on Tuesday evenings at 7pm early June to mid-August. Bring something to sit on. Free shuttle buses whisk visitors from the visitor center to the parade site (✆ **703/289-2500**). Nearby is the 49-bell **Netherlands Carillon** (✆ **703/289-2500**). You can climb the tower (kids under 12 must be with an adult) or tiptoe through 15,000 blooming tulips in the spring. Enjoy a concert by guest carillonneurs, usually on Saturday and holidays during April, May, and September from 2 to 4pm. In years past, the concerts were held on Saturday, from 6:30 to 8:30pm, June through August. Just north of Arlington Cemetery, at **Fort Myer,** visit the caisson platoon stables of the Old Guard, which counted George Washington as one of its members. The horses, used in processions and presidential funerals, can usually be viewed Monday through Friday from noon to 4pm. Drive here or take a taxi from the Arlington Cemetery Metro or visitor center. Nearby, the **Old Guard Museum** (www.mdw.army.mil/oldguard) contains displays dating from the Revolutionary War era. The museum is open Monday through Saturday from 9am to 4pm and Sunday from 1 to 4pm.

Arlington, VA (west side of Memorial Bridge). ✆ **703/607-8000.** www.arlingtoncemetery.org. Free admission. Apr–Sept daily 8am–7pm; until 5pm the rest of year. Metro: Arlington Cemetery. You can also walk across Arlington Memorial Bridge (from near the Lincoln Memorial), or board a Tourmobile downtown or at the cemetery's visitor center.

Korean War Veterans Memorial ★ **Ages 2 and up.** After years of squabbling and disagreement over its design, the Korean War Veterans Memorial was unveiled in July 1995. Since then, it has been hailed as a tour de force. On a 4-acre parcel southeast of the Lincoln Memorial and across from the Vietnam War Veterans Memorial (with your back to Lincoln, it is to the right of the Reflecting Pool), the stainless-steel statues of 19 poncho-draped soldiers on the march make a powerful statement, drawing the viewer into the action. In the background is a black granite mural wall with the etched faces of support troops. The faces were culled from actual photos of Korean War veterans.

Southeast of Lincoln Memorial, French Dr., and Independence Ave. ✆ **202/426-6841.** www.nps.gov/kowa. Free admission. Daily 24 hr. Park staff on duty 8am–7:30pm (summer extended hours). Metro: Smithsonian (Independence Ave. exit); or Foggy Bottom, and then walk.

Vietnam Veterans Memorial ★★ Moments **Ages 10 and up.** The Wall, 140 panels of polished black granite stretching almost 500 feet, honors the nearly 60,000 men and women who died or remain missing as a result of the Vietnam War. Names are listed chronologically, from the first casualty in 1959 to the last in 1975. Although many leave the site misty-eyed, children too young to know anything of the Vietnam War will probably be bored. Vietnam veteran Jan Scruggs initiated the project in 1979, and since its opening on November 13, 1982, the memorial has been one of the most-visited sites in Washington. Nearby is the Vietnam Women's Memorial, a bronze sculpture of three women and a wounded soldier, which was dedicated in November 1993.

Northeast of the Lincoln Memorial, near 21st St. and Constitution Ave. NW. ✆ **202/426-6841.** www.nps.gov/vive. Free admission. Daily 24 hr., with rangers on duty 8am–7:30pm (summer extended hours). Metro: Foggy Bottom (walk east on H or I sts., turn right at 21st St., and walk for 6 or 7 blocks).

World War II Memorial **Ages 10 and up.** A 7½-acre parklike setting with fountains and a rainbow pool at the east end of the Reflecting Pool (btw. the Washington Monument and Lincoln Memorial) honors the 16 million who served in the American armed forces during WWII, those who gave their lives, and those at home who supported the war effort. The granite and bronze bases of the memorial plaza are inscribed with the seals of the armed services. Highlights of the war years are depicted in 24 bas-relief panels. Two pavilions mark the north and south ends of the plaza, which visitors can access via ramps. Granite benches hug the curvilinear walls—a good place to reflect, and also to rest your weary dogs and let the kids romp. The 56 granite pillars, representing each state, territory, and the District of Columbia at the time of the war, are arranged according to the year each entered the Union. Sculpted into the Freedom Wall at the western side of the memorial are 4,000 gold stars. They symbolize the 400,000 American soldiers who died during the war. That's a lot of casualties. The memorial is pleasing enough, but also a reminder that we have learned little about the idiocy of war in the intervening years.

17th St. NW (btw. Washington Monument and Reflecting Pool). © **202/426-6841.** www.nps.gov/nwwm. Free admission. Daily 24 hr., with rangers on duty 8am–7:30pm (summer extended hours). Metro: Foggy Bottom or Smithsonian; then a 15-min. walk.

NATIONAL CATHEDRAL

Washington National Cathedral Moments **Ages 4 and up.** Because the cathedral (officially named the Cathedral Church of St. Peter and St. Paul) is one of the few sights in Washington not close to a Metro station, I suggest taking a taxi, a Metrobus, or the Old Town Trolley. The sixth-largest religious structure in the world turned 100 in 2007. Did you remember to send a card? It perches on a parcel known as "the close," on Mount St. Alban, and is visible from several vantage points inside and outside the city. The top of the tower is 676 feet above sea level—that's mighty high, given Washington's zero elevation. Construction began in 1907 on the Gothic-inspired cathedral, but not until 1990, with the completion of the twin west towers, was the cathedral officially consecrated. Pick up an illustrated guide in the Cathedral Museum Store detailing the history and architecture before exploring on your own, or take the 30-minute guided tour weekdays between 10 and 11:30am and 1 to 4pm; Saturday from 10 to 11:30am and 12:45 to 3:30pm, and Sunday between 1 to 2:30pm (© **202/537-6207**). Tours begin every 15 to 20 minutes. No tours are given Thanksgiving, Christmas, and Easter.

The **Space Window,** 1 of more than 200 stained-glass windows in the cathedral, is dedicated to the Apollo 11 mission. Can your kids pick out the moon rock? Viewing the **Rose Window** in the North Transept at dusk is a religious experience in itself. The vaulted ceiling above the 518-foot-long nave is 102 feet. But everything is kid size in the charming **Children's Chapel,** with its tiny chairs and pint-size pipe organ, scaled for a 6-year-old.

The **Pilgrim Observation Gallery** has a fantastic view of Washington beyond the flying buttresses and gargoyles. The gallery is open Monday through Saturday from 10am to 4pm and Sunday from noon to 4pm.

Let your youngsters loose to run around, or meander with them, through nearly 60 magnificent acres of beautifully landscaped prime real estate. Enjoy a family picnic, perhaps, and then stop in at the **Bishop's Garden** (open daily during daylight hours) south of the cathedral. It's modeled on a medieval walled garden. Dried herbs, teas, gifts, and books are sold in the **Herb Cottage.** At the **Greenhouse,** on South Road, you can purchase growing herbs and plants. The Museum Shop, Herb Cottage, and Greenhouse are open daily, except December 25 and January 1, from 9:30am to 5pm (© **202/537-6267**).

The **Flower Mart,** held the first Friday (10am–6pm) and Saturday (10am–5pm) in May, features plants and garden items along with rides, puppet shows, and other activities for kids. More than 50 vendors sell food items, jewelry, and crafts. Free shuttles run from the Tenleytown Metro both days (© **202/537-3185**). **Family Saturdays** (kids 4–8) are workshops that include a tour of the cathedral and an art project; these are held once a month from 10 to 11:30am and noon to 1:30pm. The cost is $6 per child (with an adult). Call © **202/537-02184** for reservations. In the **Gargoyle's Den** (for kids 6–12) most Saturdays between 10am and 2pm, docents help kids get a taste of cathedral arts through arts-and-crafts projects (create a gargoyle or carve a stone). The cost is $5 per group of up to four people, $1 for each additional person. For more information, call ✆ **202/537-6200;** school groups ✆ **202/537-2934.**

Listen to a short talk about the **Great Organ** and hear a minirecital most Mondays and Wednesdays at 12:30pm. Hear the **Cathedral Choir Evensong** weekdays at 5:30pm during the school year. Demonstrations of the cathedral's 10,650-pipe organ are held on Wednesdays at 12:30pm, and anyone can attend. The cathedral also hosts special concerts throughout the year. For information on Tour and Tea at the cathedral, see p. 105. At the cathedral's annual open house in September, visitors can tour the bell tower. Special **Behind the Scenes tours** are suitable for kids 11 and older and involve lots of stair-climbing. To arrange, call ✆ **202/537-6200** or write specialtours@cathedral.org.

Massachusetts and Wisconsin aves. NW. ✆ **202/537-6200.** www.cathedral.org. Suggested donations $15 per family; free admission when attending a service. Mon–Fri 10am–5:30pm; Sat 10am–4:30pm; Sun 8am–6:30pm; some extended summer hours. Metro: Tenleytown and then no. 32, 34, or 36 bus south on Wisconsin Ave. Bus: N-2, -3, -4 up Massachusetts Ave. from Dupont Circle, or take Old Town Trolley.

3 THE WHITE HOUSE & BRANCHES OF THE GOVERNMENT

Some of the sites listed below have suspended or limited their tours since the terrorist attacks of September 11, 2001, and the war with Iraq, and tour details are subject to change based on security concerns. To avoid disappointment, please call any of the federal buildings you'd like to visit before you go.

The White House ★★ **Ages 10 and up.** Self-guided tours are open to individuals (and groups) Tuesday through Thursday 7:30am to 11am, Friday 7:30am to noon, and 7:30am to 1pm Saturday (except federal holidays). Visitors must make reservations through their congressional representatives (you can look them up at www.senate.gov and www.house.gov). You must submit your name, date of birth, and Social Security number to your U.S. representative or senator, who will submit all names for security screening. Allow several weeks at least. You may make your request up to 6 months in advance. Assuming you pass muster and get your tickets, before your tour, stop first at the **White House Visitor Center,** 15th and E streets, to peruse the exhibits to enhance your visit. A White House spokesperson says that the tour is appropriate for kids 12 and over. (I think that mature 9- and 10- year-olds will get something out of it, too.) For the trivia buffs among you, the White House has no front door or back door—just a north front and a south front.

Fun Facts Birthday Greetings from the President

If a family member is celebrating an 80th (or higher) birthday, and you'd like the president to send the celebrant a greeting card, send a written request—at least 6 weeks in advance—with Gram's or Gramp's birthday and address to Greeting Office, The White House, Washington, DC 20500.

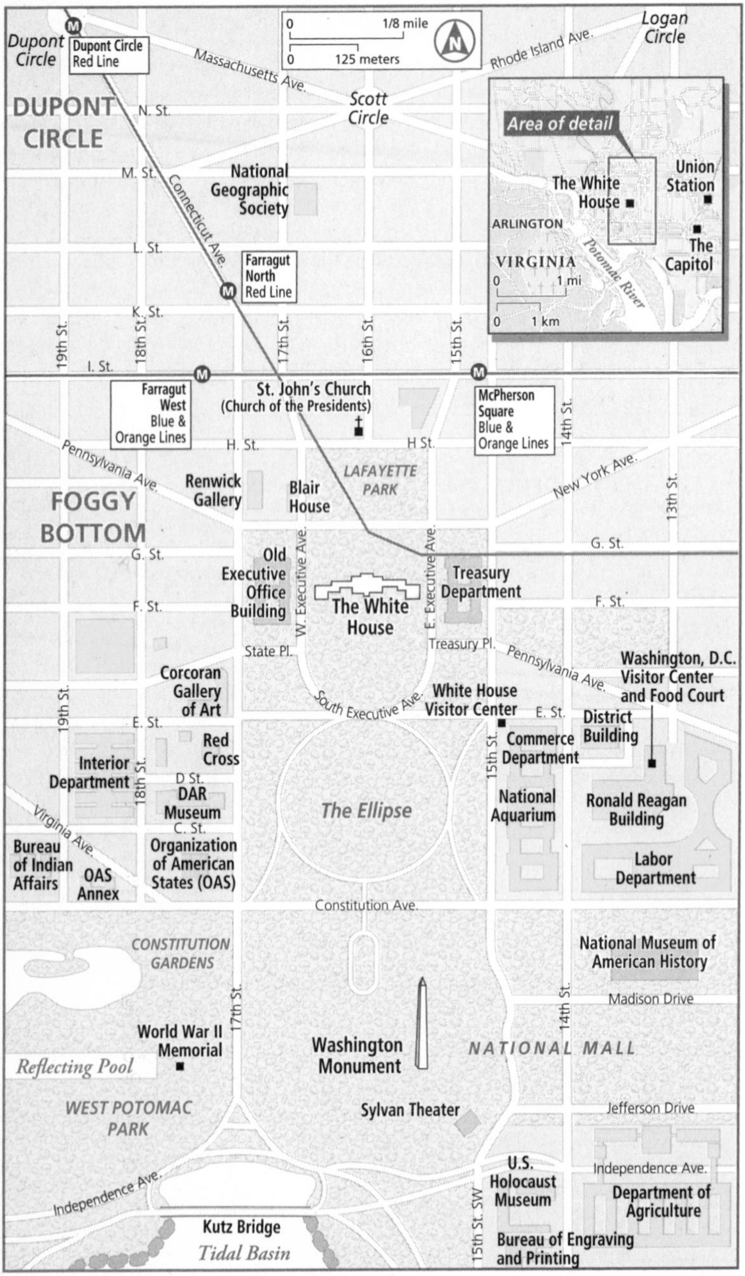
Dupont Circle
Dupont Circle Red Line
DUPONT CIRCLE
Massachusetts Ave.
Scott Circle
Rhode Island Ave.
Logan Circle
0 1/8 mile
0 125 meters
N. St.
M. St.
L. St.
K. St.
I. St.
Connecticut Ave.
National Geographic Society
Farragut North Red Line
Area of detail
The White House
Union Station
ARLINGTON
VIRGINIA
Potomac River
The Capitol
0 1 mi
0 1 km
19th St.
18th St.
17th St.
16th St.
15th St.
14th St.
13th St.
Farragut West Blue & Orange Lines
St. John's Church (Church of the Presidents)
McPherson Square Blue & Orange Lines
H. St.
H St.
Pennsylvania Ave.
Renwick Gallery
Blair House
LAFAYETTE PARK
New York Ave.
FOGGY BOTTOM
G. St.
Old Executive Office Building
W. Executive Ave.
The White House
E. Executive Ave.
Treasury Department
F. St.
State Pl.
Treasury Pl.
Corcoran Gallery of Art
South Executive Ave.
White House Visitor Center
Washington, D.C. Visitor Center and Food Court
E. St.
District Building
Red Cross
Interior Department
D St.
DAR Museum
C. St.
Commerce Department
National Aquarium
The Ellipse
Ronald Reagan Building
Virginia Ave.
Bureau of Indian Affairs
OAS Annex
Organization of American States (OAS)
Labor Department
Constitution Ave.
CONSTITUTION GARDENS
National Museum of American History
Madison Drive
World War II Memorial
Washington Monument
NATIONAL MALL
Reflecting Pool
WEST POTOMAC PARK
Sylvan Theater
Jefferson Drive
U.S. Holocaust Museum
Independence Ave.
Department of Agriculture
15th St. SW
Kutz Bridge
Tidal Basin
Bureau of Engraving and Printing

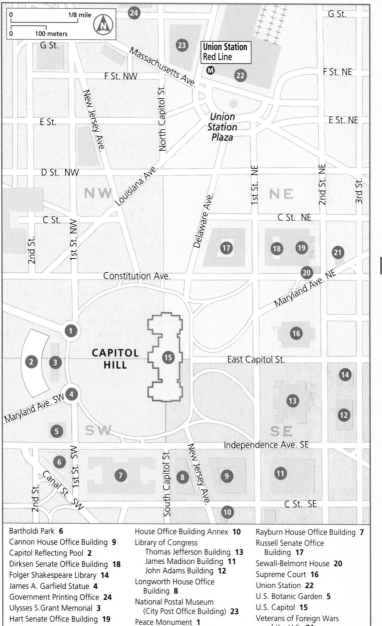

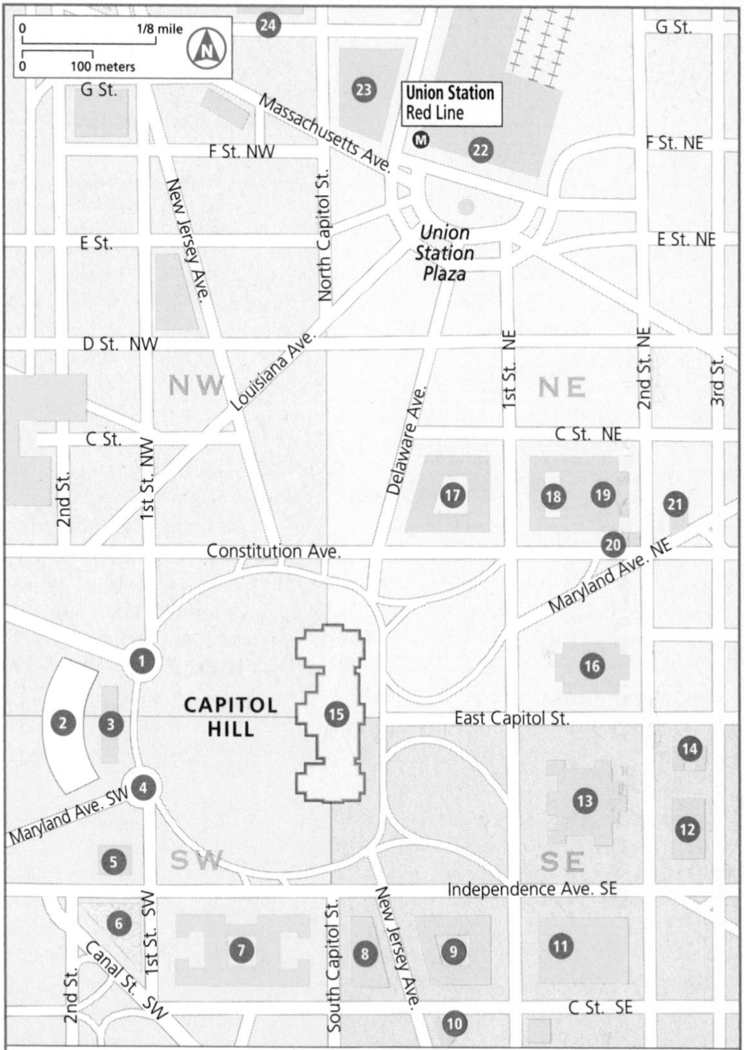

Bartholdi Park **6**
Cannon House Office Building **9**
Capitol Reflecting Pool **2**
Dirksen Senate Office Building **18**
Folger Shakespeare Library **14**
James A. Garfield Statue **4**
Government Printing Office **24**
Ulysses S.Grant Memorial **3**
Hart Senate Office Building **19**
House Office Building Annex **10**
Library of Congress
  Thomas Jefferson Building **13**
  James Madison Building **11**
  John Adams Building **12**
Longworth House Office Building **8**
National Postal Museum (City Post Office Building) **23**
Peace Monument **1**
Rayburn House Office Building **7**
Russell Senate Office Building **17**
Sewall-Belmont House **20**
Supreme Court **16**
Union Station **22**
U.S. Botanic Garden **5**
U.S. Capitol **15**
Veterans of Foreign Wars of the U.S. **21**

Fun Facts Heads Up

The rotunda's cast-iron dome (which replaced the original one of copper and wood) was begun in 1855 and finished in 1863 during Lincoln's presidency. It has a diameter of nearly 100 feet and weighs 9 million pounds. Don't get nervous: You're safe standing on the rotunda floor, 180 feet beneath it, as more than 5,000 tons of ironwork provide the girding.

Like Aaron Neville, I "tell it like it is." The 20- to 35-minute self-guided tour closely resembles a cattle roundup and takes in the ground and main public floors, including the East, Green, Blue, and Red rooms; the State Dining Room; Cross Hall; North Entrance Hall; and the Oval Room, where Franklin Roosevelt gave his fireside chats. On display, besides presidential portraits and memorabilia, are period furnishings (for the most part reflecting the Greek Revival and Victorian styles), portraits of the First Ladies, and exhibits on the day-to-day operation of the White House and its role as a national symbol.

Young children enjoy the annual Easter egg roll and the spring and fall garden tours (see "Calendar of Kids' Favorite Events" in chapter 2 for details). My granddaughter attended in 2009 and was within shouting distance of the First Lady and First Daughters. She's still talking about it. On the west side of the South Lawn lies the Children's Garden, with bronze imprints of the hands and feet of White House children and grandchildren. ***A word of caution:*** Waits of more than 2 hours in line for the Easter egg roll are not unusual. My advice: Take plenty of snacks. Call or check the website for the latest info about tickets and security. The past few years, tickets for the egg roll were given out the weekend before the (Mon) event. Check the White House website for updates; trying to reach the house by phone is next to impossible.

1600 Pennsylvania Ave. NW (visitor entrance at East Gate on E. Executive Ave.). ✆ **800/717-1450** or 202/456-7041. www.whitehouse.gov. Free admission. Closed during presidential functions. Metro: McPherson Sq., Farragut North, or Farragut West.

U.S. Capitol ★★★ **Ages 6 and up.** Even if your home is outside the United States, the Capitol will give you a sense, more than any other federal building, of what this country is all about. As you face the Capitol's East Front, the Senate side is north (right), and the House side is south (left). Flags fly over the respective sides when either is in session, and night sessions are indicated by a light burning in the dome. Presidential inaugurations have taken place here since 1801. The Rotunda is the site of state funerals for U.S. presidents (beginning with Abraham Lincoln) and heroes, military and otherwise. (In Oct 2005, Rosa Parks became the first woman, second African American, and 1 of only 30 private citizens to lie in state in the Rotunda. Parks spearheaded the civil rights movement when, in Montgomery, Alabama, in 1955, she refused to give up her bus seat to a white man.) The House Chamber is where the president delivers the State of the Union message every January. Information on committee meetings is published weekdays in the *Washington Post's* "Today in Congress" column. Call ahead if you're interested in a specific bill.

Note: Tickets are required to enter the Capitol (no exceptions!), and they may be booked in advance online (http://tours.visitthecapitol.gov) or through your representative or senators. Tickets are free and allow you to visit 8:30am to 4:30pm, Monday

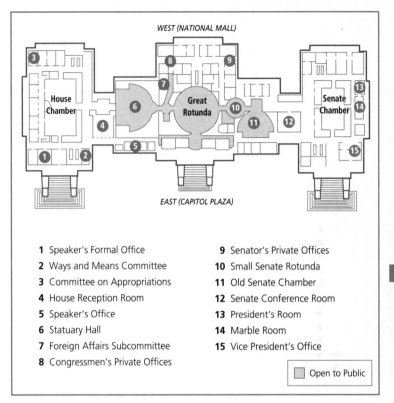

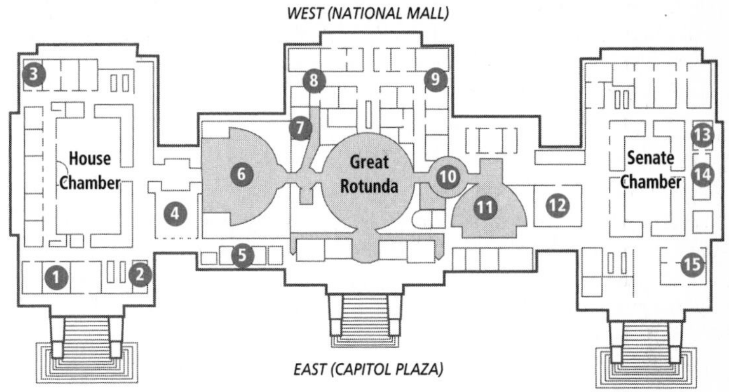

1 Speaker's Formal Office
2 Ways and Means Committee
3 Committee on Appropriations
4 House Reception Room
5 Speaker's Office
6 Statuary Hall
7 Foreign Affairs Subcommittee
8 Congressmen's Private Offices
9 Senator's Private Offices
10 Small Senate Rotunda
11 Old Senate Chamber
12 Senate Conference Room
13 President's Room
14 Marble Room
15 Vice President's Office

Open to Public

through Saturday. A *limited* number of same-day passes are available at the kiosks—two each on the East and West fronts of the Capitol. My feeling—why travel here and risk being turned away?

Because of heightened security, you will be refused admission if you have any of the following along: aerosol or nonaerosol sprays; cans, bottles, or liquids; oversized suitcases, duffle bags, or backpacks larger than 14 inches wide by 13 inches high and 4 inches deep; knives, razors, or box cutters; Mace or pepper spray; or firearms and explosives (just in case you were wondering). Strollers, cameras, and video recorders are okay. A coat-check room is available only if you have tickets for the Senate or House galleries. For up-to-date information, call ✆ **202/225-6827.**

The short but sweet half-hour tour departs every few minutes from the Rotunda every day but Sunday. ***A word to the wise***: Guides say that during peak times (Sat, around major holidays, and Mar–Sept) it is best to visit from noon to 1pm. The guides are so well scrubbed, so smooth, and so knowledgeable that they must be running for office. Encourage older kids to ask questions during the tour and then allow time for wandering around and attending a hearing or committee meeting, usually held in the morning or other times when Congress is not in session. If you have toddlers, quit after the introductory tour.

The guides do a marvelous job describing the history of **Statuary Hall,** where the House met from 1807 to 1857. Here you'll find statues of U.S. presidents, important state figures, statesmen, legislators, Supreme Court justices, and inventors. Note the bronze plaque on the floor where John Quincy Adams collapsed on February 21, 1848. He died in an adjoining room soon thereafter. Due to an acoustical anomaly, whispers can be heard across the room. Usually, the guide will demonstrate this phenomenon, to your kids' delight. If the guide forgets, ask. It's the kind of experience that sticks in a child's memory forever.

To the right of the entrance of Statuary Hall is a painting depicting the signing of the Declaration of Independence. That's Thomas Jefferson stepping on John Adams's foot—no love lost there, according to historians.

Constantino Brumidi's allegorical fresco the ***Apotheosis of Washington*** lines the very top of the dome and depicts Washington accompanied by Liberty, Victory, and Fame. The 13 figures crowned with stars represent the 13 original states. If your neck stiffens looking up at the masterpiece, pity poor Brumidi, who spent 11 months on his back to complete the painting. More than 25 years of Brumidi's handiwork is also evidenced elsewhere in the Capitol—in the frieze encircling the rotunda, the Senate reception room, the President's Room, and the first-floor Senate corridors.

The Crypt was originally intended as Washington's final resting place, but his relatives insisted on Mount Vernon. (You know how family can be.) So instead of Washington, the Crypt holds changing exhibits that describe the history and construction of the Capitol.

If you visit the **House Gallery,** the Democrats will be seated to the right of the presiding officer and Republicans to the left. Senators have assigned seats, according to seniority, but representatives do not, and a system of bells informs those who are not in attendance of what is going on. Wouldn't the kids love this when they're absent from school?

The Supreme Court met in the **Old Supreme Court Chamber** from 1800 to 1860. Thomas Jefferson was sworn in as president here in 1801, and in 1844, Samuel F. B. Morse sent the first telegraph message ("What hath God wrought?") to Baltimore from here.

If you visit the handsome **Old Senate Chamber,** built between 1793 and 1800 and in use until 1859, note the mahogany desks with inkwells and sand shakers for blotting the ink, and the handsome red carpet with gold stars. No wonder this was considered the hottest show in town for many years. When crowds overflowed the galleries, it is said that some senators politely gave their seats to ladies. In the new Senate Chamber, they now lose their seats to ladies—14 women members as of 2003.

Led by Sen. Jefferson Davis (later president of the Confederacy), Congress appropriated $100,000 in 1850 for building a Capitol extension to include new House and Senate wings. The Senate moved into its new quarters on January 4, 1859. The House convened for the first time in the new south building on December 16, 1857. Originally, the House met in what is now Statuary Hall.

Before you leave here, stroll around to the West Front for an unbroken view of the Mall, the Washington Monument, and the Lincoln Memorial.

After years of haggling, planning, stops and stalls, and escalating costs, the **Capitol Visitor Center** opened in a new three-level, underground addition (or should we call it a subtraction?) on Dec. 2, 2008. A Great Hall, an orientation theater, a 600-seat dining room, a gift shop, and skylights for viewing the dome are part of the project. And visitors can watch live video of the House and Senate floors. Included in the new center is a

Did You Know?

- The Capitol cornerstone, misplaced during work on the East Front in the 1950s, is still missing.
- Several years ago, a women's restroom was created closer to the Senate side of the Capitol to accommodate the growing number of women in the Senate. It has two stalls, two sinks, and no glass ceiling.
- Up to 10,000 visitors a day come to the Capitol.
- The 20-foot statue *Freedom,* perched atop the dome since 1863, was supposed to be nude. You can imagine what a furor that caused in the mid-1800s, so sculptor Thomas Crawford draped the figure in a flowing robe. Despite the feathers flowing from the eagle-topped helmet, *Freedom* is not a Native American. All 7 tons of her were lowered from the dome by helicopter on May 9, 1993, for cleaning and restoration, which took several months. (You have to admit, 130 years is a long time to go without a bath.)

fancy, 2-story hearing room on the House side; on the Senate side are small hearing rooms and an oversize TV-radio studio (with makeup facilities!) so senators can communicate more easily and photogenically with their constituents. The price for your representatives' add-ons? A mere $85 million. (Ever feel like screaming?) Welcome to Washington! (Wonder if less-than-scrupulous lawmakers will be humbled into cleaning up their acts?) Visitors will enter from the East Front plaza.

Morning VIP tours, appropriate for kids 10 and up, include admission to the House and Senate galleries. Usually, the House and Senate convene from noon until late afternoon, but exceptions are almost a rule.

Last-minute passes may be available if you stop at your senator's or representative's office. Call if you don't know the location (✆ **202/224-3121**). Passes are usually given to noncitizens who show their passports to the appointment desk on the Senate side, first floor, or the Doorkeeper of the House. In the summer or any other time when Congress is not in session, visitors can enter the Senate and House galleries without a special pass. Groups of more than 15 can schedule a tour up to 6 months in advance (✆ **202/224-4910**). Remember to call in advance to find out whether the building is open to visitors and what restrictions are in place.

East end of the Mall (entrance on E. Capitol St. and 1st St. NE). ✆ **202/225-6827.** www.visitthecapitol.gov. Free admission. Mon–Sat 8:30am–4:30pm; ask about extended summer hours. (Call ahead or check website, because extended hours change from year to year.) Tours every 15–20 min., Mon–Sat 8:30am–4:30pm. No tours Sun. Closed Thanksgiving, Dec 25. Metro: Capitol South or Union Station.

Federal Bureau of Investigation (FBI) building ★★ **Ages 8 and up.** ***Note:*** At press time, the FBI building was closed for extensive renovations. It was first scheduled to reopen in spring/summer 2007. This being Washington, 2007, 2008, and 2009 came and went, and no date has been set for the reopening. And nobody's talking at FBI Headquarters. (Can you imagine a company in the private sector getting away with such vague nonsense—and staying in business? What are they doing in there? I'm not sure I want to know.) Save yourself time and possible disappointment and call first.

Break Time

The **South Buffet Room** in the Dirksen Senate Office Building (1st St. NE, btw. Constitution Ave. and C St. NE) is a convenient refueling spot when exploring Capitol Hill (✆ **202/224-7196**). Getting here is half the fun if you first get permission from your senator or congressional representative to take the free subway that runs under the Capitol to this all-you-can-eat buffet. A carvery station features ham, roast beef, or turkey, and several steamer trays have additional hot main courses. Side dishes, a full salad and fruit bar, a wide choice of desserts, and (nonalcoholic) beverages are also included in the price of admission. Finish the feast at the make-your-own sundae bar. The lunch buffet costs $16 for adults and $11 for children under 10. Reservations are taken for groups of six or more. American Express, Discover, MasterCard, and Visa are accepted. It's open Monday through Friday from 11:30am to 2:30pm. High chairs and boosters are available.

J. Edgar Hoover FBI Bldg., Pennsylvania Ave. and 10th St. NW (tour entrance E St. btw, 9th and 10th sts.). ✆ **202/324-3447.** www.fbi.gov. Free admission. Mon–Fri 8:45am–4:15pm. Closed federal holidays. Metro: Archives/Navy Memorial, Metro Center, or Gallery Place.

Bureau of Engraving and Printing ★ Ages 6 and up. You can bet your bottom dollar that the buck starts here. Kids old enough to appreciate money will go gaga over the green stuff.

This 40-minute guided tour is available every 15 minutes on a first-come, first-served basis, Monday through Friday, beginning at 9am (for seasonal hours, see below). The tour is so popular that you need tickets during the months of March through August. Same-day free tickets are available at the kiosk on Raoul Wallenberg Place (15th St. SW), beginning at 8am. During the Cherry Blossom Festival, they're usually gone by 8:30am. September through February, no tickets are required. Congressional/VIP tours are weekdays at 8:15 and 8:45am only. (See chapter 2 for more information on how to get VIP tours.) ***Note:*** If the Department of Homeland Security announces a Code Orange alert on the day of your visit, the bureau will be closed.

Workers in round-the-clock shifts print about 22 million notes per day; that's about $77 billion annually. Each sheet (plain old cloth at the start) picks up color from ink-filled lines engraved in the heavy steel plates. The backs are printed first; the faces are printed the next day. At the FBI, you'll learn that counterfeiting at this level is very difficult. The bureau also prints Treasury bonds and White House invitations.

If you think that "pieces of eight" were coined by Robert Louis Stevenson for *Treasure Island,* stop between 8:30am and 3:30pm at the visitor center, where you'll find the real thing as well as electronic games and video displays related to the "root of all evil." You can also purchase a souvenir bag of shredded green. (Incidentally, the life expectancy of a $1 bill is 18 months. Easy come, easy go.)

14th and C sts. SW (enter on 14th St.). ✆ **866/874-2330** or 202/622-2000. www.bep.treas.gov. Free admission; free tickets required Mar–Aug. Sept–Apr Mon–Fri 9–10:45am and 12:30–2pm (every 15 min.); May–Aug 9–10:45am, 12:30–3:45pm, and 5–7pm. Closed federal holidays and Dec 25–Jan 1. Metro: Smithsonian.

Department of State Diplomatic Reception Rooms Ages 12 and up. Kids over the age of 12 who are interested in seeing a showcase of 18th-century and early

19th-century American furniture and decorative arts can take a fine-arts tour of the diplomatic reception rooms on the eighth floor of the Department of State. Secretaries of state, VIPs, and cabinet members have all hosted bashes here. The terrace views of the Lincoln Memorial and Potomac River aren't bad. Three 45-minute guided tours are available by reservation only, 90 days in advance.

23rd and C sts. NW (enter at 23rd St.). ✆ **202/647-3241.** www.receptiontours.state.gov. Free admission. Tours Mon–Fri 9:30am, 10:30am, and 2:45pm by reservation only. Strollers not permitted; leave them and kids under 12 at home. Closed major holidays. Metro: Foggy Bottom.

Library of Congress ★ **Ages 10 and up.** The nation's library is also the world's largest. Established as a research center for Congress in 1800, the library's first collection, then housed in the Capitol, was burned during the War of 1812. The cornerstone for the Thomas Jefferson Building section, a formidable example of Italian Renaissance architecture, was laid in 1890, and construction lasted 11 years until it was complete. (When you're on the Hill, stop to see the exterior and Great Hall of the Thomas Jefferson Building, and enjoy the view of the Capitol from the west steps.)

Anyone 18 and older can do research or browse here, with a library card from the James Madison Building, 101 Independence Ave. SE, between 1st and 2nd streets. Take a driver's license or passport to room LM140 for a temporary card. Unlike your local public library, you may not borrow any of the books that fill 650 miles of shelves in the Thomas Jefferson, James Madison, and John Adams buildings.

To get to the library's **visitor center,** enter from 1st Street SE at Independence Avenue (sidewalk level). The **Main Reading Room,** located in the Jefferson Building, is awesome. Researchers 18 and older are always welcome; others may gain entry only during the hour-long guided tour. I think you'll agree that the **Great Hall** is a sight to behold, with its soaring arches, ceilings decorated with mosaics, and marble stairways cleaned to a spit-and-polish shine. In the **Southwest Gallery and Pavilion** on the second floor, you'll find "American Treasures of the Library of Congress," a permanent exhibition of maps, rare books, and photographs. Among the treasures is L'Enfant's blueprint for Washington. You'll also see the contents of Lincoln's pockets the night he was assassinated.

But first, catch the video in the theater. Tours are Monday through Friday at 10:30 and 11:30am; 1:30, 2:30, and 3:30pm; Saturday 9:30, 10:30, 11:30am, 1:30, and 2:30pm. Most kids 10 and older should find it interesting; anyone younger (unless they're especially precocious or bookish) will think it's boring. Among the special collections housed in 20 reading rooms are children's literature and genealogy. The recently expanded gift shop invites browsers and souvenir collectors.

The **Gutenberg Bible** and **Giant Bible of Mainz** are displayed on the main floor, along with rotating exhibits of photographs, music manuscripts, prints, and posters. With very young children, skip the Jefferson Building tour and head for the Madison Building next door on 1st Street, between Independence Avenue and C Street SE. The **Copyright Office,** one of the library's departments, is located here. On the fourth floor, the copyright exhibit features one of the original Maltese falcons, masks from *Star Wars,* Bert and Ernie puppets, Barbie dolls, posters, and more. Visit any time between 8:30am and 5pm.

Capitol Hill (across from the Capitol), 10 1st St. SE (btw. Independence Ave. and East Capitol St.). ✆ **202/707-8000.** www.loc.gov. Free admission. Madison Bldg. Mon–Fri 8:30am–9:30pm, Sat 8:30am–5pm; Jefferson Bldg. Mon–Sat 8:30am–4:30pm. Closed Dec 25 and other major holidays. Metro: Capitol South.

The Pentagon **Ages 8 and up.** The world's largest office building (3.7 million sq. ft.) is the headquarters of the Department of Defense—that's the Army, Navy, Air Force,

Marines, Coast Guard, and Joint Chiefs of Staff. Any school kid can tell you that it was named for its five-sided construction. About 23,000 people work here daily, occupying offices along 18 miles of corridors.

Hour-long general public tours are conducted by active-duty servicemen. To qualify, you must apply at the Pentagon website or contact your senator (www.senate.gov) or representative (www.house.gov) from 3 weeks to 3 months in advance. Tours are Monday through Friday between 9am and 3pm; never on federal holidays or weekends. For details, call ✆ **703/697-1776** or go to http://pentagon.afis.osd.mil/tours.

If your kids are interested in the service branches' large art collection or portraits of Medal of Honor recipients, by all means bring them. Personally, I think it's rather dry stuff, and rest assured that there's no way that you or your kids will be admitted to the War Room or any place else where you can actually see what goes on here. Still, tours might interest kids over the age of 8 who have a certain fascination with the military. Please note that the tour lasts an hour and you can expect to walk 1½ miles. If your kids are still talking to you afterward, take 'em to Pentagon City to shop and eat. You may visit Pentagon Memorial Park, in memory of the victims of the September 11, 2001, terrorist attacks, on your own without special papers or prior reservations. The park, located at 1 Rotary Rd., on the west side of the Pentagon Reservation (hey, this place is huge), is open daily around the clock but I recommend visiting in daylight. The memorial features 184 cantilevered benches, one for each victim. The 59 benches facing the Pentagon represent those who died in the building; 125 benches, representing the passengers on American Airlines Flight 77, face the opposite direction so that visitors can see the engraved names of the victims against the sky. Each bench sits above a small reflecting pool. The reflected light makes the memorial visible from far away and from above. ***Note:*** Photography is okay inside the memorial; strictly prohibited inside the Pentagon. For more information on the memorial, including access, see www.whs.mil.

Break Time

You can grab a quick bite to eat at the Madison **Cafeteria** (✆ **202/554-4114** or 202/707-8300), on the sixth floor of the Madison Building. Inside is a wall of windows overlooking the city. There's a salad bar at lunch, as well as hot main dishes, carved meats, health food, pizza, fast food (fried chicken, burgers), deli sandwiches, and desserts. Prices for most main courses range from $5 to $10. ***Note:*** Posted prices reflect employees' 20% discount. Reservations and credit cards are not accepted. It's open Monday through Friday from 9 to 10:30am and from 12:30 to 3pm (snacks and drinks only 2–3pm). A coffee shop is open on the ground floor Monday through Friday from 9 to 10:30am and 12:30 to 4pm and Saturday 8:30am to 2pm. Frankly, unless you're starving or pressed for time, I suggest eating somewhere on Pennsylvania Ave.

The more formal **Montpelier Room,** adjoining the cafeteria on the sixth floor, has floor-to-ceiling windows and serves a marvelous $12 buffet lunch Monday through Friday between 11:30am and 2pm. It includes a (nonalcoholic) beverage. You may purchase wine or beer, however, and there's a dessert menu. Prime rib is featured on Friday. Reservations are required for four or more (✆ **202/707-8300**). MasterCard and Visa are accepted here. ***Note:*** This place is definitely not for very young kids.

Break Time

Hear ye, hear ye. The decision is out on the food in the **Supreme Court Cafeteria** (✆ **202/479-3246**): It might not be supreme, but it's appealing. Fresh-baked muffins are featured at breakfast; soup, sandwiches, main courses, salad bar, ice cream, and desserts are available at lunch. Most main courses range from $5 to $8. Reservations and credit cards are not accepted. The cafeteria is open to the public Monday through Friday from 7:30 to noon, and 2 to 4pm. Between noon and 2pm you'll have to make do with the vending machines on the ground floor.

Arlington, VA (across the 14th St. Bridge). ✆ **703/695-1776.** http://pentagon.afis.osd.mil. Free admission. Families of fewer than 5 people must request a public tour from their state representative at www.senate.gov or www.house.gov. Closed to individuals; group tours only by special advance request. Those 16 and older must have a photo ID. Groups of 9 or more must reserve 2 weeks or more ahead. Metro: Pentagon.

Supreme Court ★★ **Ages 10 and up.** The highest court in the nation, empowered by Article III of the Constitution to ensure that congressional, presidential, and state actions comply with the Constitution, hears about 150 cases annually.

In this imposing structure of classic Greek design, once thought too grandiose for its intention, the Supreme Court hears cases during about half the weeks from the first Monday in October through April. Only about 50 seats are open to the public, so arrive by 9am. Cases are heard Monday through Wednesday from 10am to 3pm, with a lunch-hour recess from noon to 1pm. Although children are welcome in the courtroom, no disruptions are tolerated. Phone the information office (✆ **202/479-3211**) or consult the *Washington Post's* "Supreme Court Calendar" for the schedule.

From mid-May to early July, you may attend half-hour sessions on Monday at 10am, when the justices release orders and opinions. The many rituals attendant with the justices' entrance will fascinate older children. You can tell them that "Oyez! Oyez!" is French legalese for "Hear ye, hear ye."

When the court is not in session, you may attend a free lecture (9:30am–3:30pm, every hour on the half-hour) about Court procedure and the building's architecture. Follow up the lecture with a walk through the Great Hall (Mon–Fri 9am–4:30pm) and see the 20-minute film on the workings of the Court (✆ **202/479-3211**).

On the ground floor, take a look at the imposing spiral staircases and Court-related exhibits. There's also a gift shop on this level, open from 9am to 4:25pm. From the top of the entrance steps, there's a wonderful view of the Capitol.

1st St. and Maryland Ave. NE (opposite the U.S. Capitol). ✆ **202/479-3211.** www.supremecourtus.gov. Free admission. Mon–Fri 9am–4:30pm. Closed holidays. Metro: Capitol South or Union Station.

4 MORE D.C. ATTRACTIONS

ARCHITECTURE

National Building Museum **Ages 10 and up.** Once you visit the former Pension Building, which somewhat resembles Rahway Prison on the outside and a Roman bath and Renaissance palace on the inside, you'll know why this museum is dedicated to the

Visiting the Old Post Office

Although the **Old Post Office** ★ (1100 Pennsylvania Ave. NW, btw. 10th and 12th sts.; ✆ **202/289-4224**) is no longer a working post office, families love to come here to eat, shop, and enjoy the family entertainment. Do take a few minutes from your chicken wings and peanut butter fudge to inspect the impressive architecture. Built in 1899 as quarters for the federal postal department, it suffered years of neglect. The three-level renovated complex reopened in May 1984, thanks largely to the efforts of Nancy Hanks, a former head of the National Endowment for the Arts in the 1970s. Renovation began in 1978 and took 6 years to complete.

If you do nothing else, tour the **clock tower** ★★. The vista, from the equivalent of a high-rise's 12th floor, is astounding, and the windows are covered with thin wires, so you don't have to be nervous about your little ones. On your way to the tower, stop on the 10th floor to check out the **10 Congress bells,** replicas of those at Westminster Abbey. They range from 600 to 3,000 pounds, and each one is about 5 feet in diameter. The order in which the bells are struck changes continuously, and it takes nearly 4 hours to go through all the permutations. A full peal honors the opening and closing of Congress, state occasions, and national holidays. You may attend a practice session Thursday between 7 and 9pm, but I suggest calling first. Tours of the tower are free and are conducted by the National Park Service (✆ **202/606-8691;** www.nps.gov), usually from 8am to 11pm in April through August, and 10am to 5:45pm in September through March. Meet your guide in the lower lobby near the 12th Street entrance for a ride up, up, and away in the glass elevator.

building arts. It is the only U.S. institution dedicated solely to architecture, urban planning, design, engineering, and construction, and is one of D.C.'s *ooh* and *ahh* experiences.

Statistics to stick in your suitcase: The exterior measures 400 feet by 200 feet. The interior Corinthian columns are 75 feet high, 8 feet in diameter, and 25 feet in circumference. And 70,000 bricks went into *each* column!

In 1885, Grover Cleveland was the first president to hold an inaugural ball here. In case you're planning a future event and your family room doesn't cut it, the Great Hall is available for events other than presidential social functions. It measures 316 feet by 116 feet, and the ceiling is 159 feet high. That's about 15 stories.

"Washington, Symbol and City," is the museum's signature exhibition, exploring the growth and development of the federal capital. Temporary exhibitions usually change every 6 to 8 months. **"An Architectural Wonder: The U.S. Pension Building"** details the building's history and construction. If your children are over 10 or have an interest in architecture and urban development, this is an excellent introduction to D.C. If they have zero interest, come here anyway for a quick glimpse of the Great Hall.

Tours lasting 45 minutes are conducted daily at 11:30am, 12:30, and 1:30pm. Families may drop in for free educational and fun **Discovery Cart workshops** ★★, suitable for kids 5 and older. They're held most Saturdays at 10:30am and 2:30pm; Sundays at

11:30am and 2:30pm. In 2009, these interactive programs included the five basic bridge types and using different materials to build an arch. I'm a big fan of learning by doing, and the Building Museum gets it right. All ages are welcome. Ask about Family Tool Kits (for different age groups; $5 rental fee) and free Amazing Arches activity, available most days. The Tool Kit has a tape measure, level, binoculars, compass—for hands-on learning about building and architecture. The museum hosts summer family drop-in programs (fashioning fans to resemble a building, decorating mirrors with beads and ornaments, for example). Call or email for days and times (✆ **202/272-2448;** family@nbm.org). Two or three Sundays a year, the museum's Great Hall becomes airspace, as model-plane enthusiasts gather to launch their lightweight balsa and elastic band aircraft. Call or check the website for details.

The Museum Shop, on the ground floor, has a broad selection of architecture- and design-related books, objects for the home and office, prints, and posters (✆ **202/272-7706**). Hours are Monday through Saturday, 10am to 5pm and Sunday 11am to 5pm. The **Café** (operated by the wonderful Firehook Bakery) in the Great Hall is open for sandwiches, soups, salads, desserts, and beverages Monday through Friday from 8:30am to 4:30pm, Saturday from 10am to 4:30pm, and Sunday from 11am to 4:30pm (✆ **202/628-0906**).

401 F St. NW (at Judiciary Sq., btw. 4th and 5th sts. NW). ✆ **202/272-2448.** www.nbm.org. $5 suggested donation. Mon–Sat 10am–5pm; Sun 11am–5pm. Closed major holidays. Metro: Judiciary Sq.

ARCHIVES & LIBRARIES

See also the entry for the Library of Congress in section 3, "The White House & Branches of Government," of this chapter.

Folger Shakespeare Library ★ **Ages 10 and up.** The 19th-century oil magnate Henry Clay Folger built this library for his vast collection of original First Folios and other rare books and manuscripts. Since opening in 1932, the Folger, whose neoclassical white marble facade is decorated with sculpted scenes from Shakespeare's plays, has been recognized as one of the world's most esteemed research libraries on Will (as he was known to his Elizabethan friends) and the Renaissance.

Anyone who wants to do research on 16th- or 17th-century European life—social history, geography, science, and law—need look no further than the more than 300,000 books here. To gain access to the library's materials, you must first become a "reader" (researcher); call the registrar at ✆ **202/675-0306.**

The library is home to a gem—an authentic Elizabethan theater that is open to visitors when not in use for rehearsals or performances. The highly regarded **Folger Consort** performs here regularly, and Shakespeare's birthday (Apr 23) is celebrated with an open house every year on the closest Saturday (Apr 24, 2010). Pick up a Children's Guide and Scavenger Hunt before you visit the Great Hall. Free docent-led tours are given Monday through Friday at 11am and 3pm and Saturday at 11am and 1pm. Tour the Elizabethan Garden the third Saturday of every month, 11am and 1pm, April through October. At other times, you can connect via your cellphone to a self-guided audio tour narrated by library director Gail Kern Paster. Bill's Buddies, geared to grades 3 through 12, perform excerpts from the Bard's works for groups on four weekday mornings a year. Tickets are $15.

Ask about other Shakespeare-related activities for families. For information, call ✆ **202/544-7077.** Bard-inspired mementos are on sale in the **Folger Shop.**

201 E. Capitol St. SE. ✆ **202/544-4600.** www.folger.edu. Free admission. Mon–Sat 10am–5pm. Closed federal holidays. Metro: Capitol South or Union Station.

National Archives ★ **Ages 6 and up.** This place is so popular, it's advisable to make reservations for a self-guided visit at least 6 weeks ahead (visitorservice@nara.gov). I learned the hard way recently and stood in line with other yokels (not my favorite way to pass time). A 1-hour wait is not unusual March through May, on weekends, and during the week between Christmas and New Year's. For a 1-hour guided tour, Monday through Friday at 9:45am, call ✆ **202/357-5450** at least 6 weeks in advance.

If you have any doubts about the inscription on the statue out front—"What is past is prologue"—step inside the rotunda. The building is a classical structure with—count 'em—72 Corinthian columns designed by John Russell Pope, architect of the National Gallery and Jefferson Memorial. Each of the bronze doors weighs 6½ tons (don't try slamming these!). Trivia fact: Because the building was constructed on Tiber Creek, which ran through the city, more than 8,500 pilings had to be driven into the ground before construction could begin.

I suggest viewing the 11-minute introductory film in the McGowan Theater first. Then I'd head over to main attraction, the **Charters of Freedom,** an exhibit that contains some of the most precious paper in the country: the 1297 version of the Magna Carta, the Declaration of Independence, four pages of the Constitution, and the Bill of Rights. Each night these priceless documents, already sealed in helium-filled bronze-and-glass cases, are lowered 22 feet into a bombproof and fireproof 55-ton steel-and-concrete vault. During the day, armed guards keep an eye on things.

From there, head to the Public Vaults, which, at any given time, exhibit more than 1,000 records, photos, maps, film clips, and facsimiles chronicling our nation's history. Interactives help drive the history home. The **Record of America** section in the central corridor shows the effects of time and technology on recordkeeping, from early Native American treaties to presidential websites. The intention is that each visitor will leave with a better understanding of his or her personal connection to the records housed in this building.

The National Archives is also the storehouse for 5 million photos (including Mathew Brady's Civil War snapshots); nearly 12 million maps, charts, and aerial photographs; and 91 million feet of motion-picture film. And talk about odd couples: The Archives has a photo of Elvis Presley and Richard Nixon at the White House in 1970. Thousands of old newsreels can be screened in the motion picture, sound, and video branch on the ground floor, but you have to make an appointment first.

Alex Haley began searching for his *Roots* here. So can you! Researchers must be at least 14 and have a valid photo ID, or be accompanied by a parent or guardian. Those 18 and older need a valid photo ID. Call first for details and hours. Research and microfilm rooms are open Monday through Saturday. Use the Pennsylvania Avenue entrance and stop in Room 400 for advice before you begin your quest. The **Charters Café,** on the lower level, is open Monday through Friday from 7:30am to 4pm. Books and souvenirs are sold in the **Archives Shop** (under the Rotunda), open during Archives hours.

700 Constitution Ave. (btw. 7th and 9th sts. NW). ✆ **202/501-5000** for information on exhibits and films, or 202/501-5402 for research information. www.archives.gov. Free admission. Daily day after Labor Day–Mar 14 10am–5:30pm; daily Mar 15–Labor Day 10am–7pm (last admission 30 minutes prior to closing). Closed Dec 25 and federal holidays. Metro: Archives.

ART

See first section of this chapter, "The Smithsonian Institution," for listings of the following art museums: the Freer Gallery of Art, the Hirshhorn Museum and Sculpture Garden, the National Museum of African Art, the Renwick Gallery, the Arthur M. Sackler

Gallery of Asian and Near Eastern Art, the American Art Museum, and the National Portrait Gallery.

Corcoran Gallery of Art ★ **Ages 8 and up.** Washington's oldest private museum is best known for its permanent collections of American 19th-century landscapes and Impressionist art, as well as its special exhibitions of contemporary art and photography. Exhibits change frequently but run the gamut from Andy Warhol to Mary Cassatt. The first-floor double atrium and imposing marble staircase will probably impress your little ones more than what's hanging on the walls. When you enter, ask at the information desk for a brochure aimed at 6- to 12-year-olds intended to arouse their interest in specific artworks.

Family Workshops are held on select Saturday mornings at 10:30am and noon. After a short interactive gallery tour, children move to an artist's studio (in case you didn't know, the Corcoran is also an esteemed art school) to create a take-home work. The fee is $8 per child. Tours are held Wednesday through Sunday at noon. (The museum is closed Mon–Tues.) The Corcoran School of Art offers a 4-year program to students of the fine arts and photography, and offers studio classes for children of all ages. Inquire at the information desk or call for a catalog about the Children's Workshops and Young People's Program.

In the gift shop, you'll find children's books and educational trinkets, as well as art books for all. For information on special and family events, as well as on group tours, call the education department.

The cafe is open for breakfast, lunch, snacks, and afternoon tapas, Wednesday, Friday to Sunday, 11am to 2pm, and Thursday 10am to 8pm. The popular Sunday Gospel Brunch is 10:30am to 2pm ($25 adults, $12 kids under 12).

500 17th St. NW, at New York Ave. ✆ **202/639-1700.** www.corcoran.org. Admission $10 adults, $8 seniors 62 and older, free for kids 11 and under. Wed and Fri–Sun 10am–5pm; Thurs 10am–9pm. Open on federal holiday Mon 10am5pm. Closed Dec 25 and Jan 1. Metro: Farragut West or Farragut North.

National Gallery of Art (East and West buildings) and Sculpture Garden ★★★ **Ages 4 and up.** Let's dispense with the details first. The East and West buildings are connected by an underground concourse with a moving walkway. You can enter the West Building from the Mall (Madison Dr.) or Constitution Avenue at 6th Street; you also can enter at 4th or 7th streets between Constitution Avenue and Madison Drive. The only above-ground entrance to the East Building is on 4th Street. Strollers are available at each entrance. The buildings are least crowded weekdays before noon.

Break Time

When I'm downtown and draggin', I head for the picturesque **Pavilion Cafe ★★★**, in the National Gallery Sculpture Garden (9th St. and Constitution Ave.; ✆ **202/289-3360;** www.pcdavilioncafe.com) to unwind and refuel. Glass walls overlook the fountain, reflecting pool, and flowering shrubs. How can you not like it? On warm days you can dine (or write postcards) outdoors. Personal pizzas, large salads, sandwiches, panini, and wraps are tasty and satisfying. Most items are $6.25 to $9.50. Desserts cost $2 to $6. A wide selection of beverages, including wine and beer, is available. Hours are Monday to Saturday from 10am to 7pm in summer (until 4pm rest of year), Sunday 11am to 7pm in summer (5pm rest of year).

Break Time

Any time is a good time to head for the National Gallery of Art's **Cascade Café** (they can call it a cafe, but it is still a cafeteria to me; ✆ **202/737-4215;** www.nga.gov/dining), open from 11:30am to 3pm Monday through Saturday and noon to 4pm Sundays. The line moves quickly in this bright and cheery space, with seating for 450. It's located in the East building on the Concourse level. At lunch, create your own salad or choose a premade sandwich or one with hand-sliced deli meats from the carvery, a wood-fired pizza, or a hot main dish (most items $5–$8). I am happy to report that the food has improved over the years. Kids can have a hotdog or hamburger and make their own sundaes from frozen yogurt and varied toppings. Try to snag a table near the faux waterfall. Next to the Cascade Café is a full coffee and ice cream bar that also has paninis and pastries ($4–$8). It is open Monday through Saturday from 10am to 4:30pm, and Sunday from 11am to 5:30pm, usually with extended hours in summer. High chairs are available.

The Garden Café (✆ **202/216-2480**) is located on the ground floor of the museum's West Building next to the museum shop. Come here to reflect, cool your heels, and have dessert ($6.75), or sample one of the chef's seasonal offerings amid the ferns and marble. This is probably the most "adult" of the Mall museum eateries and offers sit-down service. It's also the priciest, and reservations are recommended, so you may want to savor it sometime without the kids. A buffet tied to a temporary exhibit is $19 per person. A la carte items (soups, salads, sandwiches, a hot main dish, desserts) range from $7 to $18. It's open Monday through Saturday from 11:30am to 3pm, and Sunday from noon to 4pm for a la carte dining (4-6pm for dessert on concert days). High chairs are available, but I'd think twice about filling one, if you get my drift.

All of the National Gallery eateries accept American Express, Diners Club, Discover, MasterCard, and Visa.

The National Gallery is 1 of the 10 most popular art museums in the United States, attracting more than 6 million visitors annually. The classically inspired **West Building,** another John Russell Pope creation, houses 12th- to 20th-century sculpture and paintings within its 500,000-square-foot interior. Industrialist Andrew Mellon's collection formed the nucleus, augmented by the sizable collections of Samuel H. Kress, Joseph Widener, Chester Dale, and numerous individual donors.

Here are a few suggestions in the West Building that might appeal to your children: the Byzantine *Madonna and Child,* Giotto's *Madonna and Child,* Filippino Lippi's and/or Botticelli's *Portrait of a Youth,* Raphael's *St. George and the Dragon,* anything by El Greco (kids think he's "weird"), Holbein's portrait *Edward VI as a Child,* Fragonard's *Young Girl Reading,* Renoir's *A Girl with a Watering Can,* Copley's *Watson and the Shark,* and the Degas sculptures.

Do show them the bronze statue of Mercury on top of the fountain in the rotunda and then head for either of the lovely colonnaded garden courts. Under arched skylights, with comfortable chairs overlooking putti fountains, rest museum-weary feet (and children).

The West Building overpowers and bewilders some adults. So show the kids a few things here, then hightail it over to the less intimidating **East Building.**

At the corner of 3rd Street and Pennsylvania Avenue, aim your peepers at Frank Stella's 30-foot aluminum-and-fiberglass *Mr. Homburg.* Resembling a hard-edge spaceship, it landed here because it was too large for the National Gallery Sculpture Garden. Steel cables set in concrete anchor it to terra firma, but it still moves in the wind. Neat!

I think of the East Building as a breath of fresh air. If your kids see nothing more than Henry Moore's humongous abstract bronze resembling two upside-down cloven hooves *(Knife Edge Mirror Two Pieces)* at the entrance, and the soaring ground-level central court with its three-story-high Calder mobile and vibrant (much too large for the living room) Miró tapestry, *Woman,* you will have accomplished something. Ask the kids if they can identify the shape of the building. It's a trapezoid, which architect I. M. Pei ingeniously divided into two interconnected triangles.

Pick up a colorful self-guided tour booklet for children and their families and the quarterly publication, *NGAkids.* It lists films, activities, and artist-specific info in kid-friendly language. Before leaving home, you can see what's on tap at www.nga.gov/programs/family.html. Kids are usually drawn to Mondrian's neat grids and/or Motherwell's sloppy splotches. See what they make of the latter's inkblot, *Reconciliation Elegy.* Their answers should make for interesting conversation. Roy Lichtenstein's *Look Mickey* will strike a familiar chord, while Matisse's *Large Composition with Masks* enchants all ages.

From the upper level, climb the spiral staircase (it's only 25 steps) to the Tower level, where special works are hung. Getting there is half the fun, and kids enjoy discovering this "secret" place.

Some kids can spend days on the moving walkway and investigating the origin of the waterfall (overflow from street-level fountains) on the Concourse Level next to the Cascade Buffet.

Two-hour **Family Workshops** ★ (for parents and their children, ages 6–8 or 9–12) take place in the East Building Concourse, Education Studio, most Saturdays and Sundays, usually 10:30am to 12:30pm and 1:30 to 3:30pm. These include an artist-led tour and related hands-on projects. Information on Audio Tours for adults and kids (ages 7–12), Postcard Tours for Families (all ages), the Children's Film Program (ages 7 and up), special exhibitions, tours, lectures, films, and concerts is available at the art information desks in the West Building and the ground floor of the East Building. These programs complement the exhibitions and expose children to the fine arts (✆ **202/842-6249**). Of course, once you arrive, you can always inquire at an information desk.

If you don't make it to the East or West buildings, I direct you to one of my grandkids' favorites, the museum's **Sculpture Garden** ★★★, 9th Street and Constitution Avenue NW, open in summer Monday through Thursday and Saturday from 10am to 7pm and Friday from 10am to 9pm; Sunday, it's open from 11am to 7pm. During the fall and winter seasons, the garden closes at dusk.

My grandkids love coming here because it sparks their imaginations, and they can roam more freely than in a museum. Younger kids, especially, will find this a heck of a lot more interesting than what's indoors. Amid indigenous plantings and trees, and a fountain that, I am told, could become an ice rink, are about two dozen 20th-century sculptures. Wait until they see Claes Oldenburg's giant *Typewriter Eraser* (at 3, my granddaughter Jaymie saw it as a bagel with hair), Roy Lichtenstein's *House I,* Barry Flanagan's whimsical *Thinker on a Rock* (a rabbit), and Sol LeWitt's concrete-block *Four-Sided Pyramid.* Bet they flip over Calder's *Red Horse* and Lucas Samaras's *Chair Transformation!*

On the north side of the Mall (btw. 3rd and 7th sts). NW (entrances at 6th St. and Constitution Ave. or Madison Dr.). ✆ **202/737-4215.** www.nga.gov. Free admission. Mon–Sat 10am–5pm; Sun 11am–6pm. Summer hours are frequently extended. Closed Dec 25 and Jan 1. Metro: Archives or Judiciary Sq.

National Museum of Women in the Arts (NMWA) **Ages 8 and up.** This museum celebrates, and is a showcase for, "the contribution of women to the history of art." It opened in 1987 in this striking Renaissance Revival building, formerly the Masonic Grand Lodge. There are more than 1,200 paintings, prints, and sculptures by 400 women. In 1982, the museum's founders, Wallace and Wilhelmina Holladay, donated their collection and library—a cornucopia of artworks by women spanning 5 centuries. Come for the permanent collection, featuring artists such as Mary Cassatt, Frida Kahlo, Georgia O'Keeffe, Helen Frankenthaler, Elaine de Kooning, Käthe Kollwitz, and Judy Chicago, as well as special exhibits and programs, and kids' events requiring reservations (✆ **202/783-7370**).

Works with special appeal for young people include *Noah's Ark* in the mezzanine members' lounge and the story quilts by Faith Ringgold. A snappy self-guided tour workbook for 7- to 12-year-olds, "Artventure," is free at the information desk. Kids are invited to find decorative elements on the mezzanine, distinguish faux marble from the real thing, and examine portraits for the sitter's mood and occupation. At the information desk, unearth the latest museum doings: storytellers, hands-on activities, and folksingers. **Family Programs** ★ are held the first Sunday of the month during the school year. Kids 6 to 12, accompanied by an adult, are invited to take part in art projects, view performances, and do hands-on activities. The museum's Elizabeth A. Kasser Wing, just east of the preexisting museum, has a museum shop and two upstairs galleries, one dedicated to female artists displaying their works for the first time and the other devoted to sculpture. The **Mezzanine Café** is open for lunch and light fare Monday through Friday from 11:30am to 2:30pm and brunch on select Sundays (✆ **202/628-1068**). Or grab a bite at nearby **Capitol City Brewing Co.** (p. 88).

1250 New York Ave. ✆ **202/783-5000,** or 202/783-7996 for group tours. www.nmwa.org. Admission $12 adults, $10 seniors (60 and over), free kids in grades K–12 w/ID, NMWA members. Additional fees for selected exhibitions. Walk-in tours dependent on guide availability; group guided tours must be scheduled in advance. Mon–Sat 10am–5pm; Sun noon–5pm. Closed Thanksgiving Day, Dec 25, Jan 1. Metro: Metro Center.

Phillips Collection ★★ Finds **Ages 6 and up.** Just when you thought this awesome museum of Impressionist, post-Impressionist, and 20th- and 21st- century American and European art couldn't get better, it does.

The Sant building, the Phillips' latest addition, opened in 2006 with more gallery space, an enlarged museum shop and cafe, sculpture courtyard, 180-seat auditorium, activities room, and improved research and library facilities.

If you plan to visit on a Saturday or Sunday, paid admission is required. To save time, I encourage you to order tickets ahead through **Ticketmaster** (✆ **800/551-SEAT** or 202/397-SEAT; www.ticketmasters.com).

Children seem to take to the museum off Dupont Circle because it began as the home of the late Duncan Phillips and his family. As such, it is homey (maybe not like your home, but homey nonetheless), with elegant furniture, polished floors, and Asian rugs. Most kids react favorably to the playfulness of Klee's works, the sunny colors and good feeling of Renoir's *Luncheon of the Boating Party* and other Impressionist works, and the large color canvases of Mark Rothko. A major Georgia O'Keeffe exhibition is on view through May 9, 2010. I'll bet they'll have something to say about Alexander Calder's *Only, Only Bird,* constructed of aluminum beer and coffee cans. See if Susan Rothenberg's rich and edgy *Three Masks* is on view when you visit. More than 100 paintings, photographs, and sculpture by the likes of Degas, Calder, Avery, and other giants span the 19th to 21st centuries.

I suggest taking a general walking tour (times vary); or a 15-minute tour, showcasing a single work or artist, given Tuesday through Friday at noon. On weekends an introductory tour of the collection is offered every Saturday at noon. A tour of the current temporary exhibition is Sunday at noon.

Pay a visit to Phillips' **Young Artists Exhibition,** an ongoing display of children's art inspired by the museum's collection. The museum also offers dynamic gallery experiences for student groups, engaging children in activities that range from interactive hands-on gallery learning to play-acting about art.

When you enter, pick up a free family guide to help ignite your kids' interest in art. Those 6 to 12 are usually ripe for this experience. In the past, **Art at Home** asked children to write a poem or story about a painting to enhance their critical thinking about a particular work of art. The group programs must be prearranged (✆ **202/387-2151**). If your family is small, maybe you can hook up with another to meet the quota. The Phillips also sponsors family workshops throughout the year. Call to be put on a mailing list (✆ **202/387-2151,** ext. 247). Thursday from 5 to 8:30pm, the **Artful Evenings** program includes a musical performance or gallery talk ($5) and may appeal to children 10 and older. You can grab a light bite or dessert Tuesday through Sunday in the small cafeteria-style cafe. Then step into the courtyard to see Ellsworth Kelly's specially commissioned bronze sculpture and to commune with nature. The museum shop carries posters, stationery, postcards, and art books.

1600 21st St. NW, at Q St. ✆ **202/387-2151.** www.phillipscollection.org. Free admission Mon–Fri (donations suggested); Sat–Sun $10 adults, free for age 18 and under and museum members. Additional charge for special exhibitions. Tues–Sat 10am–5pm; Thurs 10am–8:30pm; Sun 11am–6pm. Closed federal holidays. Metro: Dupont Circle (Q St. exit).

HISTORY

See also section 1 for individual listings on the Smithsonian Building, the National Museum of American History, and the Anacostia Museum and Center for African-American History and Culture; all of section 2; all of section 3; and the Folger Shakespeare Library and the National Archives in "Archives & Libraries," earlier in this section.

Frederick Douglass National Historic Site (Cedar Hill) **Ages 10 and up.**

Here's a golden opportunity for your kids to exercise their imaginations and visualize while the ranger describes the (stored) memorabilia and talks of Douglass.

Half-hour tours are given four or five times a day and require a reservation, which you can make online at www.recreation.gov. While the tour is free, there is a $1.50 fee (per ticket). After the tour, allow time to stroll the grounds.

Abolitionist and orator Frederick Douglass purchased Cedar Hill, the 20-room Victorian home on the Anacostia, in 1877, after living on Capitol Hill for 5 years. While the furniture is in storage, large images of the rooms as they appear when furnished, as well as historic photos of the home, are on view so you can visualize the space as it will appear when everything is in place.

A short film detailing Douglass's early years as a slave, his subsequent escape to the North, and lifetime achievements is shown in the visitor center. Self-educated, this civic leader, writer, publisher, and orator carved a significant niche in American history as a spokesman for the downtrodden and oppressed.

During February, which is Black History Month, films and special programs honor this unique individual. February 14, Douglass's birthday, is marked by a wreath-laying ceremony.

From the hill leading to Cedar Hill, you can enjoy a sweeping panorama of the Anacostia River, Washington Navy Yard, the Washington Monument, and the Capitol.

1411 W St. SE. ✆ **202/426-5961** or 800/967-2283 for reservations. www.nps.gov/frdo (www.recreation.gov to reserve online). Free, but reservations ($1.50 per person fee) required. Mid-Apr to mid-Oct daily 9am–5pm; mid-Oct to mid-Apr daily 9am–4pm. Closed Thanksgiving, Dec 25, and Jan 1. Metro: Anacostia and then B-2/Mt. Rainier bus (8 blocks). Directions (from the Mall): South on 9th St. to I-395 north, to I-295 south across bridge; exit onto Martin Luther King, Jr. Ave., and turn left on W St. SE. Go 3 blocks to visitor-center lot.

Ford's Theatre and Lincoln Museum ★★ **Ages 6 and up.** On April 14, 1865, President Abraham Lincoln was shot by John Wilkes Booth while attending a performance of *Our American Cousin* at Ford's. Lincoln was carried to the house of William Petersen across the street, where he died the next morning. The incident was anything but good for business, and Ford's wasn't used again as a theater until 1968. In the interim, it was a records-processing site and Army Medical Museum before Congress coughed up the funds to restore the theater to its 1865 appearance.

Ford's Theatre reopened in July 2009 after 2 years of renovations—and I think you'll like the results. Watch a 15-minute presentation, given hourly in the theater. Most visits include a half-hour interpretive talk by a National Park ranger or member of Fords' Theatre Society (depending on availability of staff). Then you're free to tour on your own. In addition to the clothes Lincoln wore the night he was assassinated, you'll see the Derringer pistol used by Booth and the compass he used to escape to Maryland. Two of the more eerie items in the exhibit are the Lincoln life mask and plaster casts of his hands. Audiovisual displays describe Lincoln's early life, political experiences, and presidential years.

As part of your visit, cross the street to the **Petersen House** ("The House Where Lincoln Died") at 526 10th St. (✆ **202/426-6924**). It gives me the willies, but kids love it. Because the bed in the ground-floor bedroom was too short for his lanky frame, Lincoln was laid diagonally across it. The original bloodstained pillow makes a powerful impression on kids (and adults, too). In the front parlor, the clock is stopped at 7:22am, the time of Lincoln's death. In 1896, the government bought the house for $30,000; it's maintained by the National Park Service.

511 10th St. NW (btw. E and F sts.). ✆ **202/426-6924** for historic site, or 202/347-4833 for box-office information. www.nps.gov/foth. Free admission. Timed-entry tickets at ✆ **202/397-SEAT.** www.ticketmaster.com. Museum daily 9am–5pm; Petersen House 9:30am–5:30pm; theater portion of museum closed during matinees and rehearsals; box office daily 10am–6pm. Closed Dec 25. Metro: Metro Center or Gallery Place.

International Spy Museum ★ **Ages 8 and up.** The word is out on the street, and it's anything but covert: The Spy Museum is hot! The admission is steep, but not compared to amusement-park fees. The Spy Museum amuses and informs—and unlike some amusement-park rides, it won't make you sick. Near the Smithsonian American Art Museum, the Verizon Center, and the Convention Center, it's a valentine devoted largely to the characters and technology that contributed to the dissolution of the Cold War. Most kids over 10 will lap up the sugar-coated history enhanced with strong visuals, interactives, spoken narrative, and canned music. Think Mata Hari on MTV. Your kids may be too young, but surely you or their grandparents will recall the gear carried by famous TV and movie spies such as Maxwell Smart's (Don Adams, aka Agent 86) book phone, James Bond's lunchboxes, and the model tarantula featured in *Dr. No.* Among the highlights in the permanent collection are a camera-carrying pigeon, a carved Great Seal of the United States with hidden microphone (a gift from Russia, no less), vintage lock-picking tools, a World War II German encoding device, and a replica of James Bond's Aston Martin. Can his martini stirrer be far behind? Kids 12 and older can find out if they have what it takes to be an operative in Operation Spy, an hour-long interactive romp where they can decrypt a secret message, conduct a polygraph test, and crack a safe. The museum has taken certain, um, liberties, using props in some instances instead of the real things. Big deal. Your kids won't notice. Just park your disbelief with your packages at the door. This isn't the Smithsonian.

On site are a large gift shop with a super selection of T-shirts, puzzles, books, and games, and the **Spy City Cafe** (✆ **202/654-0999**), with salads, sandwiches, wraps, seven varieties of hot dogs, and photos of D.C. spy drop-off points, of which there are *many.* Most items are under $8, and there is seating for 50. **Zola** (as in Emile) is for fine dining and not suitable for youngsters (reservations recommended; ✆ **202/654-0999**). Sometimes you can pick up same-day tickets at the museum. Play it safe—and smart—and purchase tickets in advance at Ticketmaster, in Macy's, 12th and G sts. NW (✆ **800/551-SEAT** [7328] or 202/432-SEAT [7328]; www.ticketmaster.com). A little closer, please, while I whisper some highly classified info. From April to October, when the museum is open until 8pm, I suggest an early evening visit. (Oops! Guess it's no longer top secret.)

Past special activities for kids 9 to 13 included a Saturday-night Operation Secret Slumber (includes snack, light breakfast, souvenir, and Sun museum admission at a pricey $115; one adult must accompany every two junior spies.).

I thoroughly enjoy the **Spy City Tour** ★ (in conjunction with Grayline), appropriate for kids 12 and up. On Tuesdays and Saturdays, at 10am, participants are bused to 25 espionage sites around the city on a highly interactive mission. The running commentary by a professional actor is clever and informative. Tickets are $75 and include museum admission. (While I think it's overpriced, if you have the spare change, I say go for it.) **Spy at Night** is a Saturday evening program in which participants adopt the identity of an intelligence office to catch (what else?) a spy. I'd recommend it for kids 10 and older. The cost is $20. See the website for info about other special Spy activities.

800 F St. NW. ✆ **202/393-7798.** www.spymuseum.org. Admission $18 adults, $17 seniors (65 and older), $15 kids ages 5–11, free 4 and under; surcharge for special shows ($20 for Operation Spy). Daily 9:30am–6pm or 7pm; ask about extended summer hours. Closed Thanksgiving, Dec 25, and Jan 1. Metro: Gallery Place/Chinatown.

National Museum of Crime & Punishment **Ages 10 and up.** John Walsh, the host of *America's Most Wanted,* teamed up with an Orlando, Florida, personal-injury attorney/entrepreneur (what's unusual about that?) to open the new National Museum of Crime & Punishment. Few, if any, would argue that the United States lacks a rich criminal history—or more than its share of criminals. This museum sets out to document that legacy. The museum's founders set out to give a historic overview of criminal evolution beginning with the first time a caveman clubbed a neighbor over a hunk of meat (or a woman), to current-day scenarios in which a white-collar criminal eliminates a competitor over money (or a woman). The museum is chock full of strong visuals and interactives to drive home the stake, I mean, point, about man's baser side. Older kids can test their shooting skills, crack a safe, examine medieval torture devices, ogle a replica of Bonnie and Clyde's bullet-ridden car, or collect evidence for a crime lab. In the museum gift shop, Cop Shop, you can purchase a T-shirt emblazoned with an electric chair and DON'T DO IT. Hmm. While the museum claims that it does not intend to glorify criminals, there's a heck of a lot of evidence to the contrary. Some of the material may upset little ones. I wouldn't bring kids under 10 or 11 years old. And I'm not sure about those who are older (like grandmotherly-guidebook writers—don't we get more than our fill of this subject in the media?).

575 7th St. NW (btw. E and F sts.). ✆ **202/621-5550.** www.crimemuseum.org. Admission $18 adults, $15 seniors and kids ages 5–11, free 4 and under (online discounts available). Mid-March to Aug 9am–9pm; Sept to mid-Mar 10am–8pm (hours vary according to season and events). Metro: Gallery Place/Chinatown.

Old Stone House **Ages 4 and up.** Kids feel comfortable in this modest pre-Revolutionary War house in Georgetown, probably because it's small like they are. Sometimes in summer, concerts are held in the garden (enter through gate on M St.), where you may picnic (as long as you clean up when you're through). When a park ranger is on site (which is most of the time), you may tour the entire house and learn some colonial history from the ranger. A candlelight tour is held around Christmas. The on-site Eastern National Bookstore is open daily from noon to 5pm, with goods representative of the 17th and 18th century—stoneware, hand-blown glass, pottery, toys and games—as well as books on Washington, D.C.

3051 M St. NW. ✆ **202/426-6851.** www.nps.gov/rocr/oldstonehouse. Free admission. Wed–Sun noon–5pm (gardens open daily). Closed Thanksgiving, Dec 25, Jan 1, and other federal holidays. Metro: Foggy Bottom, then 7-block walk via Pennsylvania Ave. to M St.

U.S. Holocaust Memorial Museum ★★★ **Ages 10 and up.** When this museum opened in April 1993, I was among the skeptics who were certain that it could not possibly measure up to the advance media hype. I was wrong. The architecture and contents evoke a visceral reaction among visitors, regardless of religious or ethnic background. In fact, officials who track such things say that 80% of the museum's visitors are non-Jews. It would be easy to spend the better part of a day here. But I don't advise it. My personal limit is about 2½ hours before I crave fresh air and daylight.

To visit the permanent exhibition, **The Holocaust,** which occupies the majority of the museum, you need timed entry passes March through August. A finite number of same-day passes are available when the museum opens at 10am. If it's your only chance to visit and your kids are 10 and older, I say order passes in advance at www.tickets.com (✆ **800/400-9373**). The $1.75 per-pass processing fee is well worth it. You do not need passes for special exhibits ("Remember the Children: Daniel's Story" and "The Children's Tile Wall"; both suitable for children under 10) or the Wexner Learning Center.

Nearly two million visitors per year of all ages and backgrounds cross the cobblestones, once part of the Warsaw ghetto, to gaze at the photographs of those who perished. The museum planners' intended purpose has been masterfully and powerfully realized. I strongly recommend a visit here, but with some reservations: Do not bring very young children, and discuss the Holocaust with older kids before visiting. The Museum Guide, reading list, and suggested answers to typically asked questions are available at the information desk and at **www.ushmm.org**.

Mature 8-year-olds on up can, and should, see the first-floor exhibit **"Remember the Children: Daniel's Story."** Pick up a free family guide at the information desk, along with a list of the day's events and times for the 15-minute orientation video (suitable for all ages). Daniel's Story details a fictional but historically accurate German youth's odyssey from a comfortable and secure home in 1930s Frankfurt to a 1941 ghetto and then

Break Time

The itty-bitty, cafeteria-style **Museum Café** is located in a separate light-filled annex, off the museum's west entrance plaza (Raoul Wallenberg Plaza). The limited all-vegetarian, nonkosher menu (three kosher items are prepared off-site) includes bagels, muffins, knishes, panini, personal pizzas, roasted vegetable salads, matzo ball soup, PB&J, fruit, desserts, and drinks—ideal for a between-meal pick-me-up or light lunch. And you can order a bagged lunch online ($10; five-bag minimum; 3 days in advance)! With slim pickin's in this neighborhood, it makes sense if your plans include a visit to the Tidal Basin cherry blossoms or Jefferson or FDR memorials. Security screens all who enter because of the administrative offices upstairs. Most items range from $6.75 to $9. Reservations are not accepted. It's open daily from 8:30am to 4:30pm; April through mid-June, usually extended hours.

to the gates of Auschwitz. Visitors walk Daniel's path, literally and emotionally. While the experience is sobering and unsettling, it stops well short of horrific. At the end, a short film reinforces the tragic message of a family's demise due to genocide. Young visitors are encouraged to express their reactions by recording their thoughts (markers and paper provided) and posting them in a museum mailbox. Also of note: **The Children's Tile Wall ★**, on the lower level, consists of 3,300 tiles painted by American schoolchildren as a memorial to the more than one million children who died in the Holocaust. Taken as a whole, it is decorative and lovely in its simplicity. On closer inspection, it is a poignant reminder of the museum's mission. If you wish, you may light memorial candles in the **Hall of Remembrance.**

The Holocaust (permanent exhibition) is housed on the second, third, and fourth floors. The museum's planners, educators, and child psychologists concur that youngsters 10 or 11 can handle the experience. I agree, but you know best what might or might not upset your kids. Along the way, 4-foot 10-inch walls shield young visitors from the most "difficult" exhibitions. Visitors entering the permanent collection receive an identity card with the name and family history of a Holocaust victim whose fate can be traced during the tour.

After entering the **Hall of Witness,** visitors ride to the fourth floor to begin the tour. (The fifth floor, with its library and archives, is devoted to scholarly pursuits. High-school students are welcome to do research here between 10am–5:30pm. Help is provided by library staff.) The fourth floor deals with the rise of Nazism from 1933 to 1939; the third floor focuses on the persecution of minorities, ghetto life, and the death camps from 1940 to 1944. The second floor details the liberation of the camps and refugees' resettling efforts. Young people take note: Also on the second floor is the **Wexner Language Center,** where you can learn about the Holocaust at your own pace through the user-friendly interactive computer system, which uses photographs, videos, and oral histories.

After several visits, I still find the most powerful exhibits to be the huge photograph of American soldiers liberating a camp; the *Nazi Rise to Power* and other historical films; the "Tower of Faces," photos of more than 100 *shtetl* families taken between 1890 and 1941 near Vilna (now Lithuania); the Anne Frank exhibit; a railcar that once stood on the tracks near Treblinka; "Voices from Auschwitz" (memories of survivors); thousands of shoes from death-camp victims; and artwork by children in Auschwitz. Whenever I visit, it is solemnly yet appropriately quiet in the Holocaust Museum.

Wednesdays at 1pm, March through August, Holocaust survivors speak in the Rubinstein Auditorium (suitable for mature 12-year-olds and older).

The museum shop contains books on the Holocaust, personal narratives, CDs, audio- and videotapes, and several shelves of titles for young readers. From April to mid-June, the shop stays open Tuesday and Thursday until 6:30pm.

100 Raoul Wallenberg Place (15th St. SW). ✆ **202/488-0400.** www.ushmm.org. Free same-day timed passes (often gone by 10:30am) at museum box office for permanent exhibits. For passes, required for the permanent exhibition, Mar–Aug, contact Tickets.com (✆ **800/400-9373;** service charge of $1.75 per ticket). Daily 10am–5:20pm; ask about extended summer hours. Closed on Yom Kippur and Dec. 25. Metro: Smithsonian (Independence Ave. exit).

Woodrow Wilson House Museum ★★ Finds Ages 8 and up. The handsome Georgian Revival mansion, built in 1915, is just off Embassy Row in Kalorama—the only former president's residence in the District open to the public. It's also one of my favorite museums. It will turn on kids with an interest in American history. Wilson, our 28th president, lived in this stately residence for 3 years after his second term, and his widow, Edith, resided here until her death in 1961. Since then, the National Trust has maintained it.

Visitors are surprised to learn that, despite his stern appearance and demeanor, the former scholar and university president was just a regular guy—a movie buff who was a fan of Tom Mix (an early cowboy movie star) and who subscribed to *Photoplay* movie magazine. On a more sublime level, you can see Wilson's inaugural Bible, the casing of the first shell fired in World War I, a White House Cabinet chair, and a vintage 1915 elevator. Staff prefer that you make a reservation online for the 45-minute guided tour, but they accept walk-ins. The tour, Tuesday through Sunday between 10am and 4pm, offers insight into the private life of the man behind the wire-rimmed spectacles. Programs for school groups are available during the school year.

The Friends of the Wilson House is part of a consortium that sponsors the popular **Kalorama House and Embassy Tour,** which includes a stop at one or more ambassadors' private residences. The annual event is usually the second Sunday of September. For more information and to make reservations, call ✆ **202/387-4062,** ext. 18.

2340 S St. NW. ✆ **202/387-4062.** www.woodrowwilsonhouse.org. Admission $7.50 adults, $6.50 seniors, $3 students, free 6 and under. Tues–Sun 10am–4pm. Closed Thanksgiving, Dec 25, and federal holidays. Metro: Dupont Circle, Q St. exit; then walk north on Massachusetts Ave. for 5 blocks to right at 24th St. and right at S St. half a block.

SPECIAL CHILDREN'S MUSEUMS

DAR Museum ★ Ages 4–10. Do not pass Go, do not collect $200, just head for the **New Hampshire Toy Attic** on the third floor to see 18th- and 19th-century children's furniture, toys, and dolls. Dollhouse aficionados will delight in the miniature furniture and accessories. Enjoy a museum tour, crafts, and games during **Fun Family Saturdays** for kids 7 and up, every third Saturday, September to June. Reservations are strongly encouraged. If there's space, walk-ins are welcome (✆ **202/879-3240** or museum@dar.org). To introduce young ones to early American history, 1-hour "Colonial Adventure" tours for 5- to 7-year-olds are held the first and third Saturdays, September through May, at 1:30 and 3pm. Reservations are required (✆ **202/879-3341**). Kids don colonial-style garb and visit a reproduction of a one-room house where they may scribble on a chalkboard, card wool, have a make-believe tea party, and imagine what it would be like to sleep in a trundle bed right beside their parents.

The "Touch of Independence" exhibit is filled with touchable kid-size period furniture and old-style toys and dolls. Guided tours of furnished period rooms are offered (subject to docent availability) on the hour and half hour, Monday through Friday from 10am to 2:30pm and Saturday 9am to 4:30pm. Just show up. You can take a self-guided tour Monday through Friday from 9:30am to 4pm and Saturday from 9:30am to 5pm. Call or check the website for special-exhibition information.

1776 D St. NW. ✆ **202/879-3241.** www.dar.org/museum. Free admission. Mon–Fri 9:30am–4pm; Sat 9am–5pm. Closed national holidays and during DAR's annual meeting in Apr. Metro: Farragut West or Farragut North.

Madame Tussauds **Ages 8 and up.** It pains me to include this, as wax museums are my least favorite form of entertainment, but I gotta do what I gotta do, realizing that many of you will enjoy this paean to kitsch. The best thing I can say about the seventh in the Tussauds chain, without *wax*ing total negativity, is that visitors are encouraged to touch, touch, touch (the kids ought to like that). Come kiss George W. Bush if you have the stomach for it; feel J. Edgar Hoover's suit (would that he'd been portrayed in his favorite dress and red high heels); take the hand of Lincoln, appearing more depressed than you've ever seen him. Feel the sweaty face of Nixon, all full, sensual lips. (Who modeled for this? Angelina?) In the Glamour section, you can drool over Brangelina and Julia Roberts and pinch J-Lo's ample *tuchis,* if you desire. In Sports, youngsters can help Tiger Woods line up a shot (yeah, right). The most interesting section is Behind the Scenes, where you can match footprints and height with the famous and infamous and learn how the figures are created. Wind up—or down—with a sugar rush, when sweet Katie Couric interviews you as family members watch on the TV monitor. Surely you have better ways to spend your vacation time and dollars in a city brimming with real experiences.

1025 F St. NW (at 10th St.). ✆ **202/942-7300.** www.madametussaudsdc.com. Admission $20 adults 13–59, $15 kids 4–12, seniors 60 and older $18. Daily Sun–Wed 10am–4pm; Thurs–Sat 10am–6pm (except during occasional special events). Metro: Metro Center.

5 FOR KIDS WITH SPECIAL INTERESTS

AIRPORTS

Due to heightened security following the September 11, 2001, terrorist attacks and the war in Iraq, airport tours could be suspended. Call before you go.

Washington Dulles International Airport **Ages 6 and older.** Visitors are welcome to stroll around Eero Saarinen's soaring main terminal (recently renovated to twice its original size). Pick up information for a self-guided tour at the information desk inside the terminal. The drive alone is worthwhile, especially at dawn or dusk but never during rush hour, to view this stunning architectural masterpiece. To ascend a tower and watch arriving and departing flights, go to the nearby Udvar-Hazy Center of the National Air and Space Museum (see listing earlier in this chapter, p. 127).

Chantilly, VA. ✆ **703/572-2700.** www.mwaa.com. Daily 24 hr. Directions: Constitution Ave. to Theodore Roosevelt Bridge, Rte. 66 west; bear left, and follow signs to Dulles Airport only. From Key Bridge, take Rte. 29 to Rte. 66, and follow the signs.

College Park Aviation Museum ★★ **Ages 4 and up.** This Smithsonian-affiliated museum is on the site of the world's oldest continuously operating airport, which opened its doors—make that field—in 1909. Remember Wilbur and Orville? Well, they taught the first two army officers to fly here the year the field opened. Other firsts include the first testing of a bomb dropped from a plane (1911) and the first U.S. Air Mail service (1918). This is a fantastic facility with appeal for kids of all ages (count me in!). Wing it on your own, and visit the historic airport (✆ **301/864-3029**). Tours are self-guided except the last Saturday of the month at 11am and 1pm. Group tours are available for 10 or more.

Pack a picnic to eat on the grounds, or walk a short distance to the **94th Aero Squadron,** 5240 Paint Branch Parkway, College Park (✆ **301/699-9400**). Kids love this restaurant. It's decorated to resemble a war-torn French farmhouse from around World War I and faces the runway. Out front are replicas of World War II fighter planes. Every September, the airport hosts a weekend Air Fair with airplane, helicopter, and hot-air balloon rides, as well as displays and children's entertainment. Bring extra batteries for your camera. There are photo ops aplenty. Docents are especially kid-friendly, stopping to kibitz with youngsters and sometimes give them free souvenirs. (I hope I don't get them into trouble.) The Prop Shop sells—you guessed it—flight-related souvenirs and is open the same hours as the museum. Preschoolers can join the Peter Pan Club (story time and activities) the second and fourth Thursday of the month, 10:30 to 11:30am, and there's no extra charge.

1985 Cpl. Frank Scott Dr., College Park, MD. ✆ **301/864-6029.** www.pgparks.com. Admission $4 adults, $3 seniors, $2 kids 2–18, free 23 months and under. Daily 10am–5pm. Closed Easter, July 4, Thanksgiving, Dec 25, Jan 1. Groups must call at least 1 week ahead to schedule a tour. Metro: College Park and then walk 2 blocks.

THE MILITARY

See section 2 of this chapter for individual listings on Arlington National Cemetery; the Pentagon; and the World War II, Korean War, and Vietnam War memorials.

U.S. Navy Museum **Ages 6 and up.** This museum chronicles the history of the U.S. Navy from the Revolutionary War to the present. Exhibits include "200 Years of the Washington Navy Yard" and "The Navy in the Korean War." Kids gravitate to the model ships and weaponry. They can turn a sub periscope, climb on cannons, and work the barrels of antiaircraft weapons. When they tire of war games, they can board the 1950s destroyer USS *Barry,* berthed outside. You must call ahead and make an appointment to visit. Weekdays, enter at 11th Street SE (at O St.). Weekends and holidays, enter at M Street SE (at 5th St.).

Bldg. 76, 805 Kidder Breese SE, Washington Navy Yard. ✆ **202/433-6897.** www.history.navy.mil. Free admission. Mon–Fri 9am–5pm; Sat–Sun and holidays 10am–5pm. Closed Thanksgiving, Dec 24–25, Jan 1. Metro: Eastern Market or Navy Yard and then walk; taxi after dark. Some free parking at 7th and M sts. SE.

MODEL TRAINS

All aboard! As you probably know, model trains are not just for Christmas anymore. With your little cabooses in tow, try train spotting at the following locations. See also the review of the **Baltimore & Ohio Railroad Museum** (p. 279), in Baltimore, Maryland.

B&O Railroad Station Museum (Ellicott City) **Ages 4 and up.** About an hour's drive from downtown D.C., this museum is housed in the oldest railroad station in America. Catch a glimpse of life in the 19th century at exhibits that change every month

U.S. Navy Memorial & Heritage Center

There's more here than first meets the eye. After taking a family picture with Stanley Bleifeld's statue *The Lone Sailor* on the plaza, enter the belowground visitor center, which is unmistakably shiplike. *The Homecoming,* another work by Bleifeld, welcomes visitors at the entrance. Throughout the Gallery Deck are interactive video kiosks. Push a button and learn about Navy history, or retrieve information on naval ships and aircraft. If you have friends or relatives who've served in the Navy, see if they're registered in the Navy Memorial Log. If they're not, pick up an enrollment form.

Action-packed Navy-related movies play three times most days in the theater. A special "Matinees at the Memorial" series takes place one Saturday a month, April through October. In 2009, John Wayne starred in the 1944 hit, "The Fighting Seabees." Sometimes the show is canceled in favor of a Guard Drill Team performance or concert by the U.S. Navy Band. Admission is free.

Check out the **"Wave Wall,"** where 200 years of naval history are depicted in 13 panels, before picking up souvenirs in the Ship's Store, full of nautical gifts and memorabilia.

From Memorial Day to Labor Day, you might want to take in at least one of the armed forces' 8pm concerts in the outdoor amphitheater (weather permitting). Tickets are not required. Call ✆ **202/737-2300,** ext. 768.

The center is at 701 Pennsylvania Ave. NW, between 7th and 9th streets (✆ **202/737-2300**). Admission is free. Hours March through October are Monday through Saturday from 9:30am to 5pm; November through February, Tuesday through Saturday, same hours. Closed on major holidays.

or two. If you can choose only one, make it the annual **Holiday Festival of Trains** ★, late November to late January. Call or check the website for exhibits and special events the rest of the year. On permanent display is an HO-scale model replica of the first 13 miles of the Baltimore & Ohio Railroad, the nation's first. When it opened in 1827, it ran from Baltimore to Ellicott City. Train and history buffs will want to stop in the museum store for hats, shirts, books, and other choo-choo-related souvenirs. You'll need a car to get here. If you want to stay longer to explore more of quaint Ellicott City, park in one of the several metered lots within walking distance.

2711 Maryland Ave. (Main St. and Maryland Ave.), Ellicott City, MD. ✆ **410/461-1944.** www.ecborail.org. Admission $5 adults, $4 seniors and students, $3 children 2–12, free under 2. Wed–Sun 11am–4pm. Closed Easter, Memorial Day, July 4, Labor Day, Thanksgiving, Dec 24–25, Dec 31, Jan 1. Directions: Take Colesville Rd. (Rte. 29/Old Columbia Pike) north from I-495 to Rte. 144 east (Old Frederick Road–Main St.); follow signs to Historic District and museum. Short-term parking on the street and nearby lots.

Fairfax Station Railroad Museum **Ages 4 and up.** Visitors lay tracks for the N-gauge model train displays the third Sunday of every month February through November, from 1 to 4pm. But every Sunday, the public is invited to check out the quaint train depot (much smaller than a caboose) filled with Civil War and Red Cross memorabilia (Clara Barton nursed wounded soldiers at the original site after the second

Battle of Manassas). The caboose houses a permanent model train exhibit. The museum serves as a staging area for lectures, workshops, and craft shows. When you're in the area, come see the annual Holiday Train Show the first weekend in December. With a little planning, children can celebrate their birthdays with a caboose party. A small gift shop features railroad and Civil War souvenirs.

11200 Fairfax Station Rd., Fairfax Station, VA. ✆ **703/425-9225.** www.fairfax-station.org. Suggested donation $2 adults, $1 children 4–10, free 3 and under. Sun 1–4pm (permanent exhibit in caboose); model trains run 3rd Sun of every month Feb–Nov. Directions: Rte. 123 South of George Mason University to Fairfax Station Rd., 1/4 mile to museum.

SCIENCE & NATURE

See section 1 in this chapter for listings on the following science museums: the National Museum of Natural History, the National Zoological Park, and the National Air and Space Museum.

Discovery Creek Children's Museum **Ages 6 months and up.** Families are invited to drop in for science- and nature-related activities (hikes, crafts, discussions, stories, guest speakers) on Saturday and Sunday from 10am to 3pm in Glen Echo Park's former stables. Every month there's a different theme. The cost for the weekend programs is nominal: $5 for ages 2 to 64, $3 for 65 and older, free for kids under 2. Discovery Creek also has satellite locations in the area—the best known is the historic schoolhouse on MacArthur Boulevard where Discovery Creek had its start several years ago. (The schoolhouse is also available for private birthday parties.) Discovery Creek's weekday programs are geared to groups, by reservation only (✆ **202/337-5111**).

D.C. area residents, take note: Discovery Creek has programs that introduce infants, toddlers, and preschoolers to the wonders of nature. The fee for Toddler Treehouse, for example (four sessions, each 1½ hr.), is $60 for members, $75 for nonmembers. On your way in or out of the park, ride the beautifully restored 1921 Dentzel carousel. Glen Echo is also the site for performances by the Puppet Co. and Adventure Theatre. In fact, visitors with Puppet Co. and Adventure Theatre ticket stubs get $1 off. Both offer professional productions that are well worth seeing (see chapter 10). You could spend the better part of a day at this historic former amusement park.

Stables at Glen Echo Park, 7300 MacArthur Blvd., at Goldsboro Rd., Glen Echo, MD. ✆ **202/337-5111.** www.discoverycreek.org. Sat–Sun 10am–3pm. Admission $5 adults and kids 2–64, $3 seniors 65 and older, free kids under 2. Closed Thanksgiving weekend, Dec 25, Jan 1, and government holidays. Metro: Friendship Heights and then Metrobus no. 29. Directions: Massachusetts Ave. to end at Goldsboro Rd., left to MacArthur Blvd., right at MacArthur, left into park; park, and then cross footbridge.

Goddard Space Flight Center Visitor Center **Ages 6 and up.** You can reach the stars just a half-hour from downtown in beautiful Greenbelt, Maryland. And now for something new—and far out. Using computers and video projectors, **"Science on a Sphere"** ★ shows compelling images projected on a large suspended sphere. The half-hour movies (moving pictures may be closer to the truth), with music, take place six times a day. Very cool. Kids are drawn to the hands-on interactive displays in the visitor center and space-age souvenirs in the gift shop. Step outside to the rocket garden, with actual rockets and some mockups. The model-rocket launches have been popular with local families for many moons and are held the first Sunday of every month (weather permitting) at 1pm.

ICESat Rd., Greenbelt, MD. ✆ **301/286-8981.** www.nasa.gov/goddard. Free admission. Sept–June Tues–Fri 10am–3pm, Sat–Sun noon–4pm; July–Aug Tues–Fri 10am–5pm, Sat noon–4pm. Closed Thanksgiving,

Dec 25, Jan 1, and all federal holidays. Directions: Take New York Ave. to I-295 north (Baltimore-Washington Pkwy.); turn left on Greenbelt Rd. (Rte. 193), turn left at Soil Conservation Rd., and then turn left at the first gate (just before security checkpoint).

National Aquarium **Ages 1 and up.** More than 1,000 specimens are contained in 50 tanks at the oldest public aquarium in the nation. And it looked like the oldest until a 2008 makeover (some might say "Extreme") brought it in synch with the 21st century. I've always liked this place—and so do most kids—but it was rather lackluster. I applaud the new look. More than 200 species swim here—assorted salt- and freshwater fish, including sharks, an eel, an alligator, and Japanese carp. And they get along swimmingly. The piranhas, you'll be happy to learn, have their own tank. Have a late lunch with the sharks at 2pm Monday and Wednesday; piranhas, 2pm Sunday, Tuesday, or Thursday; or alligators Friday at 2pm. A visit here is an especially good option for toddler and elementary-school-age kids; older children may become bored quickly. Families can reserve a room here for birthday parties.

Note: A large multilevel aquarium in Baltimore is also known as the National Aquarium, but the two are oceans apart in content and scope. See the Baltimore entry on p. 283.

Department of Commerce (lower level), 14th St. (btw. Pennsylvania and Constitution aves. NW). ✆ **202/482-2825.** www.nationalaquarium.com. Admission (cash only) $7 adults, $6 seniors and military, $3 ages 2–10, free under 2. Daily 9am–5pm. Closed Thanksgiving and Dec 25. Metro: Federal Triangle.

National Geographic Museum ★ Finds **Ages 8 and up.** Before entering Explorers Hall, watch the short introductory videotape on the 16-panel screen to familiarize young trailblazers with the National Geographic Society's mission of "increasing and diffusing geographic knowledge." Here visitors can enjoy a variety of temporary exhibitions along with permanent exhibits and interactive displays reflecting the richness and diversity of our world. Changing exhibits focus on different aspects of the natural world—animals (prehistoric and living), climate changes, undersea and land exploration (and, of course), discoveries by National Geographic researchers and works by National Geographic photographers. Some exhibits may be too sophisticated for kids under 8, but older children enjoy the museum for its relatively intimate size. Here, complex geographic information is explained at a level that they can readily understand and appreciate through the many interactive exhibits and videos, such as "Where Did We Come From?" (evolution) and "What's Shaky and Quaky?" (volcanoes). The fascinating Geochron—world time map to the uninitiated—is shaded to show daylight and night. Look up to the 3D model of the Grand Canyon plastered to the ceiling.

At the **Mammals Kiosk,** the touch-screen reveals pictures of 700 animals and 155 vocalizations. Visitors are encouraged to "touch, play, and learn" while testing their trivial pursuit of geophysical knowledge in "Geographica," where you can also feel a tornado and walk beneath a flying dinosaur. Experience orbital flight with loved ones in **Earth Station One,** an amphitheater that several times an hour simulates an orbital flight 23,000 miles above Earth's surface. ***Note:*** Large groups are advised to call ahead (✆ **202/857-7689**).

Your kids might have to drag you away from **Global Access,** an educational, fun-to-play video game. After picking a country you'd like to know more about, choose specific topics (history, culture, flora, and fauna) from the menu. Voilà! Press a button, and the living atlas tells all. In the **Television Room,** you can watch scenes from the society's enormously popular and instructive TV series.

Wouldn't your kids like to be on the cover of *National Geographic* magazine? Sure they would! Outside the TV Room are two photo booths where they can choose to have their face plastered on a postcard-size cover.

Gaze at the Washington sky overhead in the small planetarium and then take a gander at a nearly 4-billion-year-old moon rock. Pick up past and current copies of *National Geographic* magazine, a wide and interesting selection of beautifully photographed books for the whole family, maps, videos, educational gifts, and souvenirs in the gift shop.

17th and M sts. NW. ✆ **202/857-7588.** www.ngmuseum.org. Free admission. Mon–Sat and holidays 9am–5pm; Sun 10am–5pm. Closed Dec 25. Metro: Farragut North (Connecticut Ave. and L St. exit) or Farragut West.

National Museum of Health and Medicine **Ages 10 and up.** A multiyear effort had been under way to move this hard-to-find museum (part of the Armed Forces Institute of Pathology) back to the Mall, its original site before moving uptown in 1972. Now, with Walter Reed slated to close, who knows where the museum will be in a few years?

Older kids with a strong stomach and interest in medicine or pathology won't want to miss this. Don't bring young children; they might have trouble sleeping afterward. The museum has numerous exhibits of diseased, injured, and defective body parts—some famous, such as Lincoln's skull bone and President Garfield's spine.

Permanent exhibitions include "Medicine During the Civil War," "Evolution of the Microscope," and "Human Body, Human Being," which features preserved, um, body parts (stomachs, brains, lungs, kidney stones, and so on). Show your kids the smoker's and coal miner's lungs (a far better deterrent than media ads and your nagging about the effects of smoking). The first Saturday of the month, the museum has a health-awareness program from 11am to 2pm. Information on drugs and AIDS is also exhibited. Just show up for the free docent-led tours that are led the second and fourth Saturdays of the month at 1pm. Call about group tours (✆ **202/782-2201**). Yes, there is a gift shop. No souvenir preserved brains last time I browsed. ***Please note:*** This is a military site, and the rules for admission to the grounds are strict and many. Most Metrobuses are not allowed on the grounds, so you could be dropped the equivalent of several blocks away. Call or check the website before heading there. If you're hungry after what you've viewed, the Walter Reed campus has a cafeteria and a few fast food restaurants.

Walter Reed Army Medical Center, Bldg. 54, 6900 Georgia Ave. (at Elder St. NW). ✆ **202/782-2200.** http://nmhm.washingtondc.museum. Free admission but donations are suggested. Daily 10am–5:30pm. Closed Dec 25. Metro: Silver Spring or Takoma Park, and then take a bus or taxi 1½ miles to the museum. Free parking.

Rock Creek Nature Center and Planetarium ★ **Ages 4 and up.** The nature center has exhibitions, a Discovery Room, a planetarium, a library, and an active beehive, connected by a tube to the outdoors. Gather here for guided walks and to explore the self-guided trail on your own. A free Young Planetarium show takes place Wednesday at 4pm. "The Night Sky," a show for kids 4 to 7 and their parents/adult companions, is held on Saturday and Sunday at 1pm. On Saturday and Sunday at 4pm, the "advanced" show is geared to those 7 and older. Free tickets are distributed half an hour before each show. "Exploring the Sky," a stargazing session cosponsored by the National Park Service and the National Capital Astronomers, is held one evening a month from April through November at Picnic Grove No. 13, near the Nature Center, Military and Glover roads NW. Because the time varies from month to month, call ahead.

See the section on "Parks, Gardens & Other Wide-Open Spaces," in chapter 8, for more information on the park itself.

5200 Glover Rd. NW. ✆ **202/895-6070.** www.nps.gov/rocr/planetarium. Free admission. Wed–Sun 9am–5pm. Directions: North on Connecticut Ave., turn right onto Military Rd., and then turn right onto Glover Rd.

U.S. Naval Observatory ★ Finds Ages 8 and up. On a clear night, you can see forever at the Naval Observatory. Weather permitting, you'll have stars in your eyes after peering through the 12-inch Alvan Clark refractor at celestial bodies 25,000 light-years away. Gates open for security checks selected Mondays at 8pm for the 8:30pm 1½-hour tour. Wear sturdy shoes, and be prepared to walk a distance over hilly terrain to the observatory itself. Leave backpacks, bulky items, and bags behind. Cameras are okay. Requests must be submitted online at www.usno.navy.mil at least 4 to 6 weeks in advance. Be prepared to answer questions, including the names in your party, dates of birth, daytime phone, and an e-mail address. Because this is military property, according to the website, tours "may be suspended at any time." There is some on-street parking. The closest Metro (Dupont Circle) is not so close. The N2 and N4 Metrobuses pass by, but you might miss the show because the buses are less than punctual after 7pm. If you don't have a car, I'd take a taxi.

Massachusetts Ave. (at 34th St. NW; enter the South Gate near the Embassy of New Zealand). ✆ **202/762-1438.** www.usno.navy.mil. Free admission. Selected Mon at 8:30pm. Closed federal holidays.

MEDIA

Newseum ★★ Ages 8 and up. Okay, I'm a skeptic. I pooh-poohed the pre-opening hype about this museum. I was wrong, wrong, wrong. This museum rocks! (How's that for objectivity?). A 74-foot engraving of the First Amendment introduces visitors to scores of state-of-the-art displays and interactives covering 500 years of news—media history, elections, coverage of world-changing events—in multilevel galleries, theaters, shops, a signature restaurant (The Source), and a food court. Dedicated to the Fourth Estate, it has been in the works for more years than I can count and takes the place of the original Newseum in Arlington, Virginia.

The news satellite and helicopter suspended from the 90-foot ceiling of the Great Hall will wow younger kids, as will riding in the largest glass hydraulic elevators in the world. But these are just appetizers. Start your visit in the orientation theater with the 7-minute film *What's News.* The front pages of 80 newspapers are displayed outside the Pennsylvania Avenue entrance and in the **Today's Front Pages** gallery. So if you feel out of touch, you can catch up on hometown news. Pick up a floor plan at the information desk and ask about a family activity guide (in the works).

Note: A couple of galleries are not appropriate for youngsters. The Pulitzer and 9/11 exhibits have materials that might be disturbing to young children; the museum's staff advises discretion. Otherwise, one of D.C.'s newest, most exciting attractions is clearly out to woo families. While you could spend the better part of a day at the Newseum (and I have), I believe *most* kids under 10 will snooze after an hour. But for children who dig history—and their companions—this place is a monolithic time capsule of more than 500 years of world history. Because this book deals with other sights and subjects, I've culled a few highlights that have broad appeal (besides riding the elevator, large enough for Atila and his elephants). Tour a TV studio and take your place in the audience during regularly scheduled special events. In the World News Gallery, where 80 front pages are updated daily, watch the news on large-screen monitors and learn about the dangers facing foreign correspondents (in case you've been out of touch the past 60 or so years). Step up to a touch screen in the Newsroom and assume the role of photojournalist. Play reporter or anchor on one of the interactives. Use a teleprompter, and record and send a message electronically—then watch it appear online.

In **"Race For Your Rights"** ★, a game with a hero and villain targeted at 7- to 11-year-olds, youngsters must overcome race-course obstacles by answering questions about First Amendment rights. Changing exhibits are geared to youngsters. While they're waiting for the new exhibits they can search a large wall for their favorite comic strip characters on the way to the food court. Or dine at The Source, masterminded by world-renowned chef Wolfgang Puck. The Lounge/Café portion of the restaurant is open for lunch Monday through Friday and dinner Monday through Saturday. The Food Court is open daily from 9am to 4pm.

Let's hope the Newseum spreads positive karma along with the (uncensored) news throughout D.C.—and the world.

555 Pennsylvania Ave. NW (at 6th St.). ✆ **888/NEWSEUM** [639-7386]. www.newseum.org. Admission $20 adult, $18 seniors (65 and up), $13 children 7–12, free 6 and under. Daily 9am–5pm. Closed Thanksgiving, Dec. 25, Jan. 1. Metro: Archives/Navy Memorial then walk toward Pennsylvania Ave. and left toward the Capitol (big dome), cross at 7th St., and walk 1 block to 6th St.

Voice of America **Ages 7 and up.** Between the Air and Space Museum and the Capitol, the world's largest radio station welcomes visitors to the downtown facility, where programs are broadcast worldwide, round the clock, on 26 channels in 42 languages! During the 45-minute tour, Monday through Friday at noon and 3pm, you will see the control room, hear part of a feature show, view a short film, and perhaps catch the evening news in Russian. Foreign visitors, who outnumber Americans by a wide margin, are excited when they recognize broadcasters that they listen to at home. The large mural, *The Meaning of Social Security*, was completed by Ben Shahn, for the WPA (Work Projects Administration), in 1940. Ask about the kids' version of the tour (children 7 and older), available to families on request. Reserve by phone (✆ **202/203-4990**), online (www.voanews.com), or by e-mail (tickets@voanews.com). Arrive at least 10 minutes early for security check.

330 Independence Ave. SW (enter on C St. only). ✆ **202/619-3919.** www.voa.gov. Free admission. Tours Mon–Fri noon and 3pm. Call or go online for reservations. Metro: L'Enfant Plaza or Federal Center SW.

The Washington Post **Ages 11 and older.** Groups *only* (10–30 people, with reservations made in advance) may tour one of the *Post* printing plants: Springfield, Virginia (Thurs), or College Park, Maryland (Tues). The 1-hour tours are given only in response to a written and faxed request at least 4 weeks in advance. The request must include the date and time your group wants the tour, preferred tour location, name of organization, full names of all participants, name of contact person and phone number, and special needs. Fax your request to ✆ **202/334-4963.** For more information, call the Public Relations Department at ✆ **202/334-7969.** Jeez, if you do all this, you must be very motivated.

1150 15th St. NW. ✆ **202/334-7969.** www.washingtonpost.com. Free admission, reservations required. Tour printing plants by reservation only. Metro: Farragut North or McPherson Sq.

6 ORGANIZED TOURS

For an easy way to see D.C.'s major attractions, or when you're looking for something to do without wearing out the troops, take a guided tour. Ride one of the National Park Service's **Tourmobile** trams (✆ **202/554-5100;** www.tourmobile.com), and get off as often as you like—or not at all! This is the area's largest sightseeing operation and the only one licensed to make stops at attractions on the Mall. See "Getting Around," in chapter 3, for more information on different tours available.

Martz Gray Line Sightseeing Tours (✆ **202/289-1995;** www.graylinedc.com) offers several tours—from 3 hours to 2 days—in and around D.C. and to destinations as far as Williamsburg and Charlottesville, Virginia. Martz/Gray Line departs from convenient Union Station (first parking level) and offers courtesy pickup at several hotels. I wouldn't try an all-day trip with preschoolers, who might view the confinement as an invitation to riot. Also beware of kids who get nauseated on buses. I'm particularly fond of the "Washington After Dark" tour, but I don't recommend it for families with kids under 9 or 10. The bus stops at each presidential memorial and major monument for about 20 minutes so that you can take pictures, buy a souvenir, or stop and stare. My favorite moments are spent on the steps of the Lincoln and Jefferson memorials, taking in the scene. You must walk from the drop-off point to the monument (sometimes the equivalent of several blocks). And the tour ends between 10:30 and 11pm. I suggest eating first and/or carrying a snack; all the monument concessions close early in the evening. (Last time I skipped dinner and was so hungry that I would have sold my mother for a bag of pretzels.) Martz/Gray Line also offers a multilingual tour of Washington, departing from the tour company's Union Station terminal. Advance reservations are required (✆ **202/289-1995**).

Tour D.C. (✆ **301/588-8999;** www.tourdc.com) leads group walking tours of Georgetown and Embassy Row/Dupont Circle. Mary Kay Ricks (lapsed attorney, tour guide, and author) and staff are experts at peppering their narrative with spicy scandals. History buffs, groupies, and teens might enjoy "Women, Love, and Property," a tour of Georgetown, where many influential women, such as Pamela Harriman, Jacqueline Kennedy Onassis, and Katharine Graham resided, and "John and Jackie in Georgetown," tracing the years the Kennedys lived there. Tours are spring through fall but never in July and August. Too hot! The cost is $300 and up. Tour D.C. will craft a tour that fits your group like a glove. ***Note:*** Tours are geared for adults. Children are welcome at the discretion of parents.

Tour de Force (✆ **703/525-2948;** www.atourdeforce.com), through owner/guide/historian/author Jeanne Fogle—customizes tours, via motorcoach, SUV, limo, or on foot (half-day, full-day, and multiday). The author of books on D.C.'s history, she's a native who knows her stuff and whose family has resided in the District for more than 150 years. Prices vary.

Washington Walks (✆ **202/484-1565;** www.washingtonwalks.com) offers numerous walking tours of the District's neighborhoods as well as private themed tours. How about this: The "Moveable Feast" walk takes participants on the Metro to sample snacks at local eateries. Sounds delicious to me! "In Fala's Footsteps," for kids 4 to 9, is but one of the popular family tours. (Fala was FDR's beloved Scottish terrier.) The licensed guides will tailor a tour to your liking, but give them a couple of days to plan. Tours are held April through October daily, rain or shine. Group walking tours are $10 a head, free 3 and younger. Bus tours are more. You must reserve at least 48 hours in advance. Call or check the website for more on scheduled tours and arranging private tours.

Independent guide **Anita Allingham** ★ (✆ **301/493-8568**) leads a tour of the National Zoo. Her "Illuminated Night Tour" includes stops at the Lincoln Memorial, with its unobstructed view of the eternal flame marking John F. Kennedy's grave; the steps of the Jefferson Memorial, to ogle the White House and Washington Monument; and the Kennedy Center rooftop, for an unequaled panorama of downtown and beyond. Anita is a seasoned pro, a D.C. native who has been guiding tourists around the nation's capital since 1976. She'll modify the evening tour to suit you and is also available for tailor-made walking tours (using Metro and/or taxi) and as a guide to Baltimore, Annapolis, and beyond. Call for prices.

A word of caution: If you're considering a small, lesser-known tour company, make sure that the tour guides are licensed. You don't want to hear about Washington from someone recently arrived from Minnesota who makes up commentary along the way. When in doubt, call the **Guild of Professional Tour Guides,** known hereabouts as "the Guild" (✆ **202/298-1474;** www.washingtondctourguides.com). This association of more than 200 licensed guides with 10 or more years of experience will steer you toward a guide or company that meets your specific needs.

Neighborhood Strolls

I've been pounding the D.C. pavement since I was a college student in Foggy Bottom. I can tell you unequivocally, walking is the best way to see Washington. L'Enfant laid out the city on a grid. Wasn't he clever? It's easy to find your way around (see chapter 3), and once you get the hang of subdividing the District, you'll blaze your own trails. Although the shortest distance between two points might be a Metro ride, you'll shortchange your kids and yourselves, missing some of D.C.'s charm and beauty, if you fail to explore on foot.

WALKING TOUR 1 GEORGETOWN

START: **Old Stone House.**

FINISH: **Foggy Bottom Metro.**

TIME: **2 to 5 hours (2 hr., if you don't eat or shop; up to 5 hr. or more, if you want to shop, eat, ride the canal boat, or take a cruise to Alexandria).**

BEST TIMES: **Weekdays.**

WORST TIMES: **Weekends, year-round. If you go on a weekend, start early and wind down before the thundering hordes arrive.**

Georgetown is the ideal neighborhood for strolling. Kids of all ages take to the unique hodgepodge of old and new. Remnants of the past invite exploration—the C&O Canal, historic buildings and homes, and lush parks. On the flip side, scores of up-to-date shops and restaurants—and no less than four ice cream shops—line Wisconsin Avenue and M Street, and fill The Shops at Georgetown Park (hereinafter, "Georgetown Park"), a three-tiered enclosed mall.

Wisconsin Avenue and M Street is Washington's oldest intersection. Pierre L'Enfant and George Washington set out from this crossroad one frosty October morning in 1791 and traveled east to establish the boundaries of the future District of Columbia. During the 1870s, more than 500 canal boats brought limestone, coal, flour, and other raw goods to the mills, factories, and blacksmiths headquartered along the waterfront of the Port of Georgetown. Consider the history as you browse about 500 shoe stores (only a slight exaggeration).

On weekends from spring through fall, Georgetown's permanent population of 11,000—an interesting mix of government bureaucrats, students, merchants, and blue-bloods—swells threefold, making it a primo spot for people-watching. Given that the 272-block parcel in the city's west end boasts more than 100 restaurants and bars, you'll never be more than a hop, skip, or a jump away from sustenance—everything from a bagel or burger to the haughtiest haute cuisine.

Copies of the **"Georgetown Visitors Guide and Map"** (www.georgetowndc.com) and brochures are free at the White House Visitor Center, 1450 Pennsylvania Ave. NW; the concierge desk in the Georgetown Park mall, 3222 M St. NW, at Wisconsin Avenue; the Georgetown Visitor's Center, 1057 Thomas Jefferson St. (btw. 30th and 31st St.); and most Georgetown hotels, shops, and restaurants.

Take a map and wear comfortable shoes; the area is hilly, and some sections are paved with brick or cobblestone. Your kids will be so tired at the end of the walk that they'll sleep for 48 hours. If you begin at the Foggy Bottom Metro station, at 23rd and I streets NW, it's about a 15- to 20-minute stroll to Georgetown. If you wish to save time and your stamina, take Metro to Dupont Circle or Rosslyn, Virginia, and then hop on the Georgetown Metro Connection shuttle (hereinafter, "Georgetown Shuttle"), with pickups every 10 minutes (www.georgetowndc.com). The fare is $1 (50¢ with a SmarTrip card), 25¢ for seniors 65 and older. (See chapter 3 for more details.) If you choose to walk, go north on 23rd Street toward Pennsylvania Avenue. Bear left at Washington Circle to Pennsylvania Avenue. Continue on Pennsylvania to where it dead-ends at M Street, and continue on M Street. The Old Stone House is at 3051 M St.

1 Old Stone House

The only pre-Revolutionary War building still standing in D.C. was built in 1765, and the five rooms are furnished with items typical of the late 18th and early 19th centuries. It is open Wednesday through Sunday from noon to 4pm (usually until 5pm in summer). Kids can run up and down the hilly lawn (no pesticides are used on the grass), and everyone can enjoy the magnificent flowers that bloom from early spring into October. The garden spills over with picnickers in warm weather.

When you leave, cross M Street (watch the traffic!) to Thomas Jefferson Street, and head down the hill toward the river. On your left, you'll see:

2 The Georgetown & Charles F. Mercer

One-hour cruises on these working canal boats depart several times a day between mid-April and late October. Stop at the National Park Service office in the Foundry Mall, 1055 Thomas Jefferson Street, for tickets and information. You might prefer to detour along the canal towpath, a lovely place to stroll. The water's odor can get a mite strong in summer, but most of the time, it's tolerable.

When you reach the end of Thomas Jefferson Street, you've arrived at:

3 Washington Harbour

This is a large complex of offices, private residences, restaurants, and shops fronting the Potomac River.

Walk toward the river and you'll arrive at the:

TAKE A BREAK

You could do worse than to fall into the splashy **Sequoia** restaurant, at 3000 K St. (✆ **202/944-4200;** www.arkrestaurants.com). Reservations are a necessity at peak times and for highly desirable outdoor seating (spring–Oct, weather permitting). There's no kids' menu, but burgers and pizza are always available. Sequoia may be a tourist draw, but it is also top drawer! Nearby, **Cafe Cantina** sells wraps, burritos, and pizza by the slice. **Bangkok Joe's** specializes in dumplings. The adjacent Washington Harbour Park is a splendid picnic site (no tables, but plenty of benches).

4 Scenic Promenade

Walk along the promenade and, if you face the water, you'll see Theodore Roosevelt Island straight ahead. The infamous Watergate and the Kennedy Center are to the left. Key Bridge, to the right, connects Arlington, Virginia, to Georgetown. At the far right of the promenade is Washington Harbour Park.

Exit the area onto K Street (under the Whitehurst Freeway) and walk up 31st Street (it runs parallel to Wisconsin Ave.). Go 1 short block and left at South Street. Measure your fitness level as you climb the steep hill, with attached homes banked on the right. On the left is the Ritz-Carlton Hotel Georgetown. Historic Grace Church is on the corner at Wisconsin Avenue. Turn right here. This is the southern end of M Street.

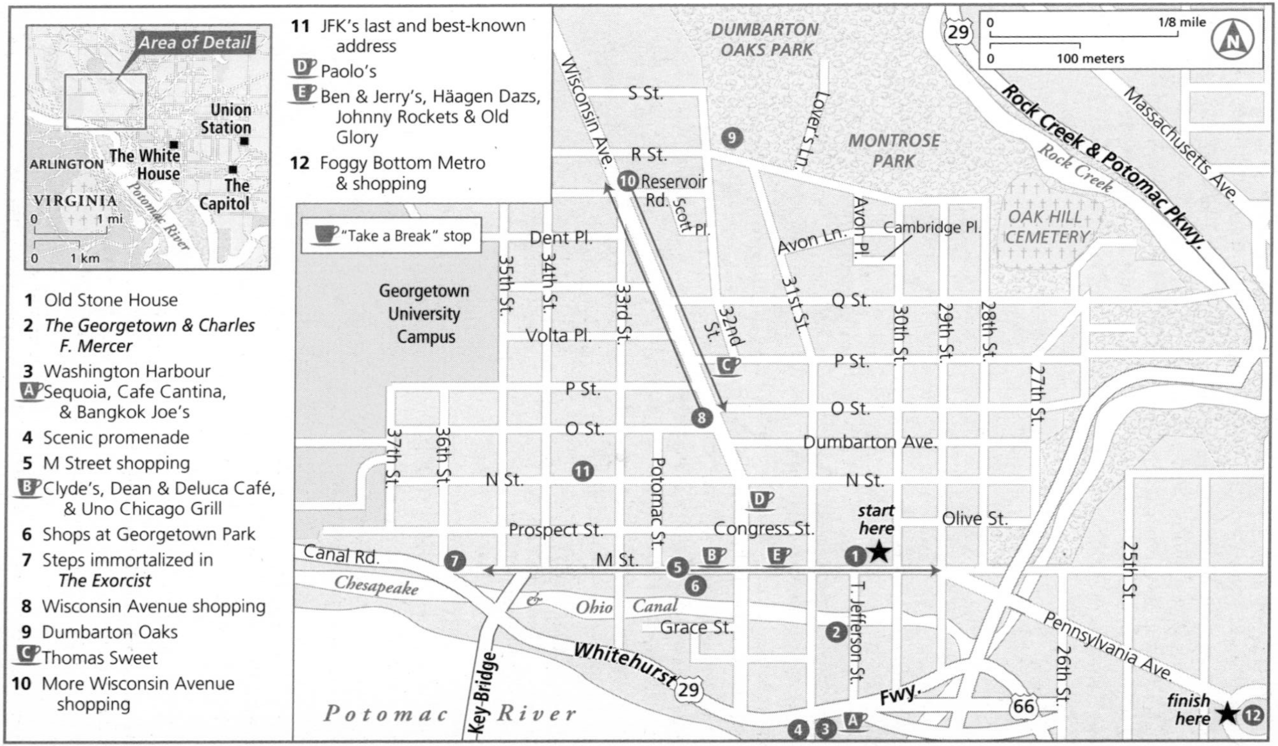
Area of Detail
Union Station
The White House
ARLINGTON
The Capitol
VIRGINIA
Potomac River
0 1 mi
0 1 km
1 Old Stone House
2 The Georgetown & Charles F. Mercer
3 Washington Harbour
A Sequoia, Cafe Cantina, & Bangkok Joe's
4 Scenic promenade
5 M Street shopping
B Clyde's, Dean & Deluca Café, & Uno Chicago Grill
6 Shops at Georgetown Park
7 Steps immortalized in The Exorcist
8 Wisconsin Avenue shopping
9 Dumbarton Oaks
C Thomas Sweet
10 More Wisconsin Avenue shopping
11 JFK's last and best-known address
D Paolo's
E Ben & Jerry's, Häagen Dazs, Johnny Rockets & Old Glory
12 Foggy Bottom Metro & shopping
"Take a Break" stop
Georgetown University Campus
DUMBARTON OAKS PARK
MONTROSE PARK
OAK HILL CEMETERY
0 1/8 mile
0 100 meters
Rock Creek & Potomac Pkwy.
Rock Creek
Massachusetts Ave.
Wisconsin Ave.
S St.
R St.
Reservoir Rd.
Scott Pl.
Lover's Ln.
Avon Ln.
Avon Pl.
Cambridge Pl.
Dent Pl.
35th St.
34th St.
33rd St.
32nd St.
31st St.
30th St.
29th St.
28th St.
27th St.
26th St.
25th St.
Q St.
Volta Pl.
P St.
O St.
Dumbarton Ave.
N St.
Olive St.
Potomac St.
Prospect St.
Congress St.
start here
finish here
M St.
Canal Rd.
37th St.
36th St.
Chesapeake & Ohio Canal
Grace St.
T. Jefferson St.
Pennsylvania Ave.
Whitehurst Fwy.
29
66
Key Bridge
Potomac River

5 M Street Shopping

A few doors below M Street, at 1075 Wisconsin, is Georgetown Tees, which sells souvenir shirts. Across the street, Banana Republic, at 3200 M St., sells stylish and pricey casual wear in adult sizes. Diagonally across this busy intersection is Benetton's two-story shop, with clothing for the whole family, at 1200 Wisconsin Ave.

> **TAKE A BREAK**
> **Clyde's** (3236 M St.), **Dean & Deluca Café** (3276 M St. NW), and **Pizza Paradiso** (3282 M St. NW) are all within 2 blocks of Wisconsin Avenue and M Street.

Serious shoppers will want to inspect:

6 Shops at Georgetown Park

Georgetown Park, at Wisconsin Avenue and M Street, is a multilevel mall with 75 shops, including H&M department store, with reasonably priced trendy clothing; Fit to a Tee, with the zaniest collection of shirts ever assembled in one place; The Hattery; Lil Thingamajigs (games, puzzles, toys); Candy Land (jelly beans and other sweets); and good old Mrs. Field's. If it's been more than 20 minutes since you've eaten, there are a number of restaurants and cafes. If your dogs are dragging, buy your tickets for the Old Town Trolley here (not to be confused with Old Town Alexandria).

If you detour a few blocks and continue walking west on M Street to 36th Street, to your right, you'll see the:

7 Steps Immortalized in The Exorcist

These steps have been immortalized in both the film and the book versions of *The Exorcist.*

Get back on track and continue your uphill exploration of:

8 Wisconsin Avenue Shopping

Walk along the west (left) side of the street. At 1208, check out Abercrombie & Fitch for stylish, durable sportswear. American Eagle Outfitters (1220) has jeans, tees, and the like for teens and adults (but the XS will fit big kids). At 1258 is Gap—adult sizes only; Gap Kids is across the street (1267). Near the corner of P Street, the inimitable Commander Salamander (1420) has leatherwear, way-out fashions, irreverent T-shirts, and jewelry. On cobblestoned P Street, west of Wisconsin Avenue, remnants of the city's 1890 electric streetcar lines are visible. See what the stars have in store, or have your palm read by Mrs. Natalie (1500). Hungry? Cafe Bonaparte (1522) is open daily for breakfast, lunch, and dinner, serving authentic French onion soup, mouthwatering crepes (with a dozen fillings, half of them sweet), and other bistro favorites.

Cross Wisconsin at Q Street for the downhill walk on Wisconsin Avenue's east side. Turn right at R Street to:

9 Dumbarton Oaks

Located between 31st and 32nd streets, Dumbarton Oaks was the site of the 1944 Peace Conferences. The small museum of pre-Colombian art and magnificent grounds never disappoints. Robert Woods Bliss and his wife, Mildred, avid collectors of pre-Colombian and Byzantine art, used Dumbarton Oaks as a country retreat between 1920 and 1940. They donated their collection and the property to Harvard University, which housed the art in eight glass pavilions designed by Philip Johnson.

All ages enjoy the formal gardens and grassy expanses on the 10-acre site. It's especially beautiful spring through fall, when a riot of seasonal flowers blooms behind rows of boxwood hedges. Game time: See if your kids can locate the 10 reflecting pools, nine fountains, Roman-style amphitheater, and orangery among the broad terraces and twisting paths. (See "Parks, Gardens & Other Wide-Open Spaces," in chapter 8, for more information.)

> **TAKE A BREAK**
> Anchoring the southeast corner at Wisconsin Avenue and P Street is **Thomas Sweet,** an ideal spot to take a break at an institution that's on the endangered species list (an old-fashioned ice cream parlor).

Head back to Wisconsin Ave., and head up the east side of the street for:

⑩ More Wisconsin Avenue Shopping

On the east side of the street, Piccolo Piggies (1533) sells attractive, distinctive children's clothing. Appalachian Spring (1415) has kaleidoscopes, finger puppets, wooden toys, and baby gifts among its stunning collection of American crafts. At 1319 Wisconsin, Betsey Johnson draws well-heeled teens and their fashion-conscious moms for au courant duds. Farther on Wisconsin, you'll come across Gap Kids and Baby Gap (1267), and Wet Seal (1225), filled with well-priced fashions for preteen and teen girls.

Head south on Wisconsin to N street. Turn right on N, and go to no. 3307:

⑪ John F. Kennedy's Last & Best-Known Residence

JFK resided at seven Georgetown addresses between 1947 and his presidency. He met his future wife at a Georgetown dinner party in 1951. 3307 N St. NW was home to the Kennedys, from shortly after Caroline's birth, in 1957, until JFK's inauguration and move into the White House, on January 20, 1961. After her husband's assassination, Mrs. Kennedy returned to the house at 31st and O streets, owned by her parents.

> **TAKE A BREAK**
> Ready to take another break? Stop for a plate of pasta, chicken, salad, or pizza at the trendy **Paolo's** (1303 Wisconsin Ave., at N St.), or try one of the places mentioned above.

When you've had enough, you can catch the Georgetown Shuttle on Wisconsin Avenue or any no. 30 Metrobus (Shipley Terrace or Congress Heights) along Wisconsin Avenue or M Street back to the:

⑫ Foggy Bottom Metro & Shopping

If you'd like to fit in a little more shopping, retrace your steps east across M Street to the Metro. Local teens flock to Urban Outfitters (3111), which has on-the-fringe and off-the-wall clothing and home furnishings. Get a makeover or replace tired cosmetics at Sephora (3065). A few doors down, at 3005, is Déjà Blue, with thousands of pairs of broken-in (okay, they're secondhand) jeans. On the south side of M Street, you'll find a large Barnes & Noble bookstore, at 3040 M (at Thomas Jefferson St.). The megastore has a large children's section and cafe.

> **TAKE A BREAK**
> As you're winding down your tour of Georgetown, satisfy your sweet-tooth cravings with a takeout sundae in a cone at **Ben & Jerry's** ice cream (3135 M St.). Or cross the street if you are a **Häagen-Dazs** fan (3120). Next door to Ben & Jerry's is **Johnny Rockets** (3131), for diner-style burgers, fries, shakes, and '50s music. **Old Glory** (3139) has great barbecue and ribs.

Continue on M Street to Washington Circle, bear right to 23rd Street, and then turn right at 23rd to the Metro. Enjoy your nap!

START:	**Washington Monument.**
FINISH:	**Constitution Gardens.**
TIME:	**4 hours or more. Take snacks or sandwiches, as you will be limited to vendor fast food, unless you deviate several blocks to a food court or sit-down restaurant. Take a stroller for children under 5. There are benches and grassy knolls along the way, but with kids under 8 or 9, you may want to carve this into smaller pieces.**
BEST TIMES:	**Anytime during daylight hours is the right time. Start in the morning, if you want to ride to the top of the Washington Monument.**
WORST TIMES:	**Evenings are the worst times to go.**

Start on the monument grounds between 15th and 17th streets NW, between Constitution and Independence avenues (behind the White House and Ellipse). Walk toward the humongous obelisk, one of the most instantly recognizable edifices in the world. If you've arrived on a nice day—and Washington has many throughout the year, but especially between April and November—get outdoors and enjoy this loopy trail of the monuments and memorials.

❶ Washington Monument

Pick up free timed-entry passes in the morning. To avoid disappointment, order them ahead (see p. 146). Weather permitting, hand the kids the camera, ask them to lie on their backs, and shoot up. (If you try it, you may not get up.)

Walk west toward the Lincoln Memorial, and cross 17th Street to the:

❷ World War II Memorial

You'll find it at the east end of the Reflecting Pool (that's the end nearest the U.S. Capitol). Ask your kids what they think of the Field of Stars and Memorial Plaza. Who's got the camera?

Walk south and cross Independence Avenue to:

❸ The Tidal Basin

Pretty, huh? Even without the cherry blossoms, it's a sight for sore eyes. Photo op!

If this were a clock, you'd be standing at 12 o'clock. Straight ahead is the Jefferson Memorial at 6 o'clock. Walk clockwise (south) and around the perimeter of this glorified pond to the:

❹ Boat House

Here you can rent a paddleboat mid-March through mid-October, weather permitting. Fuel up with ice cream or a snack from one of the vendors here.

Continue clockwise toward 6 o'clock and over the Outlet Bridge to the:

❺ Jefferson Memorial

This is my personal favorite of all the presidential monuments and memorials. Go in to the memorial itself to read the inscriptions, take pictures of ol' TJ, and take a look in the bookshop, especially inviting to history buffs. Spend some quiet time lolling on the steps, admiring the view—and taking pictures, of course.

Continue around the "clock" path that hugs the Tidal Basin, across the Inlet Bridge to the:

❻ Franklin Delano Roosevelt Memorial

The planners designated this as the exit, but they won't consider you disrespectful or un-American if you see it in reverse, beginning at the south end. Because the bookshop is here, stop to inspect the interesting history books and FDR memorabilia, so you don't have to backtrack. Take some photos of the magnificent fountains, granite walls, and 3-foot sculpture of Fala, FDR's beloved Scottie. Let the kids run around. There is nothing to break. Grab a snack and make a pit stop before you leave.

Exit at the north entrance, heading north through West Potomac Park, until you reach Independence Avenue. Cross Independence Avenue to the:

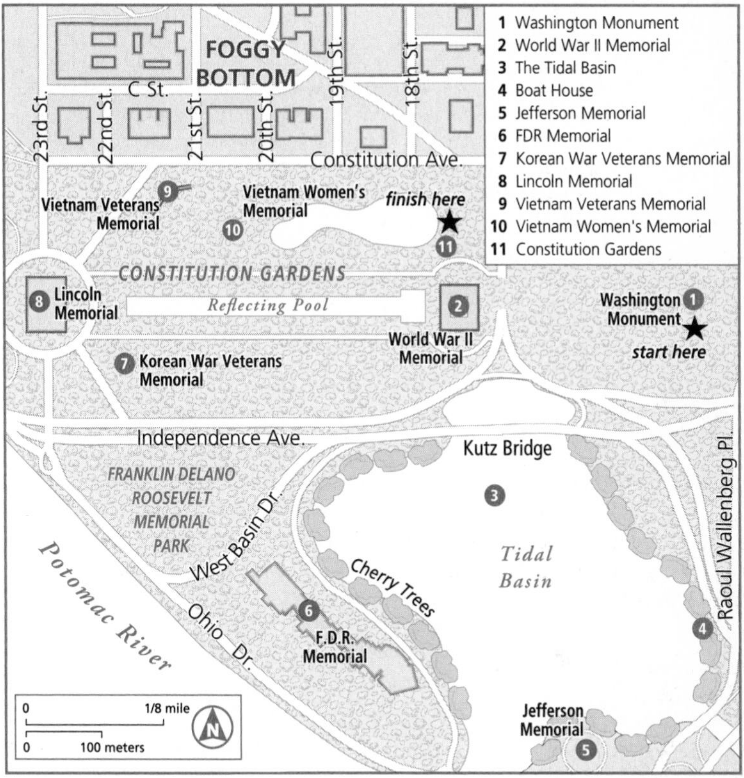

7 Korean War Veterans Memorial

Are your kids impressed by the steel statues of 19 soldiers on the march? One can hope.

Walk a short distance to the Greek temple look-alike, where a very large man sits brooding. You've arrived at the:

8 Lincoln Memorial

After looking around inside, rest on the steps and aim your camera across the National Mall toward the Capitol. Not a bad view, eh? If you're here at dusk, walk around to the back of the memorial to watch the sunset.

Walk down the steps, and head left to the:

9 Vietnam Veterans Memorial

People from all over the world pay their respects at the low-slung black granite walls honoring the nearly 60,000 soldiers who died in the Vietnam War. The victims' names are inscribed chronologically from the first casualty in 1959 to the last in 1975. Since opening in 1983, it remains one of the most-visited sites in Washington.

Walk toward the Reflecting Pool and the nearby:

10 Vietnam Women's Memorial

Small but poignant, it is dedicated to the 7,500 women who served in the Vietnam War.

Head east toward 17th Street and the pond in this parklike parcel known as:

11 Constitution Gardens

With any luck, you'll see some turtles and frogs. In spring, you may see some baby ducklings, along with Mom and Dad.

The closest Metro is Smithsonian, about a 10-minute walk west.

WALKING TOUR 3 DUPONT CIRCLE

START: Dupont Circle Metro.

FINISH: Kramerbooks and Afterwords Cafe (1517 Conn. Ave. NW, btw. Dupont Circle and Q St.).

TIME: 2 hours or more. As always, bring snacks or sandwiches and water. There are numerous restaurants near the Metro—both formal and casual—but not along the route.

BEST TIMES: Anytime during daylight hours is good.

WORST TIMES: Evenings are the worst time for this tour.

This is a good choice any time of the year. Because some of this route is uphill, I suggest bringing a stroller, if your child is 5 or under. It won't be fun if you have to schlep your kid piggyback-style, and you can always use the stroller for shopping bags and snacks. Start at the Dupont Circle Metro and take the escalator (or elevator) to the street. Then head for the:

❶ Fountain (in Dupont Circle)

Take pictures of one another and/or the colorful characters who hang out in this city park. The fountain was designed by Daniel Chester French, the same dude who sculpted Lincoln's statue at the Lincoln Memorial.

After exiting the south end of the park, cross the traffic circle onto New Hampshire Avenue. Walk south 1 block to 1307 New Hampshire Ave. and the:

❷ Heurich Mansion

Nice piece of Romanesque Revival real estate, huh? The former home of local brewer Christian Heurich is command central for the Historical Society of Washington, D.C.

Cross New Hampshire Avenue, make an immediate right at 20th Street, go half a block, and then turn left at O Street, past Victorian-style row houses. Go right at 21st Street, to Massachusetts Avenue, to ogle the:

❸ Walsh McLean House

The Indonesian Embassy, at 2020 Mass Ave., was formerly the family home of Evalyn Walsh McLean, the society hostess and owner of the cursed Hope Diamond (p. 134).

Head north on Massachusetts Avenue 2 blocks and then west on Q Street to 23rd Street and the:

❹ Bison Bridge

Kids like the four humongous bronze beasts at this bridge (officially, the Dumbarton Bridge) spanning Rock Creek Park. According to the Smithsonian, it was bison that roamed the West, not buffalo, which are indigenous to Africa and Asia.

If you're feeling ambitious, continue on Q Street for several blocks into Georgetown. Otherwise, walk north on 23rd Street 1 block to Sheridan Circle; then turn left around the circle to Massachusetts Avenue. Go 2 long blocks and bear right at S Street. Pass the statue of Irish patriot Robert Emmet to 2340 S St. and the:

❺ Woodrow Wilson House

The 28th president is the only U.S. president buried in D.C. (at the National Cathedral) and the only one to live in Washington after vacating the White House. Put that in your trivia pipe and smoke it! Stop here with older kids, especially those with an interest in history.

Next door, at 2320 S St., is the:

❻ Textile Museum

Stop here, if the spirit moves you, for the extensive collection of historic and contemporary rugs and textiles.

Retrace your steps back to Massachusetts Avenue, head south to Dupont Circle, and turn left 1 short block around the circle to Connecticut Avenue. Go left (north) to 1517 Connecticut Ave. and:

> **TAKE A BREAK**
> **Kramerbooks & Afterwords Cafe.** At this Washington, D.C. institution, you can browse books to your heart's content and have dessert or a meal.

From here, it's only a block to the Metro.

8 For the Active Family

Museums are marvelous mind-expanders, but little people (and big people, too) grow restless after too much hard-core enrichment. To prevent fatigue and brain strain, stagger periods of sightseeing with visits to places where kids can romp, roam, and let off steam. (We all know what happens to steam that's pressurized too long.) You won't have far to look for these kinds of places, because downtown and its environs are chock-full of parks, open spaces, playgrounds, and recreational areas. And the largest front yard in the neighborhood—the National Mall—is just a Frisbee toss away from many downtown attractions.

1 PARKS, GARDENS & OTHER WIDE-OPEN SPACES

GARDENS & PARKS

Battery Kemble Park In a residential area not far from the C&O (Chesapeake and Ohio) Canal, this mile-long park boasts flowering dogwood trees in spring, a beautiful fall display of autumn leaves, and good sledding and cross-country skiing in winter. In recent years, this has become doggy central. During your stroll, notice how many pets resemble their owners. If you're allergic, I advise staying away. You can fly a kite; take a nature walk; picnic; and play football, baseball, or soccer on one of the fields. ***Note:*** The terrain is hilly and best avoided if you suffer from physical limitations or respiratory ailments.

Chain Bridge Rd., btw. Nebraska Ave. and MacArthur Blvd. NW. ✆ **202/426-6841.** Free admission. Daily dawn–dusk. Metro: Tenleytown station, then 1¾-mile walk north on Wisconsin Ave. to Tenley Circle. Right onto Nebraska Ave. Left on Chain Bridge Rd., then left into the park. Driving directions: Take Canal Rd., turn right onto MacArthur Blvd., and then turn right onto Chain Bridge Rd. The entrance and small parking area are about midway btw. MacArthur Blvd. and Nebraska Ave. Additional parking on side streets.

Brookside Gardens ★ A visit here is like a breath of spring year-round. In addition to formal and natural-style landscaping on 50 acres (part of Maryland's park system), Brookside is known for its azaleas, roses, 11 types of gardens, and other seasonal displays. If you're in the area between May and mid-September, between 10am and 4pm, don't miss the annual butterfly show in one of the twin conservatories, where more than 30 species flit around, sometimes landing on visitors. The experience is indescribable, and admission of $6 for adults, $4 for kids (3–12), free 2 and under, is well worth it. Even babies take to the winged beauties, but you'll have to carry your little ones, as strollers are not allowed in the Conservatory. ***Note:*** Come between 2 and 4pm, when it's less crowded. The theme for the **Children's Garden** changes periodically. Children's programs for kids 3 and up include Saturday morning Story Time in the Visitor Center, with nature stories and related crafts projects. As part of the Weekend Discoveries program, youngsters are invited to take part in projects rooted around various plants and flowers. Call for information on these and other special events (✆ **301/962-1400**). The

Children's Garden invites tots to tread along a stone path leading to a tea party, inspect a gnome's house, and stack wood (blocks).

Many of the 2,000 volumes in the horticultural library are geared to young people, but these must be used on site. Stop in the **Visitors Center Children's Classroom,** with kids 2 to 7, for hands-on activities, self-guided tour info, games, books, and puzzles. Hours are Tuesday to Friday, September through June, 2 to 5pm; July and August, 9am to 5pm. At Saturday Story Time, October through mid-December at 10am, kids ages 3 to 6 hear a nature-related story and take part in a related hands-on activity. It's free. No reservations required. Visit if time permits, but leave pets, food, and drinks behind.

1800 Glenallan Ave., Wheaton, MD. ✆ **301/962-1400.** Fax 301/949-0571. www.brooksidegardens.org. Free admission; fee for special exhibits. Gardens daily sunrise–sunset. Conservatories daily 10am–5pm; visitors center and gift shop Mon–Sat 9am–5pm, Sun noon–4pm. Metro: Glenmont; then taxi. Directions: Take Georgia Ave. north from the Beltway, and turn right on Randolph Rd.; after 2 blocks, turn right at Glenallan Ave. On-site parking.

C&O Canal National Historic Park (Finds) If you have a car, this park is well worth the half-hour or so drive from most downtown locales. Go during the week or early on weekends, bring a brown-bag lunch, and plan to spend the better part of a day. Orient yourselves at the **Great Falls Tavern Museum,** a short walk from the entrance. Join a nature walk with a park ranger. Park rangers conduct nature walks and special programs, including hiking and bird watching. The cliffs attract rock climbers, and the river is a favorite for kayaking and fishing.

Enjoy Mother Nature on foot or bike along the towpaths that extend along the old C&O Canal, from Georgetown, for 185 miles to Cumberland, Maryland. Imagine the canal in its heyday, when boats traveled through 74 lift locks to reach western Maryland. The original plan, which called for a waterway all the way to Pittsburgh, was not completed, and the canal closed after a flood in 1924. Be sure to cross the footbridges that lead to the Olmsted Island overlook. The view is spectacular, and it's a great photo op. ***Note: Be forewarned:*** No pets, bikes, or picnics are allowed on the bridges (leashed dogs are permitted in the park). Consider a ride on a mule-drawn boat (see "Rides for Children," later in this chapter) for that experience. Quench your thirst at the park refreshment stand.

Don't even think of wading in the water. Even when it looks calm, it is rocky and turbulent below the surface. Several people drown annually because they ignore warning signs. Please, please ***watch your little ones near the canal locks,*** and practice hand-holding with your junior trailblazers.

MacArthur Blvd. and Falls Rd., Potomac, MD. ✆ **301/299-3613.** www.nps.gov/choh. Admission $5 per car; $3 walk-ins and bikers. Daily sunrise–sunset. Directions: Take MacArthur Blvd. into Maryland and continue 4 miles beyond the Beltway. Park entrance is at intersection of MacArthur Blvd. and Falls Rd.

Constitution Gardens ★ (Finds) Baby ducks hatch annually, between April and June, on this park's small lake. Your little ducklings are invited to feed them, along with the turtles, fish, and the occasional frog. The park also features walks, bike paths, and a landscaped island reached by a footbridge. Kids can sail small boats, but no swimming is allowed. Have a picnic on the 14 acres and see the names of the 56 signers of the Declaration of Independence set in stone (literally). The Vietnam War, Korean War Veterans, and World War II memorials are nearby, in the western corner of the park. Park rangers are happy to answer your questions at the Vietnam Veteran Memorial, from 9:30am to 11:30pm (p. 151).

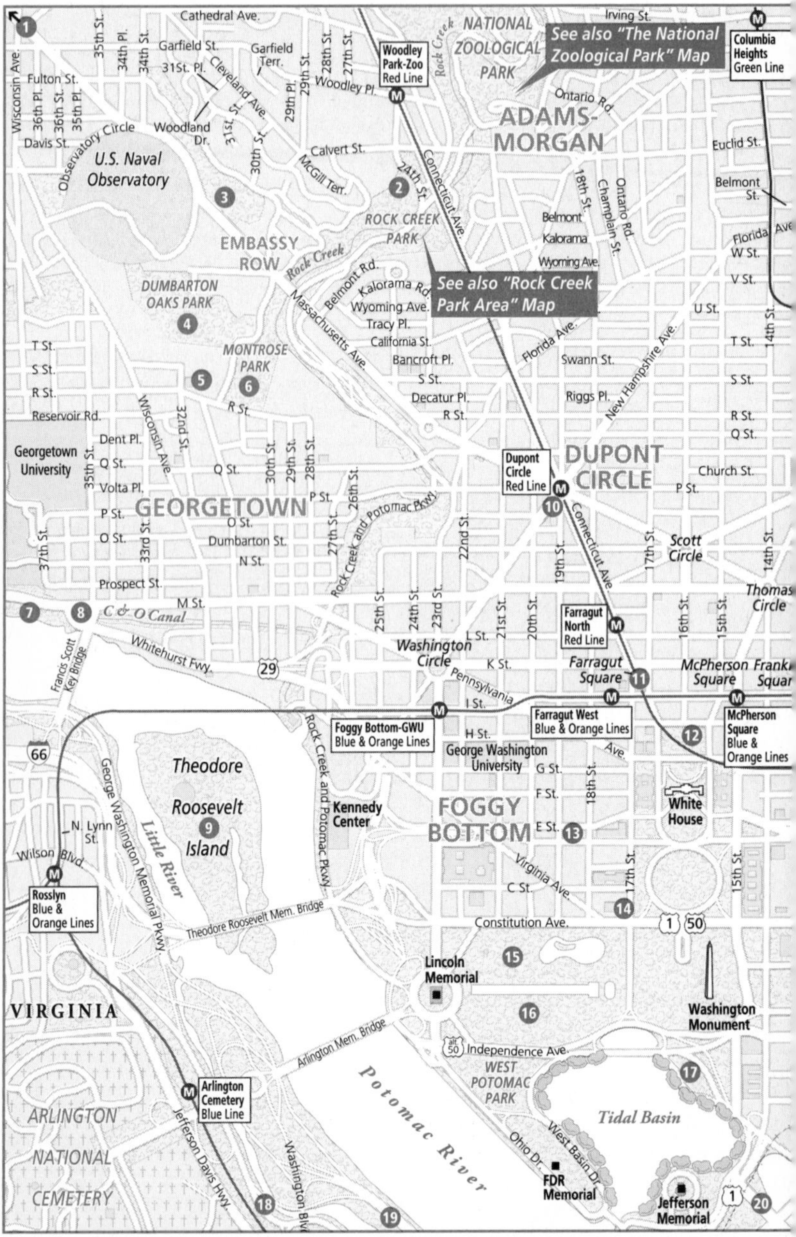
Cathedral Ave.
Irving St.
NATIONAL ZOOLOGICAL PARK
See also "The National Zoological Park" Map
Columbia Heights Green Line
Wisconsin Ave.
35th St.
34th Pl.
34th St.
Garfield St.
Garfield Terr.
31St. Pl.
Cleveland Ave.
29th St.
28th St.
27th St.
Woodley Park-Zoo Red Line
Woodley Pl.
Rock Creek
Ontario Rd.
ADAMS-MORGAN
Fulton St.
36th Pl.
36th St.
35th Pl.
Observatory Circle
Woodland Dr.
31st. St.
29th Pl.
30th St.
Davis St.
Calvert St.
McGill Terr.
24th St.
Connecticut Ave.
18th St.
Champlain St.
Ontario Rd.
Euclid St.
U.S. Naval Observatory
ROCK CREEK PARK
Belmont
Kalorama
Wyoming Ave.
Belmont St.
EMBASSY ROW
Rock Creek
Belmont Rd.
Kalorama Rd.
Wyoming Ave.
Tracy Pl.
California St.
See also "Rock Creek Park Area" Map
Florida Ave
W St.
V St.
U St.
14th St.
DUMBARTON OAKS PARK
Massachusetts Ave.
Florida Ave.
New Hampshire Ave.
T St.
S St.
R St.
Reservoir Rd.
MONTROSE PARK
Bancroft Pl.
S St.
Decatur Pl.
R St.
Swann St.
Riggs Pl.
T St.
S St.
R St.
Q St.
R St.
Wisconsin Ave.
32nd St.
Dent Pl.
Georgetown University
35th St.
Q St.
Volta Pl.
Q St.
30th St.
29th St.
28th St.
26th St.
Dupont Circle Red Line
DUPONT CIRCLE
Church St.
P St.
P St.
GEORGETOWN
P St.
O St.
Rock Creek and Potomac Pkwy.
37th St.
O St.
33rd St.
Dumbarton St.
N St.
27th St.
22nd St.
19th St.
Connecticut Ave.
17th St.
Scott Circle
14th St.
Thomas Circle
Prospect St.
M St.
C & O Canal
25th St.
24th St.
23rd St.
21st St.
20th St.
Farragut North Red Line
16th St.
15th St.
Francis Scott Key Bridge
Whitehurst Fwy.
29
Washington Circle
L St.
K St.
Pennsylvania
Farragut Square
McPherson Square
I St.
Foggy Bottom-GWU Blue & Orange Lines
H St.
Farragut West Blue & Orange Lines
McPherson Square Blue & Orange Lines
66
George Washington Memorial Pkwy.
Theodore Roosevelt Island
Rock Creek and Potomac Pkwy.
George Washington University
G St.
Ave.
F St.
18th St.
White House
Kennedy Center
FOGGY BOTTOM
E St.
N. Lynn St.
Little River
Wilson Blvd
Virginia Ave.
C St.
17th St.
15th St.
Rosslyn Blue & Orange Lines
Theodore Roosevelt Mem. Bridge
Constitution Ave.
1
50
Lincoln Memorial
Washington Monument
VIRGINIA
Arlington Mem. Bridge
alt 50
Independence Ave.
WEST POTOMAC PARK
Potomac River
Tidal Basin
Arlington Cemetery Blue Line
ARLINGTON NATIONAL CEMETERY
Jefferson Davis Hwy.
Washington Blvd
Ohio Dr.
West Basin Dr.
FDR Memorial
Jefferson Memorial
1
1
2
3
4
5
6
7
8
9
10
11
12
13
14
15
16
17
18
19
20

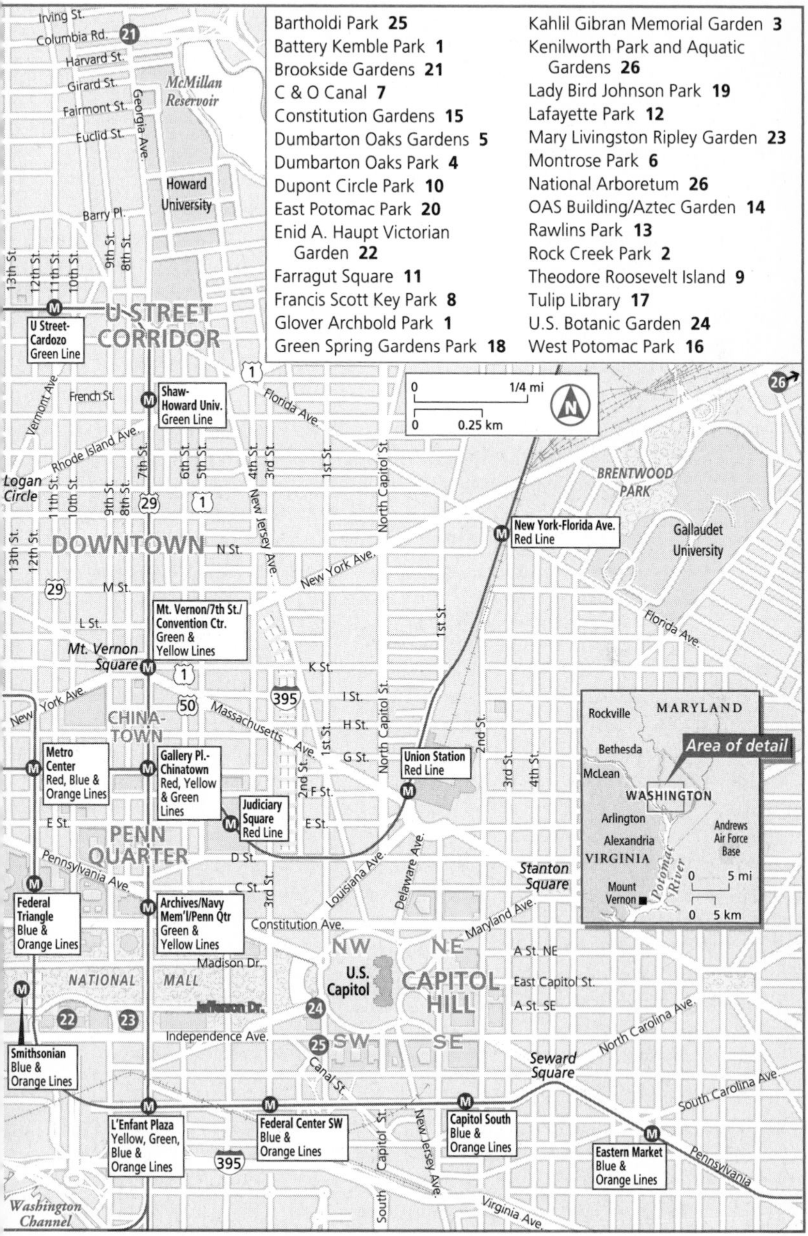
Bartholdi Park 25
Battery Kemble Park 1
Brookside Gardens 21
C & O Canal 7
Constitution Gardens 15
Dumbarton Oaks Gardens 5
Dumbarton Oaks Park 4
Dupont Circle Park 10
East Potomac Park 20
Enid A. Haupt Victorian Garden 22
Farragut Square 11
Francis Scott Key Park 8
Glover Archbold Park 1
Green Spring Gardens Park 18
Kahlil Gibran Memorial Garden 3
Kenilworth Park and Aquatic Gardens 26
Lady Bird Johnson Park 19
Lafayette Park 12
Mary Livingston Ripley Garden 23
Montrose Park 6
National Arboretum 26
OAS Building/Aztec Garden 14
Rawlins Park 13
Rock Creek Park 2
Theodore Roosevelt Island 9
Tulip Library 17
U.S. Botanic Garden 24
West Potomac Park 16
0 1/4 mi
0 0.25 km
U STREET CORRIDOR
DOWNTOWN
CHINA-TOWN
PENN QUARTER
NATIONAL MALL
CAPITOL HILL
U.S. Capitol
McMillan Reservoir
Howard University
BRENTWOOD PARK
Gallaudet University
Logan Circle
Mt. Vernon Square
Stanton Square
Seward Square
Washington Channel
U Street-Cardozo Green Line
Shaw-Howard Univ. Green Line
Mt. Vernon/7th St./Convention Ctr. Green & Yellow Lines
New York-Florida Ave. Red Line
Metro Center Red, Blue & Orange Lines
Gallery Pl.-Chinatown Red, Yellow & Green Lines
Judiciary Square Red Line
Union Station Red Line
Federal Triangle Blue & Orange Lines
Archives/Navy Mem'l/Penn Qtr Green & Yellow Lines
Smithsonian Blue & Orange Lines
L'Enfant Plaza Yellow, Green, Blue & Orange Lines
Federal Center SW Blue & Orange Lines
Capitol South Blue & Orange Lines
Eastern Market Blue & Orange Lines
MARYLAND
Area of detail
Rockville
Bethesda
McLean
WASHINGTON
Arlington
Alexandria
VIRGINIA
Andrews Air Force Base
Mount Vernon
Potomac River
0 5 mi
0 5 km

W. Potomac Park, Constitution Ave. (btw. the Washington Monument and Lincoln Memorial). © **202/485-9880.** www.nps.gov/coga. Free admission. Daily dawn–dark. Metro: Smithsonian. Limited free parking on Constitution Ave.

Dumbarton Oaks Gardens ★★ Moments Restless feet love to explore every inch of these 16-acre, formally designed gardens in Georgetown. The winding brick paths lend themselves to spirited games of hide-and-seek. Spring is glorious when forsythia, narcissus, tulips, daffodils, and flowering trees bloom. The roses and wisteria flower in late spring and summer, and fall brings forth a showy display of foliage and chrysanthemums. Strollers are allowed but could be more of a hindrance due to the gardens' many steps and levels. No visitor to Washington should leave the city without stopping here.

1703 32nd St. NW (garden entrance on R St., btw. 31st and 32nd sts.). © **202/339-6401.** Fax 202/339-6419. www.doaks.org. Admission Mar 15–Oct 31 $8 adults, $5 seniors and age 2–12; free up to 2 years, and for everyone Nov. 1–Mar 14. Mar 15–Oct 31 Tues–Sun 2–6pm; Nov 1–Mar 14 Tues–Sun 2–5pm. Foggy Bottom Metro, then Georgetown Shuttle to Wisconsin and R St., or no. 30, 32, 34, or 36 bus from Pennsylvania Ave. and 23rd St. NW, then walk 2 blocks. Directions: North on Wisconsin Ave. NW, right at R St. to entrance. Limited 2-hr. on-street parking on R, S, and 32nd sts. Mon–Fri; no time limit Sat–Sun, but you may have trouble finding a space.

Dupont Circle Park ★ Sit, sun, or stalk the pigeons at Washington's largest circular park, or pick up food from one of the many nearby takeout places and picnic on a bench. There's plenty of entertainment—intended and unintended—particularly on weekends. Enjoy the fountain, listen to boom-box and live music. Some mighty serious chess games are played here, and you're welcome to watch as long as you don't interrupt.

Dupont Circle NW (intersection of Connecticut, Massachusetts, and New Hampshire aves.). Free admission. Daily dawn–dark. Metro: Dupont Circle.

East Potomac Park ★ A one-way road outlines the 300-plus acres of man-made peninsula between the Potomac River and the Washington Channel. Depending on who's counting, 1,200 to 1,300 **cherry trees** ★★ bloom in late March or early April. The blossoms usually last 7 to 12 days, less if it's windy or if there is a freeze. Most of the trees you see have been added over the years—fewer than 200 of the original trees survive. You can find out more at the cherry trees' very own website: www.nationalcherryblossomfestival.org. The original trees—Yoshinos—have single white flowers in clusters and are marked by bronze plaques. A well-equipped playground at Hains Point attracts kids with its colorful climbing apparatus. The park is perfect for strolling, biking, or fishing, and also has picnic grounds, a public **swimming pool** (© **202/727-6523**), 24 **tennis courts** (© **202/554-5962;** www.eastpotomactennis.com), as well as one 18-hole and two 9-hole **golf courses** (© **202/554-7660;** www.golfdc.com). Call for information on the permit you'll need to use the tennis courts. No permit is needed for playing golf.

Ohio Dr. SW. Park located btw. the Potomac River and the Washington Channel. © **202/426-6841.** www.nps.gov/nama. Free admission. Daily dawn–dark. Limited free parking; it's best, however, to arrive by taxi, or hoof it from Smithsonian Metro station, if you're up to it, because streets are hard to navigate.

Enid A. Haupt Victorian Garden Named for its philanthropic donor, this 4-acre minipark covers the underground complex housing the Sackler Gallery and Museum of African Art. Seasonal flowers brighten the beds and spill from baskets hanging from the iron lampposts. In summer, the tea roses and saucer magnolias are spectacular.

An ideal rest stop when your family is museumed out, the 19th-century embroidery parterre is for admiring, not stomping on. I found out the hard way when ordered by a uniformed gent to "Kindly get off the grass." There are benches, however, for relaxing.

Maybe your kids will be so impressed by the neatness of this space that they'll take the concept home and apply it to their rooms.

A handmade brass sundial was built by David Shayt and David Todd, two National Museum of American History staffers. At the dial's corners, the four seasons appear as weather symbols. Can your offspring identify summer? (It's the Smithsonian sunburst logo.) If you're smart enough to read a sundial, whip out your protractor, and make sure that the gnomon is set at approximately 40 degrees, Washington, D.C.'s latitude.

1000 Independence Ave. SW (btw. the Freer Gallery and Arts and Industries Bldg.; also accessible from the Sackler Gallery). ✆ **202/357-2700.** www.si.edu/opanda. Free admission. Daily dawn–dusk. Metro: Smithsonian (Mall or Independence Ave. exit).

Farragut Square Noontime concerts are held some summer weekdays in this pretty park in the heart of D.C.'s business district. Brown-bag it on a nice day and watch the power bunch lunch.

912 17th St. NW. Free admission. Daily dawn–dusk. Metro: Farragut West or Farragut North.

Francis Scott Key Park Key Park fills a once-vacant eyesore of a lot just east of the Georgetown side of Key Bridge, which connects D.C. and Rosslyn (Arlington), Virginia. Featuring a wisteria-covered pergola as well as a bronze bust of Key, by sculptor Betty Dunston, it is capped by a flag with 15 stars and stripes—similar to the one that inspired Key to write "The Star-Spangled Banner." A walkway and bike path from the C&O Canal are carefully integrated into the hilltop setting, which has a commanding view of the Potomac River.

35th and M sts. NW, Georgetown. Free admission. Daily dawn–dusk. Metro: Rosslyn, then cross Key Bridge on foot. Directions: Drive to Georgetown, park on street (good luck!) or in garage at Shops at Georgetown Park (Wisconsin Ave. and M St. NW), and walk west on M St. to 34th St.

Glover Archbold Park The mix of towering trees, a bird sanctuary, and colorful wildflowers makes this long and slender 183-acre park, which stretches south from Massachusetts Avenue to Canal Road, a popular destination for families. A 2-mile nature trail begins at 44th Street and Reservoir Road. There are several others, and plenty of picnic areas, too, sprinkled throughout this park.

MacArthur Blvd. and Canal Rd. to Van Ness St. and Wisconsin Ave. ✆ **202/282-1063.** www.gloverpark.org. Free admission. Daily dawn–dusk. Directions: Take Wisconsin Ave. north, turn left on Cathedral Ave., then turn left on New Mexico Ave. Park on New Mexico.

Green Spring Gardens Park ★★ The children's garden has a bathtub filled with a water garden. A pumpkin-shaped form supports vines with turtle-shaped rocks in the center. Check out the enchanting flower bed frame. (Get it? Flower bed?) Elsewhere on the grounds are two ponds with frogs and fish and an occasional blue heron. Canadian geese and ducks visit frequently. Budding horticulturists can learn the basics of gardening in a host of hands-on workshops on Saturday afternoons and Monday holidays (when schools are closed), and throughout the summer. Adults can sign up for classes, too. The 27-acre public park is filled with native plants, 20 themed gardens, vegetable and herb gardens, and blooming and fruit-bearing trees. Permanent plant displays are housed in the greenhouse in the Horticulture Center. A historic house is open to the public Wednesday through Sunday and *may* be of interest to preteens. Generous parents take note: You can rent the gazebo outside the 1760 manor house for your child's next birthday party.

4603 Green Spring Rd., Alexandria, VA. ✆ **703/642-5173.** www.greenspring.org. Free admission, but reservations and fees required for classes. Park daily dawn–dusk; Horticulture Center Mon–Sat 9am–4:30pm, Sun noon–4:30pm; Historic house Wed–Sun noon–4:30pm. Horticulture Center closed Thanksgiving, Christmas, Jan 1. Directions: From D.C., take I-395 south to Duke St. west. Go about 1 mile to right at Green Spring (btw. Jerry's Ford and Salvation Army Thrift Shop), and then 2 blocks into parking lot.

Kahlil Gibran Memorial Garden This quiet, reflective garden honors the Lebanese-born mystical poet who spent much of his life in the United States. Here he wrote thoughtful phrases that have been devoured for decades by college kids in search of the truth and themselves. Some of Gibran's pithier musings are inscribed in the benches near the main fountain. The bronze bust of Gibran is by Washington sculptor Gordon Kray. Make your pilgrimage on foot or by taxi; neighborhood parking is sparse, and there's no Metro close by.

3100 Massachusetts Ave. NW (opposite the British embassy). www.embassy.org/embassy_row. Free admission. Daily dawn–dusk. Metro: Dupont Circle, then uphill walk or bus north on Massachusetts Ave. Directions: Drive north on Massachusetts Ave. about 1 mile past Dupont Circle. If you reach Wisconsin, you've gone too far. (***Note:*** Parking is scarce.)

Kenilworth Park and Aquatic Gardens When was the last time you saw an Egyptian lotus (said to be Cleopatra's favorite flower)? Well, it is just 1 of the more than 100,000 water plants growing on 11 acres of ponds in this sanctuary. About 75 varieties of water lilies and sand lotuses bloom from May through August. The annual Waterlily and Founders Day, held the second or third Saturday in July, showcases these exotic beauties. Except in the dead of winter, kids will see turtles, frogs, and small fish. Bring binoculars in spring; migrating waterfowl and songbirds are frequent visitors. If you come in the morning, you'll see the night-blooming tropicals, which usually close by 10am. There are picnic tables and a playground, and tours are conducted Saturday and Sunday at 9 and 11am Memorial Day through Labor Day.

Kenilworth Ave. and Douglas St. NE. ✆ **202/426-6905.** www.nps.gov/keaq. Free admission. Daily 7am–4pm (park); visitor center closes at 4pm. Plenty of on-site parking. Metro: Deanwood; then take a taxi. Directions: Take the V2 bus to Kenilworth Ave. and Polk St., and walk 1 block to gardens. (***Note:*** This is not a good neighborhood to walk through, so you might want to take a taxi.)

Lady Bird Johnson Park Although considered part of D.C., the former Columbia Island is accessible only by footbridge from the Virginia side of the Potomac River. I don't suggest it, because it's so close to the highway. The best way to enjoy the sight—a must in spring—is to drive or be driven. The park was dedicated to Mrs. Johnson in 1968 to recognize her efforts at beautifying the city and the nation. More than 2,500 dogwoods and one million daffodils create a gorgeous blanket of gold in the spring. At the south end of the park, there is a 15-acre grove of white pines, azaleas, and rhododendrons, designated as the Lyndon Baines Johnson Memorial Grove.

Adjacent to G. W. Memorial Pkwy., VA. www.nps.gov/lyba. Free admission. Daily dawn–dusk. Directions: From D.C., drive over the Arlington Memorial Bridge, take the G. W. Memorial Pkwy. south to and through National Airport, and continue north on the parkway to Memorial Bridge and D.C.

Lafayette Square Check out the statues of Andrew Jackson and Lafayette, whose heads are favorite pigeon roosting spots, in this 7-acre city park. Protesters, pigeon lovers and haters, bureaucrats, and people-watchers fill the benches and sprawl on the grass at all hours of the day and night. Depending on their ages, your kids might enjoy talking to the protesters or feeding some of the tamest squirrels in the area.

Btw. Pennsylvania Ave. and H St. NW, across from the White House. www.nps.gov/history. Free admission. Daily dawn–dusk. Metro: McPherson Sq.

Mary Livingston Ripley Garden *Finds* Trees, shrubs, annuals, perennials, and ornamental grasses pack this pleasing pocket-size garden, tucked between the Hirshhorn and Arts and Industries buildings. Tours led by a Smithsonian horticulturist are held April through October, on Tuesdays at 2pm, weather permitting. Just show up (✆ **202/357-1926;** www.si.edu/opanda).

Enter from Independence Ave. SW (btw. 7th and 9th sts). Free admission. Daily dawn–dusk. Metro: Smithsonian or L'Enfant Plaza (Smithsonian exit).

Montrose Park Come here to picnic, commune with nature, or ramble through the heavily wooded terrain. Lover's Lane (off R St.), which forms the western boundary of the park, is a cobblestone path that led to Baltimore, in the 18th century. I don't recommend your trying to reach Charm City in this manner.

R St., at Avon Place NW, Georgetown. www.nps.gov/history. Free admission. Daily dawn–dusk. Directions from Georgetown: From M St., go north on 29th St., and turn left on R St.

National Arboretum ★★ *Moments* When the azaleas bloom (usually mid-April through mid-May) this is one of my favorite D.C. destinations. Visitors are *tree*-ted to one breathtaking sensory experience after another at this 444-acre haven in northeast D.C., established by an act of Congress in 1927 to educate the public and do research on trees and shrubs. With plenty of room to roam, it's an instant favorite spot for children, regardless of age. (I know because I'm still a kid at heart.) The koi (Japanese carp) that live in the pool outside the information center approach Brobdingnagian proportions, reaching nearly 3 feet in length and weighing in at 30 pounds. For 25¢ a handful, visitors can buy food to feed the fish. The lily pads are said to be sturdy enough to support a small child, but please don't try it—those koi have big appetites.

Worth a visit at any time of year, the arboretum is most popular from late March through October. In late April and May, the azalea display (about 70,000, at last count) draws large crowds. For a Wow! experience, follow the path to the top of Mount Hamilton and drink in the breathtaking kaleidoscopic **view of the Capitol,** framed by trees. Kids can sniff the contents of the Herb Garden or get intoxicated in June and July, when 100 fragrant varieties of roses perfume the air. The medicinal, dye, Native American, beverage, and fragrance gardens are of special interest to young people, as is the knot garden, with its dwarf evergreens. Some of the specimens in the **National Bonsai Collection**—a gift from Japan to mark our bicentennial—are more than 300 years old! More than 150 species are housed in three pavilions. Don't leave without seeing the **national Capitol columns** ★★, from the Capitol's East Portico, the only things salvaged from the Capitol's original facade after renovation of the central portion in 1959. You might think that you've wandered onto Washington, D.C.'s version of Stonehenge. A picnic area, a water fountain, and restrooms are located near the state trees (pick up a map at the administration building).

Note: This place is huge, so if you didn't drive (and this is one of the few places in D.C. where a car comes in handy), seriously consider the 40-minute taped open-air tram tour, with departures at 10:30am (if not reserved by a group), 11:30am, and hourly 1 to 4pm daily. Buy same-day tickets at the tram kiosk outside the administration building. The fare is $4 for adults, $3 for seniors, $2 ages 4 to 16, and free 3 and under (child must ride on companion's lap).

3501 New York Ave. NE. ✆ **202/245-2726.** Fax 202/245-4575. www.usna.usda.gov. Admission to grounds free; fee for tram. Grounds daily 8am–5pm; bonsai collection and Japanese garden daily 10am–3:30pm; gift shop Mon–Fri 10am–3:30pm, Sat–Sun 10am–5pm. Closed Dec 25. Metro: Union Station, then taxi; or Stadium-Armory, then take a B2 bus to Bladensburg Rd. and R St. Walk east 900 ft. to the R St. gate. Directions: New York Ave. (east) and enter the service road immediately after crossing Bladensburg Rd. Plenty of free parking.

OAS Building/Aztec Garden Introduce your kids to the exotic banana, coffee, palm, and rubber trees growing on the Tropical Patio at the headquarters of the world's oldest organization of nations. Epitomizing the mission of the Organization of American States (OAS) is the Peace Tree (a fig-rubber hybrid), planted by President William Howard Taft, in 1910, at the building's dedication. Walk to the back of the building for a display of seasonal plants around the dazzling blue-tiled pool. The fellow overseeing this lush scene is the Aztec god of flowers, Xochipilli. Before you go, let your kids know that this garden is for looking, not for running around. Those 16 and older must show photo ID to the guard.

OAS Bldg., 17th St. and Constitution Ave. NW. www.oas.org. Free admission. Mon–Fri 9:30am–5pm. Metro: Farragut West.

Rawlins Park This urban pocket park near the Corcoran Gallery gets passing grades most of the year, but when the **magnolias bloom** ★★★ in April to May (depending on the weather), it rates an A-plus. The park's statue is of Civil War Gen. John A. Rawlins.

E St. (btw. 18th and 19th sts. NW). Free admission. Daily dawn–dusk. Metro: McPherson Sq. or Farragut North or West.

Rock Creek Park ★★★ The leader of Washington parks is more than a century old. The 4-mile-long, 1,800-acre parcel fills the center of northwest D.C. longitudinally. (See the "Rock Creek Park" map, on p. 205.) And it is nothing short of fantastic. If you have the time, I urge you to introduce your kids to some of its many wonders during your stay (but not after dark).

If time allows for only one stop at Rock Creek Park, make it the **Nature Center and Planetarium,** at 5200 Glover Rd. NW (✆ **202/426-6829**), where kids will find exhibits pertaining to the park's natural history and wildlife, and can meet a few of the latter. **Guided nature walks** and **self-guided trails** begin and end here. The center is open year-round Wednesday through Sunday from 9am to 5pm; it's closed holidays. Special hikes, activities, and talks geared to young trailblazers take place every month.

Stargazing is held once a month from April through November (Apr–May at 8:30pm, June–Aug at 9pm, Sept at 8pm, Oct at 7:30pm, Nov at 7pm), cosponsored by the National Park Service and the National Capital Astronomers. Programs are geared to children 4 and older. Meet at Picnic Grove No. 13, at Military and Glover roads NW. To receive the upcoming month's activity calendar, "Kiosk," call ✆ **202/426-6829.** The Park Service does a dynamite job with this program.

The historic **Peirce Mill and Barn,** near the intersection of Beach Drive and Tilden Street NW (✆ **202/426-6828**), unfortunately has been closed for several years due to internal damage to the mill (powered by a waterwheel). Here's the good news: Thanks to the efforts of The Friends of Peirce Mill, it is due to reopen during summer 2010. For current info, go to www.peircemill-friends.org. In the meantime, you can visit the Peirce Barn across the parking lot from the mill. A park ranger is usually on site to answer questions. The barn is open Saturday and Sunday from noon to 4pm. Weekday group tours are given by reservation.

At **Thompson's Boat Center** ★, across from the Kennedy Center and Watergate, you can rent a boat and paddle or row along the Potomac. Or hop on a bike, also available at Thompson's, to explore nearby Theodore Roosevelt Island (see listing below). It's open daily from February to November (closed December and January).

The Candy Cane City (Meadowbrook Recreation Center) ★ playground, located at 7901 Meadowbrook Lane (off East-West Hwy.), in Chevy Chase, Maryland, is maintained by the Maryland-National Capital Park and Planning Commission. It's a favorite

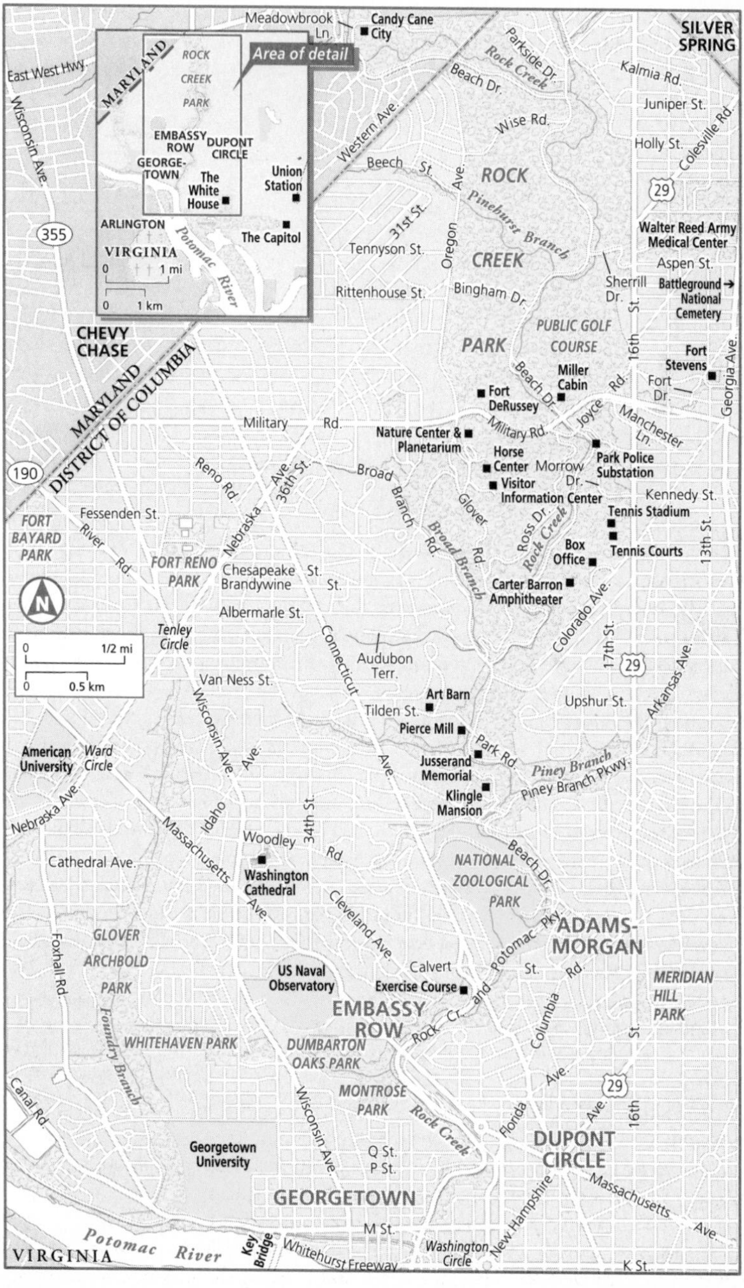
Meadowbrook Ln.
Candy Cane City
SILVER SPRING
Area of detail
MARYLAND
ROCK CREEK PARK
EMBASSY ROW
DUPONT CIRCLE
GEORGE-TOWN
The White House
Union Station
ARLINGTON
The Capitol
VIRGINIA
Potomac River
East West Hwy.
Wisconsin Ave.
Western Ave.
Parkside Dr.
Rock Creek
Beach Dr.
Kalmia Rd.
Juniper St.
Wise Rd.
Holly St.
Colesville Rd.
Beech St.
Oregon Ave.
ROCK CREEK PARK
Pineburst Branch
31st St.
Tennyson St.
Walter Reed Army Medical Center
Aspen St.
Rittenhouse St.
Bingham Dr.
Sherrill Dr.
Battleground National Cemetery
CHEVY CHASE
PUBLIC GOLF COURSE
16th St.
Fort Stevens
Georgia Ave.
Miller Cabin
Fort Dr.
Fort DeRussey
MARYLAND
DISTRICT OF COLUMBIA
Military Rd.
Nature Center & Planetarium
Joyce Rd.
Manchester Ln.
Horse Center
Morrow Dr.
Park Police Substation
Visitor Information Center
Kennedy St.
Reno Rd.
Nebraska Ave.
36th St.
Broad Branch Rd.
Glover Rd.
Ross Dr.
Tennis Stadium
Tennis Courts
Box Office
13th St.
FORT BAYARD PARK
Fessenden St.
River Rd.
FORT RENO PARK
Chesapeake St.
Brandywine St.
Carter Barron Amphitheater
Colorado Ave.
Albermarle St.
Tenley Circle
17th St.
Connecticut Ave.
Audubon Terr.
Arkansas Ave.
Van Ness St.
Art Barn
Upshur St.
Tilden St.
Pierce Mill
Park Rd.
Jusserand Memorial
Piney Branch
Piney Branch Pkwy.
Klingle Mansion
American University
Ward Circle
Wisconsin Ave.
Idaho Ave.
Massachusetts Ave.
Woodley Rd.
34th St.
Washington Cathedral
Cathedral Ave.
NATIONAL ZOOLOGICAL PARK
Beach Dr.
Cleveland Ave.
ADAMS-MORGAN
Foxhall Rd.
GLOVER ARCHBOLD PARK
Foundry Branch
US Naval Observatory
Calvert St.
Rock Cr. and Potomac Pky.
Exercise Course
EMBASSY ROW
MERIDIAN HILL PARK
Columbia Rd.
WHITEHAVEN PARK
DUMBARTON OAKS PARK
MONTROSE PARK
Rock Creek
Canal Rd.
Georgetown University
Q St.
P St.
Florida Ave.
DUPONT CIRCLE
New Hampshire Ave.
Massachusetts Ave.
GEORGETOWN
M St.
Potomac River
Key Bridge
Whitehurst Freeway
Washington Circle
K St.
VIRGINIA
190
355
29
0 1/2 mi
0 0.5 km
0 1 mi
0 1 km
N

family destination and ideal picnic spot. Little ones can climb, swing, and slide on the playground equipment while older kids and parents play softball, tennis, or basketball (✆ **301/495-2900**).

Among the park's other attractions (call or write for more information and an indispensable map) is a 1.5-mile **exercise course** for fitness enthusiasts and joggers, which begins near Calvert Street and Connecticut Avenue NW. You can rent a horse, take riding lessons, go on a ranger-led trail ride, or blaze 11 miles of bridle trails at the **Rock Creek Horse Center,** 5100 Glover Rd. NW (✆ **202/362-0117**). There is also a **golf course** off Rittenhouse Street, at 16th Street (✆ **202/882-7332**). Fulfill your day's exercise quota, and hike or bike your way through the park. Much of the sign-posted **bike route,** running from the Lincoln Memorial through the park and into Maryland, is paved and separate from traffic. On Saturday, Sunday, and holidays, Beach Drive is closed to traffic between Joyce and Broad Branch roads and Sherrill and West Beach drives. **Picnic areas** abound—some can be reserved; others require permits (✆ **202/673-7646**). **Tennis courts** (15 soft, 10 hard), at 16th and Kennedy streets NW, must be reserved from Memorial Day to Labor Day (✆ **202/722-5949;** www.rockcreektennis.com). Take the kids to see **Fort DeRussey, Fort Reno,** or **Fort Bayard,** among the 68 forts built to protect Washington during the Civil War.

5000 Glover Rd. NW (visitor information center). ✆ **202/895-6070.** www.nps.gov/rocr/home. Free admission. Open to vehicular traffic around the clock; on foot, dawn–dusk. Directions: Connecticut Ave. north to right on Nebraska Ave. Go 6 blocks into park's entrance and right at Glover Rd. (traffic light). Ample parking throughout park.

Theodore Roosevelt Island ★★ **Moments** Except for the incessant roar of jets overhead, these 88 acres of forest, swamp, and marsh, outlined by a rocky shore, are pristine and Walden-like. Hike along the 2.5 miles of nature trails of this preserve, which was once inhabited by Native Americans and now memorializes the conservation efforts of President Theodore Roosevelt. A bronze statue of the 26th U.S. president, by Paul Manship, and Roosevelt's prophetic words inscribed on granite stones can be found in the north-central portion of the island. Rabbits, foxes, muskrats, and groundhogs live in the woods, and you might spot a raccoon or two in the swamp. Bird-watchers have a field day, and so do the mosquitoes in summer—so bring plenty of insect repellent. You can also fish, but you can't picnic on the island, only on the grounds nearby. Depending on staff availability, there are guided tours on weekends, by appointment. You can't bike on the island. However, you may get to and from the island via the Mount Vernon trail and leave your wheels in the bike rack on the parking-lot side of the island. If you row over, be forewarned that your boat may "disappear." Sad but true. A handicapped-accessible fishing area is located near the island's entrance.

Off G. W. Memorial Pkwy. (btw. Key and Roosevelt bridges, on the Virginia side of the Potomac River). ✆ **703/289-2500.** www.nps.gov/this. Free admission. Daily 9:30am–dusk. Metro: Rosslyn (VA), walk 2 blocks to the footbridge at Rosslyn Circle; or, if driving, take the Theodore Roosevelt Bridge to the G.W. Memorial Pkwy. north, park on the right, and walk over the footbridge. Or arrive by rented canoe or rowboat from Thompson's Boat Center (see "Boating," later in this chapter). Ample parking.

Tulip Library If you're in town in April and you like tulips, don't miss this dazzling display—it's more colorful than the Fourth of July fireworks and doesn't make any noise. Park Service gardeners *hand-plant* 10,000 tulip bulbs from Holland every fall. Pick up a brochure from the wooden stand near the beds to help in your identification (about 100 cultivars annually) so that you can add your favorites to your home garden.

When the tulips fade, the beds are planted with annuals, making this an enjoyable spot year-round.

Near the Tidal Basin, btw. the Washington Monument and the Jefferson Memorial. www.washingtongardener.com. Free admission. Daily dawn–dusk. Metro: Smithsonian.

U.S. Botanic Garden ★★★ A visit to the Garden (at the foot of Capitol Hill) is as refreshing as lemonade on a sultry summer day. Two wings, east and west, showcase a tropical rainforest, the centerpiece of the 80-foot-high Conservatory. If I could, I'd unfold a cot and spend a week or two here.

The **visitor information desk,** at the Maryland Avenue entrance, is a departure point for docent tours.

The **west wing** focuses on plants and their relationships to humans, with many rare and endangered species. Among them is a Golden Barrel Cactus from Mexico (resembling a large, prickly globe), plants of historic note, and some genetically engineered specimens. In the medicinal garden, I was astounded to learn that the Madagascar Periwinkle (like the vinca, in many gardens) is used in treating leukemia.

The orchids are not only beautiful, but fragrant. An exception is the giant titan arum *(Amorphophallus titanum)* indigenous to Sumatra, which smells like rotting garbage (or worse) when it blooms. My advice: Stay upwind of it. The good news is that it blooms only every 2 years, the last time in July 2009.

The **east wing showcases** the interrelationship of plants and their environment. According to Native American beliefs, spirits inhabit the Saguaro cactus, indigenous to Arizona. The Garden Primeval replicates a dinosaur landscape of 150 million years ago. See if your kids can locate the fern "pups," or offshoots. Some moss resembles spruce.

Giant palms, flowering banana trees, *Dichorisandra* (electric purple lilaclike blooms), and an Asian shrimp plant with gold conical flowers resembling paper cutouts populate the jungle.

The National Garden, on 3 acres of land west of the Conservatory, contains several sections, including a Kids Garden where kids can fill a watering can and give the plants a drink, get their feet wet, sniff fragrant flowers, walk under a large leafy arbor, and get acquainted with some unfamiliar species. Rose Garden, Butterfly Garden, and a Regional Garden (plants that thrive in the mid-Atlantic). The First Ladies Water Garden features a granite fountain inspired by the Martha Washington (star) quilt pattern.

The Botanic Garden continues to add to its kid- and family-oriented programs. Lucky locals with preschoolers can sign up for Sprouts: the 1-month sessions (four different programs) are Wednesday, 10:30 to 11:30am, during which 3- to 5-year-olds (with a parent or guardian) get their hands dirty with plant-related activities. Make reservations by phone or at the website. Near the entrance, note the environmental sensor, looking like a microphone, suspended from the ceiling. It reads the light, humidity, and temperature of the building and transmits that data to a computer in the basement. Free tours of the highlights are loosey-goosey, so ask at the visitor information desk when you arrive. Free 45-minute guided tours of the conservatory are by reservation only, at least 3 weeks in advance (**✆ 202/226-4082**). Be sure to cross Independence Avenue to **Bartholdi Park ★★**, a gem unfamiliar to many who've lived their entire lives in D.C. Rest on a bench, close your eyes, and inhale the rose fragrance. Some Tuesdays at noon, USBG staff conducts a free tour, where you can learn about the garden and pick up gardening tips. Frederic Auguste Bartholdi designed the fountain for the 1876 Centennial Exhibition in Philadelphia. Sound familiar? He is better known for sculpting the Statue of Liberty.

Pickin's are slim if you get hungry here. I suggest going to the Sam Rayburn House Office Building cafeteria (16 and older must have photo ID), open to the general public 7 to 11:30am and 1 to 5pm (Independence Ave. and 1st St. SW); or the National Gallery of Art (Constitution Ave. NW, btw. 3rd and 7th sts.) for a bite at the Cascade Café (cafeteria-style) or the Garden Café (sit-down).

100 Maryland Ave. SW, at 1st St. (foot of Capitol Hill). Entrances at Maryland and Independence aves. © **202/225-8333.** www.usbg.gov. Free admission. Daily 10am–5pm; sometimes extended summer hours. Metro: Federal Center SW or Capitol South; also near the U.S. Capitol Tourmobile stop.

West Potomac Park Ask 10 D.C. residents where West Potomac Park is, and I'll bet at least 9 won't know, even though the park takes in the Lincoln and Jefferson memorials, the Korean War and Vietnam War Veterans memorials, the Constitution Gardens, and the Tidal Basin. Cherry trees are the park's main claim to fame, especially during the 2-week **National Cherry Blossom Festival** that runs from late March into April. You can write ahead for a schedule of events: National Cherry Blossom Festival, P.O. Box 33224, Washington, DC 20033-0224, or call the hot line (© **877/44-BLOOM** [442-5666]; www.nationalcherryblossomfestival.org).

Of the original 3,000 Yoshino trees, a gift from Japan in 1912, only about 200 survive. They've been supplemented over the years, and now about 1,400 Yoshinos bloom at the Tidal Basin. Most are near the 300-year-old Japanese stone lantern. While the delicate white- and pale pink–blossomed Yoshinos predominate, they now mingle with Akebonos (single pale pink flowers), the Kwanzan variety (double pom-pom-like blossoms of deeper pink), and Weeping Higans (single or double layers of petals from white to dark pink.). Blossoms last up to 2 weeks, if Mother Nature is being kind. A total of about 3,700 trees bloom in East and West Potomac Parks. Start counting! For a different perspective, rent a paddleboat (an all-new fleet in 2008) at the Tidal Basin ($10 per hour two-passenger boat, $18 per hour four-passenger). Savvy visitors reserve a month or two ahead, online at www.tidalbasinpeddleboats.com. My favorite time is dusk, when the fading light creates an otherworldly scene. Also, it's usually the least crowded time.

Approximate boundaries: Constitution Ave. to the north, Jefferson Memorial to the south, Potomac River to the west, Washington Monument to the east. © **202/547-1500.** Free admission. Daily dawn–dusk. Metro: Smithsonian; then about a 15-min. walk.

NATURE CENTERS

Science- and nature-related activities (hikes, crafts, stories) are offered on weekends in Glen Echo Park's former stables in the **Discovery Creek Children's Museum of Washington.** For details, see chapter 6.

Woodend Nature Sanctuary of Audubon Naturalist Society ★ Kids can explore self-guided nature trails in this 40-acre wildlife sanctuary and learn about conservation and the environment in special programs. Activities are geared to children 4 and older, with day and weekend family programs, classes, and field trips. For the latest stirrings, call the Voice of the Naturalist recording, updated weekly (© **301/652-1088**). Hikers and extreme walkers, take note: You can get here by taking the Metro to the Silver Spring or Bethesda stations, then a J2 or J3 Metrobus to Meadowbrook Lane. Walk north on the Rock Creek hike/bike trail 1 mile to the Woodend nature trail.

8940 Jones Mill Rd., Chevy Chase, MD. © **301/652-9188.** Fax 301/951-7179. www.audubonnaturalist.org. Free admission. Nature sanctuary daily dawn–dusk; building Mon–Fri 9am–5pm; bookstore/gift shop Mon–Fri 10am–5pm, Sat 9am–5pm, Sun noon–5pm. Closed holidays. Directions: Drive north on Connecticut Ave., turn right onto Jones Bridge Rd., and then turn left at Jones Mill Rd.

Rock Creek Nature Center ★★ Plenty of self-guided nature trails and hands-on activities distinguish this facility in the District's largest park. Guided nature walks, films, planetarium shows, and live animal presentations are scheduled throughout the year. Call ahead for specifics, and see "Gardens & Parks," earlier in this chapter. See chapter 6 for info on planetarium shows.

Rock Creek Park, 5200 Glover Rd. NW. ✆ **202/426-6829.** www.nps.gov/rocr. Free admission. Daily in summer 9am–5pm; after Labor Day Wed–Sun 9am–5pm. Directions: North on Connecticut Ave.; turn right onto Military Rd., then turn right onto Glover Rd.

OUTDOOR SCULPTURE

More than 370 outdoor sculptures decorate the D.C. landscape. Here is a handful with special appeal for kids.

National Gallery of Art Sculpture Garden ★★★ This 6-acre sculpture garden on the Mall lies west of the museum's West Building, between 7th and 9th streets, Constitution Avenue, and Madison Drive NW. I urge you to spend at least a few minutes here during your Mall crawl.

Native shade trees and curvilinear benches encircle a fountain pool (no swimming allowed). The plantings are lovely, and this heavy metal won't hurt your hearing. (For information on the sculptures, see chapter 6; for a great kids' introduction to the sculpture garden, visit www.nga.gov/kids.)

Albert Einstein Nestled in the gardens of the National Academy of Sciences at 2101 Constitution Ave. NW, Einstein's ample lap invites little ones to climb up and rest a while.

The Awakening Sadly, this statue was moved in 2009 from Hains Point, in East Potomac Park (where many could view it), to National Harbour, a huge, mixed-use, largely inaccessible development with a Gaylord resort on the Potomac River in southern Prince George's County. But I digress. This dramatic sculpture of a giant struggling to free himself from the ground has a new home. But he may well find himself home alone.

In 1993, after a car ran into the statue, the severed 17-foot arm was reattached by sculptor Seward Johnson who performed the extensive surgery. In September 2003, the statue was nearly washed away by tropical storm Isabel. Clearly, it has nine lives.

Equestrian Statue of Ulysses S. Grant Get out your camera. Outside the West facade of the U.S. Capitol, with its sweeping view of the National Mall, horse-drawn caissons flank an imposing statue of Grant.

The Lansburgh Eagle No relation to the bald eagle, *The Lansburgh Eagle,* all 800 pounds, landed with the help of a crane at 8th and E streets NW in March 1992. At last report, it was still resting comfortably in the Pennsylvania Quarter's courtyard.

Fun Facts **Did You Know?**

As you view the city's many equestrian statues, note the positions of the horses' legs. Both front legs in the air means the rider died in battle. If one front leg is raised, the rider died as a result of his wounds. If all four legs are on the ground, he died of natural causes.

The Lone Sailor The windblown sailor stands in the plaza at the U.S. Navy Memorial and Visitor Center at Market Square, Pennsylvania Avenue and 7th Street NW, where military bands give concerts on summer evenings.

Lunchbreak Located at Washington Harbor, 30th and K streets NW, in Georgetown, is a realistic workman in overalls enjoying lunch on a park bench.

Man Controlling Trade If I had sculpted this, I would have called it *Whoa, Horsey.* Michael Lantz's two massive equestrian works mirror each other on the east end of the Federal Trade Commission Building at Pennsylvania Avenue and 6th Street NW (the point of the Federal Triangle). One faces Constitution Avenue; the other faces Pennsylvania Avenue.

National Law Enforcement Officers Memorial The bronze lions, by Washington sculptor Ray Kaskey, are grouped majestically around the Judiciary Square memorial to officers who died on duty from 1794 to the present. The memorial is in the vicinity of the National Building Museum, 4th and F streets NW.

FARMS

Claude Moore Colonial Farm at Turkey Run ★ **Finds** If your kids are like most, complaining that they have it rough, take them to see how their colonial forebears lived. Watch a poor colonial family (Park Service staff in period dress) split logs, make clothes, and tend livestock. The one-room house is a real eye-opener. Kids can help the farmer harvest tobacco in August. Go on a weekday, if possible. Special events are ongoing throughout the year, such as 18th-century market fairs in May, July, and October. You can spend an authentic colonial weekend here and use a slit trench as a toilet. They've made allowances, however, and toilet paper is available if you prefer it to leaves. If you live in the area, ask about the volunteer program for kids 10 and older.

6310 Georgetown Pike, McLean, VA. ✆ **703/442-7557.** www.1771.org. Admission $3 adults, $2 ages 3–12 and seniors. AAA discount available. Large groups should call ahead. Apr to mid-Dec Wed–Sun 10am–4:30pm. Closed mid-Dec to Mar, Thanksgiving, and rainy days. Directions: Beltway to exit 44 (Rte. 193 east), and go 2½ miles to the marked access road on the left to the farm; or take the G. W. Pkwy. to Rte. 123 south, go 1 mile, turn right on Rte. 193, and then turn right into the marked access road to the farm.

Oxon Hill Farm ★ Activities abound at this working farm from around 1900, operated by the Park Service. It's not every day that kids can help gather eggs, feed chickens, and milk cows. So as not to disappoint, call ahead for the times of these special activities. Pet the animals and learn about farm life by watching seasonal demonstrations of cider pressing, corn harvesting, and sheep shearing. A cow-milking demonstration takes place two or three times a day. Say hello to Becky and Dixie, two beautiful Belgian draft horses. A highlight of the self-guided nature walk is the view of the Potomac River, Washington, and Virginia. You may also bike, hike, and picnic on the grounds. For group reservations, call weekdays between 2:30 and 4pm.

Oxon Cove Park, 6411 Oxon Hill Rd., Oxon Hill, MD. ✆ **301/839-1176.** www.nps.gov/oxhi. Free admission. Daily 8am–4:30pm. Closed Thanksgiving, Christmas, Jan 1. Directions: Beltway to exit 3A (Indian Head Hwy. south), turn right at first intersection, right onto Oxon Hill Rd., and follow it to the farm on the right.

2 OUTDOOR ACTIVITIES

BIKING

The area abounds with off-road bike paths. The 7-mile **Capital Crescent Trail** between Georgetown and Bethesda, Maryland, is paved and follows an old railroad right-of-way through scenic wooded areas. On weekends, the trail is heavily congested. For more information, call ✆ **202/234-4874** (www.cctrail.org). Other major trails include the **C&O Canal Towpath,** 23 miles from Georgetown to Seneca, Maryland; the **George Washington Memorial Parkway** ★, from the Virginia side of Memorial Bridge through downtown Alexandria, ending at Mount Vernon (with the flattest terrain of all listed); and **Rock Creek Park,** north from the infamous Watergate through northwest D.C., past the zoo, and along Beach Drive into Maryland. Parts of the route along Beach Drive are closed to traffic on weekends (see the entry on Rock Creek Park, earlier in this chapter). I biked a portion of the Mount Vernon trail recently and recommend it. There are numerous places to pull over, rest, and munch the sandwiches you remembered to bring. And the views of the Potomac and monuments are awesome. Rent bikes at Bike and Roll (www.bikethesites.com) or Big Wheel Bikes (see contact information below), both in Alexandria. A short ride through Old Town will connect you to the trail. You can go all the way to Mount Vernon, if you have the stamina.

Bookstores and bicycle shops stock maps of local trails, or you can try the **Washington Area Bicyclist Association** (**WABA;** 1803 Connecticut Ave. NW, Washington, DC 20009; ✆ **202/518-0524;** www.waba.org). A helpful site for biking in D.C. is www.bikewashington.org. Experienced cyclists who want to tackle the entire C&O Canal (which takes about 3 days, averaging 61 miles a day) can write to C&O Canal, National Historic Parks, P.O. Box 4, Sharpsburg, MD 21782 (✆ **301/739-4200;** www.nps.gov/choh).

Bike and Roll ★ (✆ **202/842-BIKE** [2453]; www.bikethesites.com) offers participants professionally guided bike tours on Trek 21-speed hybrid bikes, from March through November. Bike and Roll provides helmets, water bottles, and a handlebar bag. In the **Capital Sites Ride** ★★, cyclists visit 55 landmarks on an 8-mile circuit that takes around 3 hours. In summer, an early-morning tour departs at 7am, leaving the rest of the day for visiting air-conditioned museums and restaurants. Most of the terrain is flat and on paved and gravel trails. Along the way, guides will feed you information. Children must be 54 inches tall to ride their own bikes. Kids who measure 41 inches to 48 inches ride in a trailer or a trailer carriage (up to two kids, 100-lb. maximum combined weight) that attaches to Mom or Dad's wheels. If you're feeling skittish, you should know that families make up more than half of Bike and Roll's business, and a majority of the adult riders haven't been on a bike in years. The tours depart from the rear plaza of the Old Post Office Pavilion, 12th St. NW, opposite the Federal Triangle Metro station. (Metro: Federal Triangle). It takes around 3 hours and costs $40 for adults and $30 for kids (all ages).

If you prefer going it alone, bike rentals vary and offer several styles and extras. Bike and Roll (www.bikethesites.com) has three locations: Old Post Office (11th St. and Pennsylvania Ave. (✆ **202/842-BIKE** [2453]); Union Station ✆ **202/962-0206**); and Old Town Alexandria (One Wales Way, near King and Union sts.; ✆ **703/548-ROLL** [7655]). **Big Wheel Bikes** (www.bigwheelbikes.com) has three locations: 1034 33rd St. NW, in Georgetown (✆ **202/337-0254**); 2 Prince St., Alexandria, Virginia (✆ **703/739-2300**); and 6917 Arlington Rd., Bethesda, Maryland (✆ **301/652-0192**), where they rent hybrids, mountain bikes, 12-speeds, or tandems. The rentals average $5 to $10 an hour, with a 2- or 3-hour minimum, or $25 to $50 per day (again, depending on type of bike—basic, hybrid, or high-performance). **Fletcher's Boat House,** 4940 Canal Rd. NW (✆ **202/244-0461;** www.fletcherscove.com), rents fixed-gear bikes *only,* for $6 per hour, $25 per day. The towpath is mostly flat, so this shouldn't present a problem. Fletcher's is about a mile west of the Georgetown side of Key Bridge. The nearest restaurants are in Georgetown and on MacArthur Boulevard, which runs parallel to Canal Road. While there is a snack bar at Fletcher's, I prefer to tote snacks or a brown-bag lunch to enjoy at Fletcher's picnic area. If your kids are too young to pedal on their own, consider renting a bike child seat or trailer, but know that experts recommend that a second cyclist follow behind a bike with a child seat or trailer. Practice with the equipment before venturing out, stay on smooth surfaces away from traffic, and always give kids helmets. The equipment rents for about $20 to $25 a day at bike stores noted above.

BOATING

On a mild day (in D.C., that's usually late Mar–Nov), take to the water for a fun-filled family experience and a different view of the city. I'm willing to bet that everyone will sleep like babies afterward. Prices average $10 per hour or $30 per day. Most places are open from 9 or 10am to 5 or 6pm weekdays, with extended weekend and summer hours. Call first, because hours change seasonally. Arrive early on weekends.

Fletcher's Boat House, 4940 Canal Rd. NW (✆ **202/244-0461;** www.fletcherscove.com), rents canoes, rowboats, and kayaks. Kids must weigh 30 pounds or more (that's the smallest size life vest available). There's a large picnic area and snack bar, too. Anglers can purchase a D.C. fishing license here. **Jack's Boathouse,** 3500 K St. NW in Georgetown (✆ **202/337-9642;** www.jacksboathouse.com), rents canoes, and kayaks (single and double). **Thompson's Boat Center,** 2900 Virginia Avenue NW, at Rock Creek Parkway, Georgetown (✆ **202/333-9543;** www.thompsonboatcenter.com), rents canoes, rowing shells (but you must be certified), kayaks, and Sunfish (small sailboats) April through October.

At the **Tidal Basin** ★, Ohio Drive and Tidal Basin (near the Jefferson Memorial, roughly 15th St. and Maine Ave. SW; ✆ **202/479-2426;** www.tidalbasinpaddleboats.com), rent a pedal boat mid-March through mid-October; prices are $10 per hour for a two-seater, $18 for a four-seater. An all-new fleet, introduced in 2008, awaits your family. During the Cherry Blossom Festival and other peak times, savvy visitors reserve up to a month or two ahead online. Farther afield (or, in this case, astream), if your kids are 7 or older, they can learn to paddle their own canoes summer evenings on the C&O Canal. Bless the **National Park Service!** It offers free evening classes during the summer (although there's a nominal fee to rent equipment) at Fletcher's Boat House and Swain's Lock, off River Road, west of Potomac, Maryland. Younger kids can ride with their parents, but the rule is three to a canoe. Picnic tables are available at both sites for a light supper before the 6:30pm class begins. Call ✆ **301/299-9006** for boat-rental and class prices.

Kayaking has taken off in the past several years as a pleasurable, affordable water sport. If you're considering whitewater kayaking, you'll need some land-based training before heading out. The Potomac can be unpredictable and treacherous—no place for a wannabe lacking experience. **Atlantic Kayak,** 1201 North Royal St., Alexandria, Virginia (✆ **703/838-9072;** www.atlantickayak.com), rents canoes and kayaks, and also offers kayaking classes and tours. **Potomac Paddlesports,** 11001 MacArthur Blvd., Potomac, Maryland (✆ **877/529-2542;** www.potomacpaddlesports.com); and **Valley**

Mill Kayak School, 15101 Seneca Rd., Darnestown, Maryland (✆ **301/840-7388;** www.valleymillkayak.com), both offer classes for beginners and escorted trips.

FISHING

Thanks to the Clean Water Act, there are fish—live fish—in the waters in and around the D.C. area. Every Friday, see the "On the Move" section of the *Washington Post's* "Weekend" magazine for a listing of what fish are running and biting where. Local anglers tell me that mid-March until July is prime fishing time. Nonetheless, you'll probably catch *something* from late February through October. Cast your line for catfish, bass, and stripers from the wall along the Washington Channel at **Hains Point** or **Pentagon Lagoon,** anywhere near **Chain Bridge,** or at the seawall north of the **Wilson Bridge,** in Alexandria, Virginia.

If you want to sink your line in the **Chesapeake Bay,** board a head boat for a half or full day of fishing. Several head boats leave from the **Rod 'N Reel,** Route 261 and Mears Avenue, in Chesapeake Beach, Maryland (✆ **800/233-2080;** chesapeakebeachresortpa.com). It's about a 45-minute drive from D.C., and kids of all ages are welcome as long as someone is watching them. Prices are $55 for all ages, with a $3 discount for kids 12 and under on weekdays. Most boats go out, weather permitting, once a day at 8am and return at 3pm. Although some add a second night-fishing trip at 6pm. You can rent a rod for $5. Oh, yes, a dozen bloodworms are included with the boarding fee. Use them for best results. (My dad taught me how to fish with bologna as bait—we caught an old shoe once.)

Be sure to wear nonskid shoes for the slippery decks. Take plenty of sun block, a windbreaker or foul-weather jacket, and two coolers—one for all the fish you'll catch, and one for lunch and drinks. If you're toting your own fishing gear, leave light tackle at home. Those prone to motion sickness should take an appropriate medication a half-hour before boarding.

Many area fishers favor casting off from **Fletcher's Boat House,** at the intersection of Reservoir and Canal roads NW (✆ **202/244-0461;** www.fletchersboathouse.com). Fletcher's sells bait and tackle, rents boats, and has a snack bar. With younger kids, I'd stick to the canal here. Conveniently, you can also pick up a fishing license at Fletcher's. The cost is $10 for residents, $13 for nonresidents. Short-term visitors are better served by the $7 license, good for 14 consecutive days. For more information, call the D.C. Department of Health, Fisheries and Wildlife Division, at ✆ **202/535-2260** (www.takemefishing.org).

Please be careful when you fish the Potomac. Every year, several people drown in its unforgiving waters, which are especially treacherous and turbulent after heavy rains. Heed warning signs; they're posted for a reason. And be particularly cautious of slippery rocks along the shoreline.

HIKING

Many city and suburban parks have hiking trails (see the "Parks, Gardens & Other Wide-Open Spaces" section, earlier in this chapter), and portions of the **Blue Ridge Mountains** and **Appalachian Trail** are well within reach for a day trip. Some of the best local hiking for families is along the **C&O Canal, Theodore Roosevelt Island,** and **Rock Creek Park.** On the Maryland side of Great Falls Park, 11710 MacArthur Blvd., Potomac (✆ **301/767-3714;** www.nps.gov/gwmp), open from 9am to dark daily (closed Christmas), the 4-mile **Billy Goat Trail** ★ is a family favorite. The trail's entrance is off a towpath less than 2 miles south of the park's entrance. Section A, the first stretch, is 1.6 miles one-way and the most difficult. Tired? Return to the falls via the flatter and less challenging towpath. Just turn off at the "Emergency Exit" sign. Brave hearts can continue to sections B and C. Nobody said you have to do the entire trail on your first try. The Visitor Center is open Monday through Friday from 10am to 5pm, Saturday and Sunday 10am to 6pm (summer), 10am to 4pm (winter). A snack bar is open near the visitor center weekends.

ICE SKATING

Every few years, Washington endures a severe winter and the **C&O Canal** (✆ **301/767-3707;** www.nps.gov/choh) freezes over for skating. It's a scene straight from Currier and Ives, and one that your family won't want to miss. Skating is allowed only when the SKATE AT YOUR OWN RISK signs are posted; otherwise, forget it!

The ice-skating rink in the **National Gallery of Art Sculpture Garden,** 7th Street and Constitution Ave. (✆ **202/289-3360;** www.nga.gov), is my fave because of the setting. It is usually open from mid-November until mid-March, and hours are 10am to 9pm Monday through Thursday, 10am to 11pm Friday and Saturday, 11am to 9pm Sunday. Admission is $7 for adults; $6 for kids 12 and younger, seniors 50 and older, and students with valid ID. You can rent skates for $3; a locker is only 50¢. All sessions run 2 hours, beginning on the hour. Grab something to eat at the nearby Pavilion Café, refreshment stand, or street vendors on Constitution Avenue. In the suburbs, the **Fairfax Ice Arena,** 3779 Pickett Rd., Fairfax, Virginia (✆ **703/323-1132;** www.fairfaxicearena.com), is open year-round and offers skate rentals, lessons, and a pro shop. Don't be surprised if you run into a few Olympic hopefuls in training. In Maryland, two covered outdoor rinks—**Cabin John Ice Rink,** 10610 Westlake Dr., Rockville, Maryland (✆ **301/365-0585**), and **Wheaton Ice Rink,** at Arcola and Orebaugh avenues, Wheaton, Maryland (✆ **301/649-3640**)—attract scores of families. Both offer skate rentals and lessons. Cabin John has lockers and a snack bar, and is open year-round.

IN-LINE SKATING

If you care to schlep your in-line skates from home, you can join other scabby-knee risk-takers and head for these skating sites: Rock Creek Park (when Beach Dr. is closed to traffic Sat–Sun) and the C&O Canal trail, between Georgetown and Fletcher's Boat House (about 1.5 miles). Seasoned skaters only might want to head for the pebbly walkways on the Mall. But please don't try to blade through the museums, and always, always wear a helmet and pads.

KITE FLYING

Spring and fall are the best kite-flying seasons in the capital area. In summer, a breeze is unusual enough to attract media attention, and in winter, it's usually too chilly to enjoy kite flying. Look no farther than the Mall for the optimum kite-flying space with no overhead impediments. Otherwise, head for the nearest schoolyard or playground. The **Air and Space Museum's gift shop,** at 6th Street and Independence Avenue SW, has a mind-boggling selection of kites.

In late March, the Smithsonian sponsors an annual **kite festival** on the west side of the Washington Monument (✆ **202/357-3030;** www.kitefestival.org). If you want to enter the contest, there are two hitches: The kite has to be homemade, and it's supposed to remain airborne for at least 1 minute at an altitude of 100 feet or more. Ribbons are awarded to winners in different age groups, and trophies are given in several categories.

The children's competition usually runs from noon to 1pm. Of course, you're welcome to fly a kite (store-bought or homemade) just for the fun of it.

MINIATURE GOLF

Here is one game that junior and senior tour hopefuls (and hopeless) can enjoy strictly for fun. It doesn't cost an arm and a leg to swing a club in the scenic surroundings of Hains Point, in East Potomac Park. The **Mini Golf Course,** 972 Ohio Dr. SW (✆ **202/488-8087;** www.golfdc.com), is open daily 11am to 7pm April to November and weekends only April, September, and October, weather permitting. It's $6 per game for adults, $5 for ages 17 and under. Outside the district, try **Upton Hill Regional Park Miniature Golf,** 6060 Wilson Boulevard, in Arlington, Virginia (✆ **703/534-3437;** www.nvrpa.org).

SAILING/WINDSURFING

The **Mariner Sailing School,** Belle Haven Marina, south of Alexandria, Virginia (✆ **703/768-0018;** www.saildc.com), rents Sunfish, and larger sailboats to experienced sailors, and offers weekend and evening classes for adults. Canoes, johnboat (rowboats), and kayaks are also available. May through August, kids 8 to 15 can take a 5-day sailing course on a 14-foot Sunfish. Make reservations to ensure your spot. The Mariner Sailing School at Belle Haven Marina, 1201 Belle Haven Rd., off the George Washington Memorial Parkway (1½ miles south of Reagan National Airport), Alexandria, Virginia (✆ **703/548-9027;** www.saildc.com), rents sailboats ($30–$54 for 2 hours Mon–Fri; more Sat–Sun) and runs several week-long youth sailing camps for ages 9 to 15. The WSM fleet includes 14-foot and 19-foot boats. Weeklong courses (for different skill levels) are held from June through August. Prices vary according to boat size and the number of youths per boat. For information on sailing instruction on the Chesapeake Bay in Annapolis, Maryland (about 35 miles from downtown), see the "Annapolis" entry in chapter 11.

SWIMMING

For the location of the public pool nearest you, call the **D.C. Department of Recreation** (✆ **202/673-7660;** http://app.dpr.dc.gov). Most public pools are open from mid-June through late August or Labor Day. Frankly, they're very crowded, and most are in D.C.'s less-than-premier neighborhoods. I strongly suggest staying in a hotel with a pool or visiting one that admits outsiders.

In past years, a few hotel pools have been open to the public, if you paid for a daily pass of $10 to $15 per person per day. Like the political climate, hotel policy can change in a heartbeat. If a cooling dip at day's end is important to your family, I strongly recommend staying in a hotel with a pool. *Mar-co, Po-lo!*

TENNIS

In Rock Creek Park, the tennis courts at 16th and Kennedy streets NW are open Monday through Friday from 7am to 11pm, and Saturday and Sunday from 7am to 10pm (shorter weekend hours Nov–Apr). Courts must be reserved from April to November (✆ **202/722-5949;** www.rockcreektennis.com). Indoor court time ranges from $10 to $18; indoor time is $26 to $38. Or swing your racquet at 2 of the 24 courts (indoor, outdoor, lighted, and clay) in East Potomac Park, 1090 Ohio Dr. SW (✆ **202/554-5962**). They're open spring through fall, Monday through Friday from 7am to 10pm, and Saturday and Sunday from 7am to 8pm—with extended winter hours. Court time is $10 to $20 depending on court surface, day/time, indoor or out

3 RIDES FOR CHILDREN

BALLOON RIDES

Go up, up, and away at several locations outside the Beltway (as if there's not already enough hot air in Washington). A balloon ride does not come cheaply and is appropriate only for kids at least 8 or older, but if you're prepared to cough up the bucks, call **Maryland Ballooning** (✆ **800/585-5555;** www.marylandballooning.com) or **Balloons Unlimited** (✆ **703/281-2300;** www.balloonsunlimited.com), which has been in business since 1976. Expect a ride of an hour to an hour and a half, with departures usually near sunrise and sunset from the Virginia countryside, about an hour's drive from downtown D.C. The charge is $200 per hour for adults, $100 for children 12 and under.

BOAT RIDES

During the warm-weather months, take advantage of Washington's waterfront setting and enjoy the city from offshore with your kids: I'll bet they rate a boat ride as one of the high watermarks of their visit. Rent a pedal boat on the Tidal Basin, or a canoe or rowboat on the C&O Canal or Potomac River. For details on several D.C. boating centers, see the "Boating" and "Sailing" entries in this chapter. Also see the "Annapolis" entry in chapter 11. When boating, make sure there are appropriately sized life vests onboard for each family member, and be sure to put them on before you leave the dock.

Canal Boat Rides on the C&O Canal

Park Service guides in period dress from around 1870 will regale you with 19th-century canal lore and river songs as the mule-drawn boat makes its way along the historic waterway. The ***Georgetown*** ★★ is berthed in Georgetown, on the canal, between 30th and Thomas Jefferson streets (✆ **202/653-5190;** www.nps.bov/chob); the ***Charles F. Mercer*** is at Great Falls Park, 11710 MacArthur Blvd., Potomac, Maryland (✆ **301/767-3714**). Both operate only mid-April through October, Wednesday through Sunday. Times vary, with additional cruises Saturday and Sunday.

The *Georgetown* might look like a barge, but it is actually a boat—the Park Service told me—because it is steerable. The mules are the engine! A true barge has to be pulled and pushed; it cannot be steered. Live and learn. Anyway, the delightful and informative rides are an hour long. Leave it to the Park Service—rangers carry boxes filled with old-fashioned toys for restless little girls and boys. The cost for the ride is $5. Buy tickets at the Visitor Center, 1057 Thomas Jefferson St. NW (Wed–Sun 9:30am–4:30pm), or Great Falls Visitor Center, 11710 MacArthur Blvd., Potomac, Maryland (✆ **301/767-3714**). Reservations are not needed. Times vary, so be sure to call in advance.

Cruises

Because two sides of the Washington "diamond" are bordered by rivers—the Potomac and Anacostia—you should cast off from terra firma and see the city from the water at least once during your stay. Please note that the prices and schedules for the cruises below change frequently; call or visit the website for the most up-to-date information.

The 150-year-old steel riverboat ***Nightingale II*** (✆ **800/405-5511;** www.capitol rivercruises.com) leaves from the Washington Harbor dock in Georgetown, 31st Street and the river, for a 50-minute narrated cruise, departing hourly from noon to 9pm, April through October. The fare is $13 for adults and $6 for kids 3 to 12 (discounted if you book online), and there's a snack bar onboard. Feel free to BYO (lunch) if you like.

The luxurious 510-passenger ***Spirit of Washington*** (© **866/302-2469** or 202/554-8000; www.spiritofwashington.com) offers lunch, brunch, dinner, and moonlight cruises to Mount Vernon from Pier 4, 600 Water St. SW (at 6th Street). However, you should probably forget the dinner and moonlight cruises with kids—it's likely that the cruises will be too long, too expensive, and too boring for them to enjoy. The 2-hour lunch cruise (in the Washington Channel) aboard the carpeted, climate-controlled ship is fine if your kids will do justice to the copious buffet and dessert. Some cruises feature live music and a show. Cruises range from $42 to $86, depending on the day and meal; lunch is the best deal. For all cruises, reservations are a must (© **202/554-8000,** or 202/554-8013 for groups of 20 or more; www.spiritofwashington.com).

If food is secondary and you want to spend a fun-filled half-day on the water visiting a major sight, board the ***Spirit of Mount Vernon*** ★ (© **202/554-8000**). The cruise down the Potomac to George Washington's beautiful estate is pleasing to all ages. Cruises depart Friday through Sunday March 13 to 29 and August 28 through October 31, Tuesday through Sunday March 31 through August 23. Board at 8:15am, depart 8:30, returning midafternoon. There is a snack bar on board. Round-trip fares are $42 for adults, $40 for senior citizens, $34 for ages 6 to 11, and free for children 5 and under. Admission to Mount Vernon is included in the ticket price. You'll have ample time to look around Mount Vernon before the return voyage. You may not bring food aboard, but there's a concession stand selling all the drinks and fast food that kids' tummies can hold. There's also a food court at Mount Vernon. Arrive at the dock 1 hour before departure time. Glide by presidential monuments and the Iwo Jima Memorial, the Kennedy Center, and Georgetown on the ***Matthew Hayes*** water taxi ★, which runs several times daily from April until October (every 2 hr. 11:30am–9:30pm June–Labor Day). There are two departure points: Georgetown (Washington Harbor dock, 31st St. NW and the river) and Old Town Alexandria (Alexandria City Marina, behind the Torpedo Factory). The round-trip fare is $24 for adults, $20 for seniors, and $12 for kids 2 to 12.

The ***Miss Christin*** ★ cruises the Potomac from Old Town Alexandria to Mount Vernon from April through October (Sat–Sun only Apr and Sept–Oct; Tues–Sun the other months). The cruise departs Old Town at 11am and leaves Mount Vernon at 4pm. Fare (including admission to Mount Vernon) is $38 for adults, $30 for seniors, $20 kids 6 to 10. Potomac Riverboat Company (© **703/548-9000;** www.potomacriverboatco.com), based in Alexandria, Virginia, runs both the ***Miss Christin*** and the ***Matthew Hayes.***

In the tradition of the Parisian *bateaux mouche* on the Seine, the riverboat-restaurants ***Dandy*** and ***Nina's Dandy*** (© **703/683-6076;** www.dandydinnerboat.com) ply the waters of the Potomac daily. Luncheon, dinner, and brunch cruises depart Old Town Alexandria for a leisurely run up the Potomac past historic monuments and memorials, the Kennedy Center, Watergate, Rosslyn (Virginia), and Georgetown before heading back to port. Kids 10 and older, with the palate, patience, and pennies for a three-course lunch or five-course dinner with mostly adults, might enjoy this cruise. Or not. For more information and to make reservations (a must) phone © **703/683-6076** (www.dandydinnerboat.com). Resembling a humongous floating graham cracker, the ***Odyssey*** (© **202/488-6010;** www.odysseycruises.com) is docked at the Gangplank Marina, 600 Water St. SW. Designed to squeeze under the bridges spanning the Potomac, the glassed-in vessel accommodates 1,800 passengers. Oh, joy! Take your pick of a lunch, brunch, or dinner cruise with several price permutations. Sorry, these riverboat-restaurants don't float *my* boat. I'd rather take a no-frills cruise on a smaller boat and eat in an intimate, first-rate Old Town or waterfront Maine Avenue restaurant (for a lot less than dining with all those strangers).

Now here's a cruise worth diving for: **D.C. Ducks** ★ (✆ **202/966-DUCK** [3825]; www.dcducks.com) utilizes amphibious vehicles that transported troops and supplies during World War II. The hybrid ferries 30 visitors around several downtown sights before dipping into the Virginia side of the Potomac at the Columbia Island Marina. After a short swim, the Duck waddles ashore at Gravelly Point, across from National Airport's main runway, and heads back to Union Station over paved roads. The keels-on-wheels tours depart from Union Station, 50 Massachusetts Ave. NE, daily from mid-March to November, every hour on the hour from 10am to 4pm, and more frequently at peak times. The narrated 90-minute ride (60 on land, 30 afloat) costs $32 ($28 online) for adults, $16 ($14 online) for seniors 65 and older and children 4 to 12. Children 3 and under ride for free.

Ferry Rides

About 30 miles northwest of the District of Columbia, the ***Gen. Jubal A. Early*** ★, an old cable ferry named after an even older Confederate general, leaves from White's Ferry (✆ **301/349-5200;** http://canal.mcmullans.org), on the Maryland shore, and sails to just north of Leesburg, Virginia. The first ferries began crossing here in 1828. Kids of all ages adore the *Jubal Early,* which operates daily from 5am to 11pm, weather permitting. The ferry makes several trips per hour. The ride is 5 to 15 minutes long, depending on the current and weather. You can take your car on the ferry or go on foot ($4 one-way, $7 round-trip, $1 for foot passengers). There's a convenience store on the Maryland side. For $1.50, you can use one of the picnic tables. Take the Capital Beltway to I-270 to the Route 28 west exit, and then continue on Route 28 west; at Dawsonville, take Route 107 and follow the signs.

If you have the time, consider a visit to **Leesburg,** Virginia (✆ **703/771-2170;** www.visitloudon.org), before returning to the Maryland side of the Potomac. The town oozes charm and history. Market and Loudon streets run east and west, intersected by King Street (north and south). Stop at the Loudon Museum, 14 Loudon St. SW (✆ **703/777-7427**), for information, and browse the historic district with its brick sidewalks. Antique shops and restaurants abound in this gentle place, which is especially beautiful when the fall foliage flames in late October. At the **Leesburg Animal Park,** 19270 James Monroe Highway (✆ **703/433-0002;** www.leesburganimalpark.com), kids can feed and pet the exotic animals daily 9am to 5pm November through March, 9am to 6pm April through October. Open on Monday holidays (Columbus, Memorial, and Labor days). Admission is $8.50 per person weekdays, $13 weekends and holidays. Kids up to 2 years are free.

CAROUSELS

Families that enjoy going around together will want to take a ride on an antique carousel. Few excursions are as much fun or cost as little as these—only $1.50 to $2.50 (Carousel on the Mall). The **Carousel on the Mall** ★, 1000 Jefferson Dr. SW, in front of the Smithsonian Castle (✆ **202/357-2700**), operates, weather permitting, from 10am to 6pm March through early September and 11am to 5pm September through February. The 1940s carousel, designed by Allan Herschell, sports 58 horses, two chariots, a sea dragon, and no partridge in a pear tree.

Carousel in Burke Lake Park, 7315 Ox Rd., Fairfax Station, Virginia (✆ **703/323-6600;** www.fairfaxcounty.gov), is open April and May, Labor Day through October weekends only 11:30am to 5:30pm; Memorial Day until Labor Day daily, 11:30am to 5:30pm. **Glen Echo Park Dentzel Carousel** ★, 7300 MacArthur Blvd at Goldsboro

Road, Glen Echo, Maryland (✆ **301/492-6229;** www.glenechopark.org), has a classic 1921 Dentzel carousel. It's been my favorite since I took my kids for their first ride in the 1970s. Now they're taking their kids! Ablaze with more than 1,200 lights, the carousel has 52 carved wood figures and a 165-band Wurlitzer organ. It operates weekends from May through September, noon to 6pm. May through August it also runs Wednesday and Thursday from 10am to 2pm; in addition, during July and August you can also ride on Friday from 10am to 2pm. A park ranger gives a half-hour talk on the carousel's history Saturday at 10:30am.

Lake Fairfax Carousel, 1400 Lake Fairfax Driver, Reston, Virginia (✆ **703/471-5415;** www.fairfaxcounty.gov.), is open Memorial Day weekend to Labor Day, 7 days a week, 11am to 7pm; from Labor Day through September, weekends only, 11am to 5pm.

Lee District Park Carousel, 6601 Telegraph Rd., Alexandria, Virginia (✆ **703/922-9841**), is open Memorial Day to the day before Labor Day, Saturday 10am to 6pm and Sunday from noon to 6pm.

HAYRIDES

If you're visiting in the fall, especially around Halloween, treat your kids to a hayride at a nearby farm. Afterward, stock up on apples, pumpkins, and fresh-pressed cider while you pick the hay out of each other's hair. Call for hours and special kids' activities. Three close-to-D.C. orchards, offering hayrides and pick-your-own pumpkins as part of their all-out Halloween celebration, are **Butler's Orchard** ★, 22200 Davis Mill Rd., Germantown, Maryland (✆ **301/972-3299;** www.butlersorchard.com); **Homestead Gardens** (where you can also visit the llamas 10am–3pm daily!), 743 W. Central Ave., Davidsonville, Maryland (✆ **410/798-5000;** www.homesteadgardens.com); and **Krop's Crops,** 11110 Georgetown Pike, Great Falls, Virginia (✆ **703/430-8955**). Check the Maryland and Virginia phone books for bushels more.

TRAIN RIDES

If your youngsters have never been on a big choo-choo, board a northbound **Amtrak** train at Union Station, 50 Massachusetts Ave. NE (✆ **800/USA-RAIL** [872-7245]), and take a ride to Baltimore (only a 40-min. ride from Union Station), where there are plenty of kid-pleasing things to do. The lowest one-way reserved (off-peak) ticket from Union Station to Baltimore's Penn Station is $21 for adults and 50¢ for kids ages 2 to 15 riding with an adult (each adult can bring two children at the reduced fare). ***Please note:*** This is with advanced booking. Check the website for specials. And call too. Sometimes kids travel free, and Amtrak doesn't advertise it in a grand way. Business class and Acela Express cost more, as does travel at peak times (Fri, Sun, and holidays 11am–11pm).

Less cushy than Amtrak, and also less costly, the MARC commuter train's Penn Line (✆ **800/325-RAIL** [7245]; www.mtamaryland.com) runs from (Washington) Union Station to Baltimore Penn Station, from 5am to midnight, Monday through Friday *only.* The trip is about 45 minutes, and the fare is $7 one-way, regardless of age.

Toddlers and preschoolers delight in riding the small-scale trains in the following regional parks: **Burke Lake Park** ★, 7315 Ox Rd., Fairfax Station, Virginia (✆ **703/323-6600;** www.fairfaxcounty.gov/parks); **Cabin John Regional Park** ★, 7400 Tuckerman Lane, Rockville, Maryland (✆ **301/469-7835;** www.mc-mncppc.org/parks); and **Wheaton Regional Park** ★, 2000 Shorefield Rd., Wheaton, Maryland (✆ **301/946-6396;** www.mc-mncppc.org/parks).

9

Shopping for the Whole Family

Once upon a time, Washington, D.C. residents fled to New York and other more worldly cities to find what they wanted. Not anymore! Now even the most seriously addicted shopaholics can feed their habit in the nation's capital. Flashy multilevel malls, dependable department stores, and trendy boutiques are as much a part of the D.C. scene as cherry blossoms and government red tape. In the past decade, numerous discount stores have moved into the area, giving the full-price standbys a run for their money.

If your kids are like most (teen girls excepted), they break out in hives at the mere mention of clothes shopping. But they probably love browsing books, toys, electronics, nature-related items, and sports gear. For the kind of shopping they'll enjoy, visit one of the city's many specialty stores and museum shops.

1 THE SHOPPING SCENE

Macy's stands guard over downtown at Metro Center, 13th and F streets NW. A couple of blocks away, at 11th and F, is Swedish retailer **H&M** (for Hennes & Mauritz), a hip international chain with a second D.C. store in Georgetown and several in the suburbs. Less than a mile from Metro Center, along the Connecticut Avenue and K Street business corridor, branches of upscale national chains and specialty shops nudge one another for elbow room. Most of these stores are geared to adults, because this is the heart of D.C.'s private business sector (as opposed to the federal government). Due north, the neighborhood known as **Dupont Circle** attracts browsers and buyers with its many galleries and distinctive, one-of-a-kind boutiques. Dupont Circle and nearby Adams Morgan (whose hub is 18th St. and Columbia Rd.) have the most individualized shops. Head to either for shopping as entertainment.

Georgetown fans out from Wisconsin Avenue and M Street NW. It has always been a haven for shopping mavens and an in-place for teenagers to congregate. While their parents drop green in the fashionable clothing and housewares boutiques, kids can shop for affordable souvenir T-shirts and cool clothing at Urban Outfitters on M Street and H&M, among the 75 voguish stores at the **Shops at Georgetown Park.** While many mourn the proliferation of souvenir, record, and chain stores in Georgetown, young people lap up the goods at Gap, Banana Republic, Benetton, and Abercrombie & Fitch. Some things haven't changed, however. Georgetown is still a numero-uno draw for local and visiting teenagers, especially on weekends.

STORE HOURS Most stores in the D.C. area open Monday through Saturday at 9:30 or 10am. Closing hours are harder to pinpoint, however. Most stores are also open with abbreviated hours on Sunday and extended hours one or more weeknights. Hours can change at the manager's whim (and often do). Before setting out, call ahead to make sure the store will be open.

SALES TAX The sales tax on all merchandise (including clothing) in D.C. is 5.75%.

2 SHOPPING A TO Z

ARTS & CRAFTS

Indian Craft Shop *Finds* Although not widely known, this is an excellent source (since 1938!) for authentic, top-quality Native American arts and crafts. It is also educational. Shop for weavings, sand paintings, kachinas, fetish carvings, and elaborate basketry and jewelry from the more than 45 tribal groups within the United States that this shop represents. Don't miss the section that's devoted to the artist of the month. Then stop at the Department of the Interior Museum, across the hall (✆ **202/208-4743**) or look around the building at the many murals adorning the walls. To gain entrance to the building, you need photo ID—a passport, government ID, or driver's license. Kids need no ID, just an adult with them. Prices start at $8 for a beaded pin. Beaded necklaces start at $10. Of interest to young shoppers are books, dolls, and small stone carvings. A cafeteria on the lower level is open for breakfast and lunch. If you don't want to walk here, take a taxi; street parking is limited. Open Monday through Friday from 8:30am to 4:30pm and on the third Saturday of the month, 10am to 4pm. Closed federal holidays. Department of the Interior, 18th and C sts. NW, Room 1023. ✆ **202/208-4056.** www.indiancraftshop.com. Metro: Farragut West, and then south 6 blocks on 18th St. to C St. entrance.

Plaza Artist Materials Plaza Artist Materials has "everything your art desires," with a wide array of fine-art, drawing, and drafting supplies, and children's art kits. This is doodlers' paradise—hundreds of marking pens in enough colors to make a rainbow blush. Open Monday through Friday from 9am to 6:30pm, Saturday 9am to 5pm, and Sunday from noon to 5pm. Branch stores are located in Silver Spring, Bethesda, Rockville, Baltimore, and Towson, Maryland, as well as in Fairfax and Richmond, Virginia. 1990 K St. NW. On the 2nd level. ✆ **202/331-7090.** www.plazaart.com. Metro: Farragut West and then a 3-block walk.

Sullivan's Art Supplies ★★ *Finds* Sullivan's draws dabblers and professionals alike. The well-stocked space adjacent to **Sullivan's Toy Store** (p. 236; ✆ **202/362-1343**) has all the basic oils, acrylics, watercolors, canvasses, and brushes that a mini-Picasso or Cassatt could desire, plus craft materials. Open Monday and Tuesday 10am to 6pm and Saturday 10am to 6pm; Wednesday through Friday 10am to 7pm; and Sunday noon to 5pm. 3412 Wisconsin Ave. NW. ✆ **202/362-1343.** Metro: Tenleytown, and then walk or take any no. 30 bus 1 mile south.

Torpedo Factory Art Center ★★ Kids enjoy watching the potters, sculptors, stained-glass artisans, and other craftspeople do their thing in 84 working studios at this renovated World War I munitions plant. One-of-a-kind items are priced fairly (some would say that many are underpriced). Open daily (except for major holidays) from 10am to 6pm and the second Thursday of each month from 6 to 9pm. 105 N. Union St., Alexandria, VA. ✆ **703/838-4565.** www.torpedofactory.org. Metro: King St., and then walk 1½ miles, or take the free King Street Trolley 11:30am–10pm daily (hours may be cut back in winter).

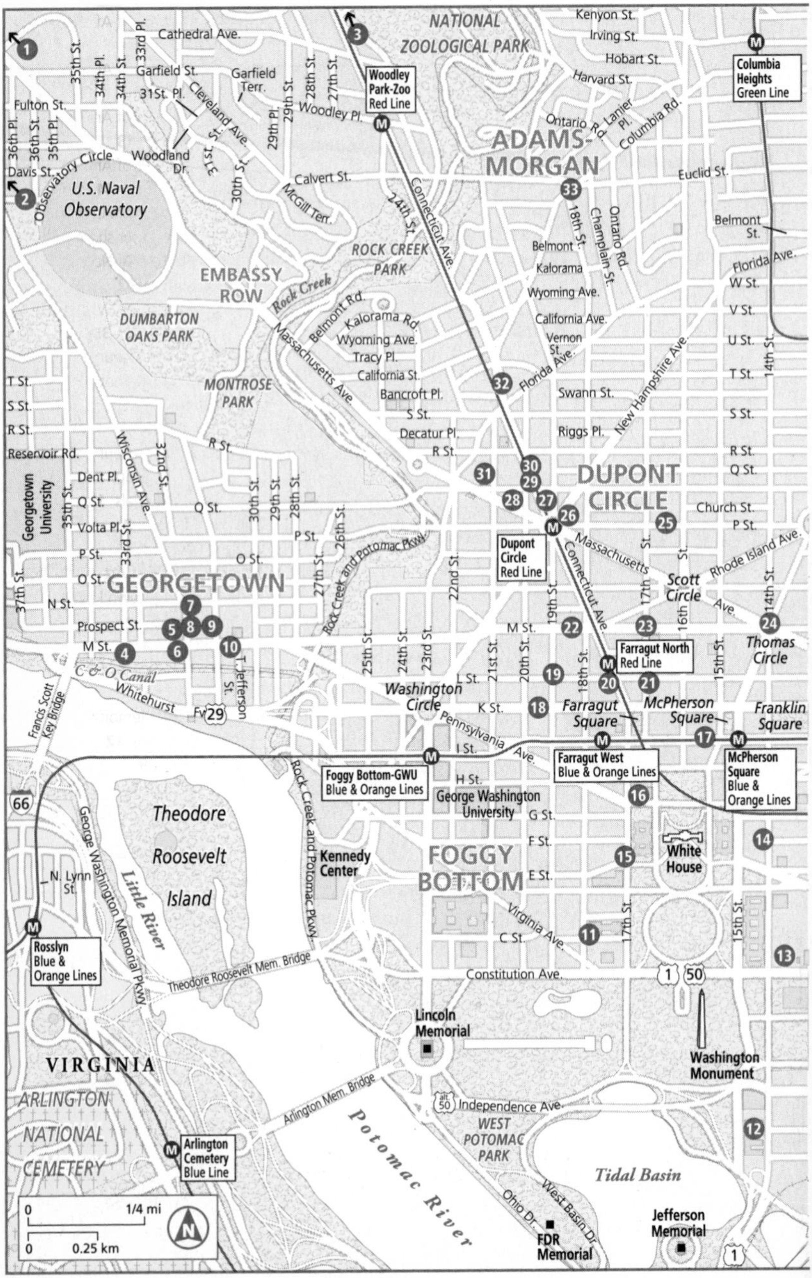
NATIONAL ZOOLOGICAL PARK
ADAMS-MORGAN
DUPONT CIRCLE
GEORGETOWN
FOGGY BOTTOM
EMBASSY ROW
ROCK CREEK PARK
DUMBARTON OAKS PARK
MONTROSE PARK
U.S. Naval Observatory
Georgetown University
Theodore Roosevelt Island
VIRGINIA
ARLINGTON NATIONAL CEMETERY
WEST POTOMAC PARK
Potomac River
Tidal Basin
Little River
Woodley Park-Zoo Red Line
Columbia Heights Green Line
Dupont Circle Red Line
Farragut North Red Line
Farragut West Blue & Orange Lines
McPherson Square Blue & Orange Lines
Foggy Bottom-GWU Blue & Orange Lines
Rosslyn Blue & Orange Lines
Arlington Cemetery Blue Line
White House
Washington Monument
Lincoln Memorial
Jefferson Memorial
FDR Memorial
Kennedy Center
George Washington University
Washington Circle
Farragut Square
McPherson Square
Franklin Square
Scott Circle
Thomas Circle
Connecticut Ave.
Massachusetts Ave.
Wisconsin Ave.
New Hampshire Ave.
Rhode Island Ave.
Pennsylvania Ave.
Virginia Ave.
Constitution Ave.
Independence Ave.
Florida Ave.
Columbia Rd.
Rock Creek and Potomac Pkwy.
George Washington Memorial Pkwy
Theodore Roosevelt Mem. Bridge
Arlington Mem. Bridge
Francis Scott Key Bridge
C & O Canal
Whitehurst Fwy
Ohio Dr.
West Basin Dr.
0 1/4 mi
0 0.25 km
N

Adams-Morgan Farmers' Market **33**
ADC Map & Travel Center **17**
Audubon Naturalist Society **3**
B. Dalton **49**
Backstage **54**
Barnes & Noble **10**, **38**
Barston's Child's Play **3**
Beadazzled **27**
Benetton **8**, **29**
Big Wheel Bikes **4**
Bike and Roll **39**
Blockbuster **25**
Blockbuster's **2**, **3**
Bloomingdale's **2**
Borders **14**, **29**
Chevy Chase Pavilion **2**
Corcoran Gallery of Art (Shop) **15**
CVS (24-hr drugstore) **24**
Dawn Price Baby **9**
Drilling Tennis **21**
Eastern Market **52**
Fairy Godmother **53**
Fit to a Tee **6**
Fleet Feet **33**
Fresh Farm Market **28**
Full of Beans **3**
Gap Kids/Baby Gap **7**
Gap **7**, **20**
Government Printing Office Store **47**
H&M **5**, **37**
Hair Cuttery **30**
Hirshhorn Museum (Shop) **41**
Hudson Trail Outfitters **2**
Indian Craft Shop **11**
Kid's Closet **22**
Kramerbooks **26**
Library of Congress Gift Shop **50**
Lord & Taylor **2**
Macy's **36**
Mazza Gallerie **2**
National Building Museum Shop **46**
National Diving Center **2**
National Gallery of Art (Shop) **45**
National Geographic Museum Shop **23**
National Museum of African Art (Shop) **42**
National Museum of Air and Space (Shop) **43**
National Museum of American History (Shop) **13**
National Museum of American Indian Art (Shop) **44**
National Museum of Asian Art (Sackler and Freer shops) **40**
National Museum of Natural History (Shop) **42**
National Museum of Women in the Arts (Shop) **35**
National Postal Museum (Shop) **48**
National Zoo (Gift Shop) **3**
Neiman Marcus **2**
News Room **32**
Old Post Office Museum (Shop) **39**
Phillips Gallery (Shop) **31**
Plaza Artist Materials **18**
Politics and Prose **3**
Ramer's Shoes **3**
Renwick Gallery of Art (Shop) **16**
Shops at Georgetown Park **6**
Ski Center **1**
Souvenir City **34**
Sullivan's Art Supplies & Toys **2**
Trover Books **51**
U.S. Holocaust Memorial Museum (Shop) **12**
Union Station **49**
Urban Outfitters **9**

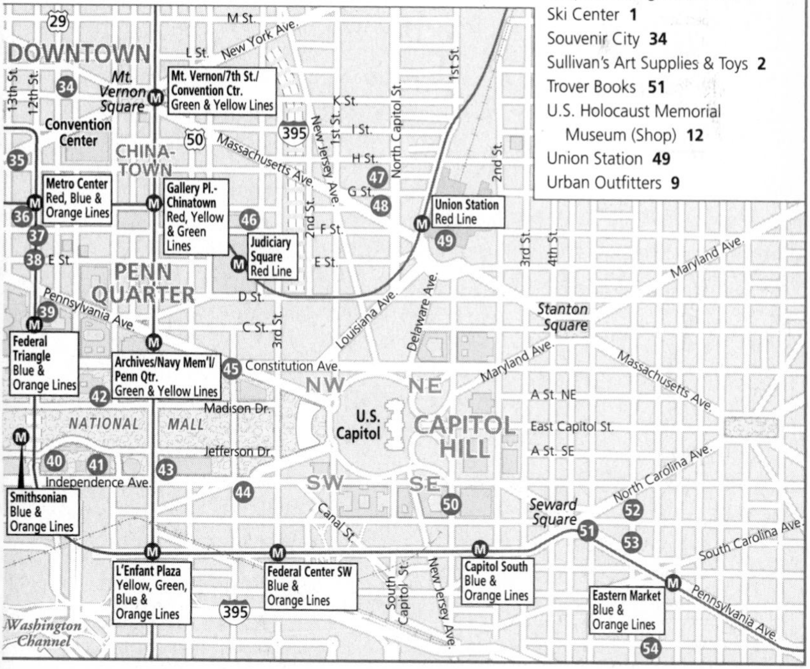

BOOKS

Although the stores listed below have a wonderful selection of children's books, don't overlook the following stores, some of which also host children's story hours: **Barnes & Noble,** 3040 M St. NW (corner of Thomas Jefferson St.; ✆ 202/965-9880); a smaller B&N store is at 555 12th St. NW (at E St.; ✆ 202/347-0176); **B. Dalton,** 50 Massachusetts Ave. NE, in Union Station (✆ 202/289-1724); **Borders,** at 600 14th St. NW (✆ 202/737-1385) and 1801 K St. NW (✆ 202/466-4999); and **Trover Shop,** 221 Pennsylvania Ave. SE (✆ 202/547-2665).

Audubon Sanctuary Shop Located at the Woodend Nature Center, on the site of the headquarters of the Audubon Naturalist Society (p. 208), this shop is just a wing's beat away from a nature preserve where youngsters can search for their favorite feathered friends. There's even a toy-filled room for your fledglings. Prices range from $5.95 to $35 for bird books (geared to different age groups), DVDs, animal puppets, puzzles, plush animals, and birds. It's open Monday through Friday 10am to 5pm, Saturday 9am to 5pm, and Sunday noon to 5pm. 8940 Jones Mill Rd., Chevy Chase, MD. ✆ **301/652-3606.** www.audubonnaturalist.org.

Borders for Kids (in Borders) ★ Finds This popular bookstore within a bookstore has a large play and performance area and an expanded program of children's events, making it a popular family destination. Storytelling takes place most Tuesdays at 10am. The glass-enclosed coffee bar is the perfect place to unwind with a new book and an espresso while the children are occupied. The hours are Monday through Saturday from 9am to 11pm, and Sunday from 9am to 9pm. White Flint Mall, 11301 Rockville Pike, North Bethesda, MD. ✆ **301/816-1067.** www.borders.com. Metro: White Flint.

Fairy Godmother ★ Finds This shoebox-size toys-and-books store on Capitol Hill is often overlooked, unfortunately. Stop in before or after you tour the Hill, or grab a bite at Eastern Market, a few doors away. In addition to a wide selection of kids' books (infants through young adults), the shop carries story tapes, toys, hand and finger puppets, and crafts. Inquire about story time and other special events. Hours are Monday thru Friday 10am to 6pm and Saturday 10am to 5pm. The Fairy Godmother rests most Sundays but is open the occasional Sunday seasonally. Ask about extended pre-Christmas hours. 319 7th St. SE. ✆ **202/547-5474.** Metro: Eastern Market.

Government Printing Office Bookstore (GPO) Perhaps you didn't know it, but the world's largest printer is right in the heart of little ole D.C. No matter how weird or way-out your kids' hobbies are, or whether they're researching a term paper or trying to decide which CD player to buy, they can probably find a book or pamphlet on the subject here. With more than 17,000 titles currently in print, the GPO is a browser's heaven and also sells photographs, prints, lithographs, and posters. Open Monday through Friday 8am to 5:30pm. 710 N. Capitol St. NW, at H St. ✆ **202/512-1800.** http://bookstore.gpo.gov. Metro: Union Station.

Kramerbooks & Afterwords ★ At this ever-popular Washington institution, you don't have to wait to get back to your hotel room to begin reading. Just step into the cafe at the rear of the bookstore ("Afterwords"—get it?) for a meal or a snack, and sink your teeth into a juicy new book. Kramerbooks stocks a respectable selection of children's books, as well as quality paperbacks and major foreign works. Kids love this place. You will, too. Open Monday through Thursday from 7:30am to 1am and round the clock from Friday 7:30am until Sunday. 1517 Connecticut Ave. NW, btw. Q St. and Dupont Circle. ✆ **202/387-1400.** www.kramers.com. Metro: Dupont Circle.

National Zoo Store Before or after visiting your family's favorite beasties in the zoo, browse the many animal-specific books for toddlers on up. Surely you will want at least one panda book as a souvenir—or commemorative stamps. Then try to resist plush toys, caps, scarves, posters, tree ornaments, and jewelry. Located near the zoo's main entrance, it's open every day but Christmas from 10am to 4:30pm. Visitor Center, Education Building, 3001 Connecticut Ave. NW. ✆ **202/633-4800.** http://nationalzoo.si.edu. Metro: Woodley Park–Zoo/Adams Morgan or Cleveland Park, and then walk 1/3 mile uphill, or take northbound L2 or L4 bus.

Politics and Prose Finds Browse the bestsellers and nonfiction at this true booklover's haunt while Junior selects something suitable for bedtime reading from the children's department. Besides an extensive collection of titles for kids of all ages, Politics and Prose hosts visits by children's book authors and has story time for preschoolers, most Mondays at 10:30am. The shop also fills mail and phone orders promptly. Open Monday through Saturday 9am to 10pm, Sunday 10am to 8pm. 5015 Connecticut Ave. NW (btw. Fessenden St. and Nebraska Ave.). ✆ **202/364-1919.** www.politics-prose.com. Metro: Van Ness, and then take L2 or L4 bus north 3/4 mile.

COMIC BOOKS

Big Planet Comics ★ Big Planet carries the latest X-Men, Disney, and Archie comics, along with vintage Nancy-and-Sluggo and Popeye for Mom and Dad. Comic cards are also available in Big Planet's quarters on one floor of a row house. Open Monday, Tuesday, Thursday, and Friday 11am to 7pm; Wednesday 11am to 8pm; Saturday 11am to 6pm; and Sunday noon to 5pm. Big Planet has branches at 7315 Baltimore Ave., College Park, Maryland (✆ **301/699-8498**); 4908 Fairmont Ave., Bethesda, Maryland (✆ **301/654-6856**); and 426 Maple Ave., Vienna, Virginia (✆ **703/242-9412**). 3145 Dumbarton St. NW. ✆ **202/342-1961.** www.bigplanetcomics.com. Metro: Foggy Bottom, and then take Georgetown shuttle or Circulator.

DEPARTMENT STORES

Nordstrom has no store in D.C. proper, but you can find stores at the following locations in the metropolitan area: the Galleria at Tysons II, 2255 International Dr., McLean, Virginia (✆ **703/761-1121**); Pentagon City, 1400 S. Hayes St., Arlington, Virginia (✆ **703/415-1121**); Montgomery Mall, Bethesda, Maryland (✆ **301/365-4111**); Annapolis Mall, Annapolis, Maryland (✆ **410/573-1121**); and The Mall in Columbia, Columbia, Maryland (✆ **410-715-2222**).

In D.C.

H&M ★★ H&M (Hennes & Mauritz), the Swedish retailer with stores in New York, Philadelphia, and Delaware (and maybe Mars by the time you read this), is known for its hip and reasonably priced merchandise under its own labels. H&M employs about 100 designers and buys in bulk to keep costs down. The merchandise in the downtown F Street location has children's sizes for toddlers on up and their families. Office wear geared to D.C.'s sartorially conservative workforce is in abundance, and the store has a maternity department. The (smaller) Georgetown store, at the Shops at Georgetown Park (✆ **202/298-6792**), has more stylish gear and caters to area teens and college students. There's also a branch at Tysons Corner Center (kids' wear; ✆ **703/556-6812**); next door, at the original Tyson's Corner (no kids' wear; ✆ **703/506-9091**); Dulles Town Center, Dulles, Virginia (kids' wear; ✆ **703/430-5520**); The Mall in Columbia, Columbia, Maryland (kids' wear; ✆ **410/740-8404**). Hours at the F Street (downtown) store are

Monday through Saturday 10am to 8pm, Sunday noon to 6pm. 1025 F St. NW, at 11th St. ✆ **202/347-3306.** www.hm.com. Metro: Metro Center or Federal Triangle.

Lord & Taylor This smaller version of New York's famous Fifth Avenue store is located 1 block from the Friendship Heights Metro stop near Chevy Chase, Maryland. You'll find high-quality children's merchandise, and most is fairly priced. Lord & Taylor's frequent sales are legendary. Open Monday through Thursday 10am to 9:30pm, Friday 10am to 10pm, Saturday 10am to 9:30pm, and Sunday 11am to 7pm. There are stores in the Maryland and Virginia suburbs as well. 5225 Western Ave. NW. ✆ **202/362-9600.** www.lordantaylor.com. Metro: Friendship Heights. Also in Kensington, Gaithersburg, Columbia and Annapolis, MD; Alexandria, McLean, Fairfax, and Sterling, VA.

Macy's In this five-story store, conveniently located at Metro Center, the salespeople are friendly and accommodating, and the selection of children's clothing is abundant and moderately priced for all age groups. If you forgot to pack something, you will find it here and not get ripped off in the process. A Ticketmaster outlet is here too. Just take the escalator upstairs from Metro. Open Monday through Saturday 10am to 8pm, and Sunday noon to 6pm. 1201 G St. NW, at 12th St. ✆ **202/628-6661.** www.macys.com. Metro: Metro Center. Also at Pentagon City and Tyson's Corner Center, VA, and Montgomery Mall, Bethesda, MD.

Neiman Marcus People with deep pockets shop for their kids' and grandkids' clothes at Neiman's. They also serve them USDA Prime sirloin steak rather than hamburger. What can I say? Occasionally I go here and pretend I'm rich. The children's departments are pricey. Send the kids to shop with well-heeled grandparents. ***Note:*** The store accepts American Express and Neiman Marcus credit cards but not MasterCard or Visa. Open Monday through Friday 10am to 8pm, Saturday 10am to 7pm, and Sunday noon to 6pm. You get 2 hours of free parking in the underground garage and limited street parking. There is also a Neiman Marcus branch at the Galleria at Tysons II, in McLean, Virginia (✆ **703/761-1600**). Mazza Gallerie, 5300 Wisconsin Ave. NW. ✆ **202/966-9700.** www.neimanmarcus.com. Metro: Friendship Heights.

In the Suburbs

Bloomingdale's A Bloomie's is a Bloomie's is a Bloomie's. Taking a cue from their famous trendsetting mother in New York, these suburban offspring do their best to satisfy the buying appetites of material girls and boys. Serious D.C. shoppers greeted the newest branch with great huzzahs when it opened in September 2007 in Chevy Chase. If you're unfamiliar with the store, I think you'll be pleasantly surprised. Sure, there are plenty of over-the-top (in design and price) imports, but most of the styles and prices are competitive. Open Monday through Saturday 10am to 8pm and Sunday noon to 7pm Other locations are at White Flint Mall, Kensington, Maryland (✆ **301/984-4600**), and Tysons Corner, McLean, Virginia (✆ **703/556-4600**). 5300 Western Avenue at Wisconsin Ave., Chevy Chase, MD. ✆ **240/744-3700.** www.bloomingdales.com. Metro: Friendship Heights.

Saks Fifth Avenue When my kids were little, I loved to shop for them at Saks, but I had to stop when their duds began costing more than mine. Now I can't afford to shop here for my grandchildren. If your kids tolerate your taste, and you can tolerate the stiff prices, head for Saks. The Metro is a short walk, and there's plenty of parking, free when you remember to validate the ticket in the store. (***Note:*** If Dad is feeling left out, just down the street is Saks' men's store, at Mazza Gallerie, 5300 Wisconsin Ave. NW [✆ **202/363-2059**].) Open Monday through Wednesday and Friday 10am to 7pm, Thursday

10am to 8pm, Saturday 10am to 6pm, and Sunday noon to 6pm. 5555 Wisconsin Ave., Chevy Chase, MD. ✆ **301/657-9000.** www.saksfifthavenue.com. Metro: Friendship Heights.

FARMERS' MARKETS

Ever since they were young, my kids have liked to wander through the outdoor markets in D.C. that sell seasonal produce, plants and flowers, homemade foodstuffs, baked goods, crafts, and secondhand stuff. If I promise to behave, they take me now—with their children. It's a great way to taste the country without leaving the city. Here are a few of our favorites.

Adams Morgan Market Locally grown produce, as well as homemade baked goods and crafts, are featured at this market. Go early for the best selection. Open first Saturday in April through late December, Saturday only, from 8am to 1pm. Columbia Rd. and 18th St. NW. Metro: Dupont Circle or Woodley Park–Zoo/Adams Morgan, and then a 15- to 20-min. walk.

Eastern Market ★★ On April 30, 2007, fire gutted part of the South Hall of this historic landmark and neighborhood meeting place. Many of us went into mourning. When a ribbon-cutting for the new market took place June 26, 2009, we rejoiced. I urge you to go. It's a D.C. treasure. You'll find everything from hog jowls and oxtails, prepared foods to go, farm-fresh produce and baked goods to plants and flowers, aged beef and seafood. Most kids like the action. Outdoors on weekends, kids over 4 or so seem to gravitate to the tables of secondhand clothes and home accessories, crafts, knickknacks, and funky jewelry. On summer weekends, when farmers' stalls line the street, there is often music and other entertainment. If you don't mind the wait, have breakfast or lunch inside at Market Lunch (p. 84). Open Tuesday through Friday from 7am to 7pm, Saturday 7am to 6pm, Sunday 9am to 5pm. 225 7th St. SE, btw. North Carolina Ave. and C St. ✆ **202/543-7470.** Metro: Eastern Market.

FreshFarm Market ★★ Every Sunday, about 30 regional farmers sell at this Dupont Circle location what they themselves have grown or made: vegetables, fruits, herbs, eggs, cheeses, flowers, and baked goods. No middlemen here! You can even pick up fragrant handcrafted soap. For info on other FreshFarm Markets (Foggy Bottom, H St., the Penn Quarter, and Silver Spring, Maryland), call or check the website. Open Sundays year-round. Late March to mid-December 9am to 1pm; January through March 10am to 1pm. 1500 block of 20th St., btw. Massachusetts Ave. and Q St. ✆ **202/362-8889.** www.freshfarmmarket.org. Metro: Dupont Circle.

FASHIONS

Baby Gap You'll have to take a brief Metro ride across the Potomac to Virginia, if you're after itsy-bitsy denim overalls and other adorable Gap label togs for newborns and infants in size newborn to 24 months. Farther from D.C. are Baby Gap stores at Fair Oaks Mall, Reston Town Center, and Tysons Corner Center (all in Virginia). The shop is open Monday through Saturday 10am to 9:30pm and Sunday 11am to 6pm. The Fashion Centre at Pentagon City, 1100 S. Hayes St. Arlington, VA. ✆ **703/416-7820.** www.shopsimon.com. Metro: Pentagon City.

Benetton Kids The Italian-based company sells comfortable, trendsetting clothing through its franchise stores all over the world. Chances are, your teenage daughters are familiar with Benetton already. This shop is devoted to kids from 6 months to 12 years. Hours are Monday through Saturday 9:30am to 9pm, and Sunday noon to 8pm. 1200 Wisconsin Ave. (at M St.) NW. ✆ **202/625-0443.** www.benetton.com. Metro: Foggy Bottom, and then a 20-min. walk or the Georgetown Connection or Circulator.

Dawn Price Baby Judging from the merchandise at this Georgetown boutique, there's nothing wrong with the local economy. You'll find everything from bibs, burp cloths, and baby announcements to designer bedding, clothing, furniture, gear, and toys to pamper tomorrow's influence peddlers. A second location is on Capitol Hill, at 325 7th St. SE (✆ **202/543-2920**). Store hours are Monday through Saturday from 11am to 7pm, Sunday from noon to 5pm. 3112 M St. (at 31 St.). ✆ **202/333-3939.** www.dawnpricebaby.com. Metro: Foggy Bottom, then Georgetown Connection or Circulator or 15-min. walk.

Full of Beans ★ Full of Beans is full of garb for girls and boys (in infant sizes to size 16). The charming neighborhood shop, which draws customers from other D.C. neighborhoods and the 'burbs, carries its own line of cotton clothing that's durable, attractive, and moderately priced. You'll also find unusual gifts—one-of-a-kind items not found in the average toy store. Full of Beans is near Ramer's Shoes (see "Shoes," later in this chapter), on upper Connecticut Avenue, so you should check out both stores before leaving the area. Beans is open Monday through Saturday 10am to 5:30pm, Sunday from 11am to 3pm. 5502 Connecticut Ave. NW. ✆ **202/362-8566.** Metro: Friendship Heights, and then a 10-min. walk.

Kid's Closet ★★ **Finds** I love this shop. It's been dressing D.C. kids for decades in durable, attractive, and well-priced clothing (Carter's, OshKosh, and Absorba, for example), in sizes ranging from 3 months to 1 year. A salesperson offers help immediately and will gladly gift-wrap your selection. Reminds me of the good old days. The store also carries accessories and must-haves, such as colorful jewelry and ballet costumes for little girls, plush toys, message tees, educational toys, and videos. Open Monday through Friday 10am to 6pm, and Saturday 11am to 5pm. 1226 Connecticut Ave. NW (at Jefferson Place). ✆ **202/429-9247.** www.kidsclosetdc.com. Metro: Dupont Circle or Farragut North.

Urban Outfitters Attention, all teens (and their parents): If you like trendy, stylish clothing and funky but functional accessories for your room, all priced so they won't eat up next year's allowance, you'll love Urban Outfitters, which has women's and men's clothing and shoes. Check out the "renewal" section—a money-saving rather than a religious experience. Open Monday through Saturday 10am to 9:30pm and Sunday 11am to 8pm. A second location is at 737 7th St. NW (btw. G and H sts.; ✆ **202/737-0259**). 3111 M St. NW. ✆ **202/342-1012.** www.urbanoutfitters.com. Metro: Foggy Bottom, and then a 15- to 20-min. walk, or the Georgetown Connection shuttle or any no. 30 bus from Pennsylvania Ave.

Why Not? ★★ **Finds** Why not, indeed! Be sure to include this upbeat shop in your visit to Old Town Alexandria. In business for close to 30 years, Why Not? stocks infant to size-14 clothing for girls, and infant through size-7 clothes for boys. But it doesn't end there. A wide range of colorful and creatively displayed toys and books fills the two-story space. A small area is outfitted with toys to keep youngsters occupied so you can shop in (relative) peace. No wonder Why Not? continues to draw shoppers from around the Beltway. Open Monday through Thursday 10am to 5:30pm, Friday and Saturday usually from 10am to 9pm (Sat hours vary seasonally), and Sunday noon to 5pm. 200 King St., Alexandria, VA. ✆ **703/548-4420.** Metro: King St., and then bus for 1½ miles to King and Fairfax sts.; walk 1 block east toward river.

FURNITURE & ACCESSORIES

In addition to the specialty stores below, try **IKEA,** with stores at 10100 Baltimore Ave., College Park, Maryland (✆ **301/345-6552**), and 2901 Potomac Mills Circle, Woodbridge, Virginia (✆ **703/494-4532**); any of the eight **Burlington Coat Factory** locations in Maryland and Virginia; or **e.a. kids** (part of Ethan Allen), in Rockville, Maryland (✆ **301/984-4360;** www.ethanallen.com), and Potomac Falls, Virginia (✆ **703/433-9001**). There's also **Great Beginnings,** Gaithersburg, Maryland (✆ **301/417-9702;** www.childrensfurniture.com).

Bellini Juvenile Designer Furniture They're not kidding about the designer part. Bellini sells top-of-the-line, European-crafted cribs, bunk beds, trundles, and bedding accessories to furnish little princes and princesses with beautiful beginnings. Open Monday through Saturday 10am to 6pm, and Sunday noon to 5pm. 12113 Rockville Pike, Rockville, MD. ✆ **301/770-3944.** www.bellini.com. Metro: Twinbrook.

Buy Buy Baby ★ This is nirvana for parents-to-be, new moms and dads, and doting grandparents. On two floors, you'll find everything, and I mean everything, for your bundle from heaven: layette items, strollers, cribs, diapers, clothing, toys, books, and then some. It's positively addictive. There's also a location in Springfield Plaza, Springfield, Virginia (✆ **703/923-9797**). Open Monday through Saturday 9:30am to 9:30pm, and Sunday 11am to 6pm. 1683 Rockville Pike (South Congressional Plaza), Rockville, MD. ✆ **301/984-1122.** www.buybuybaby.com. Metro: Twinbrook (1/2 mile from the store).

HAIRCUTS

Cartoon Cuts ★ One memory I'd like to erase: taking my kids for haircuts. They screamed and carried on like they were undergoing open-heart surgery without anesthesia. At Cartoon Cuts, today's tots get trimmed while glued to the video monitors at each station. Elephant faucets have rinsing hoses for trunks so that shampooing becomes an event instead of a dreaded chore. The shops also host birthday and karaoke parties where little snippets can be made over into their favorite rock stars. Haircuts cost $17 (entertainment included). Hours vary according to branch. Three are in suburban Maryland, and three are in northern Virginia. Check the Yellow Pages or website. Tysons Corner Center, McLean, VA. ✆ **703/748-CUTS** [2887]. www.cartooncuts.com. Metro: West Falls Church, and then bus no. 28A or 28B.

Hair Cuttery For a walk-in cut, wash, and blow-dry—$16 (wet), $24 with blow dry—you can't beat it. For kids 8 and under, it's $12 wet, $24 with blow-dry. Anyone (male, female, androgynous) with extralong hair may have to pay a little more. Men, women, and children are equally welcome. Besides the one D.C. location, there are several in the Maryland and Virginia suburbs. 1645 Connecticut Ave. NW. ✆ **202/232-9685.** www.haircuttery.com. Metro: Dupont Circle.

JEWELRY & BEADS

Beadazzled ★ There are plenty of baubles, bangles, and beads, plus everything in beadwork supplies and classes to keep you and yours from getting strung out. I love this place. It's great for browsing and shopping. The staff is incredibly good-natured and helpful. You may also purchase earrings, necklaces, and crafts that others have labored over. Open Monday through Saturday 10am to 8pm, and Sunday 11am to 6pm. A second store is located at Tysons Corner Center in Virginia (✆ **703/848-2323**). 1507 Connecticut Ave. NW. ✆ **202/265-BEAD** [2323]. www.beadazzled.net. Metro: Dupont Circle.

KITES

Air and Space Museum Store ★★ Your kids will walk on air when they see the selection of kites ($6–$100) sold here. Kites are color-coded according to degree of difficulty. Mine ("for 7-year-olds") is a breeze to fly. Launch your purchase on the Mall just outside the museum—but never in a thunderstorm. Open daily 10am to 5:30pm, with extended summer hours, usually to 7:30pm. 6th St. and Independence Ave. SW. ✆ **202/357-1387.** Metro: L'Enfant Plaza.

MALLS

What did kids do before malls? I have vague recollections of hopscotch, marbles, and stickball, but hanging out at malls is the no. 1 pastime of today's youth. You'll have no trouble keeping your little mall rats satisfied in the D.C. area—just bring lots of money. Besides these listings, there are countless malls in suburban Maryland and Virginia. (Maybe you'll want to keep this bit of information to yourself.)

The Chevy Chase Pavilion Just a block away from the Friendship Heights Metro station, this bright and compact three-tiered mall is geared more to adults than children, with upper-end stores selling apparel for men and women. Two exceptions are J. Crew, T-Mobile, and the Stein Mart chain, carrying brand-name, upscale apparel for the whole family. Who needs to shop for children's apparel when you can join the hordes at the Cheesecake Factory (free parking with validation)? Yum. If you're a fan (I am not; the coffee is bitter), grab a beverage at Starbuck's. Hours are Monday through Saturday 9am to 9pm and Sunday 10am to 6pm. 5335 Wisconsin Ave. NW, at Military Rd. ✆ **202/207-3887.** www.ccpavilion.com. Metro: Friendship Heights.

Fashion Centre at Pentagon City ★ My Virginia relatives and friends swear by the Fashion Centre (and I know some big-time shoppers). **Macy's** and **Nordstrom** are the anchors in this three-level mall, which boasts more than 160 stores. You'll find upscalers such as Abercrombie & Fitch, the Coach Store, American Eagle Outfitters, Ann Taylor, and Banana Republic.

Of special interest to the *kinder* are The Children's Place, Baby Gap, Gap Kids and Gap, Gymboree, The Limited, America!, and the Sweet Factory.

When you need a break or wear out your wallet, stop for a light bite in the Food Court, with a lucky 13 selections to choose from, or relax at one of the mall's seven restaurants. Johnny Rockets serves burgers, shakes, and other nutritious offerings that make America great. The Grill at the Ritz-Carlton holds up the high end of the spectrum. Several cafes serve moderately priced fare. Hours are Monday through Saturday from 10am to 9:30pm and Sunday from 11am to 6pm, with extended hours during the Christmas season. 1100 South Hayes St., Arlington, VA. ✆ **703/415-2400.** Metro: Pentagon City.

Mazza Gallerie While **Neiman Marcus, Saks Men's Store,** and most of the boutiquey shops at this *très* chic four-level mall will be out of reach for little people's tastes and allowances, there are some exceptions, such as **Filene's Basement** (with a kids department) and a Foot Locker store. F.Y.E. (for your entertainment) sells music, movies, CDs, and DVDs. Slip into McDonald's when a Big Mac attack hits. Hours are Monday through Saturday 10am to 8pm, Sunday noon to 6pm. 5300 Wisconsin Ave NW. ✆ **202/966-6114.** www.mazzagallerie.com. Metro: Friendship Heights.

The Old Post Office Pavilion It's nearly 200 feet from the floor to the skylit canopy of this three-level complex of retail shops and restaurants housed in a 100-year-old office building. Don't expect to do serious shopping here, but there are some novelty and souvenir shops that your kids might enjoy.

Ride the glass elevator to the tower observation deck (at the 270-ft. level) for a spectacular 360-degree view of downtown and the environs, and then inspect the 10 massive bells (a bicentennial gift from England) that are rung on state occasions. **Ticketplace** is the place to buy half-price theater tickets to many of the performances in the D.C. area. When it's time for a bite to eat, you can choose from the Bagel Express, Georgetown Deli, Greek Taverna, Pavilion Pizza, Indian Delight, Quick Pita, and Pavilion Burrito. And if your blood sugar is running low, stop at one of the ice-cream or yogurt stands for a pick-me-up.

Free entertainment—puppet shows, music, mime, singing, and dancing—is presented daily in the West Atrium. The shops are open March through August Monday through Saturday 10am to 8pm, and Sunday noon to 7pm; and September through February Monday through Saturday 10am to 7pm, and Sunday noon to 6pm. The restaurants usually stay open an hour or two later than the retail shops. There are three entrances: 10th and 12th streets NW, and Pennsylvania Avenue (at 11th St.). 1100 Pennsylvania Ave. NW. ✆ **202/289-4224.** www.oldpostofficedc.com. Metro: Federal Triangle.

Potomac Mills The Potomac Mills discount shopping mall pulls in more tourists than Mr. Jefferson's Monticello, Mount Vernon, or Paramount's King's Dominion. What does this say about mainstream America's priorities? It's not unusual for more than 30,000 salivating shoppers, credit cards in hand, to lighten their wallets in the 1.2-million-square-foot mall daily. In addition to discount outlets for many nationally known department stores, you'll find about 250 specialty shops and the warehouse-size **IKEA** for attractive, well-priced furniture (some assembly required), toys, and housewares. ***A caveat:*** Know ahead of time the average retail prices of the items you seek. It's not all bargains here, and some of the merchandise is out of season or irregular. Hours are Monday through Saturday 10am to 9pm and Sunday from 11am to 6pm. Off I-95 at 2700 Potomac Mills Circle, Prince William, VA. ✆ **703/496-9301** www.potomacmills.com. Directions: Drive south on I-95 into Virginia, and take Dale City exit 156.

The Shops at Georgetown Park This handsome multilevel complex (complete with a stylish brick Victorian interior with skylights, fountains, chandeliers, and plantings) has more than 75 upscale shops. For apparel, teens dig H&M, Express, and J. Crew. Mrs. Field's Cookies, Fit to a Tee, Sunglass Hut, and Lil Thingamajigs (toys and games) will please the kids most. Have a snack or meal from the Canal Walk Food Court or Dean & Deluca. Open Monday through Saturday 10am to 8pm and Sunday noon to 6pm. Discounted garage parking with a $10 purchase. 3222 M St. NW at Wisconsin Ave. ✆ **202/342-8190.** www.shopsatgeorgetownpark.com. Metro: Foggy Bottom.

Tysons Corner Center ★ This mall of malls is about 30 minutes from D.C. in Vienna, Virginia. Every time I turn around they're expanding. Unchecked, I fear it will take over all of northern Virginia. Among the 230 shops here are five major anchor stores: **Bloomingdale's, Nordstrom, Lord & Taylor, L.L. Bean,** and **Macy's.** Other notable emporia of interest to kids include H&M, Build-A-Bear Workshop, The Children's Place, Disney Store, Gymboree, Janie & Jack, Banana Republic, and Gap. The Food Court and more than 30 restaurants include family-pleasing T.G.I. Friday's, California Pizza Kitchen, and Silver Diner. Between the shopping, food, and eight movie theaters, you have a surefire recipe for an afternoon shopping spree followed by a relaxing (if you're lucky) family dinner and a film. There's free parking for more than 10,000 cars. You can take Metro and a bus, but I have to tell you: I don't know a soul who's done this from downtown D.C. Maybe you'll be the first. Open Monday through Saturday 10am to 9:30pm and Sunday 11am to 7pm. 1961 Chain Bridge Rd., at Rte. 7, Vienna, VA. ✆ **703/893-9400.** www.shoptysons.com. Metro: West Falls Church, and then Fairfax Connector Bus 427 (runs every 15–20 minutes).

Union Station Union Station is a top tourist draw for area and visiting families, not just a departure/arrival spot for Amtrak travelers. When you're done marveling at the magnificent architecture—lots of marble and gilt—inspired by the Baths of Diocletian from 3rd-century Rome, hunker down for something good to eat at Au Bon Pain, Café Renee, Corner Bakery Café, America, and Johnny Rockets (glorified fast food most kids love), or at one or more of the nearly three dozen eateries in the lower-level Food Court; or one of the stand-alone, table-service restaurants in or near the Main Hall. Do leave room for Vaccaro's pastries. (Love those chocolate-filled cannoli!) Nearly 75 shops are scattered between two levels. Of particular note: Alamo Flags (state, international, and novelty flags), America's Spirit (souvenirs, political memorabilia), Appalachian Spring (wooden toys, blocks and games; soft toys and baby gifts among the beautiful handcrafted items for the home), Destination D.C. (souvenirs), B. Dalton (general and local-interest books), Echo Gallery (expensive handmade dolls), Lids (hats), and Out of Left Field (sports-team clothing and souvenirs).

Still have time to kill? Buy tickets for Tourmobile, the Old Town Trolley, or a Grayline sightseeing tour. Open Monday through Saturday 10am to 9pm, and Sunday noon to 6pm. 50 Massachusetts Ave. NE. © **202/289-1908.** www.unionstationdc.com. Metro: Union Station.

Westfield Shoppingtown Montgomery For those of us who shopped here 20 and 30 years ago, it will always be Montgomery Mall. It's smaller than some of the mega-malls, which means you don't need an atlas to find your way around. Just a compass. The mall is chock full of family-oriented stores that sell quality merchandise at (usually) bearable prices. And there's a **Nordstrom,** which needs no introduction, with a "Mothers' Room" with a changing table and diaper vending machine.

Of interest to little people are The Children's Place, Gap Kids, Spencer's Gifts (12 and older, as some merchandise is racy), Gymboree (kids' wear), Stride Rite, and Border's Express.

Take your pick of about a dozen eateries in the Boulevard Cafés and five sit-down restaurants, including Legal Sea Foods. You can also catch a flick at one of the three P&G Cinemas. The mall is open Monday through Saturday 10am to 9:30pm, and Sunday 11am to 6pm. 7101 Democracy Blvd., Bethesda, MD. © **301/469-6025.** Metro: Grosvenor, and then take the no. 47 bus.

MAPS

ADC Map & Travel Center The center of the local cartophiles' universe for more than 40 years, the store has something for all age levels: wood puzzles of the continents and the United States; inflatable and traditional globes; atlases, road and street maps; and even a world wastebasket for those who want to learn some geography while filing trash. Open Monday through Thursday from 8am to 6:30pm, Friday 8am to 5:30pm, and Saturday 11am to 5pm. 1636 I St. NW. © **202/628-2608.** www.adcmap.com. Metro: Farragut North or Farragut West.

National Geographic Store Here you'll find the society's distinctive and finely detailed maps, as well as all National Geographic publications. You can also purchase globes, toys, games, puzzles, videos, DVDs, and back issues of *National Geographic* magazine. Open Monday through Saturday and holidays 9am to 5pm, and Sunday 10am to 5pm. Closed December 25. 17th and M sts. NW. © **202/857-7588.** www.nationalgeographic.com. Metro: Farragut North.

NATURE TREASURES

National Museum of Natural History Gift Shops ★★ Many locals shop at this museum store for their holiday gifts. This is one of my personal favorites. You'll find an interesting collection of books—many geared to young people—on natural history and anthropology, as well as fossil reproduction kits; shells; minerals; and attractive and distinctive clothing, crafts, and jewelry. On the ground floor is a much smaller store with puppets, activity books, puzzles, and plush animals. Open daily 10am to 5:30pm, except December 25. Extended summer hours are determined annually. 10th St. and Constitution Ave. NW. ✆ **202/633-2060.** Metro: Federal Triangle.

NEWSPAPERS & MAGAZINES

The News Room ★ Finds Still going strong after more than 30 years, the News Room is a mainstay of the Dupont Circle area. Come here for some 200 domestic and foreign newspapers and numerous magazines. The foreign-language department has books and tapes for kids who want to learn other languages. Open Sunday to Thursday 7am to 8pm, Friday and Saturday 7am to 9pm. 1803 Connecticut Ave. NW. ✆ **202/332-1489.** www.newsroomdc.com. Metro: Dupont Circle.

PERFORMING-ARTS SUPPLIES

Backstage Finds Kids with an interest in the performing arts should take a cue from Washington thespians, musicians, and dancers and go to Backstage. Under one roof is everything that professionals and amateurs need to get their act together: an award-winning selection of scripts and books, costumes, dancewear, makeup, and sheet music. Shop here for kids' costumes and dancewear (leotards, tights, and so on). I'm thinking of splurging on the Cher costume for next Halloween. Open Monday through Saturday 11am to 7pm (extended pre-Halloween hours). 545 8th St. SE (at G St.). ✆ **202/544-5744.** www.backstagebooks.com. Metro: Eastern Market.

SHOES

Georgetown has a lot of shoe stores that appeal to style-conscious teenagers. When you're shopping for their younger siblings' shoes, try the stores listed below.

Fleet Feet Adams Morgan's total sports/fitness shop carries all the top names for fleet-footed kids and adults, beginning with size 2. Open Monday through Friday 10am to 8pm, Saturday 10am to 7pm, and Sunday noon to 4pm. Limited street parking. 1841 Columbia Rd. NW. ✆ **202/387-3888.** www.dcnet.com/fleetfeet. Metro: Woodley Park–Zoo/Adams Morgan, and then walk ½ mile across Calvert Street Bridge, or take bus no. 42.

Kids Foot Locker It's never too early to pick up a wee-size Redskins jacket, sweats, T-shirt, or shorts along with kids' shoes from newborn to size 6. Some clothing to size 20 is also featured. Because there aren't any of these in D.C., you'll have to hotfoot it to Tysons Corner Center and Pentagon City in Virginia, or Prince George's Plaza, St. Charles Towne Center. The Tysons, Virginia, store is open Monday through Saturday 10am to 9:30pm, and Sunday 11am to 7pm. 1961 Chain Bridge Rd., at Rte. 7, Vienna, VA. ✆ **703/506-9020.** Metro: West Falls Church, and then bus no. 28A or 28B (runs every half-hour on the hour/half-hour).

Ramer's Shoes ★★ Finds Ramer's, the friendly neighborhood shoe store, is 1 block below Chevy Chase Circle. Come here for Keds, Little Capezio, Sebago's, Sperry's, Stride Rite, and more in sizes 0 to 4½, widths AA to EEE. Then drop in at Full of Beans for kids' duds, 2 blocks south (see the description under "Fashions"). Open Monday through

Museum Stores

Museum stores are prime sources for educational books, gift items, crafts, and souvenirs (nothing tacky here—this is quality stuff) from all over the world. The Smithsonian museum stores are usually open daily from 10am to 5:30pm, sometimes with extended hours. You can get a sense of Smithsonian museum-store merchandise at its website: www.smithsonianstore.com. Independent museum and gallery shops have varying hours, so call ahead.

- **Arthur M. Sackler and Freer Galleries,** 1050 Independence Ave. SW (✆ **202/633-4880**). Asian and African art reproductions, crafts, gifts, and books.
- **Corcoran Gallery of Art** ★, 500 17th St. NW (✆ **202/639-1790**). Art books, posters, stationery, and jewelry.
- **Hirshhorn Museum,** Independence Avenue and 7th Street SW (✆ **202/633-1000**). Contemporary art books and monographs, toys, jewelry, and some art supplies.
- **John F. Kennedy Center for the Performing Arts** ★, 2700 F St. NW (✆ **202/416-8346**). Posters, videos, books, stationery, and performing-arts memorabilia (open till 8pm).
- **Library of Congress,** 1st Street SE, between Independence Avenue and C Street (✆ **202/707-0204**). Books, books, and more books, as well as specialized library-oriented items.
- **National Air and Space Museum** ★, Independence Avenue and 7th Street SW (✆ **202/357-1387**). Flying toys (including kites); space-, flight-, and science-related books; videos; memorabilia; and freeze-dried ice cream.
- **National Archives,** 7th Street and Pennsylvania Avenue NW (✆ **202/357-5271;** open till 7pm). Books on genealogy, campaign buttons, and famous documents (replicas only!).
- **National Building Museum** ★, 401 F St. NW (✆ **202/272-7706**). Architectural toys, crafts, books, desktop accessories, and graphics.
- **National Gallery of Art** ★★, 4th and 6th streets, at Constitution Avenue NW (✆ **202/737-4215**). Posters, art books, games, stationery, and journals.

Friday 9:30am to 6pm, and Saturday 9:30am to 5:30pm. 3810 Northampton St. NW, off Connecticut Ave. ✆ **202/244-2288.** Metro: Friendship Heights, and then a 10-min. walk east on Western Ave. to Chevy Chase Circle (Connecticut Ave.); right 1 block and right on Northampton (store is a 1/2 block off Connecticut Ave.).

SPORTS GEAR

Big Wheel Bikes ★ Rent a hybrid, mountain bike, 12-speed, or tandem by the hour or day at Big Wheel's original location in Georgetown. Then pedal on the nearby C&O Canal towpath. In business since 1971, Big Wheel also sells recreational, touring, and racing bikes, and a full line of children's bikes. Open Tuesday through Friday 11am to 7pm, and Saturday and Sunday 10am to 6pm. (Call for hours Oct–Mar.) Other locations are Arlington, Virginia (✆ **703/522-1110**); Old Town Alexandria, Virginia

- **National Geographic Society,** 17th and M streets NW (✆ **202/857-7588**). Maps, toys, globes, DVDs, and back issues of *National Geographic* magazine.
- **National Museum of African Art** ★, 950 Independence Ave. SW (✆ **202/633-0030**). African-inspired accessories, crafts, toys, and tapes.
- **National Museum of American Art** ★★, 8th and G streets NW (✆ **202/357-1445**). *Masterpieces of American Art* coloring book, picture frames, and jewelry.
- **National Museum of American History,** 14th Street and Constitution Avenue NW (✆ **202/357-1527**).
- **National Museum of Natural History** ★, 10th Street and Constitution Avenue NW (✆ **202/633-2060**). Crafts, gems and minerals, dinosaur toys, jewelry, and books.
- **National Museum of Women in the Arts,** 1250 New York Ave. NW (✆ **202/783-7994**). Notepaper, books, and calendars.
- **National Postal Museum** ★, 2 Massachusetts Ave. NE. (✆ **202/633-8180**). Postal-history merchandise and stamps for collectors.
- **National Zoo,** 3001 Connecticut Ave. NW (✆ **202/633-4800**). Animal-inspired books, toys, clothing, and crafts.
- **Newseum** ★★, 555 Pennsylvania Ave. NW (✆ **202/292-6100**). Media- and journalism-inspired books, stationery, apparel; replicas of historical documents, gifts.
- **Phillips Collection,** 1600 21st St. NW (✆ **202/387-2151**). Art books, toys, and jewelry.
- **Renwick Gallery** ★, 17th Street and Pennsylvania Avenue NW (✆ **202/357-1445**). Crafts, jewelry, and how-to books.
- **U.S. Holocaust Memorial Museum,** 100 Raoul Wallenberg Place (15th St.) SW (✆ **202/488-0400**). Books, tapes, and Judaica.

(✆ **703/739-2300**); and Bethesda, Maryland (✆ **301/652-0192**). 1034 33rd St. NW in Georgetown. ✆ **202/337-0254.** www.bigwheelbikes.com. Metro: Foggy Bottom, and then a 15-min. walk or Georgetown Connection to 33rd St. Some free parking behind store.

Bike and Roll ★ The main location of this well-run operation (the same folks who offer the popular Bike The Sites tours) is at the rear plaza of the Old Post Office Pavilion. Rentals include helmet, bike tube, pump, lock, a city map, and handlebar bag. You can also rent a jog stroller, umbrella stroller, kids trailers—and wheelchairs. The minimum rate (up to 2 hours) for standard bikes is $10 or $15. Other locations are at Union Station and Old Town Alexandria, Virginia. Summer hours (late May–early Sept) are 9am to 7pm (sometimes later); March to late May and September to December, 9am or 9:30am to 5 or 6pm. 1100 Pennsylvania Ave. NW. ✆ **202/842-BIKE** [2453]. www.bikethesites.com. Metro: Federal Triangle.

Drilling Tennis and Golf Shop This shop is owned by Fred Drilling, Washington Tennis Patrons' Hall of Famer, and the staff will see that your youngster comes out swinging the right racket from the store's selection for 2- to 12-year-olds. There's no kids' clothing here, but you'll find plenty of accessories. Open Monday through Friday 9:30am to 6pm, and Saturday 10am to 4pm. 1040 17th St. NW. ✆ **202/737-1100.** www.drillingtennisandgolf.com. Metro: Farragut North or Farragut West.

Hudson Trail Outfitters Hudson Trail is a magnet for teens who are into hiking, biking, camping, and other outdoor activities. Quality gear, clothing, and accessories fill the rustic shop, and the youthful, healthy-looking salespeople are helpful and laid back. Open Monday through Saturday 10am to 9pm, and Sunday 11am to 6pm. Locations in Maryland and Virginia, too. 4530 Wisconsin Ave. NW. ✆ **202/363-9810.** www.hudsontrail.com. Metro: Tenleytown, and then 1 block south.

National Diving Center Even the youngest snorkeler can be outfitted here. The manager says that kids can snorkel as soon as they can swim, but potential scuba divers must be 12. Kids train alongside adults; there are no special kids-only classes. Besides stocking snorkeling and diving gear, the shop offers lessons (with open-water checkouts in Pennsylvania rock quarries) and diving trips off the Atlantic coast and in the Caribbean. Open Tuesday through Friday 11am to 7pm, and Saturday 11am to 6pm; closed on Sunday and Monday. 4932 Wisconsin Ave. NW. ✆ **202/363-6123.** www.dcdivers.com. Metro: Friendship Heights, then walk 4 blocks south.

Ski Center ★ Schuss down to the oldest ski shop in the area. The Ski Center has had an edge on ski stuff in the D.C. area since 1959 and can outfit all the younger members of your ski team with equipment and clothing. You can also buy or rent in-line skates here. Call for seasonal details. Open Monday to Friday 11am to 6pm, Saturday 10am to 5:30pm, and Sunday noon to 5pm (extended hours around Christmas). 4300 Fordham Rd. (at Massachusetts Ave. and 49th St. NW). ✆ **202/966-4474.** www.skicenter.com. Metro: Dupont Circle, and then northbound N-4 bus on Massachusetts Ave. to 49th St.

TOYS

Barston's Child's Play ★ This place is fun to visit. Many of the displayed toys invite touching—and you don't have to be under 3 feet tall to appreciate them. Child's Play carries Playmobil, Lego, Lundby dollhouse furniture, and Gund stuffed animals. The software, book, and art sections have been expanded in recent years. There's free parking behind the shop. Open Monday through Wednesday and Friday 9:30am to 7pm, Thursday 9:30am to 8pm, Saturday 9:30am to 6pm, and Sunday noon to 5pm. 5536 Connecticut Ave. NW. ✆ **202/244-3602.** www.barstonschildsplay.com. Metro: Friendship Heights, and then a 10-min. walk.

Sullivan's Toy Store ★★ Finds If a film crew were scouting for a typical neighborhood toy store, Sullivan's would be the ideal. A feeling of comfortable disarray pervades this Cleveland Park shop. Kids of all ages will find plenty to toy with on the well-stocked shelves. There's a huge selection of art supplies, too. The most fun can be had up front, where 60 glass jars are filled with 99¢ toys. Open Monday and Tuesday 10am to 6pm, Wednesday through Friday 10am to 7pm, Saturday 10am to 6pm, and Sunday noon to 5pm. 3412 Wisconsin Ave. NW. ✆ **202/362-1343.** Metro: Tenleytown, and then take any no. 30 bus south.

Toys "R" Us Santa's Workshop doesn't hold a candle to this megastore of toys, games, seasonal sports gear and outdoor equipment, juvenile furniture, and party supplies. Shop early or late unless you have nerves of steel and can withstand hundreds of tiny voices whining "I want!" a cappella. Open Monday to Friday 10am to 9pm, Saturday 9am to 9pm, Sunday 10am to 6pm. There are 11 other branches in suburban Maryland and Virginia. 11810 Rockville Pike, at Old Georgetown Rd., Rockville, MD. ✆ **301/770-3376.** www.toysrus.com. Metro: White Flint, then a 10-minute walk north on Rockville Pike.

T-SHIRTS

For a souvenir or gift T-shirt, check out the museum shops for top-quality shirts that wear like iron. You can also buy T-shirts from the numerous vendors blanketing the area around the National Mall. These shirts make good bargain souvenirs, but don't leave them in the dryer too long . . .

Fit to a Tee ★ This shop is crammed with oodles of souvenir and funny-message shirts for kids of all ages, in sizes infant through XXX large. If you're in a bad mood, a visit here will cheer you up. Open Monday through Saturday 10am to 9pm, and Sunday noon to 6pm. Shops at Georgetown Park, 3222 M St. NW. ✆ **202/965-3650.** Metro: Foggy Bottom, and then 15-min. walk or the Georgetown Connection shuttle to Wisconsin and M sts.

Souvenir City ★ Check out the shirts, books, paperweights, mugs, and other D.C.-inspired tchotchkes when you're downtown near the Convention Center/FBI/Ford's Theatre/MCI Center. The kids are bound to go wild over all the merchandise, so you may want to give them an "allowance" up front. This place is definitely souvenir central. Open Monday through Saturday 10am to 7pm, Sunday 11 to 6pm (usually shorter hours Oct–Mar). 1001 K St. NW (btw. 10th and 11th sts.). ✆ **202/638-1836.** Metro: Gallery Place–Chinatown and then a 3-block walk.

10

Entertainment for the Whole Family

Children's tastes in entertainment are as varied as their parents'. Some kids like watching the pros shoot hoops; others enjoy seeing lions and tigers jump through them. *Swan Lake* might transport some junior culture vultures, while their middlebrow siblings think it's far duckier to yuk it up in a comedy club. Whether your family's musical appetite runs to Beethoven, big bands, or Blitz, you won't leave the table hungry after sampling Washington's cultural smorgasbord.

Once a sleepy southern town that shut down when the last government workers left their cubicles—around 9pm (on a good night!)—D.C. now hosts so many events that you'll be hard-pressed to choose from among them. Second only to New York in the quality and quantity of our theatrical productions, musical offerings, and dance performances, we try harder!

GETTING TICKETS

Depending on availability, you can pick up half-price tickets to many events up to 4pm the day of the performance *only* at **TICKETplace** (© **202/TICKETS** [842-5387]; www.ticketplace.org), 407 7th St. NW (btw. D and E sts.; Metro: Gallery Place or Archives). A 12% service charge on the full face value of the ticket is added (so a $20 ticket costs $22.40: $20, plus a $2.40 fee). It's first come, first served. You can also purchase full-price tickets to future performances at the walk-up counter. Order tickets online at www.ticketplace.org, and you'll pay a 17% service fee, so the same $20 ticket will be $23.40 ($20, plus a $3.40 service fee). More than 60 institutions participate in this service, sponsored by the *Washington Post* and the Cultural Alliance of Greater Washington. Credit cards only, with a picture ID, are accepted. TICKETplace is open Wednesday through Friday 11am to 6pm, Saturday 10am to 5pm, Sunday noon to 4pm. Tickets for Monday and Tuesday events are sold on Sunday. Order online at www.TICKETplace.org.

Full-price tickets to many performances and sporting events are also sold through **Ticketmaster** (© **202/432-SEAT** [7328]; www.ticketmaster.com), at Macy's department stores. The flagship store is at 12th and G streets NW (Metro: Metro Center). You may also purchase tickets at Verizon Center, 601 F St. NW; Warner Theatre, 1299 Pennsylvania Ave. NW; and GWU-Marvin Center, 800 21st St., at H Street. If you know before you leave home that there's something special you want to see, you should call ahead to ensure that you get tickets.

Always ask about discounts for full-time students, persons with disabilities, and seniors. When you can't get the tickets you want through ordinary channels, there are several ticket brokers in town. They don't like being called "brokers," but that's what they are: They buy blocks of premium seats and resell them, usually with a hefty service charge attached. One that has been around a long time and is centrally located, just 4 blocks from the White House and near the Foggy Bottom Metro, is **Top Centre Ticket Service,**

Tips Rest the Troops

If you have tickets to an evening event, consider ending your sightseeing in the midafternoon and enforcing a rest period—with extra points for napping—so that everyone will be "up" for a night on the town. To find out what's going on around town, check *The Washington Post* "Style" section Monday through Saturday, "Children's Events" in the *Weekend* magazine on Friday, and the "Show" section on Sunday. *Washingtonian* magazine and the *City Paper* are other good sources for entertainment listings.

at 2000 Pennsylvania Ave. (✆ **202/452-9040**). Also try **Great Seats** (✆ **301/985-6250;** www.greatseats.com). Check the Yellow Pages and *Washington Post* classified ads for others.

The **Verizon Center,** 601 F St. NW, at 7th and F streets (✆ **202/628-3200;** www.verizoncenter.com), hosts sports events, family entertainment, and concerts by megastars. Keith Urban, Sting, the Rolling Stones, U2, and Miley Cyrus to name-drop a few, have played this giant 20,000-seat arena. For most events, kids 2 and up need a ticket. The Verizon Center, occupying an entire city block between 6th and 7th, F and G streets, is surrounded by office space, hotels, condos, shops, and restaurants.

Buy tickets at the box office (Mon–Sat 10am–5:30pm, Sun only when there is an event) or order online (www.verizoncenter.com), where you'll pay a service fee. You can also purchase tickets (with a service fee) at **Ticketmaster** (✆ **202/432-SEAT** [7328]; www.ticketmaster.com). Seats at the 200 level have the best sightlines.

Arrive an hour early to allow for security checks, a pit stop (family restrooms are on every level), and finding your seat. I suggest leaving a few minutes before the closing buzzer. (***Insider's tip:*** Head for handicap-access doors, which are open to everyone.) Dress in layers, as some performers stipulate no air-conditioning in their contracts. Also, it can feel like a giant igloo during Caps hockey games. The food, at several concessions in the center, is very pricey but adequate. Families are much better served by the neighborhood restaurants, where there is better value and more to choose from. If you want to eat before or after an event, walk 2 minutes to Chinatown (7th and H is the crossroads of D.C.'s minuscule Chinatown), or check out the slew of restaurants on 7th Street, within a few blocks of the center. For a quick hamburger, fries, and a drink, **Fuddrucker's** (p. 80) is always a safe bet with kids, as is **Five Guys,** 808 H St., at 9th St. (✆ **202/393-2900**).

1 THEATER

The **John F. Kennedy Center for the Performing Arts** (✆ **800/444-1324** or 202/467-4600; www.kennedy-center.org) leads the pack in delivering top family entertainment throughout the year. The Washington Performing Arts Society (see below), along with other cultural organizations and independent producers, contributes the lion's share of high-caliber entertainment suitable for young people. Most, if not all, offer student discounts. (Always ask presenters about student tickets when you call or go online—ticket policies have been known to change faster than the weather. And bring your kids school IDs. No ID, no discount.)

Freebies!

As part of the Kennedy Center's **Millennium Stage** project, free performances—by vocalists, musicians, actors, dancers, mimes, and performance artists—take place daily at 6pm, unless otherwise noted, in the Kennedy Center Grand Foyer (✆ **202/467-4600**). I'm not talking amateur night! Whenever I have tickets to a Ken Cen performance, I arrive early to enjoy the talent. (Sometimes it's better than what's in the theaters.) Kennedy Center for the Performing Arts, 2700 F St. NW (New Hampshire Ave. NW and Rock Creek Pkwy.; ✆ **800/444-1324** or 202/467-4600).

Daily from mid-June through September, Monday through Friday between noon and 1:30pm, catch a free concert at the Ronald Reagan Building. The series, known as **Live! on Woodrow Wilson Plaza** (btw. Constitution and Pennsylvania aves.), has featured such greats as jazz-funk vibraphonist Roy Ayers, the late, great jazz bassist Keter Betts, and blues singer Mary Lou Redmon. Local talent—dance groups, comedians, and young musicians—also perform. Buy lunch in the Reagan Building food court and enjoy it at an table with an umbrella (Ronald Reagan Bldg. and International Trade Center, 13th St. and Pennsylvania Ave. NW; ✆ **202/312-1300;** www.itcdc.com).

For more free entertainment, see "Military Band Concerts" and "The Old Post Office Pavilion," later in this chapter.

For 45 years, the **Washington Performing Arts Society (WPAS; ✆ 202/785-9727;** www.wpas.org) has been presenting world-class performances—and many are suitable for families. Think of a top recording artist, musician, choral group, or dance company, and chances are good that they have performed in Washington under the auspices of the WPAS. A season standout is the annual January Children's Concert by the Grammy-winning a cappella group, Sweet Honey in the Rock. Tickets for this fantastic live entertainment cost $12, little more than a first-run mediocre movie.

Occasionally D.C.-area theaters offer **backstage tours,** where visitors can enter rehearsal studios and dressing rooms, enjoy a demonstration of the sound and lighting equipment, and watch the hand-cranked fly lines raise and lower scenery. Maybe during your tour, the curtain will rise on your family, hogging the center-stage spotlight! At the Kennedy Center, show up at the Parking Plaza, Level A, for an hour-long tour of the theaters and public spaces. Tours are offered weekdays approximately every 10 minutes between 10am and 5pm, Saturday and Sunday from 10am to 1pm (✆ **202/416-8340**). To tour the National Theatre Monday to Friday between 11am and 3pm, the theater must be dark (no performances). Groups only, of 10 to 60 people, are welcome. Call ahead (✆ **202/783-6854**). Children are welcome, as long as they don't touch the props, lights, and anything else that might inflict bodily harm. Some of the theaters listed below offer tours and occasionally escort visitors backstage by special arrangement. Call the theaters directly for more information.

Adventure Theatre (Finds) A mix of original and familiar children's plays for 4- to 12-year-olds is presented year-round Saturday and Sunday at 1:30 and 3:30pm and weekdays between Christmas and New Years. The 2009–10 season of seven productions included original works and classics such as P.D. Eastman's *Go, Dog, Go!*, *The Red Balloon*, and *The Little Engine That Could.*

Box-office hours are Monday through Friday 10am to 4pm, and Saturday and Sunday 10am to 2pm (weekends only when there is a performance). Call to reserve tickets to individual performances. The distinctive theater, with stadium-style seating, was once a penny arcade on the grounds of a former amusement park. Cap the afternoon off with a ride on the Dentzel carousel, across from the theater. Glen Echo Park, MacArthur Blvd. at Goldsboro Rd., Glen Echo, MD. ✆ **301/320-5331.** www.adventuretheatre.org. $12 adults, $10 kids 1 year and older. Directions: Take Massachusetts Ave. north into Maryland. Left at Goldsboro Rd. Left at MacArthur (park located at this intersection). Follow signs to parking. From suburbs: I-495/95 to exit 39 (River Rd.) east (toward D.C.). Right at 5th traffic light (Goldsboro Rd.) to end. Right at MacArthur, and follow signs to Glen Echo Park parking. Closest Metro: Friendship Heights, and then take taxi (much faster) or no. 29 Metrobus to stop at MacArthur Blvd. and Goldsboro Rd.

Alden Theatre The Alden offers professional kid-pleasing entertainment—plays, puppet shows, concerts, dance and free weekend concerts—for children 3 and older, year-round in the state-of-the-art Alden Theatre. The center has an acting company for youngsters in grades 9 through 12 and summer programs too. And the theater is only a 20-minute ride from downtown (in non-rush-hour traffic) with plenty of on-site parking. Call for specific show times and directions. Order tickets online through Ticketmaster.com (✆ **703/573-SEAT** [7327]). McLean Community Center, 1234 Ingleside Ave., McLean, VA. ✆ **703/790-9223.** www.mcleancenter.org. Box office open Tues–Sat. Tickets $7–$14. Prices vary with performance; student and senior discounts by mail or at the box office. Free parking in the Community Center lot. Metro: West Falls Church (3½ miles away), and then taxi.

Arena Stage Many hit plays make it big at Arena Stage before moving to Broadway, and a roster of Arena "graduates" reads like a who's who of American theater. In one of his first roles, James Earl Jones starred here in the original production of *The Great White Hope.* In 2009, Valerie Harper starred as Tallulah Bankhead in *Looped* pre-Broadway. If you want to introduce older children to drama at its finest, you don't have to look any further. Some productions are not suitable for young people, so call the theater for an educated opinion, and check the reviews in local papers before going with your children.

The theater has undergone major renovations on its campus in southwest D.C. The projected reopening date is October 2010. (I'll eat my ticket stubs if it opens on time.) Meanwhile, performances take place at Arena Stage in Crystal City (1800 S. Bell St., Arlington, Va.) and at the historic Lincoln Theatre (1215 U St. NW) across from the U St.–Cardozo Metro station. (Before or after the show, stop next door at Ben's Chili Bowl, 1213 U St. NW, for a chili hot dog or half smoke. Awesome.)

The Target Family Fun Pack includes four tickets, four (nonalcoholic) beverages, and four snacks for $100. At least two of the four participants must be between 5 and 18 years old. For theater of this caliber, it's a great deal! With the $10-ticket program, those 30 and under can purchase tickets on Monday for performances Tuesday through Sunday. Order online (www.arenastage.org) or by phone (✆ **202/488-3300**).

Tickets for students with a valid ID (except Sat evenings) are 35% off (one ticket per valid ID). A limited number of Hottix are half-price from 90 minutes to 30 minutes before curtain time—in person at the sales office only. Maine Ave. and 6th St. SW. ✆ **202/488-3300.** www.arenastage.org. Tickets $40–$68. Metro: Waterfront Station, and then a 5-min. walk.

Capitol Steps Sophisticated kids 10 and older who are politically savvy may enjoy this irreverent comedy troupe, which began in 1981 when former Senate staffers teamed up to entertain at a Christmas party. (You never know what a Christmas party will spawn.) With rapier wit, they skewer presidents, politicos, and Washington's weird bureaucratic mentality. Their latest CD release is "Obama Mia." Performances are Friday and Saturday at 7:30pm in the amphitheater of the Ronald Reagan Building and International Trade Center. Tickets can be purchased at the D.C. Visitor Information Center, on the ground level of the building, through Ticketmaster (✆ **202/397-SEAT** [7327]; www.ticketmaster.com). 1300 Pennsylvania Ave. NW ✆ **202/312-1555.** www.capsteps.com. Tickets $39 (includes service charge). Metro: Federal Triangle or Metro Center.

The Children's Theatre Four productions for children 4 and older are staged by and for youngsters and operate under the Encore Stage & Studio. *Hansel and Gretel* and *The Velveteen Rabbit* are examples of past productions by the esteemed organization, which celebrated its 40th anniversary in 2007. TCT also offers workshops, classes, and camps for kids. Thomas Jefferson Community Theatre, 125 S. Old Glebe Rd., Arlington, VA (near Rte. 50 and Glebe Rd.). ✆ **703/548-1154.** www.encorestage.org. Adults $10, seniors and kids $8. Call for directions.

Folger Elizabethan Theatre (at the Folger Shakespeare Library) All the world's a stage in this intimate 243-seat Elizabethan-style theater (which celebrated its 75th birthday in 2007) in the shadow of the U.S. Capitol. Want your kids to ham it up with Hamlet? Then bring them to one of the three (a season) "Shake Up Your Saturdays" performance workshops (drama and improv) for kids 8 to 14 and their parents, offered on select Saturdays from 10am to noon (✆ **202/544-7077**). Docent-led tours are Monday through Friday at 11am, Saturday at 11am and 1pm. At other times, you can connect via your cellphone to an audio tour led by library director Gail Kern Paster. Tour the Elizabethan Garden at 10am and 11am the third Saturday of every month, April through October.

Ask about special weekday programs for grades 3 through 12 during the school year. You may want to bring your teenagers to a full-scale rendition of Shakespeare's plays. Lectures, poetry and fiction readings, and family and education programs also fill the playbill at the Folger, also home to The Folger Consort chamber ensemble and the annual Pen-Faulkner Awards for literature. Frolic at the Bard's birthday party open house, held annually the Sunday closest to April 23 (Apr 25 in 2010). Enjoy music, song, dance, storytelling, jugglers, and miniperformances by local schoolchildren. Arrive early: The birthday cake, in the shape of the Globe Theater, serves only 1,000.

The gift shop sells *Shakespeare for Kids* and other versions of the classics, tapes, CDs, videos, and posters. During the daily tours at 11am, you can peek in the theater. Otherwise, you have to attend a performance. Pique the kids' interest by directing them to Shakespeare for Kids at the library's website. The library and box office are open Monday through Saturday 10am to 5pm. 201 E. Capitol St. SE. (✆ 202/544-7077; www.folger.edu). Tickets $37–$53; student discounts available. Metro: Capitol South or Union Station.

Ford's Theatre As certain as a visit from Santa on Christmas is Ford's annual production of Dickens's *A Christmas Carol,* which runs from late November to early January. Many of the productions staged throughout the rest of the year are also suitable for families, with well-behaved kids 6 and older, but you should always check before going. After undergoing renovation, the theater reopened to applause in February 2009. Free same-day time-entry tickets to visit Ford's Theater National Historic Site (daily 9am–5pm; closed Dec 25) are available at the box office, daily beginning at 8:30am. It's first-come, first-served, and the limit is six per person. Or secure advance tickets ($1.50 per ticket service fee applies) through Ticketmaster.com (✆ **202/397-SEAT** [7327]). Included with *Christmas Carol* in the 2009–10 season lineup were the ever-popular musical *Little Shop of Horrors* and *The Rivalry*, a dramatization of the Lincoln-Douglass debates. Box-office hours are Monday 10am to 6pm, Tuesday to Friday 10am to 8pm, Saturday noon to 8pm, Sunday noon to 7:30pm. 511 10th St. NW, btw. E and F sts. ✆ **202/347-4833.** www.fordstheatre.org. Tickets $25–$56 (more Christmas week); ask about student and senior discounts. Metro: Metro Center.

Imagination Stage Imagination Stage, a 40,000-square-foot, state-of-the-art facility with a 700-seat theater, is the D.C. area's primo venue for introducing youngsters to live theater. The high quality of Imagination Stage's hour-long shows (musicals and plays) by professionals for young audiences, 4 and older, every weekend (year-round), weekdays in summer and around holidays, has held my grandkids' attention (and mine) numerous times. In addition to traditional seating, there are 60 cushions for little ones at the front of the stage. Kudos to founder and executive director Bonnie Fogel who began the program in 1979 for kids in her neighborhood. Imagination Stage also offers acting classes, workshops, summer programs in the performing arts, and classes for children with special needs. A shop with theater-themed gifts and souvenirs and a cafe are open daily. Performances are Saturday and Sunday during the school year, every day but Monday in summer. 4908 Auburn Ave., Bethesda, MD. ✆ **301/280-1660.** www.imaginationstage.org. Tickets $10–$21; $8 lap seats for kids under 2. Subscriptions $51–$95. Metro: Bethesda then walk 5 blocks north on Old Georgetown Rd., right at Auburn Ave. Directions: Wisconsin Ave. north to Bethesda, left at Old Georgetown Rd, go 5 blocks to right Auburn Ave. Parking in garage adjacent to theater is free on weekends.

Kennedy Center Performances for Young Audiences Under this umbrella, the Ken Cen presents musicals, plays, concerts, puppet shows, storytelling, and plays for kids 3 and up. Some performances are free (!), such as the Annual Multicultural Children's Book Festival the first Saturday in November. Performances are held throughout the year in several venues. The 2009–10 season featured The National Symphony Orchestra *Teddy Bear Concert, Peter and the Wolf,* and Galumpha's *The Human Jungle Gym* (acrobatics, dance, comedy). Call for a current brochure, or check the website.

Box-office hours are Monday through Saturday 10am to 9pm, and Sunday and holidays noon to 9pm. Kennedy Center for the Performing Arts, at the southern end of New Hampshire Ave. NW and Rock Creek Pkwy. ✆ **800/444-1324** or 202/467-4600; www.kennedy-center.org. Performances for Young Audiences subscription (3 or more performances; $45–$90). Most Youth and Family Programs tickets $ 15–$20. Metro: Foggy Bottom, and then free Kennedy Center shuttle bus.

Mount Vernon Community Children's Theatre Three major performances are presented annually by this noted ensemble in Virginia's Mount Vernon area. Classes and workshops are offered also. Reservations are advised a week or two in advance. Heritage Presbyterian Church, 8503 Fort Hunt Rd., Alexandria, Virginia. ✆ **703/360-0686.** www.mvcct.org. Prices $20 all seats.

Now This! (Finds) Every Saturday afternoon, families fill the historic Blair Mansion Inn for a delightful spinoff of the adult dinner-theater concept. Now This! includes lunch, dessert, and interactive musical entertainment, so audience participation is key. The musical-comedy improv group performs the show, especially suited to young people. Kids' birthdays are their specialty. Unlimited pizzas, hot dogs, sodas, cake and ice cream, entertainment, tax and tip is $25. Reservations are a must. Lunch is at 1pm; the show starts at 1:30pm. Plenty of on-site parking is available. Blair Mansion Inn, 7711 Eastern Ave., Silver Spring, MD. ✆ **202/364-8292.** www.nowthisimprov.com. Tickets (includes tax and tip) $25 lunch and show. Metro: Takoma or Silver Spring, and then taxi.

The Old Post Office Pavilion There's daily entertainment, usually noon to 1pm or 2 to 4pm. Consider it a smorgasbord (you're never sure what you'll get unless you check the website): choirs, acting groups, clowns, jugglers, musicians, singers, puppets, and dancers do their thing. While you're here, enjoy lunch or dinner from the Food Court, and visit the clock tower on the 12th floor of this historic building. September through February hours are Monday through Saturday 10am to 7pm, Sunday noon to 6pm; March 1 through August 31 hours are Monday through Saturday 10am to 9pm, Sundays noon to 7pm. 1100 Pennsylvania Ave. NW. ✆ **202/289-4224.** www.oldpostofficedc.com. Free admission. Metro: Federal Triangle.

Round House Theatre Round House performs plays to a mostly adult audience on its Bethesda stage just a block from the Bethesda, Maryland Metro (behind the building at 7501 Wisconsin Ave.), and plays and musicals in Silver Spring at 8641 Colesville Road next to the AFI Theatre. Special student matinees and related activities are offered for school groups. The Round House Theatre School has classes and workshops for kids from first grade through high school. The Sarah Play is comprised of high school students who produce, direct and perform one play a year. Students receive a $5 discount on all tickets. Box 30688, Bethesda, MD 20824. ✆ **240/644-1100.** www.round-house.org. Tickets: Bethesda $25–$60; Silver Spring $10 (for seniors) and $15 (general admission). Metro: Bethesda, and then walk 1 block; Spring, and then walk 1½ blocks.

Saturday Morning at the National *Finds* September through April, two free shows are given Saturday at 9:30 and 11am. The well-attended Marriott-sponsored series, begun in 1980, is as good as kids' entertainment gets. Past seasons featured puppet shows, presentations by naturalists and their animals, magicians, and celebrity readings of classic children's stories. For a Program Schedule, send a self-addressed, stamped envelope to "Saturday Morning," National Theatre, 1321 Pennsylvania Avenue NW, Washington, DC 20004. Program information is also available by phone (✆ **202/783-3372**).

I suggest arriving no later than 8:30am for the 9:30am show. If you don't make the cut, you should be good to go for the 11am show. Kill time with a croissant (or other delectable pastry) and beverage at Au Bon Pain, 700 13th St. (btw. G and H streets). The bakery opens at 8am. Tickets are handed out a half-hour before the performance, and it's strictly first come, first seated. National Theatre, 1321 E St. NW, at Pennsylvania Ave. NW. ✆ 202/783-3372. www.nationaltheatre.org. Free admission. Metro: Federal Triangle.

Shakespeare Theatre Introduce your kids 10 and over to a play by Shakespeare or one of his contemporaries, as well as other cultural events, in the 451-seat **Lansburgh Theatre** (in the Lansburgh Bldg., on happening 7th St. NW) or the 775-seat **Sidney Harman Hall** (less than 2 blocks away at 610 F St. NW). Both operate under the umbrella organization, Harman Center for the Arts, which opened in October 2007. In its 2009–10 season, the Shakespeare Theatre Company will perform four plays in Sidney Harman Hall and three in the Lansburgh. A hot ticket was *Phaedre* with Helen Mirren.

Full-time students and theatergoers 35 and under can take advantage of the Young Theatergoer Subscription—only $105 for a seven-play subscription. Students receive a

50% discount on tickets during preview week. A limited number of tickets at $10 each are available at the box office 1 hour before performances. ***Note:*** Prices for all performances are less during preview week. The *free* summertime **Shakespeare Free for All** productions take place in the Sidney Harman Hall, 610 F St. Free tickets are distributed 2 hours prior to curtain the day of the performance at the Harman Hall box office, 610 F St. For the latest, call the information hot line, at © **202/334-4790.** After a performance here, your kids might be hooked on the Bard. (Lansburgh Theatre) 450 7th St. NW. © 202/547-1122; (Sidney Harman Hall) 610 F St. NW. www.shakespearedc.org. Tickets $20–$82 (low price is for obstructed views). Seniors 20% off, 50% off Wed. noon matinee; students 50% off during preview week and 1 hr. before curtain. Metro: Archives.

Wolf Trap Farm Park for the Performing Arts (Finds) The best in musicals, groups, star performers, opera, and dance play on the stage of the sylvan 6,900-seat **Filene Center II** during the summer. *Riverdance* (will it ever go away?), Miami City Ballet, Ziggy Marley, Michael Feinstein, Smokey Robinson, Bonnie Raitt, Garrison Keillor, and numerous pop, jazz, and country stars have all performed at Wolf Trap (the country's only national park devoted to the performing arts) in recent years. Many of the performances are suitable for those with kids in tow; use your judgment. Many families pack a picnic and blanket, and opt for the less expensive lawn seats, where small children are better tolerated.

Children's Theatre-in-the-Woods has been entertaining youths from late June through early August with plays, stories, puppet shows, and clowning for more than 30 years. Two acts, appropriate for kindergarten through sixth grade, appear Tuesday through Saturday at 10 and 11:15am each week in a sylvan setting reminiscent of camp (summer, not boot). Tickets are $8 for everyone 3 and older, $10 for both shows on the same day. Reservations are required for all shows and workshops (© **703/255-1827**). Food is not allowed in the theater, but plenty of tables and grassy hillsides accommodate picnickers. I suggest bringing bug spray for the mosquitoes.

The Wolf Trap box office is open Monday through Friday 10am to 6pm, and weekends and holidays noon to 6pm. Everyone, regardless of age, must have a ticket for regular performances. 1551 Trap Rd., Vienna, VA. © **703/255-1868.** Fax 703/255-1916. www.wolftrap.org. Tickets $8–$70; some events are free. Metro: West Falls Church (Virginia), then Wolf Trap Express Bus ($3.10 [exact change] round-trip, summer only), which runs every 20 min. starting 2 hr. before the performance for all events, except opera. The last bus leaves Wolf Trap at 11pm or 20 min. after the last performance. Directions: I-495 to exit 45 (old exit 12B/Dulles Toll Road); stay on the local exit road, and then take Rte. 267 west to Exit 6 until you come to Wolf Trap. Limited free on-site parking available.

2 DANCE

Washington draws the top modern, folk, professional ballet, and ethnic dance companies from all over the world. The Kennedy Center and Washington Performing Arts Society are leading presenters. In addition, the acclaimed Washington Ballet Company, as well as numerous modern and postmodern dance groups and several student companies—many of which are springboards for tomorrow's professionals—are headquartered here. All perform regularly in the area. Tickets for performances by local groups are usually nominally priced, often $25 or less. Most of the local performing groups are also affiliated with schools that offer a wide range of children's dance classes and workshops.

Dance Place Finds Under executive and artistic director Carla Perlo's guiding light, Dance Place has been a leading presenter of contemporary and ethnic dance for more than 25 years. Dance Place pulsates year-round, with performances, classes, and workshops. Kids feel comfortable in the informal atmosphere of the performance space and are especially welcome at the many youth-appropriate performances. The June weeklong Dance Africa D.C. Festival is a multisensory treat celebrating African culture through food, crafts, music, dance, and master classes. Other highlights include the January Tap Dance Festival, performances by Carla's Kids (Dance Place's junior company), and the Youth Festival, showcasing local talent. As part of the Family Series, a child can see a performance for free with an accompanying paying adult. After-school and summer programs are open to local youngsters 7 to 13. Box-office hours are Monday through Saturday; hours vary. 3225 8th St. NE. ✆ **202/269-1600.** Fax 202/269-4103. www.danceplace.org. Tickets $22 adults, $15 students,$8 kids 2–17. Metro: Brookland.

Fairfax Ballet The Fairfax Ballet, directed by Ilona and Thomas Russell, performs a mixed-bill or full-length production in the spring and *Nutcracker* during the Christmas season. The Russells are esteemed former professional dancers who established the company's affiliated school, the Russell School of Ballet, more than 40 years ago. Performance sites and ticket prices vary. 14119 Sullyfield Circle, Ste. O, Chantilly, VA. ✆ **703/803-1055.** www.fairfaxballet.com.

Glen Echo Park Check out the contra, salsa, swing, square, or waltz classes preceding social dancing Friday evenings year-round in the old Spanish Ballroom and former Bumper Car Pavilion. Teens are welcome to join in the fun; younger kids can watch. Glen Echo Park, 7300 MacArthur Blvd., at Goldsboro Rd., Glen Echo, MD. ✆ **301/229-6022.** www.fridaynightdance.org. Cost is $5–$20 at the door. Metro: Friendship Heights, and then take no. 29 bus to stop at MacArthur Blvd. and Goldsboro Rd.

Maryland Youth Ballet (MYB) Finds The MYB, under the direction of Hortensia Fonseca and Michelle Lees, presents a superb family concert series twice a year (*The Nutcracker* in Dec. and a program of short works in mid-May) that features advanced ballet students, many of whom have gone on to successful professional careers. Performances are at the Parilla Performing Arts Center of Montgomery College in Rockville, Maryland. Get your tickets early for this spirited production of *The Nutcracker,* suitable for kids 3 and older. Call for tickets or order online (✆ **240/567-5301;** www.montgomerycollege.edu). Studio: 926 Ellsworth Dr., Silver Spring, MD ✆ **301/608-2232.** www.marylandyouthballet.org. Nutcracker tickets: $25 in advance, $20 students and seniors, reserved in advance; $25 at door. Metro: Silver Spring for the studio Rockville for performances.

Metropolitan Ballet Theatre and Academy (MBT) The MBT was founded in 1989 by former New York City Ballet ballerina Suzanne Erlon to provide training and performance opportunities to young dancers. Guest artists appear with the student company in *The Nutcracker* and in the annual Spring Dance Collection in March. All performances are held at the Robert E. Parilla Performing Arts Center, Montgomery College, Rockville. Box-office hours are Monday through Friday from 10am to 6pm. Studio: 10076 Darnestown Rd., Ste. 202, Rockville, MD. ✆ **301/762-1757.** www.mbtdance.org. Tickets $17–$22. Metro: Rockville Metro Center, and then Ride-On Bus no. 46 or no. 55 to Parilla Performing Arts Center.

Virginia Ballet Company For more than 50 years, the Virginia Ballet has been a fixture on the local dance scene. The company performs *The Nutcracker* annually at Northern Virginia Community College's Ernst Cultural Center, 8333 Little River Turnpike, Annandale, a spring concert (two performances) in May, and a single summer performance in August. Classes are ongoing at the Springfield studio. Founding artistic directors and cofounders Oleg Tupine and Tania Rousseau, well-respected dancers, ran the company's school until their deaths. Tish Cordova, ballerina with the Tulsa Ballet Theatre and a former VBC student, is the current artistic director. Studio: 5595 Guinea Rd., Fairfax, VA. ✆ **703/249-8227.** www.virginiaballet.org. Prices $15–$25. Call for directions.

The Washington Ballet Washington's resident professional ballet company presents a fall, winter, and spring series, at the Kennedy Center's Eisenhower Theater and Sidney Harman Hall (610 F St. NW). Tickets are $29 (*Nutcracker*, nosebleed section) and up. In its 2009–10 season, the company presented *Don Quixote, Genius3* (works by Twyla Tharp, Mark Morris, and Nacho Duato), and *The Great Gatsby* (choreographed by company director Septime Webre), and, for the youngsters, *Shoogie, the Tail of My Wiener Dog.* WB's Studio Company performed *Peter and the Wolf.* Programs are suitable for children over 8 (strictly my subjective opinion). The Family Series of three performances (including *The Nutcracker*) is $225 for front orchestra; prices elsewhere are lower. *The Nutcracker,* a holiday staple, is presented at George Mason Center for the Arts in suburban Virginia and at D.C.'s Warner Theatre each December. 3515 Wisconsin Ave. NW. ✆ **202/362-3606.** www.washingtonballet.org. Prices vary with the performance; discounts for groups of 10 or more.

3 MUSIC

CLASSICAL MUSIC

Washington is home to the National Symphony Orchestra, the Washington Opera, and numerous first-rate chamber orchestras and choral groups that give family and children's performances throughout the area. Guest artists also appear year-round at many sites in and around the city. Consult the *Washington Post* and *Washington Times;* or call or visit the individual presenter's websites for performance dates, times, and ticket prices, which vary widely. Some family performances are free.

D.C. Youth Orchestra This excellent youth orchestra sounds as harmonious as many professional ensembles. The spirited and talented group of young people has toured 15 countries and played for six U.S. presidents since its founding in 1960. No child is turned away from the program that instructs youngsters from 4 to 19 years old. Free concerts are one Sunday a month from October to June. Call for dates. Coolidge High School, 5th and Sheridan sts. NW. ✆ **202/723-1612.** www.dcyop.org. Free admission. Take a taxi here.

Fairfax Choral Society The youth 65-voice chorus, as well as the "parent" groups—an 80-voice chorus and 25-voice chorale—always draw an admiring crowd to performances at several northern Virginia and D.C. sites. Box-office hours are 10am to 2pm. 4028 Hummer Rd., Annandale, VA. ✆ **703/642-3277.** www.fairfaxchoralsociety.org. Tickets $35 adults, students $25 (2-ticket package). Call for directions.

National Symphony Orchestra (NSO) Finds The NSO presents about 200 concerts annually and offers several series (some geared to families). The availability of tickets for individual concerts varies. The annual **Teddy Bear Concerts** are appropriate for toddlers. The **Kinderkonzerts** (for kids 4 and up) introduce young audiences to the basic ingredients of a symphony orchestra through classics such as *Peter and the Wolf,* and new works. The NSO treats families to free concerts on Memorial Day weekend, the Fourth of July, and Labor Day on the West Lawn of the U.S. Capitol. You can also catch them at Wolf Trap's Filene Center in Virginia (p. 245) and the Carter Barron Amphitheatre, 16th Street and Colorado Avenue NW, in the summer. No cameras or recording devices are permitted at Carter Barron. The amphitheater is a 15- to 20-minute taxi ride from the White House. Or take the S-2 or S-4 Metrobus that runs on 16th Street (catch it near the White House); get off at Colorado Avenue, and walk 2 blocks. Kennedy Center for the Performing Arts, New Hampshire Ave. NW and Rock Creek Pkwy. ✆ **800/444-1324** or 202/467-4600. www.kennedy-center.org/nso. Metro: Foggy Bottom, and then free Kennedy Center shuttle.

Washington Performing Arts Society (WPAS) Washington's first presenter of cultural events—concerts by internationally acclaimed orchestras, soloists, chamber groups, and dance companies—also co-presents with other arts presenters at numerous venues. Performances by jazz and gospel singers and musicians, and contemporary dance companies usually appeal to youngsters more than solo concerts or chamber music. The annual **Children's Concert** (held in Jan, close to Martin Luther King, Jr.'s birthday) by D.C.'s own jazz/gospel group Sweet Honey in the Rock rocks! Ticket prices for the Children's Concert are $12; for other concerts, from $15 to $115 (most in the $55–$70 range). Box-office hours are Monday through Friday 9:30am to 5pm. 2000 L St. NW. ✆ **202/785-9727.** www.wpas.org. Call for directions.

MILITARY BAND CONCERTS

One of the perks of visiting Washington in the summer is enjoying the free band concerts held at several downtown venues. Call first to double-check times, because scheduling varies. During the rest of the year, watch local newspapers for information on military band concerts.

Carillon Concerts Enjoy a free concert by a guest artist playing the 50-bell Netherlands Carillon (Rte. 50 and George Washington Pkwy.; the Marine Corps War Memorial, aka Iwo Jima Memorial) near Arlington National Cemetery. In past years, concerts were held Saturdays and a weeknight May through August, from 2 to 4pm or 6 to 8pm, and on Memorial Day and July 4th. For a bird's-eye view, climb the tower if you wish, and keep a sharp eye on little ones. Experience dictates checking the days and times before setting out. Bring something to sit on. ✆ **202/433-2927.** www.drumcorps.mbw.usmc.mil. Free admission. Metro: Arlington Cemetery, and then free shuttle buses.

Marine Corps Friday Evening Parades Finds Dress parades, Friday evenings from early May through August, get under way at 2045 hours (8:45pm). Reservations are required via e-mail; there is no phone. If you pass muster, arrive by 7:15pm. Arrive after 8pm, and it's likely you'll be turned away—reservation or not. No weapons (duh!), food, or beverages except water and baby food/bottles allowed. Check the website for restrictions. U.S. Marine Barracks, 8th and I sts. SE. ✆ **202/433-6060.** www.mbw.usmc.mil/parades. Free admission. Metro: Eastern Market, and then a 10-min. walk.

Military Band Concert Series Attend a free concert by the U.S. Army Band ("Pershing's Own") year-round at venues in and around the city. Fridays, May through August, the band plays at the U.S. Capitol (West Terrace), beginning at 8pm. Call first or check the website; things can change faster than an "about face!" Multiple venues. ✆ **703/696-3399.** www.usarmyband.com. Free admission. Check Metro website (www.wmata.com) for closest Metro station to current venue.

Sunset Parade It's first come, first served for lawn seats at the Marine Corps War Memorial (aka the Iwo Jima memorial), where you'll hear the 80-member Marine Drum and Bugle Corps ("The Commandant's Own") and see precision drills Tuesday evening at 7pm from early June or July (schedule changes year to year) to mid-August. Shuttle buses run from the visitor center at Arlington Cemetery (a short walk from the Arlington Cemetery Metro stop), starting at 6pm. Iwo Jima Memorial, north end of Arlington Cemetery. ✆ **202/433-2927.** www.drumcorps.mbw.usmc.mil. Free admission. Metro: Arlington Cemetery, and then shuttle.

Twilight Tattoo Enjoy an hour of intricate military drills and precision marching along with selections by the U.S. Army Band on the Washington Monument grounds, usually one evening per week in May and June at 7pm. Call or check the website for the latest info. Arrive early and bring something to sit on. The Washington Monument, 15th St. SW, behind the Ellipse, south of the White House. ✆ **202/685-3611.** www.mdw.army.mil. Free admission. Metro: Smithsonian, then a 5-min. walk.

BLUES, COUNTRY, FOLK & JAZZ

The Barns of Wolf Trap Jazz, pop, country, folk, and bluegrass predominate from October to May on the grounds of this cozy center for the performing arts. The 200-year-old restored barn is not a place to bring babies, but the Barns invites schoolagers to come with their parents and soak up a little history with the music, dance, and performance art in this charming, rustic setting. 1624 Trap Rd., Vienna, VA. ✆ **703/938-2404,** or 703/218-6500 to charge tickets. www.wolftrap.org. Most tickets $18–$25. Kids pay full price. Metro: West Falls Church station, and then Wolf Trap Express Bus (every 20 min., beginning 2 hr. before show to 20 min. after; $3.10 [exact change] round-trip).

Blues Alley Washington's first and foremost jazz supper club for more than 40 years has reverberated to Mose Allison, Arturo Sandoval, Charlie Byrd, Nancy Wilson, Wynton and Branford Marsalis, Maynard Ferguson, Joshua Redman, and hundreds of other jazz greats. There are two shows (8 and 10pm) weeknights and sometimes three on Friday and Saturday. Reservations are taken up to 2 months in advance, and seating is first come, first served. Box-office hours are noon to 8pm. Anyone well behaved and over the age of 8 is welcome.

Dinner begins at 6pm, and you'll have no trouble gobbling up the $10 food or drink minimum. Entrees run $19 to $25; the Late Fare offerings are from $5.50 to $12. Blues Alley is smoke free. 1073 Wisconsin Ave. NW, in an alley behind M St. ✆ 202/337-4141. www.bluesalley.com. Tickets $18–$45 (students pay half Sun–Thurs 10pm show), plus $10 food or drink minimum and a $2.50 surcharge for the Blues Alley Music Society. Metro: Foggy Bottom, and then Georgetown Metro Connection shuttle; or take the Circulator or a taxi (see chapter 3).

Dubliner (Finds) The Dubliner is so fond of kids that it even has highchairs so that wee leprechauns can enjoy the spirited Irish music (jukebox all the time; live at night) and classic pub food (but not the Guinness) along with Mom and Dad at this Capitol Hill fixture in the Phoenix Park Hotel. Come for lunch or an early dinner, or Saturday/Sunday brunch from 11am to 3pm. Things can get rowdy later on. The "For the Wee Folk" menu has grilled cheese, hot dog, hamburger, and chicken nuggets (all served with fries and coleslaw) for $6.95. 4 F St. NW. ✆ **202/737-3773.** www.dublinerdc.com. Most entrees $9.95–$16 at dinner. Metro: Union Station, and then a 2-min. walk.

4 FILMS

Discovery Theater *Finds* Films, cultural events, and live performances for youngsters take place most weekdays during the school year, weekends, and in summer at this 200-seat, state-of-the-art, below-ground theater in the Ripley Center on the National Mall. Discovery Theater. Enter at kiosk, 1100 Jefferson Drive SW, btw. the Smithsonian Castle and the Freer Gallery; descend to 3rd sublevel. (Also accessible underground from the Sackler Gallery, Freer Gallery, or National Museum of African Art.) ✆ **202/633-8700.** www.discoverytheater.com. Tickets $6–$10 adults; $5–$9 kids; some free events.

The Einstein Planetarium at the Air and Space Museum *Finds* Buckle your seat belt and explore the Milky Way via *Cosmic Collisions* and *Infinity Express.* Sky Vision, the planetarium's newish dual digital projection and surround-sound system, will have you gripping your armrests. The special effects are awesome. The 20-minute "flights" to the edge of the universe are appropriate for kids 5 and older. The films alternate. *The Stars Tonight,* a free presentation daily at 11:30am, explores the D.C. skies. Einstein Planetarium, Independence Ave. and 7th St. SW. ✆ **202/633-IMAX** [4629]. www.si.edu/planetarium. Tickets $8.75, $7.25 children 2–11, $7.75 60 and older. Metro: L'Enfant Plaza.

Films on the Vern Bring chairs or a tarp or sit on your own natural padding at the Mount Vernon (2100 Foxhall Rd. NW, in D.C., not Virginia) campus of George Washington U for a free outdoor film series Wednesday evenings, mid-July to mid-August. *In Pursuit of Happyness* and *Patch Adams* starred in 2009. If it rains, the nearby Eckles Library Auditorium opens its doors. Hop on the Vern Express, a free shuttle between G.W.'s Foggy Bottom and Mount Vernon campuses. ✆ **202/242-6673.** www.gwu.edu/mvcl. Free admission. Metro: Foggy Bottom, then shuttle.

The Johnson IMAX Theater at the Natural History Museum *Finds* See beautifully photographed large-scale movies about the natural world, all in 3D! *Lions: Roar of the Kalahari, Sharks,* and *Sea Monsters*—all in 3D—were playing in late 2009. There is a $1.50 per ticket service charge, if you order tickets by phone or on the Internet. Johnson IMAX Theater, 10th St. and Constitution Ave. NW. ✆ **202/633-IMAX** [4629]. www.si.edu/imax. Tickets $8.75 adults, $7.25 ages 2–11, $7.75 60 and older. Metro: Smithsonian or Federal Triangle.

The Lockheed Martin IMAX Theater at the Air and Space Museum *Finds* If you're visiting the museum, stop at the box office first, preferably when it opens around 9:45am. The breathtaking films shown on the five-story IMAX screen frequently sell out, and after you've seen one, you'll know why. Tickets may be purchased up to 2 weeks in advance. Frankly, I think it's worth the $1.50 surcharge to order tickets by phone or online a week or so before you visit. *To Fly,* the first presentation, debuted in 1976 and still fills the house. The aerial shots, from an 1800s-era hot-air balloon, barnstormer, hang glider, and a Saturn-bound rocket, are guaranteed to knock your socks off. On the IMAX screen in fall 2009 were: *Night at the Museum: Battle of the Smithsonian* (parts of the commercial 2009 film were shot in the Air and Space Museum), *Fighter Pilot: Operation Red Flag,* which invites viewers into the cockpits of F-15s as armed-services pilots train for international missions, and *3D Sun,* stunning imagery taken from NASA spacecraft. With younger kids I'd opt for *To Fly,* with a running time of a half-hour; most films are about 40 minutes each. Lockheed Martin Theater, Independence Ave. and 7th St. SW. ✆ **202/357-1686** or 202/357-1675. www.si.edu/imax. Tickets $8.75 adults, $7.25 ages 2–11, and $7.75 60 and older. Metro: L'Enfant Plaza.

National Museum of African Art Call or check the website for a schedule of films and other events related to daily life, folktales, politics, and the art of Africa's rich and diverse culture. Films are 30 to 60 minutes long and suitable for older kids and their families. They are shown in the Discovery Theater (accessible from the NMAA) or the Learning Center Lecture Hall on the second level. 950 Independence Ave. SW. ✆ **202/357-2700.** www.nmafa.si.edu. Free admission. Metro: Smithsonian.

Screen on the Green **Finds** On 4 or 5 Monday nights in July and August the National Mall, between 4th and 7th streets, is the site of free movies, suitable for kids 10 and older who won't wander off into the perspiring sea of humanity. The show starts at dusk (8:30–9pm), for oldies and goodies such as *Close Encounters of the Third Kind* and *Rebel Without a Cause,* which played in 2009. Movie buffs of all ages cheer their favorite lines or speak them along with the actors. People start setting up camp as early as 5:30pm, so get here by 7pm, or you'll be out of luck and tripping over bodies. Bring a low lawn chair or a blanket, a picnic, if you like, and plenty of bug spray. Cold drinks and ice cream are sold. National Mall, btw. 4th and 7th sts. NW. ✆ **877/262-5866.** Free admission. Metro: L'Enfant Plaza or Archives–Navy Memorial.

5 PUPPET SHOWS

Puppet shows are given throughout the year, most frequently by the Puppet Co. (at the Puppet Co. Playhouse, in Glen Echo Park). Also see "Theater," earlier in this chapter, for addresses and phone numbers and the Friday "Weekend" section of the *Washington Post.*

Most performances are timed for 45 minutes or less, just the right length for restless tykes. Call the following puppeteers to see if they'll be presenting a show during your visit. No strings attached.

For kids who would like to learn more about this ancient craft, puppet-making classes are sometimes offered by Glen Echo Park (✆ **301/634-2226;** www.glenechopark.org), such as the week-long class for 9- to 12-year-olds in June 2009 ($250); and at Imagination Stage (✆ **301/280-1660;** www.imaginationstage.org). Blue Sky Puppet Theater conducts classroom creative dramatics workshops for youngsters (with Blue Sky puppets).

Blue Sky Puppet Theatre Blue Sky has been pulling strings since 1974 and performs hundreds of times a year at venues in and around the city—recreation centers, libraries, museums, even The National Zoo. Wolf Trap Park for the Performing Arts has hosted them in the past. Call for dates and locations, which vary from year to year. 4301 Van Buren St., University Park, MD. ✆ **301/927-5599.** www.blueskypuppets.com.

The Puppet Co. **Finds** Try to sandwich in a performance by the Puppet Co. in the Puppet Co. Playhouse, a state-of-the-art 250-seat theater in Glen Echo Park. (Hey, I recall sitting on the floor of the old facility, trying to hold onto two wriggling kids.)

Award-winning co-directors Christopher MayField Piper and Allen Stevens produce shows that win fans from 2 to 102. Each show runs 4 to 6 weeks. Performances are Wednesday through Sunday. Times vary. Call to reserve tickets. The Puppet Co. Playhouse, Glen Echo Park, 7300 MacArthur Blvd., Glen Echo, MD. ✆ **301/320-6668.** www.thepuppetco.org. Tickets $8. Directions from Washington: Massachusetts Ave. north into Maryland, left at Goldsboro Rd., left at MacArthur Blvd. and park entrance, follow signs to parking; from suburbs I-495/95 to exit 39 (River Rd.) east (toward D.C.), right at 5th traffic light (Goldsboro Rd.) to end, right at MacArthur, and follow signs to Glen Echo Park parking. Metro: Friendship Heights, and then take a taxi (much faster) or the no. 29 Metrobus to stop at MacArthur Blvd. and Goldsboro Rd.

6 STORY HOURS

Story hours at the public library or area bookstores are fun and quiet times for preschoolers and young scholars—and their parents.

Visiting authors speak, from time to time, at the following children's bookstores, which also have story hours: **Barnes & Noble,** 555 12th St. NW (at E St.; ✆ **202/347-0176**); **Borders,** 1800 L St. NW (✆ **202/466-4999**); and **Borders for Kids,** White Flint Mall, North Bethesda, Maryland (✆ **301/816-1067**). Call the individual stores for details (see the "Books" section in chapter 9). Check the monthly literary calendar that appears the third or fourth Sunday of every month in the *Book World* magazine of the Sunday *Washington Post.*

7 SPECTATOR SPORTS

Washington, D.C. is a happening sports town, with teams in everything from professional soccer to Major League Baseball. If tickets are available (which may be an impossibility for football) they're usually sold at both the sports facility and by **Ticketmaster** (✆ **800/527-6384** or 202/397-7328; www.ticketmaster.com).

Baltimore Orioles Many D.C. fans, hungry for baseball when the city was without a team, became and continue to be die-hard fans of the MLB's Baltimore Orioles. If you're a Birds fan or plan to be in Baltimore during your stay, catch the O's, from early April to October, at Oriole Park at Camden Yards. Camden Yards, 333 W. Camden St., Baltimore. ✆ **888/848-BIRD** [2473]. www.orioles.mlb.com. Most tickets $20–$75. Mon–Fri MARC train/Camden Line or 701 Express Bus from Union Station to Camden Yards; Sat–Sun and holidays, take no. 703 bus from Greenbelt Metro station.

Washington, D.C., Professional Sports Teams

Quick Fact: Washington, D.C. was without a baseball team for more than 30 years. The Senators left in 1974 to the consternation of many. Someone finally heard the long-ignored war cry of persevering fans to "Bring Baseball Back to Washington!" In 2005, the Washington Nationals played their first season at RFK. Guess it's true: Slow but steady wins the race.

Baltimore Ravens The NFL's Baltimore Ravens also have a 16-game schedule. Games are played at M&T Bank Stadium. Buses and MARC trains run from one or more D.C. locations. M&T Bank Stadium, 1101 Russell St., Baltimore, MD. ✆ **410/261-7283.** www.baltimoreravens.com. Single game tickets $60 to way, way up. Check Metro website (www.wmata.com) for closest station to game-day locale.

DC United Soccer fans from around the world applaud our MLS (Major League Soccer) DC United soccer team. The season runs from early April to mid-October, with home games at RFK Stadium. Whatever the outcome, the games are fun and high spirited. RFK Memorial Stadium, 2400 E. Capitol St. SE. ✆ **202/587-5000.** www.dcunited.com. Tickets generally $22–$50. Metro: Stadium/Armory, and then a short walk.

The Washington Capitals DC's pro hockey team plays at the Verizon Center. The fast-skating regular-season action runs from early October through April. Verizon Center, 601 F St. NW. ✆ **202/628-3200.** www.washingtoncaps.com or www.capstickets.com. Tickets $35–$350. Metro: Gallery Place/Chinatown.

Washington Wizards The NBA's (National Basketball Association) Washington Wizards preseason starts in early October. Close to 40 regular season games start early November and run through April. Games are played at the Verizon Center. It's easy to get here by Metro or car from anywhere in the D.C. area. Just hop on a train to Gallery Place/Chinatown, and walk a block. Verizon Center, 601 F St. NW. ✆ **202/628-3200.** www.nba.com/wizards. Tickets $40–$275. Metro: Gallery Place/Chinatown.

Washington Freedom The WPS (Women's Professional Soccer League) had its inaugural season in 2009, after the WUSA league folded several years ago. Drive here (no public transportation) and catch a game from early April through mid-August at the beautiful Maryland SoccerPlex. 18031 Central Park Circle Boyds, Maryland. ✆ **202/547-KICK** [5425]. www.washingtonfreedom.com. Tickets $20–$40.

Washington Nationals After more than 30 years without a Major League Baseball team, in 2005 fans resumed cheering (and sometimes booing) the Washington Nationals. The regular season goes from early April until late September at Nationals Park near the Anacostia River and the Navy Yard. 1500 South Capitol St., SE ✆ **202/675-NATS** [6287]. www.nationals.mlb.com. Tickets $5–$335 (grandstand–Lexus President's Box, respectively). Metro: Navy Yard then 1/2 block walk.

Washington Redskins D.C.'s best-known team is the NFL's (National Football League) Washington Redskins. Home games are played Sunday afternoons, with the occasional Sunday- or Monday-night game at FedEx Field. That's the good news. Now the bad: Except in rare instances, you cannot buy individual tickets; they are all purchased by season-ticket holders. The occasional ticket is available in the *Washington Post* classified ads, at Craigslist.com, or from a ticket broker (see the Yellow Pages). Expect to pay a premium from a broker. ***Note:*** *Do not drive!* I repeat, leave the car in a Metro lot and take Metro. FedEx Field, 1600 FedEx Way, Landover, MD ✆ **301/276-6000.** www.redskins.com. Ticket price varies based on success of your beg-borrow-steal method of purchase. Metro: Landover station, and then a shuttle bus ($5).

11

Side Trips from Washington, D.C.

If time permits, you might want to plan a side trip to one or more of the attractions listed below. Using your hotel as a base, you can visit most of the following in a day and be back in D.C. for the late-night news on TV.

1 THEME-PARK THRILLS

Your idea of a good time may not include losing your lunch on a giant roller coaster, but kids take a different view. Just remember, if they're under a certain height or age restriction, you'll have to ride the roller coaster with them. ***A word of warning:*** Amusement parks depend on food, beverage, games, and souvenir sales for half their revenues. Although you're a captive audience once you arrive, with a little planning, you don't have to feel like a human ATM machine once you've paid the staggering admission. One solution is to pack a cooler with drinks and snacks, and picnic outside the parks—*after* the roller coaster, of course.

Six Flags America ★ **Ages 2 and up.** Only 12 miles from D.C., Six Flags features more than 100 rides, games, shows, attractions, many water-based rides, and one of the world's largest wave pools, all in several miniparks located on a 115-acre site in Prince George's County, Maryland, just 15 minutes from the Beltway. New in 2010 is Thomas Town, a children's area based on the popular Thomas and Friends characters. Daily parades through the park by Looney Tunes characters and summer concerts are part of the entertainment.

Hurricane Harbor has 11 water rides, from mild to max thrill and wetness factors, including wave and kiddies' pools. ***Note:*** The eight roller coasters have minimum height restrictions that range from 42 inches to 54 inches.

Hearts and stomachs flip-flop on the park's **The Flip Side.** (Who comes up with these names?) Among the park's other coasters, **Superman, Ride of Steel** flies on steel tracks at speeds up to 70 mph, with a 200-foot drop. Lucky folks on the **Batwing** coaster ride at a 30-degree angle and scream their way through various twists and corkscrews. Waiting a half hour or more for the coasters (11 in all) is not unheard of, so if at all possible, visit on a weekday, and arrive early. Bathing suits are required for the water slides and pool, but you can stow your dry duds in rental lockers.

The so-called Family Rides have height, rather than age, restrictions. And you must be 36 inches or taller to ride most of the Looney Tune–inspired Kids' Rides (42 inches for The Great Chase).

The food is comprised of the usual (overpriced) suspects—burgers, hot dogs, pizza, fried chicken, and Chinese—enough salty and sweet treats to mess with your cholesterol and blood pressure levels for a while. Buy the Flash Pass ($15), and advance to the head of the line on eight of the most popular rides. Each pass is good for one person on five rides or five people on one ride. With cranky kids on a hot day, it's probably well worth it.

13710 Central Ave., Largo, MD. ✆ **301/249-1500.** www.sixflags.com. Admission adults $40 (online); $50 at the park; kids under 48 in. $25, free for kids 2 and under. Check website for specials. Weekends only May and Oct; daily Memorial Day–Labor Day. Hours vary. Metro: Addison Rd. (not a great neighborhood), and then taxi. Directions: Take I-495/I-95 to exit 15A (Rte. 214 east). The park is 5 miles on the left. Parking $15.

Paramount's Kings Dominion ★★ Ages 4 and up. Farther afield, near Richmond, Virginia, about a 2-hour drive from the District, this theme park could keep your family busy for a fortnight or two, with its 12 roller coasters, close to 40 other rides in six theme areas, water park, numerous shows, shops, and attractions. The new-in-2010 Intimidator 305, at 305 feet, is the East Coast's tallest coaster and reaches a max speed of 92 mph. (I'll meet you at the nearest snack bar when you're done.)

If you are still reading, knock yourselves out and visit **KidZville,** inhabited by Hanna-Barbera characters, or explore **Yogi's Cave** and ride the **Taxi Jam Coaster** (billed as "a child's first coaster"). Youngsters can romp in the Kidz Construction Company area and "drive" a dump truck or cement mixer. Ride the Rugrats Toonpike, and meet their fave Nickelodeon characters, SpongeBob and Dora and Jimmy Neutron among them. Eat in the cutesy **Busytown Café,** decorated with characters from the pen of popular kids' author Richard Scarry.

A word of caution: Don't ride any of the 12 roller coasters after a full meal. It's not a bad idea to take a motion-sickness pill half an hour before boarding. (Factoid to stash in your box of caramel corn: The Grizzly was modeled after Coney Island's famous Wildcat.)

At WaterWorks, open daily Memorial Day through early September, dip into the **Tidal Wave Bay,** a gigantic wave pool, or swim over to the **Surf City Splash House,** with more than 50 ways to get soaked.

Those prone to motion sickness, and those with kids old enough to ride alone, can pass the time in one of the air-conditioned shows or shops, selling mostly ho-hum, overpriced souvenirs. Lines for rides can be incredibly long on weekends and holidays, so you might want to plan around these times. ***Note:*** No refunds are given for inclement weather.

Doswell, VA (about 80 miles south of D.C.). ✆ **804/876-5000.** www.kingsdominion.com. Admission $45 ages 3–61, at least 48 in. tall in shoes; $32 under 48 in. tall and seniors age 62 and over; free for children 2 and under. ***Note:*** Discounts available online. Coupons for reduced admission are sometimes available at area supermarkets. Late Mar–Memorial Day and Sept–Oct weekends only; Memorial Day–Labor Day open daily. Hours vary. Directions: Take I-95 south to exit 98 (Doswell). You can't miss it from there. Parking $10.

2 MOUNT VERNON ★

16 miles S of Washington, D.C.

George Washington's home, just 16 miles from the District, is restored to its original appearance, down to the paint colors on the walls. If you're visiting Washington, D.C. for more than a couple of days, this should be at or near the top of your must-see list. And I urge you to earmark 5 hours or more for a visit. In summer and on weekends and holidays, the crowds are unreal. Check the line status on arriving. If it's long, tour the grounds first. November through February is the least busy time. Wear thick-soled shoes or galoshes during those months—the terrain can get muddy. GW's estate and final resting place is owned and maintained by the **Mount Vernon Ladies' Association** (✆ **703/780-2000;** www.mountvernon.org). The site is open daily April through August

8am to 5pm; March, September, and October 9am to 5pm; and November through February 9am to 4pm. Admission is $15 for adults, $14 for seniors 62 and older, $7 for ages 6 to 11, and free for children 5 and under. For a brochure, write to Mount Vernon Ladies Association, Mount Vernon, VA 22121, or go to www.mountvernon.org.

GETTING THERE

BY CAR Take any of the bridges over the Potomac into Virginia to the George Washington Memorial Parkway going south. The parkway ends at Mount Vernon. If you end up in Richmond (overshooting Mount Vernon by an hour!), turn around and head north.

BY TOURMOBILE Tourmobile buses (✆ **202/554-5100**) depart daily (mid-June to Labor Day) from Arlington National Cemetery and the Washington Monument. Round-trip fare is $32 for adults, $16 for children 3 to 11, and free for kids 2 and under. The fare includes admission to Mount Vernon. Payment is in cash or traveler's checks *only.* Departures are at 10am, noon, and 2pm.

BY RIVERBOAT If you want to make a full day of it, the ***Spirit of Mount Vernon*** riverboat travels down the Potomac from Pier 4, at 6th and Water streets SW (✆ **202/554-8000**). In 2009, *Spirit* cruises to Mount Vernon operated March 13 through 29 and August 28 through October 31, Friday through Sunday only; March 31 through August 23, Tuesday through Sunday. Board at 8:15am, depart at 8:30 a.m., and return at 3pm. There is a snack bar on board. Round-trip fares are $46 for adults, $41 for kids 3 to 11 and senior citizens, free for children 2 and under. Fares include admission to Mount Vernon.

Potomac Riverboat Company runs a water taxi service between Georgetown and Alexandria on the *Matthew Hayes* and *Miss Mallory* in April (weekends only), May (Tues–Sun), and Memorial Day to Labor Day (daily); September to Columbus Day (second Mon in Oct), it's open Tuesday to Sunday. You can travel one-way or round-trip. The fare is $26 round-trip for adults, $20 for seniors, $14 for kids 2 through 11, free 23 months and under. Departure times vary according to demand. Call ✆ **703/548-9000,** or go to www.potomacriverboatco.com.

EXPLORING MOUNT VERNON

Ever wonder how an aristocratic 18th-century American family lived? Minus the air-conditioning, you've come to the right place to find out. (Before air-conditioning was added about 15 years ago to cool down this hot attraction, the upstairs bedrooms often reached a sweltering 100°F/38°C). Poor George must have spent many a sleepless night.) Some of the furnishings are original, and the rooms are arranged as if George still lived there. About 500 of the original 8,000 acres still exist as part of the estate, and 30 are yours to explore. The plantation dates from 1674, when the land was granted to Washington's great-grandfather. Washington spent 2 years in retirement here before he died in 1799.

Like fine wine, Mount Vernon improves with age. Begin your tour in the Ford Orientation Center with a 20-minute film, "We Fight To Be Free," about the darkest days of the Revolutionary War. I recommend that first-time visitors pick up an audio tour for $6. Be sure to visit the adjacent Reynolds Museum and Education Center before or after touring the mansion and grounds. It's crammed with artifacts and memorabilia—such as GW's dentures, not wooden as many of us were led to believe. Children are usually less interested in the period furnishings than in the family kitchen and outbuildings, where everyday tasks—baking, weaving, and washing—took place.

In summer in the **Hands-on-History tent** (next to the mansion), children take part in such activities as carding and spinning wool, trying on colonial clothing, playing corncob darts, and rolling hoops. Also ask about special family programs on weekends from late May through early September.

April through October, head to **George Washington: Pioneer Farmer,** the working farm site down by the riverside. Depending on the season, kids can watch sheep shearing, ride in a wagon, or even assist in harvesting. Let's not forget that George was, first and foremost, a farmer who planted new crops and experimented with new farming techniques at Mount Vernon. Ask at the barn for an Activity Pack, a guide to the hands-on activities available.

A short walk from the mansion is the tomb where George, Martha, and other family members are buried. On the third Monday of February, a memorial service commemorating Washington's birthday, open to the public, is held at the estate. On my last visit, I unexpectedly took part in a short, moving ceremony. You too can have this singular experience. Just show up at the tomb between 10am or 2pm daily.

Also of interest are the slave burial ground and 30-minute walking tour describing slave life in Mount Vernon. Washington owned more than 300 slaves and freed more than 100 at the end of his life. Visit the re-created slave cabin. Imagine your family living in this 14-by-16-foot space. The tour is available April through October at 2pm. Tours of the gardens are given April through October at 11am. In the museum, you can view the family's personal possessions. Allow time for a stroll through the grounds and gardens—the view from the front lawn is awesome. Talk about prime waterfront property! It is said the river teemed with herring in Washington's day.

Every December, the mansion is decorated for Christmas. During the two Friday and Saturday evenings preceding Christmas, a candlelight tour is held from 5 to 8pm. The tour begins with gingersnaps and cider on the grounds. The re-enactors are superb. I heartily recommend it for families with kids 8 and older. Show up before 5pm for a good parking spot, and be forewarned—you'll do a lot of walking.

The **Shops at Mount Vernon** are rather Disneyesque, but you can pick up books on Washington (the largest collection in the nation, I hear), cookbooks, china, and other Mount Vernon–inspired housewares and crafts, and a cherry-flavored hatchet. If you're desperate (desperately hungry, that is), a food court here has outdoor seating, weather permitting. Just outside the main gate is the **Mount Vernon Inn** restaurant, open daily except Christmas. The menu is varied and the prices reasonable, with several comfort food choices that appeal to youngsters. Lunch is served every day 11am to 3:30pm; dinner is Monday through Thursday 5 to 8:30pm, Friday and Saturday 5 to 9pm (**✆ 703/780-0011;** www.mountvernon.org). Reservations are a must at the inn. Picnic, if you like, 1 mile north of Mount Vernon at scenic Riverside Park; or on your way back to D.C., stop in Old Town Alexandria (see below), where there are scores of restaurants. If you choose the *Spirit of Mount Vernon* (see above) as your mode of travel, you can eat at the onboard snack bar.

3 OLD TOWN ALEXANDRIA ★

6 miles S of Washington, D.C.

Everyone enjoys a visit to Old Town, the once-thriving colonial port on the western shore of the Potomac River. About 6 miles south of D.C., it's a picturesque parcel that invites walking, browsing, and people-watching. The area is steeped in history, with many fine restorations of 18th- and 19th-century buildings dotting its cobblestone streets. If possible, plan your visit for midweek. Some attractions are closed Monday, and weekends, the crowds are everywhere.

George Washington was a teenage surveyor's assistant when Alexandria became a city in 1749. The original 60 acres now comprise Old Town. During your visit, allow time to explore the waterfront and board a tall ship, watch artisans at work in the **Torpedo Factory Art Center,** and shop for up-to-date merchandise in old-style buildings.

The easiest way to get to Old Town is via Metro to the King Street station. Walk if you're in the mood (it's a mile and a half) or take the free King Street Trolley, daily from 11:30am to 10pm (departures are 10, 30, and 50 minutes past the hour at each terminus). It's only about a 6-mile trip by car. In rush hour, however, those 6 miles will feel like 60. Old Town's narrow streets become traffic-choked on weekends, and you won't need your car to sweep through the neighborhood anyway. *Most* of the sights are contained within 36 square blocks. But if you insist, take the Arlington Memorial or 14th Street Bridge to George Washington Memorial Parkway (which becomes Washington St.). Take a left at King Street, and continue 4 blocks to Ramsay House Visitor Center for a parking permit (good for 2 hr. at meters).

Make the **Ramsay House Visitors Center,** 221 King St. (✆ **703/838-5005;** www.visitalexandriava.com), your first stop. A faithful reconstruction of Alexandria's first house, it is open from 10am to 8pm (may close earlier in winter) every day except Thanksgiving, December 25, and January 1. Pick up brochures (available in several languages) and **Discovery Sheets,** outlining self-guided walking tours for families with kids in three age groups. (If your kids are old enough to appreciate such things, you can purchase admission tickets to historic homes and sights here).

Alexandria Colonial Tours (✆ **703/519-1749;** www.alexcolonialtours.com) offers several family-friendly tours. How's this for fun? Self-guided **Scavenger Hunts** take kids on **themed tours** through Old Town, lasting about an hour each. **Trail of the Pirates' Treasure** is geared to kids 4 to 7 (and an adult companion). Reservations are a must. The ever-popular hour-long **Ghost & Graveyard Tour** is offered Wednesday through Sunday evenings at 7:30pm from late September through November (sometimes twice on Friday and Saturday at 7:30 and 9pm) and is suitable for kids 10 and older. Call for prices and seasonal hours. From the Ramsay House Visitors Center, Old Town extends approximately 5 blocks north and south, and 3 blocks west and east (to the waterfront).

SPECIAL EVENTS

Inquire about special events, some of which require tickets, at the visitor center, or call the Alexandria Convention & Visitors Association ("The Fun Side of the Potomac"; ✆ **703/746-3300;** www.visitalexandriava.com). Additional contact info for a few events is listed below.

January

During Alexandria Restaurant Week (Jan 11–17, 2010; TBA 2011), diners enjoy a three-course prix-fixe dinner at select restaurants for $35 (a relative bargain; www.dinealexandriavA.com).

February

Festivities marking **George Washington's birthday** include the nation's largest George Washington Day parade, a 10k race, and special tours in honor of Alexandria's most famous former resident.

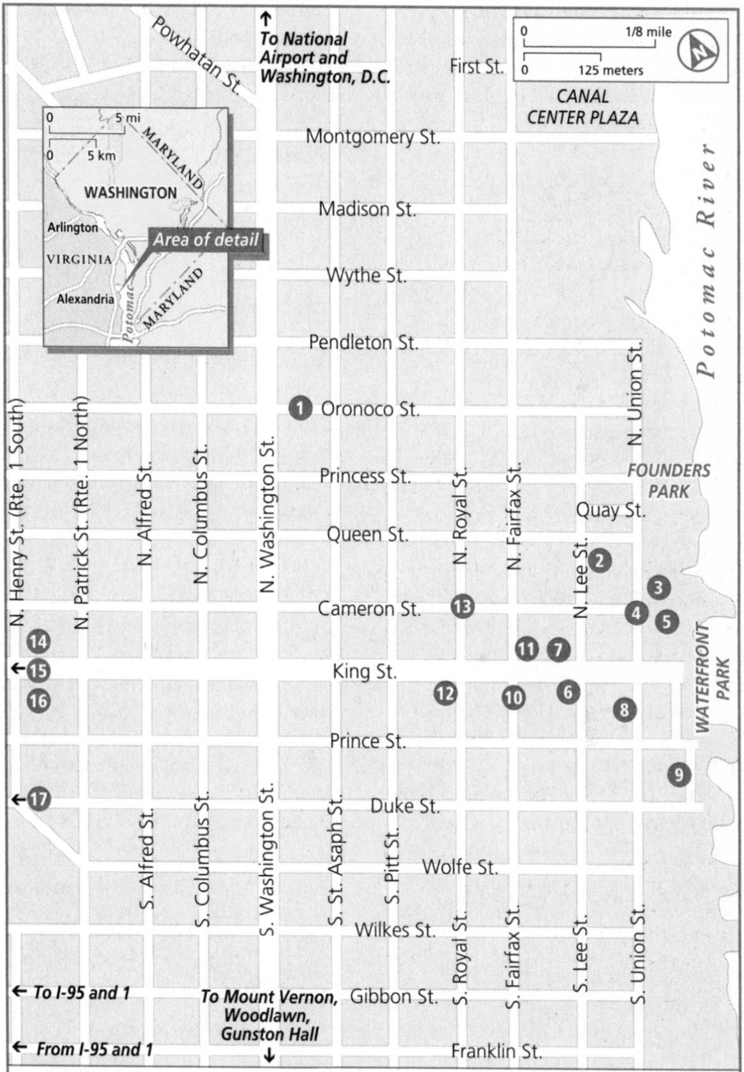

Alexandria City Dock **5**
Chadwicks **9**
Chart House **3**
Fort Ward Museum & Park **14**
Gadsby's Tavern Museum **13**
Generous George's Pizza **17**
Hard Times Café **16**
Hotel Monaco Alexandria **12**
King St. Metro **15**
Lee-Fendall House **1**
Monday's Child **2**
Ramsay House Visitors Center **11**
Riverboat Cruises **5**
Stabler-Leadbeater Apothecary Museum **10**
Torpedo Factory Art Center & Food Court **4**
Union Street Public House **8**
Warehouse Bar & Grill **7**
Why Not? **6**

MARCH

Alexandria's origin might be Scottish, but you wouldn't know it when **St. Patrick's Day** rolls around. The town grows greener than a field of shamrocks, and there's a parade and plenty of entertainment.

APRIL

Tours of historic homes and gardens are featured during the **Historic Garden** Tour one Saturday this month, 10am to 4pm.

MAY

From May to September, narrated Historic Walking Tours leave from the visitor center daily. Purchase your tickets right before the tour. The anecdotal narration about Alexandria's history interests most kids 8 and up.

JUNE

Don't miss the **Red Cross Waterfront Festival,** an outstanding family event held the second weekend of June. Boat rides and races, historic tall ships, children's games, entertainment, and food are featured at the harbor. The event draws around 100,000 people. A free shuttle ferries visitors to and from the King Street Metro station. For information, call ✆ **703/549-8300** (www.waterfrontfestival.org).

Drive or taxi over to **Fort Ward** (see listing below) on selected days for Civil War drills, concerts, and lectures.

JULY

Alexandria celebrates its founding and the nation's birthday on the second Saturday of the month at Orono Bay Park with music, activities, and fireworks set to the *1812 Overture,* played by the Alexandria Symphony Orchestra.

AUGUST

Gadsby's Tavern is the scene for music, entertainment, and food—1700s style—during **August Tavern Day Open House. Union Army Garrison Day** features authentically dressed military units in drills. Call the Fort Ward Museum and Historic Site (✆ **703/838-4848;** http://oha.ci.alexandria.va.us).

SEPTEMBER

Storytellers, jugglers, crafts, and people in period dress are featured at the **Colonial Fair.** Kids especially like the glass-blowing demonstration.

OCTOBER

The **Alexandria Festival of the Arts** takes place the second weekend of the month with artists' booths set up on King Street. Here's an excellent opportunity to mingle with the artists and purchase one-of-a-kind pieces.

Visit **Fall Harvest Family Days** at Mount Vernon—wagon rides, wheat treading (in the 16-sided barn), dancing demos (no disco, just 18th century-style), blacksmithing, beekeeping, and early-American games and music (www.visit.mountvernon.org).

Celebrate Halloween by taking your ghouls and boys (over the age of 10, please) to the 1-hour **Ghost & Graveyard Tours,** Sunday through Thursday at 7:30pm, twice on Friday and Saturday (7:30 and 9pm; ✆ **703/548-0100**).

NOVEMBER

Your kids might willingly accompany you to the **Historic Alexandria Antiques Show** (✆ **703/549-5811**), with dozens of dealers from several states showing their wares.

DECEMBER

The **Annual Scottish Christmas Walk** heralds the holiday season with bagpipers, a parade of the clans and Scottie dogs, puppet and magic shows, children's games, and, of course, food.

Visit historic Alexandria homes and a tavern, decked with holly and other seasonal decorations, during the **Old Town Christmas Candlelight Tour,** usually the second week of the month. **First Night Alexandria** is a family-focused, alcohol-free celebration held December 31, similar to those in cities across the country. About 50 acts perform on three dozen stages in and around Old Town. Admission for kids 12 and under is free; for adults, $15. Midnight fireworks at the pyramidal Masonic Temple usher in the new year. Afterward, free shuttle buses take revelers to area garages where parking is also free (provided you sport a First Night badge; www.firstnightalexandria.org).

EXPLORING OLD TOWN

Note: To get to Old Town sights and restaurants (unless otherwise noted), take Metro to King Street Station, then walk 1 to 1½ miles, or hop on the free King Street Trolley daily from 11:30am to 10pm. The trolley departs the Metro station and the Torpedo Factory (King Street and the Potomac River) every 10, 30, and 50 minutes past the hour.

Take younger children to **Waterfront Park,** where they can run loose, feed the pigeons, and look at the boats. Board the 125-foot schooner ***Alexandria,*** a classic Scandinavian cargo vessel berthed here. Tour the decks, the main salon, and a stateroom of this tall ship Saturday and Sunday from noon to 5pm. The tour is free, but donations are appreciated.

Bring your lunch, if you wish, and take a narrated cruise of the Alexandria Waterfront and beyond aboard the Potomac Riverboat Co.'s fleet (✆ **703/548-9000;** www.potomacriverboatco.com). The ***Miss Christin*** cruises from Old Town to Mount Vernon. The fare, which includes admission to Mount Vernon, is $38 for adults, $30 for seniors, and $20 for kids 6 to 10. Cruises cast off from the Alexandria City Marina, Union and Cameron streets, behind the Torpedo Factory. Departures are several times daily from May until early September, and weekends only in April, most of September, and all of October. Also see "Cruises," in chapter 8.

Everyone enjoys a stroll through Old Town's quaint streets to browse the area's enticing shops. Of special interest to kids are **Why Not?,** 200 King St., with children's clothing, some toys, books, and gift items; and **Monday's Child,** 218 N. Lee St., with kids' fancy clothing, shoes, and toys. ***Note:*** Some properties are closed on Monday.

Fort Ward Museum and Historic Site **Ages 2 and up.** This 45-acre park, a short drive from Old Town, boasts an extensive Civil War research library and is the site of one of the forts erected to defend Washington during the Civil War. Explore the fort, six mounted guns, and reproduction of an officer's hut. Civil War weapons and other war-related exhibits are displayed in the museum. Picnic areas surround the fort, and outdoor concerts are given every Thursday during the summer. Every year during **Living History Day** (usually the hottest day in Aug), visitors flock to the Civil War encampment, where uniformed regiments perform drills. Tell the kids: No battles allowed. Ask about soldier-led tours, Civil War artillery and signal corps demonstrations, and the Christmas Open House.

4301 W. Braddock Rd. ✆ **703/838-4848.** http://oha.alexanria.gov/fortward. Free admission; donations appreciated. Apr–Oct, Tues–Sat 9am–5pm; Nov–Mar Tues–Sat 10am–5pm Sun noon–5pm. Park open daily 9am–sunset. Metro: King St. or Braddock Rd. Directions: I-395 south to Seminary Rd. exit, left at 4th light (Alexandria Hospital/North Howard St.), and right at West Braddock Rd. to entrance on left. Free parking next to museum.

Gadsby's Tavern Museum ★ **Ages 10 and up.** For a meaningful Old Town experience, especially for history buffs, I suggest a stop at this tavern, visited by Washington,

Madison, and Jefferson (but not recently), which is now a museum of colonial furnishings and artifacts.

Notice that there are two buildings. The first was built around 1770 and operated as a tavern run by Mary Hawkins. The second building was built around 1792. John Gadsby took it over in 1796 and ran it as the City Hotel. In 1802, Gadsby took over the lease of the first building and turned it into a coffeehouse. Gadsby hosted two birthnight (birthday) balls for George Washington and his date, Martha, in 1798 and 1799. Contrary to popular opinion, GW never slept here. Today the ballroom is used for weddings and historic reenactments.

Half-hour tours are conducted 15 minutes before and after the hour. October through March, the first tour is at 11:15am and the last is at 3:15pm. April through October, the first tour is at 10:15am, and the last is at 4:15pm. Sunday tours are between 1:15 and 4:15pm year-round.

In the dormer room in the 1770 section of the museum, kids can try out the straw mattresses and rope beds. Very lumpy and scratchy! **Gadsby's Tavern,** on the newer building's first floor, is open for lunch and dinner, and offers half-price children's portions of some entrees. Strolling musicians entertain evenings and during Sunday brunch. Reservations are recommended (✆ **703/548-1288**).

134 N. Royal St. ✆ **703/838-4242.** www.gadsbystavern.org. Admission $5 adults, $3 ages 5–12, free for children under 5. $1-off coupon at website. Apr–Oct Tues–Sat 10am–5pm, Sun–Mon 1–5pm; Nov–Mar Wed–Sat 11am–4pm, Sun 1–4pm.

Lee-Fendall House **Ages 8 and up.** Many Lees have called this home over the years, but Robert E. never hung his clothes in the closet. Alexandria's only Victorian house museum was built in 1785. The original structure was renovated in 1850. Younger kids will probably like the antique dollhouse collection and boxwood garden better than the home, which serves as a museum of Lee furniture and memorabilia. The half-hour tour paints an impressionistic picture of family life in the Victorian age. Take time to enjoy the garden and lovely grounds. Lectures, educational programs, and special events are ongoing throughout the year. In February, families can learn about Valentine's Day in the 19th century (and make a valentine). Call for information on other special events; reservations are required.

614 Oronoco St. ✆ **703/548-1789.** www.leefendallhouse.org. Admission $5 adults, $3 ages 11–17, free for children 10 and under. Wed–Sat 10am–4pm; Sun 1–4pm.

Stabler-Leadbeater Apothecary Museum ★ Finds **Ages 8 and up.** The second floor was once the site of a large wholesale drug (no, not that kind) operation that processed herbs and medicines for 500 other apothecary shops. I find this one of Old Town's most interesting and unusual sites. View the hand-blown medicine bottles, medicinal herbs and potions, and bloodletting paraphernalia. I encourage you to take the docent-led tour given every 20 to 30 minutes. I bet you'll learn a lot. Pick up a souvenir or two in the small gift shop.

105–107 S. Fairfax St. ✆ **703/838-3852.** www.apothecarymuseum.org. Admission $5 adults, $3 ages 5–12, free under 5. Apr–Oct Sun–Mon 1–5pm, Tues–Sat 10am–5pm; Nov–Mar Wed–Sat 11am–4pm, Sun 1–4pm.

Torpedo Factory Art Center ★★★ Finds **Ages 4 and up.** This is a must-see for all ages, and there's a lot of history here, too. The Torpedo Factory was just that—a navy-built torpedo shell–case factory, around World War I. These days, the only thing fired up is the clay. Observe sculptors, painters, weavers, potters, and numerous other craftspeople and artisans doing their thing. You also get to talk to the artisans and buy their wares. Because most items are priced reasonably, it's an excellent opportunity to stock up on one-of-a-kind gifts. Kids seem most fascinated watching clay take shape on the potter's wheel. Self-guided tours, available at the information desk, will help you structure your visit. Alexandria Archaeology, in Studio 327 on the third floor, showcases many artifacts from the 10,000-year history of the land now called Alexandria. All the sensory overload may stimulate your appetite. If it does, go out the back door to the large food court with reasonably priced fare and indoor and outdoor seating.

105 N. Union St. ✆ **703/838-4565.** www.torpedofactory.org. Free admission. Torpedo Factory Fri–Wed 10am–6pm, Thurs 10am–9pm; Alexandria Archaeology and Research Lab Tues–Fri 10am–3pm, Sat 10am–5pm, Sun 1–5pm. Closed Thanksgiving, Dec 25, Jan 1, Easter, July 4.

WHERE TO STAY

Hotel Monaco Alexandria ★ Stay in the heart of Old Town at the Hotel Monaco Alexandria. Walk to all the historic sights, bike along the Potomac, cruise to Mount Vernon for the day (the marina is a few blocks away), and watch artists at work in the Torpedo Factory. Catch the free King Street Trolley to the King Street Metro and cross the river to D.C.'s attractions in less than a half-hour. At check-in, kids can borrow a goldfish to keep them company during their visit. And what child could resist Doggie Happy Hour, Tuesday and Thursday evenings 5 to 8pm, spring through fall? (For more information, see chapter 4, p. 72.)

480 King St., Alexandria, VA 22134. ✆ **703/549-6080.** www.monaco-alexandria.com. 241 units. $159–$599. Kids 17 and under stay free in parent's room. Crib complimentary. Rollaway $15. Extra person $25. AE, DC, DISC, MC V. Valet parking $20 (with in-out privileges). Metro: King St., then complimentary shuttle. **Amenities:** Restaurant; on-site fitness center; indoor pool (with an adult); 24-hr. room service. *In room:* LCD flatscreen TV, DVD player, hair dryer, Wi-Fi.

WHERE TO DINE

Very Expensive

Chart House ★ SEAFOOD/BEEF What distinguishes this Chart House is its prime waterfront location—almost like dining on a luxury yacht. Though expensive, the food is consistent, and the servers are professional and attentive. An ideal setting for a special-occasion dinner, the Chart House welcomes kids of all ages, although I don't want to dine there with anybody's kids who are under 6 or so. The fried coconut shrimp is sensational, and the Chart House also turns out tasty, if uninspired, fish and beef. Unlimited trips to the copious salad bar, with about 40 items, and served bread are both included in the main-course price. Or make a meal of salad for $16 (that's a lotta lettuce!). The kids' menu has six items for average price of $10. Or maybe they'll be happier munching an appetizer of coconut shrimp with plum dipping sauce.

1 Cameron St. ✆ **703/684-5080.** www.chart-house.com. High chairs, booster seats, kids' menu. Reservations recommended. Main dishes lunch $7–$17; most dinner items $15–$27; kids' menu items $9–$11; Sun brunch $26 (1 entree, unlimited salad, cocktail). AE, DC, DISC, MC, V. Lunch Mon–Sat 11:30am–3pm; dinner Mon–Thurs 4–10pm, Fri–Sat 4–11pm, Sun 2–10pm; brunch Sun 10:45am–2:15pm.

Moderate

Union Street Public House AMERICAN Try the burger topped with cheddar on toasted rye, ribs, hero sandwich, or a N'awlins-style po' boy at this lively and inviting pub known for consistently good food and service. More adventurous? Try the New Orleans–style fare (Creole chicken, gumbo, jambalaya, and the like) or one of the nightly specials. Sample one of the local beers while you're here. Little ones can order from the kids' menu, with six items from $3.95 (hot dog) to $6.95 (grilled salmon). Fish and chips are $5.95 and yummy.

121 S. Union St. ✆ **703/548-1785.** www.usphalexandria.com or www.unionstreetpublichouse.com. High chairs, booster seats, kids' menu. Reservations not accepted. Soups, salads, sandwiches, and small plates $8.95–$14; most entrees $14–$23. AE, DISC, MC, V. Mon–Thurs 11:30am–10:30pm; Fri–Sat 11:30am–11:30pm; Sun 11am–10:30pm (brunch served Sat–Sun 11am–3pm). Metro: King St., and then free King Street Trolley or 1-mile walk.

Warehouse Bar & Grill SEAFOOD/CAJUN This popular steak and seafood house, with its warm mahogany bar and cozy ambience, is known mainly for its seafood and Cajun cuisine. Often, it combines the two effectively, as in the crawfish and shrimp beignets (dinner appetizer for $8.95). Nobody's stopping you from getting two orders in lieu of an entree. The crab cakes and seafood sampler are highly recommended by friends living in Old Town. If you have room, dip into the bread pudding for dessert. Reasonably priced, surprisingly good steaks are on the menu too. The kids' menu features pint-size portions of pasta, chicken nuggets, or fish nuggets.

214 King St. ✆ **703/683-6868.** www.warehousebarandgrill.com. High chairs, booster seats, kids' menu. Reservations recommended. Lunch $6.95–$17; most dinner main courses $10–$20; kids' menu $5.95. AE, DISC, MC, V. Mon–Thurs 11am–10:30pm; Fri 11am–11pm; Sat 11am–11pm; Sun 10am–9:30pm (Sun brunch 10am–4pm).

Inexpensive

Chadwicks AMERICAN Eat in or carry out at good old reliable Chadwicks, a stylish pub opposite the waterfront, between Duke and Prince streets. The salads, burgers, homemade soups, and Sunday brunch—served until 4pm—are all standouts, and kids always receive VIP treatment. This isn't fine dining, but the food is above average and served with a smile. The servers are usually friendly and accommodating. Diners 10 and under can order from their own menu, which includes hamburger/cheeseburger, pizza, grilled cheese, chicken tenders, spaghetti, and PB&J. Kudos to Chadwicks for fighting inflation—the prices have changed little over the years. There's some street parking, and a pay lot ($5) is across the street.

203 S. Strand St. ✆ **703/836-4442.** www.chadwicksrestaurants.com. High chairs, booster seats, kids' menu. Reservations accepted. Most main courses $6.95–$17; kids' menu items $2.95–$4.95. AE, DISC, MC, V. Mon–Sat 11:30am–1am; Sun 10am–1am (Sun brunch 10am–4pm).

Eamonn's ("A Dublin Chipper") ★★ SEAFOOD This place is bare-bones casual and seating is limited. Having said that, the fish and chips (thick-cut French fries), served in a paper cone, are outstanding, hence the Eamonn's company prayer (posted everywhere), "Thanks be to cod." And here's incentive from the owners to get your kids to try the fried cod: "Get your wee ones to eat fish—and the cone is on us! You shape their world—don't forget their palates." Hear, hear! Diners can choose from among seven dipping sauces. I prefer the Marie Rose with fish. You'll find your own favorite. ***Note:*** Nothing but malt vinegar will do on the "chips." There are a handful of side dishes and, if you have room, fried candy bars (Snicker's, Milky Way, Mars). I don't think so.

728 King St. ✆ **703/299-8384.** www.eamonnsdublinchipper.com. High chairs. Main dishes: $4–$8. MC, V. Mon–Wed and Sun 1:30–10pm, or Thurs–Sat 1:30–11pm (or later).

Generous George's Pizza ★★ PIZZA/PASTA Although 2 miles from Old Town, GG's is a destination in itself, which has been pleasing families for more than 30 years. A foursome (but no starving teenagers) can enjoy superior pizza and a beverage in a supercasual, funky 1950s setting and escape for $45. And you won't have to "shush" your little pepperonis. If you're adventurous, try George's ingenious (and tasty) Specialty Pizzas, such as barbecue chicken or taco style ($12 for personal size, $18 for regular, $20 large). There is also a selection of sandwiches/subs, pasta dishes, and salads. The kids' menu, for children 11 and under, includes a personal pizza with two topping (kids can make it themselves Mon–Fri only), chicken dinosaurs (shaped chicken nuggets), and mac and cheese. All items are under $7.

3006 Duke St., Alexandria, VA (2 miles from Old Town). ✆ **703/370-4303.** www.generousgeorge.com. High chairs, booster seats, kids' menu, crayons, balloons. Reservations accepted for groups of 20 or more (call 24 hr. ahead). Most items $11–$19. AE, DISC, MC, V. Sun noon–10pm; Mon–Thurs 11am–10pm; Fri–Sat 11am–11pm. From Old Town, drive west on Duke St. 2 miles, or take a taxi.

Hard Times Cafe Value AMERICAN One could live on Hard Times' onion rings, but it'd be a shame not to leave room for the chili. Kids usually prefer the milder, tomatoey Cincinnati variety (with a hint of cinnamon) to the spicy, mostly meat Texas style. They may go for the Elvis sliders (three mini-cheeseburgers) or they can order PB&J, hot dogs, a burger, or spaghetti off the kids' menu. All come with fries or apple sauce and a drink (nonalcoholic). You can also get vegetarian chili and Terlingua Red Chili (Texas-style, with a kick). The chili burger is sensational. Ask about daily specials. There's limited metered street parking, as well as free evening and weekend parking in the rear lot. Don't forget the Hard Times when in Arlington, or Clarendon, Virginia; or Bethesda, Rockville, or College Park, Maryland.

1404 King St., at West St. ✆ **703/837-0050.** www.hardtimes.com. High chairs, booster seats, kids' menu. Reservations for 10 or more. Main courses $7–$9; kids' menu items $4. AE, MC, V. Sun–Thurs 11am–11pm; Fri–Sat 11am–midnight.

4 ANNAPOLIS

35 miles NE of Washington, D.C.

Set off with your crew for Annapolis, the jewel of the Chesapeake. Annapolis is less than an hour's drive—as the gull flies—from downtown D.C. (except at rush hour!). Judging by the upturn in the number of tourists the past several years, it's clear that the secret is out. Explore the many facets of this friendly, charming 18th-century seaport on the Severn River, dubbed "the sailing capital of the United States." Annapolis is home to the U.S. Naval Academy, the Maryland State House, St. John's College, beautifully maintained historic homes, fine shops and restaurants, and about 30,000 pleasure boats.

GETTING THERE

BY BUS Monday through Friday only, bus transport is available to the New Carrollton Metro and D.C. via Dillon's Bus Service (✆ **410/647-2321;** www.dillonbus.com). It's not much help to visitors, because the buses carry commuters from Annapolis to D.C. in the morning and make return trips between 3 to 7pm. But if you can figure a way to utilize this service, do so. It's a bargain. The D921 (D is for Dillon) bus carries passengers from Annapolis to New Carrolton Metro. One-way fare is $3.50. From Annapolis to D.C. take the D922 and D950—only $4.25 each way. Call or check the website for departure times and to find the most convenient departure point.

BY CAR Annapolis is easily reached from D.C. (in non-rush-hour traffic) in about 40 minutes by car via U.S. 50, an eastern extension of New York Avenue. If you leave D.C. after 3pm on a weekday, you'll be in the thick of commuter traffic. Don't make the trip on Friday after 1pm mid-May through September—beach traffic is horrendous. Take the Rowe (rhymes with *cow*) Boulevard exit off U.S. 50, and follow the signs to Annapolis.

PARKING ***Warning:*** Most street parking is at meters, in effect from 10am to 7:30pm daily. Don't cut corners. I think the meter maids hide under the cars and ticket as soon as the EXPIRED sign pops up. Some spaces are for 15 or 30 minutes only. If you can't find a metered spot near City Dock, or if you want to avoid the hassle of looking, try the Hillman Garage (closest to the downtown action), with entrances on Duke off Gloucester and Main streets, or Gott's Court Garage, Northwest Street off Church Circle (behind the West St. Visitor Center). Both cost $1 an hour with an $8 max. If you strike out, head back to the Navy–Marine Corps Stadium (Rowe Blvd. and Taylor Ave.), where all-day parking costs $5 (more during special events). The lot is open between 10am and 9pm (extended hours during special events). The Navy Blue Shuttle departs for the historic district on the hour and half hour (Mon–Fri 6:30am–8pm; Sat–Sun 10am–6pm). The State Shuttle (for state government workers but open to the general public) runs about every 5 minutes during peak rush hour times and every 15 minutes at other times (Mon–Fri *only* 6:30am–8pm). Both are free.

BY METRO Take the Metro Orange line to New Carrollton or the MARC commuter train from Union Station (Mon–Fri only) and then take a cab (about $50).

INFORMATION

Stock up on brochures at the (seasonal) City Dock Information Booth, in the heart of town. It's open daily April through early October from 9am to 5pm. But sometimes it's closed for no apparent reason. More comprehensive information on lodging, sights, dining, and special events is available from the walk-in Annapolis **Visitors Center** at 26 West Street, next to Gott's Garage, off Church Circle, open daily from 9am to 5pm (✆ **888/302-2852** or 410/280-0445; www.visitannapolis.org). A touch-screen video guide there dispenses information about sights and special events.

To see Annapolis from the Chesapeake Bay, stop at City Dock or call for information on **Watermark Cruises** (✆ **410/268-7600;** www.watermarkcruises.com). ***Hint:*** To see Annapolis at its least crowded, plan on arriving before noon, especially on weekends and May through October.

SPECIAL EVENTS

Note: For information on special events, call ✆ **410/280-0445** or visit www.visitannapolis.org unless otherwise noted.

January

Kids 10 and older (with a parent) can attend Opening Day of the **Maryland General Assembly** at the State House on State Circle (✆ **410/841-3810;** www.maryland.gov).

April

The Ballet Theatre of Maryland presents its spring **Dance Concert** at this time of the year (✆ **410/263-8289;** www.balletmaryland.org).

May

During **Commissioning Week,** in late May at the Naval Academy, the public is invited to dress parades and a stunning air show by the Blue Angels, celebrating the graduation of the Naval Academy's first class (seniors, to us civvies). Walk tall and bring bottled water, because it's usually hot (✆ **410/293-1000;** www.usna.edu). A festive **Memorial Day Parade** wends its way through the Historic District to the City Dock.

Annapolis Marriott Waterfront **17**
Annapolis Sailing School (Kidship) **16**
Banneker-Douglass Museum **3**
Cafe Normandie **8**
Cantler's **24**
Chesapeake Children's Museum **1**
Chick and Ruth's Delly **10**
City Dock **20**
Gotts Court Garage **2**
Governor's Mansion **7**
Helen Avalynne Tawes Garden **5**
Hillman Garage **2**
History Quest **13**
Jug Bay Wetlands Sanctuary **1**
Kunta Kinte Memorial **19**
Market House **15**
Maryland State House **9**
Navy-Marine Coprs Stadium **5**
Newman Street Playground **18**
Pirate Adventures on the Chesapeake **16**
St. Anne's Church **6**
St. Clair Wright History Center **14**
Scotlaur Inn **10**
Susan Campbell Park **22**
U.S. Naval Academy Visitors Center **23**
Visitors Center **4**
Visitor Information at City Dock **21**
Welcome Center **14**
William Paca House and Gardens **11**

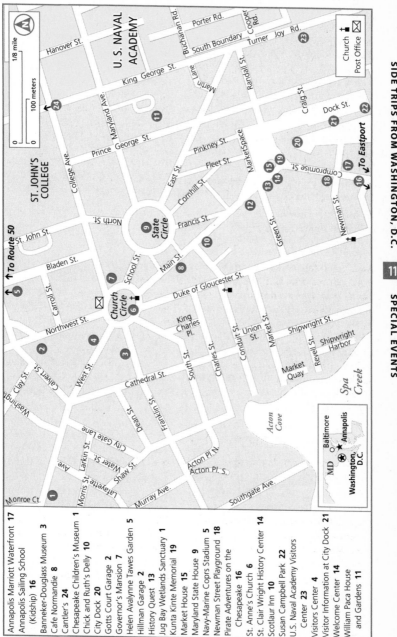

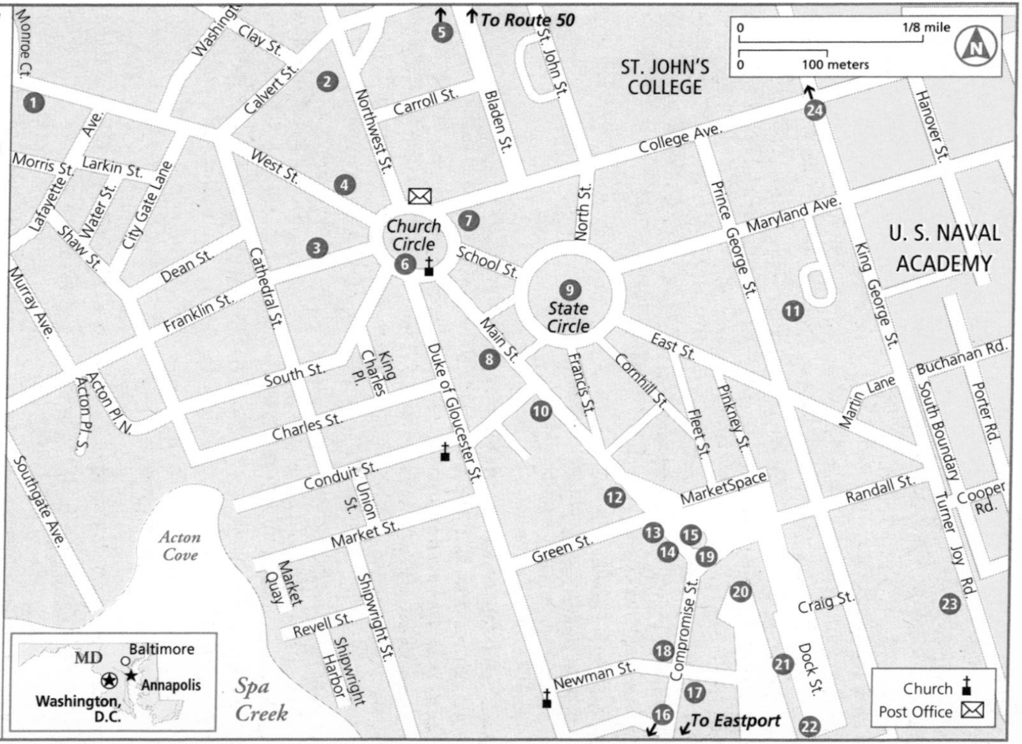

Bring lawn chairs or something soft to sit on, and enjoy the waterfront **Summer Serenade Concert Series** at City Dock, most Tuesday evenings at 7:30pm through mid-August (✆ **410/293-0263;** www.usna.edu). A **Fourth of July Celebration** with oodles of family fun takes place at City Dock and the Naval Academy. At 9:15pm, fireworks over the Severn River cap the Fourth.

August

Crab pickers by the bushel scuttle over to the **Rotary Crab Feast** (it's the world's largest crab feast), usually the first Friday night of the month, at the Navy–Marine Corps Stadium (✆ **443/951-0340;** www.annapolisrotary.com). The **Maryland Renaissance Festival** kicks off at the Anne Arundel County Fairgrounds in Crownsville (20 min. from downtown Annapolis) and runs through October (✆ **800/296-7304** or 410/266-7304; www.rennfest.com).

September

Navy football kicks off this month in the Navy–Marine Corps Stadium. Even when Navy loses, the games and halftime shows are colorful and inspiring. Your kids are sure to enjoy the march-on by the Brigade of Midshipmen before the game and the precision drills and entertainment at halftime (www.navysports.com). Come to the **Anne Arundel County Fair** at the county fairgrounds in Crownsville. Ages 16 and older cost $5, ages 6 to 15 is $2, 5 and under are free (✆ **410/923-3400;** www.aacountyfair.org).

October

The **U.S. Sailboat and Powerboat shows** draw boating enthusiasts from all over the world to City Dock on succeeding weeks (usually the second and third weeks, Thurs–Mon; ✆ **410/268-8828;** www.usboat.org). It's not for tiny tots, and strollers are discouraged. The **Ballet Theatre of Maryland,** a regional professional company, presents its annual fall performance at Maryland Hall for the Creative Arts (✆ **410/263-8289;** www.balletmaryland.org). The **Annapolis Symphony Orchestra Youth Concert** features works accessible to young people. Before the performance, players from the brass, wind, string, and percussion sections demonstrate the range of their instruments for little ears (✆ **410/263-0907;** www.annapolissymphony.org). The annual **Halloween Concert,** hosted by the Naval Academy, invites kids and adults to come in costume for a Halloween sampling of spooky organ selections and a light show at the Naval Academy Chapel (✆ **410/293-8497;** www.usna.edu).

November

The Saturday of Thanksgiving weekend, **Santa Claus** arrives (by boat, of course) at City Dock (✆ **410/280-0445**).

December

Treat your kids to a performance of *The Nutcracker* by the Ballet Theatre of Maryland (✆ **410/263-8289;** www.balletmaryland.org) or *The Messiah* by the Annapolis Chorale (✆ **410/263-1906;** www.annapolischorale.org), both at Maryland Hall for the Creative Arts. Colonial Players presents *A Christmas Carol* annually (✆ **410/268-7373;** www.cplayers.com). Enjoy a **Child's Colonial Christmas** at the London Town Publik House and Gardens in Edgewater (✆ **410/222-1919;** www.historiclondontown.com). Take part in the **Grand Illumination** at City Dock, where the community Christmas tree is lit and carolers serenade. Bundle up and go early to the **Christmas Lights Parade,** usually the second Saturday of the month, sponsored by the Eastport Yacht Club and visible from several spots in and around City Dock. Scores of local boaters spend months festooning their rigs with lights, greenery, and costumed mates (✆ **410/263-0415;** www.eastportyc.org). Bid adieu to the old year and welcome the new one at the alcohol-free, family-oriented **First Night Annapolis** celebration, featuring performances by musicians, mimes, choral groups, and dancers in storefronts and public buildings throughout downtown, at the Naval Academy, and at St. John's College. Special kids' entertainment starts at 3pm on New Year's Eve, and at midnight, fireworks light up the harbor. Adults and kids age 5 and older are $15 (www.newyearsannapolis.org).

EXPLORING ANNAPOLIS

Weekends and holidays, bench seats are scarce at **Susan Campbell Memorial Park,** fronting Ego Alley, Spa Creek, and the Chesapeake Bay. Even so, it's a great place to stroll and enjoy the panoramic view of the harbor and beyond. Plan your day as pleasure craft parade up Ego Alley. A ceremony commemorating the arrival of *Roots* author Alex Haley's ancestor, Kunta Kinte, aboard the slave ship *Lord Ligonier* on September 29, 1767, is held annually at City Dock, where there's a life-size statue of Mr. Haley reading a book to three children. Along the adjacent seawall, plaques contain quotes from *Roots.* Take a minute or two and read the powerful messages.

Despite a small-town population of 36,000, Annapolis encompasses 16 miles of waterfront. The views from the water are awesome, so board one of the **cruise boats** or water taxis berthed at the dock; or **learn to sail**—it's a breeze at one of the area's sailing schools. Sightseeing, shopping, and restaurants are all an easy walk from the heart of the historic district.

For an introduction to "the Sailing Capital of the U.S.," **Discover Annapolis Tours** offers visitors 350 years of history and architecture in an hour-long tour aboard minibuses with big windows. With little ones (and old ones), this is an easy way to view the sights. Bring your camera for the stop at Governor Ritchie Overlook, with its sweeping views of the Severn River and Naval Academy. Tours depart from the Visitors Center, 26 West Street (half a block from St. Anne's Church), several times a day. The cost is $18 for adults, $9 for kids 11 to 15, $3 for kids 3 to 10, and free for kids 2 and under. Call for departure times (✆ **410/626-6000;** www.discover-annapolis.com).

Take an **audio tour** (lasting about 1 hr. and 15 min.), narrated by Walter Cronkite, or reserve a specialized tour at History Quest, 99 Main St. (✆ **410/267-6656**). You also can take an **African-American Heritage** tour, with narrative about the African-American experience in Annapolis. For a **guided walking tour** of the historic district, State House, U.S. Naval Academy, and St. John's College, led by knowledgeable tour leaders in period dress, call the **Historic Annapolis Foundation** (✆ **410/267-7619;** www.annapolis.org) or **Three Centuries Tours** (✆ **410/263-5401;** www.annapolis-tours.com).

Hike up **Main Street** from City Dock to Church Circle. Regrettably, national chains have moved in with a vengeance, forcing many mom-and-pop stores to bite the dust. Stop at **History Quest,** maintained by the **Historic Annapolis Foundation,** at 99 Main St. (✆ **410/267-6656;** www.annapolis.org). Check out the free museum and watch the video on the second floor for an overview of Maryland's state capital—history, architecture, and cultural attractions. You can also purchase tickets here for several tours.

A. L. Goodies is still at 100 Main St. for souvenirs, T-shirts, fudge (skip the cookies—they look better than they taste), and a large and entertaining greeting-card selection (on the second floor). **Avoca Handweavers,** at 141 Main St., stocks beautiful woolens and gifts from the British Isles for the whole family. The clan plaid trousers and kilts and hand-knit sweaters for kids are hard to resist. **Snyder's Bootery,** facing Conduit Street, has a huge selection of boat shoes (or it will order your size). Across from Snyder's is **Chick and Ruth's Delly,** an Annapolis institution since the 1950s and open nearly round the clock (see "Where to Dine," later in this section).

Encircling the Maryland State House on **State Circle** are some of the town's premier shops and galleries, often overlooked by visitors. At **Annapolis Pottery,** where browsers can catch potters at work, a dazzling assortment of attractive, well-priced dishes and accessories is for sale, and special orders are taken. Another gem is the **Maryland Federation of Art Gallery,** housed in a restored building dating from 1840, at 18 State Circle. Solo and small-group exhibits of multimedia works change every 4 weeks and include three national shows per year.

Maryland Avenue, with its many home-design and accessory boutiques, antique shops, and galleries, is more reminiscent of "old" Annapolis and, therefore, worthy of investigation. The commercial section runs from State Circle to Prince George Street.

KidShip Sailing School **Ages 8 and up.** Before you go overboard for sailing, this is a good place to start. KidShip is part of the Annapolis Sailing School (in business for more than 40 years and the largest sailing school in the country). In 2 days of concentrated instruction, alternating between the classroom and the school's fleet of 24-foot Rainbow sloops, families can learn enough to skipper a small boat. June through August, **KidShip** offers beginning sailing instruction for kids 8 to 15 in 2-day weekend (Sat–Sun 9am–4pm) and 5-day (half- and full-day) courses. Intermediate and advanced courses are available too. Call or visit the website for current prices.

601 6th St. ✆ **800/638-9192** or 410/267-7205. www.annapolissailing.com. Ask about packages with hotel room.

Banneker Douglass Museum **Ages 8 and up.** This little-known museum, housed in a Victorian Gothic church built in 1874 by former slaves, is located off Church Circle. Anyone interested in American history and the African-American experience should take a few minutes to visit the edifice, named for Frederick Douglass (abolitionist, orator, author and activist) and Benjamin Banneker (1731–1806), an astronomer, farmer, surveyor, almanac writer, and mathematician who is best known for assisting Maj. Andrew Ellicott, the surveyor chosen by President George Washington, to establish the boundaries of the District of Columbia in 1791. A permanent exhibit with interactive displays showcases the contributions of Maryland's most important African Americans: Banneker, Douglass, Harriet Tubman, and Thurgood Marshall. Changing exhibits are devoted to African-American history in Maryland.

84 Franklin St. ✆ **410/216-6180.** www.bdmuseum.org. Free admission. Tues–Sat 10am–4pm.

Chesapeake Children's Museum **Ages 2–10.** I hate to be the one to drag your family away from the waterfront, but this hands-on museum, the brainchild of executive director Debbie Wood several years ago, is a worthwhile detour for those traveling with young children, especially preschoolers. The building is on 5½ acres of parkland and lies on Spa Creek Trail. Nature walks make use of the woodland and wetland habitats.

Indoors, youngsters try on foul-weather gear and climb aboard an anchored minitug, peer into an osprey nest, fashion clay molds of duck tracks, or try on costumes and entertain on a pint-size stage. Many are content to watch and touch the diamondback terrapins or role-play in the dental office.

The Minnows room, for infants and toddlers, is filled with soft, safe playthings. The museum holds story times, special events, classes in art and movement, and talks for parents on child-related topics. ***Note:*** Children must be accompanied by an adult.

25 Silopanna Rd. ✆ **410/990-1993.** www.theccm.org. Admission $3, free for children under 1. Open Thurs–Tues 10am–4pm year round; Wed for groups only. Directions: Rte. 50 east to exit 22/Aris T. Allen Blvd./Rte. 665, which flows into Forest Dr.; go left at 4th light, Hilltop Lane; turn left at next light, Spa Rd.; go right at Silopanna Rd., and left at stop sign into lot.

Watermark Cruises **Ages 2 and up.** If you're first-timers, the 40-minute narrated cruise on the double-decked *Harbour Queen* provides a pleasing introduction to the waterfront sights, including the Bay Bridge and Naval Academy. The cruise operates late March through November (weather permitting) with several departures daily, more on weekends. The *Miss Anne* (actually, there are two *Miss Annes!*) tours Spa Creek from April through October, with several departures daily at quarter of and quarter after the hour. Drinks and snacks are available on board all boats.

Special events, offered a few times a season, include cruises to three historic lighthouses—Thomas Point, Sandy Point, and Baltimore Harbor. Reservations are required. Watermark also arranges private parties.

City Dock. ✆ **410/268-7600.** www.watermarkcruises.com. $12 adults, $5 kids 3–11, free 2 and under. Daily Apr–Oct dawn–dusk; Mar and Nov–Dec, weather permitting.

Jug Bay Wetlands Sanctuary Finds **Ages 4 and up.** This is an incredible spot for anyone with an interest in the natural world and/or Chesapeake Bay ecology. It's about a half-hour from Annapolis, but it's well worth the ride. At seven environmentally themed workstations in the visitor-friendly laboratory, hands-on activities encourage youngsters to learn about the wetlands ecosystem.

Most weekends, Jug Bay offers seasonal outdoor workshops—hiking, birding, and such—on 7 miles of wetlands paths. Nature lectures (many of which are appropriate for kids with their families) are also given most Saturdays and Sundays. Summer Science Camps for kids in 5th through 12th grades are always well attended. Please note that Jug Bay is open on a limited basis by reservation only. No reservation is required to hike the Glendening Nature Preserve, open daily 9am to 5pm; closed Sunday December to February.

1361 Wrighton Rd., Lothian. ✆ **410/741-9330.** www.jugbay.org. Admission $5 adults, 3 seniors and under age 18. By reservation only Wed and Sat–Sun (except Sun Dec–Feb) 9am–5pm. Directions from D.C.: Take the Beltway to Rte. 4 east/south, 11 miles to right at Plummer Lane, then right on Wrighton Rd.; go half a mile to entrance on left. Call or check the website for directions from Annapolis. Free on-site parking.

Maryland Hall for the Creative Arts **Ages 6 and up.** Maryland Hall, which offers year-round workshops in the fine arts as well as demonstrations, exhibits, and performances, is less than a 10-minute ride from downtown Annapolis. The Annapolis Symphony (✆ **410/269-1132**), Ballet Theatre of Maryland, and Annapolis Youth Orchestra (once a school) all make their home here. You can catch each of them several times annually.

801 Chase St. ✆ **410/263-5544.** www.mdhallarts.org. Admission varies. Directions: Rte. 50 east to Rowe Blvd. exit., turn right at bottom of ramp, right at 2nd light (Taylor Ave.); proceed to traffic circle (West St.), go a third of the way around, turn right on Spa Rd., and take 1st left (Greenfield).

Maryland State House **Ages 8 and up.** The oldest state capitol in continuous legislative use served as the nation's capitol from November 1783 to June 1784. In this building, George Washington resigned his commission in 1783, and the Treaty of Paris was ratified. The stained-glass skylights are by Louis Comfort Tiffany. Guided half-hour tours are scheduled between 9am and 5pm daily.

State Circle. ✆ **410/974-3400.** www.mdarchives.state.md.us. Free admission. Mon–Fri 9am–5pm, Sat–Sun 10am–4pm.

Newman Street Playground ★ **Ages 2 and up.** Local school kids helped plan these humongous wooden play structures. You can picnic here or seek shade and rest during your tour of Annapolis. Weekdays, September to June, during school hours, the park fills with students from the elementary school that backs onto the park.

Newman and Compromise sts. (Marriott side of City Dock). Free admission. Daily during daylight hours.

William Paca House and Gardens (Moments) **Ages 6 and up.** William Paca, a signer of the Declaration of Independence and governor of Maryland during the Revolution, built this five-part Georgian mansion between 1763 and 1765. In the early 1900s, the house became a hostelry for legislators and visitors to the U.S. Naval Academy. When the wrecker's ball threatened in 1965, the Historic Annapolis Foundation stepped in and restored the house and 2-acre garden to their former grandeur. Older kids generally find the house of interest, and *everyone* delights in the garden, with its intricate terraces and waterway. The flower enclosure is abloom from March to November. A self-guided audio tour costs $1. Or join a guided tour, several times a day. Metered street parking is nearby; the Hillman Garage (Main St.) is within walking distance. Save $1 on each admission to a Historic Annapolis property and on audio tours of Annapolis by reserving online.

186 Prince George St. ✆ **410/990-4543.** www.annapolis.org. Adults $8, seniors $7, kids 6–17 $5, 5 and under free ($1 discount online). Mon–Sat 10:30am–5pm; Sun 12:30–5pm. Abbreviated winter hours. Closed Thanksgiving, Dec 24–25.

Pirate Adventures on the Chesapeake **Ages 2 and up.** Pirate Crabby welcomes kids boarding the 35-foot *Sea Gypsy IV* with a booming "Hello, mates!" All summer and weekends spring and fall, the 75-minute "pirate" cruise plies Annapolis Harbor several times daily, weather permitting. Kids dress up in pirate garb, listen to seafaring songs, and search for treasure buried beneath a well-marked buoy. The highlight for most is an encounter with a pirate. That's when the little tars get to fire the hydraulic water cannons. Without even knowing it, children learn something about map reading, local ecology, pirates, and commerce on the Chesapeake. Preschoolers through third graders especially go overboard for this splashy cruise.

Annapolis City Marina, Severn Ave. (behind Carrol's Creek restaurant). ✆ **410/263-0002.** www.chesapeakepirates.com. $18 for 3 and over, $10 2 and under. Discounts for groups of 30 or more. Reservations required. Directions: From downtown Annapolis, cross Spa Creek bridge, turn left at Severn Ave., go through STOP sign to left at 3rd St. Park in lot next to Sea Gypsy berth. Overflow parking at Annapolis City Marina parking lot, 410 Severn Ave. at 4th St., then walk 1 block to Sea Gypsy.

Helen Avalynne Tawes Garden ★ **All ages.** This delightful 6-acre garden depicts Maryland's varied landscape, from the Appalachians in the western part of the state to the ocean beaches of the Eastern Shore. It reminds us of the necessity to value and conserve our precious natural resources.

Weekdays, pick up a booklet at the garden display in the lobby, and check out the great blue heron and Baltimore oriole (the state bird, not a baseball player) before beginning your walk. More than likely, the most interesting thing to younger kids will be the Texture, Taste, and Fragrance Garden, which invites visitors to "taste and see if you can identify" certain herbs. I'm partial to the gazebo and nearby pond. Monday to Friday, the gift shop is open 9am to 3pm, and the cafeteria is open 7:30am to 3pm.

Behind Department of Natural Resources, 580 Taylor Ave., at Rowe Blvd. (across from the stadium). ✆ **410/260-8189.** www.dnr.state.md.us/publiclands/tawesgarden.html. Free admission. Garden daily dawn–dusk; lobby exhibits Mon–Fri 8am–5pm (closed holidays).

U.S. Naval Academy ★ **Ages 6 and up.** Before visiting, check security restrictions via phone or online. It's only a 5-minute walk from City Dock in downtown Annapolis to the Naval Academy, founded in 1845. Hours change seasonally for the hour-long guided walking tour that departs from the Armel-Leftwich Visitor Center adjacent to the Halsey Field House inside Gate 1.

Try to see the short film *To Lead and to Serve* before you begin your tour. The gift shop bears checking out, as does the view of downtown from the riverfront promenade behind the building. Depending on security restrictions, you may be able to visit several buildings on your own. In **Lejeune Hall,** across from the visitor center, you'll find cases of trophies and photographs of the academy's athletic achievements. Close by is **Dahlgren Hall,** where a chrome yellow biplane "flies" from the ceiling. The navy's ice hockey team plays here. Pick up a snack at the **Dry Dock Restaurant** (✆ **410/293-2873**), open from 8am to 9pm.

It's a hop, skip, and jump across the Yard, as the academy grounds are called, to the awesome **Navy Chapel** and **John Paul Jones's crypt.** Nearby is the Naval Academy Museum, **Preble Hall** (✆ **410/293-2108**), filled with 200 years of naval art and artifacts. The ground-floor **Gallery of Ships** delights all ages. Many of the ships are original builder's models. The museum is open Monday to Saturday, 9am to 5pm; Sunday 11am to 5pm. From the seawall at the **Robert Crown Sailing Center,** you might see boatloads of plebes learning to sail. Most will never board a sailboat at any other time in their lives, yet they are all required to learn the basics.

In Bancroft Hall, the "dormitory" for all 4,300 midshipmen, tomorrow's officers chow down on 2,000 pounds of meat and 7,000 quarts of milk daily. If you're touring on your own, arrive at Bancroft Hall at noon (weekdays, weather permitting, and at the discretion of the Academy) for **noon meal formation** ★—in my mind, the highlight of an academy visit. Would your kids be willing to line up like this for their lunch? Athletic teams practice in the afternoon on the fields behind Bancroft. Stroll the beautiful grounds, and walk along the **Dewey seawall** for a wide-angle view of the Chesapeake Bay. In season, catch a band concert in the gazebo. After **Commissioning Week,** in late May or early June, it's fun to watch the procession of weddings (one an hour!) from the lawn opposite the chapel.

Many athletic events are free and open to the public. For information and tickets, call the **Naval Academy Athletic Association** (✆ **800/US-4-NAVY** [874-6289]; www.navysports.com).

Please note that everyone 16 and over must have a photo ID to be admitted to the U.S. Naval Academy grounds.

Visitor Gate at foot of King George St. ✆ **410/293-1000.** www.usna.edu. www.navyonline.com. Free self-guided tour; guided tour $9 adults, $8 seniors (62 and older), $7 for children in 1st–12th grades, free for children under 1st grade. Visitor center daily Mar–Dec 9am–5pm; Jan–Feb 9am–4pm. Tour hours vary seasonally. Call ahead. Closed Thanksgiving, Dec 25, Jan 1. Group tours by appointment year-round. Directions: Rte. 50 east to Rowe Blvd. exit.; proceed on Rowe about 1 mile to left at College Ave., and right at King George St. to Gate 1. Limited 2-hr. street parking on adjacent streets and at City Dock.

WHERE TO STAY

If you're planning an overnight stay, take your pick of historic inns, B&Bs, and luxury hotels. Hotels outside the historic district often offer complimentary shuttle service. For a brochure describing B&Bs in Annapolis, write the **Annapolis Association of Licensed Bed and Breakfast Owners,** P.O. Box 744, Annapolis, MD 21404, or check out the **Annapolis, Maryland Bed and Breakfasts** website, www.azinet.com/annaarea.html.

Expensive

Annapolis Marriott Waterfront ★ Overlooking the harbor and Spa Creek, the Marriott enjoys a prime downtown location, as does **Pusser's Landing** restaurant and dockside bar/lounge. A children's menu at lunch and dinner offers a handful of reasonably priced items, or the kids can fill up on one of the light-fare offerings. Scores of Annapolis eateries (not to mention shopping and sightseeing) are within a few blocks. Room service is available, and the hotel has an exercise room with fitness equipment. The second floor is a smoking floor. All other floors are nonsmoking. Two rooms and the top-floor suite have Jacuzzis. Regrettably, the hotel paved over the swimming pool several years ago to gain parking. When there are big doings at the Naval Academy and during October's boat shows, this place is booked a year ahead.

80 Compromise St., Annapolis, MD 21401. ✆ **800/336-0072** or 410/268-7555. www.annapolismarriott.com. 150 units. $249–$449 (waterfront suite) single or double. Cribs and rollaways free. AE, DISC, MC, V. Ask about special packages and promotions. Valet parking $19 per 24-hr. period (in-out privileges). **Amenities:** Restaurant; 2 bars; concierge (weekends only); basic fitness center; room service (breakfast and dinner only). *In room:* A/C, TV, hair dryer, high-speed Internet and Wi-Fi (fee).

Moderate

Scotlaur Inn Roll out of bed onto Main Street—literally! Stay at what could be the world's only "Bed and Bagel," and enjoy a full complimentary breakfast in Chick and Ruth's Delly downstairs. The 10 distinctive rooms in the family-owned and -operated establishment all have private bathrooms (some with shower only, so be sure to ask if you must have a tub) and modem hookups. The rooms are small, but the Victorian furnishings, antique bookcases and books, and dynamite location more than compensate. They haven't built structures with such thick walls in many moons. When you go downstairs for breakfast, ask Ted to do magic tricks for your kids. You won't have to ask twice.

165 Main St., Annapolis, MD 21401. ✆ **410/268-5665.** www.scotlaurinn.com. 10 units. $95–$120 per room (higher during special events). Cribs free; rollaways $15 per night. Ask about special winter rates. MC, V. Garage parking $10 per night (coupon for 1-time 50% discount). Pets accepted, with advance notice. **Amenities:** Restaurant. *In room:* A/C, TV/VCR, Wi-Fi, hair dryer.

WHERE TO DINE

Annapolis has scores of restaurants in all price ranges. For a recommendation, ask a shopkeeper or local (usually dressed more casually then visitors; almost always in boat shoes or walking shoes).

Moderate

Cafe Normandie COUNTRY FRENCH I would have no problem dining at this cozy, plant-filled bistro several times a week. Don't try all these at one sitting, but I can personally recommend the cream of crab soup, French onion soup, Caesar salad (with grilled chicken or blackened fish), veal and fish main courses, sautéed soft-shell crabs, and crepes (seafood or ratatouille). Breakfast is served Saturday and Sunday from 9am to noon. Wrap up with a fruit- or ice cream–filled crepe. If your kids are finicky, they're bound to dig the crepes.

185 Main St. ✆ **410/280-6470.** www.restaurant.com. High chairs, booster seats. Reservations recommended. Lunch and dinner main courses $9.95–$26. AE, MC, V. Mon–Fri 11am–11pm; Sat–Sun 9am–11pm.

Cantler's Riverside Inn ★★ SEAFOOD You can't visit Annapolis and not go to Cantler's. It'd be a crime not to dig into the local delicacy, steamed Maryland blue crabs (in season May–Oct), at this down-home restaurant on Mill Creek. Be prepared: The harvest the past few years has approached pitiful, and market prices averaged $100 a dozen for jumbos in 2009. Pitiful! When they're that expensive, I order the lump crab cake. Grab a seat on the deck, covered patio, or inside. Get here early on the weekends—that means by noon for lunch and before 5pm for dinner if you don't want a horrible wait. The crabs and steamed clams (when available) are the best around. I also recommend the vegetable crab soup, and soft-shell or crab-cake sandwich. The kitchen also serves up fried chicken and steak for non–crab eaters. The kids' menu has nine sandwiches and main dishes, all of which come with a vegetable and fruit or fries. ***Note:*** The steamed crabs are heavily doused with spicy Old Bay seasoning. You may want to scrape some off before the little ones dig in.

Take the kids underneath the restaurant for a peek into the shedding boxes. This is where the Maryland blue crabs do their striptease (with no privacy) to become the sought-after delicacy, soft-shell crabs. Call for directions—it's about a 10-minute ride from downtown Annapolis.

458 Forest Beach Rd. ✆ **410/757-1311.** www.cantlers.com. High chairs, booster seats. Reservations not accepted Fri–Sun; accepted for groups of 10 or more Mon–Thurs. Most items $10–$26 (not including crabs). AE, DC, MC, V. Sun–Thurs 11am–11pm; Fri–Sat 11am–midnight.

Inexpensive

Chick & Ruth's Delly (Finds) DELI/AMERICAN The **Dellyland Delight kids' menu** (for those 10 and under) offers breakfast fare and sandwiches with potato chips or french fries. Of course, you'll treat them to one of the oversize sodas or shakes that they won't be able to finish (that's where you come in). I love the well-seasoned "delly" (home) fries on the breakfast platters, which are served all day. The 44 tasty sandwiches (try the Main Street, if you can't decide) are named for Maryland pols and locals. You can also get everything from a hot dog or hamburger to a Caesar salad and homemade vegetable crab soup. You gotta love the funky decor, fountain treats, and cheeky servers at this friendly eatery that has served four generations of Annapolitans. And the servers don't seem to mind cleaning up after little ones. Join the locals reciting the Pledge of Allegiance weekdays at 8:30am and weekends at 9:30am.

165 Main St. ✆ **410/269-6737.** www.chickandruths.com. High chairs, booster seats, kids' menu. Reservations not accepted. Most items $7–$9; kids' menu items $4–$6 MC, V. Sun–Thurs 6:30am–11:30pm; Fri–Sat 6:30am–12:30am. Closed Thanksgiving, Dec 25, and Dec 31.

Kilwin's ★ ICE CREAM & CANDY I discovered Kilwin's in Sarasota many years ago. Imagine my joy when a branch opened a few years back on Main Street, just 3 miles from my home and office. Come here for a single-scoop cone, a hot fudge sundae (regular size or in a huge waffle cone for gluttons), homemade fudge, or another of Kilwin's fantastic candies. My children and grandkids seem to have inherited the dominant family gene for loving sweets. But we all need dairy products in our diets. If you're gonna splurge, might as well do it on the real thing. (I expect to pack on 10 or more pounds before writing the next edition of this book.)

126 Main St. ✆ **410/263-2601.** www.kilwins.com. Most items under $6. AE, DISC, MC, V. Daily 10am–10pm.

5 BALTIMORE

38 miles NE of Washington, D.C.

Where to start? Only an hour's drive or 40-minute train ride from D.C., Charm City offers families an abundance of sights and experiences. You could easily spend several days in Baltimore and leave begging for more. Birthplace of Babe Ruth, H. L. Mencken, Cal Ripken, and our national anthem, the city is enlivened by its rich ethnic heritage. Baltimore is also a big sports town, supporting both the Baltimore Ravens (NFL football) and Orioles baseball.

The **Inner Harbor,** a revitalized complex of businesses, sightseeing attractions, shops, restaurants, and hotels built around the city's natural harbor, is always abuzz. The Baltimore Orioles play in Oriole Park at Camden Yards (see "Exploring Baltimore," later in this section), frequently to sellout crowds. The Baltimore Ravens play at PSI Stadium next to Oriole Park.

During your visit, try steamed blue crabs, harvested spring through fall from the Chesapeake Bay. When the local pickin's are slim, they're brought in from the Carolinas and Gulf states. Baltimore also boasts the best corned beef between New York City and Miami Beach and multiethnic neighborhoods and restaurants.

GETTING THERE

BY BUS Greyhound (✆ **800/231-2222**) provides frequent service between the Washington bus terminal at 1st and L streets NE and 2110 Haines St., in Baltimore. The current fare Monday through Thursday is $11 one-way and $22 round-trip; Friday through Sunday $13 one-way, $24 round-trip. Children 2 through 11 pay half price (one child per paying adult). There are many different fares, for example: what day of week you travel, refundable versus nonrefundable tickets, and so on.

BY CAR To get to Baltimore from D.C., take I-95 to I-395 north to Pratt Street; make a right and another right at President Street. You'll find many parking lots near the harbor.

BY TRAIN Frequent daily train service via Amtrak (✆ **800/USA-RAIL** [872-7245]) is available between Washington's Union Station and Baltimore's Penn Station. Fare for a family of four (two adults and two kids 2–15) is $102 round-trip, reserved coach. The trip takes about 40 minutes. Baltimore's Penn Station is a short taxi ride from the Inner Harbor.

Less expensive than Amtrak is the **MARC commuter train, Penn Line** (✆ **800/325-RAIL** [7245]; www.mtamaryland.com). It's a glorified subway car, but the price recommends it. The fare from D.C.'s Union Station to Baltimore's Penn Station is only $7 per adult one-way, free for up to two kids 5 and under with each paying adult (additional children pay full fare), but bear in mind that it operates weekdays only.

INFORMATION

For maps and information on sightseeing and walking tours, contact the **Baltimore Area Convention and Visitors Association,** 401 Light St., Baltimore, MD 21202 (✆ **800/282-6632**; www.baltimore.org). A **visitor center** is located at 401 Light St. (at E. Conway St.) at the Inner Harbor.

Getting around the harbor (the National Aquarium, Fells Point, Fort McHenry, the American Visionary Art Museum, Federal Hill, Port Discovery, and Little Italy) is easily

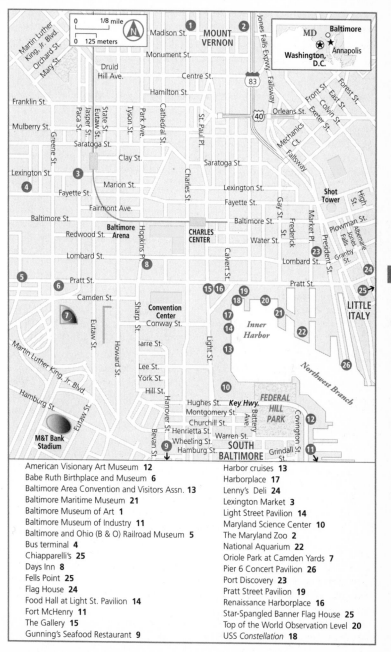

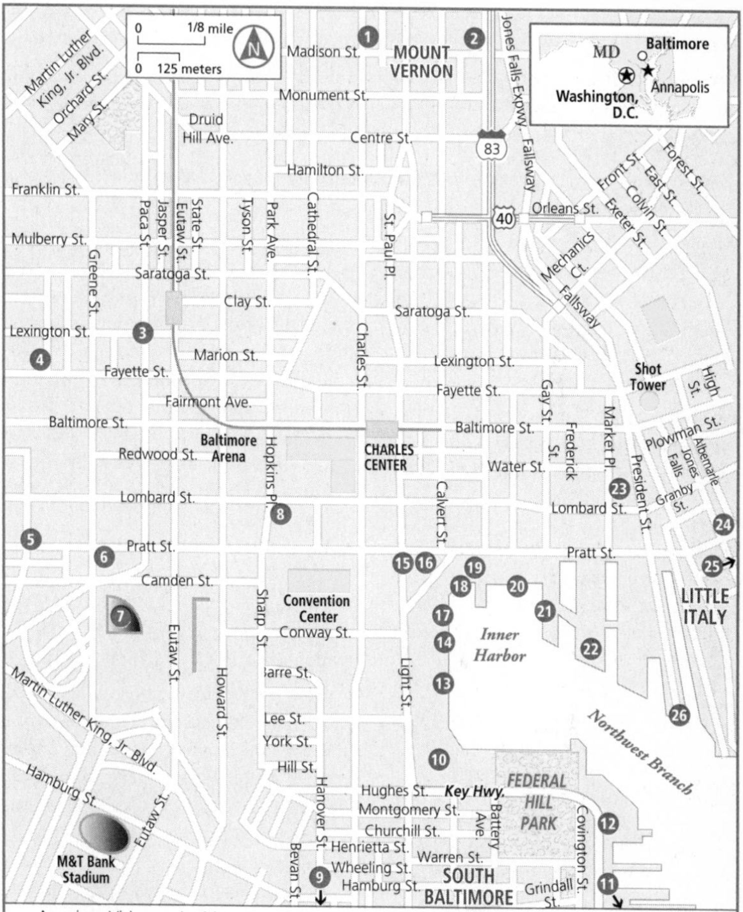

American Visionary Art Museum **12**
Babe Ruth Birthplace and Museum **6**
Baltimore Area Convention and Visitors Assn. **13**
Baltimore Maritime Museum **21**
Baltimore Museum of Art **1**
Baltimore Museum of Industry **11**
Baltimore and Ohio (B & O) Railroad Museum **5**
Bus terminal **4**
Chiapparelli's **25**
Days Inn **8**
Fells Point **25**
Flag House **24**
Food Hall at Light St. Pavilion **14**
Fort McHenry **11**
The Gallery **15**
Gunning's Seafood Restaurant **9**
Harbor cruises **13**
Harborplace **17**
Lenny's Deli **24**
Lexington Market **3**
Light Street Pavilion **14**
Maryland Science Center **10**
The Maryland Zoo **2**
National Aquarium **22**
Oriole Park at Camden Yards **7**
Pier 6 Concert Pavilion **26**
Port Discovery **23**
Pratt Street Pavilion **19**
Renaissance Harborplace **16**
Star-Spangled Banner Flag House **25**
Top of the World Observation Level **20**
USS *Constellation* **18**

done by water taxi. The 11 blue-and-white boats crisscross the harbor on several routes year-round, weather permitting. Boats stop at landings every 15 to 18 minutes. Tickets ($9 adults, $4 kids 10 and under; cash or check only) are good for unlimited, all-day use. For more information, call ✆ **800/658-8947** or 410/536-3901 or go to www.thewatertaxi.com.

SPECIAL EVENTS

Note: For event information, call ✆ **800/282-6632** (www.baltimore.org), unless otherwise noted.

January

Ring in the New Year at the Inner Harbor and watch the dazzling pyrotechnic display at midnight. For a chilling experience, watch ice carvers create spectacular sculptures.

February

Bring older kids to the American Craft Council: **Baltimore Show.** More than 500 artisans sell their wares in Festival Hall at one of the largest and most prestigious craft shows in the country (✆ **800/836-3470;** www.craftcouncil.org).

March

Musicians and other performers entertain at Harborplace around **St. Patrick's Day.**

April

Enjoy contemporary band music at the **Easter Sunday Music Fest** in the Harborplace Amphitheatre. The Easter Bunny greets children throughout Harborplace and the Gallery on Easter Sunday afternoon.

May

The **Preakness** horse race (part of the Triple Crown) is celebrated with concerts, parades, and balloon festivals the third week of May preceding the race at Pimlico (www.preaknesscelebration.org).

June

Summer ethnic festivals take place June to September, but not every weekend. Admission is free, but bring your wallet and appetite. Call the visitor center for the dates of the Polish, German, Italian, and other festivals. Enjoy music Friday, Saturday, and Sunday all summer at the Harborplace Amphitheatre's **Summer Concert Series.** Head for **Citysand** in the Harborplace Amphitheatre, where architects work with kids to sculpt elaborate sand creations. Pay tribute to the Stars and Stripes on **Flag Day** (June 14) at **Fort McHenry** (✆ **410/962-4290;** www.nps.gov/fomc).

July

Baltimoreans celebrate the **Fourth of July** with daytime entertainment and a dazzling fireworks display at the Inner Harbor. A summer concert series takes place every Friday, Saturday, and Sunday night in the amphitheater. **Artscape** is the third weekend of the month along Mount Royal Avenue and showcases the visual and performing arts with exhibits (including artwork by youngsters), hands-on activities, musical performances, street entertainment, and international foods—outdoors and in tents (www.artscape.org).

August

Who can resist the free entertainment weekends and lunchtime weekdays dished out by fire eaters, unicyclists, jugglers, and clowns at the **Inner Harbor?** Show your appreciation with a tip. These folks work hard for the money.

September

Bookworms from several states wriggle over to meet and greet local authors, attend workshops, and listen to speakers at the annual **Baltimore Book Festival,** held Friday evening, all day Saturday and Sunday the last weekend of the month at Mount Vernon Place (www.baltimorebookfestival.com).

October

The **Fells Point Funfest** (first weekend) attracts kids of all ages to its colorful street festival. Clowns, jugglers, and musicians entertain, and children's games, tempting snacks, and crafts are always within easy reach (www.preservationsociety.com).

November

What would Thanksgiving be without a parade? Follow the floats and cartoon characters from Camden Yards to Market Place on the Saturday before Turkey Day for the **Thanksgiving Parade.**

December

The **Annual Lighted Boat Parade** illuminates the harbor as more than 50 boats in holiday finery file past. In a **Merry Tuba Christmas,** traditional carols are played by an orchestra of tubas and euphoniums in the Harborplace Amphitheatre (www.harborplace.com). The **New Year's Eve Extravaganza** at the Baltimore Convention Center is a perfect way for the entire family to bid adieu to the old year: no booze and plenty of entertainment, with fireworks at midnight over the Inner Harbor (www.baltimorefunguide.com).

EXPLORING BALTIMORE

American Visionary Art Museum ★ **Ages 6 and up.** There's some really weird stuff going on here, and it's utterly captivating. I imagine that if Hieronymus Bosch and Monty Python joined forces to create an art museum, this is what it would look like. Most of the self-taught artists are outsiders—jailbirds, religious visionaries, and certifiable wackos. Because many of the paintings, drawings, sculptures, and assemblages are so off center that they're in the next galaxy, they grab children with their stripped-bare honesty and lack of pretension. No climbing, please, on the 55-foot whirligig in the outdoor plaza. Be sure to see the outdoor sculptures.

The July 4th "Big Kabooooom!" family day features a pet parade, pie-eating contest, and activities such as the Mr. Potato Head Beauty Contest—only $1 admission. Check out one of my favorite museum shops (at one of my fave museums) for funky stuff that you won't find in the Smithsonian. The popular **Joy America Café,** atop the museum, closed for a spell and is due to reopen—maybe in time for your visit. I myself look forward to getting reacquainted with an old friend.

800 Key Hwy. ✆ **410/244-1900.** www.avam.org. Admission $14 adults, $8 students age 5 and older (through grad school w/ID), $10 seniors, free for children 6 and under. MC, V. Tues–Sun 10am–6pm. Closed Thanksgiving and Dec 25. Directions: Take I-95 north to exit 55, and turn left onto Key Hwy.; continue 1½ miles to Covington St. Metered parking on Covington St. and Key Hwy.

Baltimore & Ohio Railroad Museum **Ages 2 and up.** The museum is on the site of the country's first train station, Mount Clare, where the first passenger ticket was issued in 1830. Check out the HO gauge (btw. regular size and miniature) train display on the second floor: The detail is astounding. In the roundhouse, you can wander through the locomotives, freight and passenger cars, and cabooses. The comprehensive exhibits are a must-see for little toots who get steamed up over trains and railroad history. In the backyard, train rides on the diesel Montclair Express are offered once a day Wednesday to Friday, 3 times each Sat, and twice on Sunday, April through December. Half-hour movies on railroad history run on weekends, and a museum store stocks books, train memorabilia, clothing, and whistles. Grab a light meal or snack in the **Iron Horse Café** or snack at a picnic table in good weather. All aboard!

901 W. Pratt St. (at Poppleton). ✆ **410/752-2490.** www.borail.org. Admission $14 adults, $12 seniors, $8 ages 2–12, free for children under 2. Mon–Fri 10–4; Sat 10–5, Sun 11–4. Directions from D.C.: Take New York Ave. east to I-295 north, to I-95 north, to I-395 north (Martin Luther King, Jr. Blvd.); go left at Lombard, and go 3 blocks to left at Poppleton to free museum parking. Directions from Pratt St. (Baltimore Inner Harbor): Go north 1 block to Lombard St., cross MLK Blvd. (do not get on MLK), proceed 3 blocks to 1st light, and turn left (Poppleton) to free museum parking.

Baltimore Maritime Museum **Ages 4 and up.** Kids will get an idea of how sailors live and work on a guided tour of the lightship *Chesapeake,* the submarine USS *Torsk,* the 327-foot Coast Guard cutter *Taney,* and the 7-foot Knoll Lighthouse, which once stood at the mouth of the Patapsco River. All are docked at/near Pier 3.

Pier 3, Inner Harbor, Pratt and Gay sts. ✆ **410/396-3453.** Admission Admiral (60 and older) $8, Captain (15–59) $10, Petty Officer (6–14) $5, Stowaway (5 and under) free. Mar–Oct, 10am–5:30pm, Nov–Feb 10am–4:30pm.Closed major holidays. Directions: Take I-95 north and follow signs to Inner Harbor.

Baltimore Museum of Art ★★ **Ages 8 and up.** Maryland's largest art museum is noted for its decorative arts, furniture, and paintings. And it's all free. The Cone Collection is one of the world's outstanding modern-art collections, with works by Matisse, Picasso, Cézanne, Van Gogh, and Gauguin. The Levi and Wurtzburger outdoor sculpture gardens brim with contemporary pieces.

The modern-art wing houses a prestigious collection of 20th-century art in 16 galleries. Changing exhibitions augment the permanent collection. **Gertrude's,** the on-site restaurant, has seating indoors and on the terrace (✆ **410/889-3399**). Summer jazz performances take place in the sculpture garden, where picnicking is welcome. Special family programs are ongoing. The museum store is worth a stop.

Art Museum Dr., at North Charles and 31st sts. ✆ **443/573-1700.** www.artbma.org. Free admission. Wed–Fri 10am–5pm; Sat–Sun 11am–6pm. Closed major holidays. Directions: Rte. I-295 north to Russell St. exit., right at Pratt, and left on Charles to Art Museum Dr.

Baltimore Museum of Industry ★ Finds **Ages 4 and up.** This museum is dedicated to the industrial history of Baltimore and is housed in the former Platt Oyster Cannery on the Inner Harbor. Kids can pretend they work on an assembly line at the Children's Motorworks section, or become workers in an 1883 Oyster Cannery. Children gravitate to the turn-of-the-20th-century drugstore, a replica of George Bunting's apothecary (he invented Noxzema, in case you didn't know), complete with a soda fountain. In other parts of the museum, visitors encounter a meat-packing exhibit and a 1920s garment-loft workshop. Come for the outdoor farmers' market Saturday from 9am to 1pm, June through October.

Special hands-on activities in the Cannery and the Children's Motorworks are for groups only.

1415 Key Hwy. ✆ **410/727-4808.** www.thebmi.org. Admission $10 adults, $6 seniors, students, children 5 and older; free for children 5 and under. Workshops extra. Tues–Sat 10am–4pm; Sun 11am–4pm. Closed Thanksgiving, Dec 24–25, Jan 1. Directions: I-95 to Ft. McHenry exit and then follow signs to Key Hwy.

Fort McHenry National Monument and Historic Shrine ★ **Ages 4 and up.** Francis Scott Key was so moved on the night of September 11, 1814, as the British fired on Fort McHenry (missing their target repeatedly, I might add), that he wrote a poem that became our national anthem in 1931. Visit the spot where the bombs were "bursting in air" while Key was waxing poetic from a boat in the harbor. A 16-minute orientation film plays on the half-hour from 9am to 4pm. The flag change is at 9:30am and 4:20pm. Pretty stirring, I think. The gun collection and underground dungeons are of special interest to most kids. The waterfront park is an idyllic spot for watching Old Glory snapping in the breeze and boat traffic on the Patapsco River and Chesapeake Bay. The first or second weekend in September, the annual Defenders' Day event features marching troops, military encampments, and fireworks. Show up on Flag Day (June 14) for free fireworks. Keep an eye out for the two ghosts in War of 1812 uniforms that reportedly haunt the fort.

East Fort Ave. (at the very end). ✆ **410/962-4290.** www.nps.gov/fomc. Free admission to the grounds; admission to Star Fort $7 16 and over, free for age 15 and under. Daily Sept–May 8am–5pm (last entry 4:45pm); June–Aug 8am–7:45pm. Directions: Take I-95 north to exit 55/Fort McHenry (before the tunnel), to left on Lawrence St., turn left on Fort Ave.; continue 1 mile to park.

The Gallery **All ages.** During your visit to the Inner Harbor, browse The Gallery, a pleasing, four-level mélange of shops and restaurants that is part of Harborplace (see below). The Gallery has a soaring, light-filled atrium that evokes the outdoors. The big draws for families are the Children's Place, Foot Locker, Gap and Gap Kids for clothing, and GameStop for video games.

When hunger strikes, head for the fourth-level food court, where McDonald's fries and burgers are sure kid-pleasers. (Five Guys burgers and fries, across the street in the Pratt St. Pavilion, are far superior.) You'll also find Moun Wok, Salad Works, and Sbarro. Or cross the street to the Pratt and Light Street Pavilions for more choices.

200 E. Pratt St.; Pratt, Light, and Calvert sts., at the Inner Harbor. ✆ **800/HARBOR-1** (427-2671) or 410/332-4191. www.harborplace.com. Mon–Sat 10am–9pm; Sun 11am–7pm; some extended summer hours. Directions: Take I-95 north and follow signs to Inner Harbor.

Harborplace ★ **All ages.** Baltimore's top tourist draw at the Inner Harbor consists of two pavilions (Light and Pratt sts.) and a mall (the Gallery) that do their seductive best to lure visitors into their shops, restaurants, and food stalls. The **Light Street Pavilion** is primarily food oriented. Kids love the second-floor Food Hall, which boasts a wide array of American-style and ethnic fast food. Weather-permitting, chow down on a bench overlooking the harbor. For sit-down service, try Johnny Rockets (1950s-style diner). Lee's Ice Cream is made locally. Check out the Best of Baltimore (Charm City souvenirs) and The Flag Shop. At the information kiosk, find out about special events, which, in the past, have included rowing regattas, band concerts, and crab races.

Shoppers head for the **Pratt Street Pavilion,** filled mostly with restaurants. Pig out at the following sit-down restaurants: Pizzeria Uno, the Cheesecake Factory, Tír Na Nóg Irish Bar & Grill, and Five Guys (fast-food burgers, fries, and soft drinks). The air is always festive around Harborplace. Without spending a cent, you can have a rich time watching the other tourists, strolling the waterfront promenades, and window-shopping.

Pratt, Light, and Calvert sts. ✆ **410/332-4191.** Shops and Food Hall: Mon–Sat 10am–9pm; Sun 11am–7pm (extended hours Sat–Sun in summer); restaurants with separate entrances stay open later. Directions: Take I-95 north and follow signs to Harborplace.

Lexington Market ★★ (Finds) **All ages.** Skip breakfast; it's pig-out time! The former open-air market, named for the Revolution's first battle, opened in 1782. Back then, farmers arrived with produce, game, fowl, and dairy goods. The first shed was raised in 1803, and the market grew in fits and starts. Fire destroyed it in 1949. Two brick buildings opened in 1952. Today, after further renovation in 2002, about 130 merchants hawk produce, seafood, poultry, and a variety of prepared foods and baked goods from row upon row of stalls in two buildings. An information kiosk is located in the center of the Arcade, the site of entertainment and special events such as the annual chocolate and ice cream festivals. Seating for 500 is available on the Arcade's second level. Free concerts take place Friday and Saturday noon to 2pm.

Recommendations (diligently researched over many years) include Polock Johnny's sausage sandwiches (with the works), Barron's Deli for corned beef, Faidley's for crab cakes and other seafood, Park's Fried Chicken, Utz potato chips, and Berger's for doughnuts and the best cookies in the area.

400 West Lexington St. (btw. Paca and Eutaw). ✆ **410/685-6169.** www.lexingtonmarket.com. Mon–Sat 8:30am–6pm. Directions: Take I-95 north to Russell St. exit; Russell becomes Paca; continue 5 blocks. Ample garage and lot parking; limited street parking.

Maryland Science Center ★★ **Ages 2 and up.** Time passes quickly in this facility, established by the Maryland Academy of Sciences. Scores of hands-on exhibits invite kids of all ages to touch, explore, and learn. Enter a distorted room, make friends with a computer, and delve into physics, geology, and the human mind.

The third-floor **Kids' Room** features a jungle gym and slide, plant and animal specimens, and a dress-up corner. It's open daily 12:30 to 4:30pm. See (reconstructed) dinosaurs that once called Maryland home in the Dinosaur and Earth Sciences Hall. Kids can try their hand at digging for archaeological finds in the Dark Pit.

Because this is Maryland, it would be fitting to follow the Blue Crab (exhibit) with live crabs, fish, diamondback terrapins (the University of Maryland mascot), and walk across a huge floor map of the Chesapeake Bay.

Watch a movie on the five-story-high **IMAX** screen, or reach for the stars in the **Davis Planetarium.** Both are recommended for kids 4 and over. Several movies alternate in the IMAX theater, and planetarium shows air twice a day on weekdays and numerous times on weekends. On most Thursdays and Fridays at 7:30pm, a double feature is shown in the IMAX. Timed tickets are sold at the box office.

Admission includes all exhibits, one IMAX movie, and a planetarium show. (***Note:*** Sometimes timed tickets are required for special exhibits, at an additional cost.) Strollers are allowed in the museum but not in the theaters.

Weather permitting, you can ride the 1912 Herschell-Spillman carousel next to the science center daily in summer (noon–midnight), weekends the rest of the year. The figures on this creation include horses, dogs, pigs, and roosters. Rides still cost $1.25.

Inner Harbor, 601 Light St. (at Key Hwy.). ✆ **410/685-5225.** www.mdsci.org. Admission $11–$25 depending on age and package chosen (museum, planetarium, Demo Stage, IMAX movie). Tues–Thurs 10am–5pm; Fri 10am–8pm, Sat 10am–6pm (till 8pm in summer), Sun 11am–5pm (10am–6pm summer). Closed Thanksgiving and Dec 25. Directions: Take I-95 north and follow signs.

The Maryland Zoo ★★ **Ages 2 and up.** Come see why this is rated among the top zoos in the country. The Maryland Zoo has long been an innovator in trading cages for natural habitats. Animal lovers benefit by coming face to face (well, almost) with their favorite creatures. With fewer barriers, kids leave with a greater appreciation of the interdependence of *all* living things.

Be a voyeur and watch from the underwater viewing station at **Polar Bear Watch** as Alaska and Magnet (polar bears) go through their aquatic antics.

Visit the zoo's newest exhibit, Prairie Dog Town, and the more than 100 species inhabiting the **Maryland Wilderness** section of the Children's Zoo. Your little bipeds can climb into a huge oriole's nest, scale a tree, or crawl through an acrylic tunnel under a dam. In the **Maryland Farmyard,** kids are invited to ride a pony, pet a sheep, breeze down the silo slide, or watch a cow-milking demonstration. Lunch with the Kodiak bears at 2pm, or watch the African black-footed penguins dive for raw fish at 3pm. In the **Chimpanzee Forest,** designed as part of a species-survival plan, you and your little monkeys can watch the chimps swing from a fire hose vine and frolic in their very own play area. The well-placed observation platforms allow visitors to feel almost at one with the chimps. Year-round, the zoo typically has free activity booklets and special family events. Be sure to ask about these and summer programs. One perk of a summer visit is you can ride a camel ($4). Cap your visit with a ride on the antique carousel and Zoochoo Train.

Druid Hill Park. ✆ **410/366-LION** (5466). www.marylandzoo.org. Admission $15 adults 12–64, $10 ages 2–11, $12 seniors 65 and over, free for children under 2. $2 discount if purchased online. Daily 10am–4pm. Directions: Take I-95 north to I-695 west (toward Towson) to I-83 south (Jones Falls Expy.). Exit 7 west off the expressway to Druid Park Lake Dr., and follow signs to the zoo. Plenty of free parking.

National Aquarium ★★ **Ages 2 and up.** Enter this multistory aquarium towering over the harbor via the dramatic pavilion entry. A 35-foot waterfall flows through pools with turtles and frogs, representing the water that cascades from the Allegheny Mountains in western Maryland to the Chesapeake Bay. Set aside at least 2½ to 3 hours, preferably *early or late in the day,* to do justice to the main Aquarium Building and Marine Mammal Pavilion. Admission is by timed-entry tickets. Whenever possible, steer clear of midday (about 11am–3pm) and weekend crowds. To avoid disappointment, always order tickets ahead (see details below). Don special glasses for the 4D immersion shows (sights, sounds, smells, and the occasional misting), sure to wow all but the toddlers in your party. **"Jellies Invasion"** draws attention to imbalances in the world's oceans. **"Animal Planet Australia: Wild Extremes,"** feasts your eyes on cockatoos, lorikeets, and flying foxes (a fruit bat) in a realistic rock-gorge habitat like those in the Northern Territory. Freshwater crocs are no threat here. Owing to wide expanses of glass, the smallest in your party will have a clear view of the animals in this stunning exhibit.

The steamy and exotic South American **Rain Forest,** where small animals and tropical birds roam freely, is still a highlight. Visit the puffins next to the rainforest. The **Atlantic Coral Reef** has more than 800 species. The coral is plastic, but the fish don't mind.

Very young kids who might be bored in the main aquarium will wake up in the **Marine Mammal Pavilion,** with its many interactive displays. One allows you to mimic whale sounds. Bottlenose dolphins cavort several times a day during entertaining half-hour shows in the 1,300-seat pavilion with two multiscreen video monitors. Sit back a few rows or risk an unscheduled shower.

The seals are fed several times a day outside the main aquarium. Call for feeding times, because they are not "sealed" in stone. Check the sign over the lobby information desk to find out when the sharks dine.

Pier 3, 501 E. Pratt St. (adjacent to Harborplace). ✆ **410/576-3800.** www.aqua.org. Timed-entry tickets required. Admission $25 adults, $24 seniors 60 and over, $15 ages 3–11, free for children 2 and under. Purchase advance tickets after 3pm a day ahead through www.aqua.org. Or order tickets up to 3 months ahead through Ticketmaster (✆ **202/432-SEAT** [7328] or 410/481-7328). Sun–Thurs 9am–5pm; Fri 9am–8pm; Sat 9am–6pm. Hours vary slightly seasonally. Closed Thanksgiving and Dec 25. Directions: Take I-95 north and follow signs to Inner Harbor. Garage across the street.

Oriole Park at Camden Yards **Ages 6 and up.** Take them out to an Orioles ball game, *if* your young ones are old enough to sit still through nine or more innings. Even when the game is lackluster, it is a thrill to be in this magnificent structure, where Cal Ripken, Jr., broke records and played his last game in 2001. For my money, the view of downtown Baltimore, perfectly framed beyond the outfield, beats an O's ninth-inning home run with the bases loaded. If the game is boring, check out the overflow memorabilia from the Babe Ruth Museum (see entry below).

You could do worse than to patronize the numerous and varied food concessions, but, as always, the pickins are pricey. I prefer to eat before or pack a picnic to enjoy pregame at one of the tables provided for such purposes on the Eutaw Street corridor, between the warehouse and the ballpark. Seats at the park are roomy, and best of all, restrooms are abundant. Tickets are a hot commodity, so order early. Ask about special events and promotional giveaways, many of which are geared to young people. You can purchase tickets over the phone or at the O's website (see below). There is plenty of parking in nearby lots on game days. Feel free to bring reusable bags of food and drink, however, no coolers or backpacks are allowed in the stadium.

Main gate at 333 W. Camden St. ✆ **888/848-BIRD** [2473]. www.orioles.mlb.com. Admission (most seats) $20–$85. Tours of the stadium offered daily; call for times, which vary (✆ **410/685-9800**). To charge tickets in D.C., call ✆ **202/432-SEAT** [7328]. Early Apr–early Oct (later, if the O's make the playoffs). Directions: Take I-95 north to Rte. 395/downtown or I-295 north, and follow signs to stadium. For information on public transportation to the games, call ✆ **800/543-9809** or 410/539-5000.

Babe Ruth Birthplace and Museum and Sports Legends at Camden Ages 6–14. Stand in the very room where George Herman Ruth, Jr., drew his first breath in 1895. The Sultan of Swat's career record of 714 homers remained unbroken for more than 40 years, until Hank Aaron settled the score in 1974, to be unseated by Barry Bonds' 756th homerun on Aug. 7, 2007. Displays in this downtown row house chronicle the Babe's life. Don't miss the photo of 3-year-old slugger Babe Ruth playing ball. In The Locker Room, kids can try on uniforms from their favorite pro and collegiate teams. Lots more stuff is displayed 3 blocks east (just follow the baseballs painted on the sidewalks) at the 22,000-square-foot Sports Legends museum at historic Camden Yards at Oriole Park, 301 W. Camden St. My staff of experts tells me this is one of the top sports museums in the country, folks. Among the exhibits and interactives, you'll find plenty of Orioles memorabilia, too, like Cal Ripken's last home-run ball (Sept. 23, 2001).

216 Emory St. ✆ **410/727-1539.** www.baberuthmuseum.com or www.sportslegendsatcamdenyards.com. Admission Birthplace (Babe Ruth Museum): $6 adults, $4 seniors, $3 kids 3–12; Sports Legends adults, $6 seniors, $4 kids 3–12; combined ticket $12 adults, $8 seniors, $5 kids 3–12. Apr–Oct daily 10am–6pm (until 7pm on Oriole home-game days). Nov–March daily 10am–5pm. Closed Thanksgiving, Dec 25, Jan 1. Directions: Take I-95 north to Rte. 395/downtown; at fork, take Martin Luther King, Jr. Blvd., turn right on Pratt, go 2 blocks, and turn right on Emory; go 1 block to museum. Limited free parking; also street parking.

Port Discovery ★★ Finds Ages 2–10. Trace your kids against the "magic" wall of a glass booth, help them fly a virtual plane, watch them climb the Empire State Building, and cheer them on as they explore Kid Works, a maze full of opportunities for climbing, jumping, and sliding. Families also applaud the Dreamlab, and Check out Wonders of Water, which demonstrates in terms they can understand (building a fountain, listening to water chimes), how humans interact with water—and the repercussions of their actions. Sensory delights await kids in Sensation Station, Down on the Farm, and other innovative interactives at this "kid-powered" museum. Visit The Diner, an authentic '50s-style hash house where kids can pretend to cook and serve their parents. Let them loose in the fully enclosed Soccer Field. Kids between 2 and 10 seem to get the most from a visit, but it's not unusual for older siblings and parents to get involved. One area is devoted to kids from birth to 4 years—with soft surfaces and plush toys. Occupying a former fish market, Port Discovery is stimulating, educational, and, most of all, fun. Show up when it opens on weekends and during school vacations. Save time in line at the box office by ordering tickets ahead at Ticketmaster (✆ **800/551-7238;** www.ticketmaster.com). There's a McDonald's off the first-floor atrium level. A better bet: Head for the Rams Head Tavern, one of the sit-down restaurants across the court at Market Place.

35 Market Place (at Lombard St.). ✆ **410/727-8120.** www.portdiscovery.org. Admission $13 (ages 3–102), free for kids 2 and under. Mon–Sat 10am–5pm (closed Mon Oct–May); Sun noon–5. Directions from D.C.: Take I-95 north to I-395, and turn right at Pratt; follow signs. Plenty of garage parking at Discovery Park Garage ($7 Sat–Sun with museum validation), entrance Lombard St. at Market Place.

Star-Spangled Banner Flag House **Ages 4–14.** Almost everyone has heard of Francis Scott Key. But how many of you know who Mary Pickersgill was? It seems that the commander of Fort McHenry during the War of 1812 entrusted Mary with creating a garrison flag 30 by 42 feet. Not just any flag would do. The order was for a flag that the British would have no trouble seeing from a distance. When the flag outgrew Mary's bedroom, she pieced it on the floor of a nearby malt house. Mary delivered the goods in about 6 weeks, and it inspired Key to write our national anthem in 1814. Stroll down Pratt from the Inner Harbor to this brick row house, built in 1793. You can't miss the glass flag window (an exact replica of the original) before viewing many of Mary's personal possessions. If you want to see the flag itself, you'll have to go to the Smithsonian's National Museum of American History.

844 E. Pratt St. (at Albemarle St.). ✆ **410/837-1793.** www.flaghouse.org. Admission $7 adults; $6 seniors, students with ID, and military with ID; free for kids 5 and under; all kids free (w/paying adult) 2nd Sun of month. Group rates are available. Tues–Sat 10am–4pm (last tour at 3:15pm).

Top of the World Observation Level **Ages 4 and up.** On a clear day you can see forever—well, almost. Would you settle for the harbor, the O's stadium, and north to Towson 13 miles away?

Inner Harbor, 27th floor of World Trade Center, 401 E. Pratt St. ✆ **410/837-VIEW** [8439]. www.bop.org. Admission $5 adults, $4 seniors, $3 kids 3–12, free 2 and under. Sept–Memorial Day Wed–Sun 10am–6pm; Memorial Day–Labor Day 10am–8pm daily. Directions: Take I-95 north and follow signs to Inner Harbor (next to National Aquarium).

USS Constellation **Ages 4 and up.** The USS *Constellation,* built in 1854 and retired in 1945, was the last navy ship powered entirely by sail. The crew grants landlubbers permission to come aboard and tour the majestic sloop of war (handicap accessible) daily. Special activities take place on weekends. One day a year, in early September, the ship is towed toward Ft. McHenry and returned facing in the opposite direction. Known as the Annual Turnaround, it's done so the ship will weather evenly on both sides. Call about guided tours for groups of 10 and more.

Inner Harbor. Pier 1, btw. Pratt and Light St. Pavilions. ✆ **410/539-1797.** www.constellation.org. Admission $10 adults, $8 seniors, $5 kids 6–14, free for kids 5 and under. Daily Apr–Oct 10am–5:30pm; Nov–Mar 10am–4:30pm. (***Note:*** Last tickets sold half-hour before closing.)

CRUISES

Of the numerous cruise boats plying the Inner Harbor during the warm-weather months, here are a few that are particularly appealing to tiny tars.

Harbor Cruises **Ages 2 and up.** With older kids, you may want to take one of the numerous 60-minute and longer cruises (with food, entertainment, and holiday themes) on the *Inner Harbor Spirit.* Offered year-round, with additional cruises added April through October.

Inner Harbor, corner of Light and Lee sts. ✆ **800/695-BOAT** [2628] or 410/727-3113. www.harborcruises.com. Directions: I-295 north to right at Pratt, right at Light St., right at Lee St., and right into Harbor Court (hotel) garage. Big boats are just across the street.

WHERE TO STAY

Expensive

Renaissance Harborplace ★★ Any closer to the harbor, and you'd be swimming. The Renaissance's location is prime, and rooms (some with harbor views) are spacious and well appointed. The hotel recently underwent a major renovation. As my son might say, "it's stylin'." Suites and parlor suites are available, at a higher rate, of course. **Watertable,** the hotel's new restaurant and lounge overlooking the harbor, welcomes families with well-behaved kids to enjoy fresh and seasonal fare that showcases local seafood. The hotel is attached to the **Gallery,** a multilevel mall with scores of shops, restaurants, and food stands. Harborplace is just across Pratt Street and reachable by a skywalk from the hotel. Both have more than their share of restaurants. The concierge will secure tickets for local attractions and help you plan your sightseeing activities. Always ask about special packages and discounted rates.

202 E. Pratt St., Baltimore, MD 21202. ✆ **800/535-1201** or 410/547-1200. www.marriott.com/city/baltimore-hotels. 622 units. Mon–Fri $359 and up double; Sat–Sun from $199. Children 17 and under stay free in parent's room. Cribs and rollaways free. AE, DC, DISC, MC, V. Self-parking $26; valet parking $36. **Amenities:** 3 restaurants (formal, coffee shop, and ground-floor cafe); lounge/bar; concierge; health club; indoor pool; sauna; room service. *In room:* AC, TV, hair dryer, minibar.

Moderate

Days Inn ★ Value Just 3 blocks from the Inner Harbor, 2 blocks from Oriole Park at Camden Yards, and 4 blocks from the aquarium, the Days Inn is a good buy for families, especially if you're able to take advantage of one of several special packages usually offered on weekends. A free fridge and microwave are available upon request to cut down on the cost of eating out. High-speed wireless and in-room Nintendo are complimentary. A fitness center and business center are onsite. **Hopkins Bar and Grill,** the hotel's windowed (lots of natural light!) restaurant, features Maryland crab cakes and American fare—and a kids menu. It's open for breakfast, lunch, and dinner weekdays, and breakfast and dinner on weekends. An outdoor heated pool is open from Memorial Day to Labor Day.

100 Hopkins Place, Baltimore, MD 21201. ✆ **800/325-2525** or 410/576-1000. www.daysinnerharbor.com. 250 units. $119–$269 double. Age 18 and under stay free in parent's room. Cribs free, rollaways $10 per night. Ask about special family and weekend packages. AE, DISC, MC, V. Self-parking $20. **Amenities:** Restaurant; bar; concierge; fitness center; outdoor poolroom service. *In room:* A/C, TV, hair dryer.

WHERE TO DINE

Baltimore has many family-friendly restaurants in all categories and price groups. For more suggestions, go to **www.baltimore.org**.

Expensive

Chiapparelli's ★ ITALIAN Bring the bambinos for heartily sauced pastas (nothing subtle or bland here), seafood, and veal at this Little Italy fixture, still going strong since 1940. Create a meal from fried calamari or clams casino and Italian wedding soup (with spinach, pasta, and meatballs). Be warned: The portions are huge, especially the pasta.

The large house salad, drenched in a creamy garlicky dressing, is meal sized. Personal pizzas, panini, salads, subs (cold cuts, sausage and pepper, meatball) at lunch are $6 to $9 and large enough for small appetites to share. At dinner, add $2 for "lighter" fare; most entrees run $18 to $20. The children's menu (all items $6) has spaghetti with meatballs, ravioli, pizza bread, or chicken tenders and fries.

237 S. High St. ✆ **410/837-0309.** www.chiapparellis.com. High chairs, booster seats, kids' menu. Reservations recommended. Most lunch main courses $7–$11; most dinner main courses $16–$18; kids' menu items $6–$8. AE, DC, MC, V. Sun–Thurs 11:30am–9pm; Fri–Sat 11:30am–11pm.

Moderate

Gunning's Seafood Restaurant SEAFOOD This is Brooklyn, Maryland (not to be confused with Brooklyn, New York), and it's hard-shell crab territory, so roll up your sleeves and dig into a pile of steamed crabs while the waitresses "Hon" you to death. If picking crabs seems too much like work, try Gunning's award-winning crab cakes or one of several other seafood offerings. Gunning's is also known for its fried green pepper rings. Try 'em (you'll thank me). A kids' menu features hamburgers, hot dogs, and ice cream for dessert. Eat in one of the dining rooms, the large enclosed "garden" room, or outdoors in the crab garden when the weather cooperates. Crabs are also available for carryout. ***Tip:*** Buy the largest crabs—less work and more meat.

3901 S. Hanover St. ✆ **410/712-9404.** High chairs, booster seats, kids' menu. Reservations required for 8 or more. Main courses lunch $7–$16, dinner $17–$30; crabs $65 and up a dozen, depending on size; kids' menu items $6.50. AE, DISC, MC, V. Mon–Thurs 11am–10pm, Fri 11am–11pm; Sat noon–11pm; Sun noon–9pm. Directions from D.C.: I-95 or I-295 to I-695/Glen Burnie, exit 6A/N Linthicum; go 3½ miles to 2nd traffic light, and turn and left (Hanover), 1 block to restaurant.

Inexpensive

Lenny's Deli DELI Lenny's location might leave something to be desired, but such a minor irritation disappears with the first bite into a corned-beef sandwich (order it extra lean or regular). The pastrami is as good as it gets. Don't forget a pickle—half done or well done (sour)—to go with your corned beef. Lenny's also offers a selection of subs, chicken (rotisserie and fried), and more than a dozen side dishes—from mashed potatoes and macaroni and cheese to knishes and kosher pickles. It's strictly cafeteria style and no frills. Come here to drool over the corned beef or pastrami, not the decor. Lenny's has free Wi-Fi, so you can check e-mail while you slobber mustard on your shirt. The original Lenny's is still thriving in Owings Mills.

1150 E. Lombard St. ✆ **410/327-1177.** www.lennysdeli.com. Reservations not accepted. Most items $6–$9. AE, DISC, MC, V. Mon–Sat 7:30am–6pm; Sun 8am–5pm.

12

Fast Facts

1 FAST FACTS: WASHINGTON, D.C.

AMERICAN EXPRESS There's an American Express Travel Service office at 1501 K St. NW, entrance on 15th St. NW (✆ **202/457-1300**).

AREA CODES Within the District of Columbia, it's 202. In Northern Virginia, it's 703. In D.C.'s Maryland suburbs, it's 301. You must use the area code when dialing any number, whether it's a local 202, 703, or 301 phone number.

AUTOMOBILE ORGANIZATIONS Motor clubs will supply maps, suggested routes, guidebooks, accident and bail-bond insurance, and emergency road service. The **American Automobile Association (AAA)** is the major auto club in the United States. If you belong to a motor club in your home country, inquire about AAA reciprocity before you leave. You may be able to join AAA even if you're not a member of a reciprocal club; to inquire, contact AAA (www.aaa.com). AAA has a nationwide emergency road service telephone number (✆ **800/AAA-HELP** [222-4357]). In Washington, AAA's downtown office is near the White House, at 1405 G St. NW, between 14th and 15th streets (✆ **202/481-6811**).

BUSINESS HOURS Offices are usually open weekdays from 9am to 5pm. Most banks are open from 9am to 3pm Monday through Thursday with some staying open until 5pm; 9am to 5pm on Friday; and sometimes Saturday mornings. Stores typically open between 9 and 10am and close between 5 and 6pm from Monday to Saturday. Stores in shopping complexes or malls tend to stay open late, until about 9pm on weekdays and weekends, and many malls and larger department stores are open on Sundays. (See chapter 9, p. 220, for more specific information about store hours.)

DRINKING LAWS The legal age for purchase and consumption of alcoholic beverages is 21; proof of age is required and often requested at bars, nightclubs, and restaurants, so it's always a good idea to bring ID when you go out. Liquor stores are closed on Sunday. District gourmet grocery stores, mom-and-pop grocery stores, and 7-Eleven convenience stores often sell beer and wine, even on Sunday.

Bars and nightclubs serve liquor until 2am Sunday through Thursday and until 3am Friday and Saturday.

Do not carry open containers of alcohol in your car or any public area that isn't zoned for alcohol consumption. The police can fine you on the spot. Don't even think about driving while intoxicated.

DRIVING RULES See "Getting There," p. 19.

ELECTRICITY Like Canada, the United States uses 110 to 120 volts AC (60 cycles), compared to 220 to 240 volts AC (50 cycles) in most of Europe, Australia, and New Zealand. Downward converters that change 220 to 240 volts to 110 to 120 volts are difficult to find in the United States, so bring one with you.

EMBASSIES & CONSULATES All embassies are located in the nation's capital, Washington, D.C. Some consulates are located in major U.S. cities, and most nations have a mission to the United Nations in New York City. If your country isn't listed below, call for directory information in Washington, D.C. (✆ **202/555-1212**) or check **www.embassy.org/embassies**.

The embassy of **Australia** is at 1601 Massachusetts Ave. NW, Washington, DC 20036 (✆ **202/797-3000;** usa.embassy.gov/au). Consulate locations include New York, Honolulu, Houston, Los Angeles, and San Francisco.

The embassy of **Canada** is at 501 Pennsylvania Ave. NW, Washington, DC 20001 (✆ **202/682-1740;** www.canadianembassy.org). Other Canadian consulates are in Buffalo (New York), Detroit, Los Angeles, New York, and Seattle.

The embassy of **Ireland** is at 2234 Massachusetts Ave. NW, Washington, DC 20008 (✆ **202/462-3939;** www.irelandemb.org). Irish consulates are in Boston, Chicago, New York, San Francisco, and other cities. See website for complete listing.

The embassy of **New Zealand** is at 37 Observatory Circle NW, Washington, DC 20008 (✆ **202/328-4800;** www.nzembassy.com). New Zealand consulates are in Los Angeles, Salt Lake City, San Francisco, and Seattle.

The embassy of the **United Kingdom** is at 3100 Massachusetts Ave. NW, Washington, DC 20008 (✆ **202/588-7800;** www.britainusa.com). Other British consulates are in Atlanta, Boston, Chicago, Cleveland, Houston, Los Angeles, New York, San Francisco, and Seattle.

EMERGENCIES Call ✆ **911** for police, fire, and medical emergencies. This is a toll-free call. (No coins are required at public telephones.)

If you encounter serious problems, contact the **Travelers Aid Society International** (✆ **202/546-1127;** www.travelersaid.org.), a nationwide, nonprofit, social-service organization geared to helping travelers in difficult straits, from reuniting families separated while traveling, to providing food and/or shelter to people stranded without cash, to emotional counseling. Travelers Aid operates help desks at Washington Dulles International Airport (✆ **703/572-8296**), Ronald Reagan Washington National Airport (✆ **703/417-3975**), and Union Station (✆ **202/371-1937**).

GASOLINE (PETROL) At press time, in the Washington region, the cost of gasoline (also known as gas, but never petrol), hovers around $2.40 a gallon. Taxes are already included in the printed price. One U.S. gallon equals 3.8 liters or .85 imperial gallons. Fill-up locations are known as gas or service stations.

HOLIDAYS Banks, government offices, post offices, and many stores, restaurants, and museums are closed on the following legal national holidays: January 1 (New Year's Day), the third Monday in January (Martin Luther King, Jr., Day), the third Monday in February (Presidents' Day), the last Monday in May (Memorial Day), July 4 (Independence Day), the first Monday in September (Labor Day), the second Monday in October (Columbus Day), November 11 (Veterans' Day/Armistice Day), the fourth Thursday in November (Thanksgiving Day), and December 25 (Christmas). The Tuesday after the first Monday in November is Election Day, a federal government holiday in presidential-election years (held every 4 years, and next in 2012).

For more information on holidays see "Calendar of Events," in chapter 3.

HOSPITALS If you don't require immediate ambulance transportation but still need emergency-room treatment, call one of the following hospitals (and be sure to get directions): Children's Hospital National Medical Center, 111 Michigan Ave. NW (✆ **202/476-5000**); George

Washington University Hospital, 900 23rd St. NW, at Washington Circle (✆ **202/715-4000**); Georgetown University Medical Center, 3800 Reservoir Rd. NW (✆ **202/444-2000**); or Howard University Hospital, 2041 Georgia Ave. NW (✆ **202/865-6100**).

HOT LINES To reach a 24-hour poison-control hot line, call ✆ **800/222-1222;** to reach a 24-hour crisis line, call ✆ **202/561-7000;** to reach a 24-hour rape crisis line, call ✆ **202/333-RAPE** (7273).

INSURANCE For information on traveler's insurance, trip-cancellation insurance, and medical insurance while traveling, please visit www.frommers.com/planning.

INTERNET ACCESS Washington, D.C., is lacking in Internet cafes, probably because everyone here carries her own personal connection with her, via Blackberry, laptop, iPhone, or some other form of PDA. I know of only one public Internet cafe: In Dupont Circle's **Kramerbooks and Afterwords** bookstore, 1517 Connecticut Ave. NW (✆ **202/387-1400**), which has one computer available for free Internet access, with a 15-minute time limit. Also see "Staying Connected" in chapter 3.

LEGAL AID If you are "pulled over" for a minor infraction (such as speeding), never attempt to pay the fine directly to a police officer; this could be construed as attempted bribery, a much more serious crime. Pay fines by mail, or directly into the hands of the clerk of the court. If accused of a more serious offense, say and do nothing before consulting a lawyer. Here the burden is on the state to prove a person's guilt beyond a reasonable doubt, and everyone has the right to remain silent, whether he or she is suspected of a crime or actually arrested. Once arrested, a person can make one telephone call to a party of his or her choice. International visitors should call their embassy or consulate.

MAIL At press time, domestic postage rates were 28¢ for a postcard and 44¢ for a letter. For international mail, a first-class letter of up to 1 ounce costs 98¢ (75¢ to Canada and 79¢ to Mexico); a first-class postcard costs the same as a letter. For more information go to **www.usps.com**.

If you aren't sure what your address will be in the United States, mail can be sent to you, in your name, c/o General Delivery at the main post office of the city or region where you expect to be. (Call ✆ **800/275-8777,** for information on the nearest post office.) The addressee must pick up mail in person and must produce proof of identity (driver's license, passport, and so on). Most post offices will hold your mail for up to 1 month, and are open Monday to Friday from 8am to 6pm, Saturday from 9am to 3pm.

Always include zip codes when mailing items in the U.S. If you don't know your zip code, visit www.usps.com/zip4.

NEWSPAPERS & MAGAZINES Washington's preeminent newspaper is the *Washington Post,* which is sold in bookstores, train and subway stations, drugstores, and sidewalk kiosks all over town. These are also the places to buy other newspapers, like the *New York Times,* and *Washingtonian* magazine, the city's popular monthly full of penetrating features, restaurant reviews, and nightlife calendars. For up-to-the-minute news, check out the websites of these publications: www.washingtonpost.com, www.nytimes.com, www.washingtonian.com.

Also be sure to pick up a copy of *Washington Flyer* magazine, available free at the airport or online at www.fly2dc.com, to find out about airport and airline news and interesting Washington happenings.

PASSPORTS See www.frommers.com/planning for information on how to obtain a passport. See "Embassies & Consulates," above, for whom to contact if you lose yours while traveling in the U.S. For other information, please contact the following agencies:

For Residents of Australia Contact the **Australian Passport Information Service** at ✆ **131-232,** or visit the government website at www.passports.gov.au.

For Residents of Canada Contact the central **Passport Office,** Department of Foreign Affairs and International Trade, Ottawa, ON K1A 0G3 (✆ **800/567-6868;** www.ppt.gc.ca).

For Residents of Ireland Contact the **Passport Office,** Setanta Centre, Molesworth Street, Dublin 2 (✆ **01/671-1633;** www.irlgov.ie/iveagh).

For Residents of New Zealand Contact the **Passports Office:** ✆ **0800/225-050** in New Zealand, or 04/474-8100; or log on to www.passports.govt.nz.

For Residents of the United Kingdom Visit your nearest passport office, major post office, or travel agency; contact the **United Kingdom Passport Service** at ✆ **0870/521-0410;** or search its website at www.ukpa.gov.uk.

For Residents of the United States To find your regional passport office, either check the U.S. Department of State website or call the **National Passport Information Center** toll-free number (✆ **877/487-2778**) for automated information.

POLICE In an emergency, dial ✆ **911.** For a nonemergency, call ✆ **202/727-1010.**

SMOKING The District is smoke-free, meaning that the city bans smoking in restaurants, bars, and other public buildings. Smoking is permitted outdoors, unless otherwise noted.

TAXES The United States has no value-added tax (VAT) or other indirect tax at the national level. Every state, county, and city may levy its own local tax on all purchases, including hotel and restaurant checks and airline tickets. These taxes will not appear on price tags.

The sales tax on merchandise is 5.75% in the District, 5% in Maryland, and 4.5% in Virginia. Restaurant tax is 10% in the District, 6% in Maryland, and varied in Virginia, depending on the city and county. Hotel tax is 14.5% in the District, varied 5% to 8% in Maryland, and averages about 9.75% in Virginia.

TIME The continental United States is divided into **four time zones:** Eastern Standard Time (EST; this is Washington's time zone), Central Standard Time (CST), Mountain Standard Time (MST), and Pacific Standard Time (PST). Alaska and Hawaii have their own zones. For example, when it's 9am in Los Angeles (PST), it's 7am in Honolulu (HST), 10am in Denver (MST), 11am in Chicago (CST), noon in Washington, D.C. (EST), 5pm in London (GMT), and 2am the next day in Sydney.

Daylight saving time is in effect from 1am on the second Sunday in March to 1am on the first Sunday in November, except in Arizona, Hawaii, the U.S. Virgin Islands, and Puerto Rico. Daylight saving time moves the clock 1 hour ahead of standard time.

TIPPING Tips are a very important part of certain workers' income, and gratuities are the standard way of showing appreciation for services provided. In hotels, tip **bellhops** at least $1 per bag ($2–$3, if you have a lot of luggage) and tip the **chamber staff** $1 to $2 per day (more if you've left a disaster area for him or her to clean up). Tip the **doorman** or **concierge** only if he or she has provided you with some specific service (for example, calling a cab for you or obtaining difficult-to-get theater tickets). Tip the **valet-parking attendant** $1 every time you get your car.

In restaurants, bars, and nightclubs, tip **service staff** and **bartenders** 15% to 20% of the check, tip **checkroom attendants** $1 per garment, and tip **valet-parking attendants** $1 per vehicle.

As for other service personnel, tip **cab drivers** 15% of the fare; tip **skycaps** at airports at least $1 per bag ($2–$3 if you have a lot of luggage); and tip **hairdressers** and **barbers** 15% to 20%.

TOILETS You won't find public toilets or "restrooms" on the streets in most U.S. cities but they can be found in hotel lobbies, bars, restaurants, museums, department stores, railway and bus stations, and service stations. Large hotels and fast-food restaurants are often the best bet for clean facilities. Restaurants and bars in resorts or heavily visited areas may reserve their restrooms for patrons.

VISAS For information about U.S. Visas, go to **http://travel.state.gov** and click on "Visas." Or go to one of the following websites:

Australian citizens can obtain up-to-date visa information from the **U.S. Embassy Canberra,** Moonah Place, Yarralumla, ACT 2600 (✆ **02/6214-5600**), or by checking the U.S. Diplomatic Mission's website at **http://usembassy-australia.state.gov/consular**.

British subjects can obtain up-to-date visa information by calling the **U.S. Embassy Visa Information Line** (✆ **0891/200-290**) or by visiting the "Visas to the U.S." section of the American Embassy London's website at **www.usembassy.org.uk**.

Irish citizens can obtain up-to-date visa information through the **Embassy of the USA Dublin,** 42 Elgin Rd., Dublin 4, Ireland (✆ **353/1-668-8777**); or check the "Visas to the U.S." section of the website at **http://dublin.usembassy.gov**.

Citizens of **New Zealand** can obtain up-to-date visa information by contacting the **U.S. Embassy New Zealand,** 29 Fitzherbert Terrace, Thorndon, Wellington (✆ **644/472-2068**), or get the information directly from the website at **http://wellington.usembassy.gov**.

VISITOR INFORMATION **Destination D.C.** is the official tourism and convention corporation for Washington, D.C., 901 7th St. NW, 4th Floor, Washington, DC 20001-3719 (✆ **800/422-8644** or 202/789-7000; www.destinationdc.org). Before you leave, order a free copy of the bureau's *Washington, D.C. Visitors Guide,* which covers hotels, restaurants, sights, shops, and more and is updated twice yearly. At the ✆ **202/789-7000** number, you can speak directly to a staff "visitor services specialist" and get answers to your specific questions about the city.

Be sure to consult Destination D.C.'s website, where you can read and download the visitors' guide, along with the latest travel information, including upcoming exhibits at the museums and anticipated closings of tourist attractions. The website is also an excellent source for maps, which you can download and print from the site or order for delivery by mail.

Once in D.C., you can stop by Destination D.C.'s offices on 7th Street NW (Metro: Gallery Place/Chinatown, H St. exit) to pick up the visitors guide and maps, and to talk to visitors services specialists. Office hours are Monday to Friday, 8:30am to 5pm.

If you're arriving by plane or train, you can think of your airport or the train station as visitor information centers; all three Washington-area airports and Union Station offer all sorts of visitor services. See "Getting There & Getting Around," in chapter 3, for details.

The **D.C. Chamber of Commerce Visitor Information Center** (✆ **866/324-7386** or 202/289-8317; www.dcchamber.org; click on "Visiting DC," then "Visitor Information Center") is a small bureau inside the immense Ronald Reagan International Trade Center Building, at 1300 Pennsylvania Ave. NW. To enter the federal building, you need to show a picture ID. The visitor center lies on the ground floor of the building, a little to your right as you enter from the Wilson Plaza, near the Federal Triangle Metro. From March 15 to Labor Day, the center is open Monday through Friday, 8:30am to 5:30pm, and on

Saturday from 9am to 4pm; from Labor Day to March 14, the center is open Monday through Friday 9am to 4:30pm.

Also look for business improvement district (BID) offices and their patrolling "ambassadors," who dispense information, directions, and other assistance in their individual neighborhoods. Among the most established are: the **Downtown D.C. Business Improvement District (Downtown D.C. BID),** 1250 H St. NW (✆ **202/638-3232;** www.downtowndc.org); the **Golden Triangle Business Improvement District (Golden Triangle BID),** 1120 Connecticut Ave. NW (✆ **202/463-3400;** www.gtbid.com); and the **Capitol Hill Business Improvement District (Capitol Hill BID),** 30 Massachusetts Ave. NE, inside Union Station's garage (✆ **202/842-3333;** www.capitolhillbid.org).

National Park Service information kiosks are located inside or near the Jefferson, Lincoln, FDR, Vietnam Veterans, Korean War, and World War II memorials and at the Washington Monument (✆ **202/426-6841** or 202/619-7222; www.nps.gov/state/dc for all national parklands in D.C., or www.nps.gov/nama for National Mall and Memorials Park sites).

The **White House Visitor Center,** on the first floor of the Herbert Hoover Building, Department of Commerce, 1450 Pennsylvania Ave. NW (btw. 14th and 15th sts.; ✆ **202/208-1631,** or 202/456-7041 for recorded information), is open daily (except for Thanksgiving, Christmas Day, and New Year's Day) from 7:30am to 4pm.

The **Smithsonian Information Center,** in "the Castle," 1000 Jefferson Dr. SW (✆ **202/633-1000,** or TTY 202/633-5285; www.si.edu), is open every day but Christmas from 8:30am to 5:30pm; knowledgeable staff answer questions and dispense maps and brochures.

Take a look at the D.C. government's website, **www.dc.gov**, and that of the nonprofit organization Cultural Tourism D.C., **www.culturaltourismdc.org**, for more information about the city. The Cultural Tourism D.C. site, in particular, provides helpful and interesting background knowledge of D.C.'s historic and cultural landmarks, especially in neighborhoods, or in parts of neighborhoods, not usually visited by tourists.

Check out the websites and blogs of www.washingtonpost.com, www.washingtonian.com, www.dcist.com, and www.ontaponline.com for the latest commentary and information about Washington happenings. Refer to the box titles "Best Washington, D.C., Websites," in chapter 1, for more sources.

2 AIRLINES

MAJOR AIRLINES

Air France
www.airfrance.com

Air Jamaica
www.airjamaica.com

AirTran Airways
www.airtran.com

Alaska Airlines/Horizon Air
www.alaskaair.com

American Airlines
www.aa.com

Avianca
www.avianca.com

British Airways
www.british-airways.com

Cape Air
www.capeair.com

Continental Airlines
www.continental.com

Delta Air Lines
www.delta.com

A Primer on D.C.'s Airports

Three airports serve the nation's capital: Reagan National (in Virginia, and closest to D.C.), Dulles (also in Virginia and a bit of a trek), and BWI (Baltimore–Washington International, south of Baltimore, Maryland).

RONALD REAGAN WASHINGTON NATIONAL AIRPORT (REAGAN NATIONAL OR "NATIONAL") For convenience, National is the airport of choice for domestic flights. The number of international flights is limited. Landing at night, the view of the monuments and Capitol—*c'est magnifique.* Reagan is less than 5 miles from the White House. Under the best of circumstances (between 9pm and 4am), it's a short drive or taxi ride to downtown D.C. But frequent traffic tie-ups have caused many a passenger to miss a flight. If you rent a car, you might overshoot the turn-off for D.C. (The traffic patterns near the airport are daunting.) If you can handle walking one-quarter to one-half a mile with luggage, Metro is the way to go. Covered pedestrian bridges connect the Metro station and the terminal. The stunning glass-and-steel main terminal designed by Cesar Pelli has 54 skylighted domes and a five-story glass wall overlooking the Potomac River. If you've got time to kill, the view from Gate 43 is primo. In the vast commercial space, 40 shops, 25 eateries, and 30 retail carts vie for travelers' wallets. There's even a meditation room near the baggage claim area so that you can compose yourself if your flight out is canceled or delayed. Of course, the best parking spaces—112 of them right next to the terminal—are reserved for VIPs—senators, congressional reps, and local politicians.

For airport information, call ✆ 703/417-8000 or visit www.mwaa.com.

Finnair
www.finnair.com

Frontier Airlines
www.frontierairlines.com

Iberia Airlines
www.iberia.com

JetBlue Airways
www.jetblue.com

Korean Air
www.koreanair.com

LAN Airlines
www.lan.com

Lufthansa
www.lufthansa.com

Midwest Airlines
www.midwestairlines.com

North American Airlines
www.flynaa.com

Northwest Airlines
www.nwa.com

Qantas Airways
www.qantas.com

South African Airways
www.flysaa.com

Southwest Airlines
www.southwest.com

Spirit Airlines
www.spiritair.com

Swiss Air
www.swiss.com

TACA
www.taca.com

United Airlines
www.united.com

USA 3000
www.usa3000.com

WASHINGTON DULLES INTERNATIONAL AIRPORT (DULLES) Located in Chantilly, Virginia, about 30 miles and a 35- to 45-minute ride to downtown D.C. in non-rush-hour traffic, Dulles handles most of the area's international flights. The main Eero Saarinen–designed terminal is an architectural marvel. It is also huge. There is a second midfield terminal; a third is on its way, but no one is saying when. I find Dulles to be a hassle because, in most instances, passengers must ride mobile lounges to board planes, adding to travel time—and overall crankiness. Call ✆ 703/572-2700 or visit www.mwaa.com.

BALTIMORE–WASHINGTON INTERNATIONAL AIRPORT (BWI) One of the nation's busiest airports, BWI is a few miles south of Baltimore, Maryland and 34 miles to the heart of downtown D.C. Mid-morning to mid-afternoon and evenings after 7pm, it's about a 45-minute ride. I find BWI to be the most user-friendly of the three airports. On the downside, you might wait a fortnight for your luggage. On the plus side, Southwest (with close to 200 flights daily to more than 30 nonstop U.S. destinations) flies here, and is the best and most reliable airline on the planet, in my opinion. BWI sports a two-level observation gallery, with computerized interactive displays and a Smithsonian Museum Shop. If you're early for your flight, sink into one of the comfortable leatherette chairs in front of the 147-foot-wide window and marvel at the takeoffs and landings. By punching a flight number into one of the computer displays, your kids can learn the altitude, speed, and location of the plane of their choice. For airport information visit www.bwiairport.com.

US Airways
www.usairways.com

Virgin America
www.virginamerica.com

Virgin Atlantic Airways
www.virgin-atlantic.comBudget Airlines

3 MAJOR HOTEL & MOTEL CHAINS

Best Western International
www.bestwestern.com

Clarion Hotels
www.choicehotels.com

Comfort Inns
www.ComfortInn.com

Courtyard by Marriott
www.marriott.com/courtyard

Crowne Plaza Hotels
www.ichotelsgroup.com/crowneplaza

Days Inn
www.daysinn.com

Doubletree Hotels
www.doubletree.com

EconoLodge
www.econolodge.com

Embassy Suites
www.embassysuites.com

Fairfield Inn by Marriott
www.farfieldinn.com

Four Seasons
www.fourseasons.com

Hampton Inn
http://hamptoninn1.hilton.com

Hilton Hotels
www.1hilton.com

Holiday Inn
www.holidayinn.com

Howard Johnson
www.hojo.com

Hyatt
www.hyatt.com

InterContinental Hotels & Resorts
www.ichotelsgroup.com

La Quinta Inns & Suites
www.lq.com

Loews Hotels
www.loewshotels.com

Marriott
www.marriott.com

Motel 6
www.motel6.com

Omni Hotels
www.omnihotels.com

Quality Inn
www.QualityInn.com

Radisson Hotels & Resorts
www.radisson.com

Ramada Worldwide
www.ramada.com

Red Carpet Inns
www.bookroomsnow.com

Red Lion Hotels
www.redlion.rdln.com

Red Roof Inns
www.redroof.com

Renaissance
www.renaissancehotels.com

Residence Inn by Marriott
www.marriott.com/residenceinn

Rodeway Inns
www.RodewayInn.com

Sheraton Hotels & Resorts
www.starwoodhotels.com/sheraton

Super 8 Motels
www.super8.com

Travelodge
www.travelodge.com

Vagabond Inns
www.vagabondinn.com

Westin Hotels & Resorts
www.starwoodhotels.com/westin

Wyndham Hotels & Resorts
www.wyndham.com

4 CAR-RENTAL AGENCIES

Advantage
www.advantage.com

Alamo
www.alamo.com

Avis
www.avis.com

Budget
www.budget.com

Dollar
www.dollar.com

Enterprise
www.enterprise.com

Hertz
www.hertz.com

Kemwel (KHA)
www.kemwel.com

National
www.nationalcar.com

Payless
www.paylesscarrental.com

Rent-A-Wreck
www.rentawreck.com

Thrifty
www.thrifty.com

INDEX

See also Accommodations and Restaurant indexes, below.

General Index

Accommodations

Restaurants

NOTES

NOTES